THE BRITISH
IMAGINATION

Also by Peter Watson

HISTORY

The German Genius: Europe's Third Renaissance, the
Second Scientific Revolution and the Twentieth Century
Ideas: A History from Fire to Freud
The Modern Mind: An Intellectual History
of the Twentieth Century
Wisdom and Strength: The Biography
of a Renaissance Masterpiece
From Manet to Manhattan: The Rise of the Modern Art Market
The Age of Nothing: How We Have Sought
to Live Since the Death of God
Convergence: The Idea at the Heart of Science
The French Mind: 400 Years of Romance, Revolution and Renewal

INVESTIGATIVE JOURNALISM

War on the Mind: The Military Uses and Abuses of Psychology
Twins: An Uncanny Relationship
The Caravaggio Conspiracy
Sotheby's Inside Story
The Medici Conspiracy: The Illicit Journey of Antiquities
from Italy's Tomb Raiders to the World's Greatest Museums
Fallout: Conspiracy, Cover-Up and the
Deceitful Case for the Atom Bomb

FICTION

The Nazi's Wife
Landscape of Lies
Crusade
Stones of Treason
Capo
Gifts of War (The Kissing Gates)
The Clouds Beneath the Sun
Madeleine's War

THE BRITISH IMAGINATION

A History of Ideas from Elizabeth I to Elizabeth II

PETER WATSON

**SIMON &
SCHUSTER**

London · New York · Amsterdam/Antwerp · Sydney/Melbourne · Toronto · New Delhi

First published in Great Britain by Simon & Schuster UK Ltd, 2025

1 3 5 7 9 10 8 6 4 2

Simon & Schuster UK Ltd
1st Floor
222 Gray's Inn Road
London WC1X 8HB

www.simonandschuster.co.uk
www.simonandschuster.com.au
www.simonandschuster.co.in

Simon & Schuster Australia, Sydney
Simon & Schuster India, New Delhi

A CIP catalogue record for this book
is available from the British Library

Hardback ISBN: 978-1-3985-1388-4
eBook ISBN: 978-1-3985-1390-7

Typeset in Sabon by M Rules
Printed and Bound in the UK using 100% Renewable Electricity
at CPI Group (UK) Ltd

The authorised representative in the EEA is Simon & Schuster Netherlands BV,
Herculesplein 96, 3584 AA Utrecht, Netherlands. info@simonandschuster.nl

MIX
Paper | Supporting
responsible forestry
FSC® C013604

The history of Britain is arguably the most important 'national' history precisely because it has been the most intertwined with, and influential upon, other histories worldwide, in all their dimensions – political, economic, social and cultural.
– NORTH AMERICAN CONFERENCE ON BRITISH STUDIES: *Report on the State and Future of British Studies in North America*

British history is perhaps the best single avenue of inquiry into the large processes of 'globalization' in all its many dimensions – political, economic, social and cultural. As creators of the first 'world system' and the first world market, and as the originators of industrialism, the British occupy a unique position in human history.
– NORTH AMERICAN CONFERENCE ON BRITISH STUDIES: *Report on the State and Future of British Studies in North America*

British history is an ostensibly local history that 'extends itself into Oceanic, American and global dimensions' on nothing less than a 'planetary scale'.
– J. G. A. POCOCK, quoted by ANTOINETTE BURTON

Hear, oh, BRITANNIA! potent Queen of ideas,
On whom fair Art, and meek Religion smiles,
How AFRIC'S coasts thy craftier sons invade
With murder, rapine, theft – and call it Trade!
– ERASMUS DARWIN

Imagination, a licentious and vagrant faculty, unsusceptible of limitations, and impatient of restraint ...
– DR SAMUEL JOHNSON

England cannot afford to be little.
– WILLIAM HUSKISSON, Secretary for War and Colonies

To carry back to distant centuries the ideas of the century in which one lives is of all sources of error the most fertile.

– MONTESQUIEU

Current beliefs must not be allowed to exercise a censorship on the past: the worldview of any cultural group merits attention on its own terms. Only by accepting this scale of values, will the ... complex network of beliefs of any society be fully appreciated.

– CHARLES WEBSTER

Look at the Genesis myth. Once you have eaten of the Tree of Knowledge you can't go back. It suggests that power can enslave and that knowledge can enslave as well ... The key example in liberal humanism is the idea that knowledge liberates. I think that knowledge normally simply enhances human power.

– JOHN GRAY

Knowledge brings power to us all.

– JENNY UGLOW

*Im*perfection is one of the dogmas of Christianity.

– GEORGE LEVINE

English history is in a sense early American history.

– CHARLES HOMER HASKINS

Facts show truth to be a *living* thing, that grows, moves and expands.

– NEIL MACGREGOR

This dubious practice of explaining history from the standpoint of self-righteous indignation.

– DAVID KOPF

Nations should privilege the teaching of their own past (and, within reason, gloss it).

– JANAN GANESH

Every human achievement, every human society, is to be judged by its own internal standards.

– ISAIAH BERLIN

Curiosity about difference should apply to the past in general. The 'Middle Ages' or 'Ancient World' ... are not just stepping stones to the 'modern' present we know ... the Greeks and Romans did not think of themselves as 'ancient' and 12th-century people did not imagine themselves to be living in an in-between period of time ... Presentism, at its worst, encourages a kind of moral complacency and self-congratulation. Interpreting the past in terms of present concerns usually leads us to find ourselves morally superior ... Our forebears constantly fail to measure up to our present-day stand-ards ... we must question the stance of temporal superiority that is implicit in the Western ... historical discipline ... this temporal feeling of superiority applies more to the Western past than it does to the non-Western one.

– LYNN HUNT, President, American Historical Association

One of the intellectual and moral responsibilities of being an adult, as I see it, is to be able to hold more than one reality in your head at the same time.

– ZADIE SMITH

Where imperialism is routinely stripped and operated on under hal-ogen lamps, the history of collaboration is still in shadow.

– A. P. THORNTON

If we do not think to ask, 'Why did they think that?', we know less about the past than we think.

– A. P. THORNTON

In history, as in all serious matters, no achievement is final, since 'history' is contemporary thinking about the past.

– R. G. COLLINGWOOD

It is precisely by thinking about how a past society without our concepts dealt with what we understand using the concepts that it did not have that we come to understand that society better.

— ROBIN OSBORNE

Poetry is the art of uniting pleasure with truth, by calling imagination to the help of reason.

— DR SAMUEL JOHNSON

Were it not for imagination, Sir, a man would be as happy in the arms of a chambermaid as of a Duchess.

— DR SAMUEL JOHNSON

Imperialism doesn't stop being necessary just because it becomes politically incorrect.

— MICHAEL IGNATIEFF

So far from being a ghost of Empire, the Commonwealth was largely the creation of the leaders of successful national liberation movements.

— ARNOLD SMITH, first Secretary General of the Commonwealth

CONTENTS

Smalltime Latecomer: Self-Inflicted Wounds; 'Despiser of Learning'

When Her Majesty Queen Elizabeth II died in September 2022, her passing brought to an end a long period of British history which had lasted more than 400 years, since the accession of her namesake, Queen Elizabeth I, in November 1588. During that time, Britain's intellectual and creative life had flourished as never before. Having been a small, underpopulated, out-of-the-way backwater, riven by tumultuous usurpations of this king and that and repeated ructions against Rome, it was only under the first Elizabeth that the country finally started to make its way in the world and steadily began to acquire ambition. It would in time become one of the leading nations of 'the West', a modern concept embracing the more prosperous countries and civilisations grouped mainly around the North Atlantic in Europe and the Americas. By the time Elizabeth II was laid to rest, the world was entering a 'post-Western' phase, with non-Western countries, led by China and Russia, but including India and nations in Africa and the Middle East, beginning to make economic and political and cultural progress, while the West, though still prosperous, no longer could be said to dominate the affairs of the world. During the seventy-year reign of Queen Elizabeth II forty-nine former colonies gained their independence as stand-alone states.

Though this seems like a new situation, and in some ways it is, it is in other ways a return to much earlier times. In the tenth century AD, the famous Arab geographer Alī al-Masʿūdī had this to say about the peoples of 'Urufa', as Muslims then called Europe: 'The warm humour is lacking among them; their bodies are large, their natures gross, their manners harsh, their understanding dull, and their tongues heavy ... The farther they are to the north the more stupid, gross, and brutish they are.'[1] His slightly later colleague Ṣāʿid ibn Aḥmad, *qadi* of the Muslim city of Toledo in Spain, wasn't much more impressed. According to Bernard Lewis, the great Islamic scholar, in 1068, two years after the Battle of Hastings, Ṣāʿid wrote a book in Arabic on the categories of nations. He found that there had been eight nations that had contributed most to knowledge – including the Indians, Persians, Greeks, Egyptians and, of course, the Arabs. On the other hand, he found that the north Europeans 'have not cultivated the sciences [and] are more like beasts than like men ... they lack keenness of understanding and clarity of intelligence'.[2]

In fact, if any single nation could be said to lead the world in antiquity, it was China. In seafaring, the magnetic compass and the stern post rudder, dating from the fourth century AD, were accompanied by the anchor, canvas sails and pivoting sails. At the same time there was another side to the medieval Chinese elite, a more abstract metaphysical cast of mind which found expression in the scholar-bureaucrat, chosen by written examinations where candidates' names were pasted over and replaced by numbers so that examiners could not identify who was who, to ensure that talent and not lineage counted.

The Indian mathematician Aryabhata calculated pi as 3.1416 as early as 499 AD. He understood that the earth was a sphere spinning on its own axis. The earliest evidence for the alphabet in India dates from the third century BC. A second innovation of the Indians was the invention/creation of Hindu numerals, which was also an achievement of Aryabhata. Later, it was the Indians who introduced the concept of nought, o, though the Mayans also had a concept of 'emptiness'.

The Arabic word for o, *zephirum*, is the basis for both our words 'cipher' and 'zero'. Among Arab philosophers al-Razi and Ibn Sina stand out. Al-Razi, known in the West by his Latin name, Rhazes, was the first chief physician of the great hospital at Baghdad. In choosing the site, he is said to have hung up shreds of meat in different places, selecting the spot where putrefaction was least. Ibn Sina again is known in the West by a Latinised name, Avicenna. His most famous work was *Al-Qanun* (*The Canon*), in which he codified some 760 drugs. *The Canon* also pioneered the study of psychology, in that Ibn Sina observed a close association between emotional and physical states, the beneficial role of music, and the effect of the environment in medicine (i.e. rudimentary epidemiology).[3]

Arab civilisation achieved a further glory in Spain to rival that in Iraq, with the high point coming in the last half of the tenth century. By that point, Cordova, the capital, was on a par with Baghdad and Constantinople as one of the three great cultural centres of the 'known world'. It had paved streets, where each house undertook to mount a light outside at night. There was a regular postal service, coins in gold and silver, gardens galore, a whole street of bookshops, and seventy libraries.

So far as influence on Western thinking is concerned, the greatest achievement of Muslim Spain was in the *falsafah* of Ibn Rushd, otherwise known as Averroës. Averroës was the first person to notice that no one is ever afflicted with smallpox twice, the beginnings of the idea of inoculation, but it is as a philosopher that he had most influence. His most important argument was that not all the words of the Qur'an should be taken literally. When the literal meaning of the text appears to contradict the rational truths of philosophers, he said, those verses are to be understood metaphorically.

By the twelfth century, however, long-term, systemic change was under way. This was the great era of the Crusades, cathedral-building and the foundation of universities across Europe. There are many theories why this great change took place then, ranging from the continent's variable climate, which demanded more clothing and more furniture, stimulating calculation and the development of science, to the number of natural peninsulas (Iberia, Italy, Greece) fostering greater nationalism and therefore more competition, to the spread of Christianity and its associated language, Latin, which all in the church could speak, promoting greater communication and greater cooperation. Another theory was that the plague of the fourteenth century had a differential effect, in that the 'die-off' rate was less in western Europe than in the Middle East or Asia. Finally, there was the steady growth of technology in Europe: the water mill from the sixth century; the plough from the seventh; the crop rotation system from the eighth; the horseshoe and the neck harness from the ninth. In the same way, the employment of the mill proliferated to other uses, from beer-making in 861, through tanning in 1138 and paper-milling in 1276, to the blast furnace in 1384.[4] Watermills and windmills had transformed corn-grinding and metallurgy, and spectacles and the clock were invented. In other words, there was nothing sudden but a steady take-off of Europe.

These changes would lead, in time, to the Renaissance, the great flourishing of European painting, literature and philosophy, first in Italy, then in France and Spain. England, meanwhile (there was no Britain then), had been conquered by the French in 1066; the English language had, to an extent, been sidelined (Richard Rolle, generally held to be the first significant poet to use what is recognisably English, died in 1349); and the country had been mired in the Hundred Years War with France (1337–1453), which had overlapped with the tumultuous fifteenth century when, of the eight kings who occupied the throne of England between 1399 and 1509, two were murdered, five were deposed in one way or another, two were exiled, and five were captured and imprisoned (Henry VI was imprisoned and recaptured three times, as well as suffering a mental breakdown). Two of the kings ascended the throne as young children, with all the danger and opportunity that implied. And all this without counting the number of times rebellions were threatened, or the people who were executed – beheaded or burned – for their part in trying to overthrow one king or another. The Hundred Years War finally came to an end only for the so-called Wars of the Roses to break out two years later in 1455, lasting until 1487. William Shakespeare was to write five plays about these turbulent times.

In the late Middle Ages, a small number of English priests did display an international bent, and visited Cordova, Toledo and other areas of Arab learning, such as Antioch, familiarising themselves with – and in some cases collecting – humanist manuscripts: John of Oxford (d. 1200), Alfred of Sarechel (*fl.* 1215), Daniel of Morley (*c.*1140–*c.*1210). Many of them were associated with Hereford Cathedral, rather than Oxford or London. And others, like Robert Grosseteste (*c.*1186–1253) and Roger Bacon (*c.*1219/20–*c.*1292), had shown an early interest in science, both visiting the university at Paris. Later, individuals such as Humphrey, Duke of Gloucester (1390–1447), brother of Henry V, bought many humanist manuscripts which he donated to Oxford colleges. In other words, there was an interest in learning, in nature, in philosophy beyond the church, and through John Wycliffe ('the morning star of the Reformation') and others, the beginnings of a reaction against Rome. But England's intellectual and imaginative elite cannot be said to have been anything other than thin on the ground.

And this is reflected in the fact, too often overlooked, that England was small. Just how small is highlighted by Table 1. Until the late eighteenth century Britain's population was about a third that of France and Germany, half that of Italy, and 30 per cent smaller than Spain.

Table 1 Population of selected countries at selected dates (figures in millions)

	1000 AD	1400	1500	1600	1700	1800	1900
France	5.0	11.0–14.0	15.0	18.5	21.5	31.0	41.5
Germany	3.0	9.6	12.0	16.0	15.0	25.0	65.0
Italy	7.0	7.0–10.0	10.5	13.0	13.5	20.0	37.0
Spain	6.5	4.5	6.8	8.2	8.7	14.7	20.2
Britain	0.8	2.8–3.0	4.0	6.0	8.5	21.0	45.0

And then, of course, came the reign of Henry VIII, his six wives and his 'Great Matter' with Rome, culminating in the Dissolution of the Monasteries, when two thirds of the 900 religious houses in England were alienated and hundreds of libraries were vandalised, their contents taken by 'ignorant nobles' who sold off historically important artefacts for profit or used manuscripts 'to scrub their boots, sold them to grocers and soap sellers and sent away whole ships full'. 'The dispersal of England's literary heritage,' said John Bale, who compiled a history of English writers around the time of the Dissolution, 'seriously undermined the nation's reputation among Europe's elite', producing the idea that the English were 'despisers of learning'.[5]

And after Henry came Mary Tudor, known to history as 'Bloody Mary' on account of the hundreds of heretics she had burned at the stake or beheaded (280 according to one account). To this point, English history reads like a list of self-inflicted wounds.

All that was about to change. It would take time but during Elizabeth's reign there would be, as several observers, then and since, have noticed, an increasing coherence of England and, more than that, a sense of its 'gathering greatness', as ideas began to flourish like never before. This had a great deal to do with London, where we begin. England might be small but not London. Not only was it large, a home to the Court, an intellectual powerhouse, but, unlike Paris, Vienna, Rome, Madrid or Berlin, it was a port. No one knew it at the time, but England's all-important 'blue-water destiny' beckoned.

PART ONE

THE ELIZABETHAN MIND:
THE GREAT RE-SET

'A More Intense Englishness'

arly in 1593, Queen Elizabeth I, then aged fifty-nine, embarked on a translation – from Latin into English – of *The
Consolations of Philosophy* by Boethius, the sixth-century
Roman consul, who, like her, combined a life in power and politics
with a wider interest in ideas. The translation was an extraordinary
enterprise, more than a hundred pages long, but she completed the
work in thirty hours; according to contemporaries, 'she just seems
to have dashed it off ... It is what she did for leisure when she was
taking a break from running the country.'[1]

Out of Henry VIII's three legitimate children to survive infancy,
both Edward and Mary were exceptionally intelligent. Elizabeth
was no different. She was an accomplished linguist, fluent in Latin,
French, ancient Greek, Spanish and Italian, and translated works
into and out of those languages all her life, often giving them as gifts
to others in her circle. On formal visits to Oxford and Cambridge
she conversed easily with the professors in Latin. She received an excellent education from several eminent humanist scholars – William
Grindal and Roger Ascham among them – and in recent years the
University of Chicago has published all her works in three modern
editions, each close to 500 pages: her speeches, poems (103 of them),
prayers, *sententiae* (proverbs, aphorisms) and her letters, rich in elegant rhetorical flourishes, as was typical of the times. These show
her, in the words of one modern historian, to have been 'a significant
author in her own right'. And so, in addition to being 'The Pirate

Queen' (the Spanish view), 'The Heretic Queen' (the Vatican view), 'The Faerie Queen' (Edmund Spenser's view), 'The Virgin Queen' (the Hollywood/BBC view), we can also add 'The Learned Queen', the title of a recent study.

As Anne Boleyn's daughter, Elizabeth was the living focus of her father's break with Rome, of the Reformation itself. She had seen what her siblings had made of their opportunity to govern the realm, and how between them Edward and Mary had thrown their subjects this way and that. She herself had been imprisoned for a time. This made her neither doctrinaire nor dogmatic.

An early achievement was the Elizabethan Settlement, implemented beginning in 1559, only a few months after Elizabeth's accession. The Settlement did not create Anglicanism as we know it – that came later. But it *was* a settlement, a set of arrangements which effectively brought the English Reformation to a close, and is why this book begins where it does, with a re-set in English life. The Settlement remained in place for some time and then, after further disruptions, which we shall come to, it was revived in a form that we can recognise today. It consisted of the following three elements:

- The Act of Supremacy, which in 1558 re-established the Church of England's independence from Rome. Elizabeth was named 'governor' rather than head, as more suited to a queen than a king.
- The Act of Uniformity, passed in 1559, which reintroduced Cranmer's 1552 *Book of Common Prayer*. This laid down the liturgical services of the church, in which allowances were made so as to appeal to both those Catholic-inclined and those who preferred Lutheran ideas. In particular, greater latitude was allowed in regard to belief about the 'real presence' of Christ in the Eucharist and traditional priestly vestments. Church attendance on Sundays and holy days was made compulsory with fines attached to non-observance. But the revised *Book of Common Prayer* removed the denunciation of the bishop of Rome, which had been in the Edwardian version, and it also deleted the so-called Black Rubric or Declaration on Kneeling, whereby it was held that to kneel was not to 'adore' (implying idolatry); it was

more a form of respect since the bread and wine remained as natural substances.

- The adoption in 1571 of the Thirty-Nine Articles as a confessional statement, together with a book of homilies – they were basically a set of sermons which laid out certain specifics as an aid to salvation. One set of articles described the exact authority of the church, another the errors people should seek to avoid, a third the exact nature of the incarnation of Jesus Christ. As modern law contracts would say, this was all developed 'for the avoidance of doubt'.

Elizabeth's own views were fairly conservative; she did not believe in the doctrine of transubstantiation, disliked married clergy, was more or less Lutheran as regards the 'real presence' in the Eucharist, and disliked candles in procession and the elevation of the host during Mass. The wording during the Communion service was that the bread was to be eaten *in remembrance* that Christ died'. (Italics added.) The general tenor of the Elizabethan church was Calvinist, though the settlement did implicitly acknowledge that, at parish level, unlike at Court in London, or at Canterbury, Catholic priests and traditionally minded laity were still present in great numbers. The queen was disappointed by the iconoclasm of the more extreme Protestants. She thought there should still be a division between the chancel and the rest of the church.

One gets the impression that the queen – born in 1533 – was mentally exhausted by the seemingly endless wrangling during her father's and her siblings' reigns and, without giving away too much, felt that enough blood had been shed and it was time to move forward: this was the re-set, but Protestantism did not become the majority religion in England until the 1580s.

The genius of the Elizabethan Settlement was its vagueness, says the historian Richard Helgerson. It is sometimes presented as a sensible attempt to find a 'third way' in religion 'that was neither in thrall to Luther nor the pope'. Luther's pessimism, his conviction as to humankind's chronic need to rely on God in all things, never appealed to people who would become famously industrious Puritans.[2]

John Jewel, who became bishop of Salisbury on his return from exile during Bloody Mary's reign, wrote *Apologia ecclesiae anglicanae* in 1562, which provided the backbone of this English 'third way' for half a century. He argued that the church should rely only on Scripture and the writings of the ancient fathers, ignoring all the other niceties of faith that separated Lutherans from others. The teaching of John Calvin in Geneva during the 1550s did influence Protestantism across stretches of the Netherlands and Switzerland, and parts of France and Germany. The Geneva Bible, predominantly the creation of English exiles toiling there during their Marian exile, together with Calvin's own *Institutes of a Christian Man*, also enjoyed a wide influence, but Elizabeth was deeply sceptical about the Geneva ascendancy in general and, moreover, could never get it out of her head that it had given birth to John Knox's *First Blast of the Trumpet against the Monstrous Regiment of Women*.

Calvinism's extraordinary doctrine of predestination, that everyone had been singled out 'in the mind of God' before birth for 'election or damnation', never caught on in the Church of England. What did catch on was for many clerics to take advantage of the Edwardian settlement's adoption of clerical marriage, many of them taking the opportunity to legitimise their liaison with their 'housekeepers'.

Elizabeth was twenty-five at her accession in November 1558. On the small side, pale-skinned, a golden redhead, with brown eyes and exceptionally long fingers, she would prove a popular and much-admired queen, and her reign, as we shall see, was distinguished as a renaissance of cultural and political achievement. When she acceded, she inherited more than sixty royal residences, though she only ever made use of about half a dozen of those – Whitehall (the largest, all 23 acres of it), Hampton Court, Greenwich, Richmond, St James and Windsor Castle – and she travelled around them in a regular order: Whitehall for Christmas, for example, and Windsor for Easter and the Maundy ceremony when she would wash the feet of poor women (the same number as her age) and offer them gifts. St George's Day (23 April) was also spent at Windsor.

Her Court consisted of more than a thousand people and its central element was the Presence Chamber, a great hall where she held her audiences and where the great entertainments took place. With so many people in attendance, security was tight, and all her meals were ceremoniously checked for poison (dinner being held around noon). The palaces were also home to a great library, the queen being an avid reader, very interested in history. Ceremony was paramount, her arrival anywhere always greeted by a fanfare of trumpets. By custom, the queen's head was meant to be higher than anyone else's at all times, though given her diminutive height this must have often caused protocol problems. No one was supposed to turn their back on the monarch; she expected – and received – flattery and liked a certain flamboyance in the appearance and character of her close courtiers. Around her – and across all Europe – there was constant speculation as to whether she really was a virgin queen.

'THE KINGDOM OF OUR OWN LANGUAGE'

Historians have noted that a profound psychological change came over England during Elizabeth's reign, more fundamental even than the other important changes that occurred in politics, exploration and social affairs. This was a time, these historians say, when English men and women began to feel their Englishness *more intensely* than ever before as the sovereign state and the Crown finally triumphed during those years over the church and as a self-contained national unit came into being. Moreover, it was 'not the tacitly accepted necessity it had been for some time, but the consciously desired goal'.

Intellectually, Roger Ascham helped lead the way. He was a forceful but somewhat puzzling man.[3] Born around 1515, in Yorkshire, Ascham studied at St John's College, Cambridge, then the largest and most learned college of either university, where he was elected a fellow and where he became known for his beautiful handwriting (despite the recent invention of printing, manuscripts were still in wide use). By 1540, when the Regius professorship of Greek was established (after the Dissolution of the Monasteries), he was lecturing there on both mathematics and Greek, which latter he had taught himself. He achieved prominence to begin with as the author of *Toxophilus* ('Love of the Bow', 1545), his first book, which on the surface is about archery but was really an argument for the development of English eloquence as a prominent feature of the Protestant Reformation. More specifically, *Toxophilus* is a thinly veiled allegory promoting *vernacular* rhetoric as a weapon in the cause for the 'utter destruction of papistrie and heresie'.[4]

And this is what interests us, in that a major novelty of the book was that Ascham had 'written this Englishe matter in the Englishe tongue for Englishe men', arguing in it for the deliberate and active self-fashioning of oneself and noting that, before Virgil and Horace corrected it, Latin was as rude and barbarous as English, just as Homer had similarly reformed Greek.[5] Ascham was urging his fellow English shining lights to flex their muscles and their imaginative powers. More than that, Richard Helgerson has identified around Ascham a whole cohort – or generation – of like-minded Elizabethans who responded to his call to arms. They include Philip Sidney, Fulke Greville, Francis Bacon, Walter Raleigh and Christopher Marlowe, but first among them was Edmund Spenser, who, in a letter sent in 1580 to his friend Gabriel Harvey, a Cambridge professor and Latin specialist, said: 'Why a God's name may not we, as else the Greeks, have the kingdom of our own language', a sentiment identical to Ascham's.

GRAMMAR SCHOOLS GALORE

Under Elizabeth, there were energetic attempts to improve education in England; new ideas were introduced, new theories of learning which were intended to apply right across the social spectrum. Basically conservative, their main aim was to inculcate social unity and the official state religion, the details of which, of course, were relatively new. But they also tapped into humanist theories about 'active citizenship'. Elizabeth's reign saw the introduction of a massive number of new grammar schools across England, designed equally for the clergy, the 'gentle' classes and the children of the wealthy merchant class.[6] By its end, according to Freyja Cox Jensen, England had 360 grammar schools, one for every 12,000 people living in the country, 'a greater provision than existed even in Victorian times'. Bishops were tasked with reporting every year on the schools within their remit, in order to identify candidates for the church and civil service. (The plan of Richard Barnes, bishop of Durham, for education 'according to ability irrespective of class', did not catch on.)

Elizabeth's reign contributed to a widening understanding of what learning was. More and more it began to matter to the self-image (and therefore the self-confidence) of the 'gentle' classes, forming an important part of the changing psychology in Elizabethan society that we have already alluded to. Baldassare Castiglione's *The Courtier* was translated into English by Sir Thomas Hoby in 1561, spreading notions of civility, civic duty and 'active service'. A university education was no longer enough; more and more a gentleman must add to his accomplishments through foreign travel and, in many cases, by further study at one of the Inns of Court. The Inns, known colloquially as Britain's 'third university', were reformed and enlarged during Elizabeth's time on the throne, to provide for their growing clientele.

Beyond schooling, however, and important as that was, intellectual life in Elizabethan England found expression in a number of developments which mainly took place in London. London was then a city of about 200,000, up from 50,000 at the beginning of the century.[7]

'CUNNING PRINCEPLEASERS': THE CULT OF ELIZABETH – FLATTERY AND FAVOUR

We may begin with the Court. As mentioned above, the Court consisted of somewhere between 1,000 and 1,500 people but the intellectual and artistically creative elite was much smaller than that. A belief current at the time held that only the Court offered that milieu of sophisticated leisure which could allow poetry to flourish – courtly style and habits of mind were held to be particularly congenial to the distinctive features of poetry, and courtly manners had a direct bearing on the development of poetic style. In *The Arte of English Poesie* (1589), the controlling assumption of the author, George Puttenham (1529–90), a critic with a somewhat lascivious private life, is that to be a good poet entails being a proper courtier.[8] And to assure that poets may thrive as 'cunning princepleasers', Puttenham offers 'norms' for their art drawn from approved standards of courtly conduct. Proper courtiership, he insists, assures a command of poetic decorum since the courtier – whose social survival relies on wit, judiciousness and poise – 'hardly needs to learn what is or is not desirable in poetic style'. Puttenham is, in fact, not above suggesting that the poetic life is no more than an extension of good courtiership. 'While the *Arte of English Poesie* is ostensibly a treatise on poetry, it is at the same time one of the most significant arts of conduct of the Elizabethan age.'[9]

In his dedicated examination of the Elizabethan courtier poets, the American historian Stephen W. May argues that the Elizabethan courtier class, which dominated national patronage and intellectual and social power, was understood by contemporaries to consist of people who were given access not just to the royal household, nor even to the Presence Chamber, but to the very Privy Chamber of the queen. On these grounds, he says, the list of 'courtier poets' who meet this criterion comprises thirty-two of whose work we have examples.[10]

This list yields a number of familiar names (Dyer, Greville, Harington, Raleigh, Sackville, Sidney) and a number who are not nearly as familiar to us, at least as poets (Ascham, Bacon, Cecil, Hatton, Heneage, Mildmay). Interestingly, what the Earl of Surrey and Thomas Wyatt had introduced to English poetry during Henry VIII's reign had no immediate counterpart at Elizabeth's Court; 'there was little lyricism, less love'. Most of the verse, we are told, was occasional, mildly celebratory or commendatory and tried to be classical in its learned humanism.

Despite the poets' access to the throne, we mustn't be too high-minded about courtier poetry. Two phrases need to be borne in mind. One is 'The most important fact about Elizabeth I was her sex'. And two, as Roy Strong – among others – put it, the cult of Elizabeth grew out of 'an inexhaustible craving for flattery fed by an insatiable appetite for favour'. Both were equally important, but most important of all was the fact that with the Court being the apogee of life for anyone of talent and ambition, access to the courtiers was the crucial element in intellectual/social/political life, which in a way could hardly be distinguished, and for anyone who wasn't born into the top elite, patronage was really the only way to secure advantage, and the ultimate source of patronage was of course the queen herself.[11]

This accounts for so much in Elizabethan times, where the queen's sexual status, her marital status and her theological status overlapped in ways that were unique to her, to the realm and to the psychology of the nation, as we shall repeatedly see. It means, for instance, that the use of (inevitably ambiguous) erotic language in the process of patronage negotiations could not help but be ever-present *and* an ever-present source of anxiety, not least from an inherent uncertainty about sincerity. Texts addressed to patrons often used an intimate vocabulary in which the relationship between courtier/poet and patron was presented as loving and honest, and freely given. Yet the pursuit of a Court career could not be had without the heavy cooperation of others. In Strong's words: 'As a result, it is often impossible to tell whether the speaker of a poem is in love or seeking political favour.' This makes reading courtier poetry both endlessly fascinating and endlessly irritating.

Overlapping with the courtier poets and helping to define the intellectual culture of the realm were a number of literary circles grouped around prominent individuals. The most eye-catching were those gathered around Robert Dudley, Earl of Leicester, around Sir Philip Sidney, around Robert Devereux, Earl of Essex, and around Ben Jonson.

Intensely intellectual and politically astute, Leicester was the patron of the Puritan movement, and he helped enforce the Act of Supremacy, found Oxford University Press and install Alberico Gentili as professor of international law at Oxford. Very interested in translation, Leicester encouraged more than a hundred books, which were dedicated to him. Fascinated by history and theatre, he had his own company of players and musicians and was the principal patron of Nicholas Hilliard, the miniaturist. His circle of scholars included John Dee, Philip Sidney and Gabriel Harvey.

Those at the centre of the Sidney circle encompassed his brother Robert, his sister Mary, Countess of Pembroke, a significant poet and translator, and his friends Fulke Greville, sonneteer, biographer of Sidney and another favourite of the queen, and Sir Edward Dyer, also a poet. Sidney was exceptionally newsworthy as he was a brilliant military leader in the Protestant cause, 'a leading hope for the faith'. Generally held to be the next greatest writer of sonnets after Shakespeare, his sprawling love poem *Arcadia*, while written to his lover, was dedicated to his sister.

Essex, politically ambitious, was loosely related to the queen in that his great-grandmother was Elizabeth's aunt; he and his circle were famously obsessed by Tacitus because of his exploration of republicanism, obviously a touchy subject with Elizabeth. Many of Essex's poems are bitter and pessimistic, written when he was in the Tower of London awaiting execution for an attempted *coup d'état*. Essex also acted as a patron of the painter Isaac Oliver and encouraged the development of limning.[12] Essex's intellectual concerns included an interest in navigation and the links between Ramism and Protestantism; he believed in self-improvement through academic endeavour.

Ben Jonson's circle called themselves variously the 'Tribe of Ben' or the 'Sons of Ben' and met, first, at the Mermaid tavern and later the Devil's Head. They included the poet Robert Herrick and Richard Lovelace, another poet who was in and out of prison for his political activities.

All that said, and as important as those circles were in setting the imaginative and intellectual tone of the reign, and while the whole genre of courtier poetry was the most typical exemplar of Elizabethan high culture, emphasising how the Court took centre stage, the best single instance of the cult of Elizabeth, that all-important mix of flattery and favour, without which sixteenth-century English society cannot be fully understood, was produced by someone helped by Leicester but largely excluded from the charmed circle, at least for much of the time. This was Edmund Spenser, whose masterpiece was *The Faerie Queene*.

In a way *The Faerie Queene* came out of nowhere, just as Spenser himself came out of nowhere. He was born in 1552 near the Tower of London to poor parents who may have been connected with the Lancashire family of Le Despensers, 'an house of ancient fame' from which the Northamptonshire Spencers were also descended.

Despite his poor background, Spenser was educated at Pembroke College, Cambridge as a sizar, or paid scholar who waited on others at mealtimes. He remained in Cambridge for seven years, in the process becoming exceptionally accomplished in the New Learning, the Greek and Latin classics, the philosophy of Plato and Aristotle and the poetry of Theocritus and Virgil. Among the friends he made there were Gabriel Harvey, a fellow of Pembroke who introduced Spenser to Sidney. Through his friendship with Sidney, Spenser was introduced in London to Leicester, Sidney's great-uncle, and through him gained access to the best society available in the capital.

Robert Dudley, Earl of Leicester, was a favourite of Elizabeth I, even for a time *the* favourite (for years he was regarded as her suitor, during which time his apartment at Court was next to hers). Deeply involved in the domestic and foreign politics of the day, alongside William Cecil and Sir Francis Walsingham, the queen's spy chief, Leicester was also a candidate for marriage to Mary, Queen of Scots. He was Elizabeth's master of the horse, a privy counsellor and Lord Steward of the royal household. During the Armada he was in command of the land forces. He was a backer of Drake on his voyages of plunder. Spenser fitted in neatly and naturally for a time. Also for a time, he fitted in naturally to the circle of poets and young men of learning that included Sidney, Dyer, Greville, Harvey and others. Known as the Areopagus, they were dedicated to the reform of English poetry, advocating that more allowance be made for foreign works.

In the winter of 1579 Spenser published his *Shepheards Calendar*, with a dedication to Sidney. This was a series of twelve pastoral poems in the style of Virgil, taking the form of dialogues between shepherds who pass the time discussing love, old age and, inevitably, religion. Some of the verses attack the zeal, sloth and pomp of worldly clergy, one is devoted to courtly praise of the queen. Its eloquence and fluency made it at once what many considered the most accomplished poem that had appeared since the death of Chaucer.

Not long afterwards, and now a much better-known figure, Spenser travelled to Ireland as private secretary to Lord Grey of Wilton and he was to remain there – amid growing turbulence, rebellion and bloodshed – for the rest of his life. It was there that he made the acquaintance of Sir Walter Raleigh, an acquaintanceship which soon ripened into an intimate friendship. It was during a visit from Raleigh when, sitting under the shade 'of the green alders of the Mulla's shore' (in real life, Lake Killnemullah), Spenser read aloud the first books of *The Faerie Queene* to him. Raleigh was so delighted that he insisted Spenser accompany him to London where Edmund was able to read his great work to Her Majesty. She was no less enchanted by the work than Raleigh was, as Spenser had the chance to explain its structure as a huge, sprawling romantic epic – pastoral, chivalrous, ethical and above all allegorical.

The action takes place far away in the unreal fairyland of medieval chivalry, replete with incidents that have been described as 'either highly improbable or frankly impossible', using archaic or deliberately unfamiliar language, a world populated by plants which speak, healing fountains, magic mirrors, dragons, satyrs, knights and giants, together with several winding digressions. Gloriana, the Queen of Fairyland, holds a solemn twelve-day festival during which she commands her knights to undertake twelve adventures, where the knights are commissioned to champion the cause of people in distress and right the wrongs that have been done to them.

It was an extremely successful attempt to match the cultural accomplishments of Greece and Rome and at the same time was authentically English in its reliance on English medieval traditions.[13] It is clear from the narrative that the symbolic lover of the queen is none other than the people of England, the only marriage in the book being between the Thames and the Medway, which itself represents a mystical union between the prince and the subjects. The queen loved it when it was read to her, not least because of its flattering lines picturing her as Gloriana. She offered Spenser an annual pension there and then.

We can't leave it there, however. In an account of the many virtues of the Elizabethan age, we cannot overlook the fact that Spenser's ultimate fate was not at all what it might have been. He returned to Ireland and, on the queen's recommendation, became sheriff of Cork. Now the acknowledged prince of living poets, nonetheless his time in Ireland was turbulent. The native Catholic Irish loathed the Protestant English, opposition grew and, in the autumn of 1598, a bloody uprising, known as Tyrone's Rebellion, broke out in which peasants attacked and set fire to the castle where Spenser and his family lived; they barely escaped with their lives. When Spenser finally made it back to London he was in severe distress and 'prostrated' by the hardships he had endured. Moreover, his view about the queen had changed – among other criticisms of her, he now thought she could have been more generous with her pension. Broken psychologically, broken-hearted and in poverty, Spenser died in January 1599 in a tavern in King Street, Westminster. He was buried close to the tomb of Chaucer in Poets' Corner in Westminster Abbey, his fellow poets bearing the pall, the Earl of Essex paying the funeral costs. Spenser was forty-six.

Poetry was by no means the only cultural activity of the Court, of course. Other forms of entertainment included pageants, masques and straightforward plays. Elaborate Accession Day tilts were designed to honour the queen but at the same time they were major public spectacles – the Whitehall Tiltyard was a permanent structure that could seat 10,000–12,000 spectators. The predominant aim of the pageants was to reinforce the cult of the queen in which her image was 'to make her feminine nature acceptable to the people'.[14]

The cult of the queen was surely both a conscious and an unconscious response to the sexual, social and theological dilemma of an unmarried virgin in such a precarious position of power. As Stephen Greenblatt put it, not entirely ironically:

> The gorgeous rituals of praise channeled national and religious sentiments into the worship of the prince, masked over and thus temporarily deflected deep social, political and theological divisions in late sixteenth-century England, transformed Elizabeth's potentially disastrous sexual disadvantage into a supreme virtue and, in the same movement, metamorphosed a pack of dangerous, phallic-aggressive fortune seekers into gentle knights kneeling at the foot of the faerie Queene.[15]

The reality was very different. As Elizabeth entered the new century, she was a rapidly ageing, tired and lonely old lady 'kept going', in

Greenblatt's words, 'by a will of iron and unflagging determination'. By dodging and leaving unresolved many crucial issues, this remarkable woman was able to fashion the crown into a multivalent yet ambiguous symbol, 'which managed to hold the hearts and minds of all its peoples'.

LEARNING AND LICENCE

Away from the Court (although, as we have seen, it was in some ways impossible to get away from the influence of the Court), there were nonetheless several important formal and less formal intellectual/ imaginative developments in the Elizabethan era.

Arguably the most immediate institution in cultural and intellectual matters were the Inns of Court. The four Inns – Gray's Inn, Lincoln's Inn, Middle Temple and Inner Temple – were voluntary legal societies. Located just west of the old City of London, between High Holborn to the north and the Thames to the south, the Inns made (and still make) up the heart of London's legal district.[16] Today their sole function is to call (train) men and women to the English bar, but their origin is obscure, beginning sometime in the fourteenth century, perhaps as temporary accommodation for lawyers or legal apprentices, hence the term 'inn'. They varied in the extent to which they conformed to or resisted the religious tempers of the time, as shown by this contemporary doggerel:

> Inner for the rich,
> Middle for the poor,
> Lincoln's for the gentleman,
> And Gray's Inn for the whore.

Despite these differences, Jessica Winston says that the Inns are more alike than not and by 1558, when Elizabeth took the throne, they were expanding in more or less the same way as each other. Several poets – Barnabe Googe, Thomas Lodge – dedicated their works to the Inns, Shakespeare alluded to them in *Henry IV Part 2* and Ben Jonson famously characterised Inns of Court men as a group when he dedicated *Every Man out of His Humour* (c.1600), a play about 'characters' and 'types' at the Inns of Court, confessing that he understood Inns of Court men but not how they varied from Inn to Inn.[17]

In 1602, Edward Coke, a lawyer we shall meet again, observed that the Inns were the 'most famous university for [the] profession of law only' while George Buck, antiquarian and master of the Revels under James I, said they were the main reason why London, next to Oxford and Cambridge, was 'the third university of England'.[18] Lawyers attended the Inns for seven years, together with a series of 'learning vacations', and these, along with communal dining ('eating law'), fashioned a distinctive cast of mind, producing a raft of influential legal figures: Thomas More, Nicholas Bacon, William Cecil, Francis Bacon, Coke himself and Simon D'Ewes.[19] Part of this distinctive cast of mind can be put down to the fact that, in early modern England, the language of common law was a specialised tongue, a mix of French and English, interspersed with Latin terms, and known as 'law-French'.[20]

The Inns were expensive and scholarships were not available, meaning they were more socially homogeneous than the universities and this too helped their distinctive mindset. As they were tolerant in religious matters, recusant Catholics could often be found there. To an extent, they became finishing schools as well as law schools and it was here, rather than among the more academic religious souls of Oxford and Cambridge, that future members of Parliament, magistrates and administrators got to know each other in their formative years. They 'drank, diced and misbehaved'. 'Revelling' was a tradition and the Inns were often, in Jonson's words, places of 'humanity and liberty ... learning and licence'.[21]

The Revels were in fact a traditional season of merry-making which lasted from All Saints' Eve (31 October) to Candlemas (2 February). Every year, a 'prince of misrule' was elected to lead the celebrations, which played an important role in encouraging English theatre and, it should be said, provided Shakespeare with one of his most distinguished audiences.[22]

The literary activities of members were especially noteworthy, in part because the Inns were congenial to men who thought the social and literary world of London was more agreeable and better fitted their wider concerns than the relatively narrow study of law, so that the Inns became in time among the most important centres for imaginative and literary activity in the capital. Among the poets and playwrights who belonged to an Inn may be numbered Thomas Sackville, Thomas Lodge, John Donne, John Marston, George Whither and John Ford. Inns of Court men wrote plays and masques for performance by colleagues; they mounted their own productions and patronised the theatres of the capital, happily removed from the teeming crowds of Fleet Street and the City. Winston quotes Thomas Churchyard, writing in 1580 and praising the intellectual culture of London: 'Here dwells the sages of the world and all the Muses nine', and he goes on to mention the Inns for special commendation: they are 'where wit and knowledge flows'.[23] By no means every man of the Inns was 'literary' – translations were popular, and books on horsemanship were not unknown.

Several lawyers from the Inns of Court also contributed to a revolution in historical writing, beginning around 1580.[24] There were five of them: Raleigh, Stow, Camden, Bacon and Selden, who together produced a whole complex of changes in the purpose, content, method and style of historical writing, and especially so in five areas: one, an attack on authority; two, the appeal to experience; three, the rationalisation of utility (pragmatism); four, the extension of the quantitative method, most significantly in the expansion of libraries; and five, the new emphasis on original research, examining consumption and production.[25] In doing this, English history writing was catching up with the writing of French and other European historians.

It is also worth pointing out, given the current climate of opinion, that some plays of the time consisted of commentary on contemporary politics, and in particular the dangers of empire and imperial expansion, which, it was widely feared, would lead to stagnation at home.

The full extent of the intellectual and cultural impact of the Inns may be had from Winston's calculation that, between 1558 and 1642, 'over one hundred major and minor writers were members of an Inn.'[26]

Gresham College

After the Inns of Court, the most important new institution of learning in London, and in England, was Gresham College. Sir Thomas Gresham, who studied briefly at Cambridge and whose father had benefitted from the dissolution of the monasteries, was the financial advisor to Queen Elizabeth and her representative in Amsterdam. He absorbed the advanced commercial arrangements there, ideas which he brought to Britain, becoming the founder of the Royal Exchange, England's first commercial building, which, after its opening by the queen in 1571, was granted the right to sell alcohol and luxury goods, making it the centre of social and financial activity, with apothecaries, barber-surgeons and practitioners of physic (medicine) among the clientele.

Gresham's son had died tragically young, leaving him heartbroken, and when he himself died in 1579, in his will he bequeathed all the revenues from the land and buildings comprising the Royal Exchange, and also his great house in Bishopsgate Street, jointly to the City of London and the Company of Mercers. In return, they were charged with supporting from the revenues of the Royal Exchange seven professors, with generous stipends, who were to be lodged in his mansion house and there to read public lectures in their respective faculties of law, rhetoric, divinity, music, physic, geometry and astronomy. Since Lady Gresham, who was given use of the house until her death, did not die until December 1596, it was not until 1598 that the seven professors were installed in full possession of Sir Thomas's mansion house, now become Gresham College, and commenced the reading of their lectures.

The opening of Gresham College was the culmination of a long effort in Elizabethan England to bring about the establishment of a permanent endowed foundation which would offer instruction and further research in the mathematical sciences in particular and provide a convenient rallying point for all who were concerned with promoting progress in the practical application of these sciences to useful works. Lectureships in medicine had, early in the sixteenth century, been founded at Oxford and Cambridge, and a lectureship in surgery in connection with the Royal College of Physicians had been founded by Baron Lumley in 1583. But for astronomy and geometry, the first enduring recognition came with the creation of those subjects in Gresham's foundation (which also established almshouses for eight poor men).[27] Not until 1619, says Francis Ames-Lewis, were the Savilian professorships of astronomy and geometry established at Oxford, and the early incumbents of these posts were all taken from the men then holding these chairs at Gresham College. The lectures were given in English in the mornings, and in Latin in the afternoons, so that educated visitors from around Europe would be able to attend and understand what was being said.[28]

Some idea of the intellectual networks that existed then can be had from the experience of William Petty, the third Gresham professor of music, who, with John Graunt, a haberdasher, was stimulated by the conversations at Edward Lloyd's coffee house in Lombard Street to develop an interest in mortality statistics and demographics, this being another aspect of mathematics, as music was then. This would eventually lead to the development, in Petty's case, of life insurance and, in Graunt's case, of epidemiology.[29]

Lloyd himself was also interested in what are now called statistics and he would go on to found *Lloyd's List*, the daily newspaper about the shipping industry that flourished all the way down to 2013, and still continues as a quarterly. Although insurance is not often regarded as an aspect of intellectual history, marine and fire insurance, which both became accepted procedures in Elizabethan London, were nonetheless important imaginative innovations.[30]

Other intellectual and imaginative initiatives included the Society of Antiquaries, founded in the mid-1580s by Matthew Parker and William Camden (see below) together with some thirty-five others who petitioned the queen to allow the formation of a society based on the idea of the Italian academies. Their aim was to establish a forum for the study of Britain's history and antiquarian artefacts. No formal petition was ever granted, though Ames-Lewis says meetings were held anyway, usually on Fridays, with Anglo-Saxon literature as the subject for discussion. The society, obviously enough, was a natural outgrowth of Parker's enthusiasm for national monuments and the society's aims stressed the preservation of manuscripts and rare books relating to English history and antiquities. It was closed by James VI and I in 1604 but reopened a decade or so later. Education more generally fell out of fashion under James, especially for women. Bathsua Makin (1600–75), known as England's most learned lady, presented him with a book of poems in six languages, whereupon he is said to have remarked: 'But can she spin?'[31]

Thomas Linacre had died well before, in 1524, but the Royal College of Physicians, which he had helped to found, was still going strong and in 1582 set up the Lumleian lectures on medical matters, which began two years later and would continue into the seventeenth century. This was in fact an era when lectures became relatively common – scientific lectures were given regularly in Leadenhall Chapel, cosmography lectures in Blackfriars, while Deptford was a centre for the study of hydrography and navigation.

THE POLITICAL EDGE TO THEATRE: MAKING GREATNESS FAMILIAR

Shakespeare's tragedies and comedies and histories began in the playhouses of Shoreditch and Southwark, performed by 'rogues and vagabonds' to 'an assembly of tailors, tinkers, cordwainers, sailors, old men, young men, women, boys, girls and such like'. This is Richard Helgerson, again, who also reminds us that the fathers of other playwrights – Chettle, Greene, Kyd, Marlowe, Munday and Peele – were respectively a dyer, a saddler, a scrivener, a shoemaker, a draper and a clerk. More than that, the Burbages, who built the theatre and eventually supplied Shakespeare with his leading actors, had been joiners. Helgerson's point is that the particular social and dramatic configuration of Elizabethan imaginative life changed decisively sometime around 1600.[32] For Richard Burbage, the crucial event was the reopening of the Globe in 1599 and the Fortune in 1600, followed soon after by the emergence of a third company at the Boar's Head and Rose. Then there was the increasing prominence around the turn of the century of a new generation of playwrights, including Jonson, Chapman, Dekker, Marston and Middleton. From 1590 on, what had been essentially a players' theatre was becoming an authors' theatre.[33] What seems to have happened in the late 1580s and early 1590s is a shift in the weight of production and recognition

towards the new non-player writers. Over and above this, and together with printed texts being used increasingly, Marlowe, Nashe,
Greene and their fellow university wits tried to project themselves
out of the 'base company' of theatrical clowns and into the 'orbit' of
gentility.[34] Which meant that the theatre of the day 'was excessively
concerned with status'. Shakespeare was no exception to this.[35]
Indeed, in most Elizabethan literature status is a prime concern.[36]
One might even say that status is never very far away in any early
English literature, and according to the New Historicists – a trend
in scholarship coming on stream relatively recently – Shakespeare's
plays participate in a continuing tradition of radical protest about
status, one that leads from the Peasants' Revolt in the fourteenth
century down to the Sacheverell riots in the eighteenth, directed at
Dissenters and Presbyterians. It has been suggested that, over the
years, there has been an ongoing relation of sorts between popular
revolt and theatre and, certainly, recent New Historicist scholarship
has stressed the political edge of Shakespeare rather than the purely
aesthetic.[37] Some historians have proposed that it is this quality
which defines him as 'the national poet.'

And this may be why, so the theory goes, the clown dominates
much of Elizabethan theatre. Falstaff, says Helgerson, is in part the
clown. 'There is a parallel between the order of the theatre and the
order of the state. The clown ruptures this, as does Falstaff.' While
Shakespeare, on the one hand, tends to legitimate heredity and the
preservation of an aristocratic order, plays put on by other playwrights, like *Sir Thomas Wyatt* (1602) by John Webster and Thomas
Dekker, and the 1599 offering of *Sir John Oldcastle*, written by
Michael Drayton and others, each offer as hero a man of the people
at odds with the Crown. The latter play, apparently, was written specifically to correct Shakespeare. Shakespeare's history plays, as more
than one critic-historian has pointed out, are concerned 'above all'
with the consolidation and maintenance of royal power. Moreover,
we may say that, in a society where even aristocrats had to repeatedly
underline their superior social status by playing at being aristocratic,
it is scarcely surprising that the theatre should become a school for
social advancement and the actor become the very model of 'self-
fashioning mankind' and a more intense Englishness.[38]

Helgerson's verdict is just one among many. But he is exceptionally clear. 'From the 1570s on, the younger Elizabethans had been driven in their writing of England by a sense of national inferiority, or national barbarity. Shakespeare's history plays present, as do none of the other texts, a prominently royal image of England.' In making 'greatness familiar', Shakespeare stood, and still stands, for royal Britain. And in establishing the new genre of the national history play, which contributed so much to the consolidation of central power, it also contributed to the emergence of the playwright – Will Shakespeare himself – as both gentleman and poet.[39] Status again.

The Increasing Coherence of England

A nd not only status. We see here, in the plays – by John Webster, Thomas Dekker and Michael Drayton, rather than Shakespeare – the emergence of an interesting intellectual distinction: that between the monarchy and the nation, which again has been addressed by Richard Helgerson, who sees this view also epitomised in the works of Christopher Saxton, William Camden, Michael Drayton (again) and Edward Coke.

Christopher Saxton (c.1540–c.1610) was a Yorkshireman. He was a cartographer who is remembered as the person who produced the first county maps of England and Wales, which in time led to the first atlas of any country. Map-making became possible through advances in surveying and in printing, especially from engraved copper plates. The atlas – which had a variety of symbols to show buildings and settlements, rivers, hills and mountains (though with no information as to height or exact location) and of course place names – was published in 1579, containing thirty-five maps, each bearing the arms of Elizabeth I and Thomas Sackford, Saxton's patron. He was given a monopoly to sell them for ten years.

There was an appetite for what Saxton was doing because a national history could arise only after its coherence as a territorial entity had been established. With the arrival of territorial coherence, 'the British countryside became a geopolitical unity'.[1]

William Rockett argues that an entirely new enterprise of scholarship was required to define the historical parameters of this new order, and 'the provinces as well as Britain's topographical character were discovered in the endeavour of seeking and explaining the ancient origins of the nation's institutions'. John Leland, one-time librarian to Henry VIII, was the first person in Britain to conceive of a national history incorporating particular provincial localities.[2] His plan was to include histories of the aristocracy and the kings of England, biographies of English authors, descriptions of the adjacent islands and 'a work of historical topography in as many books as there were counties in England and Wales'. Leland's idea was intended as an honour to the king, 'for the recovery of the nation's sovereignty from Roman usurpation'.

Rockett records that Leland inspired a generation of 'journeying scholars' who hoped instead to illustrate the *provincial* origins of some at least of the nation's institutions. Among them were the respective Kentish and Cheshire historians William Lambarde and William Smith, in addition to John Norden, John Speed and Camden. Their comprehensive surveys included Lambarde's unfinished topographical dictionary, Smith's *Particular Description of England*, Speed's *Theatre of the Empire of Great Britain*, Norden's unfinished *Speculum Britanniae* and Camden's *Britannia*.[3]

Camden's manuscripts survive in profusion, in the British Library, the Bodleian, Cambridge, Yale, the Folger Shakespeare Library in Washington, DC, and elsewhere.[4] He studied at Oxford without taking a degree, and later became undermaster and, after 1594, headmaster at Westminster School. He failed to get a fellowship at All Souls because he was opposed there 'by the Popish faction'.[5]

Camden was aware that some Europeans thought Elizabethan England backward in certain respects and, beginning in 1571, he started touring the British provinces in the school holidays and for four years after, whenever his duties at Westminster would permit. On his journeys he recorded his observations of both natural and geographical interest, 'with a good eye for Plinyesque curiosities'.[6] His main purpose, however, was a topographical survey, which also identified the contours of Britain's *political* geography, the idea being that in framing the narrative of *Britannia*, he wanted to find a way to explain Britain's national origins. It was a work of recovery rather than discovery.

The first edition appeared in 1586 and in it he sought to describe his wanderings in a series of tours encompassing all the counties, beginning in the south-west with Cornwall and Devonshire and then moving north. In the course of this he built up a massive collection of documentary and archaeological materials, as well as compiling descriptions of counties which together provided a coherent core of the national past. The result was a clever topographical eye-witness report, rather than a simple calendar or chronicle: the link between local materials and the decisive events of the nation's past was very innovative.

Camden drew attention to the physical remains of the Saxon, Danish and Norman eras as well as the Roman, making imaginative use of coins, inscriptions and works of monumental art found in churches and across the countryside.[7] He grasped that it would be impossible to describe Britain's origins without attempting to recover ancient Celtic and Roman equivalents of the English names with which they had been replaced. For him, ancient place names had a unique importance, representing the earliest traces of British civilisation and Camden went so far as to learn Welsh as well as Old English, and studied ancient texts such as Ptolemy's *Geographia*.[8] He used the Antonine Itineraries (fifteen 'road maps' of Britain compiled in the first and second centuries AD), to correlate ancient and contemporary sites and to identify ruins whose names had been lost.

Britannia opens with a chronological survey of Britain's main historical divisions – British, Roman, Saxon, Danish and Norman; it closes with descriptive surveys of Scotland and Ireland. The best-known part is probably the county tours, which make up the central section. Here, Camden moves from town to town along a course shaped by topographical contours, always keeping a look-out for the remnants of antiquity and using chronicles and other documents and artefacts to explore the history of hamlets, town walls, gates, bridges, churches, castles, parishes and bishops' sees.[9] Within this, Camden organised his fifty-two county itineraries, incorporating the Danmonii – the tours of Cornwall and Devon – proceeding to the Durotriges (Dorsetshire), the Belghae (Somerset, Wiltshire and Hampshire) and so on. The twelve Welsh counties are linked to the Silures, the Dimetae and the Ordovices. Stuart Piggott, the eminent archaeologist, thought that the achievement of *Britannia* was 'to elucidate the ancient British topography in order to enable Britain to take her rightful place at once with the world of antiquity and that of international scholarship'.[10] Before *Britannia* there was no organised antiquarian effort; fifteen years after its publication there were two such bodies, the Society of Antiquaries and the Surrenden Society, together with a network of amateurs collecting across the country.

Wyman Herendeen compares Camden to Spenser and Drayton, as does Helgerson, and this is the central point.[11] Whereas the early maps of *Britannia* had contained the royal coat of arms, suggesting that the land belonged to the Crown, later maps had no such features and in so doing paralleled a characteristic of Michael Drayton's poem *Poly-Olbion*, first published in 1612. This aspect, says Helgerson, in an interpretation that has been contested, but which remains very persuasive, is that in *Poly-Olbion*, thirty songs written in Alexandrine couplets, instead of elaborate coats of arms we find, as Drayton himself puts it, 'every mountain, forest, river and valley, expressing in their sundry postures their loves, delights, and natural situations'.[12] In other words, Drayton's Britain is 'peopled' by its natural and man-made landmarks. 'Its streams are nymphs, its hills shepherds, its differing regions rival choirs. *Its only crowns are worn by towns and natural sites.*' (Italics added.) Moreover, Drayton's frontispiece is an allegorical personification of Great Britain, 'a goddess-like woman dressed in a map'.

What Helgerson is getting at here, and it chimes with what was happening in the theatre, is that chorography was a threat to the Crown. For fifteen years the Society of Antiquaries met as a private organisation, independent of any official authority, to read papers on English institutions, customs and topography. But when its members presented a petition to the queen requesting formal recognition, they were refused. The maps and map-making, Helgerson maintains, had marginalised the Crown and in so doing impugned royal authority. Quite bluntly, he says: 'Chorography had become a dangerous political activity.'[13] Traditionally, to be loyal to England was to be loyal to the monarch but the chorographers presented a very different image. 'To them England is Devonshire, Stafford and York, Cripplegate Ward and St Michael's Mount.'[14] Loyalty here means *loyalty to the land*, its counties, villages and towns. 'Even to its uninhabited geo-graphical features.' Still other maps included the coats of arms of the inhabitants – 295 of them for the county of Dorset, for example.[15] Local particularity, Helgerson insists, represents resistance to royal encroachment.

The very title, *Poly-Olbion* ('Many Albions'), represents the multiplicity of Drayton's idea. In keeping with this attachment, *Poly-Olbion* described many claims to sovereignty. 'The Dart, the Parret, the Severn, the Lug, the Thames, the Trent, the Humber and the Teis, Dean Forest, Malvern Hill, the Vale of Evesham and the Isle of Man are all called king or queen.'[16] But none exercises rule beyond a narrow region. *Poly-Olbion* recognises we are all part of two communities, the local and the national.

Helgerson's argument is that the whole business of chorography, from Saxton to Camden and Drayton, is to make the land visible and in so doing to explain and describe what, exactly, England *is*. Just as Spenser, in *The Faerie Queene* and his other work, was at pains to show what the English language could do, and in praising the monarch place the language in effect and by implication above her, so the chorographers were identifying the exact limits of the land and in so doing showing that the British people, the detailed extent of the land and its history, were also more – much more – than the Crown.

Nowhere near as well known today as William Camden, or Edmund Spenser, still less William Shakespeare (there exist after all to this day a Camden Society, a Spenser Society and a Shakespeare Society), is Edward Coke (1552–1634). Yet his list of accomplishments is no less impressive and intimately affects our lives even today. The son and grandson of prosperous barristers, he was educated at Norwich Free Grammar School and then Trinity College, Cambridge, though, like so many others, he left without taking a degree. He went on to Clifford's Inn, one of the Inns of Chancery, to study law. He was called to the bar in April 1578.

Through his Norfolk connections he became associated with the Howard family, the family of the Dukes of Norfolk and Earls of Arundel, Arundel being invested with what was called a 'liberty', meaning that he was empowered to install his own officials, run his own prison and administer justice. Coke made the most of these connections to acquire a roster of important and high-profile cases. This well-connected success at the bar soon led him into Parliament and, in June 1592, at the relatively young age of forty, he became Solicitor General, and not long after that Speaker of the House of Commons. This all added to his glitter. He was a notoriously difficult man, but his abilities were plain for all to see. An added level of opportunity and difficulty came from his high-level contacts with the Cecil family. While their influence helped him land the position of Attorney General, the Cecils were political rivals of Robert Devereux, the 2nd Earl of Essex, the queen's one-time favourite who in 1601 attempted a *coup d'état* against the Crown and was beheaded for treason. Before that, however, in the early 1590s, Essex and the Cecils struggled ceaselessly for the queen's approval, during which Essex had his own candidate for Attorney General: Francis Bacon. Bacon and Coke would become fiery rivals in the years ahead but in this case of the Attorney General Coke won hands down. The queen dismissed Essex with the salty comment that 'even Bacon's uncle [Lord Burghley] thought Bacon the second-best candidate'.

Coke had many fiery exchanges in and out of Parliament, and always championed Parliament over the Crown. And this is what links him to Saxton, Camden and Drayton: his masterpiece, *The Institutes of the Lawes of England*, confirms that the monarch is subject to the laws of the land. Coke's purpose in these four volumes was to provide a coherent alternative to Roman law and replace it with English common law. The most important was the first part, entitled *Commentary upon Litleton*, copies of which were famously exported to the United States early in the colonial era.[17] It has been criticised on several grounds, for 'repulsive pedantry' and 'overbearing assertions' as well as inaccuracies, but no one doubts that the jurisprudence contained in the *Institutes* has been very influential. Coke's central thesis is that the judges of the common law are most suited to making law, followed by Parliament, and it ensues from this that *the monarch was not exempt*; he or she was bound to follow any legal rules. Whereas Roman law, used on most of the European continent, was based on *a priori* reasoning and principles, for Coke the attraction of his argument was that judges 'would bathe themselves in law', vastly more so than other people, and this familiarity would lead to 'a sensible set of judgments and principles'. His point was that the judges' intimacy with the historical list of precedent would over time ensure that the law would be predictable and certain, so that abuses would be avoided. For Coke, the law owed nothing to God and was nothing more than a contract between the people.

Not everyone was convinced. Thomas Hobbes argued that lawyers had no special skills above anyone else and that the law should be understood through the king's instructions. For him the job of judges was to 'validate' what the king said.

Coke's ideas and arguments went some way to creating contract law and establishing judicial independence. Educated foreigners thought that Coke's *Institutes* were 'barbarous' but it cannot be denied that, despite their narrow and uncompromising arguments, Coke built a coherent defence of English liberties, which ultimately protected the people from the encroachment of royal absolutism, then so prevalent across the rest of Europe. It was in the *Institutes* that Coke used the famous phrase that a house of an Englishman 'is as a castle'.

And this is the point of considering the works of Saxton, Camden, Drayton and Coke together. They can be seen as the very first changes in thought – independent of each other though they were, in different areas, but linked conceptually – about the relationship between the monarchy and the country that would lead towards the circumstances that would bring revolution and civil war into view.

London's Literacies Lead
England's 'Gathering Greatness'

Outside these more formal institutions and entities, however, the whole urban imagination of Elizabethan England – London in particular – was far more intellectually minded than had occurred before or it is usually given credit for. Deborah E. Harkness has described this evolving world in detail.[1]

The scientific revolution, and the Royal Society, were still some way off (though Gresham College was one of the precursors to the Royal Society). Yet, in Elizabeth's London, ordinary Londoners, native and foreign-born, engaged in collaboration and competition of 'natural knowledge' which, Harkness says, had an urban, rather than a 'gentlemanly' sensibility, which would so mark the early Royal Society. She makes it seem inevitable that the 'densely overlapping obligations, ties and community affiliations' of London could not but lead to what we now call science.[2] There were three important features of this sensibility.

'First, men and women living in the city expected that their work would be publicly known even if it were not published formally, because it would be studied and evaluated by other Londoners, especially those involved in similar occupations or trades.' Harkness identifies this as the proto-public sphere. For example, trade associations, such as the Grocers' Company or the Barber-Surgeons' Company, were very keen to be involved in overseeing the quality of goods together with the services provided by their members. They took care to police any individuals outside the company who might sabotage their honour or privileges.[3] The urban sensibility also encouraged a belief that there was such a thing as expertise, and that it should be recognised and 'exploited to benefit particular individuals and the city as a whole'. There was a multitude of experts in London – from ale makers to zookeepers, as Harkness puts it – who could provide specialist assistance. Finally, the density factor also made it clear that work done in collaboration with others 'was both necessary and desirable'.

Harkness's main argument is that the urban sensibility was an ideal environment for new ideas about the natural world to surface, and she identifies 'hundreds' of men and women of 'all nationalities' who were involved 'in the work of science, medicine and technology in London'. Among those is the barber-surgeon George Baker, who 'extracted teeth, set bones and performed surgical procedures in his shop at the gates of the Royal Exchange'. The Antwerp native Lieven Alaertes and Londoner Thomasina Scarlet 'established lucrative medical practices in the city', specialising in obstetrical and gynaecological complaints, 'despite the best efforts of London's College of Physicians to force women out of the medical market'. One of the queen's personal doctors, the Portuguese Roderigo López, was famous long before accusations that he had tried to poison her made him notorious, part of his celebrity stemming from the fact that he saw patients 'accompanied by an entourage of African servants'.[4]

Harkness does admit that there were few scientific breakthroughs in Elizabethan times. Instead, the significance of such figures lay in the *organisation* of their communities, the way they settled disputes, and, perhaps most of all, 'the value they placed on the acquisition of various literacies (including mathematical, technological and instrumental literacies)'. The point of these literacies, for her, was that they led to an increasingly 'hands-on' exploration of the natural world: Elizabethan London created a great mass of practically minded technicians. And she identifies one particular area which illustrates her point. This was the 'downtown neighborhood of Lime Street', where Dutch, French, Flemish and English naturalists – including botanists, apothecaries and entomologists – were all located.[5]

Thomas Penny, physician and entomologist, assembled a 'dried garden', *hortus siccus*, with plant specimens kept between sheets of paper. Gardens in town often doubled as laboratories for flowers and insects. Ortelius, the Flemish cartographer, was notably jealous of his nephew John Coles's garden. Coles and Ortelius, Harkness tells us, also collected fossils. 'Coles actually believed that shell-marks in stone were made by animals that had once inhabited the earth and had died out.'[6] She notes there was an early concept of genetics in Lime Street when it was noted that plants of one colour gave rise to 'offspring' of different hues.[7]

Every Elizabethan neighbourhood boasted an apothecary, bonesetter, physician, surgeon, midwife, herb woman, urologist and cataract specialist, often grouped around the parish church.[8] Harkness tells us: that an alewife by the Smithfield Bars sold purging medicines and administered pregnancy tests; that a barber-surgeon's son-in-law, Richard Hottoffee, specialised in head wounds at the King's Head and Castle pub in New Fish Street; that one Alice Skeres was renowned for her cough treatments; that people consulted Matthew Desilar, a French silk weaver, for 'heart pain'.[9] There was plenty of argument over the effectiveness of medicines, and this is Harkness's point: the arguments used empirical data as much as possible – this was a new approach.[10]

The Royal Exchange was another bustling area of the urban mentality. There, mathematical instruments – astrolabes, quadrants, astronomers' staffs – could be found in abundance. Certain neighbourhoods also specialised in instruments: St Botolph Aldgate in compasses; St Margaret Westminster in clocks; St Paul's in engravers. In Blackfriars they crafted scales to weigh merchandise. Instruments then were like laptops today, Harkness says, with a dazzling array of products available.[11] London was the centre of what she calls vernacular maths. This reflected a demand in the London of that time for mathematical literacy, because problems were increasingly being approached by calculation rather than trial and error.[12] The year 1596 saw the publication of a record number of maths books, and Harkness provides a list of Elizabethan mathematical authors.[13] John Dee, who we shall meet more fully in a later chapter, was probably England's most famous maths philosopher. He regarded 'things mathematical' as lying somewhere between the natural and the supernatural.[14] And mathematical literacy took a turn for the better in 1588 when the Cambridge-trained physician Thomas Hood became the first public lecturer in the subject. Because of the imminent problems with the Spanish Armada, many of those who attended his lectures were military men.[15]

At the beginning of Elizabeth's reign, experience alone had formed the basis of navigational skill, with pilots never varying the trade routes they had always followed and which they had known since they were young apprentices. By the end of the reign, voyages of exploration had reached Asia and the Arctic (see Chapters 5 and 10), and the initial disasters and losses had diminished as, over the years, new technologies using the new maths and astronomy were introduced. The impetus to innovate derived very often from abroad and the sense that England needed to keep abreast of its continental rivals (even women were allowed to register patents at this time, so keen were people to make improvements). Traditional navigational methods meant that a pilot had to be familiar with his route if he was to arrive safely. But for merchants to expand their profits and pay off investors, those merchants needed access to new markets in Asia and elsewhere, areas controlled by the Spanish and Portuguese. New routes could only be accessed by exploration of uncharted waters.[16]

Spanish navigational knowledge arrived in England via Stephen Boroughs, who, in 1560, returned after working for a time at the *Casa de contratación* in Seville, and he grasped clearly the need for England to catch up with continental developments. He had with him a Spanish manual, which was translated as *The Arte of Navigation* (1561), making it the first English-language navigation book. It included sections on new instruments, and highlighted the importance of mathematical techniques. Later, in 1588, Anthony Ashley's *Mirror of the Sea* was published, it being a translation of a Dutch manual by Lucas Janszoon Waghenaer. Commissioned by the Privy Council on behalf of the Lord High Admiral, Lord Howard of Effingham, it incorporated the new Dutch sea charts of western Europe, the North Sea and the Baltic, the most accurate ever produced. Most significant of all, says Harkness, was the acceptance in the 1590s of Gerard Mercator's thirty-year-old method allowing for the curvature of the seas, 'marking the beginning of the end of the old system of plain charts'.

PLAT THE POLYMATH

In among all this excitement of new literacies, a lesser-known figure emerges who, says Harkness, compares and contrasts with Francis Bacon. This is Hugh Plat (1553–1608). A graduate of both Cambridge and Lincoln's Inn, he was certainly a bit of a polymath, his interests ranging from agriculture and horticulture to metallurgy. He wrote ten books but the crucial thing about them is that they were based on what we would now call personal research, Plat using the word 'experiment' and taking detailed notes of his horticultural and agricultural investigations, in which he carefully assessed the credibility of witnesses, and talked to those who had observed phenomena where he himself was not present. Plat described such things as the brewing of beer without hops, and the preservation of food in hot weather and at sea.

Harkness's central point about Plat, however, is that he wrote about experimentation *before* Bacon; in fact he experimented on himself, testing an ointment that might be good for his knee, and testing another oil on his eye, which was inflamed (he tested this on his family as well). Plat did not go unrecognised: he was to earn a knighthood from James I.[17]

Despite there being a woman on the throne, Oxford and Cambridge remained resolutely closed to women. In fact, in 1561 Elizabeth banned even wives or other female family members from attending within the college precincts, in order to prevent them from 'distracting' those engaged in academic study. This was, nonetheless, the beginning of Oxbridge's return to pre-eminence, with the numbers of students in the Elizabethan years rising to nearly double those earlier in the sixteenth century. New colleges were founded: Jesus at Oxford in 1571, Emmanuel and Sidney Sussex at Cambridge in 1584 and 1596, while improvements in cataloguing produced Thomas James's monumental *Ecloga Oxonio-Cantabrigiensis* (a collection of manuscript catalogues in Oxford and Cambridge colleges) in 1600.

This may be put alongside the fact that a growing number of students left without taking a degree: roughly half the student body attended because 'it was fashionable to do so'.

The universities were also vital in the perpetuation of another characteristic of the age: the Latin culture of Elizabethan England. Latinate learning was by no means new but, as James Binns points out, the 'Elizabethan years witnessed a flowering of English Latinity that marked the culmination of centuries of learned endeavour. Inspired by the humanist movement, England's Latin writers consciously emulated a fluid, classical style, moving away from the drier style that had lingered.'[18]

Nearly all the important debates among learned men within England were conducted in Latin. Within these Latin intellectual circles, a topic of enduring aesthetic interest was the issue of Ciceronianism. So-called golden-age Latin was increasingly taken up as the most preferable form of prose, one effect (which sounds strange to us) being that writers would never use words that had not existed in the first century BC. Many guides were published during Elizabeth's reign to encourage the writing of elegant Latin, one of the best being Gabriel Harvey's *Ciceronianus*, published in 1577, where he is at pains to show that, although Cicero was the best Latin writer, there was no shortage of others equally eminent, mentioning Caesar, Livy, Sallust, Pliny and Virgil, but going on to make the point that modern scholars were not less eminent, in particular Ramus, Erasmus and the German Johann Thomas Freigius. As a result, Latin in the Elizabethan years developed into a fluid and graceful style 'that was commonly preferred over classic Cicero'.[19]

Besides the attractions of style, Latin had two other advantages. Its greater vocabulary and more developed syntax made it the language of choice for serious scholarly writing on any topic; and second, it enabled English scholars to join in European intellectual circles. One in every ten works published in Elizabeth's England was in Latin. Elizabeth's reign also saw more than 170 English translations of ancient Greek and Latin classics, 'making the old learning accessible to anyone who wanted it'.[20] This was, in fact, the great age of classical translations. Translation was considered so necessary to a proper, classical education that it became a literary art in its own right.

Bacon to Milton: Science, Equal
Qualities and the Causes of Quarrel

F rancis Bacon (1561–1626) was fairly unsuccessful while both
    Edward Coke and Queen Elizabeth were alive, as we have
    seen, but that changed on the accession of James I (and James
VI of Scotland) to the throne of England in 1603. Intellectually,
Bacon was an intermediary figure in the sense that he lived his entire
life between the publication of Copernicus's *De Revolutionibus* and
Newton's *Principia Mathematica*. But he was not intermediate in
any other sense: he was a radical thinker who used the scientific findings of his own day to move philosophy forward to accommodate the
recent discoveries, and in so doing anticipated much of the world that
Newton would finally identify. He was also a member of perhaps the
greatest generation of English people ever to have existed.

Bacon, like Coke, was born into a well-connected family – Bacon's
father was Lord Keeper of the Seal, charged with the physical protection of the Great Seal, used to certify royal documents, while his
mother, Anne, was daughter of a one-time tutor to the royal family.
She was extremely well educated herself, being fluent in Greek, Latin,
French and Italian, and a great letter writer and translator. Bacon
was educated at the family home in Hertfordshire before going on
to Trinity College, Cambridge at the age of twelve. Like Coke he
then read for the law, in his case at Gray's Inn. He also served in the
diplomatic corps in France.

Under James he made steady progress, to king's counsel, Solicitor General, Attorney General, a member of the Privy Council, Lord Keeper of the Seal (like his father before him) and, in 1617, Lord Chancellor, a cabinet office responsible for the functioning and in-dependence of the courts. But in 1621 he was charged with bribery, something he never denied, though it was normal practice for the time to accept gifts in return for some favour. He spent four days in the Tower, which seems to suggest his offence was not serious, but he felt it a disgrace and never held public office again. He devoted the remainder of his life to working on what had become a lifelong project: the reform of learning and the establishment of a society dedicated to the discovery of experimental scientific knowledge that would be *useful*. He wrote histories and essays where the 'mathemat-ical plainness' of his style was a major component of their attraction, and he criticised the vogue for Ciceronianism merely for the sake of it. Dr Johnson said that 'a dictionary of the English language might be compiled from Bacon's works'.

Of his many works the two that stand out are *The New Atlantis* and *The Great Instauration*. The former is a utopian-philosophical novel in the manner of Plato and Thomas More, describing an island with a central organised research facility (as we would say) where specially trained investigators collect data, conduct experiments, and (most importantly from Bacon's point of view) apply the results to produce 'things of use and practice for man's life'. He was especially set against the form of knowledge practised by the scholastics, split-ting hairs over increasingly recondite subjects, and also, to an extent, the humanists' dogged interest in ancient knowledge and wisdom, rather than new ideas and discoveries.

Socrates had equated knowledge with virtue but for Bacon, a man of the world as well as a philosopher, it was to be associated with power – he had a very practical view of knowledge, and this in itself changed beliefs about and attitudes to philosophy. For Bacon, the practice of science became an almost religious obligation and, since his view was that history is not cyclical but progressive (an important innovation), he looked forward to a new, scientific civilisation. This was his concept of 'The Great Instauration' or Great Renovation, 'a total reconstruction of the sciences, arts, and all human knowledge, raised upon the proper foundations'. Bacon shared the view of many contemporaries that knowledge could only be built up by the observation of nature (rather than through intuition or 'revealed' knowledge), starting from concrete data rather than abstractions that had just occurred to someone.

Bacon was convinced that the understanding of the High Middle Ages and of the Renaissance – that the study of nature would reveal God, by disclosing the parallels between man's mind and God's – was wrong. Matters of faith, he felt, were appropriate to theology but matters of nature were different, with their own set of rules. Bacon's view had a major influence on the fledgling Royal Society.

The second part of *The Great Instauration* was entitled 'The New Organon'. In it he examined some of the ways human beings obfuscate their thinking (we limit our knowledge to the immediate world around us and are too ready to generalise from there; we get too attached to theories which appeal to us, despite contravening evidence). And then there was his notion of 'induction', that thought proceeds – or should proceed – by abstracting from a few examples the underlining principle or similarity, which should then be tested by experience. This was a very influential view, with luminaries across Europe like Leibniz, Diderot and Voltaire lauding him, though others – Spinoza, Hegel and more recent theorists – have suggested he was a colossus with feet of clay.

Bacon was very imaginative. Sarah Irving has shown, for instance, that he understood very early that science and empire would be linked intimately, believing that it would reflect God's will if man exerted his influence over as much of the world as possible.[1] He also had a lot of fingers in a lot of pies, so that wherever you turn in Jacobean society you stumble against him. For example, Thomas Hobbes – who we shall come to – served as Bacon's secretary for a couple of years. William Harvey, who discovered the circulation of the blood (see below, this chapter), was his physician, at least for a time (they didn't get on). One of the strangest links is that between Bacon and Shakespeare (they were almost exact contemporaries), which has teased historians for generations, where some think that Bacon actually had a hand in the Bard's plays.

The latest Shakespeare scholarship, however, concentrates on two more substantial matters. First, there has been a concerted effort – given the influence of the so-called New Historicism – to situate Shakespeare more firmly and more specifically within his time. That is, while conceding that Shakespeare was a genius, 'a man for all time', as Ben Jonson was to say, recent historians have taken it upon themselves to show that Shakespeare's plays respond – increasingly clearly – to the contemporary issues of his day. A good example is *Henry VIII*, a play produced in 1613, well into the Jacobean era, in which Shakespeare collaborated with John Fletcher, a prolific playwright whose reputation matched Shakespeare's in their day. In the play, the author(s) specifically emphasise the king's authority in such a manner as to please the king himself. This is shown in small details, which also reveal that Shakespeare was familiar with the royal Court. At one point in the play, one male character – a gentleman – remarks to another that he

> must no more call it York Place, that's past;
> For since the cardinal's fall, that title's lost;
> 'Tis now the king's, and called Whitehall.[2]

In particular, says Mark Rankin, *Henry VIII* specifically displays Henry's success in overcoming the factions at Court and controlling policy. The central political context of the play is the fact of James's belief in the divine foundation of his monarchy.[3] Into this, the play shows us a historically conservative faction of nobles around Henry. The faction is led by Thomas Howard (the Duke of Norfolk) and his son, the Earl of Surrey (the father of the poet). The main purpose of the faction is to counsel the king against the advice of Cardinal Wolsey. In the conclusion to the plot, the dialogue frequently highlights how Henry comes to 'know' or 'love' himself. This 'assertive version' of Henry, Rankin says, 'is calculated to impress James, whose own writings insist that the dynastic example of his Tudor predecessors be understood properly'. Wolsey's fall is a result of factional manoeuvring but the central argument of the plot is always a positive reflection of the king's ability to successfully manage the outcome of events.[4] Behind it all, of course, was the continuing debate about the legitimation of English Protestant orthodoxy.[5]

The second aspect of modern Shakespeare scholarship concerns the Bard's contemporaries. In fact, 'Shakespeare's Contemporaries' is a course taught across many universities now and even the Royal Shakespeare Company includes a section on Shakespeare's contemporaries on its website.[6] All this highlights, as Patrick Murray puts it, that the theatrical milieu of that time included the 'prodigious talents' of Christopher Marlowe, Thomas Kyd, John Webster, Thomas Middleton and John Ford, producing a more mature and nuanced view of early modern drama, in which collaboration and competition are elements in the mix.[7] In particular, theatre historians have drawn attention to Middleton as 'our other Shakespeare',[8] not to mention the so-called University Wits (John Lyly, Thomas Lodge, George Peele, Robert Greene, Marlowe and Thomas Nash).[9] Marlowe, for example, is said to have provided the most significant non-Shakespearean figures in the theatre, in plays such as *Doctor Faustus, Tamburlaine* and *The Jew of Malta*, which 'tackle head on' the three central elements of sex, religion and death.[10]

THE POETS' WAR

Still on the subject of Shakespeare's contemporaries, and what they reveal about the Jacobean world, we may briefly consider the 'poets' war'.[11] For two years, between the autumn of 1599 and the autumn of 1601, a small group of English writers fought a more or less vicious conflict in London's public and private theatres.[12] 'While the war may not have lasted long or involved many soldiers it is historically important, the first record of these writers' mutual commentary and criticism.'[13]

This Shakespeare is a figure more culturally embedded than many readers will be used to imagining. Besides him, the war involved Ben Jonson, John Marston and Thomas Dekker, though the main protagonists were Jonson and Shakespeare, and the main thrust is that a series of plays produced close to one another should be seen as argument and response, a reflection of the fact that Jonson and Shakespeare in particular were both friends and rivals, and that Jonson, who could be generous (calling Shakespeare a man for all time), could also be very aggressive and full of himself. At the heart of the dispute was Jonson's feeling that Shakespeare's comedy is too comic and not biting enough.

In specific opposition to Shakespeare, 'Jonson designed comical satire to displace romantic comedy'. The central point is that the images of 'a slow, learned Jonson and a quick-witted Shakespeare' were ultimately derived from their own criticism of each other in the poets' war.[14]

These moves and countermoves produced a Jonson as a figure of judgement and a Shakespeare as a figure of 'open-ended subjectivity'. James Bednarz concludes therefore, as have others in the New Historicist school, that Shakespeare is to be understood not as a remote creator, synonymous with theatre itself, but as an engaged partisan. This was, Bednarz notes, a decisive moment in the contest that sees Shakespeare and Jonson as mighty opposites 'upon whose antagonism our conception of literature depends'.[15]

Jonson, born eight years after Shakespeare in 1572, lived much longer, well into the reign of James's son Charles, dying in 1637. Well educated in the classics, well read and cultured, his father was a Protestant landowner who had suffered at the hands of 'Bloody Mary'. He didn't lose his life, but he did lose his lands, and was imprisoned, only being freed on Elizabeth's accession, after which he joined the church. He died a month before Ben was born. Despite the late turn in his father's life to the Protestant Church, Jonson converted to Catholicism in 1598, meaning that some of his early plays were accused of 'popery'.

Jonson also had a more exuberant personality than Shakespeare, and was never one to avoid a fight, either in politics, his personal life, or more generally speaking intellectually. Part of his education took place at Westminster School, where one of his teachers was William Camden. His intention to go to Cambridge was stymied by his stepfather, who insisted he follow in his footsteps and become a bricklayer. This not being quite what he wanted for himself, Jonson soon escaped to the Netherlands, volunteering as a soldier.[16]

Returning to England he found work as an actor (not a very good one, according to some). One of his early performances was as Geronimo in *The Spanish Tragedy* (c.1586) by Thomas Kyd, generally held to be the first revenge tragedy in English literature.

(Revenge tragedies – not formally named as such until the early twentieth century – were popular dramas driven by an excitement that everyone could understand as motivation and, because there was a lot of action, more often than not ending in death all around.)

By 1597, Jonson could call himself a playwright, working for Philip Henslowe, the best-known theatrical producer of the day, and a year later he delivered his first offering, *Every Man in His Humour*, where, we are told, Shakespeare was in the cast. *Every Man* did well, Jonson thereafter being referred to as the father of English comedy. His riotous exuberance never went away, however, and in 1597 he was jailed in Marshalsea prison on account of a play he composed together with Thomas Nashe, called *The Isle of Dogs*, which was banned for its seditious nature. The very next year Jonson was in prison again, after killing a fellow actor in a duel. Jonson never went for long without being sent to jail, often because of this or that disrespectful topical allusion in his plays and, we are told, he was a bit player in the Gunpowder Plot of 1605.

On the accession to the throne of James VI and I, who was himself a poet and a writer of scriptural exegeses and political and theological treatises, Jonson adroitly adapted to the particular form of theatre that was the new king's taste: the masque. Jonson would eventually conceive around a score and more masques. This genre, now extinct, was an amalgam of words, music and dancing, put together as spectacle. These were sufficiently popular for Jonson to be awarded a pension in 1616, the year Shakespeare died, so he must have been leading a more settled life.[17]

In 1618, Jonson set out to walk to Scotland. Not much has been known about this extraordinary venture but a few years ago an account of it was found by literary sleuths and the whole journey recreated. Even in this, it seems, his egoism was to the fore, for he anticipated receiving 'the enthusiastic and lavish reception that was everywhere lauded on him'. It took him ten weeks to get to Edinburgh and when he arrived there, he lodged with John Stuart, a cousin of the king, which would seem to confirm that he was now not quite the rumbustious outcast he hitherto had been. He also lodged with William Drummond of Hawthornden, who was Scotland's premier poet at the time. Drummond remarked dryly later that Jonson was 'a great lover and praiser of himself, a contemner and scorner of others', so perhaps not that much had changed.

Jonson's classical learning runs through his poetry, and his translations from Greek or Roman classics. Best known is *The Forest*, an imaginative collection where in one poem, for example, drinking is employed as a metaphor for love, and in another a lover 'sends his beloved a garland of roses, which are returned smelling of her'.[18] One is never sure when and where he has his tongue in his cheek.

As a poet, Jonson was compared and contrasted with John Donne. Whereas Jonson represents the swagger of poetry, its grace and clarity of expression, Donne, in contrast, represents the so-called metaphysical school of poetry, with its reliance on strained, twisted metaphors and sometimes indeterminate phrasing.

Like Jonson, Donne (1572–1631) was rather more than a poet. Equally well educated, he was a soldier, a member of Parliament, and dean of St Paul's Cathedral from 1621 until his death. He was of Welsh descent on his father's side, and his mother was a great-niece of Thomas More. Educated, from the age of eleven, at both Oxford and Cambridge, he was unable to graduate on account of his recusant Roman Catholic beliefs (his religion prevented him from taking the Oath of Supremacy). In 1592, at the age of nineteen or twenty, like Coke and Bacon he was admitted to Lincoln's Inn. Later, in 1596, he fought in skirmishes against the Spanish, alongside the Earl of Essex and Sir Walter Raleigh, at Cadiz. As a result, Donne was appointed chief secretary to the Lord Keeper of the Great Seal, Sir Thomas Egerton.

His poetry was notable for its eroticism and, as Albert Smith says, 'eroticism seems to have been important to him'. In 1601 he secretly married Anne More, an act which, upon discovery, destroyed his prospects at Court, and brought about his imprisonment in Fleet jail. He wasn't in prison long but was estranged from his father-in-law until 1609, and only then was he able to receive Anne's dowry. Not that he was then leading the sort of life he had led before: he and Anne lived peaceably in Surrey, with Anne giving birth to twelve children in sixteen years of marriage.[19]

In 1602, Donne was elected to Parliament, but it was

unremunerated. Success began to come in 1610 and 1611, when he composed two anti-Catholic works, *Pseudo-Martyr* and *Ignatius His Conclave*, the second of which satirised the Jesuits. These works pleased the king, but he refused to reinstate Donne at Court, recommending instead that he 'prove' his conversion was sincere by taking holy orders. Donne followed the king's advice, was awarded an honorary doctorate in divinity from Cambridge in 1615 and became royal chaplain. Before too long, he was appointed dean of St Paul's. As well as being properly remunerated, this was a high-profile position, which he occupied until his death in 1631.

Donne was also like Jonson in that he had decided views about the layered nature of English society, the corruption in the legal system, what he saw as the weak level of its literary figures, and in particular the capital's 'pompous courtiers'. His poetry is highly satirical about a community 'populated by fools and knaves', combined with an intensity that plumbs the paradoxes of faith.[20] In aesthetic terms, Donne often uses extended and even complicated metaphors, to conjoin quite different ideas, ideas that most people do not see as in any way linked. For Donne this heterogeneity is part of the point, but this can and does bring about a notorious ambiguity for which his work is famous.

As a result of this approach, which is by no means to everyone's taste, Donne's reputation has gone through more twists and turns than that of any other major figure in English literature. During Donne's own lifetime his poetry was treasured within a small circle of admirers, who read it in manuscript, while later on he became well known as a preacher. Immediately after his death, his works were printed and had a powerful following, but at the Restoration his writing went out of fashion and taste remained unchanged for several centuries. Only at the end of the nineteenth century did his poetry find a new audience among the avant-garde.

So it is clear that Donne is not for everyone. In his biography, Izaak Walton argued that Donne changed after he was appointed to St Paul's, that that was the making of him. A new biography by Katherine Rundell, published in 2022 to much acclaim, argued that he can only be appreciated properly if the sonic qualities of his work are assimilated, that he himself was a great actor and orator, hence his success as a preacher: his poetry needs to be read aloud to properly make its mark.[21] For many readers, Donne is still what Ben Jonson said of him: 'the first poet in the world in some things'. There is an exhilarating unpredictability about Donne's world 'in which wariness and quick wits are at a premium'.

Donne's world is constantly changing, made up of brief moments which we must grasp and try to make the most of. His love poetry is no different.[22] In one case he shows how two people can remain as one while they are separated. They must find images to preserve their unity: 'Like gold to airy thinness beat'. Or this, where he imagines the twin legs of compasses, one that circles, the other that remains rooted to its spot:

> Such will thou be to me, who must
> Like th' other foot obliquely run;
> Thy firmness makes my circle just,
> And makes me end, where I begun.

He never wrote for publication – fewer than eight complete poems were published while he was alive. When he took holy orders, he worried that his duties would be too much for him. But his celebrity as a preacher was such that the king came to hear him, or he was called to Court, and no fewer than 160 of his sermons have survived.

The English Civil War (1642–5) – as might be expected – impacted directly on the lives of English intellectuals, in particular on John Milton, Thomas Hobbes and William Harvey. Milton worked in the service of the Puritan and Parliamentarian cause, Harvey as physician to the king, attending to the monarch and his forces in Oxford, though he was also attacked by a mob of citizen-soldiers, while Hobbes fled into exile in Paris.

The first man to make the most of the scientific revolution in politics was Thomas Hobbes (1588–1678), the son of a vicar in Malmesbury, Wiltshire, in the west of England. Hobbes was never a fellow of the Royal Society, as John Locke was, but he did send in scientific papers to the society, and he carried out his own experiments in physiology and mathematics.[23] (His friend John Aubrey, in his famous book *Brief Lives*, described Hobbes as being 'in love with geometry'.) Hobbes acted as assistant to Robert Boyle and amanuensis to Francis Bacon and met both Galileo and Descartes. He had an entirely materialistic view of the world, and developed the important doctrine of causality, the idea that the world is 'an endless chain of cause and effect'.

Hobbes produced his works in the immediate aftermath of the English Civil War. Like Machiavelli, he assumed that men are reasonable and yet predatory, and he built a case for the absolute authority of the sovereign. Hobbes, however, considered that a sovereign could be either a monarch or an assembly (though he preferred the former), and he placed the ecclesiastical power firmly *under* the secular power. *Leviathan* (the biblical monster, 'which alone retained the wolf-like potential of man's primeval condition') is one of the great books of political theory and contains the most comprehensive description of Hobbes's ideas, though he wrote several other books in which he reveals just what a heavy price he is willing to pay for order.

Leviathan was published in 1651. In it, Hobbes was dogmatic, didactic, dogged. He insisted that Oxford and Cambridge were producing too many clergymen, with not enough positions for them, making them 'alienated intellectuals' whose frustration would become an 'acid' which, he forecast, would play a role in revolution.[24] His attempt to be 'scientific' is everywhere apparent. Underneath it all, he believed that truth is just as discoverable in politics as it is in physics, biology or astronomy: 'The skill of making and maintaining Common Wealths consists in Certain Rules, as doth Arithmetique and Geometry; not (as Tennis play) in practice only ...' Hobbes argues openly that the state is a mere artificial contrivance for furthering the interests of the individuals who comprise it. He denies the Aristotelian belief that man is a social animal and argues that no society exists before the 'covenant of submission'. Instead, he begins with the axiom that the natural condition of man is war. In the first part, on human knowledge and psychology, his survey of what was known at the time leads him to conclude (controversially enough, then) that nature has made men 'so equal in faculties of body and mind' that, 'when all is reckoned together, the difference

between man and man is not so considerable as to prevent competition between them ... So that in the nature of man we find three
principall causes of quarrel. First, Competition; secondly, Diffidence
[by which Hobbes meant fear]; thirdly, Glory.' The consequences of
this are not good. Life, he famously remarked, is 'solitary, poore,
nasty, brutish, and short'.[25]

For Hobbes this means that, to avoid this primitive condition
of perpetual war, men must submit to a common authority. Since
the main law of nature is self-preservation, it follows that men are
obliged to 'conferre all their power and strength upon one man, or
upon one assembly of men that they may reduce all their wills ... to
one will'. This is what he means by the great Leviathan, a form of
mortal God (as he put it) who alone has the power to enforce contracts and obligations. For Hobbes this contract is supreme.

Hobbes is not blind to the totalitarian nature of his system (as
we would call it) and he concedes that it may be unpleasant to live
under. He simply insists that it is far preferable to the alternative.
Of the three kinds of commonwealth – monarchy, democracy and
aristocracy – Hobbes comes down firmly on the side of the first,
and for clear reasons. In the first place, the personal interests of the
monarch will tend to coincide with the public interest, and he can
after all always consult whom he pleases and 'cannot disagree with
himself'. In response to the criticism that monarchs will always have
favourites, he concedes 'they are an inconvenience' but adds that
they will tend to be few, whereas 'the favourites of an assembly are
numerous'.

Hobbes knew that his book would be ill received and he was not
disappointed. Indeed, he fled to France because he felt he was in such
danger from the Puritans. He alienated the Parliamentarian Puritans
because of his theory of 'servile absolutism', and he alienated the
Royalists because, although he believed in absolute monarchy, he
did not base his views on divine right. A parliamentary commission
was appointed to examine *Leviathan* and only the intervention of
Charles II saved Hobbes from persecution. Today, we do not find
Hobbes anywhere near as objectionable as his contemporaries did –
because, for the most part, we actually live by many of the precepts
he devised.

Similarly, Hobbes's argument in his 1655 book *De Corpore* that no intangible 'spirit' or soul existed, together with Descartes's reconfiguration of the soul as a philosophical as opposed to a religious notion, was an important step in the seventeenth-century shift in the locus of the essential self – from the humours, to the belly and bowels, to the brain – and the birth of a recognisably modern view of personhood. For many years – for hundreds of years – man had little doubt that he had a soul, that whether or not there was some 'soul substance' deep inside the body, this soul represented the essence of man, an essence that was immortal, indestructible. But beginning with Hobbes, talk about the self and the mind began to replace talk about the soul.

William Harvey, born at Folkestone in 1578, was a 'humorous but precise man'. He studied for five years at King's School, Canterbury, and then went up to Cambridge in 1593 at the age of fifteen. Like Newton he did not shine early on; however, after graduation at nineteen, he immediately set out for Italy, and for Padua, showing he must already have had some interest in medicine.

There he studied under Fabricius, a famous teacher of the day. Sixty-one when Harvey arrived, Fabricius was just then refining his understanding of the valves of the veins, though he also showed that the pupils of the eye responded to light. Fabricius's own knowledge was dated but he did stimulate in Harvey a great enthusiasm for medicine, which he took back home in 1602, having gained his doctorate. He went back to Cambridge, this time to earn an MD, which was necessary if he wanted to practise in Britain. He set up shop in London and, within barely a decade, was appointed a lecturer at the Royal College of Physicians.

There is written evidence – the written evidence of his own spindly hand – that he was teaching the doctrine of the circulation of the blood within a year of his arrival at the Royal College, in 1616. Harvey, we now know, had been lecturing on the circulation of the blood for a good twelve years before he committed himself to print. When his great classic, *The Movement of the Heart and the Blood*, appeared in 1628, Harvey was already fifty.

His observations were nothing if not thorough. In *De motu*

cordis et sanguinis, to give the book its Latin title, he refers to forty animals in which he had seen the heart beating, including fish, reptiles, birds, mammals and several invertebrates. The book is only seventy-eight pages long, much more clearly written than either Newton's or Copernicus's masterpieces, and its argument is plain enough for even the layman to grasp: all the blood in the body moves in a circuit and the propelling force is supplied by the beating of the heart. In order to make his breakthrough, Harvey must have deduced that something very like capillaries existed, connecting the arteries to the veins. But he himself never observed a capillary network. He saw very clearly that the blood passes from arteries to veins 'and moves in a kind of circle'. But he preferred the idea that arterial blood filtered through the tissues to reach the veins. It was only in 1660 that Marcello Malpighi, using lenses, observed the movement of the blood through the capillaries in transparent animal tissues.

Harvey's discovery of the circulation of the blood was the fruit of some beautiful observation. He used ligatures to show the direction of the blood currents – towards the heart in veins and away from the heart in arteries. And he calculated the volume of the blood being carried, to show that the heart was capable of the role he assigned to it. In particular, he showed that the amount of blood which leaves the left side of the heart must return, since in just under half an hour the heart, by successive beats, delivers into the arterial system more than the total volume of blood in the body.

It was because of Harvey, and his experiments, that people came to realise that in fact it was the blood which played the prime role in physiology. This change in perspective created modern medicine. Without it, we would have no understanding of respiration, gland secretion (as with hormones) or chemical changes in tissues.

His other major work was *On Animal Generation* (1651), on which he laboured for several years to prove that 'all life comes from the egg'; it was based on his work with hunting carcasses, mainly hinds and does. This resulted in the first definitive statement against spontaneous generation, which was a very popular theory until that point, some arguing that mud or excrement could 'generate' life forms. From 1632 on, he had accompanied King Charles I wherever

he went as 'Physician in Ordinary', an anything but ordinary position, because the king's passion for hunting provided Harvey with
many deer carcasses, the dissections of which furnished him with
many of his ideas. During the Civil War he spent time with the king
in Oxford. His lodgings were attacked by a mob and many of his
records ransacked. But he also treated the wounded and was made
warden of Merton College in 1645. The king's surrender in Oxford
that year brought on his retirement from public life.[26]

Milton (1608–74), born a bit late to be properly a part of this great
generation, is best remembered now for his epic, blank-verse masterpiece, *Paradise Lost* (1667). But, like Donne, he was much more than
a poet. Highly educated, highly intelligent, highly cultured, he spoke
several languages, including Latin, Greek, Hebrew, French, Spanish,
Italian, some Dutch and Old English, and to begin with he shone
as a pamphleteer during the increasingly personal rule of Charles I,
and its collapse into constitutional confusion and war. During that
era, Milton evolved from being a dangerously republican radical
and heretic, to the point where he became an official spokesman for
Oliver Cromwell's regime.[27]

The son of a composer and scrivener (someone who wrote for a
living, mainly in legal or business matters), John Milton was born
in London, near the Mermaid tavern (the site of a drinking club frequented by Jonson and Donne). Educated, like Jonson, at St Paul's
School, he then went up to Christ's College, Cambridge, graduating
in 1629 as fourth of twenty-four honours candidates. He stayed at
Cambridge for another three years, for a Master of Arts degree,
hoping to become an Anglican priest. During his time at Cambridge,
he penned a few shorter poems, the first to be published being his
'Epitaph on the Admirable Dramaticke Poet, W. Shakespeare'.

The intention to take holy orders didn't work out and instead he
embarked on an artistic and intellectual tour of France and Italy.
That lasted for more than a year, and during his travels he encountered a number of well-known intellectuals, including Hugo Grotius,
a Dutch legal philosopher, playwright and poet, in Paris; Galileo,
then under house arrest in Florence; Cardinal Francesco Barberini,
the distinguished antiquities and art collector and patron in Rome;

and Lukas Holste, a Vatican librarian who allowed Milton to inspect first-hand the church's great collection.

Returning to England in August 1639, he found trouble was brewing in the first so-called Bishops' War. This was a religious quarrel in Scotland about the standing of bishops and a new *Book of Common Prayer*. This provided the opportunity for Milton's first blast of polemics, *Of Reformation Touching Church Discipline in England* (1641), where he poured vitriol on the High Church policy of William Laud, archbishop of Canterbury, which Milton felt 'smacked of Catholicism'. This was followed in 1644 by another polemic, *Of Education*, which advocated radical changes to the curriculum of the universities. Milton had sought advice for this from Samuel Hartlib, a polymath of German origin who had settled in England and was known then as an 'intelligencer'. (This was a term used about a cohort of men all over Europe who kept in close contact with each other, exchanging information on the latest new ideas, in particular new instruments – such as calculators, seed machines and siege engines.)

Following the Parliamentarian victory in the Civil War, Milton now published his arguments in defence of the republican principles represented by the Commonwealth. This was *The Tenure of Kings and Magistrates* (1649), which argued for the right of the people to 'hold their rulers to account'. It also, implicitly, sanctioned regicide. Having shown his convictions, he was now appointed Secretary for Foreign Tongues (this was in March 1649), in which office he was responsible for the English Republic's foreign correspondence in Latin and other languages. Later that year he published again, this work being *Eikonoklastes*, an explicit defence of regicide, and was produced in reply to the *Eikon Basilike*, a sensational best-seller widely attributed to Charles I himself, which represented the king as an innocent Christian martyr. The debate continued when, a little later, the exiled Charles II and his entourage published their defence of monarchy, *Defensio Regia pro Carolo Primo*, which was actually written by the Heidelberg-trained Frenchman and leading humanist Claudius Salmasius. Not letting up, in February 1652 Milton released his Latin defence of the English people, *Defensio pro Populo Anglicano*, which eventually became known more popularly as the

First Defence. In these publications, Milton's splendid Latin prose and his obvious wide learning quickly brought a European reputation. Still not done, that same year he wrote Sonnet 16, addressed to 'The Lord Generall Cromwell' beginning, 'Cromwell, our chief of men ...' In 1654 his second defence of the English nation appeared, *Defensio Secunda*. This praised Cromwell but insisted he must abide by the principles of the Revolution. As a result of these several contentious works, there were many personal attacks on Milton, though he was now beginning to lose his sight and was forced to dictate his works to others, among whom was the fellow poet Andrew Marvell.

Soon after Cromwell's death in 1658, the English Republic started to crumble into rival factions, military and political, and Milton's response, first, was *A Treatise of Civil Power*, attacking the very idea of a state-dominated church, and second, *Considerations Touching the Likeliest Means to Remove Hirelings*, the target of which was the corrupt practices of the church. He continued publishing and, at the Restoration in May 1660, fearing for his life, Milton disappeared into hiding, A warrant was issued for his arrest and his writings were burned publicly. He thought it would be safe to re-emerge after a general pardon was passed but he was arrested in any case and imprisoned for a short while before friends intervened, including Marvell, by now an MP.

And it was only now, after all these polemics and counterpolemics, in 1667, that *Paradise Lost* appeared. He had started work on it six years before, when his second wife died (he married three times). He was by now completely blind, dictating it to a number of aides, and he followed it up with *Paradise Regained* and *Samson Agonistes*, both appearing four years later, in 1671.

Paradise Lost is an epic, its grand imaginative sweep taking in the creation of the world and Satan's attempts to subvert God's masterpiece, humankind. Consisting of 10,000 lines of blank verse, its timing was all important. As a well-read man, Milton was aware that the astronomers Copernicus, Johannes Kepler and Tycho Brahe had developed their ideas about the sun and the planets and, though they had not yet been widely assimilated into the modern worldview, they were already causing serious concern for the biblical understanding of the earth and the heavens, and at the same time casting doubt on the theoretical existence of giant crystal balls on the surfaces of which the planets were alleged to move in regular but complicated ways. Milton was familiar with Francis Bacon's books and beliefs, and was mathematically literate, all of which gave him a lot in common with the circle of early scientists who would soon gather together to found the Royal Society.

Paradise Lost begins by announcing that its subject is nothing less than the story of Adam and Eve and their sensational fall from grace in their search for knowledge, which God, as most people would have known, had expressly forbidden them from pursuing. At one level the book can be seen as undermining God's authority while its attitude to Satan and sin is not altogether hostile. Other topics include divorce and the desirability of sexual appetites; there is a weighing of the suitability of God's son to sacrifice himself for humankind, and a discussion of different languages and where they come from. Above all, betrayal is examined, arising when Eve accepts the recommendation of Satan, camouflaged as a serpent, and eats from the forbidden tree of knowledge. Like many masterpieces, this one swings between the familiar and the fresh, weaves new detail into old foundations and vice versa. So, as well as being a poem about the Bible, jumping off from Genesis, it can also be understood as a work of high scholarship, with much new material that was intended to make readers uncomfortable; there are arguments both for and against empire.[28]

And there are also some very human, very modern touches. For example, though Eve loves Adam, she is also aware that he may stifle her. Elsewhere, Satan is depicted as protean – Milton wants us to beware being taken in by the way people change or pretend to change. And Milton is staunchly Protestant – Adam has no need of churches or paintings to help him love God. Across the thousands of lines, the twists and turns, the overlaps and appositions are assembled into a luscious, succulent undergrowth of images, allusions and insights. Nor can the allegories of the Civil War be overlooked, or the barbs aimed at the monarchy, pressed into an all-embracing bundle. No summary can do justice to this extraordinary imaginative achievement.[29]

*

As one historian has it, whereas Milton was the 'singer' of Puritanism, John Bunyan (1628–88) was the storyteller. From a modest artisan family in Elstow in Bedfordshire, Bunyan was passionately religious, even in an intensely religious age, and was forced to spend several years in prison because he could not stop himself preaching when it was illegal for anyone except ordained clergymen in the Church of England. He had an enormous store of energy, which was directed inwards as much as outwards, and reflected in his two main works of genius, *Grace Abounding to the Chief of Sinners*, 1666, and *The Pilgrim's Progress*, published in two parts in 1678 and 1684.

Where the earlier book is a work of spiritual autobiography, *The Pilgrim's Progress* is less didactic and more of a novel, at least the second part is, though it consists mostly of isolated moments rather than a smooth narrative with events running into one another. There are three main events, with a vision of the Heavenly City inspiring the pilgrim to follow his various tribulations. In the first he is surrounded by darkness and ignorance in the Valley of the Shadow of Death, then he is mocked by Vanity Fair (everything the Puritans despised), and finally he suffers the oppressiveness of the Doubting Castle, which represents the sins everyone fears they will fall into. Enlisting the aid of Psalm 23, Christian, the hero of the story, finally conquers against the odds, aided by others who are in a similar predicament and who realise above all that they need each other. As Richard Greaves has said, '*Progress* presents a permanently attractive image of confronting the never-ending threats and confusions that attack the self both from within and without,' with Christian succeeding to a 'condition of permanent peace'. And this, combined with its vivid style, and forceful but colloquial ease, has ensured its perennial popularity.[30]

Early Thinking about 'Impire', Race and Slavery

'Empire' and 'colonialism' have become very loaded words in the twenty-first century. Unlike Milton and Bunyan, major colonial figures such as Cecil Rhodes have been the subject of sustained campaigns to have their statues taken down from positions of prominence, as their reputations are drastically rewritten. In universities, schools and colleges whole academic disciplines have been subject to 'decolonisation', which means different things in different places and at different times, but basically involves alleging that certain areas of study – even mathematics and the practice of debate itself – reflect what critics maintain are centuries of dominance by mainly white western European and North American individuals, usually men, who share a set of assumptions that, in effect, consciously or unconsciously put non-white and non-European, non-Western peoples, their interests and practices, at a disadvantage.

Despite the contemporary criticisms of empire, the reality itself grew slowly in Britain. This is surprising in view of the fact that, during Elizabeth's reign, there were many spectacularly successful voyages of oceanic exploration by a small group of wildly forceful English mariners, whose dash and swagger, not to mention their bloody violence, combined romance and criminality to an extent rarely seen on the high seas. The adventures of Martin Frobisher,

Francis Drake, Walter Raleigh and John Hawkins, to mention only the most egotistical, in their campaigns to plunder the Portuguese and Spanish fleets and raid the islands of the Caribbean, changed Britain's view of itself, and the world's view of Britain. Most of the names just mentioned were knighted and joined the roster of the queen's heroes. But there is no escaping the fact that they were corsairs, privateers – pirates, no less – pushing their piracy, as often as not, in the queen's own name. Claire Jowitt has written a whole book on England's 'culture of piracy', in which she maintains that England's pirates considered themselves braver than merchants and more financially astute than 'gentlemen', and they believed collectively that to further her aims England had to 'scrap and plunder' its way ahead. Piracy, Jowitt says, could be dismissed, camouflaged or reasoned away as 'adventure', as money-making adventures.[1] Shakespeare's plays of the 1590s and 1610s are replete with casual references to piracy, she points out; it was the accepted norm, though it is also true that at least three Elizabethan dramas presented piracy as antithetical to English values.[2]

Despite all the activity, legal, quasi-legal and downright illegal, in 1603, when Elizabeth 1 died, England had added not a single square inch of overseas territory to what it held in 1558, when the queen acceded to the throne.

EMPIRE AS A 'GOOD THING': ENGLAND'S GATHERING GREATNESS

The Elizabethans were naturally familiar with the word 'empire' because of its classical usage, the consensus then being that empire was a 'good thing', because Rome had helped to civilise the ancient Britons. New thinking about empire and colonisation emerged in the 1570s. This was partly provoked by the decline of the cloth trade in the last half of the sixteenth century together with the increasing interest in the profitable trade in gold, ivory and pepper in west Africa, which were part of a growing fascination throughout Europe for luxury goods. An added factor was the increase in commercial conflict across the 1550s and 1560s, when English mariners sought to muscle in on the trans-Atlantic trading networks fashioned by the

Spanish and Portuguese, following their discoveries in the Americas, and where, under the Treaty of Tordesillas, the pope had apportioned the Americas into two, one under Spanish authority, the other under Portuguese. The English, led by Queen Elizabeth herself, who was excommunicated by the pope in February 1570, further isolating an already isolated realm, regarded the treaty as nothing more than a stich-up and argued, ever more loudly and convincingly, that such an injunction – by the pope or anyone – could not be sustained merely by fiat; only continued presence, and fruitful occupation of the land itself, could confer sovereignty. And so, the following decades, lasting into the early seventeenth century, saw a period of piracy waged across the north Atlantic, in which England sponsored rather more plunder than it suffered.

The men who comprised this swaggering team of opportunists were not just obsessed with treasure – their spirit of adventure took in knowledge, collecting, painting, counting, reporting. They were called merchant adventurers but merchant warriors applied equally well. And there was definitely a sense of their *collective* existence which Susan Ronald puts down to their concern with 'England's gathering greatness'.[3]

The two men who emphasised England's growing enthusiasm in regard to empire were John Dee and Richard Hakluyt. Dee had a sizeable ego and ambition to match, and that ambition showed when he composed *Of Famous and Rich Discoveries*, where he revealed that he had at his fingertips a vast amount of historical, geographical and hydrographical knowledge of the northern and eastern regions of the globe, where he felt further searches for northern passages that had not been tried could be attempted. His underlying aim was that Englishmen should 'proceed upon the farther discovery of that part [of the globe] which yet is least known to Christian men'. Another starting place was the classical world and here we need to return to the fact that the elite at that time were all extremely well educated about that classical world. And that told them that, centuries before, Britain had been a colony in Rome's empire and the result had been wholly good, because the Romans had civilised the Britons. At the same time, in a classical education, as David Armitage points out, liberty and empire are irreconcilable. 'So widespread was knowledge of classical history among the generally well educated as well as the more technically learned, that the problem of how to achieve empire while sustaining liberty became a defining concern of British imperial ideology from the late sixteenth century on.[4]

Probably the greatest intellectual attempt to run these two ideas together – of the civilising effects of empire, and the reconciliation of liberty and empire – was that mounted by the two Richard Hakluyts. Both had an interest in expanding England's reach, but it was the younger man, the nephew of the older one, who was to make an impressive and decisive impact by collecting and collating as many reports of voyages of all the Elizabethan seamen as he could locate.[5]

Born six years before Queen Elizabeth I acceded to the throne in 1558, Richard Hakluyt junior was marked, says his biographer, with an indefatigable industry. He developed an obsession – there is no other word – with the English colonisation of America and set about acquiring an ever more magnificent collection of accounts of voyages of exploration and attempted settlement. In order to do so, he learned Latin, Greek, Spanish, French, Portuguese and Italian, no small investment. What spurred him was a realisation that the Spanish and the Portuguese had been making substantial profits from a century of overseas ventures in the East as well as the West.[6] Hakluyt's work was so thorough, and his energy so insistent, that his books became an inspiration for England's policy makers, including the queen. By the end of the 1580s, says Peter Mancall, Hakluyt had achieved international acclaim as one of Europe's greatest authorities on overseas exploration and as the most important promoter of English settlement of North America.[7]

Then, in September 1580, Drake returned from his circumnavigation of the globe. This was some time after Ferdinand Magellan's voyage of 1519, but even so it was a magnificent achievement and Drake's return marked the start of a new age of possibilities.[8]

Or it did for those like Hakluyt, impatient for adventure and worried by the very existence of Catholicism. Hakluyt published the second of his three important books, *The Principall Navigations, Voiages and Discoveries of the English Nation*, after he had been to Paris and immersed himself among many like-minded French travellers. His third book, what came to be called the *Discourse on Western Planting*, was not originally intended to be published. Instead, it was to be privately read by the queen and her advisors, including Sir Francis Walsingham, her spy chief, as the basis for a secret government exploration initiative. In this, Hakluyt was impatient to show that America 'had everything England needed'.

Hakluyt's work paid off. Six months after he had passed the *Discourse on Western Planting* to the queen, in 1584, she handed Raleigh the right to 'discover, search, fynde out and view such remote heathen and barbarous lands Countries and territories'.[9]

FULFILLING THE DIVINE WILL

Nicholas Canny makes the telling point that when Adam Winthrop, who lived in Groton Manor, Suffolk, filled out his diary, beginning in 1586 and continuing uninterrupted until 1619, he made not a single entry that concerned English long-distance voyaging.[10] 'People had no inkling that they were living on the threshold of some great enterprise,' Canny points out, or on the verge of a new age.[11]

Colonisation was, in effect, predicated on two ideas. The first was basically Elizabeth's view, that the only authority for colonisation was the continued occupation and use of new lands, not the pope's fiat or any monarch's proclamation; and the second was Providentialism, 'the belief that England was fulfilling the divine will'.[12] Another submission sought to justify the English authorisation of the Virginia Company to invade what was after all a territory with a long-established ruler, and this was based on Sir Edward Coke's claim that all infidels were *perpetui enemici*, 'perpetual aliens', 'for between them, as with devils, whose subjects they be, and the Christians, there is perpetual hostility, and can be no pease'. By no means everyone accepted this and fewer still were prepared to endorse Coke's grander argument, that the common law of the English people was 'identical with the law of nature'. But, as Anthony Pagden points out, the legitimacy of the conquest of Virginia was never seriously challenged until the eighteenth century.

Thus, from very early days there was an attempt by the British to separate themselves from other nations involved in empire-building. On this account, the English only settled on vacant lands, with the consent of the native population, whereas the Spanish invaded territories 'rightly occupied by legitimate if primitive rulers'.[13] Virginia, for example, was presented as a new Canaan, with several ministers referring to different parts of the Bible (Joshua 17:14, 2 Samuel 7:10) as justification for occupying the new lands, in the hope of converting the 'heathens' from their worship of 'the diuille'.[14] This quest for legitimation as regards the occupation of already occupied colonies was to be an enduring issue over time, and leads directly to the arguments of John Locke, by far the most influential advocate of empire.

'ALL THE WORLD WAS AMERICA'

Locke was very much involved in the whole colonial enterprise. Secretary to the Lord Proprietor of Carolina between 1668 and 1671, he was also secretary to the Council of Trade and Plantations, 1673–4, and a member of the Board of Trade from 1696 until 1700. More than that, he put money into the Royal African Company (trading in slaves) and the Merchant Adventurers, trading with the Bahamas, and on top of it all he was landgrave of the government of Carolina, originally a German title but in this context virtually a viceroy for confirming and settling titles to land in the early colony. Locke's most fundamental arguments concerned the phenomenon based on a segment in Roman law known as *res nullius*. Here, the idea is that all 'empty things', which notably include unoccupied lands, are the common property of everyone until they are put to some (generally agricultural) use.[15]

Locke's *res nullius* argument had two aspects. In the first place, America, said Locke, was essentially in the same condition as all the world was before the creation of humanity. This reasoning led to his famous remark, 'In the beginning all the world was America.' What he had in mind particularly was the absence among the Amerindians of any form of commercial exchange. They were still in a state of nature, 'though a very late stage of it'. As a result, Locke concluded that they were clearly not equal to a fully fledged civil society 'in the original Greek and Roman sense'.[16]

Locke's second argument turned to the original inhabitants' right to own not only their land but whatever is produced on that land.

Locke maintained that it was *labour*, work, which transformed a commodity 'from the state of nature into the domain of private ownership'. This meant, for example, that a deer is the Indian's 'if he has killed it'. The problem with the hunter and the gatherer, for Locke, was that they could not achieve a surplus in this way. 'With the invention of money, property becomes mobile but the Indians did not have money; they did not have a commercial society.' Therefore, Locke said, they had no legal right to the goods of the land 'beyond that needed for immediate survival'. Robert Cushman, organiser of the *Mayflower* voyage in 1620, put it pithily, brutally so: the Indians, he said, 'run over the grass as do also the foxes and wild beasts', doing nothing to add value by 'maturing, gathering, ordering etc.', and therefore they did not own the land any more than the foxes did.[17]

Locke's view did not lack criticism. Roger Williams, a London-born Puritan minister, who founded Providence Plantation – later Rhode Island – argued bluntly that forest-clearing and slash-and-burn agriculture *were* a form of improvement and pointed to the king's hunting grounds in England, where the monarch claimed property rights for a practice little different from that of the aboriginals in America.[18]

There was, as it turned out, a marked anti-imperial impetus among some European humanists who, in the sixteenth century, comprised the main body of critics of overseas activity.[19] One who cautioned against overseas involvement was George Buchanan, arguably Scotland's greatest early humanist, a superb teacher but a difficult man who was forced into exile for his uncompromising Lutheran views. In exile, he taught at the University of Coimbra, in Portugal, where Montaigne was a pupil, and where Buchanan did not entirely escape the Inquisition. But his Portuguese stint did give him an inside track on the Portuguese colonial experience, then much older than Britain's, and that introduced him to the diseases spread by colonial travel and the pollution that followed. He also claimed that the gold and silver discovered in the colonies undermined the political system in the long term by making it more dependent on international relations and, not least, in an age of sail, on the weather.

This is well worth pointing out: that resistance to empire is every bit as long-standing as the enthusiasm and self-congratulation that have had far more attention.

SPECULATIVE GEOGRAPHY

Traditionally, the European discovery of America has been regarded as one of the most intellectually exciting events ever. Like many aspects of the early encounters, however, this view has been challenged more and more in recent decades.

We can begin in a less contentious but nonetheless intellectually interesting way by saying that, though the discovery seems exciting to (some of) us, in the twenty-first century, that is not quite how it was viewed at the time. Sebastian Sobecki is just one who has pointed out that, judging by early names for America, medieval and Tudor writers often failed to recognise the New World as either new or indeed a single world. What had been discovered was variously known as Asia, Paradise, Atlantis, the Fortunate Isles, Norumbega or the 'elusive isle of Brazil'.[20] In his two 1507 maps of the world, the German cartographer Martin Waldseemüller (*c.*1470–1520) assigns the name 'America' to what is now South America because he believed that the new land was first visited by the Florentine explorer Amerigo Vespucci (1415–1512), 'whose accounts were at the time outperforming in popularity those linked to Christopher Columbus (1450/51–1506)'. The term 'America' gained popularity only in the second half of the sixteenth century, following Gerard Mercator's projections of 1538.[21] Spain did not adopt the name 'America' until as late as 1758 and the English also struggled with it. John Dee always used the term 'Atlantis' for America.

The fact is that there was in Europe a strong tradition of what we might call 'speculative geography', much of it taken from post-Roman writers, such as Augustine (354–430), who thought that the ocean was too vast to be crossed 'because God had placed it as a boundary to prevent humans ever reaching Paradise', which, for a time, was believed to lie on the edges of Asia. The vastness of that continent became apparent only with the voyages of Marco Polo (1254–1324). This was the first *mundus novus*, or new world.[22]

There were of course many myths and legends about voyages to – and discoveries made in – the Atlantic, dating back to St Brendan, the Irish abbot, whose desire to see Paradise took him and sixteen fellow monks far across the ocean in the sixth century. A sketch of a map made in 1570 by Abraham Ortelius, the Antwerp-born cartographer and creator of the first modern atlas, and used by Francis Drake in his circumnavigation of the globe (1577–80), shows a massive *Terra australis*, immediately south of the Strait of Magellan, extending west to New Guinea and east to Madagascar. On the north-east coast of the Pacific, there is also shown a northern passage to the Atlantic.[23]

THE CONCEPT OF COMPLEXION

In her examination of *The Elizabethan Mind*, Helen Hackett says that, in common with many people throughout history, Elizabethans defined themselves *against* those they considered 'other', to use an ugly but convenient modern term. The Irish, she says, were seen as 'wild and primitive', the Italians and Spaniards were vilified as 'too' sophisticated, to the point of decadence, while the people of Africa were variously described as 'Moors', 'blackamoors', 'Negroes' or 'Ethiopians', terms that reflected some understanding that Africa was inhabited by diverse populations.[24]

But the central term used in describing people in Elizabethan times was 'complexion', which did not mean then exactly what it means now. When both the Prince of Morocco and Portia in *The Merchant of Venice* refer to the former's 'complexion' they mean his disposition as well as the tone and colour of his skin. Complexion meant not only the natural colour, texture and appearance of the skin, especially of the face, but also a combination of the four 'humours' of the body, mind, disposition and temperament. A book published in 1576, entitled *The Touchstone of Complexions*, offered its readers a guide to 'the exact state, habit, disposition, and constitution of [someone's] own body outwardly' together with 'the inclinations, affections, motions and desires of his mind'.[25]

Because widespread travel was now more available, views about the body started to change. The central conception until then was 'humoralism'. Mark Dawson argues that the demise of humoralism was a necessary prerequisite for racism. In traditional Christianity every individual was considered to be in some way deformed by original sin, 'humanity was fallen', while Adam – the original perfect example – had the favoured ruddy complexion owing to the vivid redness of the earth. (James I, a vain man, was convinced he looked like Adam.) In the Bible, beauty is inevitably red and white. On Sundays, sermons were given with the admonition 'Know thine own complexion and always strive to keep the colour you were born with'. Paler-skinned people were thought of as phlegmatic, black hair covered a 'hot' brain, Christ 'adores' the sanguine. (As Jesus is shown growing in paintings, he gets ruddier and grows fairer.)

In Elizabeth's Britain, Christianity and civility were considered more important than race. Astrologers were asked to verify paternity, likening a child's humours to its parents. This was known as astro-humoralism. Milk was regarded as whitened blood.

Across the world, black peoples were distinguished from tawnies; Africans preferred beautiful whites to serve them, and would rub spittle on the skin of white faces to see if the colour would come off. White and ruddy complexions were favoured among the early Americans. James VI may have thought he looked like Adam but the English thought that God looked like them. Sex and skin complexion were not regarded as set at birth. In the theatre the convention was that nobles were shown by actors who had 'better' bodies.

There were several explanations for why the Indians – native Americans – were tawny. One view held that they were born white but went about almost naked in sunny climates, another that their mothers bathed them in walnut leaves, and yet another that they used the fat or grease of eagles or racoons. But their darkness meant they were naturally melancholic. Far eastern and far western people were both tawny and must therefore be related.

George Best, a proto-scientist very interested in climate, who accompanied Martin Frobisher, the privateer, on some of his voyages of exploration, also took an interest in skin colour, and wrote that he had observed 'an Ethiopian as black as coal brought into England, who taking a fair English woman to Wife, begot a Son in all respects as black as the father', concluding that this was not due to climate darkening the skin, but that 'this blackness proceedeth rather of some natural infection'. He then turned his attention to a parallel set of beliefs based on what we can call Christian geography, and the medieval TO map scheme, in which the three continents of the known world at that point – Europe, Asia and Africa – were separated by the (horizontal) Mediterranean Sea and the (vertical) River Nile, forming a T-shape, encircled by ocean, and in which the city of Jerusalem formed the very centre. This scheme remained valid until well into the Elizabethan period. The further significance of the TO maps was that the three continents were often identified with the three sons of Noah, regarded then as the progenitors of the human race after the disaster of the Flood. The population of Asia was held to be derived from the descendants of Shem, Europe from Japheth and Africa from Ham. George Best understood that all three of the wives of the sons of Noah were white and so they can only 'have begotten and brought forth white children'. Blackness, Best went on to argue, 'thus came into the world through the covetous sin of Cham' (that is, Ham, the progenitor of all Africans). On this account, while Noah's sons were in the Ark, he had forbidden them from 'carnal copulation'. But Ham, 'expecting that the first-born child after the Flood would inherit the earth', copulated with his wife, and for this 'sin against his brothers, father and God', Ham had to be punished. The fruit of this union in the Ark, Chus, was therefore made 'so black and loathsome, that it might remain a spectacle of disobedience to all the world'. Best therefore concluded that 'the cause of the Ethiopian blackness, is the curse and infection of blood, and not the distemperance of climate'.[26]

MUTUAL AMITY

It is also the case that in English trading voyages to Africa, particularly further north than west Africa, intercultural relations were carried out, as Helen Hackett says, in a spirit of 'mutual amity and respect'. In 1585, for example, Elizabeth's ambassador to Morocco, Henry Robert, arrived there and was received 'with all humility and honour', staying for three years and enjoying regular audiences with the king and/or his viceroy. In 1553, the king of Benin received an English party in his great hall and, noting the reverence he was held in by his people, the English themselves kneeled before him. He greeted them and, speaking in Portuguese, granted them huge quantities of pepper.[27]

The English also encountered Africans across the ocean, including in the Spanish colonies in and around Panama. In 1572, for example, Francis Drake formed an alliance with the so-called Cimarrons, a grouping of African slaves who had escaped from their Spanish masters and were waging guerrilla war against them. Drake sought to accommodate the Cimarrons and he and his men developed a growing respect for their black allies, since they depended on them for local knowledge and resourcefulness (such as how to catch an otter and prepare it for table).[28] Not that the Cimarrons were treated as wholly equal – their servitude was expected.

Katherine George has chronicled the changing accounts of Africans, from the fifteenth to the seventeenth centuries. She shows how initially critical views of 'Negroes' as 'bestial' were gradually replaced by more positive views, with 'an increased regard for accuracy of reporting, and an unprecedented sympathy for the primitive and his culture'.[29]

By this stage there were more than a few Africans living in England, mainly in London, and mainly, it seems, as servants – not slaves – in well-to-do households. Historians have debated the significance of three documents issued in the name of Elizabeth I in 1596 and 1601 in which she ordered the transportation of 'Negros and blackamoors' out of England, 'of which kind of people there are already here too many'. The latest research confirms that these were not, as originally thought, general edicts of expulsion: one of them is a draft, never acted upon, and the others were part of an apparently shady deal between the government and a Lübeck merchant to whom a debt was owed. But, as again Helen Hackett points out, the documents confirm the presence of Africans in Elizabethan England, in which some at least are treated as commodities and others with hostility. But once more this is not the whole picture. It became a regular occurrence, for example, to bring black Africans – from Guinea, say – to England to learn the language and then return them to their places of origin to act as interpreters/brokers in trade deals. 'Evidently some English merchants had confidence in the intellectual abilities of Africans and their potential as useful collaborators.[30]

Slavery had no legal status in England and the country had a reputation abroad as a place free from the practice. In 1587, Hector Nunes illegally purchased an 'Ethiopian' from a Cornish merchant, but when he tried to force him to 'tarry and serve' him an English court ruled he had no right to do so.[31] The latest research shows that there were at least 450 Africans living in England and Scotland between 1500 and 1640, in a population of some 5½ million. They worked mainly as maids, gardeners and porters. Interracial marriages took place, 'suggesting acceptance and integration into the community'.

RACE ON STAGE

Both playwrights and audiences were ever more fascinated by the characters of other races. In plays performed from 1550 to 1621, from before Elizabeth's reign to well after it, some forty-five characters, variously referred to as 'Africans', 'Negros', 'Moors', 'Ethiops' or 'Indians', have been identified on the London stage. Moors had appeared regularly in Henrician masques, mainly as examples of exoticism. But in the Elizabethan theatre, says Helen Hackett, the Moor was shown as charismatic and compelling 'and usually the cleverest character on stage ... He was endowed with agency and interiority, which he revealed to the audiences in soliloquies.'[32]

Shakespeare's first play with a Moorish character, *Titus Andronicus* (1592), was a great success, in which Aaron is marked by his evil brilliance and cool self-control. In a callous trick he persuades Titus that if he chops off his hand and sends it to the emperor, his sons' lives will be spared, only for a messenger to return with their severed heads, at which Aaron later recalls that he had 'laughed so heartily'.[33] His gratification lies in inflicting suffering and causing political disruption. The hot sun of the south has once more made Aaron melancholic, cold-hearted and full of sinister intentions – his character is explained by geohumoralism. A sketch of a 1595 performance of the play confirms that Aaron was depicted on stage just as he is described in the text, as 'raven-coloured'. The play's treatment of him takes an interesting turn when Tamora gives birth to their child, and it is black. She orders Aaron to kill the child, who, as the nurse says, is 'a joyless, dismal, black and sorrowful issue'. Aaron will have none of it, insisting that his son will live, and he goes on to proclaim the 'supremacy of blackness'.[34]

Othello (1604) draws together many conventions regarding the stage Moor that had developed through the late Elizabethan period.[35] This time, however, it is not the Moor who is the scheming, malignant villain but Iago, who compares himself to the devil who 'will the blackest sins put on'. Othello is repeatedly referred to as a Moor, suggesting north African heritage, but also several times as 'black', like a sub-Saharan African, and most of these references are negative. Othello speaks of his own blackness, blaming it for his supposed loss of Desdemona's affections, though she insists that 'my noble Moor / Is true of mind' and is incapable of jealousy because 'the sun where he was born / Drew all such humours from him'. Of course, she is proved horribly wrong.

Over the course of the play, Othello passes through most of the diverse mental states that Elizabethans attributed to Africans, from elevated and dispassionate, to self-righteously and relentlessly vengeful, to bestial. However, he lacks one quality commonly attributed to Africans: intelligence, which Shakespeare transfers to the wily Iago. Othello's downfall is his 'free and open nature', which Hackett says is unusual in an early modern stage Moor, such that he 'Will as tenderly be led by th' nose / As asses are'.

A HIERARCHY OF CIVILISATIONS

It can never be forgotten that, in some ways, there was nothing 'equal' in the English and European encounters with different people. Whatever their actual feelings – and those were clearly very varied – as Michael Adas points out, it was always the Europeans who went out to the peoples of Africa, Asia and the Americas, and never the reverse (though, as we shall see later in this chapter, Barbary pirates did attack the coast of northern Europe).[36] William Smith, a British merchant/explorer, found that, to Africans, his ship was a 'marvel' of design and workmanship. His assistant, who was black, and was familiar with the ship's instruments, had nothing but contempt for the Africans. It was competence that counted, not race.

Throughout the period of the great voyages of discovery, religion remained the single most important source of the Europeans' sense of their own superiority, but material culture, and especially technology and science, were other influential factors, an important part of the 'civilising mission' that justified for many their attitudes to African people. European travellers and missionaries took pride in the superiority of their technology and in their understanding of the natural world.[37] On this score, monumental architecture, sailing vessels and even housing were often more critical than astronomy or mathematics. By the eighteenth century, and certainly by the nineteenth, most European thinkers had come to the view that the control over nature made possible by Western science and technology showed that their ways of thought corresponded much more closely to the way the world worked than those of any other people, past or present.[38] It wasn't far from there for many people to judge that the material backwardness of African societies underlined their inferiority, and it wasn't far from *there* to the view (a) that slavery was justifiable, and (b) that the low level of development in Africa meant that its inhabitants needed to be protected.[39]

Adas also underlines the point that Muslims, Chinese and Indians were never 'discovered' like African or American civilisations were. They had been known about, and in the case of Muslims experienced, for years. For Adas ethnocentrism is the term best associated with the early encounters with African peoples, rather than racism.

To begin with, he points out, travel was arduous and dangerous. Diseases were prevalent, climates were inhospitable, European clothing was unsuited to tropical zones, local languages were unknown and, where writings existed, they were invariably forbidden to foreigners, all of which meant that few travellers stayed anywhere for long, and observations were confined to patterns that could readily be observed: marriage customs, modes of warfare, religious ceremonies. Travellers responded in one of two ways, he says. In the case of religious beliefs or philosophical systems, 'they resorted to general, often fantastical, descriptions. Matters scientific and technological they often ignored altogether.[40] At the same time, the superiority of

European weapons was also self-evident. The Africans had nothing to match the arquebuses, which instilled fear in them.

Nor should it be forgotten that, in the early years of expansion, many of Europe's technological advantages were less apparent than they would later become, and in some cases, in such endeavours as cotton textile and porcelain manufacturing, the Europeans were actually behind their Asian rivals. The Chinese, like many Europeans, were also keen on alchemy and astrology, so they were not so different intellectually.

Explorers did register that Africans, in contrast to the Amerindian peoples, were able to work iron and some commented on the high quality of utensils and weapons produced. But they also noted the small plots of land cultivated by the average African and noted the lack of draught animals and ploughs. These low levels of productivity led some to assume there was a natural 'indolence' to the African.[41]

What Europeans found in Asia was quite different. India's spices and textiles had found a ready market for centuries. China's overall achievements in monumental architecture were considerable and impressive. The Arab *jahazis* and Indian *kotias* were equipped with lateen rigging similar to the Portuguese caravels. So naval technology was rarely cited as evidence of European superiority.[42] The conquest of even small Asian kingdoms was beyond Europe at this stage – the armies of Ming or Mughal empires being much larger than Europeans'. Asia's technological lead over Europe was still considerable and India and China had both built up a body of writing in philosophy, medicine, astronomy, mathematics and physics. And again, unlike in Africa, the Chinese and Indians were quite happy and self-confident enough to make their writings available to European travellers.[43]

But then a raft of inventions began to separate Europe out from everyone else, beginning with the odometer, to measure distance, in the 1520s, and continuing with the single and later the compound microscope (1590s and 1650s), the thermometer (1592), the telescope (1608), devices for reading the pulse (early 1600s), the barometer (1643) and the air pump (1650s).[44] And so, although all the newly discovered civilisations could be condemned for not being Christian – their major 'error' in most people's eyes – there did emerge a hierarchy of non-Western peoples: Chinese, Indian, African.

WHITE SLAVERY

Long before Britain sought to colonise the Americas, it had to come to terms with the fact that, in 1600, the great land-based empires of the East – the Chinese, Russian and Ottoman polities, together with the Safavid Empire in Persia and the Mughal Empire in India – were infinitely more powerful. Each of them would continue to expand, with the Habsburgs' and Napoleon's imperial ambitions only adding to the mix. The sheer ubiquity of empire elsewhere needs bearing in mind when considering the shortcomings of British behaviour and thinking in the years ahead. So too do the routine levels of cruelty that were common then, so different from our own day. There were in Britain hundreds – literally hundreds – of offences which we would now regard as trivial (such as stealing a handkerchief) which carried the death penalty, often by the relatively slow and deliberately cruel ritual of burning at the stake.

However, it was not the Atlantic but the Mediterranean that was the early site of contention, rarely written about, with the so-called Barbary powers – Morocco, Algiers, Tripoli and Tunisia, the last three each a province of the Ottoman Empire – all sponsoring corsairs who, in the early seventeenth century, between them seized more than 800 English, Welsh, Scottish and Irish trading vessels. It has been calculated that some 12,000 British subjects were captured – and enslaved for life, or ransomed – during these years and that in all 20,000 Britons fell foul of Barbary corsairs. These corsairs provoked widespread anxiety, but the threat was not confined to the Mediterranean. Between 1610 and the 1630s, Cornwall and Devon lost a fifth of their shipping to north African corsairs. In 1625 alone almost a thousand sailors and/or fishermen from Plymouth were seized, 'mostly within 30 miles of the shore'. But not everyone was seized at sea. At that time the Algiers fleet was strong enough to mount occasional raids on the West Country, the Channel Islands and part of southern Ireland.[45]

After 1680, according to Linda Colley, the forceful sultan of Morocco, Moulay Ismail, systematised corsairing as a weapon of state finance, European states having to pay to redeem their captured nationals.[46] Between 1670 and 1734, British official records show that at least 2,200 captives were shipped back to Britain. White captives, it is known, were sold at the slave market in Souk el-Glizel, in Tunisia.[47]

It is not necessary to go on. 'The point is', as Colley says, 'that slavery at this early stage was not viewed in Britain as racially restricted. Before 1730, at least, the face of slavery – as far as Britons and other Europeans were concerned – was sometimes white.' Barbary slavery, she says, became a nationwide concern at this point, 'to an extent that was not true of black slavery until much later in the eighteenth century'.[48] Well before 1730, a watershed we shall come to, the people of Britain and Ireland were exposed to far more information about white Barbary slavery than about any other version of slavery. Barbary captivity was referred to in popular ballads and in the numerous sermons preached every weekend, when appeals were made for money to ransom captives.

It is therefore no exaggeration to say that the existence of white slavery involving Britons 'was taken for granted' at that time. And, as Colley concedes, 'to some extent, this must have made acquiescence in black-slave-trading easier'.[49]

A New View of Atlantic Slavery

The Transatlantic Slave Trade Database, compiled and refined over the last decades, has allowed historians to refine their estimates of the regions of Africa that supplied captives to the Americas and the timing of their departures. On the downside, Atlantic history, focused as it has been, primarily on the Americas and Europe, has tended to *distort* the study of slaving activities within Africa by focusing more on the captives sold by traders into the ocean than on those *retained by slavers within Africa*, sometimes leaving the impression that Atlantic-oriented slaving was of greater geographical spread and significance in Africa than it actually was.[50] (Italics added.)

In Atlantic history, slavers – European, African, or mixed race –
typically appear as morally questionable figures who accumulated
riches for narcissistic and unproductive ends. Yet in African
economies, slavers represented a progressive force in that they
generally transformed social, economic and labour systems, to
produce growth, and sometimes even developments, from which
they also personally gained ... One could think of slaving there in
a very general way as an African historical equivalent of Europe's
industrial revolution.[51]

While key to Atlantic history, African slavery was not principally
Atlantic oriented ... Only a portion, *perhaps relatively few*, of
Africa's captives crossed the Atlantic ... Recent published estimates of the total of Africa's *many slave trades* suggest Atlantic
slaving accounted for roughly a *quarter or less* of the captives
generated within the continent.[52] (Italics added.)

These comments, all made recently by leading historians from North
American or European universities, and specialising in the fairly new
discipline of Atlantic history, throw into relief some of the recent wild
controversy surrounding slavery and race. Here is another revealing
quote from another specialist, David Richardson: 'European contact
with Africa and with enslaved Africans *long predated colonisation*
of the Americas. For more than a millennium, enslaved Africans had
crossed the Sahara to be sold in Christian as well as Muslim markets
in the Mediterranean basin. That trans-Saharan flow would continue
until almost the dawn of the twentieth century.'[53] (Italics added.)
Thus the general trend of recent research is clear: many Africans
were victims of the slave trade, but others were willing and successful
participants in a lucrative business arrangement.

We saw just now how the most common experience of slavery that
British people would have had, until the early eighteenth century, was
as slaves themselves. And as Linda Colley aptly put it, this no doubt
affected attitudes in one of at least two ways. It may have made individuals who had been victims themselves more sympathetic to other
victims; or it may have made them feel exactly the opposite: that if they
could be enslaved, what was so wrong about it happening to others?

PART TWO

From the Royal Society to the Royal Academy, from the Scientific Revolution to the Industrial Revolution

Blue-Water Destiny

The achievements of the later Tudor dynasty were considerable, despite the turbulence. The Elizabethan Settlement, and the peace that it engendered, made economic progress possible, which was perhaps the most immediately important accomplishment. Not so obvious, but in the long run equally salient, was the challenge to authority in the Reformation, and the short reign of Edward VI, the great age of radical Protestantism, in which the relaxation of censorship allowed imagination to flourish. One result of this was that popular science was encouraged, in Elizabeth's reign in particular. Improvements in mathematics, navigation and geography, many derived from John Dee, also helped commercial expansion, as we have seen. Alongside this was the work of William Fulke, founder of scientific meteorology, which helped to reduce superstition.[1] Reginald Scot's epoch-making *Discoverie of Witchcraft* (1584) undermined beliefs in alchemy and astrology.

Christopher Hill makes the point that the growth of science, the *popularisation* of science, and the collection of information from the increasing number of overseas voyages, could not help but create a critical mass of people, experiments, instruments and ideas that were new and, taken together, amounted to what later historians would call 'a paradigm shift', of which the revolution was one fruit. That critical mass extended from the Gresham professors to the circle around William Gilbert, whose *De Magnete* ('On Magnetism', 1600) was 'the first physical treatise ... based entirely on experiment', which Galileo much admired and which prepared the way for Newton.[2]

None of these men owed anything to the universities, which failed to provide modern scientific education, whereas Gresham College immediately adopted logarithms, introduced by the Scottish land-owner and mathematician John Napier in 1614. In fact, under Henry Briggs, first professor of geometry at Gresham, the college became a leader in science, its effectiveness being shown by the fact that Richard Delamain, a joiner, learned enough from attending Briggs's lectures to become a teacher himself and invent the slide-rule. Edmund Gunter, who followed Briggs at Gresham, also invented a number of instruments to facilitate calculation and helped devise the log-line to assess distances travelled at sea.[3] Not that Gresham's was the only venue of note. There was a widespread appetite for learning, with lectures common at Surgeon's Hall, the College of Physicians and the Society of Apothecaries, and at the Inns of Court (anatomy, surgery, mathematics), while there were lectures on navigation for mariners at Sir Thomas Smith's house (paid for by the East India Company).[4]

The Effect of the Armada on Imagination

The original motivation for the great innovations that were at-tempted in those days lay – for Puritans – in the books of Daniel and Revelations, 'which provided a rich vocabulary for the terminal struggles between Christ and Anti-Christ'. Protestants at the time were acutely conscious that, from an initial state of bliss, society had entered a period of catastrophic decline. However, the Reformation was a turning point, and they were able *in theory* to look forward to a glorious future. Diverse biblical texts were assimilated to give a vivid impression of a new age, a period of perfect harmony after the Thirty Years War and Civil War.[5]

The fly in the ointment, from the scientists' point of view, was Archbishop Laud, the arch-episcopalian, who drove some into exile and some into silence. Perhaps it was because he suspected that more and more men around these new scientific institutions were losing their respect for the authority of classical antiquity, and showing 'a new critical freedom' with regard to sacred texts. In a similar vein, in 1577 Richard Willis, bishop of Winchester and a fellow of All Souls, had noted that geography had ousted grammar, poetry, logic, astrology and Greek in terms of popular works.[6]

Government did not get behind science and scientists anywhere near as much as merchants did. The Royal Navy's medical standards lagged far behind those of Sir Walter Raleigh, for instance. (This was to have practical consequences: doctors favoured Parliament's side in the Civil War, so its troops got better medical treatment than the king's.)[7]

What is clear is that Francis Bacon saw that something new was happening in society as well as in science. The new philosophy held with the Book of Daniel that it was part of God's plan that 'the opening of the world by navigation and commerce, and the further discovery of knowledge should meet in one time'.[8] Thus, says Hill, 'Bacon gave a co-operative programme and a sense of purpose to merchants, artisans, and philosophers, each of whom hitherto had seen only in part'. In this new scheme of things, Bacon said, the philosopher must cooperate with the craftsman.[9] And this is what Bacon's *The Great Instauration* is all about, 'the attempt to *restore* the commerce of the mind *with things* to its original perfection, as close to it as possible'. (Italics added.) He was speaking for and to people to whom, for centuries, 'the dogma of the helplessness of fallen humanity had been axiomatic'. Following the Armada, when the English suddenly grasped that they were a force to be reckoned with, a nation equal to any other, the expansive power of science and industry brought about a renewed confidence among Puritans, above all that England was a chosen nation, that Providential history was about to deliver a golden age led by merchants and artisans (that is, practically minded scientists). In this respect Bacon was close to Raleigh and Coke, who both wanted free trade.[10]

At this point, Samuel Hartlib enters – or re-enters – the story. Hartlib, German-Polish, originally came to Britain from Elbląg in Poland as a merchant, but all his life he was passionate about mathematics and science. He would soon become friendly with Robert Boyle and Henry Oldenburg, both founders of the Royal Society.[11]

This internationally minded group of Bacon followers was complemented by John Amos Comenius, a Czech theologian and pedagogue, one of the earliest advocates for modern education and that it be available to all. He was much travelled, advising Protestant governments across Europe. In 1641 the English Parliament invited him to be part of a commission investigating educational reform. The war interfered with that but, like the others considered here, Comenius's other great interest was in furthering Baconian ideas. In his new educational system, rote learning would be replaced by the use of experiment, observation and practice in the teaching, in particular, of languages and science.[12]

The plans and inventories of several colleges were made available for Comenius's inspection, with a view to one of them becoming a universal college 'which would make England the centre of European learning'. Chelsea College was expected to be singled out, the very building that would be given to the Royal Society by Charles II in 1667.[13] Comenius's major work, originally entitled *Pansophia Prodromus*, was translated as *A Reformation of Schools* (1642), and to it he added a series of sixteen 'handbooks', on such topics as advice to parents on preschool education, a new alphabet for young children and a survey of empirical knowledge.[14] The Comenian group, the Hartlib group and Gresham College may all be regarded as having given birth to the Royal Society.

Bacon brought all these things together: Copernicus had 'democratised the universe', destroying the hierarchical structure of the heavens, while Harvey had democratised the human body by 'dethroning the heart'; and of course Hobbes proclaimed that all men were equal.

Hill provides a long list of important thinkers influenced by Bacon (George Hakewill – who paid for the building of Exeter College, Oxford – Walter Raleigh, William Petty, John Milton, Thomas Goodwin, Richard Overton) and as the Laudian censorship broke down, the works of Bacon, Coke, Raleigh and others were more freely published, discussed and commented on. The Barebones Parliament (July 1653) had a Committee for the Advancement of Learning.[15] The collapse of censorship gave people more freedom to speculate and imagine. This was, then, we may say, the Baconian moment.

APPETITE FOR INNOVATION:
HARTLIB AND HIS ELEVEN COLLEGES

Charles Webster, in his magisterial book *The Great Instauration: Science, Medicine and Reform, 1628–1660*, which examines the English intellectual world immediately after Francis Bacon's death, puts all this in context with his concept of what he calls 'The Spiritual Brotherhood', an agglomeration of ideas and projects that went much further than those considered so far. Hartlib, for instance, conceived a project called the Office of Address, which had two basic aims: to serve as an international correspondence centre where intelligence about new discoveries could be exchanged, and to direct the efforts of inventors along lines suggested by Gabriel Plattes. Plattes was passionate about agriculture and roamed England inspecting different practices, and he had his own project, *Macaria*, in which he advocated the creation of a 'Colledge for Inventions in Husbandrie'. Another proposal, also associated with Hartlib, was the Office of Communications, which was intended as a 'Centre and Meeting-Place of Advices, of Proposalls, or Treaties and of all Manner of Intellectual Rarities'.[16] Hartlib was appointed 'Agent for Universal Learning' and paid for his troubles like a college professor. But he was far more creative than the average professor – over time he came up with a list of no fewer than eleven new colleges, which included a university in London, a 'Seminary for Plantations and Churches Beyond Seas', a college for 'Conversions or Correspondency of Jews and Advancement of Oriental Languages and Learning', one for 'Verulamian Experimental Philosophy', and one for 'all Foreign Churches'.[17] He was by no means a Little Englander.

Not all of these came to anything, but they underline the sheer appetite for innovation and a widespread enthusiasm for paradigm change. There were adventurous plans for free ports and 'Noble Schools', specialising in the skills necessary to run the state (husbandry, administration of justice, monetary policy). In William Petty's first publication, *The Advice of W.P. to Mr Samuel Hartlib* (1648), he envisaged a 'Nosocomium Academicum', a teaching hospital, staffed by unmarried men, who would have the leisure to visit patients twice a day.[18] William Harvey endowed the College of Physicians with property on which to establish a Museaeum Harveianum, which opened in 1654.[19]

At Oxford itself, the Oxford Experimental Club was better known then than now. It was centred on John Wilkins, an astronomer, head of both Trinity College, Cambridge (on Cromwell's say-so) and Wadham College, Oxford. Author of *The Beauty of Providence*, Wilkins was known as an advocate of what he called 'experimental divinity'. The Oxford Club was another of the outfits that would give rise to the Royal Society, and its rules date its formation to 1651. Webster cites the membership as forty-three, with thirty-two going on to become fellows of the Royal Society.

Amid all this widespread concern for intellectual innovation, the position of the universities continued to be anomalous. The bishops opposed research there and even Bacon in *New Atlantis* had imagined Salomon's House as a separate research institute, showing that he anticipated that their resistance would prevail. At the same time, others called for the universities to provide laboratories, not just libraries, and William Dell, the radical master of Gonville and Caius College, Cambridge, advocated a rash of state-maintained universities to be established in London, York, Bristol, Exeter, Norwich and elsewhere.[20] When the scientists were ejected from Oxford by the Restoration in 1660 (254 from Corpus Christi alone), they reassembled at Gresham College (where else?). Four of the twelve founding members of the Royal Society were Gresham professors.

PHILOSOPHY BASED ON EXPERIMENT

So change was untidy and piecemeal. Nonetheless, Hill points out that while in 1663 a bishop could still deny any Copernican theory, by the end of the century the archbishop of Canterbury himself was a 'Baconian'. John Ray, the botanist who identified the species as the basic unit of taxonomy, was born in 1627, and said in 1690 that, during his lifetime, 'vain and empty scholasticism had been replaced by a new and solid philosophy based on experiment'.[21] Robert Boyle, author of *Usefulness of Experimental Natural Philosophy*, conceded that gentleman scientists 'must converse with tradesmen in their workhouses and shops', adding that 'it was unworthy of a philosopher to refuse to learn from a craftsman'.[22]

And this puts into context the foundation of the Royal Society, which came into being in the wake of the Restoration. Oxford and Cambridge were still largely unchanged, keeping themselves free of scientists. Because of their radical links, Hartlib and the minister and pamphleteer John Dury, who had an interest in alchemy and distillation, did not become founder members, and Robert Boyle, who *was* a founder member, cut ties with them. They and people like them were attacked because of their Parliamentary connections, and an informal divide was opened up between 'High' and 'Vulgar' Baconians.[23] The first history of the Royal Society, published in 1667 by William Sprat just a few years after its founding in November 1660, largely ignored the part played by Gresham College or Parliament. And in fact, the early society went through two phases. In its first years, echoing what Boyle had said, and despite the fact that many of the fellows were 'gentlemen', the society, Hill says, 'became more utilitarian than Bacon would have wished'.[24] In Robert Hooke's *Micrographia*, notwithstanding its sensational examination of small bodies under a magnifying glass, published in 1665, the preface had 'a blatant emphasis on the profit motive'.[25] After that, however, the science of the society was more and more dominated by abstract mathematics, much at variance with Bacon's vision of science as working for the glory of God and the 'relief of man's estate'.

But that is not the complete picture either. As we shall see later on, and as Sprat was the first to point out, the Royal Society, despite its developing interest in abstract mathematics, evolved an ideal prose style as one of 'mathematical plainness ... the language of artisans, countrymen and merchants'. Scientists, Sprat said, wrote plainly and straightforwardly because they were writing for 'men that are simple and unlearned'. The Puritans, the Levellers and the Diggers, politico-religious dissidents, likewise learned to master the usage of merchants and artisans 'because it was for them that they wrote'. This was important. Eventually, it would give rise to the language of Defoe and Swift.[26]

Experiments in the Tower

Alongside Bacon and the natural theologians, in this ever-changing
world and the discovery of *beyond* (which, as we will see, encompassed three main elements: stars beyond the giant crystal balls
that were once thought to support the heavens, which Galileo's observations had dispensed with; the New World beyond the oceans;
and experimentation beyond the narrow hair-splitting of the scholastics), there was no shortage of other figures, and other types of
figure – adventurers, historians, even poets – who were also seeking
and achieving change. One notable personage we may consider in
this capacity was Walter Raleigh, who was as much a Baconian as
a merchant-adventurer or merchant-warrior. More even than that,
Hill argues that Raleigh was involved, in one way or another, in
the six major intellectual/cultural changes that came about during
the later part of the sixteenth and the first half of the seventeenth
centuries. These were: the decline in the power of the Crown in relation to Parliament; the adoption of an aggressive foreign policy; the
extension of economic liberalism; the redistribution of taxation; the
beginning of religious toleration; and the triumph of modern science.

Raleigh, as the heir to Sir Philip Sidney and his group, had close
links with Dee, Hakluyt, Thomas Bright, the inventor of shorthand,
and Thomas Hariot, one of the mediators of algebra, and was an
effective patron of scientists and navigators. In fact, Raleigh was
eager to make sure each of his voyages could be considered a scientific expedition. He sent Hariot in 1585 as a surveyor to Virginia.
Hariot's *Brief and True Report on the New Found Land of Virginia*
was much admired by Hakluyt, who reprinted it, the book being
one of the earliest examples of a large-scale economic and statistical
survey, including a description of 'marketable commodities' as well
as 'a very sympathetic account of native religion and customs'.[27]
Many scientific works were dedicated to Raleigh, who was a pioneer,
not only in navigation, but in naval medicine, dietetics and hygiene.
Even when he was in the Tower – three times, for displeasing the
queen in one way or another – he conducted chemical and medical
experiments, trying to distil fresh from salt water, to find ways of
keeping meat fresh at sea and seeking remedies against scurvy.[28]

Most of Hakluyt's works were dedicated to Raleigh, including *The Principal Navigations*, in which the view was expressed that the reduction of the American Indians 'to civility, both in manners and garments' would engender a new market which, if successful, would mean that England need not worry about capturing markets in Europe.[29] War against Spain, Hakluyt maintained, was essential to preserve England's independence but also 'to bring salvation to millions of American Indians who had, within living memory, been subjugated to popery and Spanish cruelty'.[30]

Richard Hakluyt, through his copious writings, was to become the spokesman of a newly self-conscious nationalism in England, which is explored more fully in the chapters which follow. In fact, after the defeat of the Armada, a massive propaganda campaign was begun to convince a critical mass of people that England's destiny now lay in grandiose adventures beyond the oceans, and Hakluyt started assembling facts on Baconian lines, reprinting Hariot's works among others, an ingenious format which provided adventure stories for those at home, and instruction manuals for those at sea.[31] Hakluyt was essentially Raleigh's publicity agent, the main message being that England would flourish as never before by the increase of trade in overseas lands to an extent never seen. The introduction to England of potatoes and tobacco-smoking are also attributed to Raleigh, both of enormous economic impact.[32] Hakluyt was to become, in effect, the chief spokesman and propagandist for and of *beyond*.

Making himself the spokesman for the interest of merchants, Raleigh had grasped the commercial importance of sea power. Coke and Milton were great admirers of – and much influenced by – Raleigh, whose significance here is that he employed a secular and critical approach to the study of world history which was in large part a study of biblical history, and which in book form became a best-seller (it was printed in three times as many editions as Shakespeare's *Works*).[33]

After Bacon and Raleigh, Coke. He went out of his way to promote *laissez-faire*. With his help, lawyers began to recognise the existence of a 'lawmerchant', a separate body of customs accepted by merchants; the common law that was beginning to claim sole jurisdiction over contracts made beyond the sea, and agreements – financial and otherwise – in England. This replaced the Admiralty courts and in so doing, also diminished the king's authority. Essentially, in systematising and liberalising law through his *Institutes*, Coke adapted it to the needs of commercial society, rather than for the benefit of the Crown.[34] This is, in effect, the creation of political economy.

Bacon, Hartlib, Wilkins, Raleigh and Coke, and the others considered here, each helped to undermine traditional beliefs in the eternity of the old order in church and state and helped show that the link between freedom of thought and freedom of economic activity was fundamental.[35]

UNLIKELY EMPIRE

There are many candidates for the single most consequential idea/ moment in history: printing, gunpowder, the Reformation, the French Revolution, farming, ethical monotheism, Christianity, Marxism, natural selection, experimentalism, industrialisation, the market, nationalism, the control of fire (leading to baking, ceramics, steam power and metallurgy), the soul, justice. This list is by no means exhaustive, and so far as Britain is concerned, none of them will do.

The essential arc of British history – intellectual and creative history, just as much as political, economic and military history – is of a small, indeed tiny, country sequestered on the north-west coast of Europe that over the centuries would forge the largest and most unlikely empire the world has seen. As the North American Conference on British Studies report mentioned at the beginning of this book had it: 'The history of Britain is arguably the most important "national" history precisely because it has been the most intertwined with, and influential upon, other histories worldwide.'

The key idea in this development was nothing less than a new conception of the universe, starting with the work of Copernicus, Brahe, Kepler and Galileo, all non-Britons. There were two consequences of their ultimate discoveries that there are many more stars in the sky than had been thought before the invention of the telescope, and that they are much further away and not scattered about some giant crystal balls high in the sky. One consequence was theological, the other more everyday. The post-Copernican, post-Galilean picture of reality 'replaced the prevailing conception of the world as a finite, closed and hierarchically ordered whole' with 'an *indefinite and infinite universe*' (italics added), held together by laws governing the motions of basic components that are all placed on the same level of being in the world.[36]

This was all neatly summarised by the Russian-French historian of science, Alexandre Koyré, in his evocatively titled book *From the Closed World to the Infinite Universe*. The world people lived in was no longer a small, narrow place of limited attributes and extent, but rather much, much larger and open-ended. This was a massive psychological breakthrough, especially for the religious imagination. A knock-on effect of this, as Christopher Hill has pointed out, was that by 'breaking the hard walls of the universe ... astronomers began to create a climate of opinion in which it seemed less likely that God would intervene in the day-to-day affairs of mankind'.[37] Allied to this new understanding of the heavens was the implication that God would not interfere to anoint monarchs, which seriously undermined the notion of the divine right of kings.

This was particularly resonant in Britain, in England above all, because English culture exemplified three crucial features of this breakthrough in thinking. First, the idea that God was now, in some way, more remote from the world found expression in the tumultuous nature of the English Crown. Though, in theory, monarchs ruled by divine favour, that could hardly bear much scrutiny when England's kings and queens were constantly being deposed and the throne usurped.

At the same time, and underlining the point, Henry VIII had broken away from the closed Catholic world of the Roman church and, in a sense, paralleled what Copernicus and Kepler had done in astronomy, moving the world on beyond Catholicism to fashion new forms of religion. The methods were very different, of course, but the motives and effects were similar, creating a less hierarchical, less centralised, more varied world.

Nor was that all. The previous century – slowly to begin with but with increasing vigour – had seen the opening up of the Atlantic

Ocean. The Americas had been discovered and the world was no longer confined to the relatively small landmass of mainland Europe and the enclosed sea of the Mediterranean. Here, too, there was a new world of *beyond*, which held out the promise of new experiences, new understanding, different hierarchies. As we shall see, Britain was not at the forefront of this development, at least not to begin with, but it soon caught up, being perfectly placed geographically to make the most of the oceans that were now known to cover vast expanses of the surface of the world. And, lacking a large hinterland, which would need protecting by an expensive army, England found it only too easy to turn its face to the seas. What had been seen as a colossal barrier by St Augustine, who thought there was nothing beyond the oceans, was now the route to a new beyond.

The third area of *beyond* brings us back to Francis Bacon and the scientific revolution. Until the sixteenth century, the main intellectual mode throughout Europe had been scholasticism, a somewhat inward-looking method of inquiry that compared one ancient manuscript with another to produce new syntheses now and then, though rarely with any new facts or observations. Various early academics did advocate observation and experimentation, and some foreign manuscripts were brought to Britain from the continent, mainly from Constantinople, Sicily and Spain. Despite what Deborah Harkness has to say about Hugh Plat (above, page 41), it was Bacon who first advocated with force that the humanist classics were not the last word and that observation and experimentation should be put on a solid basis. His specific aim was to create new knowledge and compile a history of trades, which would assemble the experiential knowledge of experts and specialist artisans for the benefit of all. His advocacy allowed people to create new ways of finding out new things, with new processes and devices, enabling them to go *beyond* what their forefathers and teachers had taken for granted.[38]

Bacon emphasised the weakness of humanism and drew attention to the advancements being made in mathematics and astronomy – navigation, in effect – by the English, as their explorations of the oceans paid off. And he pointed out that after its success against the Armada, England could consider itself the equal of other nations, despite their much larger populations.

This, then, is the era when modern Britain and the modern world were born: amid the general, liberating discovery of *beyond*, where navigation became the crucial workhorse in generating a new open-mindedness. These advances spawned the idea of a 'blue-water destiny'. It was this which enabled the imperial adventure that, for all its faults, would give rise to what we might call the cosmopolitan imagination, amplifying creativity – though that is no small thing – to enable curiosity, inspiration, ingenuity and, above all, *resourcefulness*; to expand, taking in the entire globe as no one had done before, and giving rise to what Gerard Delanty has called 'world openness'. This is what distinguishes the British imagination.[39]

Proving how imagination could be practically useful, that knowledge was power, was an immense task, but the consequences of this intellectual evolution marked a startling change in England's world position. One of the most important figures in this transition was Isaac Newton.

Newton, Locke, Willis:
From Soul to Mind to Brain

I saac Newton is still known to us as the man who conceived the modern notion of the universe, as held together by gravity. But, in recent decades, a second – and very different – Newton has emerged: a man who spent years involved in the shadowy world of alchemy, in the occult search for the philosopher's stone, who studied the chronology of the Bible because he believed it would help predict the apocalypse that was to come. He was a near-mystic who was fascinated by Rosicrucianism, astrology and numerology. A generation after the appearance of his famous book *Principia Mathematica*, Newton was still striving to uncover the exact plan of Solomon's temple, which he considered 'the best guide to the topography of heaven'. Perhaps most surprising of all, the latest scholarship suggests that Newton's world-changing discoveries in science might never have been made but for his researches in alchemy.

The paradox of Newton is a useful corrective. Born in 1642, he grew up in an atmosphere where science was regarded as a quite normal interest. This is already very different from the world inhabited by Copernicus, Kepler or Galileo (who died in the year Newton was born), where religion and metaphysics mattered most. At the same time, Newton shared with them certain heroic qualities, in particular an ability to work almost entirely on his own. This was just as well because much of his ground-breaking work was carried out in forced isolation in 1665 when London was devastated by the plague and he sought refuge in the village where he was born, Woolsthorpe in Lincolnshire. Newton was fortunate in having an uncle wealthy enough to send him to grammar school at Woolsthorpe and afterwards, in 1661, to Trinity College, Cambridge.

Newton was fortunate in more general ways, too. At first, he was interested in chemistry, rather than mathematics or physics. But at Cambridge he started reading Euclid and attended the lectures of Isaac Barrow, a mathematician who was key in the development of calculus, and became acquainted with the work of Galileo and others. The early seventeenth century was a time when mathematics became modern, taking a form that resembles what it has now. Gottfried Leibniz (1646–1716) and Nicholas Mercator (1620–87) were near-contemporaries of Newton (1642–1727), and René Descartes (1596–1650), Pierre de Fermat (1601–65) and Blaise Pascal (1623–62) not long dead by the time he graduated. It is no criticism of Newton's genius to say, therefore, that he was fortunate to be the intellectual heir of so many illustrious predecessors.

Of his many sparkling achievements we may concentrate on his theory of gravitation. As J. D. Bernal points out, although Copernicus's theory was accepted widely by this time, 'it was not in any way explained'. One problem had been pointed up by Galileo: if the earth really was spinning, as Copernicus had argued, 'why was there not a terrific wind blowing all round, blowing in the opposite direction to that in which the earth was rotating, from west to east?' At the speed at which the earth was alleged to be rotating, the wind generated should destroy everything. There was at that stage no conception of the atmosphere, so Galileo's objection seemed reasonable. Then there was the problem of inertia. If the planet was spinning, what was pushing it? Some people proposed that it was pushed by angels but that didn't satisfy Newton. Aware of Galileo's work on pendulums, he introduced the notion of centrifugal force. Galileo had begun with the swinging pendulum before moving on to circular pendulums. And it was this, the circular pendulum, which led to the concept of centrifugal force which, in turn, led Newton to his idea that it was gravity which holds the planets in formation, while they swing around perfectly freely.[1]

The beauty of Newton's solution to the problem of gravity is astounding to modern mathematicians, but we should not overlook the fact that the theory was itself part of changing attitudes in wider society. Although no one any longer believed in astrology, the central problem in astronomy had been to understand the workings of the divine mind. By Newton's day, however, the aim was much less theological and rather more practical: the calculation of longitude. Galileo had already used the satellites of Jupiter as a form of clock, but Newton wanted to *understand* the more fundamental laws of motion. Though his main interest was in these fundamentals, he was not blind to the fact that a set of tables – based on them – would be very practical.

The genesis of the idea has been recreated by historians of science. To begin with, G. A. Borelli (1609–79), an Italian, introduced the notion of something he called gravity, as a balancing force against centrifugal force – otherwise, he said, the planets would just fly off at a tangent. Newton had grasped this too, but he went further, arguing that, to account for an elliptical orbit (identified by Kepler), where a planet moves faster the closer it gets to the sun, the force of gravity 'must increase to balance the increased centrifugal force'. It follows that gravity is a function of distance. But what function? The breakthrough came with Edmund Halley (1656–1742). A passionate astronomer, he had sailed as far as St Helena to observe the heavens of the southern hemisphere. Halley, who helped pay for the printing of *Principia*, urged scientists to work on the proof of the inverse square law. Beginning with Kepler, several scientists had suspected that the length of time of an elliptical orbit was proportional to the rate of change of the radius, but no one had done the work to prove the exact relationship. At least, no one had published anything. In fact, Newton, sitting in Cambridge, hard at work on what he considered the much more important problems of prisms, had already solved the inverse square law but, not sharing the modern scientist's urge to publish, had kept the results to himself. Goaded by Halley, however, he finally divulged his findings. He sat down and wrote *Principia*, 'the Bible of science as a whole and in particular the Bible of physics'.[2]

Principia Mathematica is not an easy book to read but there is a clarity of understanding that underlies the more complex prose. In explaining 'the system of the world', by which he meant the solar system, Newton identified mass, density of matter – an intrinsic property – and an 'innate force', what we now call inertia. In *Principia* the universe is, intellectually speaking, systematised, stabilised and demystified. The heavens have been *tamed* and have become part of nature. The music of the spheres has been described in all its beauty. But this has told man nothing of God. Sacred history has become natural history.

Newton's other great body of work was in optics. Optics, for the Greeks, involved the study of shadows and mirrors, in particular the concave mirror, which formed an image but could also be used as a burning glass. In the late Middle Ages lenses and spectacles had been invented and later still, in the Renaissance, the Dutch had developed the telescope, from which the microscope derived.

Newton had combined two of these inventions – into the reflecting telescope. He had noticed that images in mirrors never showed the coloured fringes that stars usually had when seen directly through telescopes and he wondered *why* the fringes occurred in the first place. It was this which led him to experiment with the telescope, which in turn led on to his exploration of the properties of the prism. Prisms were originally objects of fascination because of their link to the rainbow, which, in medieval times, had a religious significance. However, anyone with a scientific bent could observe that the colours of the rainbow were produced by the sun's light passing through water drops in the sky. Subsequently it had been observed that the make-up of the rainbow was related to the elevation of the sun, with red rays being bent less than purple ones. In other words, refraction had been identified as a phenomenon but was imperfectly understood.

Newton's first experiments with light involved him making a small hole in the wooden shutter to his rooms in Trinity College, Cambridge. This let in a narrow shaft of light, which he so arranged that it struck a prism and was then refracted on to the wall opposite. Newton observed two things. One, the image was upside down, and two, the light was broken up into its constituent colours. To him it was clear from this that light consisted of rays, and that the different colours were affected by the prism to a different extent. Previously, light was believed to travel *from* the observer's eye *to* the object being observed. But for Newton light was itself a kind of projectile, shot this way and that from the object looked at: he had in effect identified what we now call photons. In his next experiment, he arranged for the light to come in from the window and pass through a prism; this cast a rainbow of light on to a lens which, in turn, focused the coloured rays on to a second prism which cancelled the effect of the first. So, given the right equipment the white light could be broken up and put back together again at will. As with his work on the calculus, Newton didn't rush into print but once his findings were published (by the Royal Society) their wider importance was soon realised. For example, it had been observed since antiquity (in Egypt especially) that stars near the horizon take longer to set and rise sooner than expected. This could be explained if it were assumed that, near Earth, there was some substance that caused light to bend. At that stage there was still no understanding of the concept of the atmosphere, but it is to Newton's credit that his observations kick-started this notion.[3]

Despite Newton's interest in astrology and occult science, the men of the time did feel that they were taking part in something new, in a venture that needed defending from its critics, and in that they took as their guiding spirit Francis Bacon, rather than some figure from antiquity. There is little doubt too that knowledge was being reorganised in new and more modern ways. Peter Burke, for example, has described this reorganisation in the sixteenth and seventeenth centuries. The word 'research' was first used in Etienne Pasquier's *Recherches de la France* in 1560, which also showed an awareness of the *need* for research. Libraries were revamped in the seventeenth century, with a more secular layout, with subjects like mathematics, geography and dictionaries being promoted at the expense of theology.[4]

THE PROPHET OF THE BUSINESS COMMONWEALTH

The rise of English and Dutch prosperity in the seventeenth century was a long-term consequence of two developments: a change in the salinity of the Baltic Sea which drove the herrings into the North Sea, boosting the catch there and augmenting the fishing industry of the countries that rimmed that body of water. More importantly, it emphasised the pivot away from the Mediterranean as the Atlantic Ocean opened up, following the discovery of America and the development of trade with the Indies and India. As a result, the politics of the new nation states changed too, with trade rivalries beginning to take precedence over religious or dynastic feuds. The general increase in prosperity and the growth of mercantile influence on government produced a greater emphasis on property and more concern with the freedoms that should be allowed for individual business initiatives. It was this set of circumstances that produced the philosophy of John Locke.

'John Locke is the prophet of the English business commonwealth, of the rule of law and toleration.'[5] It was from the political speculation of Locke (1632–1704) and the actual working out in England of the principles of toleration and limited monarchy that the French thinkers of the Enlightenment drew their inspiration. Like Hobbes, Locke wrote on political philosophy but also on human nature, in *An Essay Concerning Human Understanding* and *Two Treatises of Government*. This is one reason why his books were so influential: both aimed to fit political organisation into a wider system of understanding, and both tried to do so scientifically. The idea of political economy was gaining ground.

Locke studied medicine and was a fellow of the Royal Society, and his patron was Lord Shaftesbury, Chancellor of England. As we have seen, Locke helped draft the constitution of Carolina.[6] He was a very practical, cautious soul, who disliked abstractions, and thought that truth was probable rather than absolute, making him not untypical of the people then coming to power in England. In his scheme of things, political power should be as far from 'divine right' as can be imagined. He thought it was foolish to claim that God passed power to Adam and then through his descendants to today's royal representatives. After all, he observed tartly, on that basis we are *all* descendants of Adam, and it is impossible today to know who is who. He disagreed fundamentally with Hobbes in that he thought man's natural state was not war but the use of reason. By their nature, he says, men are equal, as Hobbes had insisted before him, but for Locke that is not enough. He goes on to make a distinction between liberty and licence. Without licence, he says, liberty is no different from the continual warfare Hobbes so feared. Therefore, the purpose of civil society is the use of reason to avoid 'the inconveniences of the state of nature which follow from every man being made a judge in his own case, by setting up a known authority to which everyone may appeal and which everyone ought to obey'. Princes and kings, he says, can have no place in this scheme, 'for no man is exempt the law'.

Locke reflected the new situation in England more than ever when he went on to argue that the reason men come together to live in society, with laws, is for the preservation of their property. Since men are 'driven' into society, it follows that the power of that society 'can never be suffered to extend further than the common good'. And this common good can only be determined by standing laws, statutes, that all are aware of and agree to, and *not* by extemporary decrees of, say, an absolute sovereign. Moreover, these laws must be administered 'by indifferent and upright judges'. Only in this way can the people (and rulers) know where they are.[7] Finally, Locke gave voice to the main anxiety of the rising commercial classes in England, that no power can take from a man his property without his consent. 'A soldier may be commanded by a superior in all things, save the disposal of his property.' In the same way, a man has property in his own person, meaning that his labour is his property too. The most important consequence of this, Locke says, is that people can only be taxed with their consent.

This is in some ways the final break regarding the divine power of kings. The connection between the state and the individual is, for Locke, a purely legal and economic convenience, relating only to the practical aspects of existence. In other words, and very bluntly, the state had absolutely no part to play in matters of belief or conscience. Where religion was concerned, Locke was a great advocate of tolerance (he devoted two works to the subject, his *Thoughts Concerning Education* and *Letters Concerning Toleration*). Tolerance, he says, should arise from the very obvious fact that different minds have different aptitudes, as is evident from the way different children grow up within the same family. Moreover, the principles of Christianity, he says, demand nothing less than toleration. 'No man can be a Christian without Charity, and without that faith which works not by force but by love . . .' The church, he insists, must be an entirely voluntary association; and it goes without saying that a person's religion should not affect his or her civil rights: 'The care of each man's salvation belongs only to himself.'[8]

As with much of Hobbes's *Leviathan*, Locke's views today seem little more than commonplaces – again because we take them so much for granted. But they were very new in Locke's own day. The idea that government should derive its authority from the governed, which implied that it should last only so long as the people wanted it, was breathtaking. 'At a time when kings ruled for a lifetime, this offered the prospect of change, even of revolution.'[9]

The growth of doubt, what Richard Popkin has called 'the third force in seventeenth-century thought', occurred in four stages. These were what we may call rationalistic supernaturalism, deism, scepticism and, finally, full-blown atheism. Atheists arose in England and France in the wake of Newton's discoveries.* In England, 'from All Souls [College, Oxford] to the Royal Society there was an outpouring of atheism in print such as the country had never seen before'.[10] There was a street referred to as 'Atheists' Alley' near the Royal Exchange in London (probably so named because the coffee houses there were frequented by the newly knowledgeable 'men of the world', including unbelievers). John Redwood, in his history of the pamphlet war, tells us that the bookshops began to 'teem with pamphlets, tracts and broadsheets

---

* Newton himself, who was an Arian – that is, he did not believe in the divinity of Christ – thought that God was 'immanent' in space and time, existing everywhere, and that matter alone had been created. This was in effect a return to the old Platonic doctrine of emanation.

dealing with the atheist scare'.[11] The theatres too were frequently home to atheist satires.[12]

After the scientific discoveries of Copernicus, Galileo and Newton, the area of scholarship which most affected beliefs about religion was biblical criticism. The first major attack on the scriptures had come as early as the twelfth century, when the Jewish scholar Aben Ezra challenged the tradition that Moses was the author of the Pentateuch. Britain was not exactly immune to this train of thought, which was a Europe-wide phenomenon, but the two Englishmen who stood out were Hobbes, who showed that the books of Joshua, Judges, Samuel and Kings were written long after the events they described, and Thomas Burnet, a Yorkshireman who was master of the Charterhouse and who, in his *Archaeologiae and Theory of the Visible World* (1736), calculated the amount of water that fell in the forty days of the Flood. He found it insufficient by a long way to drown the earth, and to inundate the highest mountains.[13]

THE BIRTH OF PSYCHOLOGY

The underlying fault-line shaking out these disparate developments was the reconceptualisation of the soul as the mind, with the latter increasingly understood by reference to consciousness, language and its relationship with this world, in contrast to the soul, with its immortality and pre-eminent role in the next world.[14] The man mainly responsible for this approach, again, was Locke, in his *Essay Concerning Human Understanding*, published in 1690. In this book, Locke himself used the word 'mind', not 'soul', and referred to experience and observation as the source of ideas, rather than some 'innate' or religious (revelatory) origin. He asked his readers to 'follow a *Child* from its Birth and observe the alterations that time makes', rejecting all innate ideas. Locke took it as read, however, that the mind did contain certain innate powers, such as a capacity for reflection, 'the internal Operations of our Minds, perceived and reflected on by our selves'.[15] Experience of the physical world, he said, gives us sensations (his examples included 'yellow', 'heat', 'soft' and 'bitter'). We reflect on these experiences and analyse them to form our ideas.

Locke argued that motivation was based on experience – nature – which helped form the mind, rather than derived from some transcendent force operating on the soul. He saw action as a response to the pleasure or pain accompanying sensations and that opened up the possibility of a deterministic/mechanistic view of motivation. This was a key ingredient in the birth of psychology, even if that term was not used much yet.

One unsettling effect of this was to further remove God from morality. Morality has to be taught; it is not innate. In the same way Locke removed 'the will' as an ingredient of the soul and explained it as simple choice, arrived at after reflection on the sensations the mind had received. Arguably most important of all, he said that the self, the 'I', was not some mystical entity relating to the soul, but an 'assemblage of sensations and passions that constitutes experience'.[16] Common sense now but breathtaking then.

Meanwhile, medical language was moving away from the terminology of the humours, and madness began to be explained as a 'failure of the mind', understood as housed in a bodily organ, the brain. The brain, in fact, had been explored as early as the 1660s, by Thomas Willis, a fashionable doctor and an Oxford professor, one of the generation of early scientists who, with Wren, Hooke and Boyle, was in at the birth of the Royal Society. Willis had carried out numerous dissections of brains – of humans and dogs mainly – and had developed a new way of extracting the brain from the skull, from underneath, which helped preserve the shape intact. His careful dissections, and some clever staining techniques, helped to show that the brain was covered in a fine network of blood vessels, and that the ventricles (the central spaces where the cortex was folded in on itself) had no blood supply and were unlikely therefore to be the location of the soul, as some believed. His book *The Anatomy of the Brain and Nerves* (1664) did much to move the seat of the passions and the soul from the heart, making him famous in the process. He invented the term 'neurologie', which he called the doctrine of the nerves. He dedicated his book to Gilbert Sheldon, archbishop of Canterbury, to highlight to everyone that he wasn't an atheist.[17]

A New Home for Imagination

A s time has gone by, and scholarship has expanded and deepened, the influence of Francis Bacon and the Royal Society has been discovered to have widened into other areas in very marked ways, beyond the worlds of Wren, Hooke and Boyle.

Barbara J. Shapiro is just one who has noted that there was a substantial shift in prose style following the arguments of Bacon and the practices introduced by the Royal Society and that this was a change which affected the writing of history, law and philosophy, but in particular led to a revised attitude to the literary arts and poetry.[1] Hitherto, poetry had been salted with rhetoric, but this was now increasingly seen as a barrier to precise factual statement, something that the introduction of newspapers during the Civil War, with their need for unbiased and plain – non-rhetorical – reporting, only encouraged. 'Good utterance', as it was called, had at its height produced the elaborate, luxuriant imagery of Edmund Spenser, and the unlikely but striking metaphors of John Donne, but these were no longer seen as apposite.

This change in attitude was seen first and most clearly in the law, especially in regard to legal proof. Trial by ordeal and trial by battle, though widespread in medieval times, could hardly be seen as attempts to try cases by rational means.[2] In England the rejection of these procedures led to the development of trial by jury. Initially, jurors, men of the neighbourhood, were assumed to know the facts of the case 'and to incorporate their knowledge in the verdict'. By the sixteenth century, however, jurors were no longer so likely to be familiar with the case and juries came increasingly to rely on the use of witnesses. And it was this development – the use of witnesses – that linked the law to the developments in science. People could see that the indeterminacy of verdicts in criminal trials was not too dissimilar from the probability discovered in mathematics. This realisation, that the actions of human beings were in the realm of probability – that is, there are some things we can never know with certainty – was a major observation or discovery of the seventeenth century, which culminated in Locke's *Essay Concerning Human Understanding* (1690).[3] This laid emphasis on the integrity, skill and purpose of the reporter, the number of witnesses, the internal consistency and the presence or absence of opposing testimony in evaluating evidence.[4]

These notions clearly rubbed off on history-writing, as historical testimony – often in the form of documentation – was increasingly used and evaluated, a good example being its use in witchcraft trials. As a result, by the end of the seventeenth century, a common set of beliefs had emerged in England about the nature of truth, the methods for attaining it, 'and the degree of probability or certainty that might be attributed to the findings produced by those methods'.[5]

Thomas Hobbes in many ways echoed Bacon's views, showing a growing hostility to the scholastic logic and rhetorical elaboration that he saw all around him. As such, it might be expected that Hobbes would fall in line with Locke, but no. Hobbes – who after all had himself translated Homer – held that poetry exemplified one of the central and traditional functions of language, 'to please and delight ourselves and others by playing with words, for pleasure or ornament'. For Hobbes, ornament found a proper home in poetry, so long as its 'resemblance to truth' was not stretched beyond the limits of the probable, which is where 'judgement' came in. Another important figure here was Thomas Sprat, who famously drew attention to the Royal Society's efforts 'to separate the knowledge of Nature from the colours of Rhetoric, the devices of Fancy, or the delightful deceit of Fables'.[6] The society's own statutes were bluntly worded: 'In all Reports to be brought into the Society, the Matter of Fact shall be barely stated, without any Prefaces, Apologies, or Rhetorical flourishes.'

Locke's approach in effect allowed for the hospitable coexistence of the new natural philosophy with poetry, eloquence and literature, and in particular the neo-classic style of the literary canon that characterised many late seventeenth- and early eighteenth-century writers and thinkers – in what came to be called the Augustan Age. In this growing separation of history from poetry, the role of the former was to deliver the specific truth of fact, not the 'universal truths' of poetry.[7] Even William Camden, an exact contemporary of Bacon, observed that he would use plain language in his works and would steer clear of the 'Nosegay of flowers' all too common in the 'Garden of eloquence'. Then again, in law, Matthew Hale, one of its most distinguished practitioners and a judge under Oliver Cromwell, declared himself 'a great Enemy of All Eloquence or Rhetoric in Pleading', on the grounds that such 'arts' would only confuse and corrupt jurors by 'bringing their Fancies and biassing their Affections'.[8]

THE EXPERIMENTAL IMAGINATION

Many Puritans felt just the same, that eloquent language was 'mere embellishment which too easily detracted from the essential argument'. Concerned as they were with a faith that stressed practical morality over doctrinal purity, the merely 'ornamental prose' of Sidney or Donne simply was not applicable to the needs of the new generation. Abraham Cowley, though he was inspired to become a poet on reading his mother's copy of *The Faerie Queene*, was influenced much more by Bacon and Hobbes, and thought that heroic poetry should not be like 'some farfetched Fairyland' inhabited by witches and giants and other 'imaginary creatures'. Dryden felt even more strongly. Much influenced by the neo-classical French poet and critic Boileau, his views also overlapped with those of Hobbes and Sprat, in that he sought a literary style that laid heavy emphasis on clarity of expression, and narrative 'shorn of fantasy and myth'. Dryden, a fellow of the Royal Society, said he saw poetry as 'a lively imitation of truth', and confessed that the best poetic style was a mean somewhere between 'ostentation and rusticity'. Locke, another FRS, preferred 'facility, clearness and elegancy in expression' while

Joseph Addison advocated a natural way of writing with 'beautiful simplicity'.[9] Tita Chico says this is part of what she calls 'The Experimental Imagination', whereby 'science was made intellectually possible because its main discoveries and technologies could be articulated in literary terms', with literary writers 'using scientific metaphors to make the case for the epistemological superiority of literary knowledge'.[10]

All this was aided by the fact that, as Shapiro tells us, towards the end of the seventeenth century poetry was 'losing its association with truth'.[11] This is a big thing to say but she insists that, increasingly, 'we hear comments that poetry, like rhetoric, was designed to foster falsehood'. This did not in itself herald the end of poetry, but views *were* changing and quite radically. Locke, for instance, went so far as to say that he thought it best to 'stifle poetic expression' in children, as it was 'a pleasant air but barren soil', at best an idle pastime. Newton felt poetry 'was a kind of ingenious nonsense'.[12]

This reshaping of literary tastes and values was no passing matter, for it brought into being new literary forms of which three were to prove the most significant: the narrative of travel and discovery, the novel and the newspaper.

THE READING REVOLUTION

These developments were all part of something which the Cambridge historian Tim Blanning says also came into being at this time – 'the public', which he calls 'a new cultural space ... Alongside the old culture, centred on the courts and the representation of monarchical authority, there emerged a "public sphere", in which private individuals came together to form a whole greater than the sum of the parts. By exchanging information, ideas, and criticism, these individuals created a cultural actor – the public –which has dominated European culture ever since.'

Blanning himself concentrates on three innovations: the novel, the newspaper and the concert. In the late seventeenth and early eighteenth centuries there was a 'reading revolution', he says, and he quotes scores of memoirs of the time to support this argument. In Britain, for example, the number of books published rose from about 400 per year in the early seventeenth century, to 6,000 a year by 1630, 21,000 in 1710 and fully 56,000 by the 1790s.

Blanning says that the chief attraction of the novel was its realism, imagination masquerading as factual *reportage*, and though many were 'trivial and lachrymose', some novelists, for example Samuel Richardson, expressed a more serious aim, to investigate 'the great doctrines of Christianity under the fashionable guise of an amusement'. Another effect of the novel, and its concern with the here and now, was to push centre stage family relationships and women, partly because most middle- and upper-class women enjoyed more leisure than their menfolk.[13]

So far as newspapers and periodicals were concerned, it was during the last decades of the seventeenth century that the transition from sporadic to regular publication occurred in several European cities – Antwerp, Frankfurt, Turin, as well as Paris and London. By the 1730s in London, there were six dailies and by the 1770s there were nine, with a combined circulation of 12,600,000. Even those who couldn't read kept up; they gathered in one of London's 551 coffee houses, 207 inns or 447 taverns,* where the newspapers were read out loud.[14]

THE REPUBLIC OF LETTERS

This picture is also amended somewhat by Jonathan Israel's discussion of 'learned journals', which came into existence at this time. 'Overwhelmingly orientated towards recent developments in the world of thought, scholarship and science, they did much to shift the focus of the cultivated public's attention away from established authorities and the classics to what was new, innovative, or challenging, even when such innovation arose in distant lands and unfamiliar languages.' Whereas previously, it took people years to find out about books which had appeared in a language different to their own, now they knew about them 'within a matter of weeks'.[15]

---

* These figures were eclipsed by those in the Holy Roman Empire, where there were more than a thousand newspapers and periodicals by the time of the French Revolution.

Defoe and Bunyan were the first, among English writers at least, to exist outside what writer and co-founder of *The Spectator* in 1711 Richard Steele called 'the circumference of wit', to mean that predominantly aristocratic society of writers who obtained patronage. 'If one inspects the memoirs ... of the many self-educated men who achieved distinction in the eighteenth and early nineteenth centuries, one finds almost invariably that their earliest contact with culture was through *Pilgrim's Progress*, the Bible, *Paradise Lost*, *Robinson Crusoe*.'[16]

One important effect of this, says Arnold Hauser, was the emancipation of middle-class taste from the dictates of the aristocracy. 'It forms the historical starting point of literary life in the modern sense, as typified not only by the regular appearance of books, newspapers and periodicals, but, above all, by the emergence of the literary expert, the critic, who represents the general standard of values and public opinion in the world of literature.'[17] Blanning adds: 'This public taste was especially strong for historical, biographical and statistical encyclopaedias.'[18]

Periodical publishing was also proving a growth business. In the tenth issue of *The Spectator* Joseph Addison wrote: 'My Publisher tells me that there are already Three thousand of them distributed every Day: so that if I allow Twenty Readers to every Paper, which I look upon as a modest computation, I may reckon about Threescore thousand Disciples in *London* and *Westminster*.' The print run of *The Spectator* later rose to between 20,000 and 30,000, on some accounts, giving a 'circulation', on Addison's calculations, of roughly half a million (the population of England in 1700 was a little over 6 million). This was later reflected in a rise in newspaper readership: between 1753 and 1775 the average daily sale of newspapers practically doubled.

The republic of letters was accompanied by the commonwealth of learning as, across the turn of the eighteenth century, divisions appeared between the 'dominions of learning', the fledgling disciplines and the realm of conversation. Newton played a role here. Robin Valenza tells us that *Principia Mathematica* was the book everyone wanted to own but no one had read, with Newton keeping back part of his writing for close colleagues who had the mathematics to understand fully what he was saying, such colleagues comprising a kind of 'mathematical sanctum'. In fact, mathematicians of the time often kept back parts of their 'proof' so as to prevent their ideas being stolen.[19] Other writers deliberately wrote in Latin to confine their readers to the 'learned'. 'Learned' no longer implied a familiarity with the Bible and there was a 'mathematics boom' alongside a growing realisation that some subjects, like physics, were inherently difficult for some people, and that that was what universities were partly for, as the home of 'difficult' knowledge, with its own language.[20] Moreover, it was increasingly understood that literature could no longer offer general learning, as there was too much differentiation.[21] As a result, knowledge of literature came to be regarded as a separate form of learning.

THE RISE OF THE NOVEL

But we are running ahead of ourselves. Early accounts of voyages to newly discovered, distant and exotic lands were widely read, the best-known account being Richard Hakluyt's *The Principal Navigations, Voyages, Traffiques and Discoveries* (1589). So strong was his material that he too found it easy to adopt a straightforward, clear style. Moreover, the sheer topicality of the genre meant that it appealed equally to scholarly, professional and general audiences, who were all gripped by its plain, direct prose.[22]

With Hakluyt having the effect he did, perhaps we should not be surprised by the introduction of the imaginary voyage, but Jonathan Swift's *Travels into the Remote Nations of the World by Captain Lemuel Gulliver* and Daniel Defoe's *Robinson Crusoe* were both highly successful and also formed part of a new trend in fact-oriented fiction. And it was not far from there to a form which combined fact and fantasy to create a new order – the novel. Ian Watt, in his book *The Rise of the Novel*, argues that the novel also grew out of John Locke's epistemology, that experience is what counts above all in providing new knowledge and food for the imagination, one effect being that this brought about a 'self-conscious rejection of the romance'. In the work in particular of Defoe, realistic individuals are situated in realistic settings, and Defoe himself assumes the role of a 'reliable and truthful reporter', reporting what he presents as, *à la* Locke, first-hand experience.²³ When *Robinson Crusoe* was first published in 1719, many thought it was a real account of a real place.

Defoe, it is now clear, is a more important figure in British history than he is usually given credit for. Besides being 'Father of the English Novel', he was a pioneer in economic thought and, arguably, the nation's first journalist. Recently, it has been shown just how much he was involved with the new learning, the sciences promulgated by the Royal Society. In fact, he embodies perfectly the imaginative link between the arts and the sciences at that time, and his ideas show well the influence of Bacon on the wider scene of English intellectual life. While *Robinson Crusoe* enjoys the distinction of being published in more editions than any other book in English, except the Bible, Defoe's other books range from *An Essay on Projects* (1697) to *A General History of Trade* (1713) and *A General History of Discoveries and Improvements, in Useful Acts* (1725–7), all titles that might well have been penned by Bacon.

In *Crusoe*, Defoe endows his hero with the Baconian mentality of observation and experiment, 'learning step-by-step from his mistakes the whole process to bake bread, to make baskets, pots, clothes and other artefacts'. He keeps a Baconian tabulation of the weather, 'observes the tides, and maintains a diary of all remarkable events – as recommended by the Royal Society'. 'Crusoe works not just as a scientist but as a Christian, sharing the belief of many seventeenth-century scientists ... that the study of the created world would give insight into the divine order.' 'Travel had from the start been an important aspect of the new philosophy: it was one of the means whereby Bacon's demand for personal observation and collection of data could be realised. In Defoe's travel books we have,' Ilse Vickers says, 'perhaps the author's most practical application of the fundamental tenets of the New Sciences ... Defoe uses and adapts the Royal Society's directions for travellers by sea to write his propaganda piece for colonization of South America.'²⁴

Defoe became a student at the Academy for Dissenters in Newington Green, to the north of London, from around 1674 to around 1679, under Dr Charles Morton, who had been a scholar at Wadham College, Oxford in the early 1650s, and would later be appointed vice-president of Harvard. This, as we now know, was in the run-up to the creation of the Royal Society and by then Oxford itself could boast several scientific benefactions. It was during Morton's time there that the Oxford Experimental Philosophy Society – Wilkins's group at Wadham, which included Seth Ward (mathematician and astronomer), Sir Christopher Wren (scientist and architect), John Wallis (mathematician), William Petty (anatomist and economist), Walter Pope (astronomer) and Robert Boyle (physicist and chemist) – changed its meeting venue from Petty's rooms to Wilkins's in Wadham. Many of these men were among those who met on 28 November 1660 at Gresham College to discuss the foundation of the Royal Society. There is little doubt that Morton, living in Wadham, would have been influenced by the intellectual society around him, and passed this on to Defoe.

The main concern of the dissenting academies like Morton's was to reproduce the standard of education of the traditional universities, all the while stressing a *practical* approach to learning, and a good example of this utilitarian ethos was the decision to include science in the teaching they offered. In his eagerness to spread the good word, Morton delivered all his lectures in English and even made English itself a subject to be studied. What the school essentially offered was a fusion of Baconian and Puritan ideals, shown above all in Morton's introduction of practical work into the classroom.[25]

Defoe seems to have been temperamentally suited to the new sciences and the Baconian approach. Instead of 'wasting time' studying the classical languages, he recommended instead, in his own writings, that men study practical, useful subjects 'related to the business of life'. Defining the 'compleat scholar', he identified a student who, for four years and more, attended a private academy, not a university, and in that time, he said, the student became a mathematician, a geographer, an astronomer, a philosopher – in a word, or two words, a complete scholar 'and all this without the least help from the Greek or Latin'.[26]

Defoe's argument, following Bacon and expanding on him, is that the traditional education system produces pedagogues unfit for real life outside the precincts of the university, 'dullards' as Morton characterised them: ''Tis better to copie nature than Bookes: as the best

Painters imitate Nature, not copies.'[27] In this Defoe and Locke were in complete agreement: 'The knowledge of things, not words, make a scholar.' In *Moll Flanders*, Defoe's conceit is his insistence that he has only 'edited' what Moll herself has put in 'her own Memorandum'. In his *Journal of the Plague Year*, the conceit is that it is an eye-witness report of the 1665 plague, though Defoe was about five at the time and too young to have witnessed the events described. Which means that the 'feel' of Defoe's books is much the same whether fiction or fact. His *A Tour through the Whole Island of Britain* is a travel book full of precise observations of both nature and socio-economic life in Britain that could have been written by Crusoe.

Being practically minded, Defoe was no less interested in educational projects, and not least for women. 'We always thought', he writes in one periodical, that 'Woman had the quickest and justest Notion of things at first sight,' but adds, 'though we have unjustly rob'd them of the Judgement, by denying them early Instruction'. He goes on to outline a curriculum for women's colleges which includes not only music and dancing, but modern languages, polite conversation and 'especially history'.

As others did, Defoe put forward a scheme for a university in London, practical ideas for the protection of battered women, a project to prevent women 'being sent to mad-houses by their husbands', and ideas about how to stop the street robberies then plaguing the capital. Clearly, he had much in common with people like Samuel Hartlib and so it is no surprise to find that he often showed in his writing a familiarity with the *Philosophical Transactions of the Royal Society*. Ilse Vickers quotes him as saying that 'being addicted to Experimental Philosophy, a Man is rather assisted than Indisposed, to be a good Christian'.[28]

Defoe wasn't alone in his endeavours, as other writers of fiction presented themselves or their characters as real historians or reporters. Isaac Bickerstaff, actually Jonathan Swift, was later named as editor of *The Tatler* by founder Richard Steele, while the invented 'Roger de Coverly' was also written about as a real person in *The Spectator*. In his account of *The Clubs of Augustan London*, Robert Allen describes several phantom societies and satiric portraits of fictitious clubmen (Borachio, Magpye and Nutbrain, the 'High-flyers' at the Swan Tripe-Club).[29] Imaginary characters showed that there was still scope for imagination but, nonetheless, the taste now was for fiction to sound like fact.[30]

The periodical press, which was to be such a feature of eighteenth-century life in Britain, grew out of the newspaper, which had originated in the Thirty Years War and Civil War, and this development, too, had a clear effect on prose. Although the early news sheets were every bit as partisan as the later ones would become, the newspaper always earned its basic credibility from the accuracy of its reporting. At the very start, during the Thirty Years War, English newspapers were limited to providing foreign news only, using letters and dispatches written by continental observers of varying credibility. Only with the collapse of Parliament's ability to control publications at the outbreak of the Civil War could newspapers include domestic news, and it was now somewhat easier to check the validity of what was printed.

During the Interregnum and Restoration, when governmental authority was restored and strengthened, the spread of news periodicals was curtailed. Fortunately, two stylish diaries produced during that time – those of the bibliophiles Samuel Pepys and John Evelyn – conveniently fill in the gaps, to an extent: war, the navy, 'music and women' in Pepys's case, an early concern with the environment in Evelyn's (he was worried England didn't have enough trees for its navy, and hated the smog of London). But when the press revived across the turn of the eighteenth century, accuracy retook centre stage and once more a plain, no-nonsense, functional prose was what was needed, again conforming very much to the preferred style of the Royal Society: clarity, not ornamentation; factual, objective reporting.[31]

Dryden, Dunciad, Defiant Daughters

I f one had to select the greatest 'maverick' in British imaginative history, one strong candidate would have to be Aphra Behn (1640–89). Not only did she have a riotous variety of careers and interests – alleged spy, beauty, traveller in foreign lands, playwright, short-story writer, novelist – but the style with which she lived her life 'out loud', with a bawdy intelligence, reveal her as ahead of her time in the most interesting ways, not quite fitting into the Royal Society's preferred manner of doing things. Certainly, she is one of those people most welcome at any dinner party game.

Probably born in or near Wye in Kent, though nothing is certain, she often described herself as the daughter of a gentleman who 'became the lieutenant-general of six and thirty islands, besides the continent of Surinam'. Few contemporaries shared this view and John Dryden considered her as low-born. She certainly arrived in Surinam, a new English colony on the north-east shoulder of South America, in 1663, staying on a plantation, where she soon took part in the political squabbles of the territory. Adventures in Antwerp followed; by this time, she had married, apparently to a German named Johann Behn, who may have died aboard ship (there is a lot of 'may' and 'apparently' in Aphra's early life). She may have been on a spying mission in Antwerp, operating under the pseudonym Astrea, mixing with the family of an executed regicide. She floundered in Antwerp and may have been forced to undertake other intelligence missions to make ends meet.

This mysterious beginning did not in any way hamper her main career as a writer, in particular of bawdy plays, reflected in their titles, *The Forc'd Marriage*, *The Amorous Prince*, *The Dutch Lover*, *Lust's Dominion*, *The Debauchee*, often mocking male pretensions. Some of them were successful, some weren't and some were set to music by Purcell. She often depicted liberties, formed friendships with bisexual and homosexual writers or lawyers, usually with reputations for republicanism and freethinking, and her poems and plays were equally full of drunken rakes, 'impassioned whores', almost prefiguring Hogarth on the stage. In one poem 'leering trees' looked down on copulating mortals. Her works were more explicitly sexual than those of any other woman of her age, so much so that at first people were convinced they were written by a man. She looked at sex from the point of view of power, not love.

The women who had preceded her in the theatre – Katherine Phillips, Frances Boothby – only ever wrote one or two plays but Behn had at least nineteen staged, which reflected and bounced off contemporary politics – the Interregnum and Exclusion Crisis – just as much as Dryden's were to do. Certain of her works were admired by James VII and II when he was Duke of York and during the Exclusion Crisis and the Popish Plot she at times became a propagandist for Charles II. One of her works was dedicated to the king's mistress, the actress Nell Gwyn; in another she lampoons – from a distance – Titus Oates, fabricator of the Popish Plot.[1]

Her works became associated with libertinism and freethinking but in *Love-Letters* she achieved what one biographer called an important landmark in the epistolary novel (see below), although even here it was an 'extraordinary analysis of erotic arousal'. Like Dryden and others, she was published by Jacob Tonson. She also wrote a number of 'Pindaricks', poems based on the work of Pindar, the fifth-century BC Greek poet, an essentially loose form divided into three sections: strophe, antistrophe and epode. Not even that does justice to the variety of her work: she produced translations from two French texts that popularised the new Copernican science, *Discovery of New Worlds* and *The History of Oracles* (both 1688), from Bernard de la Fontenelle's originals. All this shows Behn's range from the excesses of libertinism to classicism and though her reputation was to suffer mightily in the Victorian century (her writing was regarded as 'not suitable' for a woman), more recently she has been appreciated for *Oroonoko*, her 1688 novel set in Surinam.

Prince Oroonoko is the grandson of an African king, and trained for battle. During one of these battles a general takes an arrow for Oroonoko and is killed. In paying his respects to the general's daughter, Imoinda, Oroonoko falls in love with her, but so does the king, who forces her to become his wife. Oroonoko and Imoinda meet secretly to consummate their relationship but are discovered and consigned to slavery, though the king tells Oroonoko that Imoinda is dead. Later, Oroonoko is captured by a European slave trader and taken to Surinam where he is sold to a Cornishman who, unknown at first to Oroonoko, is also the owner of Imoinda, and they are reunited, living as husband and wife. When she becomes pregnant, they petition for a return to their homeland but are fobbed off, until they decide on revolt. This is disastrous all round. Rather than return to slavery, Oroonoko kills Imoinda and disembowels himself and, weakened, is captured and dismembered.

There has been much debate as to how realistic the story is, where the name Oroonoko comes from, possibly from a French novel Behn is known to have read, possibly a homophone for the Orinoco River, which flows through Surinam. Oroonoko is black but has a Roman nose and long straight hair, so it has been conjectured that Behn had a pre-scientific idea of race, and that she didn't oppose slavery, instead accepting that powerful groups would always enslave the less powerful. Also, Johan Behn, allegedly her husband, was a slave trader – would she have been opposed to slavery as an institution? The story was published in 1688, at the height of the Exclusion Crisis, and may be seen more as a support for royal qualities rather than racial ones. Whatever the truth, it is certainly one of the first European novels to show Africans in a multi-dimensional and sympathetic manner.[2] It followed Dryden's plays *The Indian Queen* (1663) and *The Indian Emperour* (1665), which also introduced foreign cultures in a more sympathetic way than hitherto.

The poet and dramatist John Dryden (1631–1700) said of himself: 'I know I am not so fitted by Nature to write Comedy: I want the gayety of humour which is required to it. My Conversation is slow and dull, my humour Saturnine and reserv'd; In short, I am none of those who endeavour to break Jests in Company, or make reparties.' In other words, he hardly presents himself as good company. And yet, despite this, some historians speak of the 'Age of Dryden', and the span of his life certainly helps us move forward with purpose: he lived through the Civil War, the Protectorate, the Restoration, the reopening of the theatres after the Puritan ban, the Great Plague and the Great Fire of London, the Exclusion Crisis and the Glorious Revolution, the Popish Plot and the Rye House Plot; he has been described as the greatest poet of the seventeenth century after Donne and Milton, 'the greatest dramatist after Shakespeare and Ben Jonson' and perhaps the greatest translator of all, especially of Virgil; he is generally recognised as having perfected the heroic couplet in poetry; he was elected to the Royal Society to help improve its writing style; he epitomises the evolution of the writer from a pleaser of patrons to a pleaser of the public; he was a frequenter of that new institution, the coffee house. He *sounds* like good company.

Born in Northamptonshire, the eldest of fourteen children, to a family of Puritan gentry, he was sent to Westminster School in London where he wrote his first poem. At Cambridge Dryden came top of his year at Trinity College. His family sided with the Commonwealth but in his first published poem, in 1649, he showed royalist inclinations. During the Protectorate, he obtained employment with Cromwell's Office of Latin Secretary, possibly because his cousin was Lord Chamberlain. Certainly, at the funeral of Cromwell in 1658 Dryden processed with both Milton and Marvell.

Dryden is best known today as a satirist, his two greatest works of this genre being *Mac Flecknoe* and *The Medall* (both 1682), though *Absalom and Achitophel* (1681) also contains a number of satiric portraits. *Mac Flecknoe* is one of two great satires against rival poets (the other is Pope's *Dunciad*, see below). It was an attack on Thomas Shadwell ('Mr S———l'), who saw himself as the heir to Ben Jonson, but who Dryden castigates as dull and unfunny, contrasting him with such characters as Spenser's Faerie Queene (holiness) and Satan in *Paradise Lost* (pride). *Absalom and Achitophel* is about the

Exclusion Crisis but mediated through biblical terms. The Exclusion
Crisis saw the Earl of Shaftesbury lead a campaign to bar the Duke of
York – brother of Charles II and a Roman Catholic – from succeeding to the throne, in favour of the king's illegitimate (but Protestant)
son, the Duke of Monmouth. In the poem, Absalom is Monmouth,
Absalom's false friend Achitophel stands for Shaftesbury, who tries
to persuade Absalom to revolt against his father, David (Charles
II), and Dryden makes his sympathy with the Duke of York clear,
despite this not being the majority view, and despite the famous
opening lines:

> All humane things are subject to decay
> And, when Fate summons, Monarchs must obey.

Dryden's two greatest plays are *Marriage à la Mode* (1673) and
All for Love (1677). *Marriage* is a comedy (with songs) set in Sicily
and, in summary, the plot sounds like a pantomime but is redeemed
in performance by its wit and its agreeable ending. It features two
unrelated plots, both about love affairs where the thwarted lovers
triumph in the end. In one plot, Palmyra and Leonidas are raised
together and fall in love but it turns out they are from different stations in life, precluding marriage. Later, after a series of deceptions,
it further turns out they are of the same station after all and can
wed. In the other plot, Rodophil and Doralice are getting tired of
one another after a few years of marriage and each is drawn to their
friends' partners, Rodophil to Melanthe and Doralice to Palamede.
After several scenes of 'noises off', with secret assignations repeatedly
sabotaged by absurd coincidences and pratfalls, the men conclude
that, since it is clear they both like the same kind of woman, they
might as well stay as they are. *Marriage* is still performed today and
is a striking example of the use of the heroic couplet, in which the
metre – iambic pentameter – rhymes and the action/thrust/idea is
completed (hence heroic) in the two lines. Dryden, for example, had
a fear and contempt for the rising middle class of England:

> The Knack of Trades is living on the Spoyle;
> They boast ev'n when each other they beguile.

At the Restoration, in *Astrea Redux* (1660) and *To His Sacred Majesty* (1661), Dryden welcomed Charles II, for which he was made the first Poet Laureate and, later, Historiographer Royal, the official chronicler of the Court, a French innovation initially. Dryden also wrote a number of operas. In his later years, however, he became known as a translator, justifying the age he epitomised as the Augustan Age. His translations of Virgil – the *Aeneid* in particular – are regarded as his masterpiece.

At the same time Dryden attracted more than his fair share of criticism and satirical derision, partly for his efforts, as one criticism had it, for 'turning himself into a public event' (i.e., showing off), for his pedantry and dogmatism on occasions, for his arrogance, for his plagiarisms, for being a turncoat (as when he converted to Catholicism), for opportunism (as when he sought and failed to capture the provostship of All Souls College, Oxford), for his propaganda masquerading as history (this was directed at *Annus Mirabilis*, his 1667 poem about the events of the previous year – the Plague, the Fire of London and the Anglo-Dutch War), and for being a 'ventriloquist' for James II. In his poem *The Hind and the Panther* (1687), also in heroic couplets, which apparently accompanied his conversion to Catholicism, the Roman church is presented as a 'milk white' hind, the Church of England as a panther, and the Presbyterians as a wolf – satire is not always subtle. He was attacked mercilessly for trimming his sails to the Catholic wind and was forced to leave the Royal Society for failing to pay his dues.[3] His sister was the grandmother of Jonathan Swift.[4]

The quarrel of the Ancients and Moderns had been going on for hundreds of years, at least since Dante and his followers delved into the works of the great philosophers and poets of antiquity and concluded that, despite all the exciting progress made by the physical sciences, Christendom had not until then generated anyone to equal Homer or Virgil, Aristotle or Horace.

Dryden entered the quarrel from time to time, generally being a consistent Modern. The Moderns, he argued, 'have the greater perspective and wisdom', though he also thought that 'progress is not linear but cyclical', with its regular 'ups and downs'. The most persistent and the most distinguished of his opponents, however, according to Michael Werth Gelber, was his distant relative, the young Jonathan Swift, who staunchly took the part of the Ancients.[5] In Dryden, Swift unearthed all that upset him among the Moderns, and he assaulted the older man in both *A Tale of a Tub* and *The Battle of the Books* (both 1704).

Swift conceded that the Moderns, whether they are historians or literary figures, could from time to time uncover forgotten texts and clarify outdated syntax, but historical criticism in itself he regarded as pointless or even dangerous. Swift was given to exaggerated circumlocutions but in this case he meant that scholarly investigation – of attribution, say, or dates of composition – 'merely adds to the boredom in the world'.[6]

In *The Battle of the Books*, various actual books in St James's Library, in St James's Palace, where one of Swift's adversaries was librarian, suddenly come alive and start scrapping, the ancient authors skirmishing with the moderns, with, at the same time, the authors butchering the critics in a deliciously silly and quite over-the-top uproar. Swift derides Dryden for his deplorable taste, likening him to the 'prime productions' of 'the Grub-Street brotherhood'.*

Swift has been described as 'nothing less than the first widely popular author of the print era'. Certainly, *Gulliver's Travels* (1726) was the best-selling fictional book of its century. But first *A Tale of a Tub*, which is an allegory of the Reformation and outlines the fate of three brothers, Peter (named after St Peter – i.e., Catholicism), Jack (John Calvin) and Martin (Luther). 'Tub' is a mocking reference to what was a common Dissenter's pulpit, a beer barrel. Swift was himself a clergyman so although *Tub* was initially published anonymously, the account could be regarded as a sermon by him. His main aims in *Battle* and *Tub* are to criticise what he saw as arrogance, the assertion that the present time was the equal of the achievements of the past – in other words the sin of pride – and to assess the threat

---

* Grub Street was a real London street that ran from Fore Street, now near the Barbican Centre, to Chiswell Street, now in Islington. The street took its name from a refuse ditch that ran alongside but, over time, it became the bohemian home for low-end apartments, hack writers, small-time publishers, and brothels.

posed by the competing religious stances. In the latter book, the Ship of State is threatened by a whale (for which, read Hobbes's *Leviathan*), and Swift's conceit is that a book be thrown over the side of the ship to distract it. The three brothers have each been given a coat in their father's will (representing the Bible), with instructions not to change it. But of course they do and the book narrates their various fates.

Samuel Johnson found *Tub* more than hilarious, a work of true genius which he much preferred to *Gulliver's Travels* because, as he put it, once one imagines very big people (in Brobdingnag) and very little people (in Lilliput), the rest follows more or less obviously, involving little in the way of original thinking. Though to an extent correct, this did not stop *Travels* being wildly successful.[7]

Swift's personality has been the object of much inquiry and speculation. He was well connected, in being distantly related not just to Dryden but also to Sir Walter Raleigh and Sir William Davenant, Poet Laureate and actor (in Dryden's plays), who was himself a godson of Shakespeare. Swift was born in Dublin and educated at Trinity College there. Trinity had been founded by Queen Elizabeth in 1592, on the site of an ancient monastery, as a sister college to St John's, Cambridge and Oriel, Oxford. To begin with, Swift was much in favour of the Glorious Revolution and supported the Whigs. Later, after bouts of ill-health and living in London for a time, and because he did not get the religious preferment he hoped for (Queen Anne disliked him), he rallied to the Tories and became part of their inner core.[8]

In London, he became very friendly with Alexander Pope, with whom he often lodged, and with John Gay and John Arbuthnot, who together arranged for publication of *Gulliver's Travels*. Eventually he was made dean of St Patrick's Cathedral in Dublin, an office created in 1219, and a position not in the gift of the monarch. He pamphleteered until the end of his life, the best known being *A Modest Proposal* (1729), another completely over-the-top argument of mock-righteousness for solving the problem of famine and undernourishment in Ireland, by proposing that the children of the poor be sold to the rich, to be eaten as food, thus preventing them becoming 'a burthen' on the Commonwealth.

Swift lost none of his acerbity in old age (he died at seventy-eight) but throughout he had shown an unusual ability for, as one critic has said, 'testing the limits of sexual propriety', even sexual abnormality, and 'as a compulsive cruiser of Dunghills ... Ditches and Common-Shores with a great Affectation [*sic*] for everything that is nasty'.[9] William Hogarth, for example, illustrated *Gulliver's Travels* with a frontispiece showing the diminutive citizens of Lilliput inserting a massive syringe-like 'Lilypucian fire engine' into 'Lemuel's bare posterior' as punishment for 'urinal prophanation of the royal palace'. And this was by no means Swift's only scatological/androsodomy satire.

The government made several attempts to silence Swift but in effect he silenced himself. In 1731 he composed his own obituary, which was published before his death in 1745, and in 1742 it is thought he suffered a stroke, losing the ability to speak; he quarrelsomely ended friendships of long standing (as with Irish playwright Richard Brinsley Sheridan), and was eventually found to be of 'unsound mind'.

The man with whom Swift often stayed when he was in London, and who helped him publish *Gulliver's Travels*, was just as unusual as he was but in a quite different way. And the first thing to say is that Alexander Pope didn't, in fact, live in London. When Alexander – who had been born in the year of the Glorious Revolution – was four, the restrictions imposed on Roman Catholics under William III prohibited 'papists' from living within 10 miles of Hyde Park Corner. His parents (his mother was a sister of Samuel Cooper, the painter) had therefore moved to Hammersmith and then to Binfield, Berkshire, out towards Reading.

Alexander Pope was a poet, translator, horticulturist, publisher and a popular subject of contemporary portraiture. During his lifespan four British monarchs reigned, two of them foreigners, William III and George I. A fifth monarch, also a foreigner, George II, was on the throne when Pope died.

During that time, power – socially, politically and economically – shifted from a patrician to a moneyed class. Mainly because of Pope a new audience for literature emerged and expanded with many more ways for authors to earn a living. But the changing circumstance that affected Pope the most can be put down to the increasing displacement of serious literature from the centre of the culture (or as the culture liked to think of itself) to a position where it was just one form of entertainment among all the rest.[10]

We should never forget how difficult it was in Pope's early years for Roman Catholic families like his to educate their children. Roman Catholic schools were prohibited by law, though a few managed to get by by stealth. In Pope's case he was at first taught by a priest, then went to a boarding school that, we are told, 'had to change premises at least once to evade the authorities'. From twelve on he was an autodidact, submerging himself in the works of the Greek and Roman poets, the neo-Latin poets and his English predecessors. He loved travel books – Montaigne, Jonson, Israel Silvestre's book on Roman gardens. His own earliest published works were even then ambitious – a modernisation of Chaucer, a translation of Homer – some of them edited by Sir Richard Steele, who was publishing *The Tatler* just then. Pope kept portraits of Chaucer, Spenser, Milton and Dryden in his bedroom to keep him, as he said, 'always humble'. He once said he hoped that 'Slav'ry be no more', but his relatives were involved in the trade and he himself invested in the South Sea Company.[11]

He really came to public attention with three notable works: *An Essay on Criticism*, published anonymously in 1711, when he was only twenty-two, and which argued that criticism is an art, a thesis 'which brought him the attention of the literary men'; *The Rape of the Lock* (1712), which, in addition, 'gained him the attention of the "Town"'; and *Windsor-Forest* (1714), which thrust him into the political world just then boiling with the factionalism surrounding the Peace of Utrecht (1713) which ended for close to fifty years England's recurring wars with France.

An Essay on Criticism is a work to which Samuel Johnson ascribes in his life of Pope 'such extension of comprehension, such nicety of distinction, such acquaintance with mankind, and such knowledge both of ancient and modern learning as are not often attained by the maturest age and longest experience'.[12] *The Rape of the Lock*, Pope's second great triumph, is set in 1711, the year the *Essay* was published anonymously. It recounts the story of a gathering in that same year, possibly brought about by negotiations between two families whose offspring are contemplating marriage, when the heir of a distinguished Roman Catholic family cuts off as a trophy the lock of hair which 'curled down invitingly' over the shoulder of Arabella Fermor, heiress of a second prominent Roman Catholic line. This event, which to us seems tame, even romantic, caused estrangement between the two families, and Pope was asked by a friend 'to write a poem ... to laugh them together again'.

Highlighting the triviality of the incident, he nonetheless acknowledges its significance for those involved, but goes on to paint a picture of merchants, judges and juries hurrying home of an evening: 'And wretches hang that jurymen may dine.' Everywhere, he is saying, there is a stubborn self-centredness. 'Contemporary London was fascinated – excited and appalled – to find itself the centre of such-well written and caustic attention and from then on Pope was a marked man.'[13]

Pope's diminutive and crippled shape (he was 4 feet 6 inches high, having been trampled on by a cow as a boy and separately contracted tuberculosis of the spine) made him, as he told a friend, 'the little Alexander the women laugh at'. This 'did not preclude', says Elizabeth Wallace, 'his entertaining the usual aspirations of young men in the springtime of their lives'. Being too direct towards women was hardly advisable in one so vulnerable to ridicule or worse, and proposals of marriage, given his condition, completely off the cards (when he did admit his feelings to Lady Mary Wortley Montagu, she collapsed in laughter).[14] Despite his condition, he was energetic and known to translate between forty and fifty lines of Greek before he got up. His translations – of the *Iliad* and *Odyssey* in particular – were both a commercial and an artistic/intellectual success.

After *The Rape of the Lock*, his next great achievement was his 'War with the Dunces'. *The Dunciad* may have been conceived after he was visited at his Twickenham home by his close friend Swift, with whom he went back over the virtually incessant attacks heaped on him since his first published works, aimed not least at his crippled body. No doubt Swift, but also Gay and Arbuthnot, all fellow members of the Scriblerus Club (which we shall come to soon), urged him to deride the pedantry and want of talent among his critics, who they were all agreed were in the ascendant.

There were several versions of *Dunciad*, the first a blast at the 'pop' literature, popular in particular in the grimier tenements of the capital, for which Pope blamed 'the cultureless Hanoverians' and their corruption of the traditional aristocracy.[15] Next came *The Dunciad Variorum*, which has a Prolegomenon by 'Scriblerus' which satirises the arrogant tediousness of academics and the 'Empire of Dulness' they inhabit. Pope was also taken aback by the turn to scientific thinking, thanks to Bacon and the Royal Society, by the enhanced stature which it had acquired over the years and which, he felt, had provoked an optimism about the human condition which he regarded as 'entirely misplaced'. And he criticised the ascendant Whig society for its egotistical swaggering and acquisitive nature. 'He went to his grave hating the new class who, he said, worshipped "the goddess of getting-on"'. Perhaps his greatest mark was to achieve for literature the right to be accounted 'a principal cultural institution'.[16]

In August 1716, Jonathan Swift wrote to Pope asking him, 'What think you, of a Newgate pastoral among the thieves and whores there?' The idea of a 'pastoral' set in Newgate prison – in existence since 1188 near one of the gates in the ancient wall around London, but rebuilt after the Great Fire of 1666 in a style deliberately intended to look 'repulsive', so as to deter miscreants – is immediately ironic and satiric, as we have come to expect of Swift. But it was John Gay who took up the challenge.

Gay's family were merchants and mayors in Barnstaple in Devon, he himself being apprenticed to a silk merchant there, an occupation he soon abandoned for a career as a playwright in London, where he did indeed compose a number of pastorals, and formed friendships with Swift, Pope and William Congreve, who helped him to stage his early efforts. Swift also helped him gain a position with the Earl of Clarendon, then the new British ambassador to the elector of Hanover. Like Swift, Gay would be disappointed not to obtain a position at Court. But he did acquire a number of distinguished patrons besides Clarendon, among them the Duke of Chandos, at whose house, Cannons, a celebrated musical salon, Gay met George Frideric Handel (1685–1759), the baroque composer, born in Halle in Brandenburg-Prussia but who, after several years moving around Italy and Germany, had settled in London in 1712.

In the early 1720s, Handel wrote three very successful operas, including *Tamerlano*, and, most notably, the anthem 'Zadok the Priest', composed for the coronation of King George II, with words taken from the Bible (this piece has been played at every coronation of a British monarch ever since, including that of Charles III in May 2023). Handel's music was extraordinarily popular in London, as was the Italian opera in general. Despite this, *The Beggar's Opera* is an attack on both Handel and the fashion for high opera, and it also draws on Locke's ideas about natural liberty. The success of this work was unprecedented – it ran for sixty-two performances at Lincoln's Inn Fields at a time when a week's run was regarded as a riotous success. It worked through Gay's desire 'to produce a comedy of incongruities', by being a parody of high opera, and by drawing parallels between high and low life. Instead of Handel-type songs, it employed common ballads and popular ditties (sixty-nine of them in forty-one rapidly changing scenes) that anyone in the audience could hear whistled in the streets any day of the week, and instead of relaying high drama set among the high and mighty, it is set amid thieves, highwaymen and whores. Characters talk in high-falutin politer ways, while discussing such subjects as shoplifting.[17] It appears there was no enmity between Gay and Handel, and they both continued to gather at Cannons. But the fashion of high Italian opera did somewhat abate after *Beggar's* and Handel went on to concentrate more on oratorio. (*Messiah*, with its famous 'Hallelujah' chorus, was composed in 1741.)

Where there *was* enmity in Gay's opera, it was directed at the Whig politician Sir Robert Walpole, now generally regarded as Britain's first prime minister (from 1721 to 1742) and the class interest he represented. In *Beggar's*, there are references to Walpole as 'Robin of Bagshot, alias Gorgon, alias Bluff Bob, alias Carbuncle, alias Bob Booty' (a character in the work).[18] In the song by Macheath, the captain of a gang of robbers and an inveterate womaniser (a parody of Walpole), 'How Could I Be Happy with Either' is a reference to Walpole having to choose between his wife and his mistress.

The achievement of *The Beggar's Opera* is to make us laugh, which it does well, but also to evoke a feeling of uneasiness among those laughing. 'We are placed in the uncomfortable position', says William McIntosh, 'of having to come to terms with two worlds. The world within the play is crowded with criminals on every level, but so is the world without.'[19]

Two years after *Beggar's*, Gay wrote *Polly*, which was set in the West Indies, where Macheath has been sent under a sentence of transportation (the Transportation Act had been introduced in 1717) but has escaped and taken to piracy, while another character from *Beggar's* has set up as a white-slaver and shanghaied Polly Peachum, yet another original character, to sell her to a plantation owner. Like Macheath, Polly escapes and in her case marries a Carib king or chief. Prime Minister Walpole prevailed on the Lord Chamberlain to ban the play. It did not reach the stage for fifty years.

The Augustan Humanists

The very concept of 'Augustan literature', or 'Augustan culture' has come under attack recently. For example, in *The Practice of Satire in England, 1658–1770*, Ashley Marshall examines some 3,000 satiric works, now easily available through such sites on the Internet as Early English Books Online, and this shows, she says, an 'unparalleled number of modes emerging, developing and sometimes disappearing' between 1660 and 1770, that satire was by no means always as abrasive as it has been made to sound, and that to begin with it was written by 'insiders for insiders' but as the eighteenth century lengthened that all changed.

That first point is certainly true. Beyond satire, in the eighteenth century, there was a rapid development of the novel, of melodrama, the poetry of personal experience (pointing towards romanticism), mercantilism, capitalism and the triumph of trade. Books fell dramatically in price, newspapers began and multiplied, sermon collections were popular, as were books of etiquette, magazines and periodicals. But authors were writing for an immediate audience, not for posterity, and in all forms of literature – poetry and novels, as well as drama and the press – literature was in *constant dialogue*. Satire became gentler as the eighteenth century progressed, evolving towards comic didacticism, perhaps, as Brooke Allen says, because satirists had less to be angry about. The Licensing Act of 1737, which in essence established a government censor over the stage, 'ended by softening the dramatic fare in London'.[20]

But Swift, Pope and Gay did help to form what someone else calls the imaginative central nervous system of the century: they were pessimistic about the possibility of moral or social progress; they believed that human nature is unchanging and knowable; they had a hierarchical view of society and of literature; they had an elegiac veneration for the past and a profound sense of the importance of history; they believed that a person's primary obligation is to concern him- or herself with serious moral questions; they were suspicious of any kind of simplification or mechanisation of man's nature, believing in his uniqueness, his free power of choice, his depravity, but also his ability to understand his corrupt nature and to achieve some measure of redemption by self-knowledge. The 'Augustan humanists', as they were called by Paul Fussell, were conservative, opposed to mechanism, rationalism, relativism, the new science, the new sentimentality, commercialism, art as self-expression, and facile utopian views of man and society. In their vision, man is an inevitably social, inevitably incomplete, inevitably tragic creature, tragic because of his potential dignity, for all his littleness.[21] They set the scene for a literature, indeed an entire culture, that would be as political as it ever would be but which, in the process, contributed to a growing latitudinarianism.

Kit-Kat and Scriblerus

On the evening of 18 December 1679, John Dryden was physically attacked in Rose Alley, by the Lamb & Flag pub, Covent Garden, by a gang of men and 'nearly done to death'. His offence, it seems, was an attack in his poem 'An Essay upon Satire' on the king, Charles II, one of the king's mistresses and the Earl of Rochester, a notorious rake who was the individual responsible, it is thought, for initiating the assault.[22]

This was a disgraceful enough event, for which no miscreant was ever identified, despite Dryden offering a £50 reward. But what interests us most at this distance was that the great man was just then on the way back to his home from an evening spent at Will's Coffee House, in Russell Street. The work of the German historian-philosopher Jürgen Habermas, as well as that of Tim Blanning, has helped bring attention to the emergence of the 'public sphere' across the turn of the eighteenth century, and the fact that there were three central locations for this: the coffee house, the club and the so-called moral weeklies.

Habermas used Britain as a 'model case' as the prototype for his now famous thesis that a novel form of bourgeois public life developed in the century preceding the French Revolution, and he used the history of the coffee house in post-Restoration London as his prime example of the social form this public sphere took. In this influential account, the coffee house is portrayed as a social space dedicated to 'high-minded' discourse on a wide range of affairs; it is also assumed to be open to any man who wanted to participate in the discussion conducted therein, regardless of social rank.[23]

We have records of a score and more of coffee houses in London at this time. Will's, which is mentioned often in Pepys's diary, was the home of the 'Wits', centred around Dryden, whose other members included William Wycherley, dramatist author of *The Plain Dealer*, though Swift thought the conversation sadly lacking.[24] Button's, also in Russell Street, took over from Will's after Dryden died, and was frequented by Addison and Steele, of *Spectator* fame, Charles Davenant, Alexander Pope and Ambrose Philips. Button's was named, in the fashion of the times, after the head waiter. The stock-jobbers gathered at Jonathan's in Exchange Alley, near the Royal Exchange. Garraway's, also in Exchange Alley, was described by Daniel Defoe as being popular with wealthy traders from the Royal Exchange.[25]

The Temple-Coffee-House Club was an assembly primarily of botanists in which James Petiver, an apothecary and botanist, who imported many drugs from the Americas, was a pivotal member. It was one of several frequented by members of the Royal Society (another was the Grecian). It gathered on Fridays in Devereux Court, near the Temple, which runs between the Strand and the River Thames. There were as many as forty members at different times, including Hans Sloane and Tancred Robinson, a naturalist and fellow of the Royal College of Physicians, who had met Marcello Malpighi on his travels.[26]

Another coffee house, Miles's, was located in the Turk's Head tavern, in New Palace Yard in Westminster, frequented by John Aubrey, James Harrington, deviser of a scheme for a utopian commonwealth called *Oceana*, and Cyriack Skinner, an amanuensis for the blind Milton and author of a biography of the poet. Miles's was also the home of a club called the Rota. The best known of the clubs were the Kit-Cat and the Scriblerus. The Kit-Cat was the greatest political club of the day, a club for Whigs, formed in the wake of the Glorious Revolution, whose members advocated a stronger Parliament and limited monarchy, and which began meeting at the Trumpet tavern, run by an innkeeper and baker of pies called Christopher Cat. The club later moved to the Fountain tavern on the Strand (now Simpsons-in-the-Strand): its members included Walpole, Locke, Congreve, Sir John Vanbrugh, a dramatist but now chiefly remembered as an architect, Addison and Steele and a raft of aristocrats, such as the dukes of Grafton, Devonshire and Manchester. Jacob Tonson, bookseller and publisher (of Milton and Dryden and copyright owner of the works of Shakespeare), was also a member.

The Scriblerus Club returns us to Swift, Pope, Gay, Arbuthnot, Addison and Steele and Thomas Parnell, a heavy-drinking Anglo-Irish poet, who helped Pope in his translation of the *Iliad*. Formed around 1713, the notable achievement of this club was the creation of 'the learned' Martinus Scriblerus, an entirely fictional individual whose *Memoirs* mocked the pedantic learning of the day and the unthinking following of new fashions. Many ideas which appeared in works by the members of the club, such as *Gulliver's Travels*, the *Dunciad* and *The Beggar's Opera*, were first aired in its meetings. They all seem to have got on well, hilariously enjoying each other's bizarre imaginations, often journeying together to visit more occasional members. One of Scriblerus's memoirs is written 'from Nubia', another after 'Three Hours of Marriage'.

THE STRUGGLE FOR POLITENESS

Although Steele and Addison are remembered today primarily for their roles in creating and editing *The Tatler* and *The Spectator* (and later *The Guardian*), their achievements went much wider. Steele, born in Ireland the son of an attorney who died when he was but five, met Addison, the son of the dean of Lichfield, at Charterhouse School, where their long friendship began. Both went on to Oxford, though Steele left without taking a degree. Steele married at first for money, his wife's family owning property in Barbados. Before he began work on *The Tatler* (published thrice weekly from April 1709 until January 1711), he was gazetteer for the *London Gazette*, the official chronicle of government, and Commissioner for Stamps.

After he left Oxford, Addison's first distinction was by contributing the preface to Virgil's *Georgics*, Dryden's great translation of 1697. He gained government employment as Commissioner of Appeals in Excise, a sinecure left vacant by the death of John Locke. He was elected to Parliament (as was Steele), and was made secretary to the Earl of Wharton, the new lord lieutenant of Ireland, making him, in effect, secretary of state for Irish affairs. Later in life he was to write *Cato*, a political tragedy exploring republicanism, which was performed at the Drury Lane Theatre with great success, running for twenty performances.

It was while Addison was in Ireland that Steele began publishing *The Tatler*. *The Spectator* was begun two months after *The Tatler* closed down (possibly because there had been a change of government, from Whig to Tory, and Steele had been 'leaned on'). It appeared six days a week from 1 March 1711 to 6 December 1712 and was very successful, Addison estimating that he could count on 60,000 to 80,000 readers for each issue. Both periodicals had begun by featuring political, social and cultural news, and 'the pleasures of the imagination', in bringing learning 'out of closets and libraries, schools and colleges, to dwell in clubs and assemblies, at tea-tables and in coffee-houses'. But what really distinguished both papers, *The Spectator* especially so, was their attempt to elevate public taste, investigating English manners and society and establishing principles of good behaviour and genteel conduct – the Whig 'struggle for politeness', for moral reflection rather than the obsession with the news of the day, which was represented as a particularly Tory vice. 'Men should not talk to please themselves, but those that hear them.'[27] *The Spectator* also devoted a lot of its attention to literary criticism, which was to prove influential in the development of the English novel. And almost certainly, its greatest long-term contribution to British intellectual life, over the years of its publication, was its exploration of a moral economy.

Both Addison and Steele had many contacts in the new world of commerce. Addison, for example, was made Commissioner of Trade and Plantations in 1715.[28] The journals Addison and Steele founded tend now to be seen as speaking up and on behalf of the new middle class of merchant whose economic weight was beginning to have cultural effects. But what Addison and Steele also did was to ensure that this 'thrusting' new class learned the 'classical' values of politeness and restraint. This is why they were called the 'moral weeklies'.

These issues were discussed almost from the start.[29] *The Spectator* finds in the Whigs the benevolent portrayal of commercial society in which trade compensates for England's barrenness and helps a sophisticated civilisation flourish: 'Trade, without enlarging the British territories, has given us a kind of additional empire.' In the process, the identification of trade with geographic expansion transforms the purpose of commerce (and empire) from personal gain to national glory, the merchant becoming a central figure in the culture preferred by *The Spectator*.[30] Trade is seen as moral because of the growth and improvement it provides, for all. At the same time, the practice of trade 'subverts inheritance and primogeniture by basing merit on energy, work, and ability'. At all times the public good and personal salvation are 'yoked' together.[31]

In this *Spectator* the cries of London are preferred to the song of larks and nightingales – advertisement is London's natural sound.[32] But Steele also linked economic success with high culture. Art, the journal insisted, and in particular theatrical art, required wealth, while ostentatious art, grand art, grandiloquent art, requires a leisure class capable of supporting it.[33] And personal happiness is a central force for moral behaviour. On this account, wealth, achievement and status become public representations of moral goodness.

Some of these arguments sound very modern and very familiar, if not a little sanctimonious, but they were new then and the overall effect, also new, was to place middle-class commercial behaviour on a par with aristocrats' 'landed gentry behaviour ethic'. While we may smile at *The Spectator*'s foresight, or at it being so much on the ball, we should also take on board Charles Knight's comment that, in the context of the times, the paper was 'virtually silent about slave-trading or war profiteering'.[34]

EVERYTHING WHICH EXISTS IS PARTICULAR

Once begun, there was no stopping the novel, which grew in popularity and spread its wings ever further throughout the eighteenth century and into the nineteenth. There were several reasons for this. One was that realism was increasingly the defining mode of the novel. Gradually, for instance, character names became more and more individualised and moved away from the archaic, allegorising names used by Sidney or Bunyan – though to begin with, for example in *Robinson Crusoe* (1719) and *Moll Flanders* (1722), the names are not *quite* realistic but hint at some of the qualities possessed by the characters: Mr *Sin*clair, Sir Charles *Grand*ison.[35] Gone too is the need for the characters to be noble heroes or heroines – Moll Flanders is a thief, Pamela a hypocrite and Tom Jones a fornicator.

The novels also got away from the plots of mythology, history and the classics. Here they were helped by the philosophy of the day, that of George Berkeley, a bishop in the Anglican Church of Ireland, and known for his criticisms of abstraction. Everything which exists, Berkeley insisted, 'is particular' and this concern with particularity, rather than abstraction, clearly fed into the subject matter of the new novel form, which explored particularity even as it considered the theoretical whole the particularity was a constituent of.

The attempt to go beyond the doings of the 'great and the good' was of course popular especially among the new reading public. Other aspects of particularity could be explored. Now that many people had access to clocks, or even pocket watches, novels could navigate the passage of time in more realistic detail. Henry Fielding used an almanac in *Tom Jones* to ensure that his chronology was exact. In getting away from the 'great and the good', the scope of place changed: interiors mattered as never before, as did the concrete particularity of female life, women often having more leisure to read than their menfolk, as Addison had cause to observe in *The Guardian*, a short-lived follow-up to *The Tatler* and *The Spectator*.

In this way the notion of literacy began to change. Certainly, in the early part of the eighteenth century, literacy among the better off implied a familiarity with the classics, and with Latin, if not Greek.[36] Meanwhile, three quarters of the poor could not read, though some, Ian Watt tells us, had a sort of semi-literacy, in that they could 'read' shop signs. But newspaper-buying tripled in the first half of the eighteenth century with almost 44,000 newspapers being read weekly according to one estimate. Book production increased fourfold in the eighteenth century, but books were still far more expensive than a glass of ale or gin.[37]

In London in particular there were also many competing entertainments – theatres, assemblies, operas, and not least the eight hanging days at Tyburn. But booksellers continued to grow, despite all, and the 'denizens' of Grub Street increasingly turned away from hack poetry to hack novels.

Another new trend in the subject matter of novels was that literature began to contemplate trade, commerce and industry *with favour*. There was a growing self-confidence among the middle class in the eighteenth century and this too was reflected in the novel, as it concerned itself with middle-class life – visits to spa towns, for example, or to recreational gardens. As Moll Flanders put it: 'With money in the pocket one is at home anywhere.'

Puritanism also found an outlet in the novel, especially its concern with marriage and the conflict between spiritual and material values. Montesquieu had observed that women were much freer in Britain and that daughters rebelled against patriarchal fathers more so than on the continent. In any case, marriage became a much more commercial proposition in the 1700s, and this was a major theme of plotting as the century wore on. Samuel Richardson played an important role here in establishing a proper code of marriage, *Pamela: Or Virtue Rewarded* (1740) being a major epiphany in the British imagination, giving us a new stereotype of a young, inexperienced and delicate woman who resists seduction to the extent that her would-be seducer marries her, and she spends the rest of the novel winning over those who had been suspicious of her and her motives. In *Shamela*, Fielding mercilessly lampooned Richardson's book. But the other point of Richardson's story was that it provided more detail about a single amorous episode than had ever been written before. This is why it was widely popular and was, in a sense, particularity with a vengeance.

Pamela is an epistolary novel, and that was a fashion too. The postal services were improving all the time, letter-writing was more and more common, the 'Republic of Letters' was more and more established. *Clarissa* (1748), generally regarded as Richardson's masterpiece, is another story about a woman determined to keep her virtue intact. She has a problem from the beginning because her own family, newly enriched, are more concerned with bettering their status than with protecting her. After her sister spurns her lover, and he turns his attention to Clarissa, the sister and the rest of the family turn against her. The would-be lover never manages to subdue her, though he does imprison her and even rapes her, but realises she will never submit. Her fortitude is amazing and amazingly long-lived, leading to her death, an unhappy ending which many readers found distressing. There was no possibility of there being a *Clarisham*.

The pre-eminence of the British novel was in general recognised by the end of the eighteenth century, and this was especially true in the era of Jane Austen, whose books – *Pride and Prejudice, Emma, Mansfield Park* – invariably cleverly contain one character who is 'more conscious' than the others. This privileged status is usually adopted and adapted to the role of the narrator, thus ensuring that the reader never loses awareness of what, exactly, is going on. Her novels, too, are about the texture of middle-class life – marriage, money and morals.

The Enormous Conceit: Britain –
'The Dread and Envy of Them All'

When you examine British intellectual and imaginative history in the 'long' eighteenth century, between the Glorious Revolution in 1688 and the Battle of Waterloo in 1815, you find a coherent collection of innovative ideas, beliefs, attitudes and practices. First and foremost, outside the new format of the novel, you find a striking degree of Christian Providentialism, in particular a buoyant and increasingly self-confident – not to say self-important – Protestantism (though wary at times, like 1745), allied to what Linda Colley calls 'the cult of trade', marked both by enthusiasm and Dissent, welded to commercialism and a competitive mercantilism that were necessary to the business of empire, and to consumption, much intertwined with the increasingly awkward trading in slaves.

All this was helped by the enormous development of print culture, which itself benefitted from the huge population growth in the last half of the 1700s, and in turn books and pamphlets and newspapers, together with coffee houses and clubs, helped broadcast a campaigning emphasis on *improvement* throughout all walks of life, and in all territories of empire. With the opening up of so many public spaces, and so many publications of so many different kinds, there was a lively concern with politeness, polite letters and polite behaviour in particular – the convenient belief that in commercial society we 'polish' one another, in a collective attempt at harmony – and with sensibility, an aspect of politeness in which the proper appreciation of complex behavioural and aesthetic matters became of first importance for many people for the first time, given that, to begin with, eighteenth-century Britain was somewhat backward in the visual arts (unlike theatre, which was stronger than ever). Sensibility was widely explored in the continuing development of the novel.[1]

But not even this does justice to the intellectual atmosphere that imbued the nation. In Elizabethan times, it will be recalled, England, as it then was, went from being a backward, peripheral player in world affairs to one of a handful of more or less equal rival powers fighting for control of the Atlantic, and Atlantic/New World trade. During the long eighteenth century, after 1707, the newly unified Great Britain would emerge as the dominant executor right across the world, and as a result its increasing self-regard and its burgeoning self-satisfaction would eventually border on a complacent sense of superiority, even as it took a leading role in the trans-Atlantic slave trade.

It is no secret or mystery as to why this occurred. Unlike most European nations, Britain was never invaded (not since 1066). Until 1688 England and Scotland had been peripheral powers but between then and the end of the Seven Years War in 1763, the newly minted nation had triumphed in the Nine Years War with France (1688–97), the War of Spanish Succession (1701–14), the War of Jenkins's Ear (1739–48) and the War of Austrian Succession (1740–8). And these were tangible victories that brought durable gains in terms of empire, land and trade routes established.[2] Britons never experienced mass conscription, or the ravages of violence on their own soil. The Glorious Revolution of 1688 and the Financial Revolution that followed so soon after it, together with the introduction of the stock market, reinforced the earlier moves towards capitalism and worldwide trade. The union of Scotland and England in 1707 was not, as Defoe put it, 'a union of affection' but it did enable Britons to think of themselves as one people, defined against the permanent threat from a much larger – and Catholic – adversary.[3]

The union, and this ever-present looming threat from France, produced in early eighteenth-century Britain a strong, self-conscious identity, a belief that the newly minted Britons were different from others beyond their shores, and that their country was 'highly centralized, around just one beautiful language and, now that the matter had been settled so conclusively in the Glorious Revolution, Protestantism was ready to become a unifying and distinguishing force much more than before'. Not until 1829 would Catholics be allowed to vote in Britain, they were excluded from all state appointments, and from Parliament. As we have seen with Alexander Pope, they were not allowed to live within 10 miles of Hyde Park Corner, were forbidden to own weapons and denied access to the best schools. They were, as Colley says, treated as potential traitors and, in a way, as un-British.[4] And this was the so-called Enlightened age.

At the same time, the situation of Nonconformist Protestants was very different. The Toleration Act introduced in the year after the Glorious Revolution had deemed that Dissenters who accepted the doctrine of the Holy Trinity had the right to worship as they saw fit, to organise their churches and schools as they wished, and to vote.

BONFIRES AND BELLS

At the beginning of the eighteenth century, daily life for Protestants in Britain of all persuasions was, in historian David Cressy's words, something of a 'soap opera written by God, a succession of warning disasters and providential escapes' which they performed every year 'as a way of reminding themselves who they were'.[5] For example, on each 30 January until 1859 Protestants fasted and prayed in memory of Charles I's execution in 1649; on 29 May, the anniversary of the restoration of the monarchy in 1660 was marked by bonfires and bells, celebrating the end of political instability and martial rule; the first day of August celebrated the accession in 1714 of the first Hanoverian king, which secured the Protestant succession; and 5 November was, as Cressy says, 'doubly sacred' since it commemorated the anniversary of the landing in England in 1688 of William of Orange, *and* the day in 1605 when James I had been rescued from the Gunpowder Plot of Guido Fawkes, who was, of course, a Roman Catholic.

The prayer used on the last occasion was written in such a way that the devout Protestant could not help but draw the appropriate conclusion, that God watched over Britons 'with a particular concern': *'From this unnatural conspiracy not our merit, but thy mercy, not our foresight, but thy providence delivered us.'* On this account the British, it was emphasised, were special, still special. 'They had a mission, a distinctive purpose.'[6] While this powerful Protestant cement, which would last through the century, especially among the classes lower down the social scale, was also a useful propellant, anti-Catholicism did not decline as much as one might expect, given the other Enlightenment developments we shall be considering in the realms of rationalism and literacy. To be sure, religious toleration did increase, especially after the final defeat of the Jacobite cause at Culloden in 1746, and especially among the elite, and some laws were relaxed. But the position of Catholics could still remain tricky, especially so in wartime, since the nation's main enemy, France, was Catholic, even if the fighting was halfway across the world, as far away as India or Canada.

But the belief persisted that Protestant Britons were especially fortunate, blessed above all with a superior religious freedom and a deeper and more substantial prosperity, economic growth coexisting comfortably with a profound Protestant patriotism and even, Colley asserts, complacency.[7] There were claims now that Britain was an 'elect nation', another Israel. In 1719, when Isaac Watts, a Hampshire-born minister, was preparing what would become his best-selling translation of the psalms, he throughout replaced the references to 'Israel' in the original with 'Great Britain'.[8] George Frideric Handel, who had decided to settle in London, also played the game so much enjoyed by his hosts. In the anthem he composed to celebrate George II's coronation in 1727, the historical references were familiar to his newly adopted nation: 'Zadok the priest and Nathan the prophet anointed Solomon king.'

Though laws against blasphemy, obscenity and seditious libel remained on the statute books, once the Licensing Act had lapsed in 1695, the situation regarding censorship in Britain was 'light years away from that obtaining in France, Spain or almost anywhere else in *ancien régime* Europe'.[9] The English, in historian Peter Gay's view, were uniquely able to enjoy an enlightenment without *philosophes* precisely because, after 1714, there was no longer any *infame* to be crushed. It was the ideology of a post-Puritan ruling order which made England both the most modern and eventually the most counterrevolutionary state in Europe.[10]

A CULT OF ENGLISHNESS

This 'enormous conceit', embarrassing to express these days, was shown above all by the personality and career of John Wilkes, a sort of anglicised Rousseau figure, 'a rake on the make', a Londoner and Dissenter educated in Holland, a lecher who 'cheerfully' abandoned his wife, but who became a folk hero and a household name. Despite telling outrageous falsehoods, he was nonetheless a popularist of genius. Two tumults about him made his name: one was libelling the king and his minister in the *North Briton*, the paper he edited, and the other was his election to Parliament – while still an outlaw – for the county of Middlesex in 1768. Each of these was converted by his supporters and by what he wrote himself into 'contests over what was owing to Englishmen'.

Wilkes became both a symptom and a cause of an intense cult of Englishness.[11] He loathed the union with Scotland, insisted on being called an Englishman, not a Briton, and when on trial for seditious libel (at which he was acquitted, to huge public acclaim), he lectured both the judge and the jury that what was on trial with him was whether Englishness and English liberty was 'a reality or a shadow'.[12] There was no questioning his Englishness (or his Scottophobia) and although he was famously ugly, famously dishonest (embezzling funds he was charged with safeguarding) and a Nonconformist who railed against the American colonists, at fashionable dinners his health was invariably the first to be toasted. He managed to write a history of England since the Glorious Revolution and was eventually elected Lord Mayor of London, in which capacity he awarded the Freedom of the City of London to a certain Horatio Nelson. An ostentatious patriotism characterised his entire career and, as several people have remarked, it is hard not to think that Samuel Johnson had Wilkes in mind when he defined 'patriotism' in his dictionary (Chapter 11) as 'the last refuge of a scoundrel'.

On top of that not entirely attractive self-consciousness was the fact that, at the same time, apologists abandoned the appeal to the divine right of kings and replaced it with an approach instead based on a convenient divine providence showing in 'the will of the people'. Finally, the religious pluralism of the time created a sense of 'almost boundless' intellectual choice which Paul Langford says did set Britain apart.[13] Voltaire, that clever old cynic, saw the new, post-1688 Britain as a nation of many religions but only one sauce. But when he wasn't making jokes, he saw that those 'many religions' were a source of the newfound strength. 'If there were only one religion in England, there would be danger of despotism, if there were only two they would cut each other's throats; but there are thirty, and they live in peace.' Faith of any kind could no longer be expected to unify this new Britain, while 'commerce would unite those whom creeds put asunder'.[14]

Which brings us to the matter of Dissent. Both Defoe and Montesquieu felt that belief was declining, the church in trouble. But this was so only where strict adherence to the ideas and beliefs of the *established* church were concerned, whereas Dissent was rampant, hardworking, in chapel as well as church and in fact, as Roy Porter also points out, an example of this was the golden age of English hymnody. Isaac Watts (1674–1748), himself a Dissenting theologian from Southampton operating as pastor to the Mark Lane Congregational Chapel in London, and despite being banned from the universities, still managed to compose more than 700 hymns in the first half of the eighteenth century, including 'O God, our help in ages past'.[15] In the countryside the gentry might retain a residue of anti-popish prejudice but in polite society toleration was increasingly seen as a virtue. It was also aided by the fact that the Hanoverian government showed no desire to interfere in the spiritual life of the ordinary citizen.[16] England was now a premier trading nation, according to the comforting cliché, whose inhabitants could take pride in being 'a polite and commercial people'. This was partly due to Britain's domination of both the slave trade and the rising territorial expansion overseas.[17] Importantly, trade was held to be not only a source of profit, but a mark of civilisation.

AMBITIOUS EGOISTS

The church continued to rail against vice, but its complaints were answered, as early as 1714, by Bernard Mandeville, an Anglo-Dutch political philosopher, educated at the Erasmus School in Rotterdam, who published a tract that said, more or less plainly, that what makes the world go round is, indeed, vice. In *The Grumbling Hive: or, Knaves Turn'd Honest*, later reissued as the better-known *Fable of the Bees: or, Private Vices, Publick Benefits*, he imagined a successful 'hive' where all the bees are 'ambitious egoists, buzzing to get on by all possible means', all the way from honest toil to shady swindles, frauds and even outright theft:

> All Trades and Places knew some Cheat,
> No Calling was without Deceit.[18]

Mandeville's hive of course was a satirical analogy of the new commercial civilisation at large and his simple but compelling message was that the world works by self-interest, that it is self-interest and envy of others more fortunate which leads to prosperity and stability, that ingenuity, time and industry 'carry life's conveniences'.[19]

This civilisation was becoming known as mercantilism. There was and is no fully worked out systematic theory or single treatise that captures all of the views associated with mercantilism, but it can be broadly summed up as a commitment to a set of ideas about the nature and causes of wealth. These included the idea that the nature of wealth lay in precious metal used as currency, that the aim of trade was to maximise the amount of national treasure, that merchants brought power and strength to the country when they were able to export goods and, consequent to this, that state policy should be to promote export industry and protect the home market. Along with all that came a preoccupation with the size of the population as a measure of national success, and support for politically enforced monopolies, tariffs, and direct state funding for colonial expansion. Political economy is the central discipline, as William Petty had long ago claimed.

The 'savage complacency' that Linda Colley describes had by now taken hold in Britain, where the self-satisfied feelings were buoyant despite Britain being more heavily taxed than elsewhere, while there were more prisons in London than in all the other European capitals put together, and in certain areas between a third and a half of the people existed at or below subsistence levels. Alongside that, as the eighteenth century got under way, the country's reputation in the arts was less exalted than in other areas of civilisation – especially in painting and music, though achievements in language and literature, the fashion for the 'natural' garden, and the adoption of Italian and classical models in the 'Augustan' age to an extent contributed to the 'Anglomania' that gripped some foreigners. The fact that the nation – the union of Scotland and England – was new, or felt new, was also a factor in the self-regarding optimism/complacency. But William Hogarth would lead English art onwards to what Ellis Waterhouse calls the Classical Age in British painting – Gainsborough, Reynolds, Romney and Wright of Derby. In 1732, George Vertue, an antiquarian who kept forty notebooks on British painting, sculpture and engraving, concluded that the nation's art was beginning to shine as never before.

Self-confidence gave way to complacency, complacency to bombast. James Thomson, poet and playwright, author of a poem in praise of Isaac Newton, added this rhyming note of self-congratulation in 1763, the year Britain finally defeated France in what has been called 'The First World War':

> The nations, not so blessed as thee,
> Must in their turn to tyrants fall,
> While thou shall flourish, great and free,
> The dread and envy of them all.
> 'Rule, Britannia, rule the waves,
> Britons never will be slaves.'

Despite his satirical criticisms, even Hogarth, on one occasion, signed himself 'Britophil'.

There were those people – coffee house pundits as often as not – who aired their worries about the dangers that were being brought about by commercial society, by the new national debt, the new financial practices, the invention of stocks and shares and suspected double-dealing. But for others even learning was a fruit of trade. In David Hume's words: 'In rude, unpolished nations, neither learning nor trade could have developed in such conditions.' 'In these new conditions,' so the theory went, 'private spaces had to be carved out in which people felt relaxed enough to tolerate each other's opinions and value respect above righteousness.'[20] Hume's compatriot Adam Smith took this reasoning to its highest standing when he 'elevated the ego of commercial man above the civic virtues of the classical republican, dwelling particularly on the wealth, freedom and political wisdom needed to sustain a commercial polity'.[21]

And so, as many foreign commentators and visitors to Britain (which they called England) recognised, the imaginative rise of the arts north of the Channel which eventually came about, as we shall see, was due to the triumph of a commercial and urban, and polite, society, not a royal court as in Louis XV's France and Frederick the Great's Prussia. It was the political as well as the economic condition of the country – its weak monarchy, free constitution and rule of law – which helped to create a literature and performing arts which were directed not to an elite court any longer but to a public, and organised commercially, rather than being confined to a few.

Dr Johnson's Microcosm of 'Conspicuous Men'

A mid that commercially minded public, the most influential club of the second half of the eighteenth century (when there were 2,000 such entities in London) was Dr Johnson's Literary Club, which met at the Turk's Head in Gerrard Street in Soho. During its thirty years (it outlived Johnson) it brought to-gether a most distinctive raft of members. Convened for the first time in 1764, following the initiative of Sir Joshua Reynolds, to begin with it comprised nine members: Johnson himself; Reynolds; Edmund Burke; Burke's father-in-law, the physician Dr Christopher Nugent; two of Johnson's 'gentlemen friends' he had met at Oxford, Topham Beauclerk and Bennet Langton; then there were Oliver Goldsmith; the Huguenot broker Mr Anthony Chamier; and Sir John Hawkins, not the slave-trader John Hawkins we met earlier, but the author of the first history of music in the English language. What started as a limited circle of friends turned into a much larger and more formal grouping of thirty-five members by 1791, at which time James Boswell released his *Life of Johnson*. Newer members included Sir Joseph Banks, the botanist; Charles Burney, another historian of music; the actors and managers David Garrick, Richard Brinsley Sheridan and George Colman; the historian Edward Gibbon; the Orientalist Sir William Jones; the political economist Adam Smith; and the politician Charles James

Fox, a great rival of William Pitt the Younger and an anti-slavery campaigner.[1]

Whereas the Kit-Cat Club, earlier in the century, had been the domain, mainly, of aristocrats, Johnson's club consisted predominantly of souls from the literary and artistic professions. There were more wealthy and aristocratic members, but they were selected for their abilities. The Kit-Cat's political sympathies were flamboyantly Whiggish, but Johnson's coterie was politically neutral, with a number of mavericks, like Johnson himself; ardent Whigs like Fox and Reynolds; and prominent conservatives such as Goldsmith.[2] Invitations to the club confirmed status as, in Johnson's own words, 'conspicuous men'.

Recent research into Johnson, especially his early life, has shown that when he was oppressed by poverty (the lonelier part of his life, as he admitted) he dabbled in 'chymical' experiments and read assiduously among such scientists as Robert Boyle, Nehemiah Grew and Isaac Newton. Indeed, he formed friendships with no fewer than thirty-four fellows of the Royal Society, nine of whom were asked to join the Club (among them Reynolds, Jones, Sir William Hamilton and George Steevens). A. D. Atkinson, who researched Johnson's scientific interests, unearthed the fact that many of the quotations in his famous dictionary were borrowed from scientific titles, so much so that Atkinson asked not entirely rhetorically why Johnson was never elected to the Royal Society, for this was a time when it was not quite as attached to the physical sciences as it now is.[3]

Johnson himself was known above all for his dictionary. As Anthony Burgess reminds us, early writers like Chaucer, Shakespeare and Milton had no access to what we today call dictionaries. Spelling did not worry them as it does a modern author. Milton preferred *Mee* to *me* when he wanted to be emphatic, and Shakespeare often just made words up.[4] Sir Thomas Elyot had produced an English 'word-book' in 1538 and Robert Cawdrey's *Table Alphabeticall* (1604) had 2,449 words, though with none beginning with W, X or Y. In the earliest dictionaries the emphasis was on difficult words, as in John Bullokar's *English Expositor* (1616), just too late for Shakespeare, and Henry Cockerman's *English Dictionarie* (1623) which highlighted what were then called 'inkhorn terms', pedantic words, such as *gargari* ('to wash or scowre the mouth with any Physicall liquor'), and *parentate* ('to celebrate one's parents' funerals').

But the pioneer work in dictionary-making was that produced, almost single-handed, by Johnson, which built on those by Edward Phillips (1658, 11,000 words), and John Kersey (1702, 28,000 words). Nathan Bailey's *Universal English Dictionary* (1721) raised the count to about 40,000 words, and William Pitt the Elder is said to have read through it twice as if it were a novel.[5] But despite this impressive increase in the words included, the growth in literacy, and the greater availability of books and their fall in price, created a dissatisfaction with the current state of affairs. In 1746 a group of London booksellers (who often doubled as publishers then) contracted Johnson to write a dictionary and advanced him the sum of £1,575 (1,500 guineas), which, it has been calculated, would be roughly £260,000 now.

Johnson, born in Lichfield, a prosperous and even learned cathedral town in the north Midlands (also home to David Garrick, Erasmus Darwin and Anna Seward), contracted scrofula as a child. This was then known as the 'king's evil' because it was believed that being touched by royalty could cure it. The king's touch was performed in Johnson's case by Queen Anne, but it failed, and his face and body remained scarred for the rest of his life. This may explain his combative personality. He was thirty-seven at the time the dictionary was commissioned and by then he had been a schoolteacher (one of his pupils being Garrick, the future dramatic actor) and he was the author of a number of poems, a play and a biography of the actor Richard Savage, both of them working for a time as hack writers in Grub Street.

Johnson, it was said, knew more books than any man alive. He was bulky, formidable, a convinced Tory and Anglican, immensely learned with a wry, robust sense of humour – for him drinking was 'life's second greatest pleasure'.[6]

He prepared the book at a house in Gough Square (north of Fleet Street). He said he would complete the book in three years though in fact it took him seven. He had six assistants, five of them Scottish, though essentially the work was his alone. The first edition ran to 42,773 words and the real attraction of the book was his concern for precedent (as in the case of common law) which he achieved by the widespread use of literary quotations – roughly 114,000 in the first edition, including Shakespeare, Milton and Dryden, who he especially revered. Besides showing his great learning and widespread reading, and making a few mistakes, some of his definitions were also trenchant, wry, satirical, and settled a few scores along the way:

Oats: a grain which in England is generally given to horses, but in Scotland supports the people.

Irony: a mode of speech in which the meaning is contrary to the word: as, *Bolingbroke was a holy man.*

Another factor in the book's success was his meticulousness. The word 'turn', for instance, had sixteen definitions, 'time' had twenty and the definition of 'put' ran to 5,000 words over three pages.[7] There *were* critics, the Yale graduate Noah Webster among them. After the book had been exported to America, it was welcomed at first, but then Webster declared that Great Britain's language was on the decline and Americans should have their own, which in general seems to have boiled down to unnecessarily and pedantically replacing 's' with 'z' (as in 'liberalize') and 'ou' with 'o' (as in 'color').

Words, Johnson said, referring to Dryden, should 'not draw attention to themselves' – this was the true merit of a literary work.[8] Words were the 'dress' of thought. He considered that Shakespeare, with his vast range of vocabulary and 'licentious turns of phrase', often threatened propriety. Only writing and print provided stability, for pronunciation still varied greatly among literate people. He urged Boswell, the friend who was to famously write his biography, to collect a whole 'folio' of 'north-country' words, and supported William Shaw's Erse (Irish or Scottish Gaelic) grammar, at least for a time. And he left out inkhorn words such as *turbinated* or *perflation*, which, Marchioness Grey complained, 'break my teeth'.[9]

A METAPHYSICAL EMPIRE

That richness and breadth were important in the other great issue in which Johnson and the dictionary were caught up – whether, in standardising English, it could become a 'classical' language. Though this may read oddly to us today, it was very much a live issue in the eighteenth century because, after their defeat in the Jacobite rebellion of 1745, the Scots became more thoroughly integrated into Great Britain, an integration that involved government-sponsored teaching of English to Highlander children and intense pressure on Lowland Scots to rid themselves of any trace of the Scots language. Johnson's *Dictionary* was part of this development but so too was the elocution project of Thomas Sheridan, the father of the playwright Richard Brinsley Sheridan.

Sheridan senior, an Irishman, whose lectures on elocution were well attended, continually bemoaned the fact that English was not properly standardised.[10] He was not alone, says Adam Beach, and, especially following Britain's great success in the Seven Years War (1756–63), after which, it may be said, the world opened up to British expansion, and brought with it the possibility that wide swathes of the world might one day speak English, a larger imperial role was envisioned for the language.[11] As Beach puts it:

> These theorists imagined themselves transforming English, along with Greek and Latin, into the third 'classical' tongue, essentially a standard and permanent language that could withstand change across vast expanses of time and space. This English 'classical' language would be implanted around the world, becoming dominant wherever Britons colonised, displacing so-called 'primitive' languages spoken by native inhabitants. Just as the English people once were civilised and improved by both Latin and the Roman conquest, so too could Britain help other nations progress by the export of English to their colonies.[12]

More than that, Beach argues that, if English could be standardised, which was one of Johnson's aims in his dictionary, thinkers like Sheridan imagined it would become *the* building block of what he called 'a metaphysical empire', an empire of language and literature 'that would outlive the actual British empire'. The Greeks and Romans in particular, it was felt, had created metaphysical empires in that *their* languages and literatures had long outlasted their physical empires and continued to be a source of inspiration and to influence thinking centuries after their actual empires had ended. This is what Sheridan and others hoped for Britain.[13]

With standardisation, Sheridan was convinced that 'an easily accessible canon of literature' would enable subjects around the world to learn from English 'classics'. Sheridan was adamant that English be extended to include colonial subjects living outside Great Britain proper, who would be civilised by conquest, as Britons themselves had been civilised by conquest, and looked forward to a 'canon' of British 'classics' available to future generations.[14]

RAISING THE STATUS OF PAINTING

Just as the age of Charles I cannot be fully grasped other than through the eyes of Van Dyck, so the art of Sir Joshua Reynolds bears the same relation to the third quarter of the eighteenth century. Hogarth had been at the forefront of the creation of the 'modern' British style, so Reynolds arrived at the opportune time (1723) to become his heir. Reynolds had virtues as a painter but also as a historian, with a strong feeling for mass, for the solidity of bodies that is curiously missing in Gainsborough, his chief rival. Reynolds is unsurpassed in the way he composed what Ellis Waterhouse called 'the mental part' of a portrait. This appears to have been aided by the fact that he was afflicted by deafness in his prime, perhaps aiding his power of concentration.

Waterhouse considered that Reynolds contributed more than anyone else to raising the status of portrait painters in Britain, 'where the practice had been despised for half a century'. This elevation of the status of painting was a prime political objective of Reynolds's years at the Royal Academy. He had been enthralled by what he had seen in Italy, referring in one of his *Discourses* to Michelangelo's nudes as 'the language of the Gods'.

Reynolds's character set his work as quite distinct from Gainsborough. Reynolds was objective, businesslike, even cool, though he was also a man of letters, and, if anything, too earnest about 'the noble qualities of art'. He had a sympathetic character, which ensured that, in his art, he was able 'to depict people as though in a moment of being caught unobserved' (see *Mrs Francis Beckford* or *James, Seventh Earl of Lauderdale*). Hoppner and Lawrence were his most obvious disciples.[15]

By contrast, Gainsborough was far more lyrical, as Reynolds acknowledged in one of his *Discourses* (and this was an honour he would confer on no one else). For Reynolds, says Waterhouse, Gainsborough was what today we would probably call an 'impressionist' – in that he left the spectator with quite a bit of work to do, filling in the details. Gainsborough's main source of income was portraits, but his heart – he said – was really in landscape and it is true he was drawn to the fleeting effects of shadow and texture (achieved by often working by candlelight). For Reynolds mass and solidity were the main concerns, whereas for Gainsborough what mattered more was flickering evanescence, the 'play of shadow on a silk dress in movement', the light, tones and half-tones 'which are the very breath of a native English landscape, a dewy freshness', as in *The Painter's Daughters Chasing a Butterfly*.[16]

Gainsborough was based for a while in Bath, at the time a very fashionable spa, and was quickly successful, with the unfortunate result, says Waterhouse, of a fall-off in quality. By the time he went back to the capital, in 1780, he had earned the patronage of the Court (which was instinctively out of kilter with Reynolds), and his full-lengths of George III and Queen Charlotte were very successful.[17] By now Gainsborough's landscapes were developing in the pastoral dimension which would, later on, culminate in the romantic movement.

Reynolds and Gainsborough were in at the beginning of the classical age of British art, which was helped by the accession to the throne, in 1760, of a young king broadly sympathetic to the arts – and, as Waterhouse pithily puts it, 'no one with a vestige of artistic feeling had sat on the throne since the revolution of 1688'.[18] But in the middle of the century, the Royal Academy was born, and public exhibitions of pictures were staged regularly so that young artists could inspect the work of their elders and quality could become a fit subject for public discussion, something we can put down as an achievement above all of Reynolds.

A Most Eloquent and Rational Madman

Edmund Burke, a Protestant Irishman despite his mother being a Catholic, was a graduate of Trinity College, Dublin, and he was certainly one of those who lived life to the full, being a practising politician, in Parliament and in government, and a writer on all kinds of topics, from manners, to philosophy, to politics, to art. After Trinity, where he started his own club, he entered the Middle Temple but gave it up to pursue literature and politics. His first work was *A Vindication of Natural Society: A View of the Miseries and Evils Arising to Mankind*, which appeared in 1756 and in which he aired what would be one of his main concerns, how to preserve the stability of life, not to mention his distinctive 'argumentative methodology' – subjecting the ideas he disagreed with to ironical absurdity.

Burke was eloquent and opinionated on a wide range of topics, and not infrequently contradictory. Strongly in favour of a free market, of the abolition of capital punishment, of Catholic emancipation, of American independence and reconciliation, he was opposed to the slave trade and, in particular, the way the East India Company was behaving in India.[19] At the same time, he considered Africans as 'barbaric', as needing to be 'civilised'. So eloquently and forcefully did he express these opinions that Edward Gibbon assessed him as 'the most eloquent and rational madman that I ever knew'. Burke echoed one of his heroes, Sir Edward Coke, in his views about the limits to royal power, but at the same time he was opposed to democracy because he was convinced that government needed a degree of intelligence rarely found among common people, and that the concerns of minorities could only be protected by 'enlightened aristocrats'. But the two works for which he is best known – both written during a long parliamentary career, from 1766 to 1794 – are *A Philosophical Inquiry into the Origin of Our Ideas of the Sublime and Beautiful* and *Reflections on the Revolution in France*.[20]

First and foremost, Burke was fascinated by the workings of the mind, a characteristic interest of the eighteenth century, and in particular by intense experiences and whether they interfered with rationality, another defining intellectual concern of the Enlightenment. To him, it was self-evident that the emotions and instincts which form the basis of humans' aesthetic responses are self-preservation and the 'social passions', in other words, sex and general sociability. For Burke it is a concern for self-preservation which provides us with a sense of the sublime, which in his terms means that which terrifies *and* astonishes us. It is this *thrill* of danger, experienced in relative safety, which allows us to rehearse how we might behave if ever we should truly be tested. By contrast – he goes on – our appreciation of beauty is not affected in the least by the 'proportion or fitness' of things but by 'their capacity to evoke affection and tenderness, in particular by their smallness, smoothness, gradualness or variation, delicacy and mildness of colour'. For him this means that the sublime and the beautiful must be precisely opposite in their physiological working.[21]

Despite his undoubted eloquence, Burke was not without his critics. For example, he was rounded on by Mary Wollstonecraft for his depiction of the qualities of beautiful women, for what he described as their 'softness, littleness, delicacy and especially their weakness'. Wollstonecraft, a Londoner, a bluestocking, who called herself 'the first of a new genus', an independent woman of reason who fell headlong for the Swiss painter 'of awesome and terrifying subjects', Henry Fuseli, was one of the first feminists and a staunch republican, and she also responded with a rapid rebuttal of Burke's other work, *Reflections*. Burke's pamphlet was published originally on 1 November 1790, and her spirited reply, *Vindication of the Rights of Men*, was published on the last day of the same month – not bad going.[22] She understood well enough that Burke's essay was aimed more at a readership in Britain than in France and her response was not as wide-ranging or as vituperative in its opposition to his arguments as Tom Paine's would be, or Joseph Priestley's.[23] But Wollstonecraft did at least go to Paris to see the events for herself, in the process nearly being caught up in the Terror.

For Burke, in *Reflections*, 'the central agreement that guarantees a tranquil society is all the more real for being tacit'.[24] Wollstonecraft was in stark disagreement here also. She said she had spent too much of her life reading novels where men had the power and women the beauty 'and all the inequalities which went with that'. She saw a clear link between Burke's *Sublime and Beautiful* book and *Reflections*, where the beautiful is feminine and the sublime masculine, leading to the conclusion: 'We submit to what we admire, but we love what submits to us; in the one case we are forced, in the other we are flattered into compliance.'[25] Burke's overriding concern, always, was for a stable society – which revolutionary France so clearly was not – and the way out, for him, was for this difference between the genders to provide the stabilising cement. For her part, Wollstonecraft advanced a thought-out argument for coeducation. She would devote her life to the issue.[26]

THE BIRTH OF THE SHAKESPEARE INDUSTRY

The friendship between Dr Johnson and David Garrick, the famous actor-manager of the eighteenth century, was very long-standing. In 1737, so the story goes, Johnson and Garrick, schoolmaster and pupil, set out from Lichfield for London with, if the story can be believed, just a handful of pennies between them.[27] Born in Hereford to Huguenot French parents, who had fled Bordeaux when the edict of Nantes was notoriously revoked in 1685, Garrick was taken into Johnson's Edial Hall School near Lichfield, in which premises Johnson taught Latin and Greek 'to young gentlemen'. The school was funded by Samuel's wife, Elizabeth 'Tetty' Johnson, and while Garrick – again so the story goes – betrayed an early aptitude for the stage, appearing in *The Recruiting Officer*, Edial Hall only ever had three pupils and so soon closed its doors. Whereupon Johnson and Garrick, now good friends (Johnson was eight years older than his erstwhile pupil), 'set out for London to make their careers'.

Garrick's stage career dates from 1741, by which time theatre had been brought low by the turbulence that so afflicted the 1730s, not to mention the Censorship Act of 1737, which created an examiner of plays in the office of the Lord Chamberlain, and established the difference between 'legitimate theatre' and 'illegitimate' – musicals, farces and reviews, notably the machine spectaculars, with 'flying' actors, 'trapdoor tricks' and warships on wheels, fighting battles with fireworks, that had so entranced the Restoration theatre public. Garrick had no shortage of competition; this was an age of famous performers – Charles Macklin, James Quin, Samuel Foote, Colley Cibber, Margaret ('Peg') Woffington – but his mix of talents set him apart. 'He was the first actor-impresario who brought the glamour of the London stage to the attention of a national audience.'[28]

As a director-manager he also introduced a number of changes designed to help people concentrate on the play. Drury Lane, London's oldest theatre, and with Covent Garden the only place licensed to stage legitimate drama, had a capacity for about 1,000. In 1762 Garrick took away spectators from the stage itself, where their proximity to the actors had proved troublesome and obstructive rather more often than he thought helpful. Now, a much clearer line was drawn between players and audience. A while later he got rid of the large hooped chandeliers that hitherto had lit both stage and auditorium. Instead, he increased the number of footlights, and fixed batteries of lights on moving poles with reflectors, all set up in the wings.[29]

In linking himself with Shakespeare so closely, Garrick's overall aim seems to have been to establish once and for all the reputation of the stage, which had until then often been firmly linked with loose women and brothels. (This is analogous to what Reynolds was attempting in painting, and a notable achievement of the eighteenth century.)

Johnson's *Shakespeare*, appearing only after a long gestation in 1765, put Shakespeare scholarship on a new footing. 'Above all, its magisterial defence of Shakespeare's dramatic technique in the context of the sixteenth-century conventions helped secure his un-challengeable place as *the* national poet.' Or, as Roy Porter put it, the national saint.

It is a curious fact that Garrick, for some reason, was not one of the original founders of Johnson's club. Nor did he show the same respectful attitude towards the national saint as did Johnson. Many contemporaries considered that Garrick's modernisation of Shakespeare's plays was insensitive or worse, though as Porter evaluates his achievement, on the actor's retirement in 1776, 'he had restored Shakespeare to the very centre of the English stage'.[30]

SNEERWELL AND TEAZLE

One of Richard Brinsley Sheridan's better-known plays is *The Rivals*, a hilarious comedy of manners set in the elegant spa town of Bath, with its evocatively named cast of characters (Sir Anthony Absolute, Fag, Lydia Languish and Mrs Malaprop). Sheridan's other plays, especially *School for Scandal*, were also great successes, but he was well known too for being the owner of the Theatre Royal at Drury Lane. *The Rivals* premiered not at Drury Lane but at the other place, Covent Garden, where it bombed. Sheridan quickly re-jigged it and it was turned into a hit, not least for the royal family.[31] *The School for Scandal* did premier at the Drury Lane Theatre with another cast of lurid characters – Lady Sneerwell, Snake, Benjamin Backbite, Crabtree and Lady Teazle and many more engaged in another *La Ronde* of manners, of scandal, gossip – true and false as gossip must be – flirting, deceiving, gambling, drinking and not-quite fornicating, so that everyone – players and audience – is exhausted at the end.

SPREADING MAWKISHNESS

Oliver Goldsmith was not quite as witty as Sheridan but both were animated by the sentiments they deplored in an age they felt was suffocated by a spreading mawkishness.[32] Goldsmith, Irish, the son of a clergyman, was educated first at Trinity College, Dublin (where he was expelled for his part in a riot), and later studied medicine at Edinburgh. Then, after a stint exploring Europe, he settled in London. More or less penniless even then, he eked out a career by tossing out reviews for Ralph Griffiths's *Monthly Review*. This, says Paul Langford, was the first publication in Britain to offer regular reviews. Goldsmith wasn't bad as a journalist, but the ups and downs of his income did not fit comfortably with the constancy of his extravagant tastes.[33] Other periodicals he wrote for included *Busy Body* and *Bee* (which he started himself and where he released *The Citizen of the World*). But this was not enough, John Brewer tells us, 'to dispel the bailiffs and the prospect of the debtor's prison. Goldsmith's parlous finances led him into every byway of authorship – biography, translations, abridgement of such classics as Plutarch and pastiche histories of England, Greece and Rome'.[34]

Goldsmith was in London, writing, writing, writing, for the best part of a decade before he would see his name on the title page of any publication. This was for his poem *The Traveller*, and it was only following the publication of his novel *The Vicar of Wakefield*, in 1766, that he acquired independence. Even the release of this novel is a story in itself, according to Dr Johnson, who says that one morning he received an urgent note from Goldsmith, 'in great distress' because his landlady had had him arrested for non-payment of his rent. Johnson, reliable as ever, sent Goldsmith a guinea there and then, and rushed across town himself not long afterwards. There, it turned out that Goldsmith had already spent the guinea, on himself, a bottle of Madeira 'at his elbow'. Insouciantly, Goldsmith let slip to Johnson that he had written a novel. 'I looked into it', said Johnson, 'and saw its merit.' Whereupon Johnson removed himself to a book-seller he knew and sold the story for £60, handing Goldsmith the money so that he could settle his debts.

She Stoops to Conquer, Goldsmith's best-known play, is subtitled 'The Mistakes of a Night', and is another slapstick romp around the snobbery of class prejudice, love with the 'wrong' people and farci-cal mistaken assumptions (some of the characters believe the house they are in is really an inn). The play satirises – if gently – the simple sentimentality of popular morality. As Brewer puts it: 'All misun-derstandings are resolved, no one is disappointed.' Goldsmith, who earned between £400 and £500 from the play, had turned a corner. He dedicated *She Stoops* to Johnson.

ÉDOUARD DE GUIBBON

Edward Gibbon, born in Putney, then a village to the west of London, in 1737, was never very healthy as a boy but in some ways, his biographers say, that may have been to his advantage. One con-sequence was that he read a lot and imbibed an intense interest in history. Another consequence was that he was sent to Bath, a spa then known affectionately as 'the national hospital', and a very fashionable spot where, as we have seen, Gainsborough was the most famous of several resident portrait artists.[35]

After Westminster School, Gibbon attended Magdalen College, Oxford, where he converted to Roman Catholicism, much to the dismay of his father, who retaliated by dispatching his son to a staunch Protestant minister in Lausanne, Switzerland. There Edward expanded his reading, generally among continental authors, savoured the landscape and, with his father threatening to disinherit him, reconverted to Protestantism. Known there as Édouard de Guibbon, he fell for Suzanne Churchod (who would become the mother of Madame de Staël), but his father was horrified at this relationship with a 'foreigner'. Breaking off their affair, Édouard wrote: 'I sighed as a lover, I obeyed as a son.'

He published his first book in 1761, when he was twenty-four. This was *Essai sur l'étude de la littérature*, its stylish French making him a celebrity in both London and Paris. In April 1764 he embarked on a grand tour with William Guise, a future MP, and it was during this journey, over the Alps and on through Italy – taking in Lucca, Pisa, Siena, Florence and finally Rome, where he was enthralled by the 'Eternal City', as he called it – that he conceived his great work, first, a history of the city, and then of its empire. Before that came off, he worked on a number of other histories, not always finished, joined Johnson's literary club, succeeded Oliver Goldsmith at the Royal Academy as professor of ancient history, and became Whig MP for Liskeard in Cornwall.

The first volume of *The History of the Decline and Fall of the Roman Empire* appeared in February 1776, after seven years and several reworkings. Despite this, the book was an immediate critical and commercial success, bringing in close to £1,000. Volumes II and III were published five years later, in March 1781, and Volumes IV, V and VI appeared together in 1788.

The six volumes covered the years from AD 98 to 1590, taking in the empire, early Christianity and the Roman State Church, together with the history of Europe. Gibbon's main argument in the book is that the Roman Empire fell because of the advent of Christianity, so that, because of its new concerns, large sums of money that would otherwise have been used promoting the interests of the state were instead transferred to religious activities. An added factor, argues Gibbon, is that many wealthy Christians renounced their lifestyle, 'replacing it with a more or less monastic existence[,] and withdrew their support for the main policies of Empire'. Gibbon was also of the view that the emphasis placed by Christianity on peace dangerously undermined the strength of the military. As a result, ultimately, the empire succumbed to barbarian invasions 'due to the loss of civic virtue' of its citizens.

Gibbon's argument is out of favour in modern times – the financial and monastic sides of Christianity have been shown to be rather more modest in their extent and even tangential as contributing factors. But the success of the book owed as much to other factors, not least its style – 'dispassionate, detached, critical' – but also to its impressive use of sources. For example, Gibbon convincingly used primary sources to question and refine the usually accepted number of Christian martyrs. On the other hand, his direct attack on Christianity, that it caused the decay of the arts, of science and of literature, hardly sat well with the then prevailing Protestant vision.

Like Hobbes with *Leviathan*, Gibbon had anticipated criticism, and, like Hobbes, he was not disappointed, but it was his 'coherent grasp of such a vast subject' that won him such a large number of readers.

Among these distinguished men, we may mention two women. Hester Thrale was born into the well-known Welsh Salusbury family and received an excellent education. She made two very different marriages, the first to Henry Thrale, a brewer, and, after he died, to Gabriel Mario Pozzi, an Italian music teacher who had taught her own children (she had twelve). Because of her first husband's social position, she became a celebrated hostess, known for her 'wisecracks and pontifications', which is how she met Johnson, Goldsmith and Frances Burney, spending time with the latter in fashionable Bath Spa. Her friendship with Johnson was so close that when he stayed with her and her husband at their house in Streatham Park, he had his own room, where he could work.

After Henry Thrale died, members of the literary club expected Hester to marry Johnson, but instead she fell for Pozzi, a move which was generally looked upon as her marrying 'down'. She kept a diary, published after her death as *Thraliana*, and wrote some verse; a book about synonyms that was really a set of essays about words; a history, *Retrospection*, regarded as 'proto-feminist' in tone; and *Anecdotes of the Late Samuel Johnson*.

A Bishop in Petticoats

Though she was a good friend of Johnson, Garrick, Reynolds and Edmund Burke, Hannah More was not, strictly speaking, part of the club. A Bristol woman, and one of five sisters, who between them at one stage ran thirty-two schools, More travelled to London for thirty-five consecutive winters to partake of what the fashionable and literary worlds had to offer, in particular meetings of 'bluestockings', groups of women eager to explore the latest learning. With a prospective fiancé putting off their wedding three times, she resolved not to marry and he, feeling guilty, settled an annuity on her, giving her security and independence.

Over a long life she wrote verse, drama and many tracts of moral exhortation, which mostly reflected her evangelical convictions and included numerous criticisms of what she saw as the shortcomings of fashionable life in Georgian Britain, even at one point offering advice to the queen. She criticised both Jean-Jacques Rousseau and Mary Wollstonecraft on education, and Thomas Paine on radical politics, and had firm views about the role of women in society (she believed in a hierarchical and deferential society and that there were some things a woman couldn't do). She thought that the poor should be taught to read, but not to write 'as it would encourage them to be dissatisfied with their lowly situation'. But she supported William Wilberforce wholeheartedly in his efforts to abolish slavery. She was known by two nicknames, 'Saint Hannah' and the 'Bishop in Petticoats'. She was a national figure and her *Cheap Repository Tracts* – 114 short, loyalist and moral Christian tales, aimed at the lower classes – were phenomenally successful: a selection of forty-nine of them sold 2 million copies and were consumed in large quantities in Sierra Leone, the West Indies and the United States.

In her poem *Slavery*, written to help Wilberforce's bill in Parliament, she wrote:

Shall Britain, where the soul of freedom reigns
Forge chains for others she herself disdains?

FROM THE KING TO THE GUTTER

Two other members of Johnson's club, who further underline its remarkable range, were Sir William Jones and Sir Joseph Banks. Both immensely accomplished, their careers and contributions are considered separately. For now, we can complete this chapter with James Boswell and Francis Barber.

Boswell is widely known for his biography *The Life of Samuel Johnson*, but he had an interesting life of his own, which brought him up against a wide array of personalities, from Rousseau and Voltaire to David Hume and Lord Monboddo. Born in Edinburgh, in 1740, the eldest son of a judge, Alexander Boswell, Lord Auchinleck, James never enjoyed good health and modern opinion is that he suffered from bipolar disorder. He was well schooled in English, Latin, writing and arithmetic but was rarely happy, suffered nightmares and, we are told, 'was chronically shy'. He began attending Edinburgh University at the age of thirteen and although he stayed for five years, he reported being frequently depressed. He then moved on to Glasgow University where he attended the lectures of Adam Smith. After all this, he re-enrolled at Edinburgh, eventually managing to pass the law exam. Before settling down as a (not too successful) lawyer, he made the grand tour, studying for a year at Utrecht University, later meeting both Rousseau and Voltaire on his travels, making a pilgrimage to Rome and visiting Corsica.

He first met Johnson in May 1763 and recorded their conversation as follows:

BOSWELL: Mr Johnson, I do indeed come from Scotland, but I cannot help it.

JOHNSON: That, Sir, I find, is what a very great many of your countrymen cannot help.

Boswell could only attend the club when he was in London. In Edinburgh he occupied the house once lived in by David Hume, where, besides law, his journal shows that he was very taken with what he called a 'Bawdy-house' where, on one occasion, he spent the entire night with an actress named Louisa: 'Five times was I fairly lost in supreme rapture.' According to some accounts he contracted venereal disease nineteen times.

His first important engagement with Johnson was *A Journey to the Western Isles of Scotland* (1775), a travel narrative by Johnson of a three-month journey, in particular to the islands of the Hebrides. Boswell also chronicled it in his own *A Journal of a Tour to the Hebrides*, not released for another three years.

The Life of Samuel Johnson has been described by several authorities as the greatest biography ever written, certainly as a 'landmark' of the genre. Boswell kept a diary or journal from the age of twenty and so the biography of his great friend and mentor contains some vivid reconstruction of conversations, asides, and trenchant criticisms. As well as a picture of the club, it is, above all, as William Dowerling has pointed out, a *moral* history in a spiritually troubled age, an account of Johnson's 'embattled existence' at a time of scepticism and unbelief. Boswell shows us the existence in his subject of an inner world of moral stability, and that he inhabits not just a social world (though there is that) but a moral sphere, quoting early on from John Courtenay's 1786 poem on Johnson's moral character:

> By nature's gifts ordain'd to rule
> He, like a Titian, form'd his brilliant school;
> And taught congenial spirits to excel,
> While from his lips impressive wisdom fell.

Boswell also highlights that Johnson's moral sanity is balanced by many personal eccentricities 'too visible to be ignored': holding forth in drawing room or tavern, festooned in a shrivelled wig and unbuckled shoes; muttering to himself in company.[36] The book explores the idea of a moralist as an intellectual ruler and 'is, in effect, one long account of intellectual combat, with Johnson as the centre of gravity, with a growing sense of awe developing throughout the narrative, in which those who surround Johnson (who we must never forget included *six* bishops) comprise a microcosm of British society "from the drawing room to the gutter"'.[37] In fact, from the king to the gutter, since when Johnson met George III, as he himself told Boswell, 'I found his Majesty wished I should talk, and I made it my business to talk.' Even his voice was impressive – 'I wish it could be preserved as musick is written.'

Of Johnson's death, Boswell wrote, 'He has made a chasm, which not only nothing can fill up, but which nothing has a tendency to fill up. – Johnson is dead. – Let us go to the next best: – there is nobody; – no man can be said to put you in mind of Johnson.' Macaulay was to say much the same of Boswell: 'Boswell is the first of biographers. He has no second. He has distanced all his competitors so decidedly that it is not worth while to place them.'

In May 1787 Boswell attended a meeting of the Committee for the Abolition of the Slave Trade, the aim of which was to persuade William Wilberforce to lead the movement in Parliament. It appears that Boswell, who had succeeded as laird at the family estate at Auchinleck in 1782 and had petitioned the Home Secretary on behalf of three escapees from Botany Bay, had an early interest in abolition but it didn't last and in 1791 he went so far as to compose a poem in support of slavery, lampooning Wilberforce in the process.

Francis Barber, Johnson's servant, was a conspicuous individual but in a rather different way from the other figures considered in this chapter. He was black. Johnson was a fervent anti-slavery advocate, his best-known comment on the subject coming in his 1775 tract *Taxation No Tyranny*, in reference to the situation in North America: 'How is it that we hear the loudest yelps for liberty among the drivers of negroes?' Barber and Johnson – and Boswell, too, but in a different way – lead us naturally into what is surely one of the most consequential intellectual/political battles of all time in Britain: the campaign to abolish slavery and the slave trade.

'There Is No Colour in an Honest Mind'

Probably the best-known fact about Francis Barber, Johnson's manservant, is that Johnson left money and much of his property to him in his will. Johnson's first biographer, Sir John Hawkins, was incensed by this, says Gretchen Gerzina, in her account of black England in the eighteenth century. Hawkins was no less incensed by the fact that Barber was married to a white woman and had control over Johnson's manuscripts and some of his other possessions so that he needed Barber's say-so to gain access to those he needed for his biography.[1]

Thanks to Barber's links with Johnson, we know more about him than might otherwise have been the case, and this immediately throws up some of the contradictions surrounding slavery, of which there are many. Barber was born in Jamaica but was brought to England in 1752 by a Colonel Bathurst, 'who apparently owned a few slaves but abhorred slavery'.[2] When Bathurst died, he left Barber the sum of £12 and his freedom. It was Bathurst's son who introduced Barber to Johnson shortly after Johnson had lost his wife, and the arrangement suited both men. It was, says Gerzina, the beginning of a long and affectionate – though sometimes troubled – relationship. (At one point Barber left Johnson to run away to sea, but the good doctor persuaded him back.)

There were at the time, according to several accounts, some 14,000 black people, from different parts of the empire, in Britain in the late eighteenth century. Three who merit inclusion in an intellectual history were Francis Williams, Ignatius Sancho and, above all, Olaudah Equiano.

According to one account, Francis Williams was the subject of a social experiment. Born in Jamaica to a very successful property owner and free man who had negotiated certain privileges for himself (such as immunity from his own slaves giving evidence against him), Francis later wrote: 'Insula me genuit, celebres aluere Britanni', by which he appears to have meant that he was born on an island (Jamaica) but educated in Britain. According to Edward Long, in his History of Jamaica (1774), Williams was the subject of an experiment in which the Duke of Montagu was anxious to see whether, 'by proper cultivation, and a regular tuition at school and the university, a Negro might not be found as capable of literature as a white person'.[3] Williams was sent to England where he attended grammar school and Cambridge University. He returned to Jamaica soon after his father's death and appears to have spent the rest of his life 'coasting' on his father's financial coat-tails, not adding much to his fortune, and selling the occasional slave for income.

Again according to Long, it was as a writer that Williams 'made a conspicuous figure' in both Jamaica and Britain, though the only surviving work of his is a highly flattering poem of forty-six lines addressed to the governor of Jamaica on the assumption of his role. The writing of Latin verses, as is well known now, was appreciated then as a 'gentlemanly accomplishment' and highly regarded, but this work is also noteworthy for asserting both a Jamaican identity and the poet's sense of his own worth:

> Ipsa coloris egens virtus, prudentia; honesto
> Nullus inest animo, nullus in arte color.

> (Worth itself and understanding have no colour.
> There is no colour in an honest mind, or in art.)

At his death, Williams still owned sixteen slaves and he was something of an embarrassment to the staunch Jamaican plantocracy, wedded as it was to notions of white supremacy. To get round that, people were dismissive of his talents. David Hume, for example, suggested those talents were 'like a parrot who speaks a few words plainly'.[4]

Charles Ignatius Sancho (1729?–1780) could hardly have had a worse start in life. He was actually born on a slave ship while it was crossing the Atlantic Ocean – the notorious middle passage, where sometimes as many as 50 per cent of the slaves died – *en route* for the West Indies. His mother died shortly afterwards, of disease, in the Spanish colony of New Grenada and, not long after, his father killed himself 'rather than endure slavery'. Aged two, Sancho was taken to Britain by his owner and given to three maiden sisters in Blackheath 'who believed that keeping the pudgy child ignorant would render him submissive'.[5] Things got better when his neighbour, the Duke of Montagu, met him by accident and was so impressed by his intelligence that he introduced him to the Montagu library, and without success tried to get the sisters to support his education. Not long after the duke died, Sancho fled the sisters and, after some difficulty, persuaded Montagu's widow to employ him as her butler, a responsible position which he filled with such distinction that, at her death, she left him an annuity of £30 and a year's salary.

An attempt at a stage career (suggested by Garrick) was stillborn owing to a speech impediment but Sancho was rescued by the late duke's son-in-law who hired him as his valet, in 1766. He took the son-in-law to Bath where he was painted by Gainsborough, then the talk of the spa. The son-in-law also became Duke of Montagu and through him Sancho resumed his acquaintance with the Montagu library. Furthermore, the duke's status as a courtier, and as governor of Windsor Castle, brought Sancho into contact with members of the aristocracy and the royal family. To many of them, he was to dedicate his musical compositions, minuets and cotillions and dances for violin, mandolin, flute and harpsichord. Joseph Jekyll, a lawyer, an FRS and a Whig MP, who wrote the first biography of Sancho, said that Sancho's compositions were typical of the taste of the times – light and bright and cheerful. He also said that the African had written a theory of music as well as two plays, all of which are now lost.[6] Sancho later opened a grocery store in Westminster with his wife, where they had seven children – the 'Sanchonettas'.

He subsequently became known for his letters, many to the press, some written as 'Africanus', and he gained a wider celebrity when one of his letters appeared in the posthumously published *Letters* of Laurence Sterne, with whom he had collaborated, encouraging Sterne to write to alleviate the oppression of Sancho's fellow Africans. He was also, it is said, the model for the character Shirna Cambo in the anonymous 1790s novel *Memoirs and Opinions of Mr Blenfield*, which is the first instance in English literature 'when white men visit a black family in their homes as equals'.[7] Sancho died in 1780 after complications of gout; being chronically overweight didn't help either. He was the first African to be given an obituary in the British press and this seems to have encouraged one of his younger correspondents, Frances Crewe, a political hostess, to edit and publish the two-volume *Letters of the Late Ignatius Sancho, an African*, sold by subscription, which revealed that many had sought his advice on literary matters, his own writing being lauded for its 'Shandean prose style, punctuation, multilingual jokes, and word play'.[8] As Vincent Carretta notes, 'The literary quality of his *Letters* was frequently cited by opponents of slavery as evidence of the humanity and inherent equality of Africans, and even Thomas Jefferson felt compelled to acknowledge, albeit grudgingly, that "we admit him to the first place [as an author] among those of his own colour".[9]

The Interesting Narrative of the Life of Olaudah Equiano, or Gustavus Vassa, the African is, without doubt, one of the most arresting books ever written. There is only one word for Equiano – indefatigable. He tells us that he was born 'in a charming vale, named Essaka', most likely in present-day Nigeria, though he says that his native language had no word for 'ocean' since no one had ever seen one. Even the slaves in his tribe had slaves of their own, he tells us. His father, he says, was a local Igbo, an 'eminence' and indeed a slave owner. Despite this, Olaudah was kidnapped at about the age of eight, together with his sister, by slave traders. He was sold and resold several times on his journey to the coast and the ocean that would soon enough become familiar, and more than a word. He then made the middle passage on a slave ship before making landfall in Barbados, but was moved on quickly to Virginia, where he was sold to an English naval officer, Michael Pascal, who renamed him Gustavus Vassa, a name he used throughout much of his life. He travelled to England and then served aboard ship as an able seaman, taking part in several episodes of the Seven Years War. He was taught to read and write by his fellow sailors, learned some mathematics, and converted to Christianity, reading the Bible daily and eventually becoming a Methodist.

But he was canny and always on the lookout for commercial openings, and he accumulated enough cash that, in 1766, he bought his freedom. After working as a hairdresser, as a free man, he returned to the sea and a series of adventures – in the Mediterranean and Turkey, on Constantine Phipps's expedition to the Arctic (along with the young Horatio Nelson), and in the Bahamas, where he was shipwrecked. He returned to London, tried to become a missionary in Africa but was rejected by the church.

Again, he returned to the sea, this time reaching Philadelphia, where he linked up with the Quakers and the recently established schools for Africans. By this time, he was becoming well known in Quaker circles on both sides of the Atlantic and back in London he contacted a lot of the black poor, a problem that was becoming acute because most were free refugees who had retreated with the defeated British troops after the American War of Independence. He was therefore ideally placed to be appointed commissary to the Sierra Leone scheme, designed to relocate freed slaves in a locality of their own. He was now more politically engaged anyway and sent a petition to Queen Charlotte 'on behalf of my African brethren'. A year later he published *The Interesting Narrative*, which was written with such brio and charm that it proved an immediate and enduring success, going through ten editions in five years and providing him with 'a modest estate'.[10]

His life was also helped at this point by marriage to Susan Cullen, of Soham, Cambridgeshire, where they made their home and had two daughters. But Equiano kept an address in London and used it as a base to make many tours around the country, speaking about his book. He was successful but that success needs to be seen alongside a rising opposition to equality, given what equality was thought to have achieved in nearby France, where the Terror was in full swing. Nonetheless, Equiano's *Narrative* and his life continued to inspire the anti-slavery lobby.

*

Unlike Sancho and Equiano, James Somerset lacked any noticeable skill, for writing, acting or anything else, but he was, arguably, the one with the greatest cultural significance. It was through Somerset that slavery began to be abolished and through him that Granville Sharp, Lord Mansfield and William Wilberforce became household names.

Very religious, from an early age Granville Sharp took part in earnest theological controversies, biblical criticism, linguistics and antiquarianism, writing *A Short Treatise on the English Tongue* in 1767, while being self-taught in Greek and Hebrew. He became interested in slavery through his brother William, who 'had medical knowledge' and was called upon to help a certain slave, Jonathan Strong, who was seeking treatment after sustaining injuries inflicted by his owner. Sharp took up Strong's case, secured his release from prison when his owner obtained his arrest as an escaped slave, and fought off a legal challenge which accused him, Sharp, of violating the owner's property rights. He then embarked on a detailed study of the legal status of slaves in Britain, as opposed to the colonies, leading to his *A Representation of the Injustice and Dangerous Tendency of Tolerating Slavery* (1769). He took up the cases of other slaves in Britain, his efforts culminating with Lord Mansfield's celebrated judgment in the case of James Somerset (1772).

Mansfield was an immensely distinguished judge, from a Scottish Jacobite family (his brother was secretary of James's court in exile in Paris), so he wasn't always trusted. But he fulfilled many roles, both legal and political (Attorney General, Speaker of the House of Lords, even Chancellor of the Exchequer). He had handled many colonial disputes and was all for religious toleration (this was the run-up to Catholic emancipation). So, despite his Jacobite origins, he wasn't a natural radical.

Somerset was born in Africa, was bought by European slave traders and left the continent in spring 1749, reaching Virginia in May. In Virginia he was sold to Charles Stewart or Steuart, a colonial merchant who was also a customs official. In 1768 Stewart returned to Britain, taking Somerset with him. In 1771 he was baptised James Summersett at a church in Holborn. The baptismal register described him as an 'adult black', aged about thirty. This had a wider significance, says Ruth Paley.[11] At the time baptism was widely believed to confer manumission. There was no legal precedent for such a belief, but it was so widespread that many colonies had passed laws specifically repudiating it.

Somerset left Stewart's service later in 1771, in what was un-ironically called 'a singular instance of ingratitude', and refused to return. After a short gap of two months' freedom, he was seized and press-ganged on board a ship, the *Ann and Mary*, the idea being that the captain would sell him again once he reached Jamaica. Three of Somerset's (white) godparents who had witnessed his arrest immediately applied to Mansfield for a writ of habeas corpus to free him from his plight.

As noted, Mansfield was no radical. Furthermore, he believed that freeing the slaves would have a 'harshly negative' impact on the British economy, and so was reluctant to issue a formal decision and worked hard to persuade the two sides to settle, which they flatly refused to do. Only then did he agree to a hearing but even then he kept delaying the trial. Eventually, however, after several postponements, in July 1772 he delivered his judgment. The courtroom was packed, mainly with black people eager to hear what they all hoped would be a momentous decision.

It was and it wasn't.

The basic case was habeas corpus, carefully constructed to make the issue straightforward. Somerset's baptism was avoided completely, the case turning on the 'fact' that 'negro slaves' were chattel goods, that Somerset was a slave according to the laws of Virginia and Africa, and that he was detained by order of his master to be sent to Jamaica and sold. The legal point before the court was, therefore, whether slavery was legal in England and whether an English court could uphold colonial laws if they conflicted with English ones. Mansfield's 'carefully worded' judgment, however, as Paley points out, 'concentrated on the legality of forcible deportation'. This was in fact governed by a statute set down as long ago as 1679, which effectively enabled Mansfield to sidestep wider issues. And so, his judgment conceded 'an important but limited advancement in slave rights', in that, as Mansfield said, under the 1679 statute, it was confirmed that slaves were servants, rather than chattels.

Somerset was free but in fact the verdict left his wider status as a slave unresolved.

No matter. It was widely believed, then and since, that Mansfield had declared slavery to be illegal and this judgment has, says Paley, passed into Anglo-American 'legal mythology'. Somerset himself thought that Mansfield had declared slavery to be illegal and urged his fellow blacks to desert their masters. Nothing more is known of Somerset.[12]

But we do know much more about Granville Sharp. Strongly sympathetic to colonial grievances, in his *Declaration of the People's Natural Right to a Share in the Legislature* (1774), he argued for American representation in the Westminster Parliament. He also loudly opposed the use of the press-gang for naval recruitment, and in 1783 he tried, unsuccessfully, to bring a private prosecution for murder after the notorious *Zong* incident, when more than 130 African slaves were thrown overboard from the slave ship of that name, some still manacled together, in what was an attempt to defraud the underwriters. And Sharp, naturally enough, was one of the twelve founding members who created the Society for the Abolition of the Slave Trade in 1787, giving his full support for the motions for the abolition of that same trade introduced into the House of Commons by William Wilberforce, providing Wilberforce with detailed information and meeting with William Pitt. Sharp also had a hand in the establishment of the colony for freed slaves in Sierra Leone, bringing him into contact with Equiano.[13]

There was a change in intellectual climate in Britain in the last decades of the eighteenth century, Sharp keeping up the pressure though at times it felt slow. He wrote *Serious Reflections on the Slave Trade and Slavery* in March 1797, but it didn't appear for another eight years – the rearguard resistance of the West Indian interest was felt everywhere. Though earnest, Sharp wasn't entirely one-dimensional – he was also known for his trips by boat on the Thames where he formed an orchestra, in which he played the harp (albeit one of his own design). These excursions, portrayed by the painter Johan Zoffany, were attended by royalty.

Wilberforce, from Hull where his family traded with the Baltic nations, was a Cambridge graduate, and was always interested in politics and in matters relating to the merchant marine. He became interested in slavery in 1787 during a conversation with William Pitt the Younger, at Holwood in Kent, under what became known as the 'Wilberforce Oak', when Pitt urged the other man 'to make the cause his own'. Wilberforce worked on two fronts, in Parliament and – as an evangelical – on the bishops. He repeatedly introduced bills, secured a Privy Council inquiry into conditions aboard slaving ships, and at first a bill was adopted for the 'gradual' improvement of conditions. But that proved pyrrhic because 'gradual' could be warped in all directions. Nor did war with France help, hostilities coming between Wilberforce and Pitt. They were reconciled but in circumstances where, such was the unrest in Britain over France, and the disorder that 'equality' could engender, that anything to do with slavery was sidelined, at least for a while.[14]

Wilberforce was no less an evangelical than Sharp and in the late eighteenth century he formed an integral part of the Clapham Sect, a group of wealthy evangelicals who mostly lived in that part of south-west London. He used this influential group to spread his message among the elite. Further bills were passed around the turn of the century, restricting still more the overcrowding in the slave ships, but progress was even now agonisingly slow. The turning point came in 1804, when nervousness about war with France was at last receding. The abolition bill was finally passed in 1807, but Wilberforce was still not done. He helped the creation of an African Institute, to improve conditions in the West Indies, laboured to establish Sierra Leone, and tried to prevent slaves being carried on foreign ships. He also supported Catholic emancipation in 1829.[15]

But we are running ahead of ourselves again.

Eden in Edinburgh: Self-Interest, Sympathy and the 'Invisible Hand'

'For a period of nearly half a century, from about the time of the Highland Rebellion of 1745 until the French Revolution of 1789, the small city of Edinburgh ruled the Western intellect.' This is James Buchan in his excellent book *The Capital of the Mind*. 'For near fifty years, a city that had for centuries been a byword for poverty, religious bigotry, violence and squalor laid the mental foundations for the modern world ... "Edinburgh, the Sink of Abomination" became "Edinburgh, the Athens of Great Britain".' On one occasion in the seventeenth century, despite the fact that there were three mail coaches between Edinburgh and London every week, the return mail contained only one letter from London to the whole of Scotland.[1]

The eighteenth century, however, was much more sociable and it was against this background that a raft of luminaries became the first intellectual celebrities of the modern world,

as famous for their mental boldness as for their bizarre habits and spotless moral characters. They taught Europe and America how to think and talk about the new mental areas opening to the eighteenth-century view: consciousness, the purposes of civil government, the forces that shape and distinguish society, the composition of physical matter, time and space, right actions, what binds and what divided the two sexes. They could view with a dry eye a world where God was dead ... The American patriot Benjamin Franklin, who first visited Edinburgh with his son in 1759, remembered his stay as 'the *densest* happiness' he had ever experienced. The famous *Encyclopédie* of the French philosophers had devoted a single contemptuous paragraph to *Écosse* in 1755, but by 1762 Voltaire was writing, with more than a touch of malice, 'today it is from Scotland that we get rules of taste in all the arts, from epic poetry to gardening'.[2]

The immediate spur to this renaissance of the north was the rebellion of 1745. The Highland Rebellion, led by Prince Charles Edward Stuart, to re-establish the (Catholic) Jacobites as the kings of Scotland (and Britain), briefly flourished in Edinburgh, before Charles, on his way to attack London, was defeated near Derby and forced to flee back to France. This concentrated minds in Edinburgh, forcing many to conclude that their future lay with England, that religious divisions, as reflected in the royal rivalries, did more harm than good, and that what counted was the new learning rather than the old politics.[3]

Probably the best description of the Scottish Enlightenment is that it was a scheme centred around not much more than a dozen individuals who sought 'practical betterment' for themselves and their fellows – theirs was, in the words of one observer, a 'Pragmatic Enlightenment'.[4] The 'first team' comprised David Hume, Adam Smith, William Robertson, Lord Kames, John Millar, Adam Ferguson, Thomas Reid and Dugald Stewart, together with very interesting lesser but still substantial names, such as Colin Maclaurin, a friend of Newton, who was Scotland's leading mathematician and one of the founders of the Honourable Society of Improvers in the Knowledge of Agriculture in Scotland; Sir Robert Sibbald, who spearheaded the founding of the Royal College of Physicians in Scotland, in 1681; William Alexander, who wrote a history of women; William Paterson, famous as one of the founders of the Bank of England; and George Wallace, who was Scotland's most important legal critic of slavery. It was also, as John Morrell points out, a golden age for Edinburgh University, despite two thirds of the chairs being in the gift of the town council, a collection of merchants and craftsmen, and this being a time when the medical school at Glasgow rose dramatically through advances there in chemistry and botany.[5]

What is notable about this group is, first, that they were very European in outlook.[6] Their main concerns were religion, being especially critical of the prejudices of the kirk (until 1745 Edinburgh had been run in a very Puritan fashion – indeed the phrase 'ten o'clock man' reflected the fact that the elders of the kirk would tour the city's pubs at that hour, to ensure that no more alcohol was served), the mind and its powers, where our moral sense comes from, the emerging science of anthropology, the nature of human sociability and, famously, the relationship between philosophy and common sense. The Scottish Enlightenment also had a deep effect on early thinking in America.

LE BON DAVID

The most devastating sceptic was David Hume, 'Le Bon David', as the French called him when he lived there as secretary to the British ambassador, and his huge appetite for intellectual battle may be seen from the range of titles of his works.[7] These include *Of Superstition and Enthusiasm* (1742), *Essay on Miracles* (1747) and *Essay on Providence and a Future State* (1748). Hume studied religion historically and this taught him, first and foremost, that it had a lot in common with other areas of human activity. He concluded that there wasn't anything special about religion, that it had emerged as just another aspect of human activity in ancient civilisations and that it was kept alive because parents taught it to their young children, who grew up unable to think in any other ways. He argued that polytheism was the earliest form of religion and arose out of man's experiences of good and bad. Benevolent gods were attributed to good events, malicious gods to bad events. In either case, he observed, the gods took human form. On the other hand, he thought that monotheism – the more abstract form of the deity – had grown out of man's observations of nature. The great natural phenomena, strange happenings such as earthquakes, lightning, rainbows and comets, convinced men that these were the actions of a powerful and arbitrary god. Hume observed, accurately enough, that polytheism has been more tolerant than monotheism.

In particular Hume worked hard to show that the alleged proofs of God's existence were no such thing, and that the anthropomorphic conception of God was also misplaced, even absurd. 'We cannot learn of the whole from knowledge of a part – does knowledge of a leaf tell you anything about a tree?' 'Assuming that the universe had an author, he may have been a bungler, or a god since dead, or a male or female god, or a mixture of good and evil, or morally quite indifferent – the last hypothesis being the more probable.' Then there were Hume's devastating criticisms of both miracles and the 'future state'. His chief argument was that, when all is said and done, there is no unimpeachable evidence for any miracle that would be accepted by a reasonable person. Hume insisted that it was equally absurd to imagine that God would 'even the score' in a future life, making up for all the injustices in this one. The interrelations between people were too complicated, he said, and made a 'balancing of the books' impossible.[8]

In Britain, and particularly in Scotland, there was a special gloss on the way the relationship between the soul and psychology was conceived, which was known as moral philosophy. This was an ancient term, dating back to late medieval times, which reflected the view that the soul, human nature and the arrangement of social conditions were all linked, and that the study of human nature would reveal God's purposes for morality. There were those who argued that the moral sense was a faculty of the soul – this was how God showed man how to behave – but the man who grounded morality in the study of human nature was, again, Hume. Born in the Lawnmarket area of Edinburgh in 1711, the son of a Berwickshire laird, he developed a passion for literature and philosophy at college. His most important work was done while he was in his twenties, but he was never made a professor, possibly because his scepticism bewildered and even frightened Edinburgh.

In January 1739, at the age of twenty-seven, Hume published the first volume of *A Treatise of Human Nature*. This set out to provide the groundwork to establish a science of man that would provide a rational moral code.[9] Experience orders life, 'knowledge becomes belief, "something felt by the mind", *not* the result of a rational process'. On this basis, all religion – with its ultimate causes and miracles – is complete nonsense.[10] Hume thought reason was completely in thrall to passion, and to that extent all science was suspect. There are no laws of nature, he said, there is no self, there is no purpose to existence, only chaos. Likewise, he did not think it possible to explain 'the ultimate principles of the soul' but thought that there were four 'sciences' relevant to human nature: logic, morals, criticism and politics. 'The sole end of logic is to explain the principles and operations of our reasoning faculty, and the nature of our ideas: morals and criticism regard our tastes and sentiment: and politics consider men as united in society and dependent on each other.'[11]

Hume's essay 'Of the Origin and Progress of the Arts and Sciences' was the earliest presentation in Scotland describing a theory about the historical stages of human societies which also advanced what he regarded as an 'empirical' (a word he liked and used a lot) analysis of human nature. It was in this essay that he advanced the view that there are fundamental differences between men and women and, more than that, that the male treatment of the female 'is a basic index of historical progress'. Hume went on to assert, in a tendentious footnote added in the 1748 edition of 'Of National Character', that 'the non-white races are too amorphous and impoverished to exhibit sufficient regularities in their passions to serve as useful objects for the study of human nature'. He was taken to task by both Monboddo and the philosopher James Beattie, who each had ideas about the effect of climate on human societies and its effect on the different races.[12]

Though he placed the passions centre stage, Hume was a moderate man in his own habits. He found many of his contemporaries 'agreeable' and, towards the end of his life, often cooked for his friends, who included several clergymen.

THE STADIAL THEORY

In the traditional university curriculum, centred around Aristotle, the management of affairs was regarded as a branch of ethics. Until the seventeenth century, as we have seen, there was no conception of 'the economy' as an entity in its own right and in the universities politics was not yet an academic discipline. Only in the eighteenth century was there a separation of economic from moral questions. Until then the 'just price' for goods was set by guild corporations and royal representatives, not (at least not directly) by the market. The emergence of modern states in the seventeenth century – France, Austria, Prussia, Sweden – was a significant step as they sought to understand the links between population levels, manufacturing and agricultural productivity, and the variable effects of the balance of international trade. As a result, the eighteenth century saw in several of these countries (but not yet Holland or Britain) the establishment of university chairs of economics and the management of the state – political economy.

In Britain, however, men argued that human nature rather than the state should govern economics.[13] At the time, there was a general acceptance that society had entered a new stage – as we have seen, it had become 'commercial'. Commercial society, people felt, was the last (or at least the latest) stage in the progress of man. This was especially the case in Scotland, where William Robertson, Adam Smith and John Millar – and to a certain extent Adam Ferguson and Lord Kames – all divided societies for analytical purposes into four stages, the 'stadial' theory of history: hunting; shepherding; agriculture; commerce.[14]

This approach or attitude was summed up by Smith: 'Every man thus lives by exchanging, or becomes in some measure a merchant, and the society itself grows to be what is properly a commercial society.' In other words, a person's place in society is defined by what they (can) buy and sell.

Born in Kirkcaldy in 1723, Adam Smith was a sickly child but he grew up to be something of a renaissance man, familiar with Latin, Greek, French and Italian. He translated works from the French, so as to improve his English. He wrote on astronomy, philology, 'poetry and eloquence', and was professor of logic and rhetoric at Glasgow before he was appointed to the more prestigious chair of moral philosophy, in 1752. Though he lived and worked in Glasgow, he participated fully in Edinburgh life: the Glasgow–Edinburgh stagecoach arrived each day in time for early-afternoon dinner. He published *The Theory of the Moral Sentiments* in 1759, a work which Alexander Wedderburn, founder of the *Edinburgh Review*, described as disclosing 'the deepest principles of philosophy'. But it is for *The Wealth of Nations*, published in 1776, that Smith is remembered and revered around the world.

When he died, 'after a life of intellectual adventure and social prudence', a local newspaper complained in its obituary (4 August 1790) that he had 'converted his chair of moral philosophy at Glasgow University into one of trade and finance'. There is some truth in this but, because of the way Smith has been understood, and misunderstood, in the years since he lived, it is important to reiterate that he was an academic, a moral philosopher, who took a very moral view of his own work. 'Capitalism' is a term invented only at the turn of the twentieth century (as '*Kapitalismus*', by Werner Sombart, the German economist and sociologist), and Smith would not have recognised either the word or the sentiment. His grasp of finance and banking was never especially strong and towards the end of his life he expressed profound misgivings 'about the moral complexion of commercial society'. There is an irony here because Smith created an approach and a language that, ultimately, divorced economics from what most people mean by morals. But he himself felt that allowing absolute freedom of economic activity was itself a form of morality. Among other things, his book was a morally outraged attack on the monopolistic practices of the grain trade. He championed the interests of the consumer against the monopolists, identifying consumer demand as the engine for the creation of wealth.

The formation of commercial society is, as both Roger Smith and Paul Langford highlight, a new stage in the evolution of a modern view of human nature. 'The term "economic man" is a code-word for the opinion that what is called society is only an association of individuals who act in the light of rational self-interest to maximise their material profit and well-being.'[15] As well as everything else, this clearly has implications for man's psychology, and it is important to be aware of the new world of the consumer into which Smith introduced his book.

Smith's theories were especially poignant because at the time, in France, the only country where there was what we might call rival

thinking, the theories of the so-called physiocrats were very different and, as it soon turned out, nowhere near as fruitful or accurate.
The physiocrats were significant because they too encouraged the
idea that, in the eighteenth century, there was a shift to commercial society and with this went an acceptance of commerce and
exchange as important to the understanding of the laws of human
nature. However, France, much more than England, was overwhelmingly rural and agricultural and this determined the theories
of the physiocrats, the main figures here being François Quesnay
(1694–1774) and the Marquis de Mirabeau (1719–89). Their view,
argued in a series of books, was that all wealth derived from land,
from agricultural productivity. Civilisation was essentially driven
by the surplus of agricultural goods over the consumption of food
required to produce it. For Quesnay there was a 'productive class',
engaged in agriculture; there was a class of proprietors, landowners
who included both the king and the church, who received the yield
of agriculture in the form of tithes, taxes and rents; and there was
what he called in a revealing phrase a 'sterile class', which included
manufacturers, dependent on agriculture and, according to him,
incapable of producing a surplus.[16]

'PERHAPS THE MOST IMPORTANT BOOK EVER WRITTEN'

Adam Smith in effect took the opposite view, that man had advanced beyond agricultural society, to a new stage in civilisation,
commercial society. The basis of economic value, the origin of
wealth, Smith said, lay in labour, work done. This was a marked
change in that Smith did not identify any one occupational sector as
the fundamental basis of wealth – what mattered instead, he said,
was exchange and productivity, the value added in any transaction.
This approach later became what was called 'classical economics'
so it is important to reiterate here that Smith had no conception of
a discipline of economics isolated from the study of moral relations,
from the history of civilisation or from political questions about how
Britain should be governed. Smith's view was essentially the modern
one that we have today: people were to be judged by their rational
and moral qualities, and the extent to which they helped the welfare

of their fellows. Although he came to be regarded as the father of free market economics, in fact Smith believed that legislation was essential in certain areas of life, to maintain fairness and openness, and he himself lectured on jurisprudence. H. T. Buckle, the historian of English civilisation, thought *The Wealth of Nations* 'perhaps the most important book that has ever been written'. Smith's approach, his rationalism, allowed mathematics to be applied to trade and exchange. This was not always successful, but it did show that economic activity obeys certain laws or order, and we have Smith to thank for this. He is often identified with the phrase '*laissez-faire*', but this is a French term, and reflects an eighteenth-century French view of economics that did not become popular in Britain until the nineteenth century. In fact, Smith himself was always equally concerned with justice in civil society as with wealth creation. People, he felt, would always naturally pursue their own self-interest and, other things permitting, this would lead to a high-wage economy which encouraged consumption, productivity and a general and continual upward cycle. Notably, Smith believed that God had so designed human nature that the average person, besides looking out for him- or herself, also shares sympathy for others. He believed that a civic humanism could go hand in hand with a commercial society. He was anti-slavery, arguing it to be uneconomic as well as morally wrong, and many in Scotland in the late eighteenth century shared his view.[17] Benevolence was an important ingredient of the Scottish Enlightenment.

The notion of 'unintended consequences', as shown in Smith's 'invisible hand', became a central plank in the Scottish Enlightenment's contribution to political and economic modernisation and its links with morality.[18] As Adam Ferguson put it, 'nations stumble upon establishments, which are indeed the result of human action, but not the execution of any human design'.[19] This was important for both the philosopher and the general public, because for the first time it was incumbent on them to grasp the hidden link between intention and the unintended consequences of specific human actions.[20]

Francis Hutcheson (1694–1746), and not Hume or Smith, is considered by many to be the founding 'father' of the Scottish

Enlightenment. For Hutcheson, benevolence is the greatest of virtues and he further claimed that 'a tendency towards benevolence was an innate characteristic of human beings', as he set out in *An Inquiry into the Original of Our Ideas of Beauty and Virtue* (1725). It was these qualities of benevolence and virtue which the American philosopher Gertrude Himmelfarb says separates the British Enlightenment from – and puts it above – the French variety. Hutcheson, Hume and Smith were also united in that they were, as Himmelfarb also says, 'great nourishers of literature', because they were convinced that, 'by moving the reader, literature was a great moral teacher'.[21]

This mood was tempered, however, to an extent, by the unsuccessful Jacobite uprising of 1745 and the brutal Highland Clearances that then took place. Many Scots, even those who thought the union with England in 1707 was the right political and economic move over the longer term, nonetheless regretted the loss of more than a few aspects of traditional Scottish culture.

Tobias Smollett was one. Writing to a friend, Smollett's Jeremy Melford, in his epistolary novel *The Expedition of Humphry Clinker* (1771), waxes indignant at the 'humiliation and cultural devastation' wrought upon the Highlanders as he and his family travel across Scotland: 'It must be observed that the poor Highlanders are now seen to disadvantage. – They have been not only disarmed by an Act of Parliament, but also deprived of their ancient garb, which was both graceful and convenient; and what is a greater hardship still, they are compelled to wear breeches ... they are even debarred the use of their striped stud called Tartane ... prized by them above all the velvets, brocades and tissues of Europe and Asia ...'[22]

Biographer, dramatist, historian, poet and, not least, travel writer, Smollett was also author of a handful of picaresque novels, including *Roderick Random* (1748), *The Adventures of Peregrine Pickle* (1751) and *The Life and Adventures of Sir Launcelot Greaves* (1762). But the book which would have the greatest impact on the future evolution of the novel was *Humphry Clinker*. This tracks the Bramble family as its various members move from their native Wales to disparate sites across England, before travelling north to Scotland, where they discover both 'geographical and social enlightenments'.

Smollett employs a series of letters, written by different characters, so that the same events are described and evaluated by different voices. In this way Smollett can investigate individual subjectivity and 'the psychology of perception'. In this way, too, every letter writer is de facto a spectator of the other characters' actions. On top of that, moreover, the letter writers often feel the need to comment upon their own sympathetic (or otherwise) reactions, as spectators of scenes involving other spectators/characters. As Deidre Dawson says, 'The overlap with Hume isn't obvious, except to those who have read Hume.'[23]

'Agents of a Benevolent Providence':
The Laboratory of Empire 1

mportant as Scotland was, as will become increasingly clear as this narrative proceeds, Francis Bacon can count as probably the most intellectually influential Briton ever. He is all the more important because, during his lifetime, England was hardly in the vanguard of anything. As Richard Drayton has pointed out, in Bacon's own area of interest, science, or natural history as it was called then, England possessed great universities and distinguished scholars at the time, and there were four universities in Scotland, but the country still turned to Padua and Montpellier for medicine, and to Prague and Paris for mathematics and philosophy. All that would change over the next two centuries for two main reasons. One was a result of the Elizabethan Settlement, which in particular promoted the cultivation of vernacular learning, often in what we can call the practical arts and sciences, not just the arid realms of scholasticism.[1] The second reason was empire.

The travel, exploration and courage needed to cross the oceans of the world sparked a need for improvements and advances in astronomy, cartography and mathematics of all kinds but in particular, geometry (ballistics, navigation). In exploring new foreign lands, there was a need for specific measuring devices, and new and potentially dangerous strange plants had to be understood, not just for themselves but for any medicinal properties they might have.

Bacon had anticipated this: in Salomon's House in *New Atlantis*, published in 1627, he narrated that 'merchants of light' would be needed to survey foreign parts. The Royal Society went so far as to print instructions for travellers on how to look for, and collect, samples of plants, soil and insects.[2]

'A Regular Commerce with Providential Truth'

As elsewhere, Christian Providentialism played its part. The idea that God should be worshipped 'through research in the Book of Nature', together with the belief that Adam's sons had the 'right and duty' to 'study and enclose' what was conveniently seen as 'a pagan wilderness', could be justified by the Book of Genesis. Samuel Hartlib, the Prussian-born 'intelligencer' who became a staunch friend of Boyle after he settled in England, had promised Cromwell that the times were 'propitious' for humankind to 'regain those powers which Adam lost when an angry Creator had closed "the conduit pipes of Natural Knowledge"'.[3] It is impossible for us to know, today, what went on in the minds of sixteenth- and seventeenth-century travellers. Did they believe the Bible literally or were they aware that its words were just a little too convenient for the situations they found themselves in? In Ireland it was proposed that expropriated land be sold off to pay for the 'Advancement of Universal Learning'.[4]

Overall, we can say, by the late seventeenth century the pursuit of knowledge, commerce and colonies, religious piety and a nascent nationalism came together, flavouring British imperialism. More, the methodical achievements of William Harvey, Edmond Halley, Robert Hook, Robert Boyle and Isaac Newton between them suggested, as again Drayton puts it, that Britain enjoyed a regular, rather than a miraculous, commerce with Providential truth, that in fact the British were indeed agents of a benevolent Providence.[5] In the same vein, William Petty, Charles Davenant and Gregory King carried out fledgling political-economic statistical surveys in order to calculate how this Providential favour had come about. Petty, obsessed with statistics, thought this favour could even be calculated, and that an Irishman could be valued at £25 (the going rate for an adult, male, African slave) but that if England could improve the Irish state of affairs, in the future he would be worth £75 – the equal of an Englishman.[6]

The truth was: because science was and is inherently expansive in its appetite for laws that apply everywhere, it naturally helped drive Britain towards a 'blue-water destiny'.[7]

KNOWLEDGE AS REVELATION

This approach does not sit very well with today's values, but there was no shortage of critics then, either. *Gulliver's Travels* was a hilarious satire on Bacon and Petty, in which the Academy of Lagado, on the island of Laputa (which Swift himself said represented the Royal Society), is a place where science is carried out to the exclusion of all other activities that would interest ordinary people. Elsewhere, in *A Modest Proposal* (1729), Swift lampooned Petty's idea of 'political arithmetic', which he regarded as simply inhuman.[8] These objections found their supporters but for many, in a post-Newtonian world, intellectual matters, especially what we would now call 'research', were looked upon as forms of piety. 'Knowledge, associated by Christians with revelation, had absorbed a moral aura, which it bestowed in turn on those who, by education and avocation, became its servants in any corner of the globe.'[9]

The British interest was also served by the fact that experimental science was a privately run affair, unlike in France, where it was an appendage of the Crown. This meant that science in France was much more related to the immediate interests of the state and as France began to extend its empire scientists were expected to play their part. For example, the Jardin du Roi in Paris, the epicentre of French global natural history, was founded in 1635, well before its British equivalent, the Royal Gardens at Kew, in 1759.

French rivalry was one factor which spurred the Royal Society and others to marry science with imperial expansion. Another was the Jacobite uprising in 1745, which brought about the creation of the Ordnance Survey. A third was the activities and interests of Hans Sloane.

Visitors to some of London's leading cultural institutions – such as the British Library, the British Museum, Chelsea Physic Garden, the Natural History Museum – will encounter portraits and busts commemorating the contributions of Sir Hans Sloane. Rather more will be aware of his name via London's streets – Sloane Square, Sloane Avenue, Hans Crescent. This reflects the fact that Sloane's most important achievement may have been the sheer number of people he knew and could call on to support his endeavours.[10]

Born in County Down in Ireland in 1660, Sloane studied medicine in London before taking an MD degree at the University of Orange in France. Returning to London, he practised medicine, first as an assistant to Thomas Sydenham, one of the founders of epidemiology. As a youth Sloane had become very interested in plants and was elected a fellow of the Royal Society at the early age of twenty-four.

In the year he was elected to the Royal Society, he accepted an opportunity to visit Jamaica, going as personal physician to Christopher Monck, Duke of Albemarle, who had been appointed governor of the island. Sloane stayed in the Caribbean for more than a year and used the opportunity to pursue his interests in natural science, collecting specimens of some 800 plants, together with shells, molluscs and insects. His travels enabled him to explore the ruins of Spanish Jamaica, learn about the process of making sugar and observe the violence of plantation slavery close up.

His later publications reveal that he took a great interest in the island's black inhabitants. This interest, according to James Delbourgo, his most recent biographer, 'went beyond mere descriptive natural history to make several subjective judgements about blacks as a racial group'.[11] Sloane based his judgements on assumptions about who made the best slaves. Scientific studies of skin colour at that time, says Delbourgo, carried the implication 'that what was in fact a construct of law had an identifiable basis in nature: if the source of blackness could be located, enslavement would be physically justified'.[12] In his journeys across the island, collecting specimens, Sloane was often accompanied by black inhabitants, and these collecting forays became eventually, again in Delbourgo's words, 'one of the age's most spectacular works of colonial science', embodied in Sloane's two-volume *Natural History of Jamaica*, with stunning life-size engravings, published in 1701.

On his return to London, he set about establishing himself. He married the wealthy widow of a Jamaican acquaintance and began his flourishing practice as a 'society doctor', while assuming new public roles, including offices in the Royal College of Physicians, and as editor of the *Transactions of the Royal Society* (of which he eventually became president). During these years he also formed a close relation with James Petiver (*c.*1665–1718), an 'apothecary-trader' – that is, someone with an apothecary's training, but who specialised in collecting medicinal plants from all over the world and selling them on. Kathleen S. Murphy's account of Petiver's collecting shows conclusively that he, like many other naturalists at that time, believed blacks and Amerindians to be 'uniquely knowledgeable about the natural world and potentially dangerous as a result of this knowledge'.[13] By the time of his death, Petiver had acquired one of the largest and most diverse natural history collections then known in Britain.[14] He oversaw a global network of collectors, captains and surgeons on ships engaged in the slave trade.[15]

After Petiver's death, Sloane purchased the apothecary's herbarium, specimens and manuscripts. Along with the rest of Sloane's collection, these objects became the nucleus of the British Museum after his own death in 1753, 265 volumes of dried plants providing the central ingredient. The British Museum Act combined acquisition of Sloane's collections with the acquisitions of other great libraries (the Cottonian, mainly brought together after the Dissolution of the Monasteries, and the Harleian, containing legal documents and illustrated manuscripts) and set a precedent for the governance of national collections and other sorts of national cultural institutions at arm's length from government – a practice still widely followed throughout the United Kingdom.[16]

HYBRID KNOWLEDGE

A final factor in this marriage of empire and science was the occurrence of the transits of Venus in 1761 and 1769.* The study of the

---

* A transit of Venus occurs when the planet Venus crosses the sun, taking about six hours, and is important for calculating various astronomical matters, such as the size of the solar system.

1769 transit was provided with generous royal funds, made available to the Royal Society, which in turn enabled James Cook's great Pacific voyages (in particular that of the *Endeavour*, 1768–71).[17]

The figure who had the vision and the energy to pull together the British scientific effort across the disparate islands and colonies which Britain had acquired over the course of the eighteenth century was Joseph Banks, who was elected president of the Royal Society in 1778, a position he held until his death in 1820.[18] The adventure of 'the laboratory of empire' offered a golden age for the collecting of natural history specimens – new forms of mammal, exotic insects, shells, interesting minerals in the realms of distant volcanoes, for example, or, in Banks's case, shrunken heads brought back from the Pacific for the benefit of anthropological colleagues. Research, often carried out by specialists (Sloane, William Sherard, Ashton Level), was a side issue on voyages where the main aim was trade and, yes, slavery. As Drayton points out, the libraries of All Souls College, Oxford and Eton College were built with wealth derived at least in part from African slavery and West Indian sugar, while East and West Indian fortunes often 'nourished' several learned London institutions – such as the Royal Society itself, Chelsea Physic Garden, founded in 1673, the Society for the Encouragement of the Arts, Manufactures and Commerce (1754) and the Linnean Society (1788).[19]

It was also the case that, at this time, the Scottish universities, of which there were then four, at Edinburgh, Glasgow, St Andrews and Aberdeen, in contrast with England's two, took a particularly strong interest in both natural history and practical learning, rather more so than Oxford and Cambridge. The Society for Improvers in the Knowledge of Agriculture (1734) mounted concerted studies of not just natural history but chemistry in mid-century, going on to coordinate great statistical surveys in the later part of the 1700s. Medical training was at that time superior in Scotland to that in England and many Glasgow- and Edinburgh-trained surgeons, who accompanied exploratory voyages to the West and East Indies as specialist crew members, brought back specimens which were collected by James Sutherland, herbalist and intendant of the Physic Garden in Edinburgh, which boasted more than 2,000 plants, mainly with medicinal properties.

A close reading of some of the works produced at the time, exploring the plants of Brazil and south Asia, for example, shows that they were actually using indigenous, native classification systems, generally without acknowledgement. It would take time for this to be fully understood. It became known as 'hybrid knowledge' and will be explored later.[20]

In America itself, British settlers, some of whom were corresponding members of the Society of Arts, provided local specimens and observations and even Newton, to an extent, relied on astronomers across the Atlantic.[21] Britons in America also started their own natural history societies. The Boston Philosophical Society was started by Increase Mather (a graduate of Trinity College, Dublin), and concentrated on the 'rarities' of New England. Others compiled natural histories of Barbados and the Carolinas. (There were already seven universities in America and an American Philosophical Society had been founded in 1743.[22]) And to the north, in Canada, natural history specimens were supplied by the Hudson Bay Company.

In India the real start of the so-called Oriental Renaissance in scholarship properly began with the arrival in Calcutta of William Jones and the establishment of the Bengal Asiatic Society on 15 January 1784. This society was established by a group of highly talented English civil servants, employed by the East India Company, who, besides their official day-to-day duties helping to administer the subcontinent, also pursued broader interests, which included language studies, the recovery and translation of the Indian classics, astronomy and the natural sciences.

Four men stood out. The first of these was Warren Hastings (1732–1818), the governor of Bengal and a highly controversial politician, who was later impeached for corruption (and, after a trial that lasted, on and off, for seven years, acquitted), but throughout it all he energetically encouraged the activities of the society.[23] It was Hastings who ensured that learned Brahmans (a high-status Indian priestly class) gathered at Fort William to supply the most authentic texts, which illustrated Indic law, literature and language. The others in the group were William Jones, a judge, Henry Colebrooke (the 'Master of Sanskrit') and Charles Wilkins. Between them, these men accomplished three things. They located, recovered and translated the main Indian Hindu and Buddhist classics; they kick-started the investigation of Indian history; and Jones, in a brilliant flash of insight, uncovered the great similarities between Sanskrit on the one hand and Greek and Latin on the other.[24]

These men were all brilliant linguists, Jones especially. The son of a professor of mathematics, he was, on top of everything else, an accomplished poet, publishing verse in Greek at the age of fifteen, while a year later – having learned Persian from 'a Syrian living in London' – he translated Hafiz, the superb Persian lyric poet, into English.[25] When the Asiatic Society of Bengal was instituted, in 1784, Hastings was offered the presidency, but declined, and so it was offered to Jones.[26] He modelled the Bengal association on the Royal Society, with weekly meetings and 'original papers'. He brought together botanists, including one who had studied under Linnaeus, and ensured that many plants, and drawings of plants, were sent back to Kew, together with details of insects and other animals, and meteorological accounts of Sumatra and the great rivers of India.[27] Jones researched Indian laws, and Indian medical practices and beliefs, and conveyed Sir William Herschel's astronomical discoveries to the Brahmans, who were, he reported, 'highly delighted'.[28] In particular, his highly successful translation of Kālidāsā's *Sakuntalā* (Calcutta, 1789) enormously impressed Joseph Banks.

One innovation of the Asiatic Society was the invitation to 'learned natives', whether lawyers, physicians or private scholars, who would, as a first step, submit their work in writing.[29] Jones suggested circulating a short memorandum in Persian and Hindi to explain 'the design of our institution', also floating the idea of a medal, with Persian on one side and Sanskrit on the reverse, as a prize of merit. He reported that 'the learned Hindus, encouraged by the mildness of our government and manners, are at least as eager to communicate their knowledge of all kinds, as we can be to receive it'.[30] Jones advertised the existence and aims of the society in its publications and invited scholars from Europe and America to contact him with queries or requests, which proved effective, and he was soon in touch with fellow scholars in England, Scotland and Massachusetts. As Garland Cannon concluded, 'His personal research helped India to rediscover her rich past, to assist her people toward a needed national pride in a trying colonial environment.'[31]

Jones's great discovery, the relationship of Sanskrit to Greek and Latin, was first aired in his third anniversary address to the Asiatic Society. As he put it:

> The Sanskrit language, whatever be its antiquity, is of a wonderful structure; more perfect than the Greek, more copious than the Latin, and more exquisitely refined than either, yet bearing to both of them a stronger affinity, both in the roots of the verbs and in the forms of the grammar, than could possibly have been produced by accident; so strong, indeed, that no philologer could examine them all three, without believing them to have sprung from some common source, which, perhaps, no longer exists.[32]

It is difficult for us today to grasp the full impact of this insight. In linking Sanskrit to Greek and Latin, and in arguing that the Eastern tongue was, if anything, older than and superior to the Western languages, Jones was striking a blow against the very foundations of Western culture and the (at least tacit) assumption that it was more advanced than cultures elsewhere. Later discoveries, of resemblances between Greco-Roman gods and Hindu deities, and commonalities in the doctrine of Hinduism and Christianity contributed to what became known as 'Indomania' among British elite scholars.[33] This had a remarkable impact on the imperial imagination and not long after scholars were finding links between Hindu and Maori, although the Maori themselves had little time for such ideas.[34]

Nearly two decades before that, on 21 July 1768, a former east coast collier of nearly 400 tons, named the *Endeavour*, embarked from Deptford. In command was the forty-year-old James Cook, a newly appointed lieutenant in the Royal Navy.

The avowed aim of Cook's voyage was to reach the recently discovered isle of Tahiti in the South Pacific and there, on 3 June 1769, officially witness the passage of the planet Venus across the face of the sun. Cook was equipped with instruments and astronomical timekeepers provided by the Royal Society and the Board of

Longitude (a system of prizes, established in 1714, awarded to those who devised instruments for calculating longitude at sea), which were the last word in technological wizardry.[35]

Tahiti might be remote, but Cook was far from alone, being but one of 150 observers from eight countries who were collaborating in what was the first example of global international scientific co-operation. The basic idea was that, as was theoretically possible, observation would provide the opportunity to calculate the distance of the earth from the sun. The earlier transit, in 1761, had been a disappointment and the next opportunities would not come until 1874 and 1882. The transit of 1769 was a precious event.

Shortly before the *Endeavour* put to sea, Cook was joined by Joseph Banks, included on behalf of the Royal Society, and Dr Daniel Solander, an eminent Swedish natural historian and a friend and colleague of Carl Linnaeus. There were also two artists aboard.

The *Endeavour* made good time and the transit of Venus observations were duly made. They were, however, a failure. The atmosphere around the planet made it impossible to judge exactly when the transit began and ended. No matter. 'Cook's First Voyage to the Pacific', as it quickly came to be known, caught the imagination and was a popular sensation.

One reason for this was that Cook embarked with a set of secret instructions ordering him, after the transit encounter, to sail to latitude 40 degrees south and then 'search to the westward for a continental land-mass which geographers had for centuries maintained must lie in the southern oceans'. And this is how Cook discovered the east coast of New Zealand, mapped both islands, then sailed on westward and found himself on the east coast of Australia, mapping it, too, from south to north. In arriving at Batavia (now Jakarta) in October 1770, via the Torres Strait, he was able to confirm that New Guinea was not part of Australia.

Cook's achievement was remarkable because of the new standards of professional efficiency that he established. He had two British predecessors who like him had circumnavigated the globe – these were John Byron in 1764–6 and Samuel Wallis in 1766–8 – but neither had made discoveries anywhere near as momentous as his and in any case, they were disabled by scurvy. For his part, Cook had arrived at Tahiti, no more than a dot on the map in a vast ocean, and on schedule. This, Richard Drayton points out, was a feat of navigation that had never before been achieved. Cook had used the 1768 and 1769 volumes of The Nautical Almanac (prepared by the Astronomer Royal, Nevil Maskelyne), and in doing so he had totally justified the establishment of the Royal Observatory in 1675 and the passing of the Longitude Act in 1714. This is because he had beyond doubt proved that longitude could be established at sea 'by lunar distance with sufficient accuracy to make a specific landfall according to plan'.[36] Cook's other no less considerable achievement was to keep the ship's crew free of scurvy. Such a doggedly collected group of specimens, drawings and notes had never been brought back before to tempt the scientific world. Beforehand, the Pacific had hardly been investigated by science; all of a sudden it was revealed in its magnificent variety.[37]

The Admiralty, we are told, had never seen anything like Cook's account of his travels. He was promoted to commander and plans were at once conceived to settle once and for all the continuing mystery of the great Southern Continent.[38] On this further voyage (1772–5), Cook circumnavigated the globe and reached the farthest south of anyone, latitude 70° 11'. Lasting fully three years and eighteen days, once more none of his crew died from scurvy.[39]

Now it remained for the North Pacific to be explored, in particular its north-eastern limits and whether there was a route to the Atlantic around Asia or America. Cook, now lauded with honours, including being elected a fellow of the Royal Society (for his achievements in regard to scurvy, for which he was also awarded the Copley Medal), was eager to put to sea again. He left on 12 July 1776. He had with him a Tahitian, Omai, whom Captain Tobias Furneaux had brought back on HMS Adventure from the second voyage, the aim being to return him to his own people. (Omai was famously portrayed by Joshua Reynolds.) During the voyage Cook and Furneaux charted virtually all the coasts of north-west America and even sailed through the Bering Strait, to arrive at latitude 70° 44' north, very near the limit of the Arctic ice, 'a compact and frozen wall stretching east and west as far as the eye could reach'.

In the middle of February 1779, some eleven years after he had sailed for the South Seas, Cook's life was 'snuffed out' in a contretemps with the indigenous people of Hawaii. His achievement was to prove that there was no great southern continent south of the Pacific, but in showing this he had brought into view the immensity and variety of the Pacific Ocean, all recorded meticulously in journals and on charts, in pictures and in prose, 'for all men to follow after him in confidence'.[40] It was an achievement in the annals of discovery rivalled only by Columbus and Vasco da Gama.

A FORMAL EMPIRE OF PROFESSIONAL KNOWLEDGE

Beginning in the middle of the eighteenth century, a new state of affairs spread across science as the Admiralty, the War Office, the Home Office, the Board of Trade and the East India Company coordinated their patronage of the arts and sciences and various areas of learning, mainly in the form of systematic surveys and inventories of natural phenomena.[41] Richard Drayton, the doyen of this field of scholarship, identifies a new stage in British intellectual life in the 1780s, what he calls a new British idiom of Enlightened Statecraft, in which *dirigiste* polices were increasingly applied.[42] Examples included the use of Jeremy Bentham for advice on prison reform and Sir Joseph Banks, then president of the Royal Society, for advice on such things as whaling, naval stores and exploration. Similarly, the East India Company appointed Alexander Dalrymple as its hydrographer to conduct surveys of the Coromandel coast and explore new routes to China. When Lord Cornwallis was appointed governor general of India in 1786, he was instructed to send home a botanical dispatch in addition to the more usual political and military communiqués. Later, under his command, astronomical surveys were carried out in several cities and a Great Trigonometrical Survey of the subcontinent completed. The EIC also founded new botanic gardens, organised Mughal collections and carried out collections of both natural and artificial artefacts. In 1804 Marquess Wellesley, who had followed Cornwallis as governor general, noted what he saw as his duty: 'To facilitate and promote all enquiries which may be calculated to enlarge the boundaries of general science is a duty imposed on the British Government in India by its present exalted situation.'[43]

Drayton, however, is sceptical: he thought the 'cause of Knowledge' merely lent dignity to an operation which might otherwise 'have appeared as mere plunder and rapine'. This perhaps goes too far. Kapil Raj, a professor of the worldwide circulation of knowledge at the École des Hautes-Études en Sciences Sociales in Paris, argues that in the 'open air sciences' – botany, agriculture, forestry, anthropology, sciences fundamental to colonialism – knowledge was in fact 'co-produced'.[44] Even if this was so, and there are plenty of individual cases where it was so, it remains true that such knowledge would never have been produced, at that time, and in such detail, without a British presence in so many disparate areas of the world.

The Admiralty had traditionally – and not unreasonably – viewed its primary responsibility as war, but towards the end of the eighteenth century it did begin to take a systematic interest in hydrology and exploration, luring Dalrymple away from the EIC. The navy was also brought in by the Royal Society on a scheme for the transfer of plants between the Pacific, Asia and the Caribbean, a scheme close to the heart of Sir Joseph Banks. The ill-fated *Bounty* expedition of 1787–9 was followed by its more successful sequel, the *Providence* expedition of 1791–3, which achieved the goal of bringing breadfruit from Tahiti to the West Indies and thus providing cheap food for the slaves there.[45]

There are two conclusions to be drawn from this brief survey. One is exemplified by the imperial evangelical fervour found in many Britons, such as Adam Smith and Jeremy Bentham. Their 'secret idols', in Richard Drayton's words, were rational economy and rational administration, leading to John Stuart Mill, who, in *On Liberty* (1859), stated plainly that 'despotism is a legitimate mode of government in dealing with barbarians, provided the end be their improvement'.[46]

The increase in the number of local scientific societies is another measure of the success of colonial elites. They provided opportunities for the promotion of improvement locally, an important ingredient of eighteenth-century ambitions. For example, improved economic well-being was one of the fundamental purposes highlighted by William Jones in his presidential address outlining the importance of

Indian science. When, for example, the Van Diemen's Land Scientific Society was founded in 1829, 'it was "constituted ... in imitation of the Royal & other literary & scientific societies of Europe & India", and it took as one of its major goals ... "eliciting and discovering the properties and uses to which the vegetable productions of the island may be applied and ... ascertain[ing] the improvements which may be adopted in their cultivation". Its successor body, the grandly named, The Royal Society of Van Diemen's Land for Botany, Horticulture and the Advancement of Science (founded in 1843 as the first Royal Society outside Britain) urged its members to promote "the advance of Science and the progress of the Colony".'[47]

The other conclusion is that the histories of British botany, zoology, geology, astronomy, geophysics, anthropology and political economy could not have developed or exist in the way that they do now without the empire: its extraordinary worldwide geographical range bestows a cosmopolitan dimension on these areas of learning without which such fields could not exist as proper scientific entities where the proper aim is the understanding of phenomena in a universal context. Such a mixed blessing is unavoidable.

Iron, Steam, Gaslight and Moonlight

If, as was maintained in the Prologue, a crucial change in sensibility took place sometime around the twelfth century, to initiate the development of what we may call the 'Western mind', and a 're-set' took place in the reign of Elizabeth I, a no less momentous change occurred in the eighteenth century. It had three elements, apart from the exploration of empire. One was that the centre of gravity of the Western world moved away from Europe, to lie somewhere between it and North America, and this shift westward to an imaginary point in the Atlantic came about as a result of the American Revolution. The second element involved the substitution of democratic, elected governments for the more traditional and often absolute monarchies of Europe. This owed its genesis for the most part to the French Revolution, which set off a chain of other revolutions that extended through the nineteenth century and into the twentieth, and partly to the ideas worked out in America. The third element of change in the eighteenth century was the development of the factory, that symbol of industrial life, so different to what had gone before.[1]

CHIMNEY ARISTOCRATS

Why did the factory and all that it implies occur first in Britain?[2] One answer is that in England many feudal and royal restrictions which remained in place in other European countries had been swept away by the revolutions of the seventeenth century.[3] Another reason was the shortage of wood, for this forced new developments in the use of the inferior but cheaper coal for fuel.[4] We should also remember that the first industrial revolution occurred in a very small area of England, bounded to the west by Coalbrookdale in Shropshire, to the south by Birmingham, to the east by Derby, and to the north by Preston. Each played its part in what became the industrial revolution: at Coalbrookdale in 1709 Abraham Darby smelted iron with coal; at Derby, in 1721, the silk thrower Thomas Lombe designed and constructed the world's first recognisable factory; in Preston, in 1732, Richard Arkwright was born; and in Birmingham, in 1741 or 1742, John Wyatt and Lewis Paul first applied the system of spinning cotton by rollers, which Arkwright would appropriate and improve.[5]

The first factories were powered by running water, and this is why they were located in the often-remote river valleys of Derbyshire – it was only here that the streams could be relied on to have enough water throughout the year. Children from foundling homes and workhouses provided cheap labour. This was not in itself a new practice – Daniel Defoe had observed Yorkshire villages in the 1720s where women and children spent long hours at spinning machines. The new element was the factories themselves and the brutal discipline they demanded. As things stood, at least the children had what little free time they were given in the countryside. But even that changed when the steam engine took the place of water power at the beginning of the nineteenth century. This made it viable for the factory to move to the source of labour, the town, coal being as plentiful there as in the countryside.[6]

The first use of the steam engine was to pump water from mines. The deeper mines, well below the water table, needed to be drained either by bailing out with buckets or with a series of pumps. The first engine to power these pumps was invented by a Baptist ironmonger from Devon, Thomas Newcomen, in the copper mines of Cornwall, around the turn of the eighteenth century. In this early form of engine, the steam which powered the piston was condensed in the cylinder, with the piston being brought back by the suction that resulted from condensation. This worked, after a fashion, but the drawback was that the entire cylinder was cooled after each stroke by the water that was injected to condense the steam. This was where James Watt came in. A chemist from Greenock, Watt made some calculations about the efficiency of Newcomen's machine and began to wonder how the heat loss might be prevented or avoided. His solution was to condense the steam in a chamber that was connected to the cylinder but not part of it. This arrangement meant that the condenser was always cold, while the cylinder was always hot. Despite this breakthrough, Watt's engine did not function satisfactorily in Glasgow owing to the poor quality of workmanship by the local smiths. Matters were transformed when Watt found much more 'eminent casters' in Matthew Boulton's factory in Birmingham.[7]

But the industrial revolution was not only, and in fact not mainly, about the great inventions of the time. The long-term change that the industrial revolution brought about was due instead to a more profound transformation in industrial organisation.[8] As one historian of this great change has pointed out, the abundance and variety of inventions 'almost defy compilation' but they could be grouped into three categories. There was the substitution of machines (quick, regular, precise, unflagging) for human skill and effort; there was the substitution of inanimate sources of power (water and coal) for animate ones (horses, cattle), most notably engines for converting heat into work, opening a virtually unlimited supply of energy; and finally, all this meant that man could make use of new raw materials – mainly minerals – which were abundant.[9]

The point of these improvements was that they enabled an unprecedented increase in humankind's productivity and, moreover, one that was self-sustaining. In earlier times, any increase in productivity had always been quickly accompanied by a population increase which eventually cancelled out the gains. 'Now, for the first time in history, both the economy and knowledge were growing fast enough to generate a continuing flow of investment and technological innovation.' Among other things, this transformed attitudes: the idea that something was 'new' made it attractive, preferable to something that was traditional, familiar, tried and tested.[10]

The essence of the factory was that it gave the owner control over materials and over working hours, enabling him to rationalise operations which needed several steps, or several people.[11] New machines were introduced that could be used by people with little or no training – women and children included.

For the workers, factory life was nowhere near so convenient. Thousands of children were recruited from the foundling homes and workhouses. Like the adults around them, children were subject to factory supervision and discipline. This was a new experience: tasks became increasingly specialised, time ever more important. Nothing like this had existed before; the new worker had no means of either owning or providing the means of production; he or she had become no more than a hired hand.[12]

This fundamental change in the experience of work became all the more obvious when the invention of steam engines made the *factory city* possible. In 1750 there had been only two cities in Britain with more than 50,000 inhabitants – London and Edinburgh. By 1801 that had grown to eight, and to twenty-nine in 1851, including nine over 100,000, meaning that by this time more Britons lived in towns than in the country, another first.[13] 'Civilisation works its miracles,' wrote the Frenchman Alexis de Tocqueville, who visited Manchester in 1835, 'and civilised man is turned back almost into a savage.'[14]

No less important in the long run, the industrial revolution also widened the gap between the rich and the poor, helping to generate class conflicts of unprecedented bitterness. The working class became not only more numerous but also more concentrated, and therefore more class-conscious. One reason for the poverty of the working classes, certainly for the low wages they were paid, was that income was diverted to the new business classes, who were investing in the new machines and factories. These 'chimney aristocrats', as Bernd von Kleist called them, came to dominate domestic government policy throughout most of Europe in the nineteenth century.[15]

Advances in electricity and in chemistry in particular underpinned many of the new industries which comprised the industrial revolution. Electricity moved ahead after the period dominated by Newton, because it was one of those areas that Newton himself had not spent any time on and where other scientists were not intimidated. People had known that there *was* such a thing as electricity for hundreds of years, being aware, for example, that amber, when rubbed, attracted small bodies. But the first real excitement was generated by Stephen Gray (1666–1736), an apprentice dyer and amateur astronomer from Canterbury, who first noticed that the corks which he put in the end of test tubes attracted small pieces of paper or metal when the tubes (not the corks) were rubbed. By extension he found that even silk loops that led from the tubes right round his garden also had the same property. He had discovered that electricity was something that could 'flow from one place to another without any appearance of movement of matter' – electricity was weightless, what he called 'an imponderable fluid'. Gray also discovered something anomalous but basic: electricity could be stored in bodies like glass or silk where it was generated, but it could not pass through them. And, conversely, those substances which conducted electricity could not generate or store it.[16]

Electricity became the rage in Europe, and then in America, after Ewald Georg von Kleist, in 1745, tried to pass a current into a bottle through a nail. Accidentally touching the nail while holding the bottle, he received a shock. Soon everyone wanted the experience, with even the king of France arranging for a whole brigade of guards to jump as one by giving them shocks from batteries of jars. It was this idea which Benjamin Franklin took up, far away in Philadelphia. It was Franklin who realised that electricity in a body tends to settle at its natural level, when it is undetectable.[17] If some were added, it became positively charged, and repelled objects, whereas if it lost some it was negatively charged, and attracted objects. This tendency to attract, Franklin also realised, was the source of sparks and shocks and, even more impressive, he realised that this was, essentially, what lightning was, a colossal spark. He demonstrated this by his famous experiment with a kite, showing that lightning was indeed electricity, and inventing the lightning conductor in the process.[18]

In 1795 Alessandro Volta (1745–1827), professor of physics at Pavia, showed that electricity could be produced by putting two different pieces of metal together, with a liquid or damp cloth between them, thus creating the first electrical current battery. But these batteries were very expensive to produce, and it was only when Humphrey Davy, in 1802, produced the new metals sodium and potassium, at the Royal Institution in London, that electricity began to be the subject of serious experimentation. Eighteen years later, in 1820, Hans Christian Oersted in Copenhagen discovered that an electric current could deflect a compass needle and the final link was made between the science of electricity and magnetism.[19]

More important even than the discovery of electricity, in the eighteenth century and the early years of the nineteenth, was the rise of chemistry. The main area of interest, at least to begin with, was the phenomenon of combustion. What actually happened when materials burned in the air? Everyone could see that such materials disappeared in flame and smoke, to leave only ash. On the other hand, many substances didn't burn easily, though if they were left in the air they did change – for example, metals rusted. What exactly *was* air?

One answer came from Johann Joachim Becher (1635–82) and Georg Ernst Stahl (1660–1734), who argued that combustibles contained a substance, phlogiston, which they lost on burning. The name 'phlogiston' was taken from the principle of phlox, or flame. On this theory, substances which contained a lot of phlogiston burned well, whereas those that didn't were 'dephlogisticated'. Though there was something inherently implausible about phlogiston (for example, it had been known since the seventeenth century that metals, when heated, *gained* weight), there were enough 'imponderable fluids' about at that time – magnetism, heat, electricity itself – to make the theory acceptable to many. But the concern with combustion was not merely academic: gases (*chaoses*) were of great practical concern to miners, for example, who ran the risk of treacherous fire-damps and 'inflammable airs'.[20] And it was this attention to gases that eventually provided the way forward, because hitherto, in experiments on combustion of metal ores, just the weight of the ore had been measured. But when gases were taken into account, this led immediately to Mikhail Lomonosov's principle of the conservation of matter, established as fundamental by Antoine Lavoisier in 1785.

The man who showed this more convincingly than anyone else was Joseph Black (1728–99), a professor of anatomy and chemistry at Glasgow University. He weighed the amount of gas lost by such carbonates as magnesia (he was the first to identify magnesium) and

limestone when heated and found that the lost gas could be reab-
sorbed in water, with an identical gain in weight.[21]

Black was followed by Joseph Priestley (1733–1804), a
Yorkshireman whose family were in the cloth trade, a devout dissenting Calvinist with a pronounced stutter, and one of the central
figures of late eighteenth-century Britain. A chemist, as well as a
liberal political theorist who very publicly supported both the French
and the American revolutions, he had the important idea that air
was more complex than it seemed. He experimented with as many
gases as he could find, or could manufacture himself, and one of
them, which he made by heating red oxide of mercury, he called at
first 'dephlogisticated air', because things burned better in it. After
isolating the gas in 1774, Priestley went on to show, by experiment,
that 'dephlogisticated air', or oxygen as we now call it, was used up,
both in burning *and* in breathing. Priestley well realised the importance of what he was discovering for he went on to demonstrate that,
in sunlight, green plants produce oxygen from the fixed air – carbon
dioxide – that they absorbed. Thus was born the idea of the carbon
cycle – from the atmosphere (another new idea of the time), through
plants and animals and back to the atmosphere.[22]

The study of gases also led John Dalton (1766–1844), a Quaker
from the Lake District and a schoolteacher in Manchester, to his
atomic theory. He too was not primarily a chemist but a meteor-
ologist – he kept a famous meteorological diary – and a physicist.
He had a particular interest in the elasticity of fluids, and it was he
who realised that, under different pressures, and incorporating the
principle of the conservation of matter, gases of the same weight
must be differently configured. The creation of new gases, and the
studies of *their* weights, led him to a new nomenclature that we still
use – for example, N_2O, NO and NO_2. This systematic study made
him realise that elements and compounds were made up of atoms,
arranged on 'Newtonian principles of attraction and electrical
principles of repulsion'.[23] His observation of certain other chemical
reactions, notably precipitation, when, say, two liquids, on being put
together, immediately produce a solid, or a major change in colour,
also convinced him that a basic entity, the atom, was being recon-
figured. His reasoning was soon supported by the new science of

crystallography, in which it was shown that the angles between the faces of a crystal were always the same for any particular substance and that related substances had similarly shaped crystals.[24]

Humphry Davy and Michael Faraday, the latter a Londoner and a member of the Nonconformist Glassite or Sandeman Christian sect, showed that passing an electric current through salts separated out the metals, such as sodium, potassium and calcium, and that, at base, all elements could be classified into metals and non-metals, with metals being positively charged and non-metals negatively charged. Faraday further demonstrated that the rate of transport of atoms in solution was related to the weights of the substances, which eventually led to the idea that there are 'atoms' of electricity, what we now call electrons. But they were not identified until 1897, by J. J. Thomson.

It is important to say that many of the inventions which created the industrial revolution were not made by traditional scientists, the kind who frequented the Royal Society, for example. The central preoccupation of the Royal Society had always been mathematics, regarded in a post-Newton world as the queen of the sciences. In such an abstract atmosphere, the practical inventor was not always regarded as a 'proper' scientist.[25]

In marked contrast there arose in the factory towns a series of 'dissenting academies', referred to earlier, which were described as such because they originated as schools to educate Nonconformist ministers – Quakers, Baptists, Methodists – who were not allowed into the regular universities. But these academies soon broadened both their aim and their intake. Almost certainly the most influential dissenting academy was the Lunar Society of Birmingham. Its members (known agreeably as 'lunatics') met informally to begin with, in the homes of different friends. Formal meetings began around 1775. The group was led by Erasmus Darwin (1731–1802) and met monthly on the Monday nearest the full moon (that being a time when they were most likely to have moonlight to walk home by).[26]

Darwin was a physician, very much a materialist, and a benevolent man of exceedingly wide interests. His busy practice lasted for forty years but he still found time to compose a vast, 1,400-page

compendium of medical knowledge titled *Zoonomia*, create a botanical garden, which he co-founded in Lichfield, help to translate
Linnaeus, explore the building of canals and argue against the established church. Radical but not revolutionary, he was all for the free
market and the advantages of industrialisation. He was a disciple
of Locke, held innate ideas to be inherently improbable and had an
early view of evolution, believing, as he put it, that 'all warm-bodied
animals have arisen from one living filament', though elsewhere
his theory had more in common with the Frenchman Jean-Baptiste
Lamarck's view about acquired characteristics being inheritable,
than that of his own grandson, Charles.

The kernel of the society, at least in its early days, was composed
of James Watt and Matthew Boulton. Watt, as we have seen, had
found that craftsmanship north of the border was not up to scratch
and joined forces with Boulton, whose Birmingham workshops
operated to a much higher standard. Here, Boulton reassured Watt
that 'the people in London, Manchester and Birmingham are steam
mill mad'.[27] Josiah Wedgwood was another 'lunatic' and he too was
one of that new breed of men lacking much formal education but
nonetheless noted for pursuing business through enlightened thinking, with a faith in reason and engrossed by measuring, weighing,
experimenting and observing, who tended to be in favour of both
the French and American revolutions and were opposed to slavery.
Wedgwood founded the potteries that bore his name, and modelled
his ceramics on ancient Greek vases discovered in the Etruscan
countryside in Italy (he named his works Etruria). Among other
things, he invented the pyrometer (though he insisted on calling it
a thermometer), to measure high temperatures, which helped him
make the fundamental discovery that at high temperatures all materials glow in the same way – that colour measures temperature
no matter what the material is. In time this would help give rise to
quantum theory.[28] Other members of the Lunar Society included
William Murdoch, who invented the gaslight (first used in Boulton's
Soho works in Birmingham), William Small, James Keir, Thomas
Day and Richard Edgeworth, one of the inventors of the telegraph.[29]

Joseph Priestley did not arrive in Birmingham until 1780 but when
he did, he immediately established himself as the leading mind. He

also became a Unitarian minister. Unitarians were sometimes accused of atheism or deism and as a result were regarded as among the boldest thinkers of their time (Samuel Taylor Coleridge was a Unitarian, for instance).[30] Priestley was certainly bold enough in his *Essay on the First Principles of Government* (1768), in which he may well have been the first to argue that the happiness of the greatest number is the standard by which government should be judged.[31] Meetings of the Lunar Society petered out in 1791 after Priestley's house was destroyed by rioters targeting religious dissenters over their support for the French Revolution.[32]

We should not make too much of the Lunar Society's 'outsider' status. Priestley lectured before the Royal Society and won its prestigious Copley Medal in 1773 for his work on gases. The group had (intellectual) links with James Hutton in Edinburgh. Wedgwood was also close to Sir William Hamilton, whose collection of ancient vases would eventually adorn the British Museum and stimulated the idea for the graceful Wedgwood pottery. Their activities and portraits were painted by Joseph Wright of Derby and George Stubbs.

But between its members the Lunar Society had many firsts to its credit, including an understanding of photosynthesis, and its importance in the understanding of the atmosphere; they made the first systematic attempts to understand and predict weather patterns; they developed modern mints for the printing of coins and improved the presses that would make mass newspapers practicable. They were also early campaigners for the abolition of slavery.

PART THREE

THE MIND OF VICTORIAN BRITAIN

Deep Space, Deep Time, Darwin

I n the late eighteenth and early nineteenth centuries, when the philologists were attacking the very basics of Christianity – seeking to pillory the absurdities and inconsistencies of the Bible, as David Hume did, for instance – the men of science did not join in. For the most part, biologists, chemists and physiologists, despite what worldwide exploration revealed, remained devoutly religious. That even applied, again for the most part, to the practitioners of the two sciences which were to produce the most convincing evidence that the biblical chronology had to be wrong: astronomy and geology.

Astronomy underwent its greatest change since Copernicus and Newton thanks to an unlikely couple who might never have achieved what they did had not the British powers-that-be decided to invite a German to be their king. The way Richard Holmes tells the story, Joseph Banks, shortly after he was elected president of the Royal Society in 1778, began to hear stories about a gifted amateur astronomer 'working away on his own' in the West Country. The man's name was Wilhelm, or William, Herschel, a German Jew from Hanover. He was in fact the organist at Bath's Octagon Chapel, who made ends meet by giving music lessons. He also composed. He lived, in a house full of astronomical and other books, with his sister Caroline, who looked after him but whom he also described as his 'astronomical assistant'.

Herschel had been born in Hanover on 15 November 1738, twelve years before his sister. On winter nights, the children were taken out-side to view the stars. In those days before widespread light pollution the night skies were much more vivid than now.

In the spring of 1756, when William was seventeen and Caroline six, the Hanover Foot Guard were posted to England, to serve under their ally, the Hanoverian King George II. The three men of the family – father, William and his older brother Jacob – were stationed in Maidstone, Kent, returning home a year later. But the family now became embroiled in the French–German wars, even to the extent of having French troops billeted in their home. Jacob and Wilhelm escaped, fleeing back to England where they arrived together in London, penniless. They obtained employment as musicians – play-ing or teaching. Eventually, when events in Germany quietened down, Jacob decided to return home. William, however, was happier in England, and he liked English culture: novels, theatre, politics. He obtained a position as music master to the Durham militia, stationed at Richmond in Yorkshire, a most civilised regional centre.

Aware that Jacob was bullying his sister, and that she had suffered a bout of typhus, which she survived but which appeared to have stunted her growth, he spirited her away to England. He took her to Bath, having by now been appointed organist at the Octagon Chapel. Caroline spoke almost no English; her face was badly marked with smallpox scars and she was less than 5 feet tall.[1] He treated her af-fectionately but made it clear that she was now to act as the hostess. He was thirty-four, she was twenty-two.

In February 1766 he started his first Astronomical Observations Journal and began collecting and building telescopes, and it was now that he had his first big idea. At that time most astronomers consid-ered the night sky as so many stars set out like inlaid diamonds on a giant glass dome. It was realised, of course, that some stars and planets were closer to Earth than others, but it was Herschel who seems to have first conceived the idea of *deep space*.

In 1774 William built his first 5-foot reflector telescope and it was immediately apparent that he had created an instrument of unparalleled light-gathering power and clarity.[2] He could see, for example, that the Pole Star – which had been the key to navigation, and the poet's traditional emblem of steadiness and singularity for centuries – was not one star at all but two. He also focused on the nebulae, or 'star-clouds', which were a mystery.

The recognition of nebulae was relatively new then. About thirty were known in the 1740s, though by the time Herschel came on the scene, and according to Charles Messier in Paris, France's most notable astronomer and star cataloguer, that number had risen to about a hundred. Within ten years, Herschel's observations swelled it still further, to about a thousand. No one knew their composition, origins or distance. The most popular understanding was that they were agglomerations of gas, hanging about in the Milky Way, 'some loose flotsam of God's creation'.[3]

From about 1779 Herschel began to expand and deepen his astronomical enquiries in earnest. His first idea was a catalogue of double stars, several of which were known, and some of which had been catalogued by John Flamsteed (1646–1719), the first Astronomer Royal. The point about double stars was that, via parallax, they might offer a more exact clue as to how far away they were. At that point there was no real understanding of astronomical distance.[4]

A NEW PLANET

And it was while he was cataloguing double stars that, on Tuesday 13 March 1781, slightly before midnight, Herschel spotted a new and unidentified 'disc-like object moving through the constellation of Gemini'. From his observation journal it seems that he thought at first that he had found a comet, but after three or four days he began to think again, noting that the object was well defined and had no trail. That could only mean a new 'wanderer', a new planet, and indeed that is what he had found, the seventh planet in the solar system, beyond Jupiter and Saturn and the first new planet to be discovered since the days of Ptolemy (*c*.90 AD–*c*.168).[5]

For some time, however, no one could agree on what exactly Herschel had found. The Royal Society asked Messier in Paris for an opinion. Nevil Maskelyne, the Astronomer Royal at the time, was in an especial quandary. There were dangers to his credibility in acceding too quickly to what Herschel was claiming. On the other hand, it was a feather in the cap of British science (albeit one

produced by a German), which the predatory French might appropriate for their own by recognising Herschel first (and maybe even
naming the body). Eventually, Messier wrote from Paris to say that,
having himself discovered no fewer than eighteen comets, Herschel's
discovery resembled none of them. The result was that Herschel gave
a paper before the Royal Society in late April. The paper, entitled
'An Account of a Comet', said plainly that he had discovered a new
planet, which he named Uranus. He was elected a fellow of the Royal
Society immediately.[6]

THE ORDER OF THE HEAVENS

The discovery began a revolution in the popular conception of
cosmology. Astronomers from all over Europe wrote to Herschel,
asking for details of his equipment, while there were still sceptics in
the Royal Society who doubted what such equipment could actually
achieve. But one who wasn't sceptical was the king, George III,
who was himself fascinated by the heavens, and invited Herschel
to Court at Windsor to congratulate him. When they met, in May
1782, with both Hanoverians speaking English, the encounter was
a great success.

In 1784, and the year after, Herschel began to draw together his
new and very radical ideas about the cosmos, which were published
in two 'revolutionary papers' in the Royal Society's *Transactions*.
In 'An Investigation of the Construction of the Heavens', published
in June 1784, Herschel identified 466 new nebulae (four times the
number identified by Messier) and for the first time raised the possibility that many of them, if not all, must be huge, independent star
clusters or galaxies that were *outside* the Milky Way. This led him
to propose that the Milky Way wasn't flat but three-dimensional,
that we are in effect inside it, part of it, and that it is discus-shaped
with arms extending out into deep space.

In his second paper, a year later, headed 'On the Construction of
the Heavens', he began by saying that astronomy needed a 'delicate
balance' of observation and speculation if it were to proceed by
induction – mere observation was not enough. And he went on to
observe that the universe was not static, that the heavens far away

were constantly changing, that all gaseous nebulae were 'resolvable' into stars and were in reality enormous star clusters far beyond the Milky Way. In so doing he immeasurably increased the size of the cosmos – by this time his nebula count had risen to well over 900, many of which, he insisted, were larger than the Milky Way.[7] And he estimated that deep space was 'not less than 6 or 8 thousand times the distance of Sirius'. He conceded that these were coarse estimates, and they are, certainly, much less than we now know, though thoroughly outlandish for their time.

For his part, William observed, further, that the many nebulae he had identified varied in systematic ways – some were more 'compressed' than others, others appeared to be 'condensing'. He advanced the idea therefore that some nebulae were older than others, more *evolved*, that nebulae aged, matured and climaxed. The fundamental force was gravity, gradually over time compressing nebulous gas into huge, bright galactic systems, and eventually condensing into individual stars.

It was in this paper that astronomy changed its character, fundamentally, from a mathematical science concerned primarily with navigation, to a cosmological science concerned with the evolution of stars and the origins of the universe.[8] The significance of all this, of course, was as much theological as scientific. Herschel was saying there had been no special Creation, there had been a purely material origin of the earth with no divine intention needed, no Genesis. Nor was divine creation visible in any other part of the universe.

Herschel's real achievement was to reveal the philosophical significance of astronomy. He calculated that the light rays that reached his telescopes from far-away nebulae must have been, in some cases, 'two million years on their way'.[9] In other words, the universe was almost unimaginably bigger and older than anyone thought. Without him, Charles Darwin would not have been plausible.

The First Geological Synthesis

In the seventeenth century Descartes had been the first to speculate that the earth might have formed from a ball of cooling ash and become trapped in the sun's 'vortex'. The idea that physics operated on the same principles throughout the universe was a major change in thinking that could not have occurred to the medieval mind but, slowly, a view was forming that the earth itself had changed over time. Nonetheless, however the earth had formed, the central problem faced by the early geologists was to explain how sedimentary rocks, formed by deposition from water, could now stand on dry land. As Peter Bowler has pointed out, there can be only two answers – either the sea levels have subsided, or the land has been raised. The belief that all sedimentary rocks were deposited on the floor of a vast ocean that has since disappeared became known as the Neptunist theory, after the Roman god of the sea. The alternative became known as Vulcanism, after the god of fire.[10]

By far the most influential Neptunist in the eighteenth century, in fact the most influential geologist of any kind, was Abraham Gottlob Werner, a teacher at the mining school in Freiburg, Germany, who proposed that, once one assumed that the earth, when it cooled, had an uneven surface, and that the waters retreated at a different rate in different areas, the formation of rocks could be explained. Primary rocks would be exposed first. Then, assuming the retreat of the waters was slow enough, there would be erosion of the primary rocks, which would drain into the great ocean, and then these sediments would be revealed as the waters retreated still further, to create secondary rocks, a process that could be repeated and repeated. In such a way the different types of rock had been formed in a succession, the first of which produced the 'primitive' rocks – granite, gneiss, porphyry – which had crystallised out of the original chemical solution during the flood, and the last, which was not formed until all the flood waters had receded, was generated by volcanic activity – accounting for how lavas and tuff, for example, had been produced. According to Werner, volcanoes around the earth were caused by the ignition of coal deposits. Though Werner was himself in no way interested in religion his Neptunist theory fitted very well with the biblical account of the Flood, which is one reason why it was so popular and gave rise to the phrase 'scriptural geology'.

This theory had tidiness to recommend it. But it did not even begin to explain why some types of rock that according to Werner were more recent than other types were often found situated below them. Still more problematical was the sheer totality of water that would have been needed to hold all the land of the earth in solution. It would have to have been a flood many miles deep: what had happened to all that water when it had receded?[11]

The chief rival to Werner, though nowhere near as influential to begin with, was a Scot from the Edinburgh Enlightenment, James Hutton, and his Vulcanism. Best known as a geologist, Hutton was in fact a trained chemist and a qualified doctor, who may have completed his medical studies simply because that was the way to learn most chemistry.[12] At university he studied mathematics, logic and metaphysics and graduated when he was only seventeen. This smooth progression was interrupted in 1745 when rebellion broke out and, soon after, he found he had fathered an illegitimate child, no small thing in Presbyterian Edinburgh. He fled Scotland, continuing his studies in Paris, Leiden and London, and did not return to Edinburgh until 1767, twenty years after he had left it.

And what a homecoming it was. The Edinburgh Enlightenment was in full flood, and he quickly formed lasting friendships with Joseph Black, James Watt and Adam Smith.[13]

Hutton looked around him at the geological changes he could see occurring in his own day and adopted the view that these processes had always been going on. In this way he observed that the crust of the earth, its outermost, most accessible layer, is formed by two types of rock, one of igneous origin (formed by heat), and the other of aqueous origin. He further observed that the main igneous rocks (granite, porphyry, basalt) usually lie beneath the aqueous ones, except where subterranean upheavals have thrust them upward. He also observed what anyone else could see, that weathering and erosion are even today laying down a fine silt of sandstone, limestone, clay and pebbles on the bed of the ocean near river estuaries. He then asked what could have transformed these silts into the solid rock that is everywhere about us. He concluded that it could only have been heat. Water was ruled out because so many of these rocks are clearly insoluble. And so where did this heat come from? Hutton concluded that it came from inside the earth, and that it was expressed by volcanic action. This would explain the convoluted and angled strata which could be observed at many places all over the world. He pointed out that volcanic action was still occurring, and that the rivers – again as anyone could see – were still carrying their silts to the sea.

Hutton first published his theories in the *Transactions of the Royal Society of Edinburgh* in 1788. This first Hutton publication was followed by the two-volume *Theory of the Earth* in 1795, 'the earliest treatise which can be considered a geological synthesis rather than an imaginative exercise'.[14]

At the time Hutton's book appeared, the historical reality of the Flood was beyond question, as was the biblical narrative of the creation of the world, as revealed in Genesis. On this account, the length of time since Creation was still believed to be about six thousand years (based on the wording in Genesis, that it took God six days to create the world and, elsewhere, that to God a thousand years is like a single day). And though some people were beginning to wonder whether this was long enough, hardly anyone thought the earth *very* much older.

There was no question but that Hutton's Vulcanism fitted many of the facts better than Werner's Neptunism. Many critics resisted it, however, because Vulcanism implied vast tracts of geological time, 'inconceivable ages that went far beyond what anyone had envisaged before'. And so, there were many eminent men of science in the nineteenth century who, despite Hutton's theories, still subscribed to Neptunism, including Sir Joseph Banks and Humphry Davy, not to mention Hutton's friend James Watt.[15]

But Hutton (a deist) was not alone in believing that the observation of processes still going on would triumph. In 1815 William Smith, a canal builder, pointed out that similar forms of rock, scattered across the globe, contained similar fossils. Many of these species no longer existed. This, in itself, implied that species came into existence, flourished and then became extinct, over the vast periods of time that it took the rocks to be laid down and harden. This was significant in two ways. In the first place, it supported the idea that successive layers of rock were formed not all at once but over time. And second, it reinforced the notion that there had been separate and numerous creations and extinctions, quite at variance with what it said in the Bible.[16]

THE ORDER IN THE ROCKS

Objections to the biblical account were growing. Nevertheless, it was still the case that hardly anyone at the beginning of the nineteenth century questioned the Flood. Neptunism did, however, receive a significant twist in 1811 when Georges Cuvier in Paris published his *Recherches sur les ossements fossiles* ('Researches on Fossil Bones'), in which he argued that there had been not one but several cataclysms – including floods – in the history of the earth. Looking about him, in the Huttonian manner, he concluded that, because entire mammoths and other sizeable vertebrates had been 'encased whole' in the ice in mountain regions, these cataclysms must have been very sudden indeed. He also argued that if whole mountains had been lifted high above the seas, these cataclysms could only have been – by definition – unimaginably violent, so violent that entire species had been exterminated and, conceivably, earlier forms of humanity.[17]

Cuvier also observed that in the rocks the deeper fossils were more different from life forms in existence today and that, moreover, fossils occur in a consistent order everywhere in the world: fish, amphibians, reptiles, mammals. He therefore concluded that the older the stratum of rock the higher the proportion of extinct species. Since, at that time, no human fossils had turned up anywhere, he concluded that 'mankind must have been created at some time between the last catastrophe and the one preceding it'.[18]

The man who played the next major role in marrying fossils and geology was William Buckland, Oxford's first professor of geology. Born in Axminster, Devon, Buckland was the son of a rector, whose interest in road improvements led to his collecting fossil shells, which interest he passed on to his son. Ordained as a priest, Buckland nonetheless kept up his interest in geology, making many excursions on horseback. In 1818 he was elected a fellow of the Royal Society and in the same year persuaded the Prince Regent to endow an additional readership in geology and palaeontology at Oxford University, becoming the first holder of the new position.

Before he had been at Oxford for very long, some miners in 1821 stumbled upon a cave at Kirkdale in the Vale of Pickering in

Yorkshire, where they discovered a huge deposit of 'assorted bones'. Hurrying to Yorkshire, Buckland quickly established that while most of the bones belonged to hyenas, there were also many birds and other species, including animals no longer found in Britain – lions, tigers, elephants, rhinoceroses and hippopotamuses. Moreover, each of the bones and skulls was deformed or broken in much the same way and he concluded that what the miners had found was a den of hyenas. He wrote up the discovery, first as an academic paper, which won the Royal Society's Copley Medal, and then followed it with a more popular account.

His thesis was nothing if not neat. Most of the bones in Kirkdale belonged to species now extinct in Europe; such bones were never found in alluvial (riverine) deposits of sand or silt; there was no evidence that these animals had ever lived in Europe since the Flood. It therefore followed, said Buckland, that the animals whose remains the miners had found must have been interred prior to Noah's time. He argued finally that the top layer of remains was so beautifully preserved in mud and silt 'that they must have been buried suddenly and, judging by the layer of postdiluvial stalactite covering the mud, not much more than five or six thousand years ago'.[19]

THE ORDERING OF LIFE FORMS: LYELL'S SYNTHESIS

There were still problems with the flood theory, however, not least the fact that, as even Buckland acknowledged, the various pieces of evidence around the world placed the flood in widely varying epochs. In addition, by the 1830s the cooling-earth theory was gaining coherence as an explanation as to why geological activity was greater in the past than now, further fuelling the view that the earth developed, and that life forms had been very different in the past. This helped give rise, in 1841, to the idea of John Philips, professor of geology at Dublin, who identified order in the great sequence of geological formations: the Palaeozoic, the age of fishes and invertebrates, the Mesozoic, the age of reptiles, and the Cenozoic, the age of mammals.

This was based in part on the work of Adam Sedgwick and Sir Roderick Murchison, in Wales, which began the decoding of the Palaeozoic system.[20] The Palaeozoic period would eventually be shown to have extended from roughly 550 million to 250 million years ago, and during that time plant life moved out of the oceans on to land, fish appeared, then amphibians and then reptiles reached land. And it was clear from the analyses of Sedgwick and Murchison that early forms of life on Earth were very old, and that life had begun in the sea and then climbed ashore. Deluge or no deluge, all this was again in dramatic contradiction to the biblical account.[21]

The importance of the discoveries of Cuvier, Buckland, Sedgwick and Murchison, over and above their intrinsic merit, is that they brought about a decisive change of mind on the part of Charles Lyell. In 1830 he published the first volume of what would turn into his three-volume *Principles of Geology*.

Lyell attended Buckland's celebrated lectures at Oxford, but after graduation took up law at Lincoln's Inn. He had private means, so an income was not his main concern and when he was sent on the western circuit it enabled him to make geological observations as he travelled. But he never had good eyesight and, as it began to deteriorate further, he abandoned the law for geology full time, to begin what would be his life's work, developing Hutton's ideas that the processes we see around us today have always existed and have shaped the surface of the earth as we know it.

Lyell's argument in the *Principles* was contained in the (fashionably) long subtitle: *Being an Attempt to Explain the Former Changes of the Earth's Surface, by Reference to Causes Now in Operation*. Essentially, *Principles* was a work of synthesis, rather than of original research, in which Lyell clarified and interpreted already-published material to support two conclusions. The first, obviously enough, was to show that the main geological features of the earth could be explained as the result of actions in history that were exactly the same as those that could be observed in the present. Lyell's second aim, despite being a devout Christian, was to resist the idea that a great flood, or series of floods, had produced the features of the earth that we see around us.[22]

On the religious front, Lyell took the commonsense view, arguing that it was unlikely God would keep interfering in the laws of nature to provoke a series of major cataclysms. Instead, he said, *provided that one assumed that the past extended back far enough*, then the geological action that could be observed as still in operation today was enough to explain 'the record in the rocks'.

So volume one of the *Principles* took issue with the Flood and began the process whereby the idea would be killed off. In volume two, Lyell demolished the biblical version of Creation. Inspecting the fossils as revealed in the order of the rocks, he showed that there had been a continuous stream of creation, and extinction, involving literally countless species. He thought that man had been created relatively recently but by a process that was just the same as for other animals.[23]

THE ASCENDING ORDER OF LIFE IN THE ROCKS

More radical still than Lyell was Robert Chambers, yet another Edinburgh figure, whose *Vestiges of the Natural History of Creation*, published in 1844, was so contentious that he published the book anonymously. This work also promoted the basic idea of evolution, though without in any way anticipating Darwinian natural selection. Chambers described the progress of life as a purely natural process, his main contribution being to order the palaeontological record in an ascending system and to argue that man did not stand out in any way from other organisms in the natural world. Though he had no grasp of natural selection, or indeed of how evolution might actually work, he did introduce people to the *idea* of evolution fifteen years before Darwin.

James Secord, in his book *Victorian Sensation*, has explored the full impact of *Vestiges*. He goes so far as to say that Darwin was, in a sense, 'scooped' by Chambers, that wide and varied sections of (British) society discussed *Vestiges* – at the British Association of the Advancement of Science, in fashionable intellectual salons and societies in London, Cambridge, Liverpool and Edinburgh, but also among 'lower' social groups. Moreover, the ideas the book promoted passed into general discussion, being referred to in paintings, exhibitions and cartoons in the new mass-circulation newspapers, and among feminists and freethinkers. Secord's especially important point is that it was *Vestiges* that introduced evolution to a huge range of people (there were fourteen editions) and that, viewed in such a light, Darwin's *Origin of Species* did not create a crisis but resolved one.[24]

Because of these factors, and others, it has been said that there was something 'in the air' in the middle of the nineteenth century, which helped give rise to what Darwin would call natural selection. A struggle for existence had been implied by Malthus, as long ago as 1797. Each tribe in history would have competed for resources, he said, with the less successful becoming extinct.[25]

Wherever one looked in the mid-nineteenth century, then, the role played by struggle, by competition, in society and in nature, was on everyone's lips. It was hard for people not to read some sort of 'end' in this progression, 'leading', via stages, to humans, 'and thus revealing a divine plan with a symbolic purpose'.[26]

A final element in this 'climate of opinion' was the work of Alfred Russel Wallace. Wallace's reputation, and role, in the discovery of evolution, have gone through their own progression in recent times. For many years it was accepted that the paper he sent to Darwin in 1858, 'On the Tendencies of Varieties to Depart Indefinitely from the Original Type', contained a clear exposition of natural selection, such that Darwin was forced to begin a move towards publication of his own book, *On the Origin of Species*. As a result, some historians have argued that Wallace was never given the recognition he deserves and have even implied that Darwin and his followers deliberately kept him out of the limelight. More recently, however, a closer reading of Wallace's paper has shown that his idea about natural selection was not the same as Darwin's, and that it was much less powerful as an explanatory device. In particular, Wallace did not stress competition between individuals, but between individuals and the environment. For Wallace, the less fit individuals, those less well adapted to their environment, would be eliminated, especially when there were major changes in that environment. Under this system, each individual struggles against the environment and the fate of any one individual is independent of others. This difference, which is fundamental, may explain why Wallace appears to have shown no resentment when Darwin's book was published the year after he had sent him his paper.[27]

None of the foregoing, however, should be allowed to cloud the fact that when *On the Origin of Species* did appear, in 1859, it introduced 'an entirely new and – to Darwin's contemporaries – an entirely unexpected approach to the question of biological evolution'. Darwin's theory explained, as no one else had done, a new mechanism of change in the biological world. It showed how one species gave rise to another and, in Peter Bowler's words, 'the historian of ideas sees the revolution in biology as symptomatic of a deeper change in the values of western society, as the Christian view of man and nature was replaced by a materialistic one'. The most notable flash of insight by Darwin was his theory of natural selection, the backbone of the book (its full title was *On the Origin of Species by Means of Natural Selection, or the Preservation of Favoured Races in the Struggle for Life*). Individuals of any species show variations and those better suited were more likely to reproduce and give rise to a new generation. No 'design' was necessary.[28]

We must be clear about the impact of the *Origin*. It owed something to Darwin's solid reputation and to the book's being packed with supporting details – it was not produced by a nobody. Yet it also had something to do with the fact that, as James Secord has pointed out, the book resolved – or appeared to resolve – a crisis, not because it sparked one. Natural selection was, essentially, the last plank in the evolutionary argument, not the first one, the final filling in of the theory, providing the mechanism by which one species gave rise to another. The non-revolutionary nature of the *Origin* is shown by Secord's chart in his book which records that the *Origin* did not decisively outsell *Vestiges* until the twentieth century.[29]

That said, the *Origin* did promote enormous opposition. Darwin himself realised that his theory of natural selection would prove the most contentious element in his argument and he was not wrong. John F. W. Herschel (William's son), a philosopher Darwin admired, called natural selection the 'law of higgledy-piggledy', while Sedgwick (who was both a divine and a scientist) condemned it as 'a moral outrage'.[30] Many of the favourable reviews of the *Origin* were lukewarm about natural selection: Lyell, for example, never accepted it fully, and described it as 'distasteful', while T. H. Huxley did not think it could be proved.[31] In the late nineteenth century, while the theory of evolution was widely accepted, natural selection was ignored, and this was important because it allowed people to assume that evolution was 'intended to develop toward a particular goal, just as embryos grew to maturity'. Viewed in this way, evolution was not the threat to religion it is sometimes made to appear. Darwin, it should be said, was never entirely happy with the word 'selection'.

Darwin's theory certainly had a major weakness. There was no account of the actual mechanism by which inherited characteristics were passed on ('hard heredity'). These were discovered by the monk Gregor Mendel, in Moravia in 1865, but Darwin and everyone else missed their significance and they were not rediscovered and given general circulation until 1900.

PROGRESSIONISM

Darwin didn't stop with the *Origin*. No account of Darwinism can afford to neglect *The Descent of Man*. The idea of 'progressionist evolution' was everywhere in the nineteenth century, as we have seen, even in physics, with Herschel's nebular hypothesis, the notion that the solar system has condensed from a vast cloud of dust under the influence of gravity. This is one reason why, as the sciences of sociology, anthropology and archaeology began to emerge, in the mid-nineteenth century, they were united in developing within a framework of progressionism. As early as 1861, Sir Henry Maine, in *Ancient Law*, had explored the ways in which the modern legal system had developed from the early practices found in 'patriarchal family groups'. Other titles with a similar approach included John Lubbock's *Origin of Civilisation* in 1870 and Lewis Morgan's *Ancient Society* in 1877, though the most impressive, by far, was James Frazer's *The Golden Bough*, published in 1890. Early anthropologists had also been affected by the colonial experience: on several occasions, attempts were made to educate colonised populations, the aim being to convert them to the 'obviously' superior European cultural practices. The fact that these attempts had all failed persuaded at least some anthropologists that there had to be 'a fixed sequence of stages through which all cultures develop'. And it followed from this that one could not, artificially, boost one culture from an earlier stage to a later one. Lewis Morgan defined these major stages as savagery, barbarism and civilisation, a comforting doctrine for the colonial powers. The main ideas he discussed were the growth of the idea of government, the growth of the idea of the family, and the growth of the idea of property.

It was in this intellectual climate that archaeologists began conceiving the advances in regard to stone hand axes, when the 'three age system' (of stone, bronze and iron) was introduced. At first the idea of a 'stone age' of great antiquity met with great resistance. No one could accept that the earliest humans had coexisted with now-extinct animals, and it was only when Jacques Boucher de Perthes discovered stone tools side by side with the bones of extinct animals in the gravel beds of northern France that ideas began to change. But then, roughly speaking in 1860, thanks in part to publication of the *Origin*, there was a rapid evolution in opinion, and the much greater antiquity of the human race was at last accepted.

The extremely crude nature of the earliest stone tools convinced many that early man's social and cultural circumstances were equally primitive and this led John Lubbock, Baron Avebury, banker, politician, entomologist and archaeologist, to argue that there had been an evolution of society from savage origins. This was more shocking than it might seem now because nineteenth-century religious thinkers still viewed modern man as degenerate as compared with Adam and Eve before the Fall.

For many people, the crucial issue underlying the debate as to whether man was evolved from the apes revolved around the question of the soul. If man was, in effect, little more than an ape, did that mean that the very idea of a soul – the traditional all-important difference between animals and men – would have to be rejected? Darwin's *Descent of Man*, published in 1871, tried to do two things at once: to convince sceptics that man really was descended from the animals and yet to explain what exactly it meant to be human – how humans had acquired their unique qualities.

In the *Descent*, he knew that, above all, he had to explain the very great increase in mental power from apes to humans. If evolution was a slow, gradual process, why did such a large gap exist? His answer came in chapter four of the book. There, Darwin advanced the proposition that man possesses a unique *physical* attribute, namely an upright posture. He argued that this upright posture, and the bipedal mode of locomotion, would have freed the human's hands and as a result the capacity eventually developed to use tools. And it was this, he said, which would have sparked the rapid growth in intelligence among this one form of great ape. Darwin did not offer any cogent reason as to why ancient man had started to walk upright and it was not until 1889 that Wallace suggested it could well have been an adaptation to a new environment. He speculated that early man was forced out of the trees on to the open savannah plains, perhaps as a result of climate change, which shrank the forests. On the savannah, he suggested, bipedalism was a more suitable mode of locomotion.

The legacy of Darwinism is complex.[32] Its timing, certainly, quite apart from its intellectual substance, played a major role in the secularisation of European thought. Darwinism forced people to a new view of history, that it occurred by accident, and that there was no goal, no ultimate end point. As well as killing the need for God, it transformed the idea of wisdom, as some definite attainable state, however far off. This undermined traditional views in all sorts of ways and transformed possibilities for the future. To mention just two, it was Darwinism's model of societal change that led Marx to his view of the inevitability of revolution, and it was Darwin's biology that led Freud to conceive the 'pre-human' nature of subconscious mental activity. As we shall see in a later chapter, Darwin's concept of what comprises 'fitness', in an evolutionary context, has been much misunderstood, and gave rise, consciously or unconsciously, to many social arrangements that were unjust and cruel. But since the rediscovery of the gene, in 1900, and the flowering of the technology based on it, Darwinism has triumphed.

Majesty with Menace

In 1840 Joseph Mallord William Turner sent to the Royal Academy exhibition a painting of a sailing ship surrounded – almost obliterated – by massive angry brown and black and grey ocean waves, set against a fiery orange and brown sky. The ship's sails have been taken down, so strong are the winds, and its hull is rising to meet yet another massive onslaught. In the foreground, where the waves are no less lumbering, we are surprised – shocked – to see a number of minuscule arms, hands and even fingers, outlined in stark black. As we look closer, we see that some of the limbs bear iron or rope manacles, lost hopelessly – all but overwhelmed – in the swell. But the ship is not there to rescue these drowning black men. This is a painting of the *Zong* tragedy mentioned in Chapter 12, when more than 130 slaves were thrown overboard, some still in their chains. The master of the ship claimed the manoeuvre was to prevent an epidemic among them from spreading but later research showed that it was an insurance scam: a claim could only be made if they were discarded to preserve the lives of others. Turner gave the painting a long title, in the fashion of the day: *Slave Ship (Slavers Throwing Overboard the Dead and the Dying, Typhoon Coming On)*. It was quickly sold to John Ruskin, but he promptly parted with it because he found it too upsetting. As Linda Colley has remarked, this picture is both more and less than a representation of a British atrocity. Turner's intention, perhaps a little late in the day, was to mark the end of slavery and not just a single shameful episode. The abolition of slavery, as was discussed in an earlier chapter, helped to bring about major changes in attitude, one of which Turner himself embodied as much as anyone: romanticism.

Romanticism was a massive revolution in ideas. Very different from the French, industrial and American revolutions, it was no less fundamental. The first man to glimpse this new approach was Giambattista Vico (1668–1744), the Neapolitan student of jurisprudence who, with stunning simplicity, sabotaged Enlightenment ideas about the centrality of science. In 1725 he published *La scienza nuova*, in which he claimed that knowledge about human culture 'is truer than knowledge about physical nature, since humans can know with certainty, and hence establish a science about, what they themselves have created'. The internal life of humankind, he said, can be known in a way that simply does not – cannot – apply to the world men and women have not made, the world 'out there', the physical world, which is the object of study by traditional science. On this basis, Vico said, language, poetry and myth, all devised by humans, are truths with a better claim to validity than the then-central triumphs of mathematical philosophy.

Very important, if very simple, things followed from this, said Vico, but people have been too busy looking outside themselves to notice. For example, people share a nature and must therefore assemble their cultures in similar or analogous ways.[1] This made it possible, even imperative, he said, for careful historians to reconstruct the thought processes of other ages and the phases they go through.[2] He thought it was self-evident that in any civil society people should hold certain beliefs in common – this is what common sense *was*, he thought. And he found that there were three important beliefs that were shared everywhere. These were a belief in Providence throughout history and in all religions, a belief in the immortal soul, and a recognition of the need to regulate the passions. Humans, he said, have expressed their nature throughout history and so it must follow that the record of myth and poetry 'is the record of human consciousness'.[3] In saying all this, Vico transformed the human sciences, promoting them so that they were on a par with the natural sciences.

Vico's innovations were not picked up elsewhere for several

decades, and it was not until Kant that the new approach began to catch on. Kant's great contribution was to grasp that it is the mind which shapes knowledge, that there *is* such a process as intuition, which is instinctive, and that the phenomenon in the world that we can be most certain of is the difference between 'I' and 'not-I'.[4] On this account, he said, reason 'as a light that illuminates nature's secrets' is inadequate and misplaced as an explanation. Instead, Kant said, the process of birth is a better metaphor, for it implies that human reason *creates* knowledge. In order to find out what I should do in a given situation, I must listen to 'an inner voice'. And it is this which was so subversive. According to the sciences, reason is essentially logical and applies across nature equally.[5] But the inner voice does not conform to this neat scenario. Its commands are not necessarily factual statements at all and, moreover, are not necessarily true or false.

The purpose of the inner voice, often enough, is to set someone a goal or a value, and this has nothing to do with science, but is created by the individual. This was a basic shift in the very meaning of individuality and was totally new.[6] In the first instance (and for the first time), it was realised that morality was a creative process but, in the second place, and no less important, it laid a new emphasis on creation, and this too elevated the artist alongside the scientist. The artist does not discover, calculate, deduce, as the scientist (or philosopher) does. In creating, the artist invents his or her goal and then realises his or her own path towards that goal. 'Where, asked Herzen, is the song before the composer has conceived it?' Creation in this sense is the only fully autonomous activity of man and for that reason takes pre-eminence. Art was transformed and enlarged. It was no longer mere imitation or representation, but expression, a far more important, far more significant and ambitious activity. 'A man is most truly himself when he creates.'[7]

We are still living with the consequences of this revolution which, it is plain, was not confined to Britain. The rival ways of looking at the world – the cool, detached light of disinterested scientific reason, and the red-blooded, passionate creations of the artist – constitute what has been called the modern incoherence, the effects of which were momentous. For one thing, the understanding of work changed. Instead of being regarded as an ugly necessity, it was transformed into 'the sacred task of man', because only by work – an expression of the will – could man bring his distinctive, creative personality to bear upon 'the dead stuff' of nature.[8] Worldly success is immaterial.

This reversal of values cannot be overstated. To begin with, man creates himself and therefore has no identifiable nature, which determines how he behaves, reacts and thinks. And unlike anything that has gone before, he is not answerable for the consequences. Second, and arguably more shocking, since man's values are not discovered but created, there is no way they can ever be described or systematised, 'for they are not facts, not entities of the world'. They are simply outside the realm of science, ethics or politics.

It is an idea that leads to a form of literature, painting and (most vividly) music that we instantly recognise – the martyred hero, the outcast genius, rebelling against a tame and philistine society.[9] The very beginning of the romantic movement, the decade of the 1770s, saw the phenomenon of *Sturm und Drang*, 'storm and stress', a young generation of German poets who rebelled against their strict education and social conventions to explore their emotions. The best-known of these 'ill-considered' works is Goethe's *The Sorrows of Young Werther* (1774).[10]

Whereas French romanticism was essentially a reaction to the French Revolution, the British variety was a reaction to the industrial revolution.[11] Wordsworth, Coleridge and Southey famously lived in the Lake District, where Wordsworth in particular took a great interest in the poor and sought in his poetry to use the words of the common people. It is the younger romantics – Shelley, Keats and Byron – who adopt an uncompromising humanism, aware of the dehumanising effects of factory life on life in general, and even the more conservative representatives, Wordsworth and Scott, share their 'democratic' sympathies in that their work is aimed at the popularisation – even the politicisation – of literature.[12] Shelley and Keats both visited the Lakes, only to be disappointed, in Keats's case by how fashionable they had become.

At this point, poetry becomes a wholly separate literary sphere.

Coleridge and Wordsworth were scarcely Luddites – both were literate in science and had scientists as friends – but Wordsworth in particular felt that science had no interest in individuality, and the romantics saw themselves as the guardians of English, cultivating the view that poetry is received by inspiration rather than crafted by the learned, free of specialism and providing an alternative both to vocational and to conversational language, that alternative itself amounting to an intellectual discipline, so that it was legitimate for 'poetic language' to be both different and, at times, difficult.[13]

And they saw in anyone who had the power to generate a poetic form of words an echo of Plato's contention that here was some sort of divine intention. This is what Shelley meant by his famous epigram that 'poets are the unacknowledged legislators of mankind'.[14] Shelley is perhaps the classic romanticist: a born rebel, an atheist, he saw the world as one great battle between the forces of good and evil. Even his atheism, it has been said, was more a revolt against God as a tyrant than a denial of Him. In the same vein, Keats's poetry is imbued with a pervading melancholy, a mourning for 'the beauty that is not life', for a beauty that is beyond his grasp. The mystery of art is in the process of replacing the mystery of faith.

A BORROWED IMAGINATION?

Byron was probably the most famous romantic. With his background, from the family of 'a shipwrecked admiral', his fascination with the Mediterranean, with Islam, his *Hebrew Melodies*, his Armenian dictionary, he was nothing if not cosmopolitan, even losing his life for his involvement in the Greek War of Independence. In his work Byron's portrayal of the hero as an eternally homeless wanderer, partly doomed by his own wild nature, is by no means original.[15] But earlier heroes of this type invariably felt guilty or melancholic about the fact that they were outside society, whereas in Byron the outsider status becomes transformed into 'a self-righteous mutiny' against society, 'the feeling of isolation develops into a resentful cult of solitude', and his heroes are little more than exhibitionists, 'who openly display their wounds'.[16] These outlaws, who declare war on society, dominate literature in the early nineteenth century. If the type had been invented by Rousseau and Chateaubriand, by Byron's time it had become narcissistic. '[The hero] is unsparing towards himself and merciless towards others. He knows no pardon and asks no forgiveness ... He regrets nothing and, in spite of his disastrous life, would not wish to have anything different ... a peculiar charm emanates from him which no woman can resist and to which all men react with friendship or enmity.'[17]

Associated with this is another major change – the notion of the 'second self', the belief that inside every romantic figure, in the dark and chaotic recesses of the soul, was a completely different person and that once access to this second self had been found, an alternative – and deeper – reality would be uncovered. This is in effect the discovery of the unconscious, interpreted here to mean an entity that is hidden away from the rational mind, a secret, ecstatic something which is above all mysterious, nocturnal, grotesque, ghostlike and macabre. The second self, the unconscious, was seen as a way to the spiritual enlargement that was such a feature of romanticism.[18]

Furthermore, the idea of the artist as a more sensitive soul than others, with perhaps a direct line to the divine, which went back to Plato, carried with it a natural conflict between the artist and the bourgeoisie.[19] The early nineteenth century was the point at which the very concept of the avant-garde could arise, with the artist viewed as someone who was ahead of his time. Art was a 'forbidden fruit', available only to the initiated and most certainly denied to the 'philistine' bourgeoisie. And it was not far from there to the idea that youth was seen as more creative than – and as inevitably superior to – age. The young inevitably knew what the coming thing was. The latest scholarship claims to find a lot of romantic poetry 'borrowed', in that there was a big Arab-Islamic influence on the British romantic imagination, notably Byron.[20]

The next thing to say about British romantic art is that it appears to have been inspired by Edmund Burke's ideas about the sublime – the transcendent depiction of disquieting, disturbing, even menacing images, the exploration of nature's fluctuating but always awesome moods in which humans are represented as all but helpless creatures at the mercy of events. This was especially true in painting.

In one focal decade of the period – the 1790s – the threads of the preceding half century were gathered together in the hands of two young artists and woven into a new and more complex tradition: Thomas Girtin and Joseph Mallord William Turner. From an early age each had received orthodox training in the topographical/ picturesque style. But they had also come within the circle of Dr Thomas Monro, a well-known mental specialist and art patron, who is now regarded as one of the key figures in the development of English watercolours. Monro was not only a by no means negligible amateur draughtsman himself but was also a passionate admirer of John Robert Cozens, who was his patient. Cozens was the greatest of a number of painters who produced topographical studies that were also landscape paintings. During the period of Cozens's illness, Monro employed Turner and Girtin to work in his house in the evenings – this became known as 'The Monro Academy'.[21]

There were two strains in romantic watercolours. One was derived from eighteenth-century topographers, with increasingly the art of the picturesque added in. The other strain, which in the light of history can be seen as vastly more important, is that of 'total romanticism', colouring both vision and technique, at times lyrical, at times fantastic, epic, verging even on the abstract. A basic quality of the romantic vision, whether in painting or poetry, is the personal response of the artist to nature.[22]

And this links us back to the sublime, which underlies all romantic painting, oils as well as watercolours. Here we come up against the works of not just Turner and Cozens, whose paintings of the Alps show a solemn grandeur, a sheer sense of vastness, but Samuel Palmer, whose visionary pastoral scenes around Shoreham in Kent caught the magic of afternoon sunlight or the mystery of moonlight, illustrating Milton's epics – again, epic is the word. Palmer was a friend of William Blake, perhaps *the* visionary of the romantic movement, with mystical undercurrents running throughout his work, poems or paintings (born in Soho, he frequently told his parents that he had seen angels in the trees). Deeply Christian, though suspicious of the organised church, he visited London churches and Westminster Abbey for inspiration. He was more of an intellectual than many of the other romantic painters and mixed in a circle that included Joseph Priestley, Henry Fuseli, Thomas Paine and Mary Wollstonecraft, some of whose works he illustrated. Together with Wordsworth and Godwin, he had high hopes of both the French and American revolutions and was against slavery. Many of his paintings show fantastic improbable or impossible scenes, in which the figures, masses of them, are tiny in relation to the overall awesome scheme of events.[23]

And this, together with his biblical illustrations – in effect showing miracles, or the underworld – links him to John Martin. Martin, from Northumberland, loved darkness as other painters loved the light. He is primarily known for a succession of huge oil paintings, usually with very grand, again epic themes: *The Destruction of Pompeii and Herculaneum*, 5 feet by 8 feet, *The Deluge*, 8½ feet by 6½ feet, *Pandemonium*, 4 feet by 6 feet. Martin was also part of the circle that included Wollstonecraft and Godwin, together with Charles Dickens, Michael Faraday and Turner.[24]

Turner, Martin's good friend, was equally adept at watercolour and oils and had two great themes – the menacing majesty of nature, whether it be mountains or, particularly, the sea, and second, the new and potentially disruptive forces of the industrial revolution. John Ruskin, beginning with the first volume of his vastly influential *Modern Painters* (1843), claimed a very particular interpretation of both Turner and his work, arguing how new and objectionable his images were, that they were scorned by his contemporaries and their greatness only recognised later in his life. This interpretation has been called into question by more recent scholarship which finds that Turner's work was described, by one contemporary at least, 'as glorious in conception, unfathomable in knowledge and solitary in power'.[25] Ruskin thought Turner the equal of Phidias or Leonardo, 'incapable . . . of any improvement conceivable by the human mind'.[26]

His style was immediately recognisable, often so wildly impressionistic as to be virtually abstract, looking forward decades. Turner's imagination was stoked by shipwrecks, fires (he witnessed at first hand the burning of Parliament in 1834), storm, rain and fog. His *Fishermen at Sea*, a nocturnal moonlit view of the Needles off the Isle of Wight, *Dawn after the Wreck* and *The Slave Ship*, with which we began this chapter, offer what one critic described as 'a summary of all that has been said about the sea by the artists of the eighteenth century'. *Snow Storm: Hannibal and His Army Crossing the Alps*, is 85 per cent pure weather.

But then he turned his attention to the new forces of the industrial revolution, as often as not by showing these agents of change via blackened mills, polluted skies and steam locomotion, both on land and at sea. His images betray considerable ambivalence about nineteenth-century industrialism and – most important, this – its vulnerability before the superiority of the environment.[27]

The steamboat age dawned in Britain with Henry Bell's *Comet*, launched in 1812, which served the Glasgow area. The first crossing of the English Channel by steamer occurred in 1816, three years before the initial trans-Atlantic (and sail-aided) journey.[28] Turner lost little time incorporating steamers in his work. *Between Quillebeuf and Villequier* shows a number of dramatically black – filthy – steamboats on the Seine, overtaking a graceful sailing boat, its sails dropping with the absence of wind, the greyish-black plume of steam and smoke in marked contrast to the gently sloping riverbank. In *Peace – Burial at Sea*, a tribute to Sir David Wilkie, a recently deceased painter who wished to be buried at sea, the image is again awash with soot, a haunting nocturnal ensemble which, as William Rodner points out, is reminiscent of the 'great dark mass' of a packet steamer described by Dickens en route to Boston that same year, 1842.[29] The most striking aspect of this picture is its blackness. (Turner said, 'I only wish I had the means to make it blacker.')

'Turner knew that despite the many virtues of modern technology, humanity was destined to remain forever subject to the majestic power of unfathomable nature.'[30] In so far as many of his paintings came close to being abstract, this too may be regarded as an unfathomable force that would, before too long, overwhelm painting.

THE ESSAY: A NEW STYLE OF WRITING

Despite all this excellent – and in some cases revolutionary – art, Britain still lagged in the formal, central, institutionalised presentation of great paintings and sculpture to its public. Munich had opened its Alte Pinakothek in 1779, the Uffizi had opened in Florence ten years after that, and the Louvre, in Paris, formed out of the French Royal Collection, was displayed four years after the Revolution in 1793. Not only that, Britain had several times missed out on acquiring great collections around which a national gallery might be assembled. In 1777 the MP John Wilkes had argued in Parliament for the government to acquire the collection of Sir Robert Walpole (containing paintings by Velázquez, Poussin, Rubens and Rembrandt), which he thought might be housed in a special pavilion to be built in the gardens of the British Museum. No action was taken, and the collection was bought by Catherine the Great of Russia. Another chance was missed when the fabled Orléans Collection was brought to London to be sold at Christie's after the Duke of Orléans, the so-called Philippe Égalité, had been guillotined. That collection was bought by a consortium of English and Scottish dukes. A third opportunity was lost when the art dealer Noel Desenfans and his business associate Sir Francis Bourgeois offered a collection they had assembled for the king of Poland before a dispute between the Habsburg monarchy and Russia put an end to Polish independence. Again, the offer was declined, and Bourgeois bequeathed the collection to his old school, Dulwich College, which opened the paintings to the public in 1814.

Then, in 1823 another collection came on the market. This one, of thirty-eight paintings, had been assembled by John Julius Angerstein, a Russian-born banker but naturalised in Britain. Among the collection were works by Raphael and Hogarth and on the strength of this it was again proposed in Parliament that the collection be acquired for the nation. Artists like the sculptor John Flaxman also campaigned for a gallery but a tipping point on this occasion appears to have been the offer of a second collection, that of Sir George Beaumont, himself a painter, who had been taught by Alexander Cozens, and who had lent part of his farm in the Lake District to his good friend William Wordsworth. Beaumont had completed a very grand Grand Tour, where he had fallen for the paintings of Claude Lorraine and acquired Michelangelo's *Taddei Tondo*. He offered sixteen of his pictures to the nation, on condition that the Angerstein pictures also be bought and that a building be acquired to house them. A second tipping point was, just then, the unexpected repayment of a war debt by Austria (of £57,000), which helped the whole deal go through. The gallery opened in May 1824, at first in Angerstein's own home at 100 Pall Mall.

Until this point, the British public was unacquainted with the fine arts because of the restrictions on access to great collections.[31] There *were* great collections in private homes but they were usually overlooked because people were more interested in the gardens. In the months ahead of the opening of the National Gallery, however, two series of articles appeared in rival publications, the *London Magazine* and the *New Monthly Magazine*, articles which did at last foster public awareness and understanding of art. The authors, William Hazlitt and Peter George Patmore, attempted to educate the English public to appreciate the fine arts. Patmore was a somewhat gossipy writer, and the father of the poet Coventry Patmore, both of whom were friends of Hazlitt, who had more artistic knowledge and detains us rather more.

In preparing people for the National Gallery, he toured Angerstein's collection at Pall Mall, Dulwich Gallery, the Marquess of Stafford's gallery (who had bought part of the Orléans Collection), pictures at Windsor Castle and Hampton Court, Lord Grosvenor's collection and still more pictures at Wilton, Stourhead, Oxford and Blenheim. Hazlitt, who was taken to America for a short time as a boy, was a trained artist – his self-portraits are fine and delicate and show him to have been a handsome, clean-shaven, not necessarily self-confident soul who, on his return from the New World, said, 'I think for my part that it would have been a great deal better if the white people had not found [America] out. Let the others [indigenous Americans] have it for themselves, for it was made for them.'

But what we see in these articles is him working out a vocabulary for art criticism and this is part of Hazlitt's significance. He was from a family of Irish Protestants, his father an ultra-Dissenting minister who studied under Adam Smith, with a brother who trained under Joshua Reynolds. A friend of Mary and Charles Lamb, Wordsworth, Keats, Coleridge and Godwin, Hazlitt had been taught by Joseph Priestley. He earned a living as a portrait painter, commissioned at one point by Sir George Beaumont. He was chronically sullen, a passionate devotee of Burke, an unsuccessful lover, a notable user of the courts to settle disputes, but the man who, almost single-handedly, invented the essay form, 'light in tone, personal in voice, written to the moment, digressive, enlivened with opinion and quirky detail'.

In effect he adapted the painter's art of sketching to a new style of writing. In this capacity he helped to make Sarah Siddons and Edmund Kean famous on the stage, but his main interest for us now lies in the quirkiness of the subjects he wrote essays about: 'My First Acquaintance with Poets', 'On Genius and Common Sense', and such topics as patriotism, the love of nature, posthumous fame, 'the disadvantages of a classical education', the pleasures of the arrival of letters in the post, and 'why the arts are not progressive'.[32] Hazlitt's literary style became sharper and more politically interventionist as he grew older but his essential significance is his perfection of the essay form, which, though short by definition, is a style of charismatic writing that has the force and impact of the pencil or ink sketch, and reflects a cast of mind that many find attractive: serious but not solemn, stylish and allusive rather than didactic; putting wit before humour, and uncomfortable truth before solipsistic beauty.[33] He died penniless but the witty, quirky, idiosyncratic essay form – his rich legacy – lives on. Recent scholarship has also shown that he was a more important influence on John Ruskin than previously thought (see next chapter).[34]

'Astronomy and Geology Are Greater Muses than Love'

In his book *Ruskinland*, historian Andrew Hill, a trustee of the Ruskin Foundation, described John Ruskin as 'a one-man world-wide web', who 'saw – if not always clearly – how art, science, nature, history, the environment, politics, economics and industry sprang from and relied on each other'. Ruskin was, as Hill notes, 'a genius of what modish strategists now sometimes call "joining the dots"'. Joining the dots is, to an extent, what this chapter will be doing. There are a lot of them.

The first set of 'dots' is what Rachel Dickinson, master of the Guild of St George, the charity started by Ruskin for arts, crafts and the rural economy, calls 'Victoria's Victorians', a cohort of extraordinary individuals who were all born in the same year, 1819: Queen Victoria herself; Ruskin, of course; Arthur Hugh Clough, poet, author of *Through a Glass Darkly* and assiduous assistant of Florence Nightingale; George Eliot, novelist; W. P. Frith, painter; Charles Hallé, conductor and pianist; Charles Kingsley, priest, professor and author of *Westward Ho!* and *The Water Babies*; and Bernard Quaritch, Ruskin's favourite antiquarian bookseller, born in Germany but settled in London.[1]

On top of that, Ruskin had more in common with a much larger group of remarkable individuals – more dots – than those linked by the accident of their date of birth. In fact, if we add to Ruskinland what we might call Browningland – Ruskin and the Brownings being firm friends – their copious exchange of letters enables us to explore not only their friendship, and views about each other's works, but introduces us also to what they thought of the majestic hinterland that surrounded them: Thomas Carlyle, John Stuart Mill, Thomas Macaulay, James Froude, Percy Bysshe Shelley, Dante Gabriel Rossetti, Charles Darwin, Herbert Spencer, William Morris, John Everett Millais and Charles Dickens, plus Rudyard Kipling and Leslie Stephen, first editor of *The Dictionary of National Biography*. These figures were among the first celebrities to be recorded by the newly invented technique of photography, and to be caricatured in two new publications, *Punch* (founded in 1841) and *Vanity Fair* (1847).

But first the Brownings. They – Elizabeth Barrett Browning and Robert Browning – have generated enormous interest, not just for the quality of their poetry, but for their social involvement and their massive correspondence, which allows an unusual, and unusually full, picture of their mental lives to be explored – and enjoyed.

Elizabeth was six years older than Robert; she was from the north, County Durham, he was from Camberwell, then in Surrey, now a London suburb. Elizabeth never really enjoyed good health, suffering head and spinal pains, caused by a fall when she was trying to mount a pony as a child, and perhaps contracting tuberculosis in her teens, which she treated with laudanum. Both of them wrote poetry as their ages crossed into double figures, showing how highly poetry was regarded in Britain at that time. Both came from families with links to slavery – Elizabeth's had settled in Jamaica in 1655, as owners of sugar plantations. Elizabeth campaigned for the abolition of slavery, wrote abolitionist verses and was much influenced by Mary Wollstonecraft's *A Vindication of the Rights of Women*, though she also loved Voltaire and Thomas Paine. After slavery was abolished, her father lost money and was forced to sell his home. Robert's grandfather was a slave owner in St Kitts, but his father, who had been sent to work on the sugar plantation, returned home after a slave revolt, becoming an abolitionist.

Both were precocious, Elizabeth reading Pope's translation of Homer at six, almost all of Shakespeare, and the rest of the Greek and Roman classics while a child. Robert became fluent in French, Greek, Italian and Latin by the time he was fourteen. His father had a library of 6,000 books, which no doubt helped Robert become the erudite man of letters he was looked upon as in his later years. He attended the newly established University College, London, because his parents were evangelicals and Oxbridge was closed to him. Elizabeth's parents were Dissenting Protestant chapel-goers.

In the late 1830s, after several years at various locations in the West Country, occasioned by the loss of the sugar plantation, Elizabeth's family returned to London and an address in Wimpole Street. Her poetry began to mature and to attract attention. Then, in 1844, she released a two-volume book of verse, simply entitled *Poems*, and about this time too she also embarked on her enormous correspondence.

The most influential poem in the new collection was 'The Cry of the Children'. Though ill, and suffering from the recent death of her brother, Elizabeth stayed in touch with current affairs and had read with distress the reports of the Parliamentary Commissioners about the appalling conditions of child labourers in the mines and manufactories. Despite her bookish nature and cultured upbringing, she managed by the force of her intellect to produce a work which actually had some effect on the politicians of the day, and helped bring about reforms.

> For, all day, we drag our burden tiring,
> Through the coal-dark, underground –
> Or, all day, we drive the wheels of iron
> In the factories, round and round.

The *Poems* were a great critical and commercial success (on both sides of the Atlantic) but, more than that, they inspired Robert Browning to write to her. 'I love your verses with all my heart, dear Miss Barrett,' and he went on to highlight her 'fresh strange music, the affluent language'.

The contrast between them at this stage was marked. She suffered poor health, was retiring and private, but her poems were popular and critically successful. He was in robust health, dressed fashionably, was in the social swim but his poems and plays had not done well (his best received was *Strafford*, a tragedy about the downfall of an advisor to Charles I), and he lived at home and was still financially dependent on his father.

Nevertheless, Elizabeth and Robert contrived to meet, and a famous courtship was conceived, albeit in secret because Elizabeth's father wished all his children to remain dependent on him. They married secretly and honeymooned in Paris before eventually moving to Italy where they would spend their time until Elizabeth's death. As threatened, Elizabeth was disinherited when her father discovered she had married.

But the arrival of Robert in Elizabeth's life was transformative: 'worn down by a succession of griefs' and a life of pain, a woman who had never enjoyed the energetic springs of youth, all of a sudden there was a sense of wonder in the air, a completely unexpected change in her fortunes, to which she responded with one of her most famous poems, Sonnet 43: 'How do I love thee? Let me count the ways.'

An interest in Italian politics (the *Risorgimento*) and a son, 'Pen', born in 1849, all added to the new excitement in Elizabeth's being, culminating, we might say, in her verse-novel, *Aurora Leigh*, about two women of very different stations in life, one bookish and not wholly unlike Elizabeth, who successfully makes her way in London and Italy, the other an unfortunate, used by men and degraded. And this was Elizabeth's attraction, that she tackled real issues, often ugly issues of modern life, which she insisted must not be ducked, but in beautiful – and entirely apposite – language. *Aurora Leigh* was described by one critic as 'the great epic of the age'.

Robert was an enormous influence on Elizabeth. And just as he had admired her *Poems*, so she had admired – before meeting him – his collections of (self-published) dramatic monologues, *Bells and Pomegranates: Dramatic Romances & Lyrics*, which included 'The Pied Piper of Hamelin'. Robert in fact wrote little during the marriage, partly because he was busy looking after Elizabeth, who continued in poor health. He was regarded by some 'as a townsman who had never come into contact with nature'. Others claimed that 'his rhymes bruise the ear', but in later life, as a sort of philosopher, an old-fashioned sage, he was often called upon to give his views on pressing problems – those 6,000 books in his library had been built on by his experiences in Italy. And his masterpiece came at the end of his life also, after Elizabeth died. This was *The Ring and the Book*, a very long blank verse based on an account he had stumbled across, in the Florence flea market, of a seventeenth-century murder in Rome.

PREACHERS AT LARGE

In the relationship between the Brownings and Ruskin, the Brownings were the older, more established authors to whom Ruskin, at least in the beginning, paid a proper deference. In the relationship between Thomas Carlyle and the Brownings, however, the roles were reversed – the Brownings to begin with paid an almost reverential deference to their elder, who by then was 'the established sage of Chelsea', admiring the older man for his fearless rejection of compromises, which had a marked effect on the Brownings' poetry in the 1850s.[2] The Brownings and Carlyle visited Paris together and the philosopher, known for his irascibility, even got along with their young son, Pen. This despite the fact that Carlyle had little patience with many of the poets of the day, the 'miserable metre-ballad mongers' as he called them, 'twanging their harps while on every side there was man's work to be done: so many Augean stables to be cleaned, so many temples to be cleared of money-changers'.[3] He was notorious for the advice he gave to poets – both of the Brownings included – to write in prose.

The friendship between Carlyle and Ruskin appears to have begun in either 1846 or 1847. Carlyle was Ruskin's senior by twenty-five years and the friendship was not without misgivings for Ruskin's parents, who were fearful that Carlyle would 'pervert' their son – and they were right. In large part Ruskin's shift of emphasis from artistic to social problems was prompted and encouraged by his older friend.

Carlyle, born the eldest of nine children to a poor stonemason in Ecclefechan in the south of Scotland, never had it easy as a young man. 'With a bag of oatmeal under his arm, he walked the ninety miles to Edinburgh and a university education.'[4] After years of hardship, first as a schoolmaster, tutor, translator and hack writer, 'his imposing genius transported him, via America, from Craigenputtock [the estate he lived on as a boy] obscurity to London fame'.[5] This contrasted with Ruskin's background as the son of a wealthy wine merchant. Despite their poverty, Carlyle's parents were not unaware of their eldest son's abilities and, after Edinburgh, his mother took rooms at Oxford, where Ruskin had been entered as a gentleman-commoner (paying for both tuition and accommodation) and from where she could watch over her frail son.[6]

The relationship between Ruskin and Carlyle was between major, enduring and influential figures of nineteenth-century England, and this despite the fact that they were very different – Ruskin the delicate art lover, sponsor of May Queen festivals, collector of rocks, alongside the stern Carlyle, transcendental mystic, scoffer at art, populariser of German metaphysics. Their styles were dissimilar and their early interests seemed widely divergent. Carlyle's early novel *Sartor Resartus* presented itself as a commentary on the thought and early life of a German philosopher, Diogenes Teufelsdröckh, while Ruskin collected minerals, sketched flowers and wrote Byron-like poems. But there was an underlying sympathy between the men – both were of Scottish parentage, had rigid Calvinist mothers, were first intended for the ministry, and both finally lost contact with conventional Christianity.[7] And both, after abandoning their Christian ministry, became to an extent 'preachers at large' to their generation, strong denunciators of the existing state of society.

CARLYLE: REVOLUTION AND GEOLOGY

In some ways, Carlyle was quite unlike any of his contemporaries. For a start he took a great interest in the literatures and philosophies of 'abroad', in particular France and Germany, and in time would become a correspondent and friend of Goethe (despite his antipathy to poetry), whose *Wilhelm Meister's Apprenticeship* he translated. *Sartor Resartus*, as noted, presented itself as an inquiry into a (fictitious) German philosopher, but Carlyle also wrote a life of Frederick the Great and a biography of Friedrich Schiller, the playwright. And he began to study German because he wanted to read the mineralogical works of Abraham Gottlob Werner, while also taking an interest in the works of Jöns Jacob Berzelius, the Swedish chemist who did such a lot to aid our understanding of the chemical bond. On top of this, Carlyle read the astronomical works of Pierre Simon Laplace and in Paris attended the lectures of palaeontologist Georges Cuvier. He was always abreast of the latest Europe-wide developments.

He suffered with dyspepsia through most of his life, with bouts of sleeplessness and spiritual doubt, and for which sea-bathing, mostly in Scotland, was the only relief. He married Jane Welsh in October 1826 and they set up a modest home in Edinburgh. Carlyle several times applied for professorships (in moral philosophy and astronomy) at universities in Scotland and London but was always unsuccessful, even though Goethe himself wrote in his support. He was much more successful, socially at least, when he and Jane moved to Cheyne Row in London where, in time, he would earn the soubriquet 'Sage of Chelsea'. Here he set about research and writing his *French Revolution: A History*.

When the three volumes eventually appeared, in 1837, the work was a sensation. It was described as 'the epic of the century' and Charles Dickens was said to carry it around with him at all times, used its material in his own *A Tale of Two Cities* (1859) and said, as he embarked on *Bleak House*, that he had read Carlyle's masterpiece for the 500th time. Part of the enduring fascination of the book stems from Carlyle's understanding of the process of revolution, and the behaviour of crowds – or the 'mob', depending on your point of view – which he thought had certain parallels with the recent developments in geology. After all, he had learned German in the first place to study the works of Werner. In fact, as Rebecca Stott points out, Carlyle was just one of an astonishing number of Victorian writers and thinkers whose works used geological concepts and images: Ruskin, Robert Browning, Alfred Tennyson (who thought that astronomy and geology were greater muses than love), Charles Kingsley, George Gissing, Dickens, John Stuart Mill, Edward Bulwer-Lytton, George Eliot and Matthew Arnold.[8] Tennyson and Kingsley studied under Adam Sedgwick at Cambridge, William Whewell was Tennyson's tutor, Ruskin studied under William Buckland and Thomas Carlyle under Robert Jameson, all of them primarily catastrophists.[9]

Geological apocalypse dominates Carlyle's history, says Stott – 'fire, whirlwind, whirlpools and deluges surge through its pages'.[10] His narrative separates marvellous scenes of vivid narrative with 'great gulfs of darkness', parts of which he passes over very quickly, giving an impression of 'violent chiaroscuro', which the editor of the *Edinburgh Review* described as 'like reading history by flashes of lightning ... Carlyle's style is itself a revolution.' In writing in this way, Carlyle was rejecting what he dismissed as the Dryasdust school rooted in rational scientific and utilitarian 'modes of thought and feeling', which he thought could not adequately describe the 'spasmodic mutability' of the world he observed around him. Throughout *The French Revolution*, there are lurid geological metaphors and the aesthetics of the sublime, in the Burkean sense.[11]

Carlyle's reputation took a knock when in 1849 he released his 'Occasional Discourse on the Negro Question'. This was brought about by a long, lingering debate between liberals and conservatives on the proper course to be taken by British colonial policy in the West Indies. In Rodger Tarr's words, the evangelical fervour of foreign philanthropists supported *laissez-faire* expansionists 'who were determined that places like the West Indies and Africa should and would become models of British industry and achievement'. Against them were those who were convinced that the social and economic degradation at home must be a first priority.[12] The dispute quickly became dialectical and Carlyle's nationalistic concern in the 'Negro Question' became a banner for the conservative position. However, it wasn't Carlyle's nationalism that was found unacceptable but his choice of metaphor, his depiction of the West Indian 'Negro' as a 'black Quashee', 'quashee' being a slang word, sometimes referring to Sunday, the day of rest, and implying someone 'who would rather eat than work'. It was in this paper that Carlyle first used the phrase 'dismal science' to refer to economics, especially political economics. He had been arguing/preaching against Malthus for some time, but the 'Discourse' refers to Malthus only in passing. The defining sin of the 'dismal science', for Carlyle, is not its Malthusian theories of (over)population, but its eagerness to leave the world ungoverned. Convinced of the need for strong leadership in society, Carlyle saw the doctrine of *laissez-faire* as an abrogation of responsibility: 'Men need to be governed. Men need to be led.'[13] According to Carlyle, 'letting men alone' was hardly the way to run an empire and 'certainly not the way to govern the black population of the West Indies'. For him the islands were sinking into ruin because of the indolence of the free black population, and he insisted that the white landowners knew the divine will best.[14]

Carlyle was very serious in his conclusion. He saw all around him an attack on liberal capitalism. When he surveyed the social scene, it was not the slavery of the Southern United States that most disturbed him. 'The worst form of slavery was the slavery of the strong to the weak, of the great and noble-minded to the small and mean! The slavery of wisdom to folly. The folly of the modern world was armed with "ballot-boxes" and forever appealed to "Dismal Sciences, Statistics, Constitutional Philosophies and other Fool Gospels".'[15]

With all this as preamble, it comes as no surprise to find that Carlyle assumed leadership in the Eyre Defence and Aid Fund, after John Eyre, the governor of Jamaica, brutally put down a rebellion which stemmed from the fact that, though slavery had been abolished, and the apprentice scheme brought to a premature conclusion, blacks on the island were growing poorer and couldn't afford the poll tax, through which they acquired the vote. After petitioning the queen, and not receiving a satisfactory answer, and after a black man had been found guilty of trespass on a vacant sugar plantation, emphasising the disparity in land-holding, tensions boiled up and, in October 1865, led by a preacher, Paul Bogle, hundreds of black Jamaicans descended on the courthouse where the 'trespasser' had been convicted. Several people were killed and even more in the police round-up that followed.

The Eyre Defence and Aid Committee was formed in London, in which Carlyle's leadership was supported by Ruskin, Dickens, Kingsley and Tennyson. Ranged against them in the anti-Eyre Jamaica Committee, who wanted Eyre tried for murder, were John Stuart Mill, Charles Darwin, Herbert Spencer and T. H. Huxley. Eyre won the suit but was replaced as governor of Jamaica within months.[16]

The least surprising *placement* in these two groupings was surely that of Tennyson. Tennyson's poetry is not explicitly imperial in a narrow political sense, but the melancholy that was such a feature of his mood, even of his 'essential genius', as some have said, was a counterforce to the 'masculine, muscular' spirit of the progressive age of colonisation, obsessed as he was by the literature of voyage and exploration, and the 'far-away wonders' of the natural world, the 'realms of gold', displacing his discontent with England by imagining a retreat into the 'vast expanses of Empire'. But he was obsessed by the periphery of empire precisely because to him it was less valued than the centre:

> I know my words are wild,
> But I count the grey barbarian lower than the Christian child.

For Tennyson, 'the conquest of the Orient is an Englishman's duty'.[17]

Thomas Babington Macaulay was a high peak of Ruskinland, rather than Browningland, and an echo of Tennyson *avant la lettre*. His writing is known for its ringing prose and dogmatic insistence on a progressive model of British history. His father was Zachary Macaulay, a Highlander, originally a statistician, who became a colonial governor (in Sierra Leone) and abolitionist, and who helped to found London University. Tom Macaulay's mother was a former pupil of Hannah More and with this background, and because he was obviously a brilliant child, there were 'inordinate expectations' of what he might achieve. He won more than one prize at Cambridge (Trinity), including the prestigious Chancellor's Gold Medal (for poetry).

He took an interest in politics from the very start, his father being an evangelical Whig who, although he was an abolitionist, looked forward to a 'free black peasantry' rather than full equality for Africans. This would colour his son's approach. When Thomas became a member of Parliament, in 1830, at the age of thirty, for a seat in the gift of the Marquess of Lansdowne, his maiden speech was in favour of the abolition of the civil disabilities of the Jews. Thereafter he made several speeches on parliamentary reform, and was given junior posts in the government during the passage of the great Reform Act of 1832, which extended voting rights to many small businessmen and landowners and recognised the change in Britain from a rural nation to an urban one, but specifically denied the vote to women. Following this, and the passage of the Government of India Act of 1833, which restricted the activities of the East India Company and brought the subcontinent more directly under the British government's control, Macaulay accepted a position as a law member of the new Governor General's Council.

Macaulay's decision to write a history of England, one which would make his name and secure his legacy, was taken when he was in India and committed to 'Anglicising' the subcontinent 'as best as he could'.[18] But Macaulay hated 'exile' and longed to return to 'civilised' Britain. He felt that what India needed was a class of Anglicised Indians, educated to British ways, who could act as cultural intermediaries – 'Indian in blood and colour but English in tastes' – between the British and the Indians. In Indian culture, for a time, the term 'Macaulay's children' referred to people born of Indian heritage who took up Western culture as a lifestyle. But his period in India also gave him time to reflect on what he felt was distinctive about Britain – in particular, its tradition of liberty and freedom.[19]

Back in Britain in 1838, he was MP for Edinburgh and secretary of war and he addressed himself to the issue of copyright law, which was influential in the English-speaking world for many years. The two works for which he is most remembered are *Lays of Ancient Rome*, a collection of heroic and tragic poems describing the history of the classical city, and *The History of England from the Accession of James the Second*. In the *History* his message was plain: 'The history of our country during the last hundred and sixty years is eminently the history of physical, of moral, and of intellectual improvement.' The 'mob' – radicals and revolutionaries, women, people of the empire – were all confined to the margins. Only Ireland, described as an 'anomalous sister kingdom', both inside and outside the nation, in Catherine Hall's words, disturbed the forward flow of his narrative. Macaulay was of the view that Burke was the greatest figure since Milton, his enthusiasm for Britain showing in his lauding of the Great Exhibition of 1851.[20] 'He disliked the institution of slavery because it represented to him the antithesis of vaunted

English freedoms and liberties, but he had no time for Africans, free or unfree', and was totally uninterested in the Caribbean.[21] *The History of England* scarcely mentions the empire and totally evades the issue of slavery. His essays on Robert Clive and Warren Hastings put forward his conviction that Britain was a 'benevolent and reforming' imperial power.[22] 'Macaulayism' refers to his policy of introducing the British educational system to the colonies, which he worked on when he was in India, and is seen by some later critics as encouraging 'a spirit of self-denigration' among the colonised.[23]

'THE HIGHER PLEASURES AND THE LOWER PLEASURES'

Can anyone have had a better childhood than John Stuart Mill, who had helped Carlyle so much with his book on the French Revolution and joined the anti-Eyre committee? The son of James Mill, himself a Scottish philosopher, historian and economist, John Stuart was educated by his father, with the assistance of Jeremy Bentham, the noted utilitarian philosopher and abolitionist, his father's explicit aim being to raise a genius. The boy was, not surprisingly perhaps, notably precocious, reading Greek at age three and Latin at eight, enabling him to dip into Euclid in the original and learn algebra without being taught. At twelve he studied scholastic logic, and the following year was introduced to political economy, studying with the revered economist David Ricardo, a friend of his father's, who took the very young man for walks to talk about ... political economy. At fourteen he stayed in France with Bentham's brother and was introduced there to another friend of his father, the renowned French political economist Jean-Baptiste Say, and then Henri Saint-Simon, after which he corresponded with Auguste Comte.[24] No one could have been luckier.

As a Nonconformist Scot, Mill was not eligible to study at Oxford or Cambridge. Instead, he attended University College, London, and followed his father into the East India Company. He married late, to Harriet Taylor, after a friendship of twenty-one years. She was a philosopher in her own right who published her own works and helped him to the point where, later, he said the books published under his name only were really joint works.

Mill became known for a very modern set of views – equality
for women (*The Subjection of Women* was published in 1832) and
minority ethnic groups, the pursuit of happiness, proportional representation, the advancement of science and the scientific method,
plus various seminal ideas about liberty, notably fighting the 'tyranny
of the majority', freedom of speech and the 'harm principle', that the
limits to liberty be set at the point where it harms others. Despite all
this he was in favour of British rule in India, believing that 'benevolent despotism' was preferable to the available alternatives (his father
had published *The History of British India* in 1818, very critical of
Hindu culture, despite never having been there, and being unable
to speak any Indian languages; this, he insisted in his defence, only
made his views more 'objective').[25]

Mill is best known for his ideas about liberty and here he is often
grouped with John Locke. Mill tried to keep things simple: individuals are free to do as they wish provided it does not cause harm to
others. Free speech is an unalloyed good: we can never be sure that
a silenced opinion does not contain, somewhere, some element of
truth. Added to which, people are more likely to change their false
opinion if they are encouraged to air it publicly in an open exchange,
and open access also stops false belief descending into dogma.

Mill also embraced Bentham's utilitarian notion that the overall
aim in life is the 'greatest good for the greatest number' and that this
does not need any great philosophical teaching to be understood by
all. More interesting perhaps is his argument that there are higher
and lower pleasures. By the higher pleasures he meant mental, moral
and aesthetic pleasures, the lower pleasures were more physical and
sensational, and a more active life was both more pleasurable and
more virtuous than a passive one. It is more virtuous to engage in
pleasures that benefit all of society (philosophy, art) than those that
merely satisfy individual needs (games, sport): it is not an *individual's* happiness that matters but that we achieve the greatest amount
of happiness *together*. The other point to an active rather than a
passive lifestyle is that happiness is better achieved *en passant* rather
than being directly striven for. He opposed Marxism, then coming
into vogue, because he felt it decreased competition in society,
from which everyone would ultimately suffer. He also foresaw that

industrialisation would eventually pose a threat to the environment. And he was firmly in favour of the emancipation of the slaves in the United States, corresponding with several legal reformers.

A separate territory in the nineteenth-century British imagination might be called Brontëland, linking a different set of personalities, taking in the three Brontë sisters, Elizabeth Gaskell and Harriet Martineau, all of whom mixed with each other though at times fell out.

The Brontë sisters – Charlotte, Emily and Anne – respectively produced between them three memorable novels reflecting the social-moral concerns of the early nineteenth century, *Jane Eyre*, *Wuthering Heights* and *Agnes Grey*. Each wrote under a pen name to begin with, on account of the feeling in early Victorian life that 'writing' was not a fit occupation for a woman. Each of the books is about a woman and/or her family coming into distress – echoing to an extent the fate of the Brontë family itself, which was from Yorkshire – and facing the more or less traditional reversals of fortune that characterised nineteenth-century literary life.

In *Agnes Grey* we follow the fortunes of a governess in various families, where she is hardly ever treated well, but finds love in the end. In *Jane Eyre*, which is held to have had a marked impact on fiction, by exploring Jane's psychology through an 'unprecedented intensely first-person narrative', the title character is also a governess, orphaned, who serves in Thornfield Hall, the house of Edward Rochester. Rochester is a difficult man, but they grow attached to each other, though it emerges later that he is already married to a 'congenitally mad woman' who inhabits the great house where the action takes place, often behaving oddly. Disappointed and devastated, Jane leaves and almost – but not quite – accepts an offer of marriage and a life in colonial India. Returning to Thornfield Hall after some time, she finds it destroyed by a fire, instigated by Rochester's mad wife, in which he himself is injured and blinded. She declares her love for him and, despite his affliction, they are married and live happily ever after.

In *Wuthering Heights*, Heathcliff, also an orphan, is the servant with whom one of the daughters of the family who employs him falls in love, though she 'cannot' marry him because of his low status. Heathcliff later leaves and makes good and returns to the family who treated him badly to begin with, but are now fallen on hard times, and he wins possession of Wuthering Heights in a bet. He visits the daughter who spurned him, but she dies giving birth to the child of the man she married instead. No one lives happily ever after.

Of the three sisters, Charlotte was probably the greatest talent. She wrote many other novels but is well known also for her letters, her skirmishes with Harriet Martineau and her friendship with Elizabeth Gaskell, who wrote her biography, the first full-scale biography of a woman novelist, which brought out her gift of friendship above her talents as a writer. Gaskell, a novelist herself, was notable because she came from an old Dissenting family, and she and her husband, a Unitarian minister – later appointed professor of history, literature and logic at Manchester New College – took a great interest in the problems of the poor.

Gaskell's main works were *Mary Barton* and *Cranford*, the former about the relenting, declining fortunes of a poor family in a fiscal depression; *Cranford* is somewhat different, being based on Knutsford in Cheshire, where Gaskell grew up, and chronicles the lives of two lower-middle-class sisters and their efforts to keep up appearances. Whereas *Mary Barton* was relentless (and criticised for being anti the managerial classes), *Cranford* is lighter and wittier.[26]

Gaskell's *The Life of Charlotte Brontë*, published in 1857, provoked a storm of controversy, with major threats of libel from figures who felt themselves traduced, their complaints so persuasively advocated that unsold copies were withdrawn and an official apology printed in *The Times*. But it is now regarded as a seminal biography of uncommon detail, style and honesty.

One of the persuasive complaints came from Harriet Martineau, Norwich-born, a descendant of Huguenots, though she too, like Gaskell, was a 'dedicated dissenter', extremely religious, a follower of Hannah More. The failure of the family firm in 1829 had thrown her back on her own resources and she began writing in earnest, despite being more or less deaf by the age of twenty, meaning she spoke with a booming voice. A journalist of wide involvements, and indefatigable in execution, one of her interests was political economy, and in 1832 she published twenty-three *Illustrations of Political Economy*, outlining mainly the ideas of James Mill and Malthus. Aimed in simple language at the working class, they made her famous almost overnight, and she was asked to write more on both poor law and taxation, though John Stuart Mill thought what she had to say 'absurd'.

In the mid-1830s, she toured America, the experience confirming her all the more in her anti-slavery feelings, and she eventually became a correspondent for the *New York Anti-slavery Standard*. She was also a committed follower of the French sociologist and positivist Auguste Comte, and though she didn't accept all of his ideas, she did translate his *Cours de philosophie positive*, its first rendering into English, though powerfully dissenting from his subordination of women. Martineau was friendly with Wordsworth, George Eliot and Matthew Arnold, warmly welcomed Darwin's *On the Origin of Species*, wrote a novel sympathetically portraying Toussaint L'Ouverture and the Haitian Revolution, and a travel book about the Middle East, *Eastern Life*. She was as modern as Mill.[27]

Essentially, the Brontës lead us on from Jane Austen, inwardly dissecting British (mainly English) domestic life, while Gaskell and Martineau, though their lives overlapped socially with the Brontës, looked forward and outward, hinting that one day empire would end.

A Significant New View of Nature

One morning in late August 1847, while Harriet Martineau was in Egypt and Syria, researching *Eastern Life*, James Prescott Joule, a wealthy Manchester brewer but also a distinguished physicist, was walking in Switzerland, near St Martin, beneath the Col de Forclaz, in the east of the country, not too far from the Italian border. On the road between St Martin and St Gervais he was surprised to meet a colleague, William Thomson, a fellow physicist, later more distinguished as Lord Kelvin. Thomson noted in a letter the next day to his father – a professor of mathematics – that Joule had with him some very sensitive thermometers and asked if he, Thomson, would assist him in an unusual experiment: he wanted to measure the temperature of the water at the top and bottom of a local waterfall. The request was particularly unusual, Thomson suggested in his letter, because Joule was then on his honeymoon.

The experiment with waterfalls came to nothing. There was so much spray and splash at the foot that neither Joule nor Thomson could get close enough to the main body of water to make measurements. But the idea was ingenious and it was, moreover, very much a child of its time. Joule was homing in on a notion that, it is no exaggeration to say, would prove to be one of the two most important scientific ideas of all time, and a significant new view of nature.

He was not alone. Over the previous few years as many as

fifteen scientists, working in Germany, Holland and France as well as in Britain, had had a very similar thought – the conservation of energy. Four of the men – Sadi Carnot, in Paris in 1832, Marc Séguin, in Lyon in 1839, Karl Holtzmann in Mannheim in 1845, and Gustave-Adolphe Hirn, in Mulhouse in 1854 – had all recorded their independent convictions that heat and work are quantitatively interchangeable. Between 1837 and 1844, Karl Mohr in Koblenz, William Grove and Michael Faraday in London and Justus von Liebig in Giessen all described the world of phenomena 'as manifesting but a single "force", one which could appear in electrical, thermal, dynamical, and many other forms but which could never, in all its transformations, be created or destroyed'.[1] And between 1842 and 1847, the hypothesis of energy conservation was publicly announced by four 'widely scattered' European scientists – Julius Mayer in Tübingen, James Joule in Manchester, Ludwig Colding in Copenhagen and Hermann von Helmholtz in Berlin, all but the last working in complete ignorance of one another.

NATURE'S CURRENCY SYSTEM: 'CONTINUAL CONVERSION'

The men who did most, at least to begin with, to explore the conservation of energy – Joule and Thomson in Britain, Helmholtz and Rudolf Clausius in Germany – would produce interminable wrangles in the mid-nineteenth century as to who had discovered what first. Perhaps the fairest thing to say is that the discovery of the conservation of energy was a joint Anglo-German project.

Joule (1818–69), born into a brewing family in Salford, near Manchester, had a Victorian mane, hair which reached almost as far down his back as his beard did down his front: his head was awash in hair. He is known for just one thing, but it was and is an important thing and one where he conducted experiments over a number of years to provide an ever more accurate answer.

As a young man he had worked in the family's brewery, which may have ignited his interest in heat. This interest was no doubt fanned all the more when he was sent to study chemistry in Manchester proper with John Dalton. As we have seen, Dalton was famous for his atomic theory, the idea that each chemical element was made up of different kinds of atom, and that the key difference between different atoms was their weight. Dalton thought that these 'elementary elements' could be neither created nor destroyed, based on his observations which showed that different elements combined to produce substances which contained the elements in set proportions, with nothing left over.

With his commercial background, Joule was always interested in the practical end of science – in the possibility of electric motors, for instance, which might take over from steam. Joule's early reports, on the relationship between electricity and heat, were turned down by the Royal Society and he was forced to publish in the *Philosophical Magazine*, not the same thing at all. But he continued his experiments, which sought to show that work – movement – is converted into heat, by stirring a container of water with a paddle wheel, Joule writing that 'we consider heat not as *substance* but as a state of *vibration*'. Over his lifetime, Joule sought ever more accurate ways to calculate just how much energy was needed to raise the temperature of 1 pound of water by 1 degree Fahrenheit (the traditional definition of 'work'). Accuracy was vital if the conservation of energy was to be proved.[2]

And gradually people were won over. For example, Joule addressed several meetings of the British Association for the Advancement of Science, in 1842, and again in 1847. The BAAS was well established then, having been founded in 1831, in York, modelled on the German *Gesellschaft Deutscher Naturforscher und Ärzte*, and holding annual meetings all over Britain in different cities each year. But Joule needed only one individual in his BAAS audience to find what he had to say important, and that came about in the 1847 meeting, when his ideas were picked up on by a young man of twenty-one. That young man was William Thomson, but he would, in time, become better known as Lord Kelvin.

Just as Joule befriended the older Dalton, so he befriended the younger Thomson. In fact, he worked with Thomson on the theory of gases and how they cool and how all that related to Dalton's atomic theory. Joule was particularly interested in nailing the exact average speed at which molecules of gas move (movement that was of course related to their temperature). He focused on hydrogen and treated it as being made up of tiny particles bouncing off one another and off the walls of whatever container they were held in. By manipulating the temperature and the pressure, which affected the volume in predictable ways, he was able to calculate that, at a temperature of 60 degrees Fahrenheit and a pressure of 30 inches of mercury (more or less room temperature and pressure), the particles of gas were moving at 6,225.54 feet per second. Similarly, with oxygen, the molecules of which weigh sixteen times those of hydrogen: since the inverse square law applies, in ordinary air oxygen molecules are moving at a quarter of the speed of hydrogen molecules, or 1,556.39 feet per second.[3] This was an amazing feat – to pin down such infinitesimal activity – and Joule was invited to address the Royal Society and was elected a fellow, more than making up for his earlier rejection.

Joule shared a lot with Thomson, including his religious beliefs, which played an important part in the theory for some people. The principle of continual conversions or exchanges was established and maintained by God, he argued, as a basis for 'nature's currency system', guaranteeing a dynamic stability in 'nature's economy'.[4]

Thomson followed on where Joule left off. Born in Belfast in June 1824, he spent almost all his life in university environments. His father was professor of mathematics at the Royal Academical Institution in Belfast, a forerunner of Queen's University, and William and his brother James were educated at home by their father (James also became a physicist). Their mother died when William was six and in 1832 their father moved to Glasgow, where again he became professor of mathematics. As a special dispensation both his sons were allowed to attend lectures there, matriculating in 1834 when William was ten. After Glasgow, William was due to go to Cambridge but there were concerns that graduating in Glasgow might 'disadvantage' his prospects down south, so although he passed his finals and the MA exams a year later, he did not formally graduate. At the time, he therefore signed himself as William Thomson BATAIAP (Bachelor of Arts To All Intents And Purposes). He transferred to Cambridge in 1841, graduating four years later, having won a number of prizes and publishing several papers in the *Cambridge Mathematics Journal*.

'The World Cannot Go Back'

Thomson echoed Joule in his theology as well as his science. 'Although no destruction of energy can take place in the material world without an act of power possessed only by the supreme ruler, yet transformations take place which remove irrecoverably from the control of man sources of power which, if the opportunity of turning them to his own account had been made use of, might have been rendered available.'[5] God, as 'supreme ruler', had established this law of 'energy conservation' but nonetheless there were sources of energy in nature (such as waterfalls) which could be made use of – in fact, it was a mistake for Thomson if they were *not* made use of, because that implied waste, the Presbyterian's abiding sin. Finally, nature's transformations had a direction, which only God could reverse: 'The material world could not come back to any previous state without a violation of the laws which have been manifested to man.'

In purely scientific terms, however, Thomson's most important contribution was to make thermodynamics (as the conservation of energy became more formally known) a consolidated scientific discipline at the middle of the century. He got together with Peter Guthrie Tait, another Scot, and their joint work, *Treatise on Natural Philosophy* (1867), was an attempt both to rewrite Newton and to place thermodynamics and the conservation of energy at the core of a new science, nineteenth-century physics. Tait and Thomson planned a second volume of their book, never written, which would include 'a great section on "the *one* law of the Universe", the Conservation of Energy'.[6]

Thomson was much more than a scientist. It was his theories that caused Isambard Kingdom Brunel's huge and failed steamship, *Great Eastern*, to be taken out of mothballs to lay a working telegraph cable across the Atlantic (after other attempts had failed), a move that transformed communication almost as much as, and maybe more than, the Internet of today, and which, alongside his other practical achievements, would bolster the continued pre-eminence of the British Empire. He made money from his scientific and industrial patents to such an extent that he was first knighted in 1866 and then made Baron Kelvin of Largs in 1892 (the River Largs runs through the campus of Glasgow University).

Thomson's ideas were being more or less paralleled in Germany by the work of Herman von Helmholtz and Rudolf Clausius. With hindsight, everything can be seen as pointing towards the theory of the conservation of energy, but it still required someone to formulate these ideas clearly and that occurred in the seminal memoir of 1847 by Helmholtz (1821–94). In *On the Conservation of Force*, he provided the requisite mathematical formulation, linking heat, light, electricity and magnetism by treating these phenomena as different manifestations of 'energy'.[7] In making his case without any experimental evidence, Helmholtz first established a clear distinction between theoretical and experimental physics.

The Tendency towards Increasing Disorder

While Helmholtz, being a doctor, came to the science of work through physiology, his fellow Prussian Rudolf Clausius, approached the phenomenon, like his British and French contemporaries, via the ubiquitous steam engine. But Clausius's special contribution was to apply mathematics far more deeply than any of his predecessors and he was an important stage in the establishment of thermodynamics and theoretical physics. His first paper on the mechanical theory of heat was published in 1850. It is in this famous paper where he argued that the production of work resulted not only from a change in the *distribution* of heat, but also from the *consumption* of heat: heat could be produced by the 'expenditure' of work. In observing this, he stated two fundamental principles, which would become known as the first and second laws of thermodynamics.

The first law may be illustrated by how it was later taught to Max Planck, the man who, at the turn of the twentieth century, would build on Clausius's work. Imagine a worker lifting a heavy stone on to the roof of a house. The stone will remain in position long after it has been left there, storing energy until at some point in the future it falls back to earth. Energy, says the first law, can be neither created nor destroyed. Clausius, however, pointed out in his second law that the first law does not give the total picture. In the example given, energy is expended by the worker as he lifts the stone into place, and is dissipated in the effort as heat, which among other things causes the worker to sweat. This dissipation, which Clausius was to term 'entropy', is of fundamental importance, he said, because although it does not disappear from the universe, this energy can never be recovered in its original form. Clausius therefore concluded that the world (and the universe) must always tend towards increasing disorder, must always add to its entropy.[8]

This idea that heat was a form of motion was not new. In addition to the ideas of Joule and Mayer, the American Benjamin Thompson had observed that heat was produced when a cannon barrel was bored, and in Britain Sir Humphry Davy had likewise noted that ice could be melted by friction. What attracted Clausius's interest was the exact form of motion that comprised heat. Was it the vibration of the internal particles, was it their 'translational' motion as they moved from one position to another, or was it because they rotated on their own axes?

Clausius's second seminal paper, *On the Kind of Motion that We Call Heat*, was published in 1857. In it he argued that the heat of a gas must be made up of all three types of movement and that therefore its total heat ought to be proportional to the sum of these motions. He assumed that the volume occupied by the particles themselves was vanishingly small and that all the particles moved with the same average velocity, which he calculated as being hundreds – if not thousands – of metres per second (building on Joule). This brought about the objection from several others that his assumptions and calculations could not be right, since otherwise gases would diffuse far more quickly than they were known to do. He therefore abandoned that approach, introducing instead the concept of the 'mean free path', the average distance that a particle could travel in a straight line before colliding with another one.[9]

The Unification of Electricity, Magnetism and Light

Clausius was elected a fellow of the Royal Society in 1868 and awarded its Copley Medal in 1879. Others were attracted by his efforts, in particular James Clerk Maxwell in Britain. According to one of his biographers, Maxwell had a scientific idea 'that was as profound as any work of philosophy, as beautiful as any painting, and more powerful than any act of politics or war. Nothing would be the same again.' These are big things to say but in a nutshell Maxwell conceived four equations that, at a stroke, united electricity, magnetism and light and in so doing showed that visible light was only a small band in a vast range of possible waves, 'which all travelled at the same speed but vibrated at different frequencies'.[10] Physicists, says the same biographer, honour Maxwell alongside Newton and Einstein, yet among the general public 'for some reason he is much less well known'.

Maxwell was brought up for the first eight years of his life on his father's estate at Glenlair, in the Galloway region of southwest Scotland. His family were well connected – his grandfather was a composer and a fellow of the Royal Society. It became plain soon enough that James was an exceptional child, learning how to knit, bake and weave baskets.[11] Like Humphry Davy and Michael Faraday, he shared the nineteenth-century scientist's fascination with writing poetry, though none was published in his lifetime, and it is not hard to see why. One poem read:

Then $^{Vn}/_{Vt}$ the tangent will equal
Of the angle of starting worked out in the sequel.

Another actually had a graph in it.

The Vale of Urr, where Glenlair was situated, was known to its residents as Happy Valley, but when she was forty-seven and James only eight, Maxwell's mother, Frances, contracted abdominal cancer and died soon after undergoing an operation (performed without anaesthetic). It had been planned for James to be educated at home but by now his father had too many calls on his time. An aunt who lived in the capital came to the rescue and took him in, which enabled him to attend Edinburgh Academy, one of the best schools in Scotland.[12]

Because the school was almost full, James was obliged to enter a class of boys a year older than he was, who had all been at the school for months, and had established their own conventions and cliques. When they saw his rough-hewn country clothes and heard his rural accent, they picked on him mercilessly, nick-naming him 'Dafty'.

Then in his second year the speed with which he mastered geometry impressed his teachers and, no less, his classmates.[13]

In mid-nineteenth-century Britain the word 'scientist' had not yet come into common use. Physicists and chemists called themselves 'natural philosophers' and biologists called themselves 'natural historians'. Maxwell decided to enrol at Edinburgh University, to study mathematics, natural philosophy and logic. He matriculated at sixteen.

This is when he began to experiment, aided by the practice of the Scottish universities of closing from late April to early November to allow students to go home to help with the farming. He read and read and read and carried out his first experiments at Glenlair, developing an interest in electromagnetism and polarised light. When he went on to Cambridge at the age of nineteen, he started at Peterhouse but found it dull and moved to Trinity, which was more congenial and much more mathematically minded (the master at the time being William Whewell, whom we have already met). In Cambridge Maxwell joined the class of the famous (in mathematical circles) 'wrangler maker' William Hopkins, wranglers being those who gained first-class degrees in the mathematics Tripos, which all had to take. The reward for wranglers was lifelong recognition in whatever field they chose. The Tripos was an arduous seven-day affair, six hours a day, and James came second.[14] With the Tripos out of the way, he was now free to give rein to the ideas that had been brewing in his mind over his two stints as an undergraduate. One was the process of vision, particularly the way we see colours, and the other was electricity and magnetism.

In his colour research he had an early breakthrough, finding that there is a fundamental difference between mixing pigments, as one does with paints or dyes, and mixing lights, as one does when spinning a multi-coloured disc. Pigments act as extractors of colour, so that the light you see after mixing two paints is whatever colour the paints have failed to absorb. In other words, mixing pigments is a subtractive process, whereas mixing lights is additive – so that, for instance, blue and yellow do not make green, as they do with pigments, but pink. And by experiment, he was able to show that there are, in light terms, three primary colours – red, blue and green – and that it is possible to mix them in different proportions to obtain all the colours of the rainbow. This was a major advance and is the theory behind the colours in colour television, for example.

At the same time, Maxwell was getting to grips with electricity and magnetism and in 1855 the first of his three great papers appeared. Michael Faraday had thought of lines of force as discrete tentacles (analogous to the lines of iron filings that form around a magnet). Maxwell now conceived them as merged into one continuous essence, which he called 'flux' – the higher the density of flux at any particular location, the stronger the electrical or magnetic force there. And he grasped moreover that the electric and magnetic forces between bodies varies inversely as the square of their distance apart – much as Newton had said of gravity.[15] In this way, lines of force became the 'field' and *this* was the concept that set Maxwell apart and put him on a par with Newton and Einstein. More than that, though, he would build on it six years later with his concept of *electromagnetic waves*.

In between times, his father fell ill, and James was forced to spend time nursing him. But it wasn't enough: he needed a post nearer home. This cropped up when he was offered the position as professor of natural philosophy at Marischal College, in Aberdeen, which would, not much later, be incorporated into Aberdeen University. The post buoyed both father and son, but it had its drawbacks. James later wrote to a friend, 'No jokes of any kind are understood here. I have not made one for 2 months, and if I feel one coming on I shall bite my tongue.' But it wasn't all hopeless, as James found the daughter of the college principal, Katherine Dewar, exactly to his taste, proposed, and was accepted.[16]

In June 1858 he and Katherine were married and then, a few months later, he read the paper by Clausius about the diffusion of gases. The problem, which several people had pointed out, was that, to explain the pressure of gases at normal temperatures, the molecules would have to move very fast – several hundred metres a second, as Joule had calculated. Why then do smells – of perfume, say – spread relatively slowly about a room? Clausius proposed that each molecule undergoes an enormous number of collisions, so that it is forever changing direction – to carry a smell across a room the molecule(s) would actually have to travel several kilometres.

Maxwell saw that what was needed was a way of representing many motions in a single equation, a statistical law. He devised one which said nothing about individual molecules but gave the proportion which had the velocities within any given range. This was the first-ever statistical law in physics. The distribution of velocities turned out to be bell-shaped, the familiar normal distribution of populations about a mean. But its shape varied with the temperature – the hotter the gas the flatter the curve, the wider the bell.

This alone was enough to put Maxwell in the first rank of scientists. The Royal Society certainly thought so, awarding him the Rumford Medal in 1860, its highest award for physics. No less important in the long run, King's College, London, was looking for a professor of natural history. James entered his name and was appointed. King's, in the Strand, just north of the Thames, had been founded in 1828 as an Anglican alternative to the non-sectarian University College, a mile further north, which was itself intended as an alternative to the strictly Church of England Oxbridge.

Being in London meant that Maxwell could attend the Royal Society, and the Royal Institution, where he was able to cement his friendship with Faraday. And Maxwell homed in on his final great insight.[17]

In his paper 'On Faraday's Lines of Force' (1855), he had found a way of representing the lines of force mathematically as continuous fields, and he had made a start towards forming a set of equations governing the way electrical and magnetic fields interact with one another. But that was still only part of the picture. 'Picture' is in fact the wrong word here, because it is at this point that physics began to enter a world where the familiar visual analogies break down. The image of a 'field' is easy enough to imagine in itself, but Maxwell's equations could only be explained with great difficulty in ordinary language, and this came home to him – and then to everyone – in his 1862 paper where he concluded, dramatically, and using the mathematics that he had himself created, that light is also a form of electromagnetic disturbance and, moreover, could be understood as both a wave and a beam of particles. This was unheard of, inexplicable when put into language, but made sense in mathematics.[18] In fact, Maxwell derived four equations which between them 'summed up everything that it is possible to say about classical electricity and magnetism' and this is why, among physicists, if not yet the general public, he is placed on a par with Newton.[19]

As if all this were not enough, Maxwell's equations contained within them the implication that there must be other forms of electromagnetic waves with much longer wavelengths than those of visible light. Their discovery would not be long in coming.

The final chapter in Maxwell's extraordinary career was when he was invited to accept an important new professorship at Cambridge. The Duke of Devonshire, who was chancellor of the university, had offered a large sum of money to build a new laboratory for teaching and research, and to compete with the best of what then existed on the continent, especially in Germany. Cambridge was being left behind in experimental science, not just by France and Germany, but by many of the new British universities as well.

Maxwell was not overkeen to accept Cambridge's offer. His theories were so new that not everyone understood them, and he couldn't be certain of his reception more generally. But many of the younger physicists at Cambridge, who *had* kept up with his work, implored him to come, and that settled it.[20]

Darwin, Empire and the
Pre-eminence of the English Novel

O ver time, evolution and natural selection would be thoroughly assimilated intellectually, not just in Britain but across Europe and the rest of the world, to the point where, as with Freudianism in subsequent eras, the culture eventually took Darwinian assumptions for granted, whether people had read him or not. Two of the areas of cultural life where this became marked were first in painting and even more so in literature.

In painting, 'the burgeoning Victorian interest in the sciences' was seen as one of pre-Raphaelite art's 'most important contemporary contexts'.[1] To begin with, many critics had seen the remorseless detail of early pre-Raphaelite painting as analogous to science. Ruskin thought that the 'grotesque and wild forms of imagination' that characterised pre-Raphaelite paintings reflected the 'incisive scepticism of recent science', while Dante Gabriel Rossetti argued that scientific discoveries could only strengthen the poetic and pictorial importance of modern art.[2] The short-lived pre-Raphaelite periodical *The Germ* (four issues only) had several articles that emphasised and reflected on the conception of nature as articulated by recent science, in particular geology and chemistry, but also mathematics, in that the classical pyramidical arrangement of forms in Old Master paintings was criticised as 'unnatural' and repeatedly attacked in their academy. In 1836, in a lecture series at the Royal

Institution, John Constable had declared, 'Painting is a science, and it should be considered as a branch of natural philosophy, of which pictures are but experiments.'[3] Elsewhere, Euclidian geometry was understood as the basis for conventional aesthetic judgement and condemned. Instead, depicted figures, it was said, should seek to express the 'electrophysiology' that recent discoveries had shown to 'animate life'. In their writings the pre-Raphaelites made frequent reference to Bacon and Newton and suggested that 'realising' an image was a 'matter of induction' deriving from observation.

In literature, as a whole raft of more recent scholars (Gillian Beer, George Levine, Redmond O'Hanlon, Sally Shuttleworth) have pointed out, evolutionary ideas were incorporated pretty thoroughly into the great novels of the century. As one of these scholars, Gillian Beer, notes, Darwin himself had a literary bent: he revered Shakespeare's history plays, was passionate about Wordsworth and Coleridge, took copies of Milton's poetry with him on the *Beagle*. And *Origin*, as several people have pointed out, was well written, with great attention to detail, and is in its way a narrative. Just as Darwin's narrative style was shaped by those literary influences, so his books, especially *Origin* and *The Descent of Man*, but also *The Expression of the Emotions in Animals and Man*, influenced George Eliot, Thackeray, Dickens, Hardy, Conrad and many others.

Beer also makes the point that at that time there was a 'wonderful inclusiveness of generalist journals', which meant that 'philosophers, lawyers, evolutionary theorists, politicians, astronomers, physicists, novelists, theologians, poets and language theorists all appeared alongside each other, more often with the effects of bricolage, true enough ... But their lying alongside on the page encouraged the reader to infer connections between their activities by the simple scan of the eye and by the simultaneous availability of diverse ideas.'[4]

George Levine, a specialist in Victorian culture at Rutgers University, in his *Darwin and the Novelists*, provides a useful starting point: Jane Austen's *Mansfield Park*, published in 1814 (and for which she received more earnings than for any other book), in which an impoverished Fanny Price is sent from her home in Portsmouth to live with her rich aunt, whose family occupy Mansfield Park in

Northamptonshire, but whose husband also has a sugar estate in Antigua in the West Indies, the source of their wealth. Fanny is witness to, and part of, a series of adventures, despite being the poor-relation observer so close to Austen's heart. (The standard Austen plot is of lovers of unequal rank and means.) But Levine's point, in making this story a benchmark, is that the underlying assumption is that it takes place at a time when natural theology was the ortho-dox belief system in Britain – that the beauty of the natural world, and the perfect way so many different organisms are adapted to it, provides evidence both for God and for the way the characters in the book occupy their 'natural' habitats. Everyone has their place in an established, stable hierarchy.[5]

But after Darwin, things are never quite so comfortable. The most obviously post-Darwin novel was *The Water Babies*, written across 1862 and 1863, by the Reverend Charles Kingsley, chaplain to Queen Victoria, Regius Professor of Modern History at Cambridge and a friend of Darwin, who had been given an advance copy of the *Origin*. *The Water Babies* tells the story of Tom, a chimney sweep, who falls into a stream and appears to drown, causing him to enter a parallel world of other 'water babies' where he undergoes a series of moral trials, in which he succeeds gloriously, earning his way back to human status and becoming a famous scientist. The book is an attack on child labour and a story of Christian redemption but it is also a (loose) allegory of evolution, as Tom 'evolves'.

George Eliot also stands out. Born Mary Ann Evans in 1819, in the Midlands near Coventry, she was always clever and bookish, and was fortunate in her friendships (Robert Owen, Herbert Spencer, Harriet Martineau, Ralph Waldo Emerson). Her early works were translations, most notably from the German (thanks to her friendship with Thomas Carlyle): David Strauss (*The Life of Jesus, Critically Examined*, which caused a sensation in Germany, France and Britain), Ludwig Feuerbach (*The Essence of Christianity*) and Baruch Spinoza (*The Ethics*). Eliot was appointed assistant editor of the *Westminster Review*, published by another friend, John Chapman, who also published Herbert Spencer and Thomas Huxley. George Eliot was very much in the socio-intellectual swim.

In 1851 Mary Ann met George Henry Lewes, a philosopher with

an interest in physiology, also much interested in positivism, evolution and scepticism, and they decided to live together, in an open arrangement, never being wed legally, despite having three children. This may be why she chose to write as George Eliot, to prevent people prying into her life, but Lewes also spurred her interest in science and her turn to fiction: *Adam Bede* (1859), *The Mill on the Floss* (1860), *Silas Marner* (1861) and then, in 1872, *Middlemarch*. This is considered by many people, including several writers (Julian Barnes, Martin Amis), to be the best novel ever written in English.

Essentially, the book consists of two love stories, the first that of Dorothea Brookes, wealthy, bright and creative, who masks her wealth, so it won't divert any man she might meet, who helps her uncle's tenants with their cottages, and who marries the older Reverend Edward Casaubon, ostensibly to help him with the research for his magnum opus, *The Key to All Mythologies* (slightly reminiscent of Strauss's *Life of Jesus, Critically Examined*), but which quickly shows itself to be out of date because he speaks no German (Eliot, of course, was a fluent translator). Disaffected by Casaubon's coldness, and the failure of his 'research', Dorothea falls for his poor but idealistic cousin and after the reverend's death she marries him. The other story features Tertius Lydgate, a young doctor, whose wife, Rosamund Vincy, a bit of a social and intellectual snob, married him for social standing but is embarrassed when he runs into financial difficulty. He leaves town to satisfy her.

More than most other nineteenth-century novels, *Middlemarch* exemplifies the various post-Darwinian issues that so interested novelists, and it is worth saying that one has to stand back from the plotting to see properly what Beer, Levine and the others are getting at. The influence of Darwinism and other recent sciences is not evident, necessarily, on every page, but more in the overall design, and in contrast with Austen: a world in constant change; the evolutionary growth of sympathy and its distribution among the social classes (particularly evident in Dickens and Thackeray); an emphasis on gradualism and uniformitarianism, by which change can be confronted and comprehended without fear; the new significance of abundance (contrary to Malthus's dire warnings) and variety in the natural world (as opposed to sameness and hierarchy); the collapse of teleology (perhaps the most important of all, mainly involving the abandonment of a compulsory happy ending); finally, the importance of chance in all development.

In *Daniel Deronda*, only slightly less revered than *Middlemarch*, Eliot tells the story of two people, Daniel, the ward of a rich man, who may or may not be the man's illegitimate son, and Gwendolen Harleth, beautiful, flirtatious but spoilt and self-involved. The two meet in a German town and both have suffered setbacks – Daniel has failed to win a scholarship to Cambridge and Gwendolen's family have suffered financial catastrophe. By accident, when Daniel rescues a young Jewish singer from drowning, he moves increasingly in the Jewish world, while Gwendolen, in love with Daniel, fails again, this time to become a singer, lacking talent as she is told, and marries a wealthy but cold grandee, while seeking emotional succour from Daniel. Daniel has learned he is Jewish, the son of an opera singer, and he marries the woman he rescued, to Gwendolen's great disappointment. Here too we see, or are invited to see, that nothing works out as it might have done, as it probably would have done in Austen's world; that no one is completely happy, no one completely adapted to their niche in life, as Darwin took care to show; that race (or ethnic identity) does and does not matter. In a way, the book is about self-understanding and, again in Darwinian mode, does not really explore morals, as so many nineteenth-century novels of the Austen type did, in favour of a gripping story, where we cannot anticipate the end. It is Darwinian but again you have to stand back to see it.

More even than that, Levine finds the influence of James Joule and the new experiments on the conservation of energy (and the fact that the world will experience a 'heat death' in the distant future) to be reflected in *Little Dorrit*, by Charles Dickens. This tells the complicated story of Amy Dorrit, the youngest child of a sizeable family one of whose senior members is a debtor, locked up in Marshalsea debtors' prison in London, where Dickens's own father had been incarcerated. Amy can come and go to the prison as she pleases. The novel is, at one level, a searing criticism of the 'system' in Britain but also a great comic-tragic-satirical romp through the most outrageous reversals of fate, as Little Dorrit's family are discovered to be heirs to a fortune, and tour Europe in style, only to lose it all later on. Various foreigners – linked to the family by previous exploits – arrive, blackmail is attempted and thwarted, biological relationships are disputed, important information is withheld, and much else. Even summarising the storyline requires energy, but Levine argues that the main characters in *Little Dorrit* 'seem to enact a diminution of energy', along Jouleian lines. The book 'also struggled movingly against the bleakness of a world in which change is the rule and knowledge and moral meaning are separated'.[6] *Little Dorrit*, Levine says, 'shows nature resisting and indeed overwhelming the human intention'.[7]

Bleak House, no less than *Little Dorrit*, was a cornucopia of interwoven plots, based on yet another aspect of Victorian society that fascinated Dickens, in this case a legal dispute over some contested versions of the same will that had been in the courts for years, for *decades*. And it had the usual Dickens array of great character names: Harold Skimpole, Sir Leicester Deadlock, Annie Flite, Inspector Bucket, Krook, the rag-and-bone merchant. The plot essentially concerns various characters who stand to benefit from the will, should it ever be sorted out, and who, in order to benefit, need to keep hidden various less than savoury episodes in their pasts. These imperfections provide much opportunity for comedy, crime and corruption and, this being Dickens, some of the wards fall in love, despite their particular drafts of the will being mutually exclusive. And, this being Dickens, the case is finally settled – not by agreement but because the legal fees have swallowed up the entire estate. The legal profession formally complained about Dickens's exaggeration.

This plot, Levine says, may be seen as Darwinian-thermodynamic in three ways. First, our knowledge of who knows what about which version of the will in the course of the book owes nothing to revelation, but instead comes from the slow build-up, in a uniformitarian way. Second, the way the various characters are revealed as related is similar to the way Darwin gradually represented the detailed interconnections of various species in the *Origin*. And third, as the energy to fight the long-standing case dissipates as the story progresses, so this too mirrors the waning of energy in the Joule–Clausius system.

It should be said that what Beer and Levine and the others are doing does not replace more traditional methods of literary analysis, but offers a new dimension. Some have found it less convincing than others.

William Makepeace Thackeray, generally regarded as Dickens's main rival as a novelist in the mid- to late nineteenth century, is probably remembered most for *Vanity Fair* and Becky Sharpe, its amoral and wily adventuress, or *Pendennis*, with the well-meaning and likeable Arthur Pendennis ('Pen'). But many people at the time thought that Thackeray's masterpiece was *The History of Henry Esmond*, a historical novel, written as a memoir in both the third and the first person, set around the turn of the eighteenth century, in which Henry, an orphan, is taken up by a viscount who, we are invited to believe, is his real father (potential illegitimacy always being a convenient starting point/ruse). Henry takes part in various political events, including an attempt to restore James Francis Edward Stuart to the British throne (the Jacobite Rising in 1715), and forms friendships with, among others, both Addison and Steele – that is, real historical figures.

Levine describes Thackeray as a Darwinian before Darwin and states that throughout the story revolution is thwarted at every point, that the author

> is most rigorously the novelist of things-as-they-are, the most intensely sceptical about intensities and extreme actions ... The framing of the story ... is immediately calculated to minimise the disruptiveness and dangers of history and of revolution itself ... What determines the direction of history in Thackeray is not some cosmic plan or the intention of leaders, but the minutiae of ordinary life, the crossing of narrative streams – chance ... History is the story of little people and of circumstances, and it doesn't seem to make much sense.[8]

As has been said, this *does* accord with the view of history Darwin gives in the *Origin*, but does that prove that Thackeray actually was aware of the link?

One of Thackeray's admirers was Anthony Trollope, who rated him higher than Dickens and thought *Henry Esmond* was his masterpiece. Among Trollope's forty-seven novels, the Barchester Chronicles are the best known, six stories set in the mythical cathedral city of Barchester in the county of Barsetshire. One of these is *Framley Parsonage* while *The Claverings*, though not technically one of the six, is also set in the diocese of Barchester and there are minimal overlaps with Barsetshire characters.

Like many of Trollope's novels, *Framley Parsonage* and *The Claverings* feature the families of clergymen who are well connected but of uncertain wealth and where marriage and social status are central concerns. Romance and marriage, for women especially, is really the only option in life, while men at least have a career to worry about and the financial reward, and social status – for them and their putative wives – that a good career will ensure. Jilting, falling in and out of love, and reversals of financial and other fortunes occur with regularity but in deliberately unexpected ways.

The Darwinian elements in Trollope are most clearly seen in his narrators, who are close and intensely dispassionate observers of events, or in nature, in particular in relation to the hero and heroine. 'The Trollopian narrator speaks with the detachment and distance of the uniformitarian scientist, so that, in *The Claverings* for example, the hero, Harry, gets his rewards without deserving them ... Harry is almost a specimen.'[9] Harry is presented as weak, vacillating, almost hypocritical. 'He is a "hero" only in that the novel is primarily about him.' But this comes out only gradually and there is no moral commentary. This is a Darwinian atmosphere in that the gradual uniformitarianism denies both genius and heroism – what happens *evolves*, with all kinds of providential intrusions.[10]

THE PREPARED IMAGINATION

Just as Trollope gave us Barsetshire, Thomas Hardy invented, or reinvented, his semi-fictional region of Wessex for a series of novels set in the West Country. Many of his books, *The Mayor of Casterbridge*, *Tess of the D'Urbervilles*, *Far from the Madding Crowd*, concern tragic figures (and the reason for their tragic status, as we shall see, was Darwinian in genesis), struggling with their passions but at the same time with their social standing. This is most clearly seen in

The Return of the Native, which centres around six main characters, all of whom inhabit Egdon Heath (possibly based on Duddle
Heath, west of Dorchester in Dorset). The six are: Diggory Venn,
who supplies farmers with the red dye with which they mark their
sheep; Thomasin Yeobright, whom Diggory is in love with, or was,
having long given up hope of success; Damon Wildeve, a not-entirely-
reliable innkeeper, whom Thomasin plans to marry; Mrs Yeobright,
Thomasin's not-entirely-straightforward aunt, who nonetheless
wants the best for her; Eustacia Vye, a mysterious exotic beauty
of Italian descent, from whom Damon has not entirely disengaged
himself; and Clym Yeobright, newly returned from a successful
career as a diamond merchant in Paris, but who now wants to settle
down as a schoolteacher. Clym is shown to us in a more advanced
stage of development than his neighbours who never went anywhere.
Damon marries Thomasin, Clym weds Eustacia, neither marriage
lives up to its promise; Damon comes into money unexpectedly (a
far from unknown happenstance in nineteenth-century plots), which
provokes a series of accidents and coincidences, some of them deadly
(an adder's bite and two drownings).

In the course of the story, Hardy pursued a path somewhat
different from that followed by most of the anthropologists and
sociologists of the period: for example, Auguste Comte and Herbert
Spencer (whom Hardy identified as among his chief intellectual influences) insist on 'fixed successive' phases of culture.[11] But throughout
the book, Hardy reminds us of the 'native' inhabitants' power of
making sensory discriminations lost to the town-dweller: 'They
could hear where the tracts of heather began and ended; where the
furze was growing stalky and tall; where it had recently been cut ...
these differing features had their voices no less than their shapes and
colours.'[12] The work helps the reader in this way to become 'native'
again and shows, as did the *Origin*, that more evolved is no better
than less evolved.

Hardy always acknowledged Darwin as a major intellectual influence on his work 'and his way of seeing'.[13] In particular, there is
no heroism in life, 'the laws of life' do not allow it, so that plot in
Hardy is not only tragic but can also be malign. Death, for example,
is not heroic but often comes about by 'crass casualty', and that the

'persistently almost attained happy alternatives are never quite obliterated by the actual terrible events. The reader is pained by the sense
of multiple possibilities only one of which can occur.'[14] In Hardy's
work, the plenitude and abundance of the world (Egdon Heath) is
everywhere shown; at each moment in the story the world appears
complete but none of the characters occupies his or her niche as
snugly as we – or they – might wish: as Darwin said in the *Origin*,
although species evolve to occupy their unique place in the world,
none is *perfectly* adapted, there is always room for improvement,
and there always will be. Maladaptation, 'the *failure of things to be
what they are meant to be*[,] obsessed Hardy', says Beer.[15] Progress,
life, for Hardy, is to move from one unstable imperfect state to a
new unstable, imperfect state. Otherwise, we deceive ourselves. Is
this the human condition?

Beer went on to trace the relationship between John Tyndall,
the Irish physicist who early on famously predicted the greenhouse
effect, and Gerard Manley Hopkins, who, as a poet, was interested
in the scientific basis of metre, sound, colour and music. Hopkins and
Tyndall had met in the Alps in 1868, at the foot of the Matterhorn, as
Tyndall was about to set out for his third attempt on the mountain.[16]
Two years later Tyndall gave a lecture, 'On the Scientific Use of the
Imagination', in which he said, 'Newton's passage from a falling
apple to a falling moon was, at the outset, a leap of the prepared
imagination,' and that phrase stuck with Hopkins (and with Beer)
as the defining influence on Victorian consciousness. 'The prepared
imagination' exactly sums up the relationship between science and
literature in the nineteenth century.

THE PRE-EMINENCE OF THE ENGLISH NOVEL

The link between Darwinism and English literature, while clearly
deeply grounded and far-reaching, is by no means the only way to
comprehend the distinctive merits of the British nineteenth-century
imagination. A decade after Beer's ground-breaking analysis, the
Palestinian critic and professor of comparative literature at Columbia
University in New York, the late Edward Said, in *Culture and
Imperialism* (1993), argued that one of the principal purposes of 'the

great European realistic novel' was to sustain a society's consent in overseas (imperial) expansion.

Said focused on the period around 1878, when 'the scramble for Africa' was beginning, and when, he says, the realistic-novel form became pre-eminent. 'By the 1840s the English novel had achieved eminence as *the* aesthetic form and as a major intellectual voice, so to speak, in English society.' All the major English novelists of the mid-nineteenth century accepted a globalised worldview, he said, and indeed could not ignore the vast overseas reach of British power. Said listed those books which, he argued, fitted his theme: *Mansfield Park, Jane Eyre, Vanity Fair,* Charles Kingsley's *Westward Ho!, Great Expectations,* Benjamin Disraeli's *Tancred, Daniel Deronda* and Henry James's *Portrait of a Lady* (James was American but spent years in Paris and London). The empire, Said says, is everywhere a crucial setting. In many cases, he insisted, 'the empire functions for much of the European nineteenth century as a codified, if only marginally visible presence in fiction, very much like the servants in grand households and in novels, whose work is taken for granted but scarcely ever more than named, rarely studied or given density'.[17]

The main narrative line of *Mansfield Park,* to repeat, follows the fortunes of Fanny Price, who leaves the family home near Portsmouth, at the age of ten, to become a domestic at Mansfield Park, the country estate of the Bertram family. In due course, Fanny acquires the respect of the family, in particular the various sisters, and the love of the eldest son, whom she marries at the end of the book, becoming mistress of the house. Said, however, concentrates on a few almost incidental remarks of Austen's, to the effect that Sir Thomas Bertram is away, abroad, overseeing his property in the West Indies. The incidental nature of these references, Said says, betrays the fact that so much at the time was taken for granted. But the fact remains: 'What sustains life materially is the Bertram estate in Antigua, which is not doing well.' Austen sees clearly, he says, that to hold and rule Mansfield Park is to hold and rule an imperial estate in close, not to say inevitable, association with it. 'What assures the domestic tranquillity and attractive harmony of one is the productivity and regulated discipline of the other.'

It is this tranquillity and harmony that Fanny comes to adore so much. Just as she is herself an outsider, brought inside Mansfield Park, a 'transported commodity' in effect, so is the sugar which the Antigua estate produces and on which the serenity of Mansfield Park depends. Austen is therefore combining a social point – old blood needs new blood to rejuvenate it – with a political point: the empire may be invisible for most of the time, but it is economically all-important. Said's underlying argument is that Austen, for all her humanity and artistry, *implicitly* accepted slavery and the cruelty that went with it, and likewise accepted the complete subordination of colony to metropolis. He quotes John Stuart Mill on colonies in his *Principles of Political Economy*: 'They are hardly to be looked upon as countries, but more properly as outlying agricultural or manufacturing estates belonging to a larger community ... The trade with the West Indies is hardly to be considered an external trade, but more resembles the traffic between town and country.' It is Said's case that *Mansfield Park* is as important for what it conceals as for what it reveals, and in that was typical of its time.

Since then, Said's work has been built on. In some cases, he has been found to have underestimated the extent to which Austen ignored what was going on around her, that many country houses, not just Mansfield Park, had close links with sugar-rich colonial estates, that many other nineteenth-century British authors – Thackeray, Scott, Dickens – were 'wilfully silent about colonial cruelty and indifferent to enslaved people's resistance to their oppression'.[18] And the study of country houses has revealed a greater black rural presence in Britain than previously thought.[19]

On the other hand, critics have pointed out that Said underestimated the subtlety of Austen's writing and misunderstood the strength of her pro-abolitionist feeling. For example, the 'Mansfield' in Mansfield Park, they suggest, references Lord Justice Mansfield, who ruled in 1772 that slavery on English soil was unsupported by common law. And Mrs Norris, Fanny's primary source of unhappiness in *Mansfield Park*, almost certainly alludes to the brutal slave captain John Norris, who was condemned by an abolitionist historian, Thomas Clarkson, whom Austen admired.[20] Further, in another Austen novel, *Emma*, the name Hawkins (after the slaver

John Hawkins) is the maiden name of Mrs Elton, the pretentious upstart, a vulgar woman who boasts she will help improve Emma's standing but whom Emma cannot stomach.

Corinne Fowler notes that *Sanditon*, Austen's unfinished novel, contains a mixed-race character, Miss Lambe, who resembles a blood relation of Lord Mansfield, whom Austen knew. Fowler also points out that Charlotte Brontë and Thackeray wrote about 'mulatto' schoolgirls and heiresses, suggesting that such characters were 'far from minor' in Austen's and other writers' concerns and that Austen in particular, and her readers, were familiar with an aspect of history that Said 'leaves untouched: the seventeenth- and eighteenth-century black presence in British cities and country estates'.[21] One critic has therefore concluded that 'Austen is more profoundly, and more ingeniously, critical of slavery than has so far been assumed'.[22] This view was reinforced in 2021 and 2023 when new details emerged about Austen's brother Charles, a captain in the Royal Navy, who took part in the navy's anti-slavery squadron.[23]

Both Kipling and Conrad represented the experience of empire as the main subject of their work, the former in *Kim* (1901), the latter in *Heart of Darkness* (1899), *Lord Jim* (1900) and *Nostromo* (1904). Said pictured *Kim* as an 'overwhelmingly male' novel, with two very attractive men at the centre. Kim himself remains a boy (he ages from thirteen to seventeen in the book) and the important background to the story, the 'Great Game' – the political conflict between Russia and Britain across 'the roof of the world' in central Asia – is, said Said, treated like a great prank. This is not quite fair. Kim, an orphan of Irish parents, born in India and often taken as a 'native' Indian, forges a friendship with an old Tibetan Buddhist monk, but is also taken up by the British secret service and spies on Russians in the Himalayas. (So, as well as reflecting on the clash of empires, the narrative records in loving detail many aspects of Indian culture.) The fiction of Kipling, for Said, does not dramatise any fundamental conflict 'because Kipling would never face one'; for Kipling '*there was no conflict*'. For Kipling, India's best destiny was to be ruled by England. Kipling respected all divisions in Indian so-ciety, was untroubled by them, and neither he nor his characters ever interfered with them. By the late nineteenth century there were, Said says, sixty-one levels of status in India and the love–hate relationship between British and Indians 'derived from the complex hierarchical attitudes present in both peoples'.

Of all the people who shared in the scramble for empire, Joseph Conrad became known for turning his back on the dark continent of 'overflowing riches'. After years as a sailor in different merchant navies, Conrad removed himself to the sedentary life of writing fiction. His best-known books, *Lord Jim*, *Heart of Darkness*, *Nostromo* and *The Secret Agent* (1907), draw on ideas from Darwin, Nietzsche and Max Nordau (about degeneration) to explore the great fault-line between scientific, liberal and technical optimism in the twentieth century and pessimism about human nature.

Christened Józef Teodor Konrad Korzeniowski, he was born in 1857 in a part of Poland taken by the Russians in the 1793 partition of that often-dismembered country (his birthplace is now in Ukraine). His father, Apollo, was an aristocrat without lands, the family estates sequestered in 1839 following an anti-Russian rebellion. Orphaned before he was twelve, Conrad depended very much on the generosity of his maternal uncle Tadeusz. Sometime before Tadeusz died, Józef stopped off in Brussels on the way to Poland, to be interviewed for a post with the Société Anonyme Belge pour le Commerce du Haut-Congo – a fateful interview which led to his experiences between June and December 1890 in the Belgian Congo and, ten years on, to *Heart of Darkness*.

In that decade, the Congo lurked in his mind, awaiting a trigger to be formulated in prose. That was provided by the shocking revelations of the 'Benin Massacres' in 1897, as well as the accounts of Henry Morton Stanley's expeditions in Africa. *Benin: The City of Blood*, by Sir Reginald Hugh Bacon, a naval officer, was published in London and New York in 1897, revealing to the Western civilised world a horror story of native African blood rites. After the Berlin Conference of 1884 (a meeting of fourteen nations called to regulate and partition Africa among those nations), Britain proclaimed a protectorate over the Niger River region. Following the slaughter of a British mission to Benin (now a city of Nigeria), which arrived during King Duboar's celebrations of his ancestors with ritual sacrifices, a punitive expedition was dispatched to capture this city. The account of Commander Bacon, intelligence officer of the expedition, in some of its details parallels events in *Heart of Darkness*. When Bacon reached Benin, he saw what, despite his vivid language, he says lay beyond description: 'It is useless to continue describing the horrors of the place, everywhere death, barbarity and blood, and smells that it hardly seems right for human beings to smell and yet live.' Conrad avoids definition of what constituted 'The horror. The horror' – the famous last words in the book, spoken by Kurtz, the man Marlow, the hero, has come to save – opting instead for hints such as round balls on posts that Marlow thinks he sees through his field glasses when approaching Kurtz's compound. Bacon, for his part, describes 'crucifixion trees' surrounded by piles of skulls and bones, blood smeared everywhere, over bronze idols and ivory.

Conrad's purpose, however, is not to elicit the typical response of the civilised world to reports of barbarism. In his account Commander Bacon had exemplified this attitude: 'They [the natives] cannot fail to see that peace and the good rule of the white man mean happiness, contentment and security.' Similar sentiments are expressed in the report which Kurtz composes for the International Society for the Suppression of Savage Customs. Marlow describes this 'beautiful piece of writing', 'vibrating with eloquence'. And yet, scrawled 'at the end of that moving appeal to every altruistic sentiment it blazed at you, luminous and terrifying, like a flash of lightning in a serene sky: "Exterminate all the brutes!"'

This savagery at the heart of civilised humans is also revealed in the behaviour of the white traders – 'pilgrims' as Marlow calls them. White travellers' tales, like those of Stanley in 'darkest Africa', written from an unquestioned sense of the superiority of the European over the native, were available to Conrad. *Heart of Darkness* thrives upon the ironic reversals of civilisation and barbarity, of light and darkness. Here is a characteristic Stanley episode, recorded in his diary. Needing food, he told a group of natives that 'I must have it or we would die. They must sell it for beads, red, blue or green, copper or brass wire or shells, or ... I drew significant signs across the throat. It was enough, they understood at once.' In *Heart of Darkness*, by contrast, Marlow is impressed by the extraordinary restraint of the starving cannibals accompanying the expedition, who have been paid in bits of brass wire, but have no food, their rotting hippo flesh – too nauseating a smell for European endurance – having been thrown overboard. He wonders why 'they didn't go for us – they were thirty to five – and have a good tuck-in for once'.[24]

At the time *Heart of Darkness* appeared there was – and there continues to be – a distaste for Conrad on the part of some readers. It is that very reaction which underlines his significance. This is perhaps best explained by Richard Curle, author of the first full-length study of Conrad, published in 1914. Curle could see that for many people there is a tenacious need to believe that the world, horrible as it might be, can be put right by human effort and the appropriate brand of liberal philosophy. Unlike the novels of his contemporaries, H. G. Wells and John Galsworthy, Conrad derides this point of view as an illusion at best, and the pathway to desperate destruction at worst.[25] Evidence shows that Conrad was sickened by his experience in Africa, both physically and psychologically, and was deeply alienated from the imperialist, racist exploiters of Africa and Africans at that time. *Heart of Darkness* played a part in ending the Belgian king Leopold's tyranny (1885–1908) in the Congo.

The Intellectual Aristocracy

Although Conrad, who didn't speak accomplished English until he was in his twenties, turned into a master stylist, and corresponded with the likes of John Galsworthy and Bertrand Russell, he remained in essence an outsider. In 1955 Noel Annan, then a fellow of King's College, Cambridge, where he would later become provost, published a fascinating paper on Victorian *insiders*, in a collection dedicated to George Macaulay Trevelyan, the most honoured – and most widely read – historian of the day. Trevelyan's middle name was the clue to Annan's article, for he was Thomas Babington Macaulay's great-nephew, and Annan's paper, entitled 'The Intellectual Aristocracy', was a tour de force, examining – over forty-five pages, in fulsome detail – no fewer than 470 Britons, each of whom had a distinguished career in the intellectual field, and who all belonged to a few families in Britain distinguished by their imaginative accomplishments. The phrase 'intellectual aristocracy' is often used quite loosely, to indicate the most intelligent or educated in this or that locality, but Annan meant more than that, much more.

His was a quite brilliant piece of sleuthing. By 'intellectual aristocrats', he meant and identified that there was in Britain in the late nineteenth and early twentieth centuries a raft of families whose intermarriages provided the candidates for a whole range of elevated rankings in society, not only such positions as masters of university colleges, professors, fellows of the Royal Society, Royal Academy or

All Souls, newspaper editors, publishers, bishops and archbishops, and senior civil servants in London or India, but authors – novelists, historians and biographers, often of people they knew or were related to – mathematical wranglers at Cambridge, explorers, museum directors, inventors, directors of the Bank of England, Poets Laureate, members of Parliament, presidents of this or that professional body, Astronomers Royal, civil service examiners, governors of colonies, judges, headmasters and headmistresses, missionaries, senior BBC personnel, generals and admirals.

More even than that, Annan's sleuthing in the *Dictionary of National Biography*, which we shall come back to, and other journals, revealed the exact extent to which many of these individuals came from the same families, families which in many cases intermarried. They shared similar family backgrounds, often knew each other quite well and formed a coherent segment or category of British society, all of which meant that, at that time, the turn of the twentieth century, Britain could boast (if that is the right word) a series of what we might call 'intellectual superfamilies', an entire sociological class that did indeed form an intellectual aristocracy.[1]

The Quaker families – the Gurneys, Frys, Gaskells, Hoares, Hodgkins, Foxes and Barclays – had married and intermarried in the eighteenth century.[2] In the nineteenth, the Wedgwoods and the Darwins were well known for intermarrying (the 'Darwoods'), as were the Trevelyans and the Stracheys. The Macaulays, Babingtons and Conybeares were also linked, and were also linked to the Darwins, the Huxleys and the Arnolds, with the Darwins being even further linked to the Keyneses.

We may begin with Walter Bagehot (1826–77), a journalist and political commentator, an authority on the British constitution and on the money markets. The son of a banker, he was one of the first distinguished graduates of the new University College, London, and one of the founders, in 1855, of the *National Review*, a quarterly magazine which published one of the first assessments of Darwin's *Origin*. In 1858 Bagehot married Elizabeth Wilson, whose father, James, had been sent to India in the wake of the 'Sepoy Mutiny' of 1857, to help stabilise the economy. Earlier, in 1843, James Wilson had founded *The Economist* magazine, first intended to gather support for the abolition of the corn laws, though its impressive prospectus went much further, urging free-trade principles overall, reporting on practical improvements in agriculture, explaining the principle of political economy (which, as we have seen, was *the* main concern in the nineteenth century), and publishing general news from the Court of St James's, reports from the colonies, law reports and book reviews. Its success may be judged from the fact that it exists to this day with a worldwide circulation of some 1.6 million. Subsequent to his marriage to Elizabeth, Bagehot became editor of *The Economist* and remained there for seventeen years. He made the magazine a success among the educated establishment, but he was known also for two other works, *The English Constitution* (1867) and *Lombard Street: A Description of the Money Market* (1873). Bagehot's main point about the famously 'unwritten' constitution of Britain was that it contains two main elements: it is not so much a system of 'checks and balances', as people often talk about other constitutions (such as the American), but instead, the British constitution is divided into the 'dignified parts' and the 'efficient parts', where the former, in his words, 'excite and preserve the reverence of the population', while the latter are 'those by which it, in fact, works and rules'. He was, in essence, explaining the stabilising appeal of a constitutional monarchy. He thought that the mystique and pageantry of the monarchy was a sort of 'disguise' that fortified the government, and he did not think that democracy needed any more 'development'. *Lombard Street* was possibly the first attempt to describe for a general readership the workings of the Bank of England as a lender of last resort.[3]

Despite the thrust of his books, to explain the workings of the central elements in Britain's political economy, Bagehot was himself an elitist. In the third of his works, *Physics and Politics*, he outlined his theory of civilisation, that civilisations begin in conformism and military power and only later can they proceed towards modern liberalism. In the process he distinguished between the 'rude man' and the 'accomplished man', the latter of which he believed resulted from 'iterative inheritances' by means of which generations became increasingly refined. In effect, this is the process that led to an intellectual aristocracy.

THE RECEDING TIDE OF FAITH

Everyone knows that Matthew Arnold's father, Dr Thomas Arnold, was the celebrated headmaster of Rugby School, and the subject of Thomas Hughes's 1857 novel, *Tom Brown's Schooldays*, describing a generation of boys 'who feared the doctor with all our hearts'. What is rather less well known is that the son was related by marriage to the Huxleys, the Trevelyans and the Macaulays. He was hardly less elitist than Bagehot, notoriously labelling Britain's entire middle class as 'philistine'.

Matthew Arnold grew up in the Lake District, where Wordsworth was a neighbour, and later a strong literary influence. At Balliol College, Oxford, Arnold befriended his fellow poet Arthur Hugh Clough, devoted assistant to his wife's cousin, Florence Nightingale. In 1843 Arnold won the Newdigate Prize for poetry, for his ode *Cromwell*. But he did little else at Oxford – his brother later wrote, 'He read a little with the reading men, hunted a little with the fast men, and dressed a little with the dressy men.'* A noted Francophile (George Sand being one of his friends), we may say that there were five aspects to his full life. After a short spell as a master at Rugby, he went back to Oxford, to Oriel, where his father had studied and where John Henry Newman (later a Roman Catholic cardinal), another influence on his life, had also been a fellow. Then, in 1847 Arnold became personal secretary to Lord Lansdowne, a leading Whig, which brought him into London fashionable society where he was able to begin to shine and discover himself, and he fell in love for the first time, this apparently giving rise to his first attempts at poetry.

Arnold would write most of his verse in the early part of his life. In some quarters he is regarded as one of the three great Victorian poets, alongside Tennyson and Robert Browning, and this was underlined, to an extent, when he was appointed professor of poetry at Oxford in 1857, though his reputation as a poet (if not as a critic) has fallen since. His most remembered works are *The Scholar-Gipsy* and *Dover Beach*. The first, based on an earlier narrative by a seventeenth-century cleric, tells the story of a student who leaves Oxford and joins a band of gipsies and learns the secrets by which they live. *Dover Beach* (1851) likens the image of the receding tide on the beach to the withdrawing of the 'sea of faith' throughout the nineteenth century, and the new predicament of human life in a godless world.[5]

> And we are here as on a darkling plain
> Swept with confused alarms of struggle and flight,
> When ignorant armies clash by night.

Stanzas from the Grande Chartreuse, written a year later, also confronts the possibility of 'ever again inhabiting an animating faith' in the way available in earlier ages:

> Wandering between two worlds, one dead,
> The other powerless to be born.

AN ATTACK ON BRITISH PAROCHIALISM

Arnold worked as a school inspector for thirty-five years. One result of this was that he spent a lot of time on the newly installed railways, time at railway stations waiting to make his connections, many nights in small hotels. Which meant that he knew Britain close up better than any other man of letters. At that time there were no state schools at any level, but rather a collection of privately run establishments of different kinds. The position required him to act as examiner, a task he described as drudgery.

But Arnold is most remembered today as a literary, social and religious critic. He was a firm advocate of the place of literature in modern life, and of the classics, one of his best-known comments being that criticism is 'the disinterested endeavour to learn and propagate the best that is known and thought in the world'. He wanted to see critical standards given a 'cultural centrality' and to do this, he felt that British works needed to be considered and compared with the best available on the continent and, above all, with the ancient classics.

On the more social level he foresaw the difficulties that would arise with the growth of democracy, and the problem of sustaining cultural activities which had traditionally been supported by a wealthy and leisured aristocracy. He felt that what he regarded as a complacent British attitude to the 'practical man' operated against a vigorous cultural life. This was the basic argument in *Culture and Anarchy* (1869), his work which is most read today, an attack on British parochialism, in which he labelled the aristocracy 'Barbarians', the middle class the 'Philistines' and the working class the 'Populace'. He felt that for there to be full human flourishing two elements needed to be combined – Hellenism and Hebraism. 'The governing idea of Hellenism is *spontaneity of consciousness*; that of Hebraism, *strictness of conscience.*' As someone who was severe on the 'deforming power of inequality', and who felt that the 'most animating event in history' was the French Revolution, he was essentially against what he saw as British narrowness.[6]

If all this makes him sound deadly serious, it is worth adding that Arnold was as good a listener as he was talker, that he was a great phrase maker (Oxford as a city of 'dreaming spires' and the 'home of lost causes'), and that *Friendship's Garland*, a series of satirical articles put together in a Voltairean style (France again), in which Britain is seen from the point of view of a German baron, evens the balance. He felt that the dogmatism of many Nonconformists was outmoded and had put many people off the church, though he remained convinced of the value of the Anglican variety, which he described as 'a *reasonable* Establishment'. He thought that the word 'God' was a form of poetry, that the idea of God was as 'a consciousness of the not ourselves'. Essentially, he thought that high ideals, culture – classical culture most of all – and religion were united in offering spiritual consolation. In the new nineteenth-century world of science, democracy and doubt, consolation is a constant reference point.

Francis Galton's constant reference point was measurement. He had a passion for mathematics and a fervent interest in counting and comparing one thing, statistically, with another. At one point in his career, he had come across some African women with extremely large breasts and had devised a method for estimating the size of their chests by triangulation. On another occasion he became fascinated by the frequency with which people were fidgeting, and published the results.

Born in Birmingham in 1822, his mother was one of several daughters of Erasmus Darwin, making him Charles's cousin. At Cambridge he seems to have had much the same sort of time as Matthew Arnold had at Oxford – reading parties, boating parties, drinking parties – and he only scraped a 'pass' degree.[7]

So far, so very little. But 'being much upset and craving for a healthier life', Galton now chose to travel.[8] He went first to the Middle East and learned Arabic, followed by a journey of exploration to south-west Africa. He produced two books as a result, *Tropical South Africa* (1852) and *The Art of Travel* (1855). The first title was rewarded with a gold medal from the Royal Geographical Society, a fellowship of the Royal Society and an invitation to become a member of the Athenaeum, which had been founded in 1824 as a club for scientists, engineers, literary figures and artists. Settling in London, Galton began to play a part in scientific administration, fulfilling active roles in the Royal Society, the Royal Geographical Society and the British Association for the Advancement of Science.

He was interested in meteorology and in fingerprints, establishing that the pattern of a person's fingerprints did not change over a lifetime and devising a taxonomic system by which they could be analysed and catalogued. But his main interest, which seems to have stemmed from the publication of *On the Origin of Species* by his cousin, was heredity and how it affected human psychology, notably character. His first publication here was *Hereditary Talent and Character* (1865), in which he embarked on a statistical study of the entries in biographical dictionaries, with the aim of discovering the frequency with which eminent people were related to other eminent people and also inquiring into how often eminent people appeared from average or 'undistinguished' families. His methods were fairly crude, certainly by modern standards, and he found that talented children did tend to occur in eminent families more frequently than in average families, from which he concluded that, if we could so arrange things, as horses and cattle were carefully matched to create faster animals, or better yielders of milk, then we should be able to create 'a galaxy of genius' where human beings are concerned.[9]

Although his method with the biographical dictionaries was crude, he did embrace more rigorous empirical studies, looking at inheritance patterns in sweet peas (ironically, the same plant used by Gregor Mendel in his famous experiments). Galton made two discoveries, one being the rate of variation falling into a normal curve, now known as the 'bell curve', the other being rudimentary laws of probability. In another case, he installed what he called an 'anthropometric laboratory' at the South Kensington Museum, a forerunner of today's Science Museum which had been founded in 1857 with samples of those exhibits left over from the Great Exhibition of 1851 and surplus machines from the Patents Office. Galton's laboratory was equipped with instruments which allowed various measurements to be taken (height, weight, chest span, head size, arm length, hearing, visual acuity and colour sense).[10]

This enabled new mathematical approaches to be worked out, helping to produce the idea of what would come to be called correlation, but in the longer run would lead back to Galton's idea that the understanding of human genetics would engender schemes for improving the 'stock', as he put it, 'to give the more suitable races or strains of blood a better chance of prevailing speedily over the less suitable'. On the basis of this, towards the end of his life, Galton devoted himself to promoting a political programme that he called 'eugenics', which he arrived at from the Greek roots for 'beautiful/happy' and 'heredity'. What he envisaged was for a scheme of positive eugenics, not only encouraging intelligent people to marry each other but to find which diseases were hereditary so as to eliminate them. Many people who followed him, however, dwelled on negative eugenics, which for some involved even sterilising those deemed 'unfit'.

Galton was knighted in 1909 and received the Copley Medal from the Royal Society a year later, two awards which reflect the success of his career. However, some of the institutions that bore his name in his honour have removed it in recent years as eugenics has come to be looked on increasingly negatively.[11]

George Bernard Shaw, part-time acerbic music critic, had fingers in many pies. One of them was the London School of Economics, which he helped to found in 1895, together with Beatrice and Sidney Webb and Graham Wallas, a social psychologist much taken with the nature/nurture debate. Beatrice Potter, a Gloucester girl, from a family of nine sisters (and a solitary brother), was born to wealth, her father having inherited a fortune, lost it and remade it in timber during the Crimean War – at least that is what she tells us in her diary/memoir, which she kept assiduously throughout her life. In 1889 she read a series of essays, *Fabian Essays on Socialism*, edited by Shaw, and was most impressed by one of the contributions written by Sidney Webb. The Fabian Society had been established not long before, in 1884, as a socialist organisation but one dedicated to gradual reform rather than revolutionary activity.

Sidney Webb was the son of a rate collector and a sergeant in the volunteers, with one live-in servant, not as opulent as Beatrice's background but comfortable enough. He was a fiery intellectual but with worldly experience both in the civil service and abroad, mainly in Germany, and, like Marx, bloated through prodigious reading in the British Museum and London Library.[12] But Sidney, too, had an evangelical ethical sense, which led him to gradualism in social reform.

Despite Beatrice being interested in Sidney's writings, the pair were not obviously well matched. As she wrote in her diary, 'His tiny tadpole body, his unhealthy skin, cockney pronunciation, poverty, are all against him.' But they had much in common intellectually: both were interested in the creation of a science of society, then so much in fashion and, on his recommendation, Beatrice joined the Fabians. After some initial difficulty over sex – Beatrice not being physically attracted to the tadpole – they settled down together, agreeing to try to live on the £1,000 annual legacy Beatrice had, so that Sidney could devote himself full-time to writing and public work.[13]

The idea for the LSE arose when a wealthy Fabian member, H. H. Hutchinson, left the society a healthy legacy, intended to be used for socialist propaganda. Sidney suggested the funds be used instead to create a school of economics in London. He had recently visited the Massachusetts Institute of Technology in Boston and knew from his earlier travels about the École Libre de Sciences Politiques

('Sciences-Po') in Paris and thought London could benefit from a research-based institution specialising in social science and public administration. His view was that the ancient universities 'had been enervated by the divorce of thought from action'.

Lectures began in October 1895 with vocational courses such as 'railway economics', abhorred by Oxbridge but a speciality at the LSE. The school's first director was W. S. Hewins, a Conservative politician, a friend of Joseph Chamberlain and a copious contributor to the *Encyclopaedia Britannica* and the *Dictionary of National Biography*, who was enticed from Oxford. He clearly set out the range of the school's disciplines: economics, statistics, commerce, banking, finance, commercial law, political science, public administration. The LSE was formed just in time to join London University, which came into being in 1900.[14]

THE GRANDFATHERS OF SOFTWARE

John Stuart Mill could be said to have had the most illustrious childhood of all time (see Chapter 18), but much the same could be said of Bertrand Russell. Mill was his godfather, but Russell was in any case the child of Viscount and Viscountess Amberley, prominent in the social issues of the day, such as feminism and birth control.

Russell is shown in Augustus John's portrait to have had piercingly sceptical eyes, quizzical eyebrows and a fastidious mouth. He was born halfway through the reign of Victoria, in 1872, and died nearly a century later, by which time, for him as for many others, nuclear weapons were the greatest threat to mankind. He once wrote that 'the search for knowledge, unbearable pity for suffering and a longing for love' were the three passions that governed his life.

At Cambridge, Russell attended Trinity College, where he sat for a scholarship. When he read for the mathematical Tripos, the special Cambridge degree, whose origins are said to lie in the 'Tripod' medieval pupils sat on when sitting their exams, Russell graduated as seventh wrangler. Russell was exhausted by his finals, so much so that he sold all his mathematics books and turned with relief to philosophy. He said later he saw philosophy as a sort of no-man's-land between science and theology. Russell's biographer also tells us that he was never entirely at home in the company of professional mathematicians – they were too 'narrow and uncultured'.[15] In Cambridge he developed wide interests, politics being one of those interests, the socialism of Karl Marx in particular. The two people he really warmed to at Cambridge were, first, Alfred North Whitehead, who *was* a mathematician but was a 'loner' with a love of classical literature, and whose course on statics Russell took. The second was George Moore, a moral philosopher who Russell thought looked like 'Newton and Satan rolled into one'.[16] They got to know each other well because each had been accepted as Apostles.

The Apostles were an elite discussion group. Formally known as the Cambridge Conversazione Society, generally six or seven strong, they met on Saturday nights for discussion when no holds would be barred. It was regarded as a deep honour to be invited and for those involved it was, in Ray Monk's words, 'the most important part of their undergraduate lives'. It went back to the 1820s, when members included Tennyson and his fellow poet Arthur Hallam.

Russell stood several times for Parliament, but was never elected. He championed Soviet Russia, won the Nobel Prize in Literature in 1950, and appeared (sometimes to his irritation) as a character in at least six works of fiction. When Russell died in 1970 at the age of ninety-seven, there were more than sixty of his books still in print. But of all his books the most original was the massive tome that appeared first in 1910, entitled, after a similar work by Isaac Newton, *Principia Mathematica*. This book is one of the least read of all time. In the first place, it is about mathematics, not everyone's favourite reading. Second, it is inordinately long – three volumes running to more than 2,000 pages. But it was the third reason which ensured that this book – which indirectly led to the birth of the computer – was read by only a very few people: it consists mostly of a tightly knit argument expressed not in everyday language but by means of a specially invented set of symbols. Thus, 'not' is represented by a curved bar; a boldface v stands for 'or'; a square dot means 'and'; while other logical relationships are shown by devices such as a U on its side ($\supset$) for 'implies' and a three-barred equals sign ($\equiv$) for 'is equivalent to'. The book's aim was nothing less than to explain the logical foundations of mathematics.[17]

The collaboration between Russell and Whitehead was a monumental affair. As well as tackling the very foundations of mathematics, they were building on the work of Giuseppe Peano, professor of mathematics at Turin University, who had recently composed a new set of symbols designed to extend existing algebra and explore a greater range of logical relationships than had hitherto been specifiable. In 1900 Whitehead thought the project with Russell would take a year. In fact, it took ten. Whitehead, by general consent, was the cleverer mathematician; he thought up the structure of the book and designed most of the symbols. But it was Russell who spent between seven and ten hours a day, six days a week, working on it.

General reviews were flattering, the *Spectator* concluding that the book marked 'an epoch in the history of speculative thought' in the attempt to make mathematics 'more solid' than the universe itself. However, only 320 copies had been sold by the end of 1911. The reaction of colleagues abroad and at home was one of awe rather than enthusiasm.[18]

Nevertheless, Russell and Whitehead had discovered something important: that most mathematics – if not all of it – could be derived from a number of axioms logically related to each other. This boost for mathematical logic may have been their most important legacy, inspiring such figures as Alan Turing and John van Neumann, mathematicians who, in the 1930s and 1940s, conceived the early computers. In this sense, Russell and Whitehead are the grandfathers of software.

A Learned Empire:
A 'Higher Purpose' for Britain

Rather more successful than *Principia Mathematica*, at least commercially, was David Livingstone's *Missionary Travels and Researches in South Africa*, his account of his journey along the Zambezi. Published in 1857, it sold 70,000 copies when anything over 10,000 was considered a best-seller.[1] Livingstone, William Wilberforce and Charles Gordon were all hero-worshipped for their work against the slave trade, and in fact, as John Mackenzie puts it, 'Livingstone and General Gordon were essentially religious figures, presented as moral titans facing dark forces which martyred them in a Christ-like sacrifice'.[2] In general the explorers were larger-than-life individuals who, because they were in far-off places, for months or even years on end, had no choice but to get along with indigenous peoples and, for the most part, returned – if they did return – with mouthwatering stories. (Livingstone, in particular, despite his 'erratic judgement', was devoid of racial feeling, promoted Africans as evangelists, was a staunch advocate of 'native agency', learned to speak Setswana, and was completely untouched by the pseudo-science of Victorian anthropology. He was convinced he was a 'favoured instrument of providence'. In his imagination, he thought that even the industrial revolution was part of a divine plan.[3])

IMPERIALISM: THE RULE OF THE ROAD

Exploration is a good way into Britain's nineteenth-century empire because, at the start of the era, it stood alongside France, Russia, the Chinese and the Turkish empires as more or less equal great states, and because, by the late eighteenth century, exploration was, in Robert Stafford's words, 'a self-imposed expectation of the Great Powers ... the Enlightenment's voracious appetite for facts provided a powerful stimulus to discovery.' As we settle into this chapter, it is worth taking on board the words of John Darwin, arguably the greatest contemporary British historian of empire: 'Empire (where different ethnic communities fall under a common ruler) has been the default mode of political organization throughout most of history. Imperial power has usually been the rule of the road.'[4] The difference was that the power and confidence bequeathed to Britain by industrialisation helped to promote scientific curiosity and intellectual inventiveness, which spilled over into constitutional and political institutions that, in the event, were available to few others, at least then.

Of course, with the arrival of steam and electrical power, and new developments in metallurgy and chemistry, new ways of coercion and movement also evolved. With that went a sense of confidence in many parts of British society about the country's place in the world and that one of the objectives of empire was for Britain 'to afford the peoples of the world the opportunity of becoming partakers of that civilization, that commerce, that knowledge, that faith which it has pleased a gracious Providence to bless our own country'.[5]

The Victorians regarded themselves as the leaders of civilisation, sure of their ability to improve the human condition everywhere, expansion by free trade not just a necessity but a moral duty to the rest of humanity.[6] That humanity was divided into a hierarchy, according to the proven capacity of each people or nation for freedom and enterprise, with the British at the top, the Americans and other 'striving go-ahead' Anglo-Saxons a few rungs below, then the Latins, with much lower down the 'vast Oriental communities of Asia and north Africa where progress appeared unfortunately to have been crushed for centuries by military despotisms or smothered under passive religions'.[7] As Richard Drayton dryly put it, 'What distinguishes British imperialism from the late eighteenth century onwards, is this faith in its capacity and right to increase the happiness of barbarians ... Empire was now a process of preparing the rest of the world to become fully human.'[8] We have been here before, of course, with William Petty trying to improve £25 Irish and black people into £75 Englishmen. (It should be said that not everyone shared this view – Richard Cobden, a Manchester manufacturer of textile prints but also a radical politician, opposed the holding of colonies and criticised Britain's role in India as 'a career of spoliation and wrong'.[9])

The new means of coercion and movement were, of course, in themselves intellectual achievements, some of which are considered in separate chapters in this book. Coercion lies in the everyday background of empire and is a story all to itself. However, as Andrew Porter has pointed out, many people besides the British benefited from the British Empire, and this chapter will attempt to go beyond its coercive policies, always granting that for some of the descendants of its victims that is difficult to do.

It is also relevant to preface the next section by pointing out that, difficult as it may be to believe in our strident times, the doctrine of imperialism did not lose its 'respectability' until the period between the two twentieth-century world wars – 1918–39. While empire could never have existed or endured without (explicit or implicit) coercion, coercion is not the whole story.

A LEARNED EMPIRE

One of the greatest intellectual achievements of empire, or more accurately the spread of empire, in the nineteenth century, was that it made the seas safe to travel, no small accomplishment. The Admiralty's Hydrographic Department had been created in 1795 and between then and 1830 a largely maritime coastal reconnaissance, together with a parallel French input, was carried out as part of specific scientific explorations.[10] The assigning of naturalists to naval surveying expeditions also meant that the Royal Navy became an important link in a worldwide network of plant transfers that stretched from the Caribbean and Central America to the Pacific and south-east Asia.[11] Uprooted from their natural habitats, these plants were 'improved' by specialists. The knowledge of indigenous peoples was often used in these operations so that in many places a unique science – an 'imperial synthesis culture' – emerged, particularly in medicine.

In 1830 the Royal Geographical Society (RGS) was founded in London by a group whose leader was John Barrow, a geologist interested in China and a fluent Chinese speaker. The RGS was essentially an outgrowth of the Africa Society, founded by Joseph Banks in 1788 to promote the exploration of Africa and other areas. The Raleigh Club, formed by supporters of exploration who seceded from the Travellers' Club (1826), had similar aims, as did parallel organisations set up in Paris (1821) and Berlin (1828).

The memoirs of the time are full of the language of national expansion and, more than that, assumptions of moral and technological superiority over other peoples, part of an overall natural theology that saw such superiority as part of a *design* that sanctioned the 'right and duty to act at will to bring about' betterment. Under natural theology, plants, animals and everything in nature had been placed where they were by God 'for the use and instruction of human beings'.[12] Science – quantification and classification – were ways to 'improvement', the eighteenth-century mantra by now familiar to all.

An added element was that it was now seen as necessary to open up areas of Africa to provide opportunities for trade in order to fill the commercial vacuum that had been left 'fallow' by the abolition of the Atlantic trade in 1807.[13] One effect was that even humanitarians thought that the expansion of empire among Africa's former slave-trading tribes was morally justified.

At the RGS, Sir Joseph Banks's leadership role, and his aim of a 'learned empire', was taken over by Sir Roderick Murchison, a Scottish geologist, who aggressively promoted a series of scientific initiatives which continued Banks's mission to 'reconstruct' the empire after defeat by the United States. Murchison envisaged the gradual establishment of geological surveys, botanical gardens, natural history museums and universities across the empire, sending information back to the 'centre of calculation' in London.[14] Not all other scientists – Darwin, Lyell, Huxley, Wallace – were in agreement with Murchison's domineering approach, but it has to be said that his initiatives coincided with the peak of Victorian prosperity, so that many of his schemes came off and by the late 1880s, save for the poles, as Banks put it, 'there were no more worlds to conquer'. The RGS published a booklet, *Hints for Travellers* (1854), which soon became famous, showing how to be an (amateur) scientist abroad: for example, how to use a sextant, how to use a watch to fix time and the heights of mountains, and so on.

In India the Great Trigonometrical Survey, founded in 1818, and Geological Survey (1851) identified the subcontinent's geological structure, its mineral resources and geographical contours. Much of the work was done by 'pundits', native Indian officers who contributed an extraordinary (and extraordinarily successful) series of secret operations which produced much practical information for the government of the country, which the Indians themselves had never, or rarely, carried out, but these surveys also explored the details of the 'no-man's-land' between British-controlled and Russian-controlled territory. The Calcutta Botanical Gardens were established in 1786 and the Bombay Forest Department in 1847.[15]

Over the years, says Robert Stafford, an 'official mind' emerged in regard to empire that was an amalgam of the Christian belief that natural resources exist to be employed for man's improvement with the new notion that it was now within Europeans' power to remake the world, by the development of a civilising mission, whose aim was to improve native societies 'along rational lines'.[16] Explorers were usually against outright annexation, but instead settled for trading, settler and missionary activity.

Fundamentally, however sympathetic explorers might be to the indigenous people they encountered, the disparity in their situations and technological status could not be avoided altogether. The differences in technological, geological and taxonomic knowledge were stark and because of that a sense of superiority on the part of Europeans was hard to avoid. As Stafford says, there was always in the explorer encounter a mix of 'brass instruments' (both scientific instruments and gifts), assumptions of white superiority, moral high-mindedness and commercial perspective. Mapping the world, not just the seas, was a principal accomplishment of nineteenth-century European civilisation. Bacon's ideal of power and knowledge had never been more exactly realised. Some people were more uncomfortable with this than others. As, to an extent, is still true.

But it is also necessary to add that, by the 1840s, humanitarianism had come to occupy a central role in Britain's imperial identity, especially so in India. One reason for this was the corrupt and self-interested behaviour of the East India Company (EIC), which had come under attack at least from the time of Edmund Burke and would eventually see the administration of India being taken out of its hands by the government.

The humanitarian movement began not with a concern for the EIC but with a Christian anxiety about India's 'decadence and depravity', and the worry that it was a 'country of heathens'.[17] Christian evangelicals – and evangelism was prominent in Britain throughout the nineteenth century, but especially so in the first half – argued that the political change which many in government felt was needed in India, to modernise its administration, could not come about without moral reform. Allied to the belief in a Providential role for Britain, this meant, among other things, the bringing of Christianity to India.

The humanitarians were, in general, disappointed with the practical results of the abolition of slavery – others, as could have been foreseen, soon took up the trade. But humanitarians did form part of the objection to white planters receiving compensation for the 'loss' of their slaves. This was not entirely wise. In many parts of the West Indies in the 1830s, for example, it had become virtually impossible in jury trials to obtain convictions for whites for crimes against blacks, very much as was to happen in the United States later on.[18] Such was the strength of racial feeling in the West Indies that colonial revolt appeared a real prospect, and if that were to happen the assumption of direct rule might provoke violence, break the imperial tie and so 'remove the basis for intervention'.

The evangelical humanitarians didn't like it, but they had to wear it. And, in buying off the West Indian plantation owners, and developing an 'apprentice' scheme to replace slavery, the British government prevented its colonies becoming what the southern states of the USA would become in the century ahead – riven by racial conflict.

The difference between humanitarian ambition and achievement was larger than most hoped for and there were setbacks. The greater efficiency of free over slave labour (a doctrine current since at least Adam Smith) was not borne out by the Caribbean colonies' experience, the terms available to free labour usually being unattractive. It will be recalled that Elizabeth Browning's father couldn't make a go of his plantation after slavery was abolished (see Chapter 18).[19] The humanitarians' position was also weakened by material decline in the West Indies, the small number of missionary converts, the unwillingness of indigenous communities to absorb British ideas of commercial habits, and by the occasionally violent rejection of British ways such as the 1857 Indian Mutiny, the Maori Wars and the Morant Bay Rebellion. The disappointment spread, as ideas about 'insurmountable racial and cultural differences' acted on even the most compassionate, causing them to lower their sights, so that equal rights increasingly seemed unrealistic.[20]

A Providential Plan

Nonetheless, Providentialism remained strong right up until the turn of the twentieth century. In the early nineteenth, many in the United Kingdom believed that Imperial Britain had been called by God to Christianise India and in line with this in 1813, Parliament opened India to missionary initiatives but also provided an established church for the subcontinent, which formed part of the Church of England.[21] Belief in the divine governance of the world led many to a conviction (real but also convenient) that the British Empire, like other great empires in the past, formed part of a Providential plan for the world. 'The spread of British trade, the conquests by British arms, the migration of British settlers, must reflect a higher purpose.'[22] David Livingstone was just one who believed his career, and in fact the entire industrial revolution, were part of a divine plan. But then, from the 1870s on, 'it became increasingly clear that India would not become Christian'. As a result, some began to reconceptualise the Providential purpose behind the Indian Empire, 'suggesting that the purpose might be to promote dialogue and understanding between the religions of the East and West' and in this way, still, encourage moral reform movements in Hinduism or Islam. Again, convenient.

MISSIONARY PEOPLES

For many Christians, the sheer vastness, the very great diversity and extraordinary success of the expansion of empire surely indicated that it was not shaped by human hands or intention and that its ultimate ends went beyond what its human endeavours appeared to anticipate. The fact that this had all occurred in the few decades since the tumults of the French Revolution was not without significance either, so that as part of the general Providence governing the world, some nations were selected by God to be 'missionary peoples', for the global spread of divine truths.[23]

Many, especially those in the East India Company, opposed the missionary activities, believing they would antagonise Muslim and Hindu believers. Nonetheless, an Anglican bishops' college was established in Calcutta with money from the Society for the Propagation of the Gospel in Foreign Parts and the Society for Promoting Christian Knowledge, to educate young upper-caste Indians into Christian principles and promote the study of Indian languages and the translation of scriptures.[24] It was not a great success: opened in 1824, in 1835 it had only fifteen students. And this was the picture more generally. Although there was some progress in abolishing suttee – the suicide of widows by immolation – there was consistent, low-level violence against 'converts' and the government had to take steps to protect those in their employ. At the end of the century, the number of Christians in India was, according to one estimate, 492,752, or 0.2 per cent of the population.

Despite this, some die-hards were still speaking of 'Providence' as late as 1906. For them, the empire always had a higher purpose.

CHRISTIANITY, FREE TRADE, PROVIDENTIALISM: THE IMPERIAL TRINITY

One of the most contentious issues of empire, perhaps *the* most contentious, and obviously enough, concerns the relationship between the governors and the governed.[25] Can such an inequitable relationship ever be truly moral, or devoid of coercion, however slight or indirect? Edmund Burke recognised this. Speaking in Parliament on the West India Bill in December 1783, he delivered an eloquent statement on Britain's obligations 'as the possessor of power over other people':

> All political power which is set over men, and ... all privilege claimed ... in excursion of them, being wholly artificial and ... a derogation from the natural equality of mankind at large, ought to be some way or other exercised for their benefit. If this is true with regard to every species of political dominion, and every description of commercial privilege ... then such rights or privileges, or whatever else you choose to call them, are all in the strictest sense a *trust*; and it is of the very essence of every trust to be rendered *accountable*, and even totally to *cease*, when it substantially varies from the purpose for which alone it could have lawful existence.[26]

Burke was aware, as were others at the time, that the East India Company's government was 'one of the most corrupt and destructive tyrannies that probably ever existed', and its servants, 'the destroyers of India', should be reined in by imperial controls so that Indians 'should again enjoy what he understood as their traditional rights and freedoms'.[27]

Nonetheless, under the twin doctrines of Christianity and free trade, and the underpinning rationale of Providentialism, and given the sizeable disparity in technology and manoeuvrability, the British were able – broadly speaking – to satisfy themselves of the overall morality of imperialism. But they were well aware, certainly after the American War of Independence, that settlers in far-off colonies could easily stray from any path set down by London and, in fairly short order, 'bring the whole project into disarray and rebellion'.[28]

Moreover, from the mid-nineteenth century on, the increasingly apparent failure of humanitarian expectations in regard to 'non-European' capacity, and the developing theories of racial hierarchies, produced a growing pessimism.[29] Against all these changing circumstances, Burke's reservations loomed large, and the government was forced to imagine and devise more than one mechanism to safeguard its high moral tone. These mechanisms involved the concepts of: trusteeship, the protectorate and indirect rule.

THE EXPANSION OF HIGHER LEARNING

Just as many British people across the empire were never entirely comfortable with the implicit (and at times explicit) coercion involved in governing a subject people, so the members of that subject people were also conflicted, albeit in a different way. While they could hardly be enamoured of their overall status as 'colonials', they did on occasion realise that the occupying civilisation had some things to recommend it. A good example here is the establishment of the universities of Calcutta, Bombay and Madras in 1875, which, according to Robin Moore, was a turning point, bringing forward a modern mode of collaboration in India in particular. Between the establishment of the three universities and the end of the century, some 60,000 Indians matriculated, 'overwhelmingly in the arts' but 2,000 in law.[30] The universities were a popular innovation.

Elsewhere in the empire, much the same was happening. Two universities had been created in Canada in the eighteenth century, New Brunswick in 1785, and King's College in Halifax, Nova Scotia, in 1788. But, as in India, the nineteenth century saw the wider spread of higher education throughout the empire, especially in the dominions – three universities were established in Australia, six in New Zealand, three in South Africa and no fewer than twenty in Canada. (There were nine colleges/universities in the United States in the colonial era.)[31]

THE BENGAL RENAISSANCE AND THE 'OXFORD OF THE EAST'

In 1800 Marquess Wellesley, governor general of India, founded a training institution for British civil servants in India, known as the College of Fort William, in which he saw, as he put it, 'an Oxford of the East'.[32] Located in Calcutta, 'the capital of British India', it was the first European-created institution of higher learning in India to accept Indians as faculty members and to promote cultural exchange between Europeans and south Asians. By encouraging qualified Orientalist scholars to contribute to its educational programme, the college also transformed the famed Asiatic Society of Bengal and William Carey's Serampore Mission into extremely effective agencies for the revitalisation of an Indian culture.[33]

The establishment of the college – or at least its timing – was fortuitous. Between 1800 and 1830, in Calcutta, as David Kopf, a historian of Asia, tells us, the Bengal intellectual was 'a confused but optimistic individual striving to reconcile partially digested alien traits and unsatisfactory indigenous traditions'.[34] But through the college he could establish relationships with British civil servants, businessmen and missionaries both for profit and for use as windows to the West.

Kopf directs our attention in particular to the British 'Orientalists', who were in all ways a distinctive group, mainly of scholars with an interest in Asian languages, history and religion, and who were by nature more sympathetic to other cultures than many of their countrymen. They built on the insights of Sir William Jones and the eighteenth-century Orientalists whose works were considered earlier. Ever since Jones's time, there had been considerable interest in indigenous knowledge of nature (unlike in Australia, for instance), and the *Philosophical Transactions of the Royal Society* regularly published articles based on indigenous knowledge, such as the manufacture of maple syrup by Canadian or New England Amerindians, the tanning techniques of Virginian Amerindians, or the use of dyeing in Tonga.[35] Likewise, there was a greater interest in Indian medical remedies in the eighteenth century, leading to what one Orientalist described as a 'distinctive Anglo-Indian medical tradition'.[36]

Through the Orientalists, the college became the centre and scene of a vigorous uncovering of the Indian past by such scholars as H. T. Colebrooke, John Gilchrist and William Carey. It was the dedication of these men to the cause of Oriental learning that predisposed those Bengalis who were brought into contact with them to develop a corresponding willingness to come to terms with the very different challenges presented by late eighteenth- and nineteenth-century civilisation. The outcome constituted an important element in the early stages of what became known as the Bengali Renaissance.

The early generation of scholars at the college, after collecting a set of ancient manuscripts from around the country, discovered (or thought they had discovered) a Vedic golden age of 'classical' Hinduism (1200–600 BC), which they said was followed by a 'medieval' period of decline under the influence of a corrupt priesthood. Despite this being a model taken from analogous Protestant interpretations of European history, it proved acceptable to Bengali historians such as Rammohan Roy and the followers of Brahmo Samaj, a reformed version of spiritual Hinduism with elements of Judeo-Islamic faith. The intellectual aim overall was to provide native Bengalis – and by extension all Asians – with the means to inquire into the 'lost ancient roots' of their own indigenous civilisation.

In its heyday, the college did become a meeting place for British and Bengali scholars, dedicated to the study of Indian languages and literatures, and in this way contributed enormously to the awakening of the Bengali mind.[37] At the school, disputations were conducted in Indian languages in a central hall lined with stately columns, which helped reinforce Wellesley's initial idea of an 'Oxford of the East'.[38]

These figures for the creation of higher learning across the empire are also evidence of a wider truth, which Ronald Robinson and John Gallagher, in their book *Africa and the Victorians*, describe as a 'portentous fact', that the Victorians' most successful associations, with the exception of India, were with Europeans transplanted abroad, self-governing white communities in what came to be called the dominions, plus the United States.[39] This was not lost on the Victorians themselves and coloured their attitudes to Africa: most did not have the appetite for – or relish the cost of – an empire in the dark continent. Literally hundreds of anti-slaving treaties had been concluded with minor chiefs but replacing the slave trade did not prove easy. When the 'scramble for Africa' did come about, it took place, so far as Britain was concerned, to protect the routes to the East. It was India and the British Isles that, to the Victorians, were the twin centres of their wealth and their strength. This eventually gave rise, later in the century, to the 'two-empire' theory aired in John Seeley's *The Expansion of England* (1883), which examined, with self-righteous approval, the worldwide spread of English governance and, no less, its language.[40]

In a way Seeley resurrected an idea that had first been aired in the eighteenth century, that Britain's empire might match – maybe more than match – the old empires of Greece and Rome, that its language, literature and political and legal institutions might stretch across the world, perhaps in perpetuity, and not just as 'metaphysical empires' as people like Sheridan and Samuel Johnson had imagined. Seeley, a Regius professor at Cambridge, thought that in particular the dominions were most likely to rally to the 'mother country'. He had few scruples, seeing the British Empire as the sole survivor of a whole 'family of empires' – Dutch, Spanish, French and Portuguese – and believing that Britain had triumphed because it had not been caught up in Europe's 'struggles', and was doubly fortunate in that, in the nineteenth century, 'distance is abolished by science'. He did not think that the British were superior to the Indians, because they had an ancient civilisation; but he insisted the latter were very splintered as to racial and religious divisions and therefore did not have a formal state to equal other formal states in the world.

Britain may have occupied India, but Seeley did not agree that India had been conquered. He admitted that the British record on slavery was a 'stain' on its history, but in a short book (of fewer than 130 pages), it was his idea of a 'Greater Britain', a unified and coherent polity existing across many of the pink bits of the map, which attracted most attention. The expansion of England (England, not Britain) was unparalleled in history, he said, and left it at that.[41]

Britain as 'the Apex of Civilisation'

A s was noted in an earlier chapter, the publication of Charles Darwin's *On the Origin of Species*, though it created massive interest, did not so much create a crisis in thought as resolve it. This is because Darwin's book did not introduce the idea of evolution but instead the mechanism of natural selection by which evolution is made to work. Again, as stated before, Darwin had in a sense been 'scooped' by Robert Chambers in his book, *Vestiges of the Natural History of Creation*, published in 1844. The timing is relevant because the idea of evolution, that there might be a progressive development of species, implying perhaps a hierarchy, including that of races, was being developed at exactly the time that slavery was being abolished, and with it the justification for slavery.

Except that it was more complicated than that. In the intellectual climate of the times, many people could accept that slavery was morally indefensible, but that did not necessarily mean they accepted that races were equal. One event that brought this into focus was the Great Exhibition, held in the Crystal Palace at Hyde Park in 1851 (Livingstone, who would have fitted in so naturally, was navigating the Zambezi). This event was the brainchild of Queen Victoria's husband, the Prince Consort, who worked assiduously to make it a success. Though the queen had fallen hopelessly in love with her German cousin, the nation did not take him to its heart as much as it might have done, but in the exhibition, and in his work creating a 'knowledge quarter' in South Kensington (the Victoria &

Albert Museum, the Natural History Museum, the Science Museum, Imperial College, the Royal Albert Hall), he did have a major – and wholly beneficial – effect on Britain's imaginative and intellectual life. That year of the Great Exhibition, 1851, as George Stocking tells us in his history of Victorian anthropology, seemed to some people at least 'a precipice in time', an extraordinary chronological frontier.[1] In the exhibition, it was as if, he said, ancients and moderns were brought into 'absolute contact', as in a geological fault. Stocking was considering in particular an account by Dr William Whewell, master of Trinity College, Cambridge, and someone we have met before, who wandered through the exhibits and made a number of telling observations.

The Crystal Palace was a glorified greenhouse, Stocking says, 1,800 feet long 'and tall enough to enclose a group of Hyde Park's great elms'. Staged only a few short years after Engels had described the desperate *Condition of the Working Class in England* and Disraeli had lamented that the country was divided into 'two nations' with little sympathy between them, the exhibition had the opportunity to make a great impact.

And its greatest impact, Stocking says, which Whewell picked up on, was that not all men had advanced at the same pace, 'or arrived at the same point'.[2] Dr Whewell observed that all men shared a generic capacity for invention but then asked what distinguished the 'stationary' states of the East from the 'progressive' West, and above all Britain? In the line of exhibits from the Tasmanian 'savage' through the 'barbaric' civilisations of the East, north-west across the European continent towards an apex in Great Britain, what lessons were there to be learned?

It is a deep irony in British history that as one of its greatest achievements – converting itself from a slaving nation to an anti-slaving nation, ahead of and against most of the rest of the world – came to fruition, other events conspired to undo what should have been an intellectual triumph to cement the political success. But there is no doubt that the failure of the evangelicals to secure as many converts as they hoped caused them to doubt other peoples' ability to accept Christianity, or other aspects of British modernity. And this, along with the fact that some imperial subjects rejected the 'good fortune' of British rule in a series of rebellions, had a countervailing effect on the imagination. This was reinforced, to an extent, by the recently developed theories of evolution so as to increasingly cement notions of biological hierarchy, sanctioned, as it was thought, by the latest scientific research.[3]

Anthropology was considered a fairly new science in the 1860s and not entirely respectable. More to the point is the fact that Victorian anthropology is now seen as 'evidently implicated' in colonialist assumptions. As Gillian Beer phrases it, 'The confidence displayed in evolutionary patterns looks like a strategy for privileging European society ... Developmental patterns are arranged with the white-middle-class European male as the crowned personage towards whom the past world has been striving.'[4] There is no question that racial 'hierarchy' views hardened in the nineteenth century, especially the last half. We may examine the range of views via the work and ideas of two men: Herbert Spencer and Sir James Frazer.

'THE SURVIVAL OF THE FITTEST': THE RISE OF SOCIAL DARWINISM

Spencer is in some ways a familiar type in British intellectual history. He was the son of a Nonconformist headmaster and honorary secretary of a provincial philosophical society, in his case in Derby. And he was the only child of his parents' nine offspring to survive infancy. Being Derby-born, in his time he worked on the railways, suffering indifferent health, both physical and emotional, which gave him an interest in psychology and its environmental context.[5] His father being just as psychologically frail as he was, Herbert was educated by his uncle, a man of the cloth but also a Cambridge wrangler. After much travel and an unsuccessful love affair, Spencer's writings on social issues for the *Nonconformist* newspaper earned him a position on *The Economist* and he began to form friends among the likes of George Eliot, G. H. Lewes, James Froude, Charles Kingsley, John Tyndall and T. H. Huxley.

His first book, *Social Studies*, was concerned with equilibrium in society, how natural laws affect how communities live together, and it was followed in 1852 by *The Development Hypothesis*, which argued for an evolutionary model of the natural world in which cells undergo progressive change as history proceeds, so that a single cell could give rise to complex organisms over thousands of years. Charles Darwin was to say that this book and its arguments helped to crystallise his own thoughts and Spencer repaid the compliment after *Origin* was released when, in 1864, in his new book, *Principles of Biology*, he drew parallels between his own economic theory and Darwin's biological ideas, and coined a phrase that was to have wide significance: 'The survival of the fittest,' he said, 'which I have here sought to express in mechanical terms, is that which Mr Darwin has called "natural selection", or the preservation of favoured races in the struggle for life.'[6]

The phrase certainly caught on, despite being frowned upon by specialists because 'fit', apart from implying physical fitness, says nothing about heritability, which is necessary for any characteristic to be carried over generations. But it was the easy resonance with cut-throat economic competition, and Britain's seeming leadership role in that realm of activity, that caused 'social Darwinism' to become such a popular idea in the late nineteenth century, certainly in Britain but also in Europe and North America.[7]

THE SHINING GREEKS AND THE FILTHY 'PRIMITIVES'

James (later Sir James) Frazer had a series of annual lectures named in his honour, in his case at each of four universities – Cambridge, Oxford, Glasgow and Liverpool. This was only one of many honours to come his way – a knighthood, the Order of Merit, a fellowship of the Royal Society – and, in 1908, he was named as the first professor of social anthropology in Britain, at the University of Liverpool. By then he was famous for his great work, *The Golden Bough*, three volumes of which (out of four) had by then been published.

Born into a family of chemists in Glasgow, he was educated at the university there, where he received a grounding in classics *and* science before going on to Trinity College, Cambridge. James's interest in anthropology was kindled in two ways. One was by reading E. B. Tyler's 'epochal' *Primitive Culture* (1871), which offered an evolutionary perspective on the development of culture, in which the author went beyond art and technology to explore human beings' moral development. The other was the friendship Frazer formed at Cambridge with William Robertson Smith, who became one of the editors of the *Encyclopaedia Britannica* and introduced Frazer to the methods and results of the German higher criticism. Smith's own pioneering work, *Lectures on the Religion of the Semites*, showed Frazer how comparative ethnographic materials could be applied to ancient religions. Then, in 1888, Smith commissioned Frazer to write articles on 'Taboo' and 'Totemism' for *Britannica* and this stimulated him to begin research for *The Golden Bough*, the first volume of which appeared in 1890.[8]

In this work he mastered a vast range of accounts of the religious beliefs and practices of 'savages' that were extremely popular in those years, written by explorers, soldiers, missionaries and traders. Then, in perhaps his most original move, he compared these beliefs and practices to the cultures of the great classical civilisations that he had been reading about since his childhood in Glasgow, comparing 'the shining Greeks with the filthy "primitives"'. His central concern was what he termed 'sacred kingship', which he believed was central to all cultures and was the 'beginning of humanity's long struggle towards understanding itself and the world around it'. His aim, it has been said, was a covert campaign against religion.

The Golden Bough was very popular with the general public and influenced among others such authors as W. B. Yeats, Robert Graves and T. S. Eliot; as had happened with Darwin's *Origin*, the literary effect was widespread. Among other anthropologists, however, it was much less well received, Frazer being accused not of racism directly, but rather of ethnocentrism because he wrote as if all societies across the globe should be categorised – if not exactly judged – according to how well or closely they conformed to stages on the road to Western-style democracies.[9]

BACON AND EMPIRE

A final honour for Frazer was to be made a founding member of the British Academy, established in 1902. Other founding fellows included Leslie Stephen, Sir James Murray, editor of the *Oxford*

English Dictionary, Edward Cowell, first professor of Sanskrit at Cambridge, and Thomas Rhys Davids, a scholar of the Palī (Indo-Aryan Buddhist) language and one of the founders of the London School of Oriental Studies. This school was not actually founded until 1916, which might appear rather late in the context of this chapter, but its mission was to 'advance British scholarship, science and commerce' in Asia and to rival established Oriental schools in Berlin, Paris and even Petrograd. 'African' was added to its name in 1938. The school's motto is 'Knowledge is Power', neatly linking Bacon and the 'higher purpose' of empire.[10]

PART FOUR

FROM POSTCOLONIAL TO POSTMODERN TO COSMOPOLITAN

Hearts of Darkness, Hearts in Darkness

Three significant deaths occurred in 1900. John Ruskin died insane on 20 January, aged eighty-one. The most influential art critic of his day, in *Modern Painters* he had a profound effect on the appreciation of J. M. W. Turner. Ruskin hated industrialism and its effect on aesthetics and had championed the pre-Raphaelites, being splendidly anachronistic. Oscar Wilde died on 30 November, aged forty-four. His art and wit, his campaign against the standardisation of the eccentric, and his efforts to 'replace a morality of severity by one of sympathy' have made him seem more modern, and more missed, as the twentieth century has come and gone, and as the twenty-first has lengthened. Far and away the most significant death, however, was that of Friedrich Nietzsche, on 25 August. Aged fifty-six, he too died insane.

There is no question but that Nietzsche looms over twentieth-century thought, in particular his idea of 'Aryans' on the one hand, the ruling class or caste, who have the 'will to power', the vital life force necessary for the creation of values on which civilisation is based, and those who do not on the other, primarily the masses produced by democracy, whereby 'morality' springs from the resentment of the 'underclass', nourishing the values of the herd animal. The acceptance of Nietzsche's ideas was hardly helped by the fact that many of them were written when he was already ill with the early stages of syphilis. But there is no denying how influential was his philosophy, not least for the way in which, for many people, it accords with what they think Charles Darwin said in his theory of evolution. Britain had its own social Darwinists alongside those of Germany, the US and France but the eugenics movement did not succeed there to anywhere near the same extent as in Germany and the United States. Instead, what held people's attention, as the twentieth century began to lengthen, was not race but gender.

It seems odd to us today to note that the National *Anti*-Suffrage League began in 1908 with the support of many well-known women, including Mrs Humphrey Ward, the novelist, Gertrude Bell, the explorer, and Beatrice Chamberlain, the educationalist daughter of Joseph Chamberlain.[1] In its petition it garnered 337,018 signatures and by 1913 it had 270 branches with more than 33,000 members at a time when the Women's Social and Political Union (the suffragettes) had 2,000.

The anti-suffragists argued that women were not competent to run a large and complex empire, that they were 'debarred by nature' from political knowledge; they were happy for women to vote in local elections but commerce, finance and war should remain the business of men. One fear was that because there were more women than men (and this was before the First World War), in any election there would be a female majority.[2] Queen Victoria, who died in 1901, remained passionately opposed to women getting the vote.[3]

Meanwhile, among the women who did want the vote, violence was growing – breaking windows, arson, planting bombs and handcuffing themselves to railings, with as many as 250,000 attending rallies, and even marches on Parliament. There were hunger strikes and many were force-fed. As the First World War neared, many left the movement and during hostilities the campaign was halted. After the war, because so many men had been killed without having a vote, the voting age was reduced to twenty-one, and for women, who now acquired the vote for the first time, it was thirty. It was a start – the first woman to be elected to Parliament was Constance Markievicz, the daughter of an Arctic explorer, in 1918. She was an Irish revolutionary who had taken part in the Easter Rising of 1916 and been sentenced to death, though this was commuted to life in prison. Her imprisonment at Holloway, as well as the policy of the Irish Citizen Army, dictated that she did not take her seat when she was elected.

THE ADVENT OF NUCLEAR PHYSICS

On the evening of 7 March 1911, in Manchester, Ernest Rutherford, professor of physics at Manchester University, introduced those present at a talk he gave to the Literary and Philosophical Society there to what was without question one of the most consequential new ideas of the modern world. This was nothing less than the basic structure of the atom.

The events of the Manchester society usually consisted of two or three talks on diverse subjects and the meeting of 7 March was no exception. A local fruit importer spoke first, giving an account of how he had been surprised to discover a rare snake mixed up in a load of Jamaican bananas. The next talk was delivered by Rutherford.

How many of those present understood him is hard to say. He told his audience that the atom was made up of 'a central electrical charge concentrated at a point and surrounded by a uniform spherical distribution of opposite electricity equal in amount'. It sounds dry but to Rutherford's colleagues and students present it was the most exciting news they had ever heard. James Chadwick, who was to make his own mark later, said he remembered the evening all his life. 'We realised that this was obviously true, this was it.'[4]

Such confidence in Rutherford's revolutionary ideas had not always been so evident. In the late 1880s he had developed the ideas of the French physicist Henry Becquerel. In turn, Becquerel had built on Wilhelm Conrad Röntgen's discovery of X-rays. Intrigued by these mysterious rays that were given off from fluorescing glass, Becquerel, who, like his father and grandfather, was professor of physics at the Musée d'Histoire Naturelle in Paris, decided to measure other substances that 'fluoresced'. Becquerel's classic experiment occurred by accident, when he sprinkled some uranyl potassium sulphate on a sheet of photographic paper and left it locked in a drawer for a few days. When he looked, he found the image of the salt on the paper. There had been no naturally occurring light to activate the paper, so the change must have been wrought by the uranium salt. Becquerel had discovered naturally occurring radioactivity.

It was this result that attracted Rutherford's attention. Raised in New Zealand, Rutherford was a stocky character with a weather-beaten face who loved to bellow the words to hymns whenever he got the chance, 'Onward, Christian soldiers' being a favourite. After he arrived in Cambridge in October 1895, he quickly began work on a series of experiments designed to elaborate Becquerel's results. There were three naturally radioactive substances – uranium, radium and thorium – and Rutherford and his assistant Frederick Soddy pinned their attentions on thorium, which gave off a radioactive gas. When they analysed the gas, however, Rutherford and Soddy were shocked to discover that it was completely inert – in other words, it wasn't thorium. How could that be? Soddy and Rutherford gradually realised that their results 'conveyed the tremendous and inevitable conclusion that the element thorium was spontaneously transmuting itself into the [chemically inert] argon gas'. What Rutherford and Soddy had discovered was the spontaneous decomposition of the radioactive elements, a modern form of alchemy. The implications were momentous.[5]

This wasn't all. Rutherford also observed that when uranium or thorium decayed, they gave off two types of radiation. The weaker of the two he called 'alpha' radiation, later experiments showing that the 'alpha particles' were in fact helium atoms and therefore positively charged. The stronger 'beta radiation', on the other hand, consisted of electrons with a negative charge. The electrons, Rutherford said, were 'similar in all respects to cathode rays'. So exciting were these results that in 1908 Rutherford was awarded the Nobel Prize at age thirty-seven, by which time he had moved from Cambridge, first to Canada and then back to Britain, to Manchester, as professor of physics. By now he was devoting all his energies to the alpha particle. He reasoned that because it was so much larger than the beta electron (the electron had almost no mass), it was far more likely to interact with matter, and interaction would obviously be crucial to further understanding. 'I was brought up to look at the atom as a nice hard fellow, red or grey in colour according to taste,' he said. That view had begun to change while he had been in Canada, where he had shown that alpha particles sprayed through a narrow slit and projected in a beam could be deflected by a magnetic field.

All these experiments were carried out with very basic

equipment – that was the beauty of Rutherford's approach. The next major breakthrough came when he covered the slit with a very thin sheet of mica, a mineral that splits fairly easily into slivers. The piece Rutherford placed over the slit in his experiment was so thin – about three thousandths of an inch – that in theory at least alpha particles should have passed through it. They did, but not in quite the way that Rutherford had expected. When the results of the spraying were 'collected' on photographic paper, the edge of the image appeared fuzzy. Rutherford could think of only one explanation for that: some of the particles were being deflected. That much was clear, but it was the size of the deflection that excited Rutherford. From his experiments with magnetic fields, he knew that powerful forces were needed to induce even small deflections. Yet his photographic paper showed that some alpha particles were being knocked off course by as much as 2 degrees. Only one thing could explain that. As Rutherford himself put it, 'The atoms of matter must be the seat of very intense electrical forces.'[6]

This result of Rutherford's, though surprising, did not automatically lead to further insights. Instead, for a time Rutherford and his new assistant, Ernest Marsden, went doggedly on, studying the behaviour of alpha particles, separating them on to foil of different materials – gold, silver or aluminium. Nothing notable occurred. But then Rutherford had an idea. He arrived at the laboratory one morning and 'wondered aloud' to Marsden whether it might be an idea to bombard the metal foils with particles *sprayed at an angle*. The most obvious angle to start with was 45 degrees, which is what Marsden did, using foil made of gold. This simple experiment 'shook physics to its foundations'. It was 'a new view of nature ... the discovery of a new layer of reality, a new dimension of the universe'. Sprayed at this angle, the alpha particles did not pass through the gold foil – instead they were bounced back by 90 degrees on to the zinc sulphide screen. Rutherford and Marsden were quick to grasp what they had witnessed: for such a deflection to occur, a massive amount of energy must be locked up somewhere in the equipment used in their simple experiment.

But for a while Rutherford remained mystified. 'On consideration I realised that this scattering backwards must be the result of a single collision, and when I made calculations, I saw that it was impossible to get anything of that order of magnitude unless you took a system in which the greatest part of the mass of the atom was concentrated in a minute nucleus.' In fact, he had brooded for months before feeling confident he was right. One reason was because he was slowly coming to terms with the fact that the idea of the atom he had grown up with – the notion that it was a miniature plum pudding, with electrons dotted about like raisins – would no longer do. Gradually he became convinced that another model indeed was far more likely. He made an analogy with the heavens: the nucleus of the atom was orbited by electrons just as planets went round the stars.[7]

As a theory, the planetary model was elegant, but was it correct? To test his theory, Rutherford suspended a large magnet from the ceiling of his laboratory. Directly underneath, on a table, he fixed another magnet. When the pendulum magnet was swung over the table at a 45-degree angle, and when the magnets were matched in polarity, the swinging magnet bounced through 90 degrees just as the alpha particles did when they hit the gold foil. His theory had passed the first test, and atomic physics had now become nuclear physics.[8]

With the benefit of hindsight, the advent of nuclear physics, with the threat of nuclear war in the distance, may not seem like the exciting advance it appeared to Rutherford, Chadwick and their colleagues at the time. It was, in its way, though no one knew it then, a 'heart of darkness', as novelist Joseph Conrad had entitled one of his stories. His fellow novelist D. H. Lawrence had similar misgivings about a set of very different changes that he was seeing all around him more or less simultaneously and which he feared for where they would lead. These fears were aired in 1913 in his novel *Sons and Lovers*.

In 1912 Lawrence had met Frieda Weekly. Frieda, born Baroness Frieda von Richthofen at Metz in 1879, had spent some time under psychoanalysis with her lover, Otto Gross, whose technique was an eclectic mix, combining the ideas of Freud and Nietzsche. In this way Lawrence had become familiar with psychoanalytic theories of infantile sexuality, which gave *Sons and Lovers* an overtly Freudian theme: the Oedipus complex. Of course, the Oedipal theme predated Freud, as did its treatment in literature. But Lawrence's account of the Morel family, from the Nottinghamshire coalfields (Nottinghamshire being Lawrence's own home county), places the Oedipal conflict within the context of wider issues. The world inhabited by the Morels is changing, reflecting the transition from an agricultural past to an industrial future and war. Gertrude Morel, the mother in the family, is not without education or wisdom, a fact that sets her apart from her duller, working-class husband. She devotes her energies to her two sons, William and Paul, so that they may better themselves in this changing world. In the process, however, Paul, an artist who also works in a factory, falls in love and tries to escape the family. Where before there had been conflict between wife and husband, it is now a tussle between mother and son. In Lawrence's words: 'These sons are *urged* into life by their reciprocal love of their mother – urged on and on. But when they come to manhood, they can't love, because their mother is the strongest power in their lives and holds them ... As soon as the young men come into contact with women, there's a split. William gives his sex to a fribble, and his mother holds his soul.'[9] Lawrence talks freely of the link between sex and other aspects of life and in particular the role of the mother in the family. But he doesn't stop there. Socialist and modernist themes mingle in the book: low pay, unsafe conditions in the mines, strikes, the lack of facilities for childbirth, the lack of schooling for children older than thirteen, the ripening ambition of women to obtain work and agitate for votes, the unsettling effects of evolutionary theory on social and moral life, and the emergence of an interest in the unconscious. In his art studies, Paul encounters the new theories about social Darwinism. Not the least interesting aspect of the book is that Paul Morel actually predicts the First World War.

The First World War had a direct impact on many writers, artists, musicians, mathematicians, philosophers and scientists. Among those killed were the English poet Wilfred Owen, on the Sambre Canal a week before the armistice. Virginia Woolf lost her friend Rupert Brooke, and three other British poets, Isaac Rosenberg, Julian Grenfell and Charles Hamilton Sorley, were also killed.

Bertrand Russell and those who campaigned against the war were sent to jail, or ostracised, or declared mad, like Siegfried Sassoon.

The most brutally direct effects of the war lay in medicine and psychology. Major developments were made in the understanding of cosmetic surgery and vitamins that would eventually lead to our current concerns with a healthy diet. The war also brought about a more sympathetic attitude to psychiatry. There had been cases of men breaking down in earlier wars, but their numbers had been far fewer than those with physical injuries. What seemed to be crucially different this time was the character of hostilities – static trench warfare with heavy bombardment, and vast conscript armies which contained large numbers of men unsuited for war. Psychiatrists quickly realised that in the large civilian armies of the First World War there were many men who would not normally have become soldiers, who were unfit for the terror of bombardment. This intense scrutiny helped make psychiatry respectable. An analysis of 1,043,653 British casualties revealed that neuroses accounted for 34 per cent.[10]

'At no other time in the twentieth century has verse formed the dominant literary form as it did in World War I (at least in the English language)', and there are those, such as Bernard Bergonzi, whose words these are, who argue that English poetry 'never got over the Great War'.[11] In retrospect it is not difficult to see why this should have been so. Many of the young men who went to the front were well educated, which in those days included being familiar with English literature. Life at the front, being intense and uncertain, lent itself to the shorter, sharper, more compact structure of verse, war providing unusual and vivid images in abundance. And in the unhappy event of the poet's death, the elegiac nature of a slim volume had an undeniable romantic appeal.

The poets writing in the First World War can be divided into two groups. There were those early poets who wrote about the glory of war and were then killed. And there were those, killed or not, who lived long enough to witness the carnage and horror, the awful waste and stupidity that characterised the 1914–18 war. Rupert Brooke is the best known of the former group. He was handsome, with striking blond hair, a product of the Cambridge milieu that, had he lived, would surely have drawn him to Bloomsbury. Francis Cornford wrote a short stanza about him while he was still at Cambridge:

> A young Apollo, golden-haired,
> Stands dreaming on the verge of strife,
> Magnificently unprepared
> For the long littleness of life.

Quite a few of Brooke's poems were written in the early weeks of the war when many people, on both sides, assumed the hostilities would be over quickly. He saw brief action outside Antwerp in the autumn of 1914 but was never really in any danger. Several of his poems were published in an anthology called *New Numbers*. Little notice of them was taken until on Easter Sunday 1915, the dean of St Paul's Cathedral quoted Brooke's 'The Soldier' in his sermon. As a result, *The Times* reprinted the poem, which gave Brooke a much wider audience. A week later his death was reported. It wasn't a 'glamorous' death, for he had died from blood poisoning in the Aegean; he hadn't been killed in the fighting, but he had been on active service, on his way to Gallipoli, and the news turned him into a hero.[12]

Several people, including his fellow poet Ivor Gurney, have remarked that Brooke's poetry tells us more about the popular state of mind in England than about Brooke's own experience of fighting in the war at the front. His most famous poem is 'The Soldier' (1914):

> If I should die, think only this of me:
> That there's some corner of a foreign field
> That is forever England. There shall be
> In that rich earth a richer dust concealed;
> A dust whom England bore, shaped, made aware,
> Gave, once, her flowers to love, her ways to roam,
> A body of England's, breathing English air,
> Washed by rivers, blest by suns of home.

Robert Graves, born in Wimbledon in 1895, was the son of the Irish poet Alfred Perceval Graves. While serving in France he was wounded, was laid unconscious on a stretcher in a converted German dressing station, and was given up for dead. One of his poems describes the first corpse he had seen – a German dead on the trench wire whom, therefore, Graves couldn't bury, and indeed many of Graves's stanzas rail against the stupidity and bureaucratic futility of the conflict. Most powerful perhaps is his reversal of many familiar myths:

> One cruel backhand sabre-cut –
> 'I'm hit! I'm killed!' young David cried.
> Throws blindly forward, chokes ... and dies.
> Steel-helmeted and grey and grim
> Goliath straddles over him.

This is antiheroic, deflating and bitter. Goliath isn't supposed to win.[13]

Wilfred Owen, born in Oswestry in Shropshire in 1893, into a religious, traditional family, was twenty-one when war was declared. After matriculating at London University, he became the pupil and lay assistant to a vicar in an Oxfordshire village, then obtained a post as a tutor in English at the Berlitz School of Languages in Bordeaux. In 1914, after war broke out, he witnessed the first French casualties arriving at hospital in Bordeaux and wrote home to his mother vividly describing the wounds and his pity. In October 1915, after he had returned home, he was accepted for the Artists' Rifles but sailed for France on active service at the end of December 1916, attached to the Lancashire Fusiliers.

Owen's first tour of duty on the Somme was an overwhelming experience, as his letters make clear, and he went through a rapid and remarkable period of maturing. He was injured in March 1917 and invalided home via a series of hospitals, until he ended up in June in Craiglockhart Hospital outside Edinburgh. This was the famous psychiatric hospital where W. H. Rivers, one of the medical staff, was making early studies, and cures, of shell shock. While at Craiglockhart, Owen met Edmund Blunden and Siegfried Sassoon, who both left a record of the encounter in their memoirs. Owen went back to the front in September 1918, partly because he believed in that way he might argue more forcefully against the war. In October he won the Military Cross for his part in a successful attack on the Beaurevoir–Fonsomme line. It was during his final year that his best poems were composed. In 'Futility' (1918) Owen is light years away from Brooke. He paints a savage picture of the soldier's world:

> Move him into the sun –
> Gently its touch awoke him once,
> At home, whispering of field unsown.
> Always it woke him, even in France,
> Until this morning and this snow.
> If anything might rouse him now
> The kind old sun will know.

For Owen the war can never be a metaphor for anything. All that there is is the experience of battle.[14] He was killed in action, trying to get his men across the Sambre Canal. It was 4 November 1918, and the war had less than a week to go.

ECLIPSE

Between 1914 and 1918, all direct links between Great Britain and Germany were cut off. But the Netherlands and Switzerland remained neutral, and at the University of Leiden, in 1915, Willem de Sitter was sent a copy of Albert Einstein's paper on the general theory of relativity. An accomplished physicist, de Sitter was well connected, and he realised that as a Dutch national he was an important go-between. He therefore passed a copy of Einstein's paper to Arthur Eddington in London.

Eddington was already a central figure in the British scientific establishment, despite having a 'mystical bent', according to one of his biographers. Born in Kendal in the Lake District in 1882, into a Quaker family of farmers, he was educated first at home and then at Trinity College, Cambridge, where he was senior wrangler and came into contact with J. J. Thomson and Ernest Rutherford. Fascinated by astronomy since he was a boy, he took up an appointment at the Royal Observatory in Greenwich from 1906, and in 1912 became secretary of the Royal Astronomical Society. His first important work was a massive and ambitious survey of the structure of the universe. This eventually provided a figure for the distance of the farthest objects, 500 million light years away, and an age for the universe of between 10 and 20 billion years.[15]

Eddington's academic standing thus made him the obvious choice when the Physical Society of London, during wartime, wanted someone to prepare a *Report on the Relativity Theory of Gravitation*. When it appeared in 1918, this was the first complete account of general relativity to be published in English. Eddington, as we saw, had already received a copy of Einstein's report from Holland so he was well prepared, and his report attracted widespread attention, so much so that Sir Frank Dyson, the Astronomer Royal, offered an unusual opportunity to test Einstein's theory. On 29 May 1919, there was to be a total solar eclipse. This offered the chance to assess if, as Einstein predicted, light rays were bent as they passed near the sun. During the last full year of the war, Dyson obtained from the government a grant of £1,000 to mount not one but two expeditions, to Principe, off the coast of west Africa, and to Sobrel, across the Atlantic, in Brazil.

Eddington was given Principe. He reached there on 23 April and by 16 May had succeeded in getting the check photographs. On 29 May, the day of the eclipse, it began cloudy but then began to clear, just after the eclipse had begun. 'I did not see the eclipse,' Eddington wrote later, 'being too busy changing plates ... We took sixteen photographs ... But the one plate that I measured gave a result agreeing with Einstein.'[16]

The publicity given to Eddington's confirmation of relativity made Einstein the most famous scientist in the world. Einstein wrote to the Englishman, thanking him, and the Royal Society held a special session at which a full account was set out. Relativity theory had not found universal acceptance when Einstein first announced it. Eddington's observations were therefore the point at which many scientists were forced to concede that this exceedingly uncommon idea about the physical world was, in fact, true.

The Passions of Small Lives

Much of the thought of the 1920s may be seen, unsurprisingly perhaps, as a response to the First World War. Not so predictable was that so many authors should respond in the same way – by emphasising their break with the past through new *forms* of literature: novels, plays and poems in which the way the story was told was as important as the story itself. It took a while for authors to digest what had happened in the war, to grasp what it signified and what they felt about it. But then, in 1922, there was a flood of works that broke new ground: James Joyce's *Ulysses*, T. S. Eliot's *The Waste Land*, Virginia Woolf's first experimental novel, *Jacob's Room*, and that was just books published in Britain. In the same year seminal works were published in French, Italian, German and in the United States.

What Joyce, Eliot, Woolf and the others were criticising was the society which capitalism had brought about, a society where life had become a race to acquire things, as opposed to knowledge, understanding or virtue. In short, they were striking at the acquisitive society. This was in fact a new phrase, coined the year before by R. H. Tawney, in a book that was too angry and too blunt to be considered great literature. Tawney came from an upper-class family and was educated at a public school (Rugby) and Balliol College, Oxford, but he was interested all his life in poverty and especially in inequality. After university, he decided, instead of going into the City, to work at Toynbee Hall in London's East End. The idea behind

Toynbee Hall was to bring a university atmosphere and lifestyle to the working classes, and in general it had a profound effect on all who experienced it. It helped turn Tawney into the British socialist intellectual best in touch with the unions, but it was the miners' strike in February 1919 that was to shape his subsequent career. Seeking to head off confrontation, the government established a Royal Commission on the Coal Mines and Tawney was one of six men representing the labour side (another was Sidney Webb). Millions of words of evidence were put before the commission, and Tawney read all of them. He was so moved by the accounts of danger, ill-health and poverty that he wrote the first of three books for which he is chiefly known. These were *The Acquisitive Society* (1921), referred to above, *Religion and the Rise of Capitalism* (1926) and *Equality* (1931).

Tawney hated the brutality of unbridled capitalism, particularly the waste and inequalities. He served in the trenches in the war as an ordinary soldier, refusing a commission. He expected capitalism to break down afterwards. Tawney thought that in the long run capitalism was incompatible with culture. Under capitalism, he wrote, culture became more private, less was shared, and this trend went against the common life of men. The very concept of culture therefore changed, becoming less an inner state of mind and more a function of one's possessions. On top of that, Tawney also felt that capitalism was, at bottom, incompatible with democracy. He suspected that the inequalities endemic in capitalism would ultimately threaten social cohesion. He saw his role, therefore, as helping to provide an important moral counterattack against capitalism for the many like himself who felt it had been at least partly responsible for war.[1]

Not everyone was as savage about capitalism as Tawney was, but as the 1920s wore on and reflection about the First World War matured, an unease persisted. One man who caught this unease, or at least part of it, was both a banker – the arch-symbol of capitalism – and a poet, the licensed saboteur.

T. S. Eliot was born in St Louis, Missouri, in 1888, into a very religious Puritan family. He studied at Harvard, took a year off to study poetry in Paris, then returned to Harvard as a member of the faculty, teaching philosophy. In 1914 he transferred to Oxford. Shortly after, war broke out. In Europe, Eliot met two people who had an immense effect on him: Ezra Pound and Vivien Haigh-Wood. At the time they met, Pound was a much more worldly figure than Eliot, a good teacher and at that time a better poet. Haigh-Wood became Eliot's first wife. Initially happy, the marriage turned into a disaster by the early 1920s, as Vivien descended steadily into madness. Eliot found the circumstances so trying that he himself sought psychiatric treatment in Switzerland.

The puritanical world Eliot grew up in had been fiercely rational. In such a world science had been dominant in that it offered the promise of relief from injustice. And yet by 1918 the world in so far as Eliot was concerned was in ruins. For him, as for others, science had helped produce a war in which the weapons were more terrible than ever, in which the vast nineteenth-century cities were characterised as much by squalor as by the beauty the impressionists painted, where in fact the grinding narratives of Zola told a grimmer truth. Then there was the new physics that had helped remove more fundamental layers of certainty; there was Darwin undermining religion and Freud sabotaging reason itself. A consolidated edition of Sir James Frazer's *The Golden Bough* was published in 1922, the same year as *The Waste Land*, and this too showed that the religions of so-called savages around the world were no less developed, complex, sophisticated than Christianity. At a stroke the simple social-Darwinian idea that Eliot's world was the current endpoint in the long evolutionary struggle, the 'apex' of man's development (Chapter 23), was removed.[2]

Eliot's response was a series of verses originally called *He Do the Police in Different Voices*, taken from Charles Dickens's *Our Mutual Friend*. Eliot was at the time working in the colonial and foreign branch of Lloyds Bank, 'fascinated by the science of money' and helping with the prewar debt position between Lloyds and Germany. He got up at five every morning to write before going into the bank.[3] We now know that Pound worked hard on Eliot's verses, pulling them into shape, making them coherent, and giving them the title

The Waste Land (one of the criteria he used was whether the lines read well out loud). Eliot dedicated the work to Pound, as *il miglior fabbro*, 'the better maker'.

His concern in his great poem is the sterility, spiritual and sexual, that he regards as the central fact of life in the postwar world. As in Woolf's novels, Joyce's *Ulysses*, and Proust's *In Search of Lost Time*, the *form* of Eliot's poem, though revolutionary, was integral to its message. Eliot juxtaposed images of dead trees, dead rats and dead men – conjuring up the horrors of Verdun and the Somme – with references to ancient legends; scenes of sordid sex run into classical poetry; the demeaning anonymity of modern life is mingled with religious sentiments. It is this collision of different ideas that was so startling and original.

The poem is divided into six parts: 'The Epigraph', 'The Burial of the Dead', 'A Game of Chess', 'The Fire Sermon', 'Death by Water' and 'What the Thunder Said'. All the titles are evocative and all, on first acquaintance, obscure. There is a chorus of voices, some-times individual, sometimes speaking in words borrowed from the classics of various cultures, sometimes heard via the incantations of the 'blind and thwarted' Tiresias. At one moment we pay a visit to a tarot reader, at another we are in an East End pub at closing time; next there is a reference to a Greek legend, then a line or two in German. Until one gets used to it, the approach is baffling, quite unlike anything encountered elsewhere. Even stranger, the poem comes with notes and references, like an academic paper. And this is Eliot's point: if we are to turn our back on the acquisitive society, we have to be ready to work:

> At the violet hour, when the eyes and back
> Turn upward from the desk, when the human engine waits
> Like a taxi throbbing waiting,
> I Tiresias, though blind, throbbing between two lives,
> Old man with wrinkled female breasts, can see
> At the violet hour, the evening hour that strives
> Homeward, and brings the sailor home from sea,
> The typist home at teatime, clears her breakfast, lights
> Her stove, and lays out food in tins.

It takes no time at all for the poem to veer between the heroic and the banal, knitting a sense of pathos and bathos, outlining an ordinary world on the edge of something finer, yet not really aware that it is.

> There is a shadow under this red rock,
> (Come in under the shadow of this red rock),
> And I will show you something different from either
> Your shadow at morning striding behind you
> Or your shadow at evening rising to meet you;
> I will show you fear in a handful of dust.
> *Frisch weht der Wind*
> *Der heimat zu*
> *Mein Irisch Kind*
> *Wo weilest du?*

The first two lines hint at Isaiah's prophecy of a Messiah who will be 'as rivers of water in a dry place, as the shadow of a great rock in a weary land' (Isaiah 32:2). The German comes direct from Wagner's opera *Tristan und Isolde*: 'Fresh blows the wind / Towards home / My Irish child / Where are you waiting?' *The Waste Land* cannot be understood on one reading or without 'research' or work.[4]

On the surface, the form of *Ulysses* could not be more different from *The Waste Land* or *Jacob's Room*, considered later. But there are similarities, and the authors were aware of them. *Ulysses* was also in part a response to the war – the last line reads, 'Trieste–Zurich–Paris, 1914–1921.'

Born in Dublin in 1882, James Joyce was the eldest child to survive in a family of ten. The family struggled financially, but still managed to give James a good education at Jesuit schools and University College, Dublin. He then moved to Paris, where at first he thought he might be a doctor. Soon, though, he started to write. From 1905 he lived in Trieste with Nora Barnacle, a young woman from Galway who he had met on Nassau Street, Dublin, in 1904. *Chamber Music*, a collection of poems, was published in 1907, and *Dubliners*, a series of short stories, in 1914. On the outbreak of war, Joyce was obliged to move to neutral Switzerland (Ireland was then ruled by Great

Britain). During hostilities, he published *A Portrait of the Artist as a Young Man*, but it was *Ulysses* that brought him international fame.

There are two principal characters in *Ulysses*, though many of the countless minor ones are memorable too. Stephen Dedalus is a young artist going through a personal crisis (like Western civilisation he has dried up, losing his large ambitions and the will to create). Leopold Bloom – 'Poldy' to his wife Molly, and modelled partly on Joyce's father and brother – is a much more down-to-earth character. Joyce makes him Jewish and slightly effeminate, but it is his unpretentious yet wonderfully rich life – inner and outer – that makes him *Ulysses*. For it is Joyce's point that the age of heroes is over. He loathed the 'heroic abstractions' for which so many soldiers were sacrificed, 'the big words that make us so unhappy'. The odyssey of *his* characters is not to negotiate the fearful mythical world of the Greeks – instead he gives us Bloom's entire day in Dublin on 16 June 1904. We follow Bloom from the early preparation of his wife's breakfast, through his presence at the funeral of a friend, encounters with racing aficionados, buying meat and soap, drinking, an erotic scene where he is on the beach near three young women and they are watching some fireworks, to a final encounter with the police on his way home late at night. We leave him gently climbing into bed next to his wife and trying not to wake her, when the book shifts perspective and gives us Molly's completely unpunctuated view of Bloom.[5]

It is one of the book's attractions that it changes style several times, from stream of consciousness, to question and answer, to a play that is also a dream, to more straightforward exchanges. There are some lovely jokes (Shakespeare is 'the chap that writes like Synge', 'My kingdom for a drink') and some hopelessly childish puns ('I beg your parsnips'); incredible inventive language, teeming with allusions; endless lists of people and things; and references to the latest developments in science. One point of the very great length of the book is to recreate a world in which the author slows life down for the reader, enabling him or her to relish the language, a language 'that never sleeps'. In this way, Joyce draws attention to the richness of Dublin in 1904, where poetry, opera, Latin and liturgy are as much part of everyday lower-middle-class life as are gambling, racing, minor cheating and the lacklustre lust of a middle-aged man for virtually every woman that he meets. Descriptions of food are never far away, each and every one mouthwatering ('Buck Mulligan slit a steaming scone in two and plastered butter over its smoking pith'; 'He smellsipped the cordial.') Bloom has no wish to be anything other than he is, 'neither Faust nor Jesus'.[6]

A TERRIBLE BEAUTY

In 1922 Joyce's colleague W. B. Yeats was named a senator in Ireland. Two years later he received the Nobel Prize in Literature. Yeats's 57-year career as a poet spanned many different periods, but his political engagement was of a piece with his artistic vision. An 1899 police report described him as 'more or less of a revolutionary', and in 1916 he had published 'Easter 1916', about the botched Irish nationalist uprising. This contained lines that, although they refer to the executed leaders of the uprising, could also serve in the ending, as an epitaph for the entire century:[7]

> We know their dream; enough
> To know they dreamed and are dead,
> And what if excess of love
> Bewildered them till they died?
> I write it out in a verse –
> MacDonagh and MacBride
> And Connolly and Pearse
> Now and in time to be,
> Wherever the green is worn,
> All changed, changed utterly:
> A terrible beauty is born.

Yeats recognised that he had a religious temperament at a time when science had largely destroyed that option. He believed that life is largely determined by 'remote ... unknowable realities'. Yeats's career is generally seen in four phases – before 1899, 1899–1914, 1914–28 and after 1928 – but it is his third phase that marks his highest achievement. This period included *The Wild Swans at Coole* (1919), *Michael Robartes and the Dancer* (1921), *The Tower* (1928) and the prose work *A Vision* (1925). This latter book sets out Yeats's occult system of signs and symbols, which were part of his 'discovery' that his wife had psychic powers and that 'spirits spoke through her' in automatic writing and trances. In anyone else such an approach might have been merely embarrassing, but in Yeats the craftsmanship shines through to produce a poetic voice that is clear and distinctive, wholly autonomous. Yeats the man is not at all like Bloom, but they are embarked on the same journey:

> The trees are in their autumn beauty,
> The woodland paths are dry,
> Under the October twilight the water
> Mirrors a still sky;
> Upon the brimming water among the stones
> Are nine-and-fifty swans ...
>
> Unwearied still, lover by lover,
> They paddle in the cold
> Companionable streams or climb the air;
> Their hearts have not grown old;
> Passion or conquest, wander where they will,
> Attend upon them still.

'The Wild Swans at Coole' (1919)

Yeats was affected by the war and the wilderness that followed. But, like Bloom, he was really more interested in creating afresh from nature than lamenting what had gone.

> That is no country for old men. The young
> In one another's arms, birds in the trees,
> – Those dying generations – at their song,
> Those salmon-falls, the mackerel-crowded seas,
> Fish, flesh or fowl, commend all summer long
> Whatever is begotten, born, and dies.
> Caught in that sensual music all neglect
> Monuments of unageing intellect

'Sailing to Byzantium' (1928)

Yeats never shared the modernist desire to portray the contemporary urban landscape; instead, as he grew older, he recognised the central reality of 'desire in our solitude', the passion of private matters, and that science had nothing worthwhile to say on the subject. Greatness, as Bloom realised, lay in being wiser, more courageous, more full of insight, even in little ways, especially in little ways.[8]

FIRE IN THE MIST

Virginia Woolf was born in 1882 into an extremely literary family (her father was Leslie Stephen, who as we have seen was the founding editor of the *Dictionary of National Biography*, and his first wife was a daughter of William Makepeace Thackeray). Although Virginia was denied the education given to her brothers, Woolf still had the run of the family's considerable library and grew up much better read than most of her female contemporaries. She always wanted to be a writer and began with articles for the *Times Literary Supplement* (begun as a separate publication from its parent, *The Times*, in 1902).

It was with *Jacob's Room* that the sequence of experimental novels for which Woolf is most remembered was begun. The book tells the story of a young man, Jacob, and its central theme, as it follows his development through Cambridge, artistic and literary London, and a journey to Greece, is the description of a generation and class that led Britain into war. It is a big idea; however, once again it is the form of the book which sets it apart.

Jacob's Room is an urban novel, dealing with the anonymity and fleeting experiences of city streets, 'the desperate passions of small lives, never to be known'. Like *Ulysses*, the book consists of a stream of consciousness viewed through interior monologues, moving backward and forward in time, sliding from one character to another without warning, changing viewpoint and attitude as fast and as fleetingly as any encounter in any major urban centre. There isn't much plot in the conventional sense and there is no conventional narrative. Characters are simply cut off, as in an impressionist painting. 'It is no use trying to sum people up,' says one of the figures. 'One must follow hints, not exactly what is said, nor yet entirely what is done.' Woolf is describing and making us feel what life is like in the vast cosmopolitan cities of the modern world. This fragmentation, this dissolution of the familiar categories – psychological as well as physical – is just as much the result of the First World War, she is saying, as the military/political/economic changes that have been wrought, and is fundamental.[9]

MIDDLEBROW

News of these books reached many people in the 1920s by a new medium – radio. The way radio developed in Britain reflected a real fear that it might have a bad influence on levels of information and taste, and there was a strong feeling, in the 'establishment', that central guidance was needed. 'Chaos in the ether' was to be avoided at all costs. To begin with, a few large companies were granted licences to broadcast experimentally. After that, a syndicate of firms which manufactured radio sets was founded, financed by the Post Office, which levied a 10-shilling (50p) fee payable by those who bought the sets. Adverts were dispensed with as 'vulgar and intrusive'. This, the British Broadcasting Company, lasted for four years (1922–6). After that the British Broadcasting Corporation came into being, granted a royal charter to protect it from political interference.

In the early days the notion of the BBC as a public service was very uncertain. Britain was still in financial straits, recovering from war, and 1.5 million were unemployed. Lloyd George's government was far from popular, and these overall conditions led to the General Strike of 1926, which itself imperilled the BBC. A second factor was the press, which viewed the BBC as a threat, to such an extent that no news bulletins were allowed before 7.00 p.m. Third, no one had any idea what sort of material should be broadcast – audience research didn't begin until 1936, and 'listening in', as it was called, was believed by many to be a fad that would soon pass.

Then there was the character of the corporation's first director, a 37-year-old engineer named John Reith. Reith, a high-minded Scottish Presbyterian, never doubted for a moment that radio should be far more than entertainment, that it should also educate and inform. As a result, the BBC gave its audience what Reith believed was needed rather than what people wanted.

There was a crop of worries about the intellectual damage radio might do. 'Instead of solitary thought,' said the headmaster of Rugby School, 'people would listen in to what was said to millions of people, which could not be the best of things.' Another worry was that radio would make people 'more passive', producing 'all-alike girls'. Still others feared radio would keep husbands at home, adversely affecting pub attendance. In 1925 *Punch* magazine, referring to the new culture established by the BBC, labelled it as 'middlebrow'.

Editorially speaking, the BBC's first test arrived in 1926 with the onset of the General Strike. Most newspapers were included in the strike, so for a time the BBC was virtually the only source of news. Reith responded by ordering five bulletins a day instead of the usual one. The accepted view now is that Reith complied more or less with what the government asked, in particular putting an optimistic gloss on government policy and actions.[10]

Not everyone thought that Reith was a stool pigeon, however. Winston Churchill, then Chancellor of the Exchequer, actually thought the BBC should be taken over. He saw it as a rival to his own *British Gazette*, edited from his official address at 11 Downing Street. Churchill failed, but people had seen the danger, and it was partly as a result of this tussle that the 'C' in BBC was changed in 1927 from Company to Corporation, protected by royal charter. The General Strike was therefore a watershed for the BBC in the realm of politics. Before the strike, politics (and other 'controversial' subjects) were avoided entirely, but the strike changed all that, and in 1929 *The Week in Politics* was launched. Three years later, the corporation began its own newsgathering organisation.

Quite different from this 'middlebrow' development was a brand new, distinctly 'highbrow' academic degree with a difference, introduced at Oxford during the 1920s, that would have a marked effect not just on Britain, but on the rest of the world too. This was PPE, or politics, philosophy and economics. The new Oxford degree was part of widespread change after the war, including the fact that women were finally allowed to take a degree. Until then, 'Greats', or *literae humaniores*, classical languages and history (of classical civilisation), together with philosophy, was widely considered the best that Oxford had to offer. But it was not open to students who had no Greek or Latin.

Two figures who had most influence on PPE were, first, Benjamin Jowett, who remained at Balliol after he graduated, rising up the pecking order and aiming to transform the college into a place where higher education was tied to public life. He was also concerned to make education available to 'every class of Society'. In this regard he appointed Alexander Dunlop to run extramural teaching, for pupils of all ages and means. Out of this grew the further idea that a new 'Greats' degree was needed, more attuned to modern life, to train up a new generation of civil servants, where subjects other than classical civilisation and languages were needed. In this new climate, the idea arose for an honours school that would cover economics and politics and natural science, with philosophy providing the common theme. This first proposal failed, with both philosophers and scientists objecting that it was too broad. Instead, a slightly different proposal, eschewing natural science but combining economics, politics and philosophy, was given the go-ahead. In a way it was 'modern Greats'.

It was not universally popular with the hierarchy, who saw it as a 'soft option for the weaker man [sic]'. The first curriculum included a relatively traditional amalgam of philosophy, political history, political economy and an unprepared translation from French, German or Italian, but it is recorded that the course grew by 10 per cent a year between 1923 and the outbreak of the Second World War – it was popular with students from the start, forcing colleges to appoint specialised tutors. In 1929 political economy was replaced by economic theory and more statistical methods, while in the tumultuous 1930s, a more mathematical component was added to the economic strand. Students were still taught in the traditional Oxford tutorial method and during the war social studies were added, housed at the newly founded Nuffield College. There were still traditionalists who were sceptical of the degree, but it continued to be popular with pupils, especially those interested in either politics or public life.[11]

Auden, Orwell and the Age of Keynes

I t is common now to speak of an 'Auden Generation' of poets, which emerged as the 1920s gave way to the 1930s and included Christopher Isherwood, Stephen Spender, Cecil Day Lewis, John Betjeman and, sometimes, Louis MacNeice. Not all of them spoke in an identical 'Audenesque' voice – nonetheless, 'Audenesque' entered the language.

Born in 1907, Wystan Hugh Auden grew up in Birmingham (though he went to school in Norfolk), a middle-class boy fascinated by mythology and by the industrial landscape of the Midlands – railways, gasworks, the factories and machinery associated with the motor trade.[1] He went to Oxford to read biology and although he soon changed to English, he always remained interested in science, and psychoanalysis especially. One of the reasons he changed to English was that he already knew that he wanted to be a poet.

His first verse was published in 1928, by Stephen Spender, whom he met at Oxford, who had his own hand press. T. S. Eliot, by then an editor at Faber & Faber, had previously rejected one collection of Auden's poems, but the firm published a new set in 1930.[2] The collection showed that at twenty-three Auden had achieved a striking originality in both voice and technique. His background in the already decaying industrial heartland of Britain, and his interest in science and psychology, helped him to an original vocabulary, set in contemporary and realistic locations. At the same time, he dislocated his syntax, juxtaposing images in deliberately jarring ways, reminiscent of the arrhythmia of machines. There was something familiar, almost ordinary, about the way many lines ended, and this too was Audenesque:

> The dogs are barking, the crops are growing,
> But nobody knows how the wind is blowing.

Reading Auden is strangely calming, as though a 'stranger were making our acquaintance', perhaps because, in the changing world of the 1930s, his familiar, clear images were something to hold on to.[3] He was not averse to drawing his ideas from sociology and the sort of information gleaned from surveys carried out by Gallup, which started its polling activities in America in 1935 and opened an office in Britain a year later. Auden's later poems appropriated the rhythms of jazz, Hollywood musicals and popular songs (now infinitely more popular than hitherto because of radio), and he peppered his lines with references to such film stars as Garbo or Dietrich:

> The soldier loves his rifle,
> The scholar loves his books,
> The farmer loves his horses,
> The film star loves her looks.
> There's love the whole world over
> Wherever you may be;
> Some lose their rest for gay Mae West,
> But you're my cup of tea.

Auden was quickly imitated but the quality and intensity of his own poetry fell off at the end of the 1930s, after the publication of one of his finest works, 'Spain'. Auden was in Spain in January 1937, not to take part as a combatant in the civil war, as so many prominent intellectuals did, but to drive an ambulance for the Republican side, though that didn't happen.[4]

Like Auden, George Orwell feared a fascist victory in Spain and so felt obliged to fight. *Homage to Catalonia* not only conveys the horror of war, the cold, the lice, the pain (Orwell was shot in the neck), but also the boredom. It was impossible to fight off the cold or the lice, but in a brief aside Orwell says that he staved off the boredom because he had brought with him, in his knapsack, 'a few Penguins'.[5] This is one of the first references in print to a new literary phenomenon of the 1930s: the paperback book.

Clive Bell, the artist, was in no doubt about the cleverest man he had ever met: John Maynard Keynes. Many people shared Bell's view, and it is not hard to see why. Keynes's Political Economy Club, which met in King's College, Cambridge, attracted the cleverest students and economists from all over the world. Nor did it hurt Keynes's reputation that he had made himself comfortably rich by a number of ventures into the City of London, a display of practical economics rare in an academic. Since publication of *The Economic Consequences of the Peace*, his attack on the reparations demanded of Germany after the First World War, Keynes had been in an anomalous position. So far as the establishment was concerned, he was an outsider, but as part of the Bloomsbury group he was by no means invisible. He continued to correct politicians, criticising Winston Churchill, Chancellor of the Exchequer, in 1925 for the return to the gold standard at $4.86 to the pound, which in Keynes's view made it about 10 per cent overvalued. He also foresaw that as a result of the mines in the Ruhr being allowed back into production in 1924, coal prices would drop significantly, leading to the conditions in Britain which provoked the General Strike in 1926.[6]

Being right did not make Keynes popular. But he refused to hold his tongue. Following the Wall Street Crash in 1929 and the Great Depression that followed, most economists at the time believed that the correct course of action was no action. Conventional wisdom held that depressions were 'therapeutic', that they 'squeezed out' the inefficiency and waste that had accumulated in a nation's economy like poison; to interfere with that natural economic homeopathy risked inflation. Keynes thought this was nonsense. Worse, given the hardship caused by mass unemployment, it was immoral. Traditional economists based their views of inaction on Say's law of markets, after Jean-Baptiste Say, the nineteenth-century French economist. Say's law maintained that the general overproduction of goods was impossible, as was general unemployment, because men produced goods only in order to enjoy the consumption of other goods. Every increase in investment was soon followed by an increase in demand. Savings were likewise used by the banks to fund loans for investments, so there was no real difference between spending and saving. Such unemployment as arose was soon rectified, or voluntary, when people took time off to enjoy their earnings.[7]

Keynes was not the only one to point out that in the 1930s the system had produced a situation in which unemployment was not only widespread but involuntary, and far from temporary. His radical observation was that people do not spend every increase in income they receive. They spend more, but they hold back some. This may not seem significant, but Keynes saw that it had a domino effect whereby businessmen would not spend all their profits in investment: as a result the system outlined by Say would gradually slow down and, eventually, stop. This had three effects: first, that an economy depended as much on people's *perceptions* of what was about to happen as on what actually did happen; second, that an economy could achieve stability with a significant measure of unemployment within it, with all the social damage that followed; and third, that investment was the key matter. This led to his crucial insight, that if private investment wasn't happening, the state should intervene, using government credits and manipulating interest rates, to create jobs. Whether these jobs were useful (building roads, say) or merely wasteful didn't really matter; they provided cash that would be spent in real ways, generating income for others, which would then be passed on.[8]

Keynes was still outside the heart of the British establishment, and it would need another war to bring him in from the cold. Ironically, the first place Keynes's policies were tried was in Nazi Germany. From the moment he assumed office in 1933, Hitler behaved almost like the perfect Keynesian, building railways, roads, canals and other public projects, while implementing strict exchange controls that prevented Germans sending their money abroad and forced them to buy domestic products. Unemployment was abolished inside two years, and prices and wages began to rise in tandem. Germany, however, didn't count for many people. The horror of Hitler prevented them giving him credit for anything.

In 1933, on a visit to Washington, Keynes tried to interest Franklin D. Roosevelt in his ideas, but the new president, preoccupied with his own New Deal, did not fully engage with Keynes, or Keynesianism. After this failure, Keynes decided to write a book in the hope of gaining a wider audience for his ideas. *The General Theory of Employment, Interest and Money* appeared in 1936. For some economists it was sensational, and merited comparison with Adam Smith's *The Wealth of Nations* (1776) and Marx's *Capital* (1867). For others, Keynes's radicalism was every bit as odious as Marx's, and maybe more dangerous because it stood a greater chance of working.[9]

In 1937, a few months after Keynes's book was published, it seemed that the Depression was easing in the United States, and signs of recovery were at last showing themselves. Unemployment was still high, but production and prices were at last creeping up. No sooner had these green shoots begun to appear than the classical economists came out of hibernation, arguing that federal spending be cut and taxes raised to balance the budget. Immediately, the recovery slowed, stopped, and then reversed itself. Gross national product (GNP) fell from $91 billion to $85 billion, and private investment halved. It is not often that nature offers a laboratory to test hypotheses, but this time it did.[10] War was now not far away. When hostilities began in Europe, unemployment in the United States was still at 17 per cent, and the Depression was a decade old. The Second World War would remove unemployment from the American scene for generations and herald what has aptly been called the Age of Keynes.[11]

The African Survey: The Laboratory of Empire 2

In 1928, during a brief tour of Northern Rhodesia, now Zambia, Sir George Schuster, economic and financial advisor to the secretary of state for the colonies, and a former financial secretary to the government of Sudan, had this to say as a result of his travels: 'It is astounding to find each little government in each of these detached countries working out, on its own, problems which are common to all, without any knowledge of what its neighbours are doing and without any direction on main lines of policy from the colonial office.'[1]

Schuster was not alone. In fact, since 1910, a small but well-connected group of men, known colloquially as 'Milner's Kindergarten' – named for their role as civil servants across southern Africa under the high commissioner, Lord Milner (1897–1905) – had been actively advocating the idea of more systematic study of the British Empire's various territories. Despite this, there seems to have been little urgency in the matter for it was not until the Paris Peace Conference had come and gone in 1919 that anything further came to pass, when Lionel Curtis, another member of Milner's Kindergarten, and a self-assured advocate of the future of the white settler dominions, established a new institution in London. This was the Royal Institute of International Affairs (RIAF), designed to counter what Curtis felt was a no less serious 'lack of adequate knowledge' in world (not just empire) politics.[2]

Out of this, a few years later, an institute was created within 'Chatham House', as the RIAF was (and still is) colloquially known, the aim of which was 'to promote a better understanding of the distinctive character and contribution of African peoples'. This might be thought to be a little late in the day but the specific purpose of the new body, the International Institute of African Languages and Cultures, was 'to bring scientific knowledge and research in the solution of the practical problems which presented themselves in any effort to administer "primitive races"'.[3] In 1924, in his book *Christianity and the Race Problem*, the missionary Joseph Oldham had argued that doctrines of racial domination would lead the world 'directly and inevitably to catastrophe'.

As John Cell tells the story, British attitudes to Africa at the time were shaped by two schools of thought. One, dominated by thinking in much of southern, central and eastern Africa, stressed economic development 'through white initiative, capital and management of migrant black labour, the evolution of Africans "on their own lines", and segregation'. The other, centring on west Africa but also including Uganda, 'emphasised peasant production, protection of African interests and indirect rule'.[4] Both these views 'drew on a common bank of scientific and anthropological theory and shared the elementary assumption ... that Africans were different, from which it followed that they should be treated differently and had a different future, diverging on what those lines were and on the end of that evolution. Both thought the end a long way off.'[5]

This much is background. Then, early in 1929, plans began to circulate for yet another institution, this one to be based in Oxford and connected with the Rhodes Trust. Cecil Rhodes was, of course, even then a controversial figure, and much more so now, known – and castigated – for his 'white supremacist' views, notably 'equal rights for all *civilized* men'. (Italics added.)

Born in 1853 in the Home Counties, Rhodes was a poor scholar but much in awe of learning, yet it was as a swashbuckling businessman, no stranger to bribery, and a pioneer of diamond-mining in southern Africa, that he emerged as the perfect embodiment of aggressive, opportunist, imperial expansionism. In his *Confession of Faith*, published in 1877, at the age of twenty-four, he advocated the

formation of a secret society 'with but one object, the furtherance of
the British Empire and the bringing of the whole uncivilised world
under British rule, for making the Anglo-Saxon race but one empire',
which would, he fervently hoped, see the eventual recovery of the
United States into this empire, crowning everything with a 'United
States of Africa'.[6] As a politician in southern Africa (he was prime
minister of Cape Colony from 1890 to 1896), he passed draconian
laws, allowing for entrapment and police searches without warrant.
His resignation as prime minister came after his part in the Jameson
Raid was revealed, a secretive attempt by mining interests to overthrow the republic, which turned into a fiasco.

The chief responsibility of the Rhodes Trust, set up in 1902,
was the administration of the Rhodes scholarships, incorporated
in Rhodes's will, and designed to promote unity and civic responsibility among English-speaking peoples. Despite a phrase in his
will to the effect that 'no student shall be qualified or disqualified
for election ... on account of his race or religious opinions', the
scholarships – until well into the twentieth century – were available
only to male applicants from countries that are today within the
Commonwealth, the United States and Germany (the latter reflecting
a vague notion of Teutonic race unity).[7] His will also created chairs
of imperial history in the universities of Oxford and London, and the
Royal Institute of International Affairs at Chatham House.

The proposed Oxford think-tank, as we would say now, was intended as an institute of government applied to Africa, and as part
of it, the African Survey emerged from a series of conferences held
at Oxford in the summer recess of that year, 1929, which also coincided with a Rhodes memorial lecture in the autumn, delivered by
General Jan Smuts, prime minister of South Africa between 1919 and
1924. It was hoped and intended that his lecture would help define
the aims and work of the new institute and during the course of his
remarks, he did indeed say that 'a whole continent was lying at the
feet of the British Empire – and that if Oxford would, as it were, turn
its attention from the Greeks to the Negroes, it would help Africa as
nothing else could'.[8]

Not everyone was on board with Smuts – there were critics who
contrasted his views with the Afrikaners' 'pejorative' attitude to

Africans, including the view that they were 'natural' slaves. Yet the summer conferences and Smuts's lecture and presence did help to broaden ideas about the new institute's mission, so that its remit should extend beyond political science to other fields of knowledge, to include the natural, medical and human sciences. Smuts, educated at Cambridge, had helped found the League of Nations while prime minister of South Africa, but not only that: he had taken part in botanical expeditions, been president of the South African Association for the Advancement of Learning and was to be a future president of the British Association in 1931. He was a scientist as much as he was anything.

Helen Tilley tells us that, in that summer and autumn of 1929, a group of thirty-one men – politicians, Oxford dons, natural scientists and anthropologists – 'gathered behind closed doors to discuss colonial Africa's future' and that like the conference of geographers that King Leopold of Belgium convened in 1876, 'the 1929 conference had ripple effects across the African continent for decades to come'.[9]

The African Survey, as it became known, which came out of these deliberations, was planned and directed by a number of prominent scientists – Richard Gregory, second editor of *Nature*, after Norman Lockyer; Julian Huxley, brother of Aldous, professor of biology at King's College, London, passionate evolutionist and a famous radio broadcaster; John Boyd-Orr, a nutritionist; and Bronisław Malinowski, a Krakow-born anthropologist who had done fieldwork among the aboriginal peoples of Australia. What distinguished this group was that its members had a consuming interest in gathering hard, empirical scientific data across the empire. The empire, in their view, provided a 'unique laboratory' in which to examine problems relating to 'democratic states and their international association', in conjunction with 'the good government of the coloured peoples and the harmony of their relations with the white peoples'.[10]

But it was still not launched properly. Some progress appeared to have been made in that, by early 1930, the Institute of Government at Oxford was being referred to as the Institute of African Studies. But then, in mid-1931, by which time it was clear that neither American nor British philanthropists would provide sufficient funds, it was scaled down to a 'Survey of African Research'. It was only then that Chatham House stepped in and offered to serve as the survey's home, and the Carnegie Foundation finally agreed to a grant of $75,000 for the first phase.

Natural science, medicine and anthropology were at the heart of the project right from the start and in fact, says Tilley, they outstripped all other fields of interest, including economics and 'native' administration.[11] Nearly 300 scientists would serve on the survey before its publication in 1938, including meteorologists, geologists, soil scientists, botanists and forestry specialists, human and veterinary doctors, nutritionists, psychologists and anthropologists. The key foci of the survey were ecological science, soil fertility, 'native' agriculture, infectious diseases, rural health care, demographic patterns, eugenics and intelligence-testing, and witchcraft legislation.

A director was found only after a two-year search, the choice ultimately settling on Sir Malcolm (later Lord) Hailey, who had been governor of both the Punjab and the United Provinces (Agra and Oudh), and who was 'widely regarded as his generation's most distinguished Indian Civil Servant', but who knew nothing about Africa and so, it was felt, would bring a fresh mind to its problems. When the project began, the question of further European settlement in colonial Africa was still open for debate. 'By the time it issued its report in 1938, this was no longer considered relevant.' During that time, 'there was a fundamental change of outlook, from an ideology of economic self-sufficiency to one of human welfare and external aid'. Cell adds that many other naïve assumptions about race relations were also abandoned by the survey.[12]

Tilley says that the survey's reports were widely circulated, even to the governments of France, Belgium and South Africa, and became, for many people, the standard works on the continent, providing, she says, an overview of the moral, political and – in particular – the epistemological debates of the period. The final survey, published in 1938, was a massive document of 1,662 pages, with the index taking it to 1,837 pages. It quickly became a widely consulted reference work with its overall theme in favour of colonial development becoming *the* prevailing ideology in the years ahead.

Overall, we may say that the African Survey proved to be a salutary experience for most of those working in the field, as they came to realise that the African way of life was much better adapted to the environment than they thought. In regard to 'native' agriculture, for example, the simple but all-important observation was that much of the farming in Africa was actually handled by the women, who also did the cooking in the home, and so its central principle was a line drawn direct from the fields to the kitchen. A second observation was that Africa is vast, with a huge range of ecological systems, meaning that 'simple, western, scientific solutions' to Africa's problems – ploughing, fallow, fertilisers – were much too general to have applicability everywhere. Instead, what was required was 'a much greater appreciation of the sophistication of African farming solutions, closely adapted as they were to local conditions'.[13]

Studies on trypanosomiasis discovered that the Zulus had their own method of control, which consisted of two elements. One was carefully timed grass fires, which acted as a general cleanser, ridding the area of ticks, which the Zulus clearly understood as the vector of the disease. This was combined with the encouragement of very dense settlements, meaning that cattle could be reared without the fear that they would be lost to *nagana*, the animal variant of trypanosomiasis.[14] Research showed that late burning had been carried out for at least a hundred years, and that the locals had their own ideas about areas that could be called 'disease reservoirs'.[15]

In relation to African therapeutics, the situation was slightly different. While anthropologists found that there was a coherence to indigenous medical belief systems, for the very same reason doctors on the ground found it difficult to gain the trust of locals using Western medical concepts and treatments. Local healing systems were difficult to dislodge and laws that banned witchcraft and fetish belief existed uneasily alongside medical licensing laws.

In the summer of 1934, the Colonial Office received a funding proposal from the colony, as it then was, of Kenya for 'an examination of African mental capacity and "backwardness"'.[16] The driving force behind this proposal was Dr Hector Laing Gordon, a settler doctor in Kenya who was president of the Kenyan branch of the British Medical Association and a key member of the Kenyan Society for the Study of Race Improvement, founded in 1933. The research would concentrate principally on physical and environmental factors that were thought to influence 'African cerebral development, quality and reaction'. Malinowski, for one, felt that the whole idea was dubious, but that was its significance, in that it reflected a growing view, prevalent since the late nineteenth century, and among the social Darwinists, that there were inherent biological differences between the races, including in mental capacity, the most controversial of all. As Tilley says, as does Chloe Campbell, in her study of eugenics in colonial Kenya, the timing was all important: racial science was emerging in Nazi Germany, and in America studies in racial science 'dwarfed' anything done in Africa.[17]

Kenya was in some ways a key country at that time. A parliamentary commission on East Africa had been struck by the tensions in the country between those interested in white settlers' rights and those who believed equally strongly in Africans' rights, and while the commission's report favoured white rule (the whites comprising a form of 'aristocracy', as the report put it), it also 'felt obliged' to acknowledge that such 'cooperation [towards development] is not due to inherent right on account of the colour of [someone's] skin'.[18] At the same time that this came about, a group of individuals wanted an institute of research in Kenya, among them Oldham, who again stressed that hard facts about Africans should be thoroughly researched.

The problems he identified included 'native ideas regarding land tenure', 'native methods of production', 'native beliefs and customs' and 'knowledge of the native mind'. Although Oldham was not opposed in theory to the investigation of the 'biological aspects of race', he was by no means sure how 'mental superiority' could be defined, or measured, and he was especially wary, as he put it, of the 'pseudoscience' coming out of American universities, often in the southern states, and which, he felt, was 'poisoning the public mind'. At an annual church congress, in 1925, which discussed 'racial questions', Oldham reiterated the arguments in his own book,

Christianity and the Race Problem, that racial discrimination went against the teaching of the church and that what mattered most to black Africans was that they be treated equally. By no means all of the white settlers at the conference agreed.

When Oldham presented his proposals to the East African governments in Nairobi, they decided they could not afford to spend 'money to appoint an organization to study the effect of European civilization on the native mind', and instead appointed a statistician to assemble demographic data, a sensible conclusion.

Even so, Gordon continued his research, and his campaign to compare the brains and the neurology of Africans and Europeans, to see how it related to his concept of 'backwardness'. He was joined in this by a colleague, F. W. Wint, Kenya's medical pathologist. In a speech to the British Eugenics Society, in 1933, when Gordon visited Britain, he claimed to have found that an examination of 3,500 skulls had led him to conclude that the average male 'native' had a cranial capacity at least 150 cubic centimetres smaller than that of the average European.[19] He further argued that African brains ceased to develop after puberty.[20] Gordon's 'findings' reflected what we might call 'old-school eugenics' but, as Malinowski and others pointed out, it had been known for some time by then that intelligence was not related to brain size, vitiating at least some of Gordon's arguments. Louis Leakey, the anthropologist and archaeologist, challenged Gordon that his methods for measuring cranial capacity were crude and inaccurate. Huxley thought that the crucial measure was to compare brain size as a proportion of body weight, many East Africans being of relatively small stature. Huxley conceded that Gordon's research did show a difference in mental capacity but that it wasn't necessarily inherent, having to do instead with cultural factors, nutrition, disease and education, or the lack of it.

Other 'old school' ideas went the same way as mental capacity. Leakey, for example, considered it unlikely that educating Africans would lead to 'detribalisation', as some thought, or that a new type of human being would emerge as white people adapted to tropical conditions, as others also claimed. Malinowski said plainly that he thought that people like Gordon were 'scientists trying to prove their own prejudices'.[21]

Epistemic Pluralism

Overall, the African Survey, in Helen Tilley's words, confirmed the notion of 'epistemic pluralism'.[22] 'The more colonial scientists looked at the adaptations of native peoples to their environments, the more they found that, though they could be improved, by elements of modern science, the greater truth was that agriculture, nutrition [and] medicine ... were perfectly adapted to the local environment. And so, rather than the imposition of western scientific innovations and conceptions on local communities, a system of "epistemic pluralism" was found to be the most useful, in effect a rapprochement between indigenous orally transmitted expertise, and field research. Although this point was not always easy for scientists or administrators to admit, learning to accommodate and build upon Africans' vernacular knowledge could hold the key to successful development'. In essence, the survey showed that ecology and epidemiology were the key sciences, not measurement as such. And in this context, ideologies of domination receded.[23]

It might be added that, as David Mills put it, the African Survey became the 'urtext for British colonial reformers and social scientists', a 'baseline survey', and that 'within weeks of its publication it was "as familiar an object on the desks in the Colonial Office as ... the Imperial Calendar"'.[24] The survey was also a major influence on the Colonial Development and Welfare Act, passed in 1940, and in the creation of the Colonial Social Science Research Council, formally appointed by government legislation in 1944 and, importantly, the first government body (in the midst of war, moreover) to represent, organise and fund the social sciences, thus playing a key role in institutionalising the embryonic disciplines of anthropology and sociology.[25]

Perhaps most important of all, the survey brought about a change in the understanding of empire, from an emphasis on administration to one of study and understanding, from the field officer to the anthropologist. All this preceded the fashionable ideas of Clifford Geertz (see the conclusion) by two decades.

Though that all sounds progressive, in that same year, 1944, there appeared a book which reminded everyone that this new understanding/approach still had some criticisms to face up to. This was *Capitalism and Slavery* by Eric Williams (1911–81), a Trinidad and Tobago political figure, who had obtained a scholarship to Oxford, where he said he encountered a great deal of racial hostility, but completed a DPhil before taking up an appointment at Howard University, a traditional black university in Washington, DC. His 1944 title was a revised version of his DPhil thesis, which had two main arguments. One was that Britain's industrial revolution was effectively financed by profits from the slave trade, and the other was that the abolition movement was less the result of humanitarianism among the British but rather because slavery was becoming uneconomic on the West Indian plantations. Williams, a Marxist, would write other books about Caribbean history but his arguments in *Capitalism and Slavery* attracted particular attention because he went on to become prime minister of Trinidad and Tobago, leading it to independence in 1962. Much postwar scholarship has been devoted to an examination of Williams's provocative views and will be considered later.[26]

Bletchley, the Bomb and Beveridge

B ritain had declared war on Germany on a Sunday, the morning of 3 September 1939. It was a balmy day in Berlin. William Shirer, the American newspaperman who later wrote a vivid history of the rise and fall of the Third Reich, reported that the city streets were calm, but the faces of Berliners registered 'astonishment, depression'. Before lunch he had drinks at the Adlon Hotel with about a dozen members of the British embassy. 'They seemed completely unmoved by events. They talked about *dogs* and such stuff.'

Others were required to show a greater sense of urgency. The very next day, Monday 4 September, Alan Turing reported to the Government Code and Cipher School at Bletchley Park in Buckinghamshire. The town of Bletchley was in an unlovely part of England, not far from the mud and dust of the county's famous brickfields.[1]

Life at Bletchley Park was so secret that the locals took against these 'do-nothings' and asked their local MP to table a question in Parliament. He was firmly dissuaded from doing so. Turing, a shy, unsophisticated man with dark hair that lay very flat on his head, found a room over a pub, the Crown, in a village about 3 miles away. Even though he helped in the bar when he could, the landlady made no secret of the fact that she didn't see why an able-bodied young man like Turing shouldn't be in the army.

In a sense, Bletchley Park had already been at war when Turing arrived. In 1938 a young Polish engineer called Robert Lewinsky had slipped into the British embassy in Warsaw and told the chief of military intelligence there that he had worked in Germany in a factory which made code-signalling machines. He also said he had a near-photographic memory, and could remember the details of the machine, called Enigma. The British believed him and smuggled Lewinsky to Paris, where he was indeed able to build a replica. This was the first break the British had in the secret war of codes. They knew that Enigma was used to send orders to military commanders both on land and at sea. But this was the first time anyone had seen it close up. It was smuggled to London in August 1939, two weeks before the outbreak of war, by Sacha Guitry, the much-married French playwright and actor.

It turned out that the machine was extremely simple, but its codes were virtually unbreakable.[2] In essence it looked like a typewriter with parts added on. The person sending the message simply typed what he or she had to say, in plain German, having first set a special key to one of a number of pointers. A series of rotor arms then scrambled the message as it was sent out. At the other end a similar machine received the message and, provided it was set to the same key, the message was automatically decoded. All personnel operating the machines were issued with a booklet indicating which key settings were to be used on which day. The rotors enabled billions of permutations. Since the code was changed three times a day, with the Germans transmitting thousands of messages in any 24-hour period, the British were faced with a seemingly impossible task. The story of how Enigma was cracked was a close secret for many years, and was certainly one of the most dramatic intellectual adventures of the twentieth century. It also had highly pertinent long-term consequences – not only for the outcome of the Second World War but for the development of computers.

Turing was a key player here. Born in 1912, he had a father who worked in the Indian civil service and the boy was sent to a boarding school where he suffered considerable psychological damage. His experience at school brought on a stutter and induced in him an eccentricity that probably contributed to his suicide some years later. He discovered in traumatic circumstances that he was homosexual, falling in love with another pupil who died from tuberculosis. Yet Turing's brilliance in mathematics shone through, and in October 1931 he took up a scholarship at King's College, Cambridge. Turing duly graduated with distinction as a wrangler, and was elected to a fellowship at King's. He spent the mid-1930s at Princeton, where he completed his PhD. The Mathematics Department there was in the same building as the recently established Institute for Advanced Study (IAS), and so he joined some of the most famous brains of the day: Einstein, Kurt Gödel, Richard Courant, G. H. Hardy and the man he became particularly friendly with, the Austro-Hungarian Johann von Neumann. Neumann was the man who most appreciated Turing's brilliance – he invited the Englishman to join him at the IAS after he had finished his PhD. Though Turing was flattered, and although he liked America, finding it a more congenial environment for a homosexual, he nonetheless returned to Britain.[3]

Here he came across another brilliant eccentric, Ludwig Wittgenstein, the philosopher/mathematician, whose lectures were open only to a select few. Turing, like the others in the seminar, was provided with a deck chair in an otherwise bare room. The subject of the seminar was the philosophical basis of mathematics: by all accounts, Turing knew little philosophy, but he had the edge when it came to mathematics and there were several pointed exchanges.

In the middle of these battles the real war broke out, and Turing was summoned to Bletchley. To the soldiers in uniform, Turing was positively weird. He hardly ever shaved, his trousers were held up using a tie as a belt, and he kept highly irregular hours. The only distinction he recognised between people was intellectual ability, so he would dismiss even senior officers who he regarded as fools and spend time instead playing chess with the lower ranks if they showed ability.[4]

But cracking Enigma was an intellectual problem of a kind where he shone, so he was tolerated. The basic difficulty was that Turing and all the others working with him had to search through thousands of intercepted messages looking for any regularities, and then try to understand them. His response was to build an electromagnetic device capable of high-speed calculation that could accept scrambled Enigma messages and search for patterns. This machine was given the name Colossus. The first Colossus (ten versions eventually became operational) was not built until December 1943. Details of the machine were kept secret for many years, but it is now known to have had 1,500 valves and, in later versions, 2,400 vacuum tubes computing in 'binary' (i.e., all information was contained in 'bits', various arrangements of either 0 or 1). It is in this sense that Colossus is now regarded as a forerunner of the electromagnetic digital computer. Colossus was slightly taller than a man, and photographs show that it occupied the entire wall of a small room in Hut F at Bletchley. It was a major advance in technology, able to scan 25,000 characters a second. Despite this, there was no sudden breakthrough with Enigma, and in 1943 the Atlantic convoys bringing precious food and supplies from North America were being sunk by German U-boats in worrying numbers. (At the darkest time, Britain had barely enough food to last a week.) However, by dogged improvements, the time it took to crack the coded messages was reduced from several days to hours, then minutes. Finally, Bletchley's code breakers were able to locate the whereabouts of every German U-boat in the Atlantic, and shipping losses were reduced considerably. The Germans became suspicious but never imagined that Enigma had been cracked, an expensive mistake.[5]

Turing's work was regarded as so important that he was sent to America to share it with Britain's chief ally. On that visit he again met Neumann. This meeting was to result in ENIAC (the Electronic Numerical Integrator and Calculator), built at the University of Pennsylvania. Bigger even than Colossus, this had some 19,000 valves and would have in time a direct influence on the development of computers.

There is no question but that Colossus helped to win the war – or at least helped Britain avoid defeat. The 'do-nothings' at Bletchley had proved their worth. In fact, Enigma/Colossus did not break upon the world for decades, by which time computers had become a fixture of everyday life. Turing did not live to see this: he took his own life in 1954.

In a survey conducted well after the war was over, a group of senior British servicemen and scientists were asked what they thought were the most important scientific contributions to the outcome of the war. This group concluded that there were six important developments or devices that 'arose or grew to stature because of the war': atomic energy, radar, rocket propulsion, jet propulsion, automation and operational research (there was of course no mention of Bletchley or Enigma). Atomic energy is considered separately; of the others, by far the most intellectually radical idea was radar.[6]

Radar was an American name for a British invention, which came to have a great number of applications, from anti-submarine warfare to direction-finding. But its most romantic role was in the Battle of Britain in 1940, when the advantage it provided to the British aircrews may just have made all the difference between victory and defeat.

It happened because Sir Robert Watson-Watt, in the radio department of the National Physical Laboratory in Middlesex, was researching a 'death ray'. He had the bloodthirsty idea that an electromagnetic beam might be created of sufficient energy to melt the thin metal skin of an aircraft and kill the crew inside. Calculations proved that this futuristic idea was a pipe dream. However, Watson-Watt's assistant, A. F. Wilkins, the man doing the arithmetic, also realised that it might be practicable to use such a beam to detect the *presence* of aircraft: the beam would be reradiated, bounced back towards the transmitting source in an 'echo'. Wilkins's ideas were put to the test in February 1935 near the Daventry broadcasting station in the Midlands. The overseeing committee, closeted in a caravan, saw that the presence of an aircraft (though not at that stage its precise location) could indeed be detected at a distance of about 8 miles.

The next steps took place on the remote East Anglian coast. Masts some 70 feet high were erected and, with their aid, aircraft up to 40 miles away could be tracked. By now the official committee realised that ultimate success depended on a reduction of the wavelength of the radio beams. Wavelengths are measured in metres, and it was not thought practical to create wavelengths of less than 50 centimetres (20 inches). But then John Randall and Mark Oliphant at Birmingham University came up with an idea they called a cavity magnetron, essentially a glass tube with a halfpenny at each end, fixed with sealing wax. The air was sucked out, creating a vacuum;

an electromagnet provided a magnetic field, and a loop of wire was threaded into one of the cavities in the hope that it would 'extract high-frequency power' (i.e., generate shorter waves). It did.[7]

It was now 21 February 1940. Anticipating success, a chain of coastal radar stations, stretching from Ventnor on the Isle of Wight to the Firth of Tay in Scotland, had been begun, which meant that once the cavity magnetron had proved itself, radar stations could monitor enemy aircraft even as they were getting into formation in France and Belgium. The British were even able to gauge the rough strength of the enemy formations, their height and their speed, and it was this 'which enabled the famous "few", Britain's fighter pilots, to intercept the enemy with such success'.[8]

May 1940 was for Britain and its close European allies the darkest hour of the war. On the tenth of the month German forces invaded the Netherlands, Belgium and Luxembourg, followed by the surrender of the Dutch and Belgian armies, with King Leopold III being taken prisoner. Neville Chamberlain resigned as prime minister, to be replaced by Winston Churchill. On the twenty-sixth, the evacuation of 300,000 British and French troops trapped in north-west France was begun at Dunkirk.

Though the war dominated everyone's thoughts, on Saturday 25 May, two scientists in Oxford University's Pathology Department conducted the first experiments in a series that would lead to 'the most optimistic medical breakthrough of the century'. Ernst Chain, the son of a Russo-German industrial chemist, had a PhD in chemistry from the Friedrich Wilhelm University in Berlin, but had been forced to leave Nazi Germany on account of being Jewish; N. G. Heatley was a British doctor. On that Saturday they injected streptococci bacteria into mice and then injected some of the mice with penicillin. After that, Chain went home, but Heatley stayed in the lab until 3.30 the next morning. By then every single untreated mouse had died – but all of the treated mice were alive. When Chain, who had also had to relinquish his post as the distinguished music critic of a Berlin newspaper, returned to the pathology lab on the Sunday morning, and saw what Heatley had seen, he is reported to have started dancing.[9]

The age of antibiotics had taken a while to arrive. The word 'anti-biotic' itself entered the English language at the turn of the century. Doctors were aware that bodies had their own defences – up to a point – and since 1870 it had been known that some *Pencillium* moulds acted against bacteria. But until the 1920s most medical attempts to combat microbial infection had largely failed – quinine worked for malaria, and the 'arsenicals' worked for syphilis, but these apart, there was a general rule that 'chemicals' in therapy did as much damage to the patient as the microbe. This is why the view took hold that the best way forward was some device to take advantage of the body's own defences, the old principle of homeopathy.

A leading centre of this approach was St Mary's Hospital in Paddington, London, where one of the doctors was Alexander Fleming. He had dropped into the lab one day in the summer of 1928, having been away for a couple of weeks' holiday and having left a number of cultures in the lab to grow in dishes. He noticed that one culture, *Penicillium*, appeared to have killed the bacteria in the surrounding region.[10] Over the following weeks, various colleagues tried the mould on themselves – on their eye infections, for example – but Fleming failed to capitalise on this early success. Who knows what Fleming would or would not have done but for a very different man?

Howard Walter Florey (later Lord Florey, PRS, 1898–1968) was born in Australia but came to Britain in 1922 as a Rhodes scholar. In the 1930s his main interest was in the development of spermici-dal substances that would form the basis of vaginal contraceptive gels. Besides the practical importance of the gels, their theoretical significance lay in the fact that they embodied 'selective toxicity' – the spermatozoa were killed without the walls of the vagina being damaged. At Oxford, Florey recruited Chain. Chain and Florey concentrated on three antibiotica – *Bacillus subtilis*, *Pseudomonas pyocyanea* and *Penicillium notatum*. They began their all-important experiments with mice.

Encouraged by the remarkable results mentioned above, Florey and Chain arranged to repeat the results using human subjects. Although they obtained enough penicillin to start trials, and although the results were impressive, the experiment was nonethe-less spoiled by the death of at least one patient because Florey, in wartime, could not procure enough antibiotics to continue the study. So Florey and Heatley left for America. Florey spent several weeks in the US Department of Agriculture's North Regional Research Laboratory at Peoria, Illinois, where they were expert at culturing micro-organisms. Unfortunately, Florey didn't get the funds he sought and Heatley, though he found himself in the company of excellent scientists, also found them anti-British and isolationist. The result was that penicillin became an American product (the pharmaceutical companies took Florey's results but did their own trials). Without the help of the US pharmaceutical companies, penicillin would no doubt not have had the impact that it did, but the award of the Nobel Prize in Medicine in 1945 to Fleming, Florey and Chain showed where the intellectual achievement belonged.[11]

If there was a single moment when an atomic bomb moved out of the realm of theory and became a practical option, then it occurred one night in early 1940, in Birmingham. The Blitz was in full force and there were blackouts every night, when no lights were allowed, and at times Otto Frisch and Rudolf Peierls – both Jews – must have wondered whether they had made the right decision in emigrating to Britain.

Frisch had at first moved to Copenhagen with the distinguished physicist and Nobel laureate Niels Bohr, but, as war approached, he had grown more and more apprehensive. Frisch was also an accomplished pianist, and his chief consolation was in being able to play. But then, in the summer of 1939, Mark Oliphant, joint inventor of the cavity magnetron, and who was by now professor of physics at Birmingham University, invited Frisch to Britain, ostensibly for discussions about physics. Frisch packed a couple of bags, as if for a weekend away. Once in England, however, Oliphant made it clear to Frisch he could stay if he wished; he could read the situation as well as anyone, and he realised that physical safety was what counted. While Frisch was in Birmingham war was declared, so he just stayed. All his possessions, including his beloved piano, were lost.[12]

Peierls was already in Birmingham and had been for some time. A wealthy Berliner, he was one of the many brilliant physicists who had trained with Arnold Sommerfeld in Munich. Peierls had been in

Britain since 1933, at Cambridge on a Rockefeller fellowship, when the purge of German universities had begun. He could afford to stay away, so he did. He would become a naturalised citizen in Britain in 1940, but for five months, from 3 September 1939 onward, he and Frisch were technically enemy aliens. They got round this 'inconvenience' by pretending that they were only discussing theoretical problems in their conversations with Oliphant.

Until Frisch joined Peierls in Birmingham, the chief argument against an atomic bomb had been the amount of uranium needed to 'go critical', start a chain reaction and cause an explosion. Estimates had varied hugely, from 13 to 44 tons. Had this been true, it would have made the bomb far too heavy to be transported by an aircraft and in any case would have taken as long as six years to assemble, by which time the war would surely be long over. It was Frisch and Peierls, walking through the leafy but blacked-out streets of Edgbaston, the suburb of Birmingham where the university is located, who first grasped that the previous calculations had been wildly inaccurate. Frisch worked out that, in fact, not much more than a kilogram of material was needed. Peierls's reckoning confirmed how explosive the bomb was: this meant calculating the available time before the expanding material separated enough to stop the chain reaction proceeding. The figure Peierls came up with was about four millionths of a second, during which time there would be eighty neutron generations (i.e., 1 would produce 2, 2 would produce 4, then 8, 16, 32 and so on). Peierls worked out that eighty generations would give temperatures as hot as the interior of the sun and 'pressures greater than the centre of the earth where iron flows as a liquid'.[13]

A kilogram of uranium, which is a heavy metal, is about the size of a grapefruit – surprisingly little. Frisch and Peierls rechecked their calculations, and did them again, with the same results. And so, as rare as U-235 is in nature (in the proportions 1:139 of U-238), they dared to hope that enough more fissionable material might be separated out – for a bomb and a trial bomb – in a matter of months rather than years. They took their calculations to Oliphant. He, like them, recognised that a threshold had been crossed, He had them prepare a report – just three pages long – and took it personally to Henry Tizard in London, the government's head of military research.[14]

The Frisch–Peierls memorandum was considered by a small committee brought into being by Tizard, which met for the first time in the offices of the Royal Society in April 1940. The committee came to the conclusion that the chances of making a bomb in time to have an impact on the war were good, and from then on, the development of an atomic bomb became British policy. The job of persuading the Americans to join in fell to Oliphant. Strapped by war, Britain did not have the funds for such a project, and any location, however secret, might be bombed. In America, a Uranium Committee had been established whose chairman was Vannevar Bush, a dual-doctorate engineer from MIT. Oliphant and John Cockcroft, another physicist, travelled to America and persuaded Bush to convey some of the urgency they felt to President Roosevelt. Roosevelt would not commit the United States to build a bomb, but he did agree to explore whether a bomb could be built. Without informing Congress, he found the necessary money 'from a special source available for such an unusual purpose'. As this implies, the atom bomb project subsequently moved out of Britain, as the world now knows, to Los Alamos in New Mexico. Frisch, Peierls, James Chadwick and several other British physicists spent the war years there, helping to develop the bomb, among them Klaus Fuchs, an émigré German, who was also a Russian spy.[15]

The scars of the stock market crash, the Depression and the events of the 1930s ran deep. How deep may be judged from the fact that although 'planning' was anathema in some quarters, for others it wasn't strong enough. Many people in Britain and America, for example, had a sneaking respect for the way Hitler had eliminated unemployment. After the experience of the Depression, the lack of a job for some seemed more important than political freedom, and so totalitarian planning – or central direction – was perhaps a risk worth taking. This attitude also stretched to Stalin's planning which, because Russia just then was an ally, never received in wartime the scrutiny it deserved. It was against this intellectual background that there appeared a document that had a greater impact in Britain than any other in the twentieth century.

Late on the evening of 30 November 1942 queues began to form outside the headquarters of His Majesty's Stationery Office in

Holborn Kingsway. This was, to say the least, an unusual occurrence: government publications are rarely best-sellers. But, when HMSO opened the following morning, its offices were besieged. Sixty thousand copies of the report being released that day were sold out straight away at 2 shillings (10 pence) a time, and by the end of the year sales had reached 100,000. Nor could it be said that the report was Christmas-present material – its title was positively off-putting: *Social Insurance and Allied Services*. And yet, in one form or another, the report eventually sold 600,000 copies, making it the best-selling government report until Lord Denning's inquiry into the Profumo sex and spying scandal twenty years later. The frenzy that attended its publication was as important an indicator of a shift in public sensibility as was the report itself.[16]

The Beveridge report, as it became known, came about inadvertently, when in June 1941 Sir William Beveridge was asked by Arthur Greenwood, Labour minister for reconstruction in the wartime coalition, to chair an interdepartmental committee on the coordination of social insurance. Beveridge was being asked merely to patch up part of Britain's social machinery but, deeply disappointed (he wanted a more active wartime role), he quickly rethought the situation and saw its radical and far-reaching possibilities.

Born the son of a British judge in India in 1879, into a household supported by twenty-six servants, Beveridge was educated at Charterhouse and Balliol College, Oxford, where he read mathematics and classics. After Oxford, like Tawney, Beveridge went to Toynbee Hall, where, he said later, he learned the meaning of poverty 'and saw the consequences of unemployment'. In 1907 he visited Germany to inspect the post-Bismarck system of compulsory social insurance for pensions and sickness, and on his return several articles he wrote in the *Morning Post* about German arrangements came to the attention of Winston Churchill, who invited him to join the Board of Trade as a full-time civil servant.[17]

After the First World War, Beveridge became director of the LSE, transforming it into a powerhouse for the social sciences. By the outbreak of the Second World War he was back in Oxford, as master of University College. His long career had brought him many connections: Tawney was his brother-in-law; Clement Attlee and Hugh Dalton, whom he had hired at the LSE, were now in Parliament and the government. He knew Churchill, Keynes and Seebohm Rowntree, whose alarming picture of poverty in York in 1899 had been partly responsible for the 1911 legislation and whose follow-up study, in 1936, was to help shape Beveridge's own document. His assistant at Oxford, Harold Wilson, would be a future prime minister of Britain.[18]

His paper envisaged two things. There were to be a national health service, children's allowances and unemployment benefits; and benefits were to be paid at a flat rate, high enough to live on, with contributions to come from the individual, his or her employer and the state. Beveridge was totally opposed to means tests or sliding scales, since he knew they would create more problems than they solved, not least the bureaucracy needed for administering a more complex system. He was familiar with all the arguments that benefits set too high would stop people from seeking work, but he was also sympathetic to the recent research of Rowntree, which had shown that low wages in large families were the primary cause of poverty.[19]

There were two reasons for the report's impact. Beveridge's title may have been dry, but his text certainly was not.[20] 'A revolutionary moment in world history', he wrote, 'is a time for revolutions, not patching.' War was 'abolishing landmarks of every kind', he said. And so it 'offered the chance of real change', for 'the purpose of victory is to live in a better world than the old world'. His principal line of attack, he said, was on want, 'but ... Want is only one of five giants on the road of reconstruction, and in some ways the easiest to attack. The others are Disease, Ignorance, Squalor and Idleness.'[21]

The success of Beveridge's plan, as he himself acknowledged, also owed something to Keynes, but the social and intellectual change that hit Britain, and other countries, was deeper than just economics. Mass Observation, the polling organisation run by Charles Madge, a friend of W. H. Auden, found in 1941 that 16 per cent said the war had changed their political views. In August 1942, four months before the Beveridge report, one in three had changed their political views. More than anything, the Beveridge report offered hope at a time when that commodity was in short supply.

*

One of the reasons hope was in short supply was Britain's continued alliance with Stalin's Russia. Despite the Great Terror there, Stalin's regime continued to benefit from its status as a crucial ally.[22] The extent to which Stalin was appeased in the middle of hostilities is shown by George Orwell's experiences in trying to get another slim volume published.

Subtitled 'A Fairy Story', *Animal Farm* is about a revolution that goes wrong and loses its innocence when the animals in Mr Jones's farm, stimulated to rebellion by an old Middle White boar, Major, take over the farm and expel Mr Jones and his wife. Old Major, when he addresses the other animals before he dies, refers to them as comrades. The rebellion itself is dignified by its leaders (among them the young boar Napoleon) with the name Animalism and Orwell never made any secret of the fact that his satire was directed at Stalin.

The revolution on the farm is soon corrupted; the pigs, looking after their own, gradually take over; a litter of puppies is conditioned to grow up as a vicious Gestapo-like Praetorian guard; the original commandments of Animalism, painted on the barn wall, are secretly amended in the dead of night ('All animals are equal *but some are more equal than others*'); and finally the pigs start to walk on two legs, after months when the slogan has been 'Two legs bad! Four legs good!'

The book appeared in August 1945, the month that the United States dropped the atomic bomb on Hiroshima and Nagasaki, and the delay between completion and release is partly explained by the difficulties Orwell experienced in getting the book published. Victor Gollancz turned down *Animal Farm*, and at Faber & Faber, T. S. Eliot did too. In rejecting the book he wrote, 'We have no conviction . . . that this is the right point of view from which to criticise the political situation at the present time.' Orwell considered publishing the book himself, but then Secker & Warburg took it on, though not immediately, owing to the paper shortage. When the book finally appeared, the evidence of Nazi concentration camps was becoming known, with its bleak confirmation of what people were capable of doing to their fellow humans.[23]

Orwell grasped clearly that though the battle against Hitler had been won, the battle against Stalin was far from over, and so far as twentieth-century thought and ideas were concerned, was much more important.

Many of the Nazi and Japanese wartime atrocities were not fully revealed until hostilities had ended. They set the seal on six grim years. And yet, for the optimistic, there was a silver lining amid the gloom. Almost all the major belligerents in the war, including the remoter areas of the British Empire, such as Australia and New Zealand, had achieved full employment. The curse of the 1930s had been wiped out. Except among his grudging opponents, this was regarded as a triumph for the ideas of John Maynard Keynes.

Keynes had been fifty-six at the outbreak of the Second World War, and although he had made his name in the first war, his role was actually more crucial in the second. Within two months of the outbreak of hostilities, he produced three articles for *The Times*, rapidly reprinted as a pamphlet entitled *How to Pay for the War*. Keynes's ideas this time had two crucial elements. First, he saw immediately that the problem was not, at root, one of money but one of raw materials: wars are won or lost by the physical resources capable of being turned rapidly into ships, guns, shells and so forth. These raw materials are capable of being measured and therefore controlled. Keynes also saw that the difference between a peacetime economy and a war economy was that in peace workers spend any extra income on the goods they have themselves worked to produce; in war, extra output – beyond what the workers need to live on – goes to the government. Keynes's second insight was that war offers the opportunity to stimulate social change, that the 'equality of effort' needed in national emergency could be channelled into financial measures that would not only reflect that equality of effort but help ensure greater equality after the war was over. And that, in turn, if widely publicised, would help efficiency. After Winston Churchill became prime minister, and despite the hostility to his ideas from the Beaverbrook press, Keynes was taken on as one of his two economic advisors (Lord Catto was the other). Keynes lost no time in putting his ideas into effect. Not all of them became law, but his influence was profound.[24]

If Keynes had won the day in regard to the regulation of domestic economics, his experiences were to be less happy in dealing with the problems facing international trade. This was the issue addressed at the famous conference at Bretton Woods in the summer of 1944. Around 750 people attended this conference, in the White Mountains of New Hampshire, which gave birth to the World Bank and the International Monetary Fund – both part of Keynes's key vision, though their powers were much diluted by the American team. Keynes understood that two problems faced the postwar world 'only one of which was new'. The old problem was to prevent a return to the competitive currency devaluations of the 1930s which had the overall effect of reducing international trade and adding to the effects of the Depression. The new problem was that the postwar world would be divided into two: the debtor nations (such as Britain) and the creditor nations (most obviously the United States). So long as this huge imbalance existed, the recovery of international trade would be hampered, affecting everyone. Keynes, who was in brilliant form at the conference, clearly grasped that a system of international currency and an international bank were needed, so as to extend the principles of domestic economics into the international field. The chief point of the international bank was that it could extend credit and make loans (provided by creditor countries) in such a way that debtor countries could change their currency ratios without provoking tit-for-tat reprisals from others. The plans also removed the world from the gold standard.[25]

Keynes didn't have everything his own way and the plan adopted was as much the work of Harry Dexter White, in the US Treasury, as it was of Keynes. But the intellectual climate in which these problems were thrashed out at Bretton Woods was that created by Keynes in the interwar years.[26]

The end of the Second World War was the high point of Keynesian economics. Keynes had brought about an amazing change in intellectual viewpoint (not just in wartime, but over a lifetime of writings), and although he would be much criticised in later years, and his theories modified, the attitude we have to unemployment now – that it is to an extent under the control of government – is thanks to him.

The Attack on the Intellectual Elite

I n November 1948 the Nobel Prize in Literature was awarded to T. S. Eliot. For him it was a year of awards – the previous January he had been given the Order of Merit by King George VI. Between *The Waste Land* and the prize, Eliot had built an unequalled reputation for his hard, clear poetic voice, with its bleak vision of the emptiness and banality running through modern life. He had also written a number of carefully crafted and well-received plays peopled with mainly pessimistic characters who had lost their way in a world that was exhausted. By 1948 Eliot was extremely conscious of the fact that his own work was, as his biographer Peter Ackroyd put it, 'one of the more brightly chiselled achievements of a culture that was dying', and that partly explains why, in the month that he travelled to Stockholm to meet the Swedish king and receive his prize, he also published his last substantial prose book. *Notes Towards the Definition of Culture* is not his best book, but it interests us here because it was the first of a small number of works, on both sides of the Atlantic, that, in the aftermath of war, formed the last attempt to preserve the traditional 'high' culture which Eliot and others felt to be mortally threatened.[1]

The Waste Land, besides its grim vision of the post-First World War landscape, had been constructed in a form that was frankly high culture – fiercely elitist and deliberately difficult, with elaborate references to the classics of the past. In the post-Second World War environment, Eliot clearly felt that a somewhat different form of attack, or defence, was needed – plain speaking that did not risk being misunderstood or overlooked. *Notes* begins by sketching out various meanings of the term 'culture' – as in its anthropological sense ('primitive culture'), its biological sense (bacterial culture, agriculture), and in its more usual sense of referring to someone who is learned, civil, familiar with the arts, who has an easy ability to manipulate abstract ideas. He discusses the overlap between these meanings before concentrating on his preferred subject, by which he means that, to him, culture is a way of life. Here he advances the paragraph that was to become famous: 'The term culture ... includes all the characteristic activities that interest a people: Derby Day, Henley Regatta, Cowes, the twelfth of August, a cup final, dog races, the pin table, the dart board, Wensleydale cheese ... and the music of Elgar. The reader can make his own list.'[2]

But if this list seems ecumenical, Eliot soon makes it clear that he distinguishes many *levels* of such a culture. For him, culture can only thrive with an elite, a cultural elite, and cannot exist without religion, his point being that religion brings with it a shared set of beliefs to hold a way of life together – Eliot is convinced therefore that democracy and egalitarianism invariably threaten culture. Although he often refers to 'mass society', his main target is the breakdown of the family, and family life. For it is through the family, he says, that culture is transmitted.

But perhaps the most important point of culture, Eliot says, lies in its impact on politics. The power elite needs a cultural elite, he argues, because the cultural elite is the best antidote, provides the best critics for the power brokers in any society, and that criticism pushes the culture forward, preventing it stagnating and decaying. He therefore thinks that there are bound to be classes in society, that class is a good thing, though he wants there to be plenty of movement between classes, and he recognises that the chief barrier to the ideal situation is the family, which quite naturally tries to buy privilege for its offspring. He views as obvious that cultures have evolved, that some cultures are higher than others, but he does not see this as cause for concern or, be it said, as an excuse for racism (though he himself was later to be accused of anti-Semitism). For Eliot, within any one culture, the higher, more evolved, levels positively influence the lower levels by their greater knowledge of, and use of, *scepticism.*[3]

THE CENTRE OF HUMAN CONSCIOUSNESS

Eliot was joined here by F. R Leavis. Much influenced by Eliot, Leavis – being a conscientious objector – spent the First World War as a stretcher bearer. Afterward he returned to Cambridge as an academic. On his arrival he found no separate English faculty but he, his wife Queenie and a small number of critics (rather than novelists, or poets, or dramatists) set about transforming English studies into what Leavis was later to call 'the centre of human consciousness'. All his life Leavis evinced a high moral seriousness because he believed, quite simply, that that was the best way to realise 'the possibilities of life'. He thought that writers – poets especially but novelists too – were 'more alive' than anyone else, and that it was the responsibility of the university teacher and critic to show why some writers were greater than others. 'English was the route to other disciplines.'[4]

In 1948 he published *The Great Tradition* and in 1952 *The Common Pursuit*. Note the words 'Tradition' and 'Common', meaning shared. Leavis believed passionately that there is a common human nature but that we each have to discover it for ourselves – as had the authors he concentrated on in his two books: Henry James, D. H. Lawrence, George Eliot, Joseph Conrad, Jane Austen, Charles Dickens. No less important, he felt that in judging serious literature, there was the golden – the transcendent – opportunity to exercise judgement 'which is both "personal" and yet more than personal'.[5]

One man sceptical of Eliot's approach was Michael Young, an educationalist, who in 1958 produced a satire that poked fun at some of the cherished assumptions of the likes of Eliot and Leavis. *The Rise of the Meritocracy* was ostensibly set in 2034 and was cast as an 'official' report written in response to certain 'disturbances' that, to begin with, are not specified. The essence of the satire is that the hereditary principle in life has been abolished, to be replaced by one of merit (IQ + Effort = Merit), with the 'aristocracy' replaced by a 'meritocracy'. Interestingly, Young found it very difficult to publish his book – it was turned down by eleven publishers. In the end the book was published by a friend at Thames & Hudson, but only as an act of friendship – whereupon *The Rise* promptly sold several hundred thousand copies.[6]

The book is divided into two sections. 'The Rise of the Elite' is essentially an optimistic gloss on the way high-IQ people have been let loose in the corridors of power; the second section, 'The Decline of the Lower Classes', is a gleeful picture of the way such social engineering is almost bound to backfire. Young doesn't take sides; he merely fires both barrels of the argument as to what would happen if we really did espouse wholeheartedly the mantra 'equality of opportunity'. His chief point is that such an approach would be bound to lead to eugenic nonsenses and monstrosities, that the new lower classes – by definition stupid – would have no leadership worth the name, and that the new IQ-rich upper classes would soon devise ways to keep themselves in power.[7]

Barely was the ink dry on the pages of these books than they were assaulted and attacked and bombarded from all sides at once. In some ways America led the way, with the 'alternative culture' of its 'Beat' poets – William Burroughs, Kenneth Rexroth, Lawrence Ferlinghetti and Jack Kerouac – and the black writers Richard Wright and James Baldwin. They were joined from the *Francophonie* by Léopold Senghor, Aimé Césaire and Frantz Fanon and from Africa by Chinua Achebe and Wole Soyinka, writing in English. In Britain Colin MacInnes's London Trilogy (*City of Spades*, 1958, *Absolute Beginners*, 1959, and *Mr Love and Justice*, 1960) contained astute observations on the way of life of West Indians in London, who had been arriving since 1948 to work in the capital's transport system, and coincided with race riots in Notting Hill. MacInnes's books also coincided with the achievements of anthropology and archaeology in the immediate aftermath of the Second World War, which together had begun to produce results showing the basic concordance of human nature and beliefs right across the globe.[8] This too was an immensely influential view in the second half of the twentieth century, becoming the orthodoxy. Running through many works, too, was the experience of being black in a non-black world. Responses differed, but what they showed was a growing awareness that the art, history, language, the very experience of being black, had been deliberately devalued or rendered invisible in the past.

*

Britain in the 1950s did not yet have a large black population. Black immigrants had been arriving since 1948, their lives chronicled now and then by writers such as MacInnes. The first Commonwealth Immigrants Act, restricting admission from the 'New' Commonwealth (i.e., predominantly black countries), was not passed until 1961. Until that point, then, there was little threat to the traditional British culture from race. Instead, the 'alternative' found its strength in an equivalent social divide that for many created almost as much passion: class.

In 1955 a small coterie of like-minded serious souls got behind an idea to establish a theatre in London that would endeavour to do something new: find fresh plots from completely new sources, in an effort to revitalise contemporary drama and search out a new audience. They named the venture the English Stage Company and bought the lease on a small theatre known as the Royal Court in Sloane Square in Chelsea.[9] The first artistic director was George Devine, who had trained in Oxford and in France, and he brought in as his deputy Tony Richardson, twenty-seven, who had been working for the BBC. While launching the company, Devine had paid for an ad in the *Stage*, the theatrical weekly, soliciting new plays on contemporary themes, and among the 700 manuscripts that arrived 'almost by return of post' was one by a playwright named John Osborne, which was called *Look Back in Anger*.

Devine was much taken by the 'abrasive' language that he grasped instinctively would play well on stage. He discovered that the writer was an out-of-work actor, a man who was in many ways typical of a certain postwar figure in Britain. The 1944 Education Act (brought in as a result of the Beveridge report) had raised the school-leaving age and initiated the modern system of primary, secondary and tertiary education. It had also provided funds to help lower-class students attend acting schools. But in drab postwar England, there were now more students than jobs. Osborne was one of these overtrained types and so was Jimmy Porter, the 'hero' of his play.[10]

'Hero' merits inverted commas because it was one of the hallmarks of *Look Back in Anger* that its lower-middle-class protagonist, while attacking everything around him, also attacked himself. Porter is driven by 'a furious energy directed towards a void'. The structure of *Anger* has been criticised as falling apart at the end, where Jimmy and his middle-class wife retreat into their private fantasy world of cuddly toys. Despite this, the play was a great success and marked the beginning of a time when, as one critic put it, 'plays would no longer be concerned with middle-class heroes or set in country houses'. Its title helped to give rise to the phrase 'angry young men', which, together with 'kitchen sink drama', described a number of plays that, in the mid- to late 1950s, drew attention to the experiences of working-class men (they were usually men). So it is in this sense that the trend typified by Osborne fits into the reconceptualisation of culture. (See the references for other typical plays.)[11]

A somewhat similar change was overtaking poetry. On 1 October 1954 an anonymous article appeared in the *Spectator* entitled 'In the Movement'. The *Spectator* article identified five authors, but after D. J. Enright had published *Poets of the 1950s* in 1955, and Robert Conquest's *New Lines* had appeared a year later, nine poets and novelists came to be regarded as what was then known as 'the Movement': Kingsley Amis, Conquest, Donald Davie, Enright, Thom Gunn, Christopher Holloway, Elisabeth Jennings, Philip Larkin and John Wain. One anthologist, perhaps going a shade over the top, described the Movement as 'the greatest rupture in cultural tradition since the eighteenth century'. Its core texts included Wain's novel *Hurry On Down* (1953) and Amis's *Lucky Jim* (1954), and its prevailing tone was 'middlebrow scepticism' and 'ironical commonsense'.[12]

The most typical poet of the Movement was Larkin. He grew up in Coventry, not too far from Auden's Birmingham, and after Oxford began a career as a university librarian (Leicester, 1946–50; Belfast, 1950–5; Hull, 1955–85), mainly because he needed a regular job. His poetic voice, as revealed in his first major collection, *The Less Deceived* (1955), was 'sceptical, plain-speaking, unshowy', and above all modest, fortified by common sense. It wasn't angry like Osborne's plays, but Larkin's rejection of old literature or tradition, lofty ideas, psychoanalysis – the 'common myth-kitty' as he put it – does echo the down-to-earth qualities of 'kitchen sink' drama, even if the volume control is turned down. One of his most famous poems is 'Church Going', with the lines 'I take off / My cycle-clips in awkward reverence', which immediately conveyed Larkin's 'intimate sincerity', not to mention a certain comic awareness. For Larkin,

> man has a hunger for meaning but for the most part is not quite sure he is up to the task; the world exists without question – there's nothing philosophical about it; what's philosophical is that man can't do anything about that fact – he is a 'helpless bystander'; his feelings have no meaning and therefore no place. He observes

> the hail
> Of occurrence clobber life out
> To a shape no one sees.[13]

Overlapping with the angry young men, and the Movement, was Richard Hoggart's highly original *The Uses of Literacy*. Published a year after *Look Back in Anger* was first staged, in 1957, Hoggart was, with Raymond Williams, Stuart Hall and E. P. Thompson, one of the founders of the school of thought (and now academic discipline) known as cultural studies. Hoggart worked alongside Larkin, in his case as a tutor in literature in the Department of Adult Education at the University of Hull, but it was in *The Uses of Literacy* that his working-class background, his army life, his teaching in the adult education department of a provincial university, came together.

Hoggart moved against Leavis: instead of following the Cambridge tradition, he brought his attention to bear on the culture he himself knew – from the singing in working men's clubs to weekly family magazines, from commercial popular songs to the films that ordinary people flocked to time and again. He described and analysed the customs he had grown up not even questioning, such as washing the car on a Sunday morning, or scrubbing the front step.

His book did two things. It first described in detail the working-class culture, in particular its language – in the books, magazines, songs and games it inhabited. In doing so, it showed, second, how rich this culture was, how much more there was to it than its critics alleged. Like Osborne, Hoggart wasn't blind to its shortcomings, or to the fact that, overall, British society deprived people born into the working class of the chance to escape it. But Hoggart's aim was more description and analysis than any nakedly political intent. Here was another Great Tradition.[14]

Hoggart led naturally to Raymond Williams. Like Hoggart, Williams had served in the war, though most of his life had been spent in the English Department at Cambridge, where he could not help but be aware of the Leavisites. In a series of books beginning with *Culture and Society* in 1958, Williams made plain and put into context what had been implicit in the narrow scope of Hoggart's work.

Williams's basic idea was that a work of art – a painting, a novel, a poem, a film – does not exist without a context, above all a *political* background. The imagination cannot avoid a relation with power; the form art takes and our attitudes towards it are themselves a form of politics. In Marxist theory, Williams reminds us, the determining fact of life is the means of production and distribution, and so the progress of culture, like everything else, is dependent upon the material conditions for the production of that culture. Culture therefore cannot help but reflect the social make-up of a society, and in such an analysis it is only natural that those at the top should not want change. On this view, then, Eliot and Leavis are merely reflecting the social circumstances of their time, and in so doing are exhibiting a conspicuous lack of self-awareness.[15] Elites, as viewed by Eliot or Leavis, are merely one segment of the population, with their own special interests. Instead, Williams advises us to trust our own experience as to whether an artist or his or her work is relevant.

Two final assaults on the Eliot–Leavis canon came from history and from science. The historical challenge came from the British school of Marxist historians. Their achievements will be discussed more fully in Chapter 31 but the most frontal attack on Eliot, Leavis et al. may be precisely dated and located. The setting was, again, Cambridge, and the time a little after five o'clock on the afternoon of 7 May 1959. That was when a 'bulky, shambling figure approached the lectern at the western end of Senate House', a white stone building in the centre of the city. The room was packed with senior academics, students and a number of distinguished guests, assembled for one of Cambridge's 'showpiece public occasions', the annual Rede Lecture. That year the speaker was Sir Charles Snow, later to be Lord Snow, but universally known by his initials, as C. P. Snow. 'By the time he sat down over an hour later', as Stefan Collini tells the story, 'Snow had ... started a controversy which was to be remarkable for its scope, its duration, and, at least at times, its intensity.' The title of the lecture was 'The Two Cultures and the Scientific Revolution', and the two cultures he identified were those of 'the literary intellectuals' and the natural scientists, 'between whom he claimed to find a profound mutual suspicion and incomprehension, which in turn, he said, had damaging consequences for the prospects of applying technology to the world's problems'.[16]

Snow had chosen his moment. He was himself a Cambridge man, who had worked in the Cavendish Laboratory under Ernest Rutherford. He was best known as a government scientific advisor and a novelist, with a multi-volume series, Strangers and Brothers, about the decision-making processes in a series of closed communities (such as professional societies or Cambridge colleges). These were much derided by advocates of 'high' literature who found, or affected to find, his style stilted and pompous.

Snow's central point applied across the world, he said, but it was also true that it applied more than anywhere in Britain. Literary intellectuals, said Snow, controlled the reins of power both in government and in the highest social circles, which meant that only people with, say, a knowledge of the classics, history and/or English literature were felt to be educated. Such people did not know much – or even any – science; they rarely thought it important or interesting and as often as not left it out of the equation when discussing policy in government or regarded it as boring socially. He thought this form of ignorance was disgraceful and dangerous, and, when applied to government, that it failed the country. At the same time, he thought scientists culpable of often being ill educated in the humanities, apt to dismiss literature as invalid subjectivism with nothing to teach *them*.[17] He concluded by arguing that the proper administration of science, which could only come about when the literate intellectuals became familiar with those alien disciplines and dropped their prejudices, would help solve the overriding problems of rich and poor countries that bedevilled the planet.

Snow's lecture provoked an immense reaction. But from one source came withering criticism. This was none other than F. R. Leavis, who published a lecture he had given on Snow in an article in the *Spectator*. Leavis argued that the methods of literature related to the individual quite differently from the methods of science, 'because the language of literature was in some sense the language of the individual – not in an obvious sense but at least in a *more* obvious sense than the language of science'.[18] Yet it is now obvious at least that Snow was right about the importance of the electronic/information revolution and he is remembered more for his lecture than his novels.

And so, piece by piece, book by book, play by play, song by song, the traditional canon began to crumble, or be undermined. Knowing more science, or being familiar with John Osborne or black writers from the Commonwealth, did not mean necessarily throwing traditional works out of the window. But undoubtedly from the 1950s on, the sense of a common pursuit, a great tradition shared among people who regarded themselves as well educated and cultured, began to break down.

Mothers and Genes:
Biochemical Breakthrough

I n 1948 the Social Commission of the United Nations decided to make a study of the needs of homeless children: in the aftermath of war, it was realised that in several countries large numbers of children lacked fully formed families. The World Health Organization (WHO) offered to provide an investigation into the mental-health aspects of the problem. Dr John Bowlby was a British psychiatrist and psychoanalyst who had helped select army officers in the Second World War. He took up a temporary appointment with the WHO in January 1950, and during the late winter and early spring of that year he visited France, the Netherlands, Sweden, Switzerland, the United Kingdom and the United States of America, holding discussions with workers involved in child care and child guidance. These discussions led to the publication, in 1951, of *Maternal Care and Mental Health*, a famous report that hit a popular nerve and brought about a wholesale change in the way we think about childhood.[1]

It was this report that first confirmed for many people the crucial nature of the early months of an infant's life, when in particular the quality of mothering was revealed as all-important for the subsequent psychological development of a child. Bowlby's report introduced the key phrase 'maternal deprivation' to describe the source of a general pathology of development in children, the effects of which were found to be widespread. The very young infant who went without proper mothering was found to be 'listless, quiet, unhappy, and unresponsive to a smile or a coo', and later to be less intelligent, bordering in some cases on the defective. No less important, Bowlby drew attention to a large number of studies which showed that victims of maternal deprivation failed to develop the ability to hold relationships with others or feel guilty about their failure. Such children either 'craved affection' or were 'affect-less'.

The thrust of this research had two consequences. On the positive side, Bowlby's research put beyond doubt the idea that a bad home is better for a child than a good institution. It was then the practice in many countries for illegitimate or unwanted children to be cared for in institutions where standards of nutrition, cleanliness and medical matters could be closely monitored. But it became clear that such an environment was not enough, that something was lacking which affected mental health, rather in the way that vitamins had been discovered to be lacking in the artificial diets created for neglected children in the great cities of the nineteenth century. And so, following publication of the WHO report, countries began to change their approach to neglected children: adoptions were favoured over fostering, children with long-term illness were not separated from their parents when they went to hospital, and new mothers sent to prison were allowed to take their young babies with them. At work, maternity leave was extended to include not just the delivery but the all-important early months of the child's life. There was in general a much greater sensitivity to the nature of the mother–child bond.[2]

Less straightforward was the link the WHO report found between a disrupted early family life and later delinquency and/or inadequacy. This was doubly important because children from such 'broken' families also proved in many cases to be problem parents themselves, thus establishing what was at first called 'serial deprivation' and later the 'cycle of deprivation'. Not all deprived children became delinquent; and not all delinquent children came from broken homes (though the great majority did). The exact nature of this link assumed greater intellectual prominence later on, but in the 1950s the discovery of the relationship between broken homes and delinquency mediated via maternal deprivation offered hope for the amelioration of social problems that disfigured postwar society in many Western countries.

The great significance of Bowlby's report was the way it took an essentially Freudian concept – the bond between mother and child – and examined it scientifically, using objective measures of behaviour to understand what was going on, rather than concentrating on the inner workings of 'the mind'.

The inner workings of the body in more general terms also became more accessible just then too. The first the public knew about the discovery of DNA, the long-chain molecule that governs reproduction, came on 25 April 1953, in *Nature*, in a 900-word paper entitled 'Molecular Structure of Nuclear Acids'. The paper followed the familiar ordered layout of *Nature* articles. But although it was the paper that created the science of molecular biology, it was also the culmination of an intense two-year drama in which, if science really were the careful, ordered world it is supposed to be, the wrong side won.

Among the personalities, Francis Crick stands out. Born in Northampton in 1916, the son of a shoemaker, Crick graduated from London University and worked at the Admiralty during the Second World War, designing mines. It was only in 1946, when he attended a lecture by Linus Pauling, the Oregon-born biochemical engineer, that his interest in chemical research was kindled. In 1949 he was taken on by the Cambridge Medical Research Council Unit at the Cavendish Laboratory, where he soon became known for his loud laugh and his habit of firing off theories on this or that at the drop of a hat.[3]

In 1951 an American joined the lab. James Dewey Watson was a tall Chicagoan, twelve years younger than Crick but extremely self-confident, a zoology student at the University of Chicago, which influenced him towards microbiology. On a visit to Europe Watson had met a New Zealander, Maurice Wilkins, at a scientific congress in Naples. Wilkins, then based at King's College in London, had worked on the Manhattan Project in the Second World War but became disillusioned and had turned to biology. The British Medical Research Council had a biophysics unit at King's which Wilkins then ran. One of his specialities was X-ray diffraction pictures of DNA and in Naples he generously showed Watson some of the results. It was this coincidence that shaped Watson's life.[4]

There and then he seems to have decided that he would devote himself to discovering the structure of DNA. He knew there was a Nobel Prize in it, that molecular biology could not move ahead without such an advance, but that once the advance was made, the way would be open for genetic engineering, a whole new era of human experience. He arranged a transfer to the Cavendish. A few days after his twenty-third birthday, Watson arrived in Cambridge.

What Watson didn't know was that the Cavendish had a 'gentleman's agreement' with King's. The Cambridge lab was studying the structure of protein, in particular haemoglobin, while London was studying DNA. That was only one of the problems. Although Watson hit it off immediately with Crick, that was virtually all they had in common. Crick was weak in biology, Watson in chemistry. Neither had any experience in X-ray diffraction, the technique developed by the leader of the lab, Lawrence Bragg, to determine atomic structure. None of this deterred them. Their main rivals came from King's, where Maurice Wilkins had recently hired the 29-year-old Rosalind Franklin ('Rosy', though never to her face). Described as the 'wilful daughter' of a cultured banking family, she had just completed four years' X-ray diffraction work in Paris and was one of the world's top experts. When Franklin was hired by Wilkins she thought she was to be his equal and that she would be in charge of the X-ray diffraction work. Wilkins, on the other hand, thought that she was coming as his assistant.[5]

Despite this, Franklin made good progress and in the autumn of 1951 decided to give a seminar at King's to make known her findings. Remembering Watson's interest in the subject, from their meeting in Naples, Wilkins invited the Cambridge man. At the seminar, Watson learned from Franklin that DNA almost certainly had a helical structure. After the seminar, he took her for a Chinese dinner in Soho. There the conversation turned away from DNA to how miserable she was at King's. Wilkins, she said, was reserved, polite, but cold. Watson returned to Cambridge convinced the Wilkins–Franklin relationship would never deliver the goods.[6]

The Crick–Watson relationship, meanwhile, flourished. Because they were so different, in age, cultural and scientific background, there was little rivalry. And because they were so conscious of their general ignorance, they could slap down each other's ideas without feelings being hurt. In the long run that may have been crucial.

A new factor entered the situation when, in the autumn of 1952, Peter Pauling, Linus's son, arrived at the Cavendish to do postgraduate research. He attracted a lot of beautiful women, much to Watson's satisfaction, but more to the point, he was constantly in touch with his father and told his new colleagues that Linus was putting together a model for DNA. Crick and Watson were devastated, but when an advance copy of the paper arrived, they immediately saw that it had a fatal flaw. It described a triple-helix structure, with the bases on the outside – and Pauling had left out the ionisation, meaning his structure would not hold together but fall apart.[7]

Watson and Crick accepted that it would only be a matter of time before Pauling himself realised his error, and they estimated they had six weeks to get in first. So began the most intense six weeks Crick and Watson had ever lived through. They now had permission to build more models (models were especially necessary in a three-dimensional world) and had developed their thinking about the way the four bases – adenine, guanine, thymine and cytosine – were related to each other. And, from Franklin's latest crystallography, they also had far better pictures of DNA, giving much more accurate measures of its dimensions. The final breakthrough came when Watson realised they could have been making a simple error by using the wrong isomeric form of the bases. Each base came in two forms – *enol* and *keto* – and all the evidence so far pointed to the *enol* form as being the correct one to use. But what if the *keto* form were tried? Watson immediately saw that the bases fitted together on the *inside*, to form the perfect double-helix structure. Even more important, when the two strands separated in reproduction, the mutual attraction of adenine to guanine, and of thymine to cytosine, meant that the new double helix was identical to the old one – the biological information contained in the genes was passed unchanged, as it had to be if the structure was to explain heredity. They announced the new structure to their colleagues on 7 March 1953, and six weeks later their paper appeared in *Nature*. Wilkins was charitable towards Crick and Watson, calling them a couple of 'old rogues'. Franklin immediately accepted their model. Not everyone was as emollient. They were told they did not deserve the sole credit for what they had discovered.[8]

In fact, the drama was not yet over. In 1962 the Nobel Prize in Medicine was awarded jointly to Crick, Watson and Wilkins, and in the same year the prize for chemistry went to the head of the Cavendish X-ray diffraction unit, Max Perutz, and his assistant, John Kendrew. Rosalind Franklin got nothing, but in April 2023, based on new evidence, she was judged a 'co-equal' in the discovery of DNA. In 1958, the day before she was to unveil the structure of the tobacco mosaic virus, she died of ovarian cancer. Aaron Klug, who continued her research, won the Nobel Prize in Chemistry in 1982.[9]

While Crick and Watson were earning their Nobels in Cambridge, in Oxford Dorothy Hodgkin was embarked on the research that would lead to her Nobel award in 1964. Dorothy Crowfoot (1910–94) was born in Giza, near Cairo, where her father was an inspector with the ministry of public instruction for Egypt and Sudan; later, showing his wide range of interest and expertise, he would become director of the British School of Archaeology in Jerusalem. Her mother had lost all four of her brothers in the First World War. Always interested in chemistry, at the age of thirteen Dorothy attended the Royal Institution Christmas Lectures given by Sir William Bragg, who had himself won the Nobel Prize for his discovery of the X-ray diffraction method, showing how crystals could reveal the atomic structure of biological substances. She read chemistry at Somerville College, Oxford, and she co-authored her first paper in *Nature* in 1932, at the age of twenty-two. She would retain her links with Somerville but at first went to Cambridge to train further with J. D. Bernal, who had in turn trained with Bragg. She fell in love with Bernal, but he was otherwise engaged (indeed, rather busy) and since he was away a lot (he was a politically active admirer of the Soviet Union) much of the day-to-day work fell to Crowfoot. It was in this way that she would come to use chemical techniques to identify the three-dimensional structures of four biological substances – pepsin, penicillin (she worked with Chain and Florey), vitamin B12 and insulin. These identifications would lead to the award of the Nobel Prize in 1964, and would help others create treatments for a range of diseases.[10]

Her intense political interests were boosted when she met and married Thomas Hodgkin, a history graduate who had lost his job as personal secretary to the British high commissioner in Palestine through his earnest support for the Arabs and had turned communist. Dorothy was very internationally minded: she was close to Chinese and Indian scientists in particular; became chairman of the Pugwash Conference on Science and World Affairs, founded by Bertrand Russell and Albert Einstein; sat on an international commission into US war crimes in Vietnam; and corresponded with Margaret Thatcher (once her student at Somerville) about the verification of chemical test bans. In 1953 she had been deemed 'statutorily inadmissible' by the US State Department, during the McCarthy era, and a quarter of a century later, in 1987, was awarded the Lenin Peace Prize. In some ways she best exemplified Britain's intellectual life at the end of empire.

To accompany these discoveries in biology, a new form of literature began to appear in the 1970s, books about biology but with a distinct philosophical edge. They were not written by journalists, as Gordon Rattray Taylor had done with *The Biological Time Bomb*, or popularisers, such as Desmond Morris with *The Naked Ape*, but by the scientists themselves. The new literature occurred not just in Britain. In France there was Jacques Monod, a Nobel Prize-winning biologist, whose *Chance and Necessity* explored what genetics might imply for ethics, politics and philosophy. In America, in *Sociobiology: The New Synthesis*, Edward O. Wilson, the Harvard zoologist, was keen to show how much social behaviour is 'government by genes'. In Britain Richard Dawkins, at Oxford, brought us *The Selfish Gene*, which, perhaps surprisingly for non-biologists, contained a fair amount of elementary mathematics.

Dawkins, in one of his crucial passages, asks us to assume that he is an animal who has found a clump of eight mushrooms – food. To these he attaches a value of +6 units (these units are entirely arbitrary). Dawkins writes:

The mushrooms are so big I could eat only three of them. Should I inform anybody else about my find, by giving the 'food call'? Who is within earshot? Brother B (his relatedness to me is ½ [i.e., he shares half my genes]), cousin C (relatedness to me = ⅛), and D (no particular relation, which can be treated as zero). The net benefit score to me if I keep quiet about my find will be +6 for each of the three mushrooms I eat, +18 in all. My net benefit score if I give the food call needs a bit of figuring. The eight mushrooms will be shared equally between the four of us. The payoff to me from the two I shall eat will be the full +6 units each, +12 in all. But I shall also get some payoff when my brother and cousin eat their two mushrooms each, because of our shared genes. The actual score comes to $(1 \times 12) + (½ \times 12) + (⅛ \times 12) + (0 \times 12) = 19½$. The corresponding net benefit for the selfish behaviour was +18: the verdict is clear: I should give the food call; altruism on my part would in this case pay my selfish genes.

Dawkins's overriding point is that we must think of the central unit of evolution and natural selection as the gene: the gene, the replicating unit, is 'concerned' to see itself survive and thrive, and once we understand this, everything else falls into place: kinship patterns and behaviour in insects, birds, mammals and humans are explained; altruism becomes sensible, as do the relations of non-kin groups (such as races) to one another.[11] Dawkins's argument, alongside that of other biologists, such as Wilson at Harvard, sparked a resurgence of Darwinian thinking that characterised the last quarter of the twentieth century.

Peasants, Postmodernism and Poetry:
Diversity and the 'Other'

T he developments reflected in the work of Bowlby, Hodgkin, Crick, Watson and Dawkins formed part of a wider general revolution, across the world, extending from biology into psychology. Among the beneficiaries of this psychological revolution were women, though it didn't come about without a fight.

One of the early combatants in Britain (alongside numerous comrades in the United States and elsewhere) was Germaine Greer, an Australian who had settled in Britain as a graduate student and had drawn attention to herself in *Suck* magazine, decrying the 'missionary position' (she thought that women were more in control and had more pleasure if they sat on men during intercourse). Her book *The Female Eunuch* did not neglect women's economic condition, though one of only thirty chapters is devoted to work. Rather, it drew its force from Greer's unflinching comparison of the way women, love and marriage are presented in literature, both serious and popular, and in everyday currency, as compared with the way things 'really are'. 'Freud', she writes, 'is the father of psychoanalysis. It had no mother.' From Austen to Byron to *Women's Weekly*, Greer was withering in her criticisms of how men are presented as dominant, socially superior, older, richer and taller than their women. In what is perhaps her most original contribution, she demolished love and romance (both given their own chapters) as chimeras, totally divorced (an apt verb) from the much bleaker reality. In fact, she says, 'Women have very little idea of how much men hate them.'[1]

A chapter headed 'Misery' recounts the amount of medication women take and the paraphernalia of sexual aids, leading to the resentment that she argued many women feel at being saddled with such things. Her diagnosis is unstinting, and her solution demands nothing else than a radical reassessment of women, not just of their economic and psychological position vis-à-vis men but, more revolutionary still, a fundamental reappraisal of what love and romance really are. Greer had the grace to admit that she had not herself altogether shed the romantic notions she was brought up with, but makes it plain she suspects they are entirely – *entirely* – without foundation. As with all true liberation, this view is both bleak and exhilarating.[2]

Juliet Mitchell's *Woman's Estate* was hardly exhilarating. A fellow immigrant to Britain from the Antipodes, in her case from New Zealand, Mitchell also studied English at a British university, though she subsequently transferred to psychoanalysis. Her account was Marxist, claiming that although socialist countries are not very nice to women, social*ism* does not require the subjugation of women as capitalism does, with its ideology of the 'nuclear family', which succeeds only in keeping women in their place, acquiring consumer goods and breeding 'little consumers'. Mitchell went on to argue that women need to undergo two revolutions, the political and the personal, and here she took the black experience as a guide but also psychoanalysis. At the same time that women regrouped politically, she said, they also needed to raise their level of self-consciousness as black peoples had done, especially in America. Women, she insisted, have been taught by capitalism and by Freud that they are the repositories of feelings, but in fact there is no limit to their experience. She favoured small groups of six to twenty-four women joining in 'consciousness-raising' sessions, taking a leaf out of the book of the Chinese revolutionaries' practice of 'speaking bitterness'.[3]

HISTORY FROM THE BOTTOM UP

A different aspect of this psychological revolution resulted in a new kind of history produced in the 1950s, 1960s and early 1970s by a small group of British Marxist historians whose aim, like that of Greer and Mitchell, was to bring into focus areas that had been overlooked, or ignored, until then. In their case, the aim was essentially to rewrite British history from the end of the Middle Ages to the beginning of the twentieth century, 'from the bottom up' (a favoured phrase, which soon became hackneyed). Three men stand out in this history of the lower orders: Rodney Hilton, Christopher Hill and E. P. Thompson.

Rodney Hilton, professor of history at Birmingham University, was like the others a member of the British Communist Party until the events in Hungary in 1956. His main interest was in the precursors of the working class – the peasants – and besides his own books on the subject, he was instrumental in founding two journals in the 1960s, the *Journal of Peasant Studies* in Britain, and *Peasant Studies* in the United States. Hilton's aim was to show that peasants were not a passive class in Britain in the Middle Ages; they did not just accept their status but were continually trying to improve it. There was, Hilton argued, constant struggle, as the peasants tried to gain more land for themselves or have their rents reduced or abolished. This was no 'golden time', to use Harvey Kaye's words, when everyone was in his place and satisfied with it; instead, there was always a form of peasant 'class-consciousness' that contributed to the eventual decline of the feudal-seigneurial regime in England. This was a form of social evolution, Hilton's point being that this struggle gave rise to agrarian capitalism, out of which industrial capitalism would emerge.[4]

The next stage in the evolution was examined by Christopher Hill, of Balliol College, Oxford, who devoted himself to the study of the English revolution. His argument was that just as the peasants had struggled to obtain greater power in medieval times, so the English revolution, traditionally presented as a constitutional, religious and political revolution, was in fact the culmination of a class struggle in which capitalist merchants and farmers sought to seize power from the feudal aristocracy and monarchy. In other words, the motivation for the revolution was primarily economic.[5]

Like Hilton and Hill, E. P. Thompson also left the British Communist Party in 1956. Like them too, he remained convinced that English history was determined mainly by class struggle. In a long book, *The Making of the English Working Class*, one of his aims was to 'rescue' the working class from 'the enormous condescension of posterity' and render visible such neglected people as weavers and artisans. In this process, he redefined the working classes as essentially a matter of experience, notably the experience – between 1790 and 1830 – of a declining and weakening position in the world (see Chapter 15 above). Before 1790 the English working class existed in many disparate forms; the experience of oppression and the progressive loss of rights, far from resulting in their extinction, proved to be a major unifying (and therefore strengthening) force.[6]

The World Turned Upside Down, published by Christopher Hill in 1972, overlapped with Thompson's book. Hill considers the years in Britain immediately after the Civil War, a time when, as in the 1960s and early 1970s, radical political ideas and new religious sects proliferated. Hill discovered several new patterns of thought. There were many communist ideas and constitutional criticisms, all of a left-wing kind, as we would recognise them. Property laws were attacked, and squatters appeared (also typical of the 1960s and early 1970s). Church services were run along more democratic lines. Members of the congregation were invited to publicly comment and criticise sermons (several 'riots and tumult' being the result).[7]

The change in the status of women was also considerable, as evidenced not only in the higher rate of divorce but in the greater role they had in the sects (compared with the established church), with some, like the Quakers, abolishing the vow in the marriage ceremony for the wife to obey the husband, and others, like the Ranters, ceasing to regard sex outside marriage as sinful. Indeed, the Ranters' views at times were very modern: 'The world exists for man, and men are all equal.'[8]

In 1959 Basil Davidson's *Old Africa Rediscovered* appeared and soon became a classic. The book followed an explosion of scholarship in African studies, with Davidson pulling the picture together. His achievement was to show that the 'dark continent' was not so dark at all, that it had its own considerable history, which a small number of Western historians had denied, and that several more or less sophisticated civilisations had existed in Africa from 2000 BC onward.

Davidson surveyed all of Africa, from Egypt and Libya in the north to Ghana, Mali and Benin in the west, the coast of Zanj (or Zinj) in the east, and the south-central area around what was then Southern Rhodesia (now Zimbabwe). He covered the appearance of 'Negro peoples', around 5000–3000 BC, according to an analysis of some 800 skulls at a site discovered from predynastic Egypt and the evidence of early migrations – for example, from the Nile area to west Africa (the Forty Day Road). He described the Kush culture, emerging from the decadence of imperial Egypt, and the enormous slag heaps of Meroe ('the Birmingham of Africa'), about a hundred miles from modern Khartoum. Besides the palace and temples, only a fraction of which had been excavated, the slag heaps were evidence of Meroe's enormous iron-smelting capability, on which its great wealth was based. Having described the great coastal civilisations of Benin, Kilwa, Brava, Zanzibar and Mombasa, Davidson's most remarkable chapters concerned the great inland civilisations of Songhay, Jebel Uri, Engaruka, Zimbabwe and Mapungubwe, mainly because such places, remote from foreign influence, most closely represent the African achievement, uncomplicated by foreign trade and the ideas such trade brings with it.[9]

Engaruka, on the borders of Kenya and Tanganyika, as it then was (now Tanzania), had been first discovered by a district officer in 1935 but was excavated later by Louis Leakey. He found the main city to consist of nearly 7,000 houses, supporting a population, he thought, of at least thirty to forty thousand. The houses were well built, with terraces and engravings that he thought were 'clan marks'. Three hundred miles from the coast, Engaruka was well defended on a steep escarpment of the Rift Valley and, Leakey felt, dated from the seventeenth century. There were some stone structures he took to be irrigation channels and evidence of solitary burials. Later excavations showed that the city was surrounded by 8,000 acres that were once under grain, producing a surplus that was traded via roads to the north and south – villages of up to a hundred houses were grouped along these roads. Iron-using techniques spread south through this area of Africa from about 500 AD.

Davidson took care to emphasise that much remained to be discovered in Africa (as has indeed occurred). But he achieved his aim, adding to the work of such writers as Chinua Achebe (*Things Fall Apart*), Wole Soyinka and others who were showing that Africa had a voice and a history.[10]

POSTMODERN: THE REJECTION OF METANARRATIVES, THE RECOGNITION OF THE 'OTHER' AND THE ASCENT OF DIVERSITY

David Harvey, a Gillingham-born and Cambridge-educated Marxist geographer, would eventually settle down as a distinguished academic in New York but his best-known work, which, on the face of it, has little to do with geography or Marxism, was *The Condition of Postmodernity*. First published in 1980, it was reissued in 1989 in a much-revised version, taking into account the many developments in postmodernism during that decade.

Contrasting postmodernity with modernism, Harvey begins by quoting an editorial in the architectural magazine *Precis 6*:

> Generally perceived as positivistic, technocentric, and rationalistic, universal modernism has been identified with the belief in linear progress, absolute truth, the rational planning of ideal social orders, and the standardisation of knowledge and production. Postmodernism, by way of contrast, privileges 'heterogeneity and differences as liberative forces in the redefinition of cultural discourse'. Fragmentation, indeterminacy, and intense distrust of all universal or 'totalizing' discourses (to use the favoured phrase) are the hallmarks of postmodern thought. The rediscovery of pragmatism in philosophy (e.g. Richard Rorty), the shift of ideas about the philosophy of science wrought by Thomas Kuhn in 1962, and Richard Feyerabend, in 1973, Michel Foucault's emphasis on discontinuity and difference in history and his privileging of 'polymorphous correlations in place of simple or complex causality', new developments in mathematics emphasising indeterminacy (catastrophe and chaos theory, fractal geometry), the reemergence of concern in ethics, politics and anthropology for the validity and

dignity of 'the other', all indicated a widespread and profound shift in the 'structure of feeling'. What all these examples have in common is a rejection of 'metanarratives' (large-scale theoretical interpretations purportedly of universal application).[11]

Harvey moves beyond this clear-eyed summing up, however, to make four contributions of his own. In the first place, he describes postmodernism in architecture (the form, probably, where most people encounter it); most valuably, he looks at the political and economic conditions that brought about postmodernism and sustain it; he looks at the effect of postmodernism on our conceptions of space and time (this is where geography comes in); and he offers a critique of postmodernism, something that was badly needed.

In the field of architecture and urban design, Harvey tells us that postmodernism signifies a break with the modernist idea that planning and development should focus on large-scale, metropolis-wide, technologically rational and efficient urban *plans*, backed by absolutely no-frills architecture (the austere 'functionalist' surfaces of 'international style' modernism). Postmodernism cultivates instead a conception of the urban fabric as necessarily fragmented, a 'palimpsest' of past forms superimposed upon each other, and a 'collage' of current uses, 'many of which may be ephemeral'. Harvey put the beginning of postmodernism in architecture as early as 1961, with Jane Jacobs's *Death and Life of Great American Cities*, one of 'the most influential anti-modernist tracts' with its concept of 'the great blight of dullness' brought on by the international style, which was too static for cities, where *processes* are of the essence. Cities, Jacobs argued, need organised complexity, one important ingredient of which, typically absent in the international style, is diversity.[12]

A whole series of trends, Harvey says, favoured a more diverse, fragmented, intimate yet anonymous society, essentially composed of much smaller units of varied character. For Harvey, the twentieth century can be conveniently divided into the Fordist years – broadly speaking 1913 to 1973 – and the years of 'flexible accumulation'. Fordism, which included the ideas enshrined in Fredrick Winslow Taylor's *Principles of Scientific Management* (1911), was for Harvey a whole way of life, bringing mass production, standardisation of product and mass consumption: 'The progress of Fordism internationally meant the formation of global mass markets and the absorption of the mass of the world's population, outside the communist world, into the global dynamics of a new kind of capitalism.' Politically, it rested on notions of mass economic democracy welded together through a balance of special interest forces. The restructuring of oil prices, coming on top of the Yom Kippur War, brought about a major recession, which helped catalyse the breakup of Fordism, and the 'regime of accumulation' began.

The adjustment to this new reality, according to Harvey, had two main elements. Flexible accumulation 'is marked by a direct confrontation with the rigidities of Fordism'. It rests on flexibility with respect to labour processes, labour markets, products and patterns of consumption. It is characterised by the emergence of entirely new sectors of production, new ways of providing financial services, new markets and, above all, generally intensified rates of commercial, technological and organisational innovation. Second, there has been a further round of space-time compression, employing the ephemeral, the transient, the always changing. 'The relatively stable aesthetic of Fordist modernism has given way to all the ferment, instability and fleeting qualities of a postmodern aesthetic that celebrates difference, ephemerality, spectacle, fashion. And the commodification of cultural forms.' The whole approach, for Harvey, culminated in the 1985 exhibition at the Pompidou Centre in Paris, called 'The Immaterial'.[13]

Harvey, as was mentioned earlier, is not uncritical of postmodernism. Elements of nihilism are encouraged, he believes, and there is a return to narrow and sectarian politics, in which respect for others gets 'mutilated in the fires of competition between the fragments'. Travel, even imaginary travel, need not broaden the mind, but only confirms prejudices. Above all, he asks, how can we advance if knowledge and meaning are reduced 'to a rubble of signifiers'?

His verdict on the postmodern condition is not wholly flattering: 'confidence in the association between scientific and moral judgements has collapsed, aesthetics has triumphed over ethics as a prime focus of social and intellectual concern, images dominate narratives, ephemerality and fragmentation take precedence over eternal truths and unified politics, and explanations have shifted from the realm of material and political-economic groundings towards a consideration of autonomous cultural and political practices'.[14] *My* truth replaces *the* truth.

A Momentary Stay Against Confusion, and the Rehearsal of Heaven

The Irish Nobel-winning poet Seamus Heaney (1939–2013) was not usually regarded as a postmodernist, but *The Government of the Tongue*, his 1988 book of essays on poetry, did in certain ways echo some of the concerns that bothered the postmodernists too.

As a preparation and explanation of what poetry is, and seeks to be, and how it brings meaning to our lives, and what *type* of meaning, Heaney can hardly be bettered.

> [A poem] begins in delight, it inclines to the impulse, it assumes direction with the first line laid down, it runs a course of lucky events and ends in a clarification of life – not necessarily a great clarification, such as sects and cults are founded on, but in a momentary stay against confusion . . . in its repose the poem gives us a premonition of harmonies desired and not inexpensively achieved. In this way, the order of art becomes an achievement intimating a possible order beyond itself, although its relation to that further order remains promissory rather than obligatory. Art is not an inferior reflection of some ordained heavenly system but a rehearsal of it in earthly terms; art does not trace the given map of a better reality but improvises an inspired sketch of it.

In the former point, Heaney is considering the size of poetry and its relation to the size of life, both the size of an individual life and the size of 'life' in general. This is important because, of course, even a short poem can have a 'big' subject and because, as the critic James Wood has said, the idea of 'one overbearing truth' is exhausted in our time, meaning that poetry, the poetic approach, is, at least in theory, more relevant and important than ever before. And although Heaney is admirably ambitious for poetry, he is also quite content for its concerns and abilities to be on the small side, the human scale, not the superhuman (this is the postmodern overlap). He speaks of poets providing us with 'the shimmer of reality', 'cadences that drink at spots of time'. He likens poetry to the clapper in a bell. Poetry is the experience of being 'at the same time summoned and released'. He praises Auden for his 'defamiliarizing abruptness', and early Auden he likens to the shock of bare wire.

He insists the language of a poem should be 'a bolt of clarification', 'a "momentary stay against confusion" in the discovery of a firmly verified outline'. The reader is permitted the sensation of a whole meaning 'simultaneously clicking shut and breaking open', a momentary illusion that the fulfilments which were being experienced in the ear 'spelled out meanings and fulfilments available in the world.' In Sylvia Plath's verses, he says, there is a sense of 'surprised arrival'; in her later poems, there is a 'sudden in-placeness about the words and all that they stand for', which recalls Wallace Stevens's definition of poetry as 'sounds passing through sudden rightnesses'.

In discussing Philip Larkin's *The Whitsun Weddings*, Heaney says 'the concluding lines constitute an epiphany, an escape from the "scrupulous meanness" of the disillusioned intelligence'. Yet while Larkin is exemplary in the way he sifts the conditions of contemporary life, 'refuses alibis' and pushes consciousness towards an exposed condition that is neither cynicism nor despair, 'there survives in him a repining love for a more crystalline reality to which he might give allegiance. When that repining finds expression, something opens and moments occur which deserve to be called visionary.'

It is, obviously enough, in the nature of poetry to be short. But if we go along with James Wood, who has said that a poem is 'the most realised form of intention', then brevity becomes an important part of the point. Heaney's claims for poetry, for the government of the tongue (and other poets have made equivalent claims), become in this way also a claim for the poetic aesthetic, for the fact and promise of brevity. In this way poetry does not become the only way to regard life, but it does become the pithiest *and richest* way to marry experience, language and meaning. It raises – or underlines – the point that new experience, the experience of new knowledge, is, by definition, invariably brief. The knowledge stays with us, of course, but the first encounter with – and the apprehension of – such knowledge happens quickly, immediately. Immediacy equals intensity. Intensity is one of the purposes of life. Here too poetry and postmodernism come together.[15]

Sir Salman, Sir Vidia and Soyinka's Nobel: English as Lingua Franca

In an essay published in 1975, Marcus Cunliffe, a British historian educated at Oxford, who became a professor at George Washington University in Washington, DC, concluded that, so far as literature was concerned, 'by the 1960s, the old Anglo-American relationship was decisively reversed: the major contribution, in quantity and quality, was American'.[1] Cunliffe had a point, but the United States was not the only area of the Americas that was strong. By the time he was making his observations the school of Latin American magic realism had emerged, among such authors as Miguel Ángel Asturias (Guatemala), Jorge Luis Borges (Argentina), Carlos Fuentes and Octavio Paz (both Mexico), Gabriel García Márquez (Colombia), Pablo Neruda (Chile) and Mario Vargas Llosa (Peru), a primarily aesthetic response to that continent's enduring political and social problems.

At the same time, and given the main concerns of this book, the fabulous intricacies of Indian fiction merit our attention. Twentieth-century Indian novels written in English date from the 1930s at least, but recall the discussions in the eighteenth century, along the likes of Thomas Sheridan and Dr Johnson, as to whether the English language might one day form the basis of a 'metaphysical empire' on a par with Greek and Latin at that time. Among the earliest authors of note were Raja Rao and Mulk Raj Anand, R. K. Narayan and

Anita Desai, in general writing domestic stories, small-scale on the face of it, but in each one the characters are unprepared for the life of an independent India, which as often as not involves some measure of Westernisation.

There is nothing small about either the characters or the plots in Salman (later Sir Salman) Rushdie's stories. His two best-known books, *Midnight's Children* (1981) and *The Satanic Verses* (1988), are written in an exuberant, overflowing style, the images and metaphors and jokes billowing forth like the mushroom clouds of an atomic bomb. Rushdie's relationship with his native India, and with the English language, is complex. His stories tell us that there are many Indias, enough of them grim, failing, divided, wounded. English at least offers the chance of overcoming the chronic divisions without which failure cannot be conquered, and only by embarking on a fabulous journey of improbable fantasies can he hope to have what in fact are very direct messages swallowed.[2]

Midnight's Children tells the story of Saleem Sinai, born at midnight on the day India achieved independence in 1947, one of 1,001 children to be born at the same time. By virtue of this, all of them are given some magical property, and the closer their births to midnight, when 'the clock-hands joined palms in respectful greeting', the stronger their magical power. Saleem has a very large nose, which grants him the ability to see 'into the hearts and minds of men'. His chief rival, Shiva, has bloated knees, meaning he has the power of war. The book is written mainly in the form of Saleem's memoirs, but there is little in the way of traditional characterisation. Instead, Rushdie gives us a teeming, tumbling narrative, juxtaposing day-to-day politics and private obsessions (one figure works on a documentary about life in a pickle factory), all intertwined with ever more fabulous metaphors and jokes and language constructions. The best and most terrible joke comes in the central scene where the two main characters discover that they had been swapped as babies. Rushdie is challenging the meaning of the most basic ideas – innocence, enchantment, nation, self, community. And, in so doing, independence. All this is done with an 'elephantiasis' of style that emulates the Indian storytellers of old, yet *Midnight's Children* is neither Eastern nor Western. That is the point, and the measure of its success.[3]

The theme of *The Satanic Verses* is migration, emigration, and the loss of faith it often brings about in the migrant. The book begins when two Indian actors, Gibreel Farishta and Saladin Chamcha, fall to earth after an Air India jet explodes 30,000 feet above the English Channel. This naturally invokes the memory of an actual explosion, of an Air India Boeing 747 off Ireland in 1985, blown up, it is believed, by Sikh terrorists in Canada. Gibreel is the star of several Bombay 'theological' films and is so popular that for many in India he *is* divine. Saladin, on the other hand, is an Anglophile who has rejected India and lives in Britain doing voiceovers for television commercials, 'impersonating packets of crisps, frozen peas, ketchup bottles'. These two fall to earth in the company of airline seats, drinks trolleys and headsets, but land safely enough on a British beach. From then on, the book follows a series of interwoven plots, each more fantastic than the last. These episodes are never out of control, however, and Rushdie's references make the book very rich for those who can decipher them. For example, Gibreel Farishta, in Urdu, means Gabriel Angel, making him in effect the archangel whom Islamic tradition regards as '"bringing down" the Qur'an from God to Mohammed'. Saladin was also the great defender of medieval Islam against the Crusaders, who restored Sunni Islam to Egypt. Gibreel, learning Islam from his mother, encounters the notion of the Satanic Verse, in which the devil is understood to have inserted a sentence in the Qur'an, later withdrawn, but which nonetheless introduces a sliver of religious doubt. Religious doubt, then, is at the very heart of Rushdie's book.

One may even say that it plays with the very idea of the devil, of the secular *being* the devil, certainly so far as the faithful are concerned. Essentially, throughout the interlocking narratives, Saladin acts as a sort of Iago to Gibreel's Othello, 'using the thousand and one voices of his advertising days'. Under this onslaught, Gibreel is led astray, notably to a brothel, the 'anti-Mosque' in Malise Ruthven's apt phrase, falling among people who blaspheme, not just in swear-words but in the criticisms of the prophet's actual behaviour (for example, Muhammad had more wives than strict Islamic law allowed). It is certainly a challenging book. But can a book that explores blasphemy actually pursue that theme without itself being blasphemous? In exploring faith, Rushdie knew he had to deliberately provoke the faithful. At one point in the book, the Prophet issues a *fatwa* against an impious poet.[4]

Perhaps it was this above all which provoked the Islamic authorities. On 14 February 1989, Ruhollah Musavi Khomeini – better known as Ayatollah Khomeini, of Iran – issued a *fatwa* against the 'apostasian' book *The Satanic Verses*. Inside forty-eight hours, Rushdie and his wife had gone into hiding, where he would remain, except for brief forays into the limelight, for nearly ten years. Muslims in Britain and elsewhere staged public burnings of the title; 10,000 demonstrated against the book in Iran, and in Rushdie's native Bombay ten people were killed when police opened fire on demonstrators. In all, twenty-one people died over *The Satanic Verses*.[5]

Like Salman Rushdie, V. S. Naipaul's novels generally concern people living outside their native context. He himself was born in Trinidad, a second-generation Indian, moved to England to attend Oxford, and remained there afterwards, except to research a remarkable series of travel books.

Naipaul is less concerned with faith than Rushdie, having more in common with Anita Desai's fascination with modernisation and technological change, though he uses this to reflect his preoccupation with the nature of freedom. *A House for Mr Biswas* (1961) ostensibly follows the building of a house. At the same time Naipaul deconstructs Mr Biswas himself. His facility for signwriting leads him out of the prison of poverty and into a marriage where he is trapped, but in a different way. Signwriting leads to other forms of writing, letters to his son mainly. As he discovers language, like a writer discovers language, so Biswas discovers another layer of freedom. But total freedom, Naipaul implies, is not only impossible but also undesirable. Fulfilment comes from loving and being loved, a status Biswas achieves, but it is not freedom. In *The Mimic Men* (1967), the scene has shifted to England, not the ideal England that a poor Trinidadian might conceive but the drab, suburban England of the immigrant, with the endless fresh attempts to get going on a career, the chronic tiredness and the poor sense of self that comprise

modern city life. Again, freedom boils down to one struggle replacing another. The later books – *In a Free State* (1971), which won the
Booker Prize, *Guerrillas* (1975) and *A Bend in the River* (1979) – are
more nakedly political, juxtaposing political and private freedom in
deliberately jarring ways.[6]

But Naipaul, Sir Vidia as he became, was much more than a novelist. In 1981, a decade before *The Satanic Verses*, he visited four
Islamic societies – Iran, Pakistan, Malaysia and Indonesia. In *Among
the Believers: An Islamic Journey*, he found Iran confused and
angry: 'the confusion of a people of high medieval culture awakening
to oil and money, a sense of power and violation, and a knowledge of
a great new encircling civilisation ... That violation couldn't be mastered. It was to be rejected, at the same time it was to be depended
upon.' Pakistan, he found, was a fragmented country, economically
stagnant, 'its gifted people close to hysteria'. The failure of Pakistan
as a society, he said, led back time and again to the assertion of the
faith. As with Iran there was an emotional rejection of the West,
especially its attitudes towards women. He found no industry, no
science, the universities stifled by fundamentalism, which provided
'an intellectual thermostat, set low'. In all four places, Naipaul said,
Islam drew its strength from a focus on the past that prevented development, and that very lack of development meant that the peoples
of the Islamic nations could not cope with the West.[7]

He was even harder on India. He visited the country three times
to write books about it – *An Area of Darkness* (1964), *India: A
Wounded Civilisation* (1977) and *India: A Million Mutinies Now*
(1990). 'The crisis of India', he wrote in 1964, '... is that it is a decaying civilisation, where the only hope lies in further swift decay.'
In 1977 things didn't look so black, though that could have meant
that the swift decay was already overtaking the country. Though not
unsympathetic to India, Naipaul pulled no punches in his second
book. Phrases from it taken at random include the following: 'The
crisis of India is not only political or economic. The larger crisis is
of an old civilization that had become aware of its inadequacies and
it is without the means to move ahead.' 'Hinduism ... has exposed
[Indians] to a thousand years of defeat and stagnation. It has given
men no idea of contract with other men, no idea of the state ... Its

philosophy of withdrawal has diminished men intellectually, and not equipped them to respond to challenge; it has stifled growth.'[8]

The award of the Nobel Prize in Literature to the Nigerian writer and dramatist Wole Soyinka in 1986, and then to the Egyptian novelist Naguib Mahfouz in 1991, the same year that Ben Okri, another Nigerian, won the Booker Prize, shows that African writing has at last been recognised by what we may call the Western literary 'establishment'. At the same time, contemporary African writing has nothing like the same following, worldwide, as does Indian or South American literature. In his *Myth, Literature and the African World* (1976) Soyinka, who had studied in Britain and read plays for the Royal Court Theatre, did his best to make many fellow writers visible in a Western context.

Soyinka was trying to do for literature what Basil Davidson had done for African archaeology, not just in the book referred to but in his own poetry and plays. In fact, it was Soyinka's choice of literature – in particular the collective nature of theatre – that finally won the Nobel Prize for him, rather than for Chinua Achebe. (Achebe, author of *Things Fall Apart* (1958), also wrote *Anthills of the Savannah*, which was shortlisted for the Booker Prize in 1987). Soyinka was part of a generation of brilliant writers who studied at Ibadan University College in the period before independence, together with Cyprian Ekwensi, Christopher Okigbo and John Pepper Clark, some of whose works he covered in *Myth, Literature and the African World*. In that book, his secondary aim, after rendering these writers visible to an international audience, was to do two things: first, to show black African literature as its own thing, having themes in common with other great literatures. At the same time, Soyinka, in discussing such entities as Duro Ladipo's Yoruba plays, or Obotunde Ijimere's *Imprisonment of Obatala*, or Ousmane Sembène's *God's Bits of Wood*, stressed the particular strengths of African literature, the ways in which it differs from its Western counterparts. He stresses the collective experience of ritual, the way the individualism of the West is alien to African experience.[9]

This leads back to cultural studies, which remain controversial, especially among an older generation brought up to believe that 'aesthetic' values are *sui generis*, independent of anything else, help-ing us to find 'eternal truths' of the human condition. But cultural studies courses at universities are very popular, which must mean that they meet some needs of the young (they have been around too long now to be merely fashionable). The heart of the issue, and the most controversial aspect of the new discipline, is the battle for Shakespeare. Keats called Shakespeare the 'chief poet', the 'begetter of our deep eternal theme'. The new Shakespearians, if we may call them that, argue on the other hand that although the Bard wrote a remarkable number of plays, he did not, as Coleridge maintained, speak for all people, in all places, and at all times.

The first concerted attack on the conventional wisdom came in 1985, in a book edited by Jonathan Dollimore and Alan Sinfield, from the University of Sussex, which was provocatively entitled *Political Shakespeare*. It comprised a series of eight essays by British and North American scholars; by comparing the chronology of the plays with contemporary political events, the essays were designed to show that, far from transcending history and politics and human nature, Shakespeare was a child of his time. As a result, the conventional meaning of many of the plays was changed radically. *The Tempest* for example, far from being a play about colonialism in America, becomes a play about England's problems with Ireland. Published in the middle of the Thatcher/Reagan years, *Political Shakespeare* created an academic storm. Two of the academic referees who read the manuscript argued that the book should 'on no account be published'. After publication, one reviewer wrote, 'A conservative critic ... may conclude in horror that Shakespeare has succumbed to an academic AIDS, his immunology system tragically disrupted by Marxist, feminist, semiotic, post-structural, postmodern and psychoanalytic criticism.' Others found the book important and in the classroom it proved popular and was reprinted many times.[10]

The most fundamental attack on the 'canon' came in 1987 from a British academic trained in Chinese studies who was a professor of government at Cornell in America. Martin Bernal was the son of J. D. Bernal (Chapter 30 above), himself a distinguished scholar of Irish birth, a Marxist physicist who won the Lenin Peace Prize in 1953 and was author of the four-volume *Science in History*. Martin Bernal's *Black Athena: The Afroasiatic Roots of Classical Civilisation* (1987–91) is a hardly less massive, three-volume work incorporating and synthesising material on philology, archaeology, history, historiography and biblical studies which, in essence, makes the following points.

One is that north Africa, in the form of ancient Egypt – several of whose dynasties were black, in the sense of 'Negroid' – was the predominant influence on classical Greece.[11] No less controversially, Bernal also claimed that this view of classical Greece was 'standard', had always prevailed in European scholarship until it was deliberately 'killed off' by 'racist' north European scholars in the early nineteenth century, men who wanted to show that Europe, and northern Europe at that, had a monopoly on creative and imaginative thought, all as one of a number of devices to help justify colonialism and imperialism.[12]

But this is only a beginning. Bernal examined classical Greek plays – such as Aeschylus's *The Supplicants* – for Egyptian influences; he looked at loan-words, river and mountain names (Kephisos, the name of rivers and streams found all over Greece with no explanation, he derives from *Kbh*, 'a common Egyptian river name "Fresh"').[13] In a chapter on Athens, he argues that the name of the city is derived from the Egyptian *HtNt*: 'In Antiquity, Athens was consistently identified with the Egyptian goddess Nt or Neit. Both were virgin divinities of warfare, weaving and wisdom.'[14]

The second half of Bernal's book follows the writings of scientists and others in the Renaissance, men like Copernicus and Giordano Bruno, to show that they accepted the Egyptian influence on Greece much more readily than later scholars. Following the French Revolution, however, Bernal discerns a reaction by Christians against the threat of the 'wisdom' of Egypt, and a rise of 'Hellenomania'. In essence, he says, classical studies as we know them today are a nineteenth-century creation, and false.

Bernal was accused of doing more harm than good, many scholars maintaining that his ideas were no more than postmodern 'Afrocentric fantasies' and his description of Egyptians as black 'misleading in the extreme'.[15] The issue is not settled and perhaps cannot hope to be. For this is only partly an intellectual debate. Exploring the alleged racism behind the theorising was just as much part of Bernal's 'project' as was the substantive result.[16]

Less contentious and arguably more useful was Peter Fryer's *Staying Power: The History of Black People in Britain* (1984, reissued 2010). Over time, it has emerged as a standard, ground-breaking work. Fryer's aim was to painstakingly record the presence of black people in Britain, from well before medieval times, and to describe the shape of both black and Asian communities, and in doing so he described some of the imaginative individuals already reported here, plus others such as William Cuffay, a founder member of the Chartist movement, and Ira Aldridge. 'The Negro Tragedian', as his biographer called this New York-born star of what would become the Old Vic, appeared as Oroonoko, billed under his stage name as 'MR. KEENE, Tragedian of Colour' in 1831, 'Keene' being close to Edmund Kean, the British actor Aldridge had seen in his native New York. Aldridge appeared in Manchester, Newcastle, Edinburgh, Liverpool and Sunderland. Fryer says of Samuel Coleridge-Taylor, born in Holborn to a father who was a doctor from Sierra Leone, that 'his was the biggest contribution yet made by a black person to British concert music'.[17] He wrote many pieces, and the first performance of *Hiawatha's Wedding Feast* (1898) was described by the principal of the Royal College of Music as 'one of the most remarkable events in modern English music history'; Fryer says, 'this cantata for tenor solo, chorus, and orchestra was soon widely acclaimed on both sides of the Atlantic'. In fact, Coleridge-Taylor became a 'shining light' in the Harlem Renaissance in the United States, but today is largely forgotten in the country of his birth.

Fryer gave much more space to Coleridge-Taylor and Cuffay than we can devote here, and he also included a number of Asians who made their mark, including Raja Rammohan Roy, in Britain from 1830 to 1833, a philosopher, reformer and journalist, the first Brahman to visit London, where he became a friend of Jeremy Bentham.[18] Together with Dwarkanath Tagore, the grandfather of the great Bengali poet Rabindranath Tagore, Roy submitted a statement to the British Parliament, frankly giving Indian views about empire. Later he helped to found the British India Society ('for bettering the conditions of our fellow subjects – the Natives of British India').[19]

Then there was Mary Seacole, half-Jamaican but equally proud of her Scottish heritage, who, though she didn't get on with Florence Nightingale, feeling she was racially prejudiced, was first into Sebastopol, where she administered to the British army, setting up a hotel and providing refreshments and medical aid to soldiers, charging only officers. She was awarded the Crimea Medal, ending her days in London with a very healthy £2,500 estate.

More interesting, perhaps, because more surprising, was Dadabhai Naoroji, the first Asian elected to the House of Commons. Son of a Parsee priest, he was born in Bombay in 1825 and, at the age of twenty-nine, became the first Indian professor of mathematics and natural philosophy. Moving to Britain in 1855 he was appointed professor of Gujerati at University College, London. Fryer investigated several other Indian parliamentarians in Britain (Womesh Chandra Bonnerjee, Sir Mancherjee Merwanjee Bhownagree), A. M. Bose, the first Indian wrangler at Cambridge, and Shyamaji Krishnavarma, founder of the *Indian Sociologist*, a monthly published in London and Paris, which Fryer says had much influence on Indian opinion.

The Promised Marriage of Mathematics, Physics and Biology

Postmodernism was a cultural development in the evolution of thought. But evolution itself continued to fascinate and its ramifications deepen. In fact, at this time, late in the twentieth century, a great deal of theorising about genetics revised and refined our understanding of evolutionary processes. In particular much light was thrown on stages of evolutionary progress, working forward from the moment life had been created, and on the philosophical implications of evolution.

British scientists played a part in this revolution but it was a truly international effort, with much work being done in the United States, by American anthropologists in Africa, who discovered new examples of early humans, by Dutch and Spanish biologists, and not least by the discovery of the Chicxulub crater in Yucatán, Mexico, created by an asteroid or meteorite, which had slammed into the earth 65 million years ago and killed off the dinosaurs, liberating the mammals. There was also much new evolutionary thinking, again by Americans, Britons and Canadians, many of whom worked in Africa alongside, and sometimes in competition with, the Leakeys. John Maynard Smith (1920–2004), professor of biology at the University of Sussex, was regarded as the doyen of neo-Darwinists, as they came to be called, and, in conjunction with Eörs Szathmáry, a Hungarian, he summed up their thinking in his book *The Major Transition in Evolution*.[1]

Of the two founders of DNA science, James Watson took a leading role in genome research but Francis Crick veered away into what many thought would be the hottest topic in biology in the twenty-first century: consciousness studies. In 1994 he published *The Astonishing Hypothesis*, which advocated a research assault on this final mystery/problem.[2]

Consciousness studies naturally overlap with neurological studies, where there have been many advances identifying different structures of the brain, such as language centres, and where MRI – magnetic resonance imaging – can show which areas are being used when people are merely *thinking* about the meaning of words. But the study of consciousness itself is still as much a matter for philosophers as for biologists. As John Maddox, former editor of *Nature*, put it in his 1998 book, *What Remains to Be Discovered*, 'No amount of introspection can enable a person to discover just which set of neurons in which part of his or her head is executing some thought-process. Such information seems to be hidden from the human user.'[3]

It should be said that some people think there is nothing to explain as regards consciousness. They believe it is an 'emergent property' that automatically arises when you put 'a bag of neurons together'. An analogy is made with the liquidity of water. The behaviour of HO molecules explains liquidity, but the individual molecules are not themselves liquid.

In 1994 the first issue of the *Journal of Consciousness Studies* was published and at the same time a whole raft of books appeared, with the British contribution including *The Astonishing Hypothesis* but also *The Emperor's New Mind* by Roger Penrose, *The Problem of Consciousness* by Colin McGinn and *Shadows of the Mind: A Search for the Missing Science of Consciousness* also by Roger Penrose. There were two international symposia on the subject at Jesus College, Cambridge, published as *Nature's Imagination* (1994) and *Consciousness and Human Identity* (1998), both edited by John Cornwell.[4]

Thus consciousness was very much the flavour of the decade at the end of the twentieth century, and it is fair to say that those involved in the subject fall into four camps. There are those, like the British philosopher Colin McGinn, who argue that consciousness is resistant to explanation in principle and for all time. Other philosophers, like the Americans Thomas Nagel and Hilary Putnam, add that at the present time (and maybe for all time) science cannot account for *qualia*, the first-person phenomenal experience we understand as consciousness. Then there are the reductionists, some of whom point out that artificially intelligent machines are already with us and that they will soon be conscious, while others claim that consciousness does depend on the physical properties of the brain but we are nowhere near solving them. Finally, there are those such as Roger Penrose, an emeritus professor of mathematics at Oxford and a Nobel laureate, who believe that a new kind of dualism is needed, that in effect a whole new set of physical laws may apply inside the brain which account for consciousness. Penrose's particular contribution is that quantum physics operates within tiny structures, known as tubules, inside the nerve cells of the brain, to produce – in some as yet unspecified way – the phenomenon we recognise as consciousness. Penrose thinks that we actually live in three worlds – the physical, the mental and the mathematical. 'The physical world grounds the mental world, which in turn grounds the mathematical world and the mathematical world is the ground of the physical world and so on round the circle.' Many people who find this tantalising nevertheless don't feel that Penrose has *proved* anything.[5]

Crick's aim has been fulfilled. Consciousness is being investigated as never before. But it would be rash to predict that the twenty-first century will bring advances very quickly, though AI is expanding faster than even the optimists thought. On the other hand, no less a figure than Noam Chomsky, the American linguistic philosopher, has said, 'It is quite possible – overwhelmingly probable, one might guess – that we will always learn more about human life and personality from novels than from scientific psychology.'

In the years ahead, 1988 may come to be considered as a turning point so far as science is concerned. It was the year in which the Internet and the Human Genome Organisation got under way, the former helped along by Donald Davies at the National Physical Laboratory in Britain and by Tim Berners-Lee at CERN, the

European laboratory for particle physics near Geneva, who devised the special HTTP protocol. This made the Internet much easier to browse or navigate, bringing about the ultramodern world and setting the shape of the twenty-first century. In that same year, a book appeared that had the most commercially successful publishing history of any work of science ever printed. It set the seal on the public acceptance of science, but just perhaps may have marked its apogee.

A Brief History of Time: From the Big Bang to Black Holes, by the Cambridge cosmologist Stephen Hawking, had been five years in the making and owed much to the work of Peter Guzzardi, a New York editor with Bantam Books, who had persuaded Hawking to leave Cambridge University Press. CUP had been planning to publish Hawking's book, because they had published his others, and had offered an advance of £10,000 – their biggest ever. But Guzzardi tempted Hawking to Bantam, though it perhaps wasn't too difficult a choice for the scientist, since the firm's editorial board had been won over by Guzzardi's enthusiasm, to the point of offering a $250,000 advance.

In the intervening years, Guzzardi had worked hard to make Hawking's dense prose ever more accessible for a general audience. The book was released in early spring 1988 – and what happened then quickly passed into publishing history. More than half a million hardback copies were sold in the United States and Britain, where the title went through twenty reprints by 1991 and remained in the best-seller lists for no fewer than 234 weeks, four and a half years, and Hawking quickly became the world's most famous scientist.

There was one other unusual element in this story of success. In 1988 Hawking was aged forty-six, but in 1963, when he was twenty-one, he had been diagnosed as suffering from amyotrophic lateral sclerosis, ALS, also known (in the UK) as motor neurone disease and (in the US) as Lou Gehrig's disease, after the Yankee baseball player who died from it. What had been a mere clumsiness at the end of 1962 had progressed over the intervening years so that by 1988 Hawking was confined to a wheelchair and able to communicate only by means of a special computer connected to a voice synthesiser. Despite these handicaps, in 1979 he had been appointed Lucasian Professor of Mathematics at Cambridge, a post that Isaac Newton had held before him, had won the Einstein Medal, and had published a number of well-received academic books on gravity, relativity and the structure of the universe. He never allowed his disability to deflect him from what he knew were science's central concerns (he died in 2018, aged seventy-six). These involved black holes, the concept of a 'singularity' and the light they throw on the Big Bang, the possibility of multiple universes; and new ideas about gravity and the fabric of reality, in particular 'string theory'.

It is with black holes that Hawking's name is most indelibly linked. This idea was first broached in the 1960s. Black holes were envisaged as superdense objects, the result of a certain type of stellar evolution in which a large body collapses in on itself, under the force of gravity, to the point where nothing, not even light, can escape. The discovery of pulsars, quasars, neutron stars and background radiation in the 1960s considerably broadened our understanding of this process, besides making it real, rather than theoretical. Hawking worked with Penrose, and this pair first argued that at the centre of every black hole, as at the beginning of the universe, there must be a 'singularity', a moment when matter is infinitely dense, infinitely small, and when the laws of physics as we know them break down. Hawking added to this the revolutionary idea that black holes could emit radiation (this became known as Hawking radiation) and, under certain conditions, explode. He also believed that, just as radio stars had been discovered in the 1960s, thanks to radio telescopes, so X-rays should be detectable from space via satellites above the atmosphere, which otherwise screens out such rays. Hawking's reasoning was based on calculations that showed that as matter was sucked into a black hole, it would get hot enough to emit X-rays. Sure enough, four X-ray sources were subsequently identified in a survey of the heavens and so became the first candidates for observable black holes. Hawking's later calculations showed that, contrary to his first idea, black holes did not remain stable but lost energy in the form of gravity, shrank, and eventually, after billions of years, exploded, possibly accounting for occasional and otherwise unexplained bursts of energy in the universe.[6]

Martin Rees's 'anthropic principle' of the universe is somewhat easier to grasp. Rees, the Astronomer Royal and another contemporary of Hawking, offers indirect evidence for 'parallel universes'. His argument is that for ourselves to exist, a very great number of coincidences must have occurred, if there is only one universe. In an early paper he showed that if just one aspect of our laws of physics were to be changed – say, gravity was increased – the universe as we know it would be very different: celestial bodies would be smaller and cooler, would have shorter lifetimes and a very different surface geography, and much else. One consequence is that life as we know it can in all probability only form in universes with the sort of physical laws we enjoy. This means, first, that other forms of life are likely elsewhere in the universe (because the same physical laws apply), but it also means that many other universes probably exist, with other physical laws, in which very different forms of life, or no forms of life, exist. Rees argues that we can observe our universe, and conjecture others, because the physical laws exist about us to allow it. He insists this is too much of a coincidence: other universes, very different from ours, almost certainly must exist.[7]

Like most senior physicists, cosmologists and mathematicians, Hawking also devoted much energy to what some scientists call 'the whole shebang', the so-called theory of everything. This is an ironic phrase, referring to the attempt to describe all of fundamental physics by one set of equations: nothing more. Physicists have been saying this is just around the corner for decades, but in fact the theory of everything is still elusive. To begin with, before the physics revolution discussed in earlier chapters of this book, two theories were required. As Steven Weinberg tells the story, there was Isaac Newton's theory of gravity, 'intended to explain the movements of the celestial bodies and how such things as apples fell to the ground; and there was James Clerk Maxwell's account of electromagnetism as a way to explain light, radiation, magnetism, and the forces that operate between electrically charged particles'. However, these two theories were compatible only up to a point. According to Maxwell the speed of light was the same for all observers, whereas Newton's theories predicted that speed measured for light would depend on the motion of the observer. 'Einstein's general theory of relativity overcame this problem, showing that Maxwell was right.' But it was the quantum revolution that changed everything and made physics more beautiful but also more complex at the same time. This linked Maxwell's theory and new quantum rules which view the universe as discontinuous, with a limit on how small packets of electromagnetic energy can be, and how small a unit of time or distance is. At the same time, it introduced two new forces, both operating at very short range, *within* the nucleus of an atom. One, the strong force, holds the particles of the nucleus together and is very strong (it is this energy that is released in a nuclear weapon). The other, the weak force, is responsible for radioactive decay. And so, until the 1960s there were four forces that needed to be reconciled: gravity, electromagnetism, the strong nuclear force and the weak nuclear force. This would eventually lead to the so-called string revolution and the second superstring revolution, superstrings being tiny entities which tax everyone's understanding but may – *may* – show that there are far more dimensions to existence than we are normally aware of and that there is a prehistory to the universe. Here in fact all visual analogies break down and only mathematics applies, mathematics that even mathematicians find hard.[8]

New theories of complexity and even chaos (chaoplexity) were generated alongside these exciting and, for many, mystifying innovations but, at the end of the twentieth century, there was a somewhat disappointed air at their achievements. But where there does remain excitement is in the relationship of physics to biology. These achievements were summarised by Ian Stewart, professor of mathematics at Warwick University, in his 1998 book, *Life's Other Secret*. Stewart comes from a tradition less well known than the Hawkins–Penrose cosmology set, or the Dawkins–Wilson evolution set. He is the latest in a group that includes D'Arcy Wentworth Thompson, professor at St Andrews (*On Growth and Form*, 1917), and Brian Goodwin, professor at the Open University (*How the Leopard Changed Its Spots*, 1994). Their collective message is that genetics is not, and can never be, a complete explanation for life. What is also needed, surprising as it may seem, is a knowledge of mathematics, because it is mathematics that governs physical substances – the deep order – out of which, in the end, all living things are made.

Life's Other Secret is dedicated to showing that mathematics 'now informs our understanding of life at every level from DNA to rain forests, from viruses to flocks of birds, from the origins of the first-self-copying molecules to the stately unstoppable march of evolution'. Some of Stewart's examples are a mixture of the enchanting and the provocative, such as the mathematics of spiders' webs and snow-flakes, or the formation of swarms of starlings; he also explores the branching system of plants and the patterned skins of such animals as leopards and tigers.

He begins by showing that the division of cells in the embryo displays a remarkable similarity to the way soap bubbles form in foams, and that the way chromosomes are laid out in a dividing cell is also similar to the way mutually repelling magnets arrange them-selves. In other words, whatever instructions are coded into genes, many biological entities behave as though they are constrained by the physical properties they possess, properties that can be written as mathematical equations.[9]

For Stewart this is life taking advantage of the mathematics/physics of nature for its own purposes. He finds that there is a 'deep geometry' of molecules, especially in DNA, which forms knots and coils, this architecture being all-important. For example, he quotes a remarkable experiment carried out by Heinz Fraenkel-Conrat and Robley Williams with the tobacco mosaic virus. This, says Stewart, is a bridge between the inorganic and organic worlds; if the compo-nents of the virus are separated in a test tube and then left to their own devices, they spontaneously reassemble into a complete virus that can replicate. In other words, it is the *architecture* of the mole-cules that automatically produces life. In theory therefore, this form of virus – life – could be created by preparing synthetic substances and putting them together in a test tube.[10]

Perhaps most revealing are the experiments that Stewart and others call 'artificial life'. These are essentially games played on computers designed to replicate in symbolic form various aspects of evolution. The screen will typically have a grid, say, 100 squares wide and 100 squares deep. Each of these squares is allotted a 'bush' or a 'flower', say, or on the other hand, a 'slug' or an 'animal that preys on slugs'. Various rules are programmed in: one rule might be that a predator can move five squares each time, whereas a slug can only move one square; another might be that slugs on green flowers are less likely to be seen (and eaten) than slugs on red flowers, and so on. Then, since computers are being used, this artificial life can be turned on and run for, say, 10,000 moves or even 50 million moves, to see what 'A-volves' (A=Artificial).[11]

The most startling program was Andrew Pargellis's 'Amoeba', begun in 1996. This was seeded with only a random block of computer code, 7 per cent of which was randomly replaced every 100,000 steps (to simulate mutation). Pargellis found that about every 50 million steps a self-replicating segment of code appeared, simply as a result of the maths on which the program was based. As Stewart put it, 'Replication didn't have to be built into the rules – it just happened.' Other surprises included the appearance of parasites, and long periods of stasis punctuated by rapid change, all processes observed in evolution proper.[12]

Stewart's fundamental point, not accepted by everyone, is that mathematics and physics are as powerful as genetics in giving form to life. 'Life is founded on mathematical patterns of the physical world. Genetics exploits and organises those patterns, but physics makes them possible and constrains what they can be.' He ends his book by predicting a new discipline for the twenty-first century, 'morphomatics', which will attempt to marry maths, physics and biology and will reveal the still deeper patterns in the world around us and how life began.[13]

THE DEATH OF IDEALS?

As the end of the twentieth century loomed, a number of books appeared that were reflective in approach, though on a wide range of topics. In *What Remains to Be Discovered*, John Maddox, recently retired as editor of *Nature*, provided a useful corrective to the triumphalism of science, describing black holes as 'putative' only, arguing that the quantum gravity project was 'becalmed', that there was no direct evidence for the notion of 'inflation' in the early universe, and that the 'Big Bang' was not so much a theory as a model. John Barrow, an astronomer and professor of geometry at Gresham College, about which we have heard so much, thought that there was an evolutionary progress in the arts 'which has steadily relaxed the compositional constraints placed on the artist ... as the constraints imposed by convention, technology or individual preference have been relaxed so the resulting structure is less formally patterned, closer to the random, and harder to distinguish from the work of others working under similar freedom of constraint.' He thought that the arts were now developing 'asymptotically', slowing down, more and more resembling each other, and unable to develop further.[14] Robert Wright identified a 'Darwinian cynicism' in thought, marked by postmodernism which, he said, views all human communication as 'discourse of power' where 'ironic self-consciousness is the order of the day', where ideals can't be taken seriously because one cannot avoid 'self-serving manipulation'.[15] Is there not something *fin de siècle* about all this?

Our Floating World

A s this narrative crosses into the twenty-first century, there is a discernible need for a change of pace, or of approach. In theory, globalisation dates back to the nineteenth century, but it really only gathered pace in the 1990s, and as they gave way to the 2000s the new technology – in particular the Internet – snowballed as never before. Many people carped that the last half of the twentieth century was more an age of consolidation rather than invention (the motor car, the aeroplane, television, film and radio all dated back to the late nineteenth/early twentieth century) but the new technology shouldered its way into those pieces of apparatus as well. At the same time, the new technology exploded in several totally new directions, as this list shows: Amazon was born in 1994, Netflix in 1997; Google was officially launched in 1998, Wikipedia in 2001, Skype in 2003, Facebook in 2004, Twitter and Spotify in 2006; the iPhone came in 2007, Google Chrome in 2008, the same year as Tesla; Bitcoin was minted in 2009, the iPad and Instagram in 2010, and Zoom in 2011. They were breathless years especially in information technology, but of course none of these innovations was special to Britain. On the contrary, the Internet enabled – at least in theory – everyone to access information and other people almost any way they chose. These developments changed intellectual (and social) life, sometimes for the better, while at other times the effects were just embarrassing. At the same time, migration, both legal and opportunistic, has also been increasing dramatically (often aided by the ubiquitous iPhone). These twin developments have created new circumstances – intellectual and social (and political, of course) – the point being that the whole idea of the relationship between culture and nation (or nationality) is changing.

That said, the new technology is mainly the work of English-speaking individuals, Americans mostly, but not only, a pattern repeated in the number of Nobel Prizes won, and Academy Awards given in the annual Oscars ceremony. Even in the Nobel Prize in Literature, since 2000 there have been nine awards for writers in English, against three for German writers, three for French and two for Chinese. In other words, even in the twenty-first century, the predominance of the Anglophone countries continues in the intellectual and cultural fields, in so far as these measures may be taken as valid.

This predominance, if such it is, is a matter that will be addressed in the concluding chapter, but for now we shall consider a raft of intellectual achievements that occurred *in* Britain in the first decades of the twenty-first century but quite a few of which, it is important to say, were conducted by individuals who were not Britons: as we shall see, this has been a trend in the new century.

Two good examples both occurred in 2004: the building of the so-called Gherkin and the invention of graphene. The official name of the Gherkin, a gherkin-shaped skyscraper in the City of London, is 30 St Mary Axe, designed by the British architect Norman (later Lord) Foster + Partners, but commissioned by the Swiss reinsurance firm Swiss Re, and built by Skanska AB, a Swedish construction company, with engineering help from Arup, another British company, though one started by a Dane. Both architect and builders were and are exceedingly international outfits. Foster was born near Stockport, Lancashire, in 1935, to very poor parents, and he left grammar school at sixteen, did his national service in the RAF, joined a local architect's firm and attended the School of Architecture and Planning at Manchester University, paying his way by working at various part-time jobs, including selling ice cream. In 1959 he won a RIBA scholarship for a drawing of a windmill and, his self-confidence growing, he next won a fellowship to the Yale School of Architecture, where he met his future business partner, Richard Rogers, a fellow architect, and another Briton. Foster also collaborated, early on, with the American architect Richard Buckminster Fuller, creator of the geodesic dome.

Foster has since designed hundreds of buildings, including many universities and museums, several airports (Hong Kong, Stansted, Beijing, Phnom Penh), rapid transit systems, bridges (the Millau Viaduct in France, the Millennium Bridge in London), clinics and libraries, the Amaravati City Masterplan; he has restored the German Reichstag in Berlin and the Great Court of the British Museum. Foster worked with Steve Jobs until the latter's death in 2011, to design Apple's offices in Cupertino, California. He has won many awards, including the Stirling Prize in Britain. Skanska's projects include renovation of the United Nations Headquarters in New York, the World Trade Center Transportation Hub, the MetLife Stadium in New Jersey (home of the New York Yankees and New York Jets) and the Øresunde Bridge, which links Denmark and Sweden, and they are also involved in HS2.[1]

Both Foster and Skanska are known for their concern for the environment, and this is one of the features of 30 St Mary Axe. Its construction came about in distressing circumstances when, in April 1992, the IRA detonated a massive bomb near the Baltic Exchange, a market for marine and shipping insurance, damaging the building beyond repair. At first, English Heritage, the government's official advisors on architectural matters, wanted the site restored to the way it had been but then it turned out that the damage was even worse than had originally been thought, and the whole site was demolished and some of the contents sold to a company in Estonia. Meanwhile, Swiss Re wanted a consolidated headquarters for their British operations *and* a striking building. They called in Foster + Partners. At first there was a plan for a Millennial Tower, though that proved too high to escape planning restrictions. Next came the Gherkin, so called early on in a BBC broadcast when the plans became known.

Besides its overall very distinctive shape, its forty-one storeys and rounded top make it easily one of the most recognisable buildings in London. The building is a classic postmodern construction, eschewing all classical theories and ideas, and playing with shapes – curves and spirals, although the dome is the only part with curved glass. The building contains a number of energy-saving devices, such as gaps between the floors, which create shafts that act as ventilation, and there are solar panels to warm the building in winter. One mark of the building's success is that its ownership changed hands in February 2007 for £600 million, making it the most expensive building ever sold in London.

That same year, 2004, two physicists at the University of Manchester announced their discovery of graphene, or more accurately the discovery of a simple method for isolating single layers of graphite. Graphene, a word coined some time before, consists of layers of carbon one atom thick arranged in two-dimensional hexagons, making it the thinnest material that exists. It is also one of the strongest, hardest and lightest. The physicists who made the breakthrough were Konstantin Novoselov and Andre Geim. Novoselov was born, in Nizhny Tagil, Russia, in 1974, educated at the Moscow Institute of Physics and Technology and at Radboud University of Nijmegen in the Netherlands, where he was taught by Geim, also Russian, born in Sochi in 1958. He too was educated at the Moscow Institute of Physics and Technology, with postgraduate research at Nottingham, Bath and Copenhagen. He then worked on superconductivity at Radboud University.

In 2001 Geim moved to Manchester where he became director of the Manchester Centre for Mesoscience and Nanotechnology a year later. (Mesoscience is the study of materials as they vary between the solid and gaseous states.) Geim, and Novoselov, who followed him from Nijmegen to Manchester, jointly used a simple method to create graphene: they used adhesive tape ('Scotch tape') to remove the top layer from a sample of graphite, which was in fact a drawing by William Blake, Novoselov also being very interested in art and art history. (He also used drawings by Turner, Picasso and John Constable.)

Graphene has countless uses in electronic technology, in quantum physics and in materials science, and is a huge growth area. A National Graphene Institute was created in Manchester in 2015 as the national centre for graphene research (other single-atom-thick substances have since been discovered). Both men won the Nobel Prize in Physics in 2010 and were knighted two years later. Geim won the Royal Society's Copley Medal in 2013 and Novoselov the society's Dalton Medal in 2016. Geim's attitude to his identity fits the twenty-first century and one theme of this last chapter: 'Having lived and worked in several European countries, I consider myself European and do not believe that any further taxonomy is necessary.' In August 2024 it was announced that the first brain implant made of graphene was ready to be used in a clinical trial in Manchester, hopefully leading to a more flexible interface which will help in such conditions as Parkinson's disease.[2]

A parallel of sorts occurred in the establishment of DeepMind, now a British–American research laboratory in artificial intelligence and a subsidiary of Google, centred in London but with branches in Canada, France, Germany and the United States. Among its achievements are intellectual abilities which surpass human abilities in certain games, plus the assessment in March 2024 of protein structures, in particular the way proteins fold and the way they interact with DNA and RNA. DeepMind was founded by (Sir) Demis Hassabis, Mustafa Suleyman and Shane Legg. Hassabis fits the pattern being described here, being born to a Greek Cypriot father and Singaporean mother and growing up in north London; so too Suleyman, who grew up in Caledonian Road, Islington, with a Syrian father and an English mother, while Legg attended Rotorua Lakes High School on New Zealand's North Island. DeepMind was sold to Google in 2014 and is now embarked on the race for AGI, artificial *general* intelligence, which may also extend to artificial imagination, though no one really knows how to define it, or recognise it if and when it happens.[3]

Two small conferences were held at the University of Surrey in 2012, together with the establishment of the Models and Mathematics in Life and Social Science project, also at Surrey, which took up where Ian Stewart's arguments had left off, and in which the new science of quantum biology was addressed. This investigated very rapid processes within cells, some examining biological processes lasting only femtoseconds (a femtosecond = one millionth of one billionth of a second, or 10^{-15} seconds), which may play a role in genetics (mutation, and therefore evolution), photosynthesis and otherwise mysterious processes such as migrating birds' uncanny ability to navigate over vast distances. This, too, may be another new level of reality, as minuscule and mysterious as strings and superstrings. Jim Al-Khalili and Johnjoe McFadden are the names to register here, the former Iraqi-born, the latter Scottish-Irish.

Elsewhere in the 'hard' sciences – physics, chemistry and medicine or physiology – British and Commonwealth scientists have been well represented in the Nobel Prizes awarded in the twenty-first century. In physics the stand-out discovery was Peter Higgs and the 'Higgs boson'. Higgs, a Scot, and another physicist, François Englert, a Belgian, both proposed the existence of something very like what came to be called the Higgs boson in 1964, since the developing understanding of the forces and particles that made up the early universe, in which forces were very strong, needed a particle such as the Higgs to account for why these particles had mass, and therefore were affected by gravity and other forces. Only in July 2012 did the Large Hadron Collider, at CERN in Geneva, finally identify this particle. It has a mass of 125 billion electron volts, making it more than 130 times more massive than a proton, and is chargeless with zero spin; these technical terms are difficult to summarise, but the important point is that its discovery completed the so-called standard model of the universe, of particle physics. The Higgs field, which exists only instantaneously, before collapsing into other particles, has been likened to snow in a field where, depending on whether you are on skis, or snow shoes, or heavy boots, progress (mass and movement) varies. It was hoped that the discovery of the Higgs boson would help in the investigation of 'dark matter', which is more common in the universe than it should be, according to the standard model, but so far there has been little to report.[4] British physicist Mark Thomson will become director-general of CERN in early 2026.

Roger Penrose, who won the Nobel Prize in Physics in 2020, is best known for his work on black holes and singularities, with Stephen Hawking. He reported the extraordinary idea that, judging by perturbations in the cosmic wave background, there might have been earlier universes. This idea never seems to have claimed the attention it so obviously deserves.

Beyond any individual scientist, or doctor, there grew up in the early years of the twenty-first century in London a new area known as 'the Knowledge Quarter'. This is centred on King's Cross station, which is both near the British Library and a terminus for the line to and from Cambridge, which is an intellectual centre itself, but also a convenient (and cheaper) home location for scientists working at University College, Imperial College or the Wellcome Trust. It is also near the Francis Crick Institute (life sciences) and the Alan Turing Institute (data science), the headquarters of the British Medical Association and the British Museum. The Institute of Physics is also in the quarter, where GSK (formerly GlaxoSmithKline), Google DeepMind, AstraZeneca and MSD, the big pharmaceutical company, also have their operations. Britain is finally getting its answer to Silicon Valley into place.[5]

In medicine and physiology, perhaps as interesting as any single discovery by British scientists (in genetic engineering, brain physiology, cloning, hepatitis and hypoxia research) is the simple statistic that in the first two decades of the twenty-first century, twelve British medical researchers won the Nobel Prize – in other words they won in more years than they didn't. British winners were not as successful as Americans – who won twenty-nine Nobels. But if you total the number of prizes won by the English-speaking nations in physiology or medicine, the total comes to forty-seven, with Japan next, at a distant four, France with three and Germany with two. This picture will be returned to in the conclusion.[6]

Also in 2004, in May, a fire at a warehouse in east London destroyed hundreds of paintings and other artworks, which were later described as 'the most important pictures to come out of this country in the last century'. They were works by the Chapman brothers, Tracey Emin, Damien Hirst, Barry Flanagan, Chris Ofili, Paula Rego and others. The London Fire Brigade said that exploding acetylene cylinders kept firefighters at bay. It was later determined that the fire had been started deliberately by arsonists, but no one was ever charged and court cases for damages went on for years.

The biggest loss occurred to the paintings owned by Charles Saatchi – around 140 paintings in his collection went up in flames. Saatchi, born in Baghdad in 1943, was with his brother Maurice co-founder of Saatchi & Saatchi, the largest advertising agency in the world in the 1980s. Saatchi has been collecting contemporary art since at least 1969, including all the major names, and in 2008 installed an opulent gallery near Sloane Square in London. He has been especially associated with what came to be called Young British Artists, most notably in a show, *Sensation*, at the Royal Academy in 1997, which itself created a sensation. It was in this show that Damien Hirst first showed his sharks in formaldehyde, entitled *The Physical Impossibility of Death in the Mind of Someone Living*, and Tracey Emin's *Everyone I Have Ever Slept With*. Particular offence was caused by Marcus Harvey's painting of Myra Hindley, who, with Ian Brady, carried out the notorious Moors murders, killing five children in the Manchester area and burying them on Saddleworth Moor. The portrait was made up of children's palm prints.[7]

Especially remarkable about the fire, or at least the artists whose works went up in flames, were the number who, like Saatchi, had multinational backgrounds. This had applied to the two biggest names in late twentieth-century painting in Britain, Lucian Freud, born in Weimar Germany and the grandson of Sigmund Freud, the founder of psychoanalysis, who had sought exile in Britain on the eve of the Second World War, and Francis Bacon, born in Ireland in 1909, when it was part of the United Kingdom, who was descended from the first Francis Bacon's brother, Nicholas, and who also spent much time in Berlin, Paris and Monte Carlo.

Neither Freud nor Bacon ever won the Turner Prize, which says more about the prize than it does about them. It started only in 1984 and has never achieved anything like the impression or prestige of other awards, but the overlap between Saatchi's taste and that of the Turner judges was considerable and here too we see the international backgrounds of these talents: Tracey Emin's mother was a Romany; Chris Ofili's parents were Nigerian; Paula Rego, though she lived and worked in London, was Portuguese; the Chapman brothers, Jake and Dinos, had a Cypriot mother; Michael Raedecker, who works in London, is Dutch; Tomoko Takahashi, who also works in London, is Japanese; Yinka Shonibare, who works in London, is British-Nigerian; Tomma Abts is German but lives and works in London; Zarina Bhimji is a Ugandan Asian living and working in London; Lynette Yiadom-Boakye, whose parents immigrated to Britain from Ghana, paints imaginary black portraits; Heather Agyepong is a British-Ghanaian, living and working in London; Shahpour Pouyan, born in Iran, works in London. This cosmopolitan list goes on.

Britain's cosmopolitan nature is reflected in literature too. V. S. Naipaul, born in Trinidad but settled in London, won the Nobel Prize in Literature in 2001, Harold Pinter, son of east European Jews, in 2005, and the Iranian-born Doris Lessing in 2007, but these were awards given mainly for distinguished works which in each case had been published decades earlier. Kazuo Ishiguro, who won the Nobel Prize in Literature in 2017, was born in Nagasaki in 1954 and emigrated to Britain in 1960, when his oceanographer father was invited to work at the National Oceanography Centre in Southampton. His first two books, understandably enough, were set in Japan: these were *A Pale View of Hills* (1982) and *An Artist of the Floating World* (1986), both explorations of 'Japanese-ness', as he felt he was losing his Japanese identity in a rapidly changing but increasingly connected world and wasn't entirely sure how he felt about that. But he then turned more decisively away and his best-known book, *The Remains of the Day* (1989), is set in a traditional country house in England on the eve of the Second World War, when aristocratic German diplomats arrive to confer with the master of the house, a Nazi sympathiser.[8] Ishiguro was made CH in the 2025 New Year's Honours, having been knighted in 2018.

Abdulrazak Gurnah, who won the Nobel Prize in Literature in 2021, is probably the least well-known laureate in Britain. Born in 1948 in what was then the Sultanate of Zanzibar, and later part of Tanzania, he left his homeland when he was eighteen, following the overthrow of the Arab elite in the Zanzibar Revolution, by the island's mainly black population, and just a year after independence from Britain. A native Swahili speaker, Gurnah is of Arab heritage, his family originally coming from Yemen. In Britain, his refugee status would affect him deeply, and after he studied at Christ Church College, Canterbury, and then completed a PhD at the University of Kent, the diary he had kept gradually transformed into a small number of books. In the early 1980s he taught at the Bayero University Kano in Nigeria, before becoming a professor of English and postcolonial literature back at Kent. Critically, his work was well received – two of his books, *Paradise* and *The Sea*, were nominated for the Booker Prize in 1994 and 2001 respectively – but they were not a commercial success, and hardly sold at all outside Britain. Most of them dwelled on the alienation and loneliness brought on by migration and displacement, added to which, although Gurnah's stories are compassionate, using irony and humour, they are also unflinching, and have been described as 'quiet stories of people who aren't heard'. The Nobel Prize changed that to an extent – Gurnah found a market in the United States at least and *Afterlives* (2022) has been translated into Swahili. It is set in east Africa in the early twentieth century, in a country occupied by Germans, and Gurnah explores the minds of black Africans fighting for their colonial masters.[9]

Ishiguro was knighted for his work and so was Ben Okri, a Nigerian who arrived in Britain aged two, though his family moved back again, when he was exposed to the Nigerian Civil War, a major influence. He transferred to Britain a second time in 1978 to study comparative literature at Essex University. He won the Booker Prize in 1991, at the age of thirty-two, making him the youngest ever to win. This book was *The Famished Road*, its title taken from a poem by Wole Soyinka, 'Death in the Dawn': 'May you never walk / when the road waits, famished.' Okri hasn't won again, or even been shortlisted, but the books kept coming, and kept revisiting the dream world that had informed his earlier work, though he claims that Francis Bacon is another major influence. He joined the board of the Royal National Theatre and in 2021 published a major collection of poems, *A Fire in My Head: Poems for the Dawn*, covering such subjects as the refugee crisis, racism and the Grenfell Tower disaster. This extract is from 'Decolonisation', one of the poems in the collection:

> It never takes place unnoticed.
> Like a Blade before your eyes.
> It transforms those crushed with their nothingness,
> Into central performers under the floodlights of history's
>   blood-like gaze.

Much worried about the climate crisis, Okri thought art was needed
to penetrate the denial that most of us have about the urgency facing
us. After years of being ignored in the United States, in 2020 he
began to break through.

Okri has been compared with Salman Rushdie, who in turn
praised Ishiguro for *The Remains of the Day*, in particular for the
author's ability to show that he was not place-bound and could direct
his imagination in fresh directions. Rushdie, who had been knighted
himself in 2007, was in fine form as the twenty-first century got
under way. His fecundity of form was especially notable: *Shalimar
the Clown* (2005), set in Los Angeles and Kashmir, concerned an
American diplomat who is murdered by his erstwhile chauffeur,
Shalimar. Gradually, it is revealed that the diplomat 'stole' Shalimar's
intended, and he is now intent on revenge. In fact, he has trained as
a killer with a terrorist organisation. He kills the diplomat on the
day he resigns his position, and returns to India to kill his ex ...
Two Years and Eight Months and Twenty-Eight Nights (2015) is
set out as a 'mystery box' with different levels, exploring the difference between transnationalism and cosmopolitanism. *Victory
City* (2023) is an epic (a favoured form for Rushdie) framed as a
translation of a work originally written in Sanskrit, derived in part
from a fourteenth-century princess-poet, Gangadevi, who is blessed
(and cursed) with a 247-year lifespan. She 'breathes' into existence
a fantastical empire which has been described as a 'sort of feminist
utopia'. Its narrative sweep covers many generations, during which
she consorts with Portuguese adventurers, transforms people into
animals at will, until it all comes crashing down via wars and other
catastrophes brought about, not least, by religious bigotry.

These four figures can be seen against an intriguing background
that shows how Britain's literary intellectuals are changing. During
the first twenty-two years of the twenty-first century, the Booker
Prize was won by eleven writers from the Commonwealth, or with
Commonwealth associations, and two from the Republic of Ireland;
in other words, for what it is worth, non-Britons have won the prize
in more years than they haven't. Cosmopolitan.

But the most exciting new talent to emerge in the twenty-first
century, certainly one of them, is a woman who also conforms to

the pattern being outlined here. Zadie Smith was born in 1975 in Willesden, an unromantic suburb of north London, to a Jamaican mother, who had emigrated to Britain in 1969, and an English father. Educated at King's College, Cambridge, she drafted her first novel while still an undergraduate there and, on showing it to an agent, a bidding war followed. *White Teeth* (2000) was a ravishing success, an original voice – funny, ironic, mocking, knowing, fierce and gentle at the same time. Set in a very multicultural London, the story revolves around two men and their families, friends and (quite often criminal in a petty sense) associates: in other words, Willesden. The two men, Archie Jones, an Englishman, and the Bangladeshi Samad Iqbal, who met in the army and drink too much, form the central plot, Archie almost committing suicide at the very beginning of the book, then marrying the mother of his short-term girlfriend, and Samad having problems being a Muslim in the fleshpots and drinking dens of London. Intellectuals, pseudo-intellectuals and re-ligious zealots play their part, as do identical twins, as the traditional slapstick source of confusion.

Of her later books, *On Beauty* was shortlisted for the Booker Prize (she has been shortlisted twice), *NW* was set in Kilburn, not a stone's throw from Willesden, and her play *The Wife of Willesden* was roughly adapted from Chaucer's *The Wife of Bath's Tale*. Her most recent novel, *The Fraud* (2023), is her first attempt at histor-ical fiction, a courtroom drama about an imposter, set against an imperial background. As in most of Smith's work, race, identity and context are central concerns.[10]

ENGINEERS OF PARADISE

In history, historiography and non-fiction more generally, as the twenty-first century has progressed, two themes have stood out. One is a growing interest in the oceans of the world – not just the Atlantic but the Pacific, the Mediterranean and the North Sea. David Abulafia, who has written several books on the oceans, concentrates in *The Boundless Sea* (2019: over 1,000 pages long) on the respect the seas command, but also on the adventure and, as he puts it, the 'wickedness' of some seafarers. He reminds us that 'admitting that black rulers sold slaves to white merchants had not come easily to historians of the slave trade'. But he goes on to reassure us that scholarship shows that pirates really did tie red bandannas round their heads and drink rum after rum. And that Columbus wrote in his notebook: 'I have not found any monstrous men, as many expected; rather, they are all people of very beautiful appearance.'[11]

Nicholas Thomas's book *Islanders: The Pacific in the Age of Empire* (2010) was a revelation for many who had had their views shaped by Alan Moorehead, in *The Fatal Impact* (1966), which had characterised the Pacific as an 'inevitably doomed region', its indigenous cultures destined to be swept aside as a result of expanding European exploration in the nineteenth century. Instead, Thomas shows that the influential essay *Our Sea of Islands*, by the Tongan anthropologist Epeli Hau'ofa, was much nearer the mark: he argued that Pacific islanders were connected rather than separated by the sea. 'Far from being sea-locked peoples marooned on coral or volcanic strips of land waiting to be discovered by Europeans, islanders formed an oceanic community based on voyaging, movement and exchange.' They ventured as far as America, Australia, Asia and even Europe. And colonial rule generally *expanded* the 'gift-giving, diplomacy, commerce and contest' that thrived between island and tribes. Even in the 1790s, Hawaiians, Maori and Tahitians mixed and exchanged ideas. James Cook realised that Pacific islanders did not live in a state of nature: their societies engaged in trade; people sailed in great ocean-going canoes from island to island; and there were 'pre-existing, inter-island patterns of allegiance and subordination'. Their consumption patterns did change of course: by the 1820s Hawaiians were dressing in European-style clothing and living in European-style houses. One, Mahine from Ralatea, joined the mission to hunt down Fletcher Christian. He had dined with Bligh before the mutiny.[12]

Still on the subject of islands, the death in 2020 of Richard Grove, fourteen years after he suffered a catastrophic car accident in Australia, brought to a close a life that had drawn attention to the way the exploration of empire, and in particular the islands of the Pacific, had focused attention on the ecology of the globe. In two books, *Green Imperialism: Colonial Expansion, Tropical Island Edens and the Origins of Environmentalism, 1600–1860* (1995) and *Ecology,*

Climate and Empire: Colonialism and Global Environmental History, 1400–1940 (1997), Grove – who among other things founded the Centre for World Environmental History at Sussex University and the academic journal *Environment and History* – argued that plant transfers by colonial officials helped to create an early environmental awareness among the main imperial powers.

Grove, whose work won several awards, neatly introduces the other main area of historical inquiry in the early twenty-first century, namely the investigation of empire, relations between the races, and the presence of black people in Britain (black Tudors, black Edwardians, black Oxford), considered more fully in the conclusion.

Among contemporary British philosophers of note, we may begin with two men with out-of-the-ordinary lifestyles. Derek Parfit (1942–2017), born in Chengdu, western China, the son of doctors in a missionary school, at first wanted to be a monk, and prayed that his parents, who had lost their faith, would return to it. He subsequently lost his own faith and turned first to poetry. After Eton, at Oxford he gained a fellowship at All Souls, where his first paper in philosophy became famous even though he had no formal training in the discipline. His main philosophical concern was to investigate how much we are the same person over time, and what this tells us about individuality, and how self-interest is related to community interest, and what is the right role for intuition. He published only two books, *Reasons and Persons* (1984) and *On What Matters* (2011), but was widely read among all manner of readers. For example, at one Tibetan monastery, monks intersperse chanting the usual sutras with intoning memorised passages from *Reasons and Persons*. Parfit, who suffered from Asperger syndrome, a condition that interferes with social interaction, practised what he preached. He was a member of the Effective Altruism Movement, which aims to mobilise millions of dollars to improve the lives of as many people as possible. Parfit was among those who contribute 10 per cent of their earnings to the altruism movement. Worried about wasting time, he had identical meals prepared and kept duplicate sets of clothes.[13]

David Pearce (b. 1959) is a transhumanist philosopher and cofounder of the World Transhumanist Association, now known as

Humanity+. This is a better name because transhumanism is the effort to improve human cognition and lifespan by using developing technologies. Pearce is a vegan, like his parents and Quaker grandparents before him, and his particular interest is in 'paradise engineering', which aims to explore how drugs and genetic engineering can end suffering for all sentient life. One project is a 'cross-species global analogue of the welfare state', in which one aim is to 'reprogram predators' to limit predation.[14]

David Deutsch (b. 1953), born in Haifa, Israel, is a theoretical physicist who argues that information can only be expressed in terms of the transformation of physical systems. An expert on quantum theory, his book *The Fabric of Reality* (1997) was an attempt to integrate computational, epistemological and evolutionary principles, expressed through an attempted synthesis of the ideas of Karl Popper, Alan Turing, Richard Dawkins and Hugh Everett's 'many-worlds theory', which argues that the basic state of the universe depends on a quantum condition that could give rise in some circumstances to other worlds. It is clearly very technical and controversial, and not easy for non-mathematicians to understand, but equally clearly is of fundamental importance. Deutsch's 2011 book, *The Beginning of Infinity: Explanations that Transform the World*, is more accessible, arguing that the Enlightenment was, in effect, a singularity itself, the beginning of a potentially unending – infinite – sequence of 'purposeful knowledge creation' leading to an infinite cascade of explanations. But this change did not have historical beginnings; our universe is part of other universes which interact via quantum processes and this interaction may have started the Enlightenment, a startling idea. In any event, Deutsch says, since the Enlightenment we have been living in a world totally different to that which predominated beforehand, which this book has tried to make clear.

Much more accessible is John Gray (b. 1948), a philosopher at the London School of Economics and someone who flatly disagrees with Deutsch (and, it must be said, with many other philosophers and historians). Gray, the author of, among other works, *False Dawn: The Illusions of Global Capitalism* (1998), *Straw Dogs: Thoughts on Humans and Other Animals* (2002), *Black Mass: Apocalyptic Religion and the Death of Utopia* (2007) and most recently *The*

New Leviathans: Thoughts After Liberalism (2023), is a thorough-going pessimist, arguing that, in replacing religion with reason, as famously happened in the Enlightenment, we have only swapped one set of delusions for another, and this is especially true since the fall of the Soviet Union, after which those in the West thought that Russia and China were going to convert to democracy and salute the 'universal triumph of liberal values'. In what one critic described as Gray's 'cherished dystopia', he says we need to 'grow up and recognize that the future does not belong to humanity'. 'There will be monarchies and republics, nations and empires, tyrannies and theocracies; along with stateless zones where there is no government at all.' In short, we must prepare for global anarchy. Here is a typical extract: 'Modern humanism is the faith that through science humankind can know the truth – and so be free. But if Darwin's theory of natural selection is true this is impossible. The human mind serves evolutionary success, not truth. To think otherwise is to resurrect the pre-Darwinian error that humans are different from other animals.' Liberal humanism, he says, embodies the idea of human progress, but this is no more than an alternative version of the Christian idea of progress and finality. Again: 'Look at the Genesis myth. Once you have eaten of the tree of knowledge you can't go back ... The key example in Liberal Humanism is the idea that knowledge liberates. I think that knowledge normally simply enhances human power.'[15]

Gray's point is that it is a mistake to think that advances in ethics or politics can in principle be like advances in science in the sense of being cumulative. Gray is convinced it is a mistake to see cumulative development in science paralleled in human well-being and ethical behaviour, and above all and *pace* David Pearce above, he is thoroughly sceptical about attempts to better the human condition. He agrees with Karl Popper, who once accepted 'bit and piece social engineering' but thought that 'anything more ambitious is certain to founder'.

It is not only in 'high culture' (quotation marks being obligatory nowadays) that the British imagination may be said to have made its mark. In 2015 Dominic Sandbrook published *The Great British Dream Factory*, a mischievous and enjoyable romp through the extent to which the British popular imagination has rendered the nation a 'cultural superpower': from Harry Potter (400 million books worldwide), to the Beatles (1 billion albums), Agatha Christie (2 billion books), Catherine Cookson (123 million despite the unpleasant things that happen to her heroines), *Top Gear* playing in Iran, *Doctor Who* everywhere, Andrew Lloyd Webber musicals, and of course John Lennon's simple but haunting song 'Imagine'.[16]

In the performing arts, contemporary classical music in Britain in the present century offers one of the most intriguing facts: that three composers – Sir John Rutter, John Tavener and Brian Chapple – were fellow pupils at Highgate School. Two others may be added to this group: Sir Karl Jenkins and Michael Nyman. Rutter and Tavener both suffered chronic illnesses, myalgic encephalomyelitis in Rutter's case, while Tavener suffered multiple heart attacks, a stroke in his thirties, and another heart attack and a tumour in his forties. Yet both produced copious compositions. Jenkins, Nyman and Tavener were fond of jazz and rock, in addition to classical music: Jenkins had his own band, while Nyman and Tavener collaborated with the Beatles and Apple records. Jenkins's mother was Swedish, while Tavener married a Greek and later converted to Orthodox Christianity. Tavener, Rutter and Jenkins each composed religious music, mainly choral, one of Tavener's best compositions being *Song for Athene*, performed at the funeral of Princess Diana. His dramatic cantata, *The Whale*, is based on the Old Testament story of Jonah.

Each broke out in new directions. Tavener produced *Akhmatova Requiem*, a setting of fifteen poems by the Russian Anna Akhmatova using the chant system of the Orthodox Church, poems which explore Stalin's purges in the 1930s. Jenkins's 'Adiemus' series of songs uses an invented language, not unlike 'scat singing' in jazz (though it sounds much softer and more formally disciplined), while Nyman produced an opera on the improbable subject (for opera) of cloning. Rutter is even more popular in the United States than he is in Britain, while Nyman's music is probably the best known of all, since he has composed for so many films. These include *The Piano*, *The Diary of Anne Frank*, *Gattaca* and *The Cook, the Thief, His Wife & Her Lover*.

In the legitimate theatre – and according to one list, there were more than a hundred British dramatists worthy of the name in the twenty-first century – a mere three theatrical experiences stood out. One was the plays of Tom Stoppard. Born Tomáš Sträussler in Zlín, Moravia, Czechoslovakia, Stoppard never lost his bite, his wit and his uncanny ability to bring the thrust of general culture on to the boards. Building on such early triumphs as *Travesties, Jumpers* and *Rosencrantz and Guildenstern Are Dead*, he continued to face up to what he felt were the major intellectual issues of the day, with plays such as *The Coast of Utopia* (2002), a trilogy which examined Russian attitudes ahead of the Revolution there, *Rock 'n' Roll* (2006), about the role of pop music in eastern European culture, and, most recently, *Leopoldstadt* (2019), an almost autobiographical account of life in the Jewish community of Vienna in the early twentieth century. This was by no means his most successful play, but his recent work does serve to underline that Stoppard above all tries to marry emotional experience and intellectual knowledge better than, and more directly than, anyone else, highlighting what theatre *is*, or should try to be. In 2020 Hermione Lee wrote an 865-page biography of Stoppard, concluding that 'he *matters*'.[17]

Two plays that broke new ground – in one way or another – were *War Horse* (2007) and *Jerusalem* (2009). The former, based on a book by Michael Morpurgo, told the story of a family of farmers, and their horses, related by one of the horses, caught up in the First World War. What stood out in the play were the life-size models, in effect puppets of wire with humans inside them, making them breathe, sneeze, and shift from foot to foot in incredibly 'human' ways, so that they almost came alive. To be moved by an animal, and to feel its nobility, was a very startling experience.

Jerusalem, by Jez Butterworth, was set in Pewsey in his native West Country, a three-act play across a single day, St George's Day, when the local councillors have decided to evict a local ragamuffin called Johnny 'Rooster' Byron, not exactly a poet, but creatively anarchic, living in an illegal caravan in the woods, which is also home to his more or less wild, drug- and alcohol-addled friends full, as one critic had it, of 'Falstaffian energies', a tumultuous counterculture of egregious punk self-obsession, redeemed by wit and pointed social observation, aimed at themselves as much as anyone. 'Jerusalem' is used ironically, of course: there are no satanic mills in Pewsey, nor chariots of fire. This was 'the state of England' in 2009.

The year 2025 would be a neat date on which to conclude this narrative, but in fact 2022 serves us better. This was not only the year in which Queen Elizabeth died, but there were two events which together show how John Gray may be right, in that intellectual advances proceed but, at the same time, as he also said, there are no advances in morality.

On Tuesday 12 October 2022, at the Newport Street Gallery, a former scenery-painting factory, just south of the Thames in Lambeth, Damien Hirst, the self-proclaimed *enfant terrible* of contemporary artists, set fire to thousands of his paintings in public. Many people who had bought these paintings queued outside, for the 'privilege' of watching the incineration of their property. A long line snaked from the old redbrick warehouse, and a strong smell of woodsmoke clogged the nostrils of the newspaper people who had been invited to watch what one observer described as 'either an act of artistic genius or the most ridiculous publicity stunt ever conceived'. The line of people, in groups, climbed a winding wooden staircase, to a white-walled gallery with five wood-burning stoves arranged around the edges. A dozen of Hirst's assistants, including his girlfriend, in orange overalls and heat-proof gloves, lowered the paintings one by one from a central stack, into the flames.

This was a culminating act in a project that had begun in July 2021 when Hirst, who had produced 10,000 'unique dot paintings', each just 8 inches by 12 inches, allocated to each of them a 'non-fungible token' (NFT), a unique digital token encrypted with the artist's signature to verify its ownership and authenticity. Selling the NFTs for around $1,700 apiece, Hirst then offered buyers a choice: they could either exchange the NFT for the physical artwork, in which case the NFT would be 'destroyed', or they could choose to have the physical artwork burned and keep the NFT. Over half the collectors (5,149) decided to retain their physical artwork, but 4,851 opted to hold on to their NFTs with the corresponding painting set alight in a public conflagration, presided over by Hirst himself.

Many present at the incineration (some from as far afield as

Croatia) had bought two works and opted to keep one physical object and have the other burned, preferring the 'adventure', as one collector put it, 'of seeing what will happen with the value of the NFT'.

Hirst himself delivered a short speech. 'People who only believe in physical art get very upset at the idea of you burning it. But people who believe in NFTs celebrate when you burn actual paintings.' In response to a question as to whether NFTs can be considered art at all, he responded: 'Who knows what art is? It's like trying to convince people who don't believe in God that there is a God. I mean, does it matter?'[18]

With Hirst's latest initiative (after tiger sharks pickled in formaldehyde, and paintings made entirely of dots), have we crossed a line where art and money have finally coalesced, completing a journey that began a long time ago in the Renaissance? One of those in the line at Hirst's conflagration said that, having initially paid £1,700 for his dot painting in 2021, by October 2022, he had been offered £42,000 for his NFT. Others are not convinced, pointing to the collapse of various cryptocurrencies and other NFTs, arguing this is just another case of the Emperor's New Clothes, which will go the way of all such ventures.

The jury is still out on Hirst's latest scheme but what we can say is that, despite one or two setbacks, and more than one court case in which he has been accused of plagiarism and even theft, he remains a cultural phenomenon who is still, several decades on from when he first began making waves, challenging us as to what art *is*.

At the same time, only a few weeks apart, in August 2022, Salman Rushdie was preparing to give a talk, ironically about the United States being a safe haven for writers, when he was attacked by a member of the audience at the Chautauqua Institute in Chautauqua in New York state. A California-born, second-generation Lebanese immigrant leaped on to the stage and stabbed Rushdie ten times. The author was rushed to hospital by helicopter but despite treatment lost the use of one eye and one hand. It later turned out that the perpetrator of the attack had read but two pages of *The Satanic Verses*, which had been published in 1988, ten years before he was born.

Rushdie was soon back at work and, in 2024, he produced *Knife*, his account of the episode, so the attack was not the end it might have been.

A Metaphysical Empire?

I n 1995, the year Salman Rushdie won the Whitbread Prize with *The Moor's Last Sigh*, Daniel Dennett, a well-known philosopher from Tufts University in Medford, near Boston, said this, plainly, in his book *Darwin's Dangerous Idea: Evolution and the Meaning of Life*: 'If I were to give an award for the single best idea anyone has ever had, I'd give it to Darwin, ahead of Newton and Einstein and everyone else. In a single stroke, his idea of evolution by natural selection unifies the realm of life, meaning, and purpose with the realm of space, time, cause and effect, mechanism and physical law.'[1] It is hard to disagree with Dennett, but for the purposes of this book, and its concerns, the importance of evolution doesn't stop there.

Darwin's dangerous idea is a useful starting point for this concluding discussion because it exemplifies three of the four major strands of British intellectual history. Postmodernists are by and large sceptical of metanarratives, but their influence is waning and in the imaginative history of the United Kingdom four metanarratives are very clear, as this book has tried to show. One that is embarrassing in retrospect is the great change that came over Britons, from being an underpopulated non-entity, defeated and sidelined by William the Conqueror, to re-establishing the English language, to experiencing 'divine Anglophilia', with God as an Englishman, to a more 'intense' Englishness under Elizabeth I, with an increasing coherence as to what Britain was and is, to the discovery of 'beyond' and a 'blue-water destiny' after the discovery of the universe. This led to a sense of 'England's gathering greatness', as it has been called, to the 'Enormous Conceit' of being 'the dread and envy of them all' as empire gathered pace, always puffed up with an expanding Providential appetite to spread Christianity. And then on to anticipating a metaphysical empire in the late eighteenth century, to seeing the English diaspora as a 'world event', to imagining a 'Greater Britain' in the white settler dominions in the late nineteenth century, together with the idea of a 'learned empire' being a 'higher purpose' for Britain. And finally, and inevitably, even to the idea that Britain was the 'apex of civilization'.

This thread is too nationalistic for the cosmopolitan temper of our times, though there is more than a grain of truth in it, as the quotes from the North American Conference on British Studies mentioned at the start of this book show. The more substantive metanarratives may be summarised as: (1) the peculiar and idiosyncratic path of religious belief, essentially the rise and fall of religion, not excluding the perceived role of Providence, and the belief that Britain was uniquely favoured, which has transformed it from being one of the most intensely religious countries to the least (in the 2021 census, for the first time, a majority of British people described themselves as having no faith, making Britain among the half-dozen least religious countries in the world); (2) the rise and continued pre-eminence of empirical science, arguably the most important metanarrative of all; (3) the creation and increasing refinement of the concept of political economy; and (4) the adventure of empire. Of course, though each of these developments may be considered separately, for the purposes of analysis, in reality they overlapped heavily.

Is there something about living on a small, out of the way, weather-beaten island on the way to nowhere that concentrates minds or, as Linda Colley says, did the smallness and poverty of Britain generate a national extroversion? Does being aware (not statistically but existentially) that you are surrounded by bigger, vastly more populous potential enemies drive you to deeper reflection on your threatened existence, and force on you the view that you must rely on God for help? And, when you succeed against the odds, does that encourage you to believe that God especially favours you? Were the tumultuous usurpations of the English throne over a long period of time, from the thirteenth to the seventeenth centuries, responsible for the loosening of the idea of the divine right of kings more quickly and more thoroughly in England than anywhere else in Europe?

Were Britain's offshore location and small size important in another sense, namely that, without a hinterland to defend, it never needed a large standing army but instead could concentrate on its navy to explore and exploit the sea, the ever-further reaches of the oceans, and that, following the discoveries of Copernicus, Kepler, Galileo and others, the British realised that, with the world opening up as never before, as 'beyond' acquired an ever-richer meaning, not just for exploration and trade, but also for the spreading of the Christian religion, a unique Providential future beckoned? Was Britain uniquely fortunate in having a generation of swashbuckling merchant adventurers/warriors willing to embrace what we might call useful violence? Was it also fortunate in having a unique generation of early scientists who grasped that empiricism was a new way of dealing with the world? With these circumstances coming so swiftly, one after the other, is this how modern Britain may be said to have begun? Did the unusual location of London, as a capital city that was also a port – unlike Paris, Berlin, Madrid, Rome or Vienna – make England more ocean-minded than other European nations, and better seamen? After the unification of England and Wales with Scotland in 1707, and after the failed rebellion of 1745, Britain was a self-confident, self-assured, even swashbuckling Protestant nation, convinced of its Providential role to create a Christian empire. Are these the factors/context that gave rise to what we understand as the British imagination?

It is not entirely true to say that empirical science is a uniquely British idea. Empirical science, or at least an empirical approach to some aspects of knowledge, has been traced to Alexandria in the first century BC and to the Han age in China at much the same time, but it does seem clear that in the early modern period, thanks to the collective thinking of Robert Grosseteste and Roger Bacon, the empirical approach emerged in many minds in Britain, in conjunction with scepticism about the established church, producing an early realisation that 'theology and natural history must go their separate ways'. The Académie des Sciences was founded in Paris only a few years after the Royal Society, but as we have seen the British institution grew out of Elizabethan London, which was home to what we would now call practical empirical minds (including Gresham College, with its lectures in English *and* Latin, for visitors), an approach recognised by Francis Bacon, arguably the most influential Briton of all so far as ideas are concerned. And it is clear that the early fellows of the Royal Society recognised that their approach to affairs was new, not only for the production of new and useful knowledge, but also for the effect it had on literature through its preference for clear, plain language, shorn of unnecessary embellishment.

The invention and adoption of the empirical approach was of course taken up by the rest of the world but even so here is a perhaps surprising fact: the English-speaking nations still lead the world in science, in the twenty-first century. How do we know? The award of Nobel Prizes. As was mentioned in the preceding chapter, since the inception of the Nobel Prizes in 1901, the English-speaking nations have won more in the 'hard' sciences, and in literature, than any others.

Let us ask first whether Nobel Prizes can be considered a good guide to excellence in science. The Nobel Foundation now has well over a century's experience to scan the workings of the scientific world, and in practice its awards are almost never queried. It may well be that a number of deserving scientists have not yet been recognised with an award but there is almost never any opposition directed against scientists who do win. The care with which the Nobel Foundation takes its responsibilities is also shown by the fact that some awards are delayed by years, such as that for Peter Higgs in 2012, for work done in the 1960s but only then supported by experimental confirmation, fully fifty years later. Despite the predominance of the English-speaking countries, awards have gone to scientists on every continent except Antarctica, and in literature to many languages scattered across the globe. Also, as shown in Tables 2 and 3, the difference between the twentieth and twenty-first centuries, with the marked growth of awards to Japanese scientists, also tends to confirm that the Nobel Foundation has its ear to the ground.

Table 2 Nobel Prizes won by selected nations/regions in the twentieth century

Nation/region	No. of prizes in 'hard' sciences	% (to nearest whole no.)	No. of prizes in literature	% (to nearest whole no.)
USA	185	41	11	13
UK	73	16	10	12
Commonwealth countries	20	4	2	2
France	30	7	13	15
Germany	71	16	9	11
Scandinavia	26	6	14	16
Switzerland	15	3	1	1
Netherlands	11	2		
Spain	2	<1	6	7
Eastern Europe	3	<1	7	8
Russia	10	2	6	7
South America	6	1	4	5
China	2	<1	2	2
Total	454		85	

SOURCE: NOBEL FOUNDATION, STOCKHOLM, SWEDEN

The point of these figures is not to make some narrow nationalistic assertion, but to ask whether, in the context of this book, these statistics can be considered evidence that the concerns of Samuel Johnson and Thomas Sheridan, back in the eighteenth century, that the British Empire might one day give rise to a metaphysical empire on the lines of ancient Greece and Rome, has actually come about. Of course, the United States cannot any longer be regarded as part of the empire, and in any case many of those 'Americans' who won

Nobel Prizes were born elsewhere – in Europe, Russia, China, South America, India. Nonetheless, almost all of them had learned English, usually as a first language, and almost all worked in an English-language tradition, in a society that embodied many of the traditions and values – such as the common law, a bicameral political system, a predominantly Protestant religious tradition and an empirical enlightenment – that were taken to the Americas by British migrants.

Table 3 Nobel Prizes won by selected nations/
regions in the twenty-first century

Nation/region	No. of prizes in 'hard' sciences	% (to nearest whole no.)	No. of prizes in literature
USA	101	49	2
UK	29	14	4
Commonwealth countries	11	5	7
Japan	23	11	1
France	12	6	3
Germany	13	6	3
Israel	5	2	1
Scandinavia	5	2	2
Russia	4	2	1
Switzerland	4	2	
Total	**207**		**24**

What the figures show is that 63 per cent of the Nobel Prizes awarded in the 'hard' sciences were won by individuals from English-speaking nations in the twentieth century, and 68 per cent in the twenty-first century. At the same time, the proportion of literature Nobels won by English-speaking nations was 27 per cent in the twentieth century and 54 per cent in the twenty-first century, higher in all cases than any other nation. The figures, tantalisingly, also show that the English-language predominance was slightly stronger in the twenty-first century, in both science and literature, than it was in the twentieth, though it is much too early to say whether this is a genuine trend. But science/technology is, arguably, the dominant cultural element of modern societies, so this is an overall important finding.

English is the main language of the Internet, the official language for maritime traffic and air traffic, partly due to the dominance in new technologies by the United States, but also due to the fact that countries and regions of the former empire – India, Malaysia, Pacific islands, Australasia, African countries and areas of the Middle East – are all familiar with English owing to their past existence as colonies. Whatever one thinks of empire, the 'glue' of the English language is a major feature of cosmopolitan life, a tremendous boon to communication and the ease of international cooperation. It is one of two official languages for astronauts (the other being Russian).

In all, eighty-eight countries of the world (out of 193 which make up the United Nations) use English as an official, administrative or cultural language. Linguist David Crystal tells us that speaking English as a second language boosts the number of English speakers by a factor of three, English also being the language most often taught as a foreign language.[2]

The overlap between English-speaking countries and those excelling in science is also remarkable. The language of science is not universally English, of course, but it is predominantly so: the dominant learned scientific journals, *Nature*, the *Lancet*, *Science*, the *New England Journal of Medicine*, *Proceedings of the National Academy of Sciences*, *Transactions of the Royal Society*, *Scientific American*, are by no means the only science journals in the world, but again they are pre-eminent. Science and the English language are not quite as intimately linked as are the sciences and the mathematical languages, but scientists in Russia, China, eastern Europe, the Arab world and Latin America know that a lack of English on their part can inhibit their levels of state-of-the-art knowledge. The Science Citation Index reports that 95 per cent of its articles are written in English, 'even though only half of them come from authors in English-speaking countries'. Twenty-eight per cent of all books published in the world are written in English.

AN ANGLOSPHERE?

This leads naturally to the notion of the Anglosphere. This term was first used by sci-fi writer Neal Stephenson in *The Diamond Age* (1995), but it has since been made use of by such forward-looking writers as James C. Bennett, of the Foresight Institute in San Francisco, who is also interested in the new nanotechnology of molecular machines, new entities which are designed to carry out biological switching devices on a small, molecular scale. Bennett is the author of *The Anglosphere Challenge* (2004), where he envisages the eventual end of the nation state, to be superseded, to an extent, by 'Network Civilisations' linked by shared values, of which the most obvious he says, is the Anglosphere. He looks forward to a unique Anglosphere Civilisation, predominating in an 'Anglosphere Century'. This will be a time, he says, when the shared values include legal tradition (common law and precedent), attitudes about the military (no large standing armies in peacetime), freedom of speech, religion and property, fixed terms for legislatures, judicial review, trial by jury, evolution rather than revolution, empiricism, increasing racial diversity, and domestic politics dominated by two political parties. Bennett sees the Anglosphere as leading the way in the future and goes so far as to say that 'the nineteenth century was the British Century without a doubt. The twentieth century was the American Century ... If the English-speaking nations [by which he means the USA, the UK, Canada, New Zealand and Australia, but also Singapore, India, southern and eastern Africa and Guyana] grasp the opportunity, the twenty-first century will be the Anglosphere Century.' He bases this on an argument that the British colonies that retained common law and the English language have performed significantly better than areas colonised by other European powers.[3]

This is perhaps going too far too soon, but to a limited extent an Anglosphere already exists in the form of Five Eyes, the collaboration on intelligence-sharing between the US, the UK, Canada, Australia and New Zealand, and AUKUS (Australia, UK, US), the collaboration on the building of atomic submarines in the Asian theatre. There is a 'five nations passport group', an informal collaboration on the development of passports; Migration 5, collaboration on migration and visa schemes; and a technical cooperation programme among the same five nations on matters of defence and technology. Stephen Potter has examined the role of the press in the English-speaking world, mainly in the settler dominions, and shown how it took its colour from London, and from the BBC; Tamson Pietsch, in *Empire of Scholars* (2004), examined the links between the universities of the empire, showing how much they too made up a 'British world', where, to give just one example, between 1890 and 1930, the physicists J. J. Thomson and Ernest Rutherford (above, chapters 15 and 24) played a key role in nearly every physics appointment in the settler world.[4] Opinion polls show that the countries viewed most positively by citizens of the Five Eyes countries are, precisely, those Five Eyes countries. There are Royal Societies in Ireland and Scotland, six in the states of Australia, in New Zealand, Canada and South Africa. There is clearly some sort of fellow feeling among the citizens of the English-speaking peoples, as well as at government level. Included here is Dominic Sandbrook's mischievous idea that, even in popular culture (outlined above), Britain's contribution is flourishing.[5]

Does this all amount to a metaphysical empire as envisaged by Johnson and Sheridan? They could not have foreseen what actually came about, but the answer is surely, and however smug-sounding, a qualified yes.

BRITISH EMPIRE LTD

A separate metanarrative relates to political economy. Here too Britain was not the founder of the idea but shared it with the physiocrats of France. However, the line of thinkers that leads from William Petty (the subject of much recent scholarship, especially on his time in Ireland, and his efforts to encourage people to spend more money), John Graunt (new details about his statistical innovations), Charles Davenant, Gregor King, Bernard Mandeville and Edward

Lloyd to Thomas Malthus, Adam Smith, William Godwin, Jeremy Bentham, Richard Owen and John Stuart Mill, and then to William Stanley Jeavons, Alfred Marshall, Arthur Pigou and John Maynard Keynes, is probably a more impressive chain than any other nation can muster. Still more recent scholarship (for example, by Neal Wood), has extended the idea of political economy back to Tudor times, identifying an early growing interest in poverty.

Elsewhere there have been investigations of the political economy of the empire, most notably in a gargantuan study by Lance Davis and Robert Huttenback, who looked at what they termed British Empire Ltd, sifting the national income figures of no fewer than forty-one foreign countries, eighteen Indian princely states and all the countries of the empire, examining the distribution of the tax burden, the composition of shareholders and the imperial interests of MPs. Their (much criticised) conclusions were that British Empire Ltd was not a money-making enterprise, that the ownership of imperial business was concentrated in the traditional elite of London merchants, and that the middle classes bore the main burden of the cost of empire, which was, overall, 'a mechanism to effect an income transfer from the British middle classes to the British upper classes with a slight transfer to the colonies in the process'.[6]

And this metanarrative is expanded in a particularly interesting way in the form of the Oxford PPE degree. This degree, it will be recalled, was begun in 1920 and therefore celebrated its one hundredth anniversary in 2020. The landscape of the degree was outlined earlier but we return to it now, because it too may be said to help shape the Anglosphere. For not only have a surprising number of PPE graduates become government ministers (including prime ministers) but, arguably more influential, the degree itself has been replicated in 172 institutions across 33 countries. The degree is now taught in twenty-nine other universities in Britain, in France, Spain, Sweden, the Netherlands, Germany, Italy, in thirty-six institutions in North America, in South Africa, New Zealand, Australia, South Korea, in twelve universities in China and in Singapore. Of course, these degrees will vary but their way of looking at the world is recognisably similar. The real consequence of political economy has been to produce two main ways of looking at the way the world should be organised, that of liberal capitalism versus that of economic socialism. Without nineteenth-century Britain and its empire, would there have been a Marx, would there have been communism, or Soviet Russia?

Is Everything Empire? Is Empire Everything?

Lest this all sound somewhat triumphalist, and self-satisfied, let us turn to the last great metanarrative, the adventure of empire, its rise and fall. Whatever one thinks of empire, its achievements and crimes, or its crimes and achievements, the fact and extent of empire is what marks British history as arguably, and as we began this book, the most important national history of all time. Empire, says Alexander Motyl, the Ukrainian-American political scientist, in *Comparative Politics*, is a growth business: in 2006 Amazon listed 10,513 books with 'empire' in their title (in 2025 the London Library listed 12,689).[7] He says that proper attention to empire in the contemporary world only began in the 1950s and 1960s, waned in the 1970s and 1980s, but a sea change took place after 2001, when interest in the *American* Empire surged. That is not quite the interest here, though the number of books published about one empire or another is noteworthy.

One useful, convenient, more or less objective way of looking at the changing scholarship of the *British* Empire is to compare *The Oxford History of the British Empire*, five volumes, published in 1999, with the *Cambridge History of the British Empire*, published in nine volumes between 1929 and 1940. Such a comparison shows how the scholarly study of imperial history has altered, both in approach and in conclusions.[8]

Three differences are especially important. First, the assumption that there was something distinctive about the British Empire has been largely abandoned in the *Oxford History*. Moreover, 'it is seen not as a liberal and progressive force implanting British parliamentary institutions around the globe, but as the expression of a typically rapacious European power extending economic and political control'. Empire came to be justified on the basis of its contribution to the economic wellbeing of the mother country and religious and other motivations were clearly subordinated to the material ... imperial expansion was driven by a host of economic and non-economic factors – by European rivalries, by missionary enthusiasm, by a desire to find an outlet for Britain's rapidly growing population, by scientific curiosity and technological imperatives, by military calculations and needs and sometimes by accident. Nonetheless one comes away from the *Oxford History* with the impression that the Empire was essentially an instrument for adding to the wealth of Great Britain.[9]

A third conclusion is that the demand created by overseas empire hastened the technological transformation of several long-established branches of British industrial life, so that, on balance, the empire 'is seen as a positive force in the development of the British economy and a benefit to Britain'.

In the *Cambridge History*, the empire, says Philip Buckner, was seen as 'at worst a benign and usually a beneficial force promoting good government and modernization around the globe', and that even during the nineteenth century, the British 'saw themselves as reluctant imperialists responding to turbulent frontiers and ultimately as a force bringing positive good to the areas of the world which were reluctantly added to the Empire'.[10] But, in the *Oxford History*, 'these hoary myths are now firmly laid to rest'. At the same time, the *Oxford History* rejects the notion that the British were 'inherently more racist than other Europeans ... The first Englishmen to have "direct dealings with Amerindians" were "sympathetic toward Native Americans and their culture" and they "made as genuine an effort as any Europeans to overcome their inherited beliefs and prejudices and accommodate America and its peoples within their world view'. The British were a 'threat' because they arrived in larger numbers than other Europeans.

The *Oxford History* also treats the Native Americans not merely as victims but as historical actors interacting with the British, and not as 'meek witnesses' to colonisation, but instead as resisters and negotiators, 'often to great effect'. During the first half of the eighteenth century the Amerindian groups around the thirteen colonies 'secured fragile places in a global imperial system' and it was only after the independence of the US that Britain abandoned its Indian allies and left them to make terms with the new United States. Similarly, the Native peoples of Canada, New Zealand and Australia were forced to make the best terms they could with the British settlers.

The *Oxford History* is also more realistic than the *Cambridge History* about the abolition of the slave trade: it concedes there was a role for humanitarians, and humanitarianism, but abolition would not have succeeded, the *Oxford History* says, without the fact that the economics of the trade were changing. This view will be assessed shortly.

The *Oxford History* also insists on the 'wide variety of responses' of non-British people to the expansion of empire, from collaboration to various forms of resistance, both active and passive. Colonial Indian history, for example, 'cannot be reduced to a simple dialectic of domination and resistance'.[11] By the 1760s, the *Oxford History* maintains, there had developed 'a deep national commitment to Empire as an integral part of Britain's power and standing in the world and of British people's sense of who they were'.[12] By the nineteenth century, however, despite the loss of the United States, the empire was a constant source of celebration and self-regard for educated and informed people, but also anxiety; in contrast, most workers were actually 'indifferent to apathetic' in regard to empire.

HORRORS AND HEROES: THE IMPERIAL HISTORY WARS

Around the time that the *Oxford History* appeared, and since then with gathering force as the twenty-first century has lengthened, thinking about empire and slavery has snowballed, concentrating in four areas:

1. A return to whether Britain really has achieved a status as a ('self-congratulating') metaphysical empire or, as the new phrases have it, it can be seen as a 'virtual nation', or an 'oceanic entity', or even 'pseudo-empire' spread out across the world, and playing a vital role in the survival of democracy.[13]

2. The resurrection of interest in 'settler societies', what they had in common and how 'British' they were (for example, comparisons are made between Canada and New Zealand, or between Georgia in the southern US and New South Wales), in an attempt to explain their role in creating an 'Anglo-World'. In one study the role of settler societies in the creation of certain advances in anthropology is described;[14] and in another, James Belich, a New Zealander, argues that the nineteenth-century British diaspora of settlers was uniquely 'explosive', but with similarities in other respects to what happened in the colonial states of America and the white dominions, and that this is what, essentially, created the 'Anglo-World'.[15]

3. A tsunami of investigations into the shortcomings of empire, and especially the coercion and violence increasingly needed to maintain its dominance, including the role of historians themselves in avoiding, obfuscating or suppressing such details, and extending to museums, about whose collections 'lies abound'.[16] Many of these works have dwelled in great detail on the horrors of empire – the violence and corruption of the East India Company, the Benin massacres, the Mau Mau campaign in Kenya, the troubles in Cyprus – and have generally been written from the standpoint of contemporary times, with little attempt to get inside the skins and minds of the people of bygone ages: presentism, it is fair to say, has been present everywhere.

4. Finally, scholarship on trans-*Saharan* slavery.[17]

At its most extreme, several authors (Sathnam Sanghera, Caroline Elkins, Kehinde Andrews, Paddy Docherty) go so far as to say that empire must not be looked back on in any way as a 'balance sheet'; that what was good about empire can never mitigate the bad. The proof of this, Sanghera says plainly, lies in the fact that so many British have difficulty facing up to it. This is a bit like an imperial version of critical race theory, where no discussion is allowed: white people are prejudiced, racist, and always were – no argument is necessary or possible. The latest postmodern take on the subject is that 'presentism', looking at the past through the lens of the present, cannot be avoided: it is inevitable and should therefore be embraced. This too is like critical race theory, subscribing to the view that argument is impossible, that whites are incorrigible prisoners of their unconscious biases. The same goes for 'toleration', which, the postmodernists now argue, 'was perhaps fit for Europe after the Reformation but is wholly unsuited to a global and diverse world'. Kehinde Andrews, the UK's first professor of black studies, at Birmingham City University, argues that we are now living in a 'new age of empire', raging that 'racism and colonialism still rule the world' and adding that the scientific rationality of the Enlightenment laid the basis for scientific racism. Simon Gikandi, in *Slavery and the Culture of Taste*, seeks to show how slavery influenced the expression of high culture throughout Enlightenment Europe.[18]

Against that, some authors, like Nigel Biggar, emeritus Regius Professor of Moral and Pastoral Theology at Oxford, in his book *Colonialism: A Moral Reckoning*, have tried instead to calibrate as exactly as possible the opposite approach – that is, offering what he says is a balanced account of the extent to which the empire was 'driven by greed and the lust to dominate', how far it was based on the theft of land, and to what extent it may be accused of genocide. Others like Robert Tombs argue that 'one can blame everything on the Empire as long as one forgets everything else'. The empire, he insists, was a 'joint creation' of rulers and ruled, 'which gave it unusual legitimacy in the eyes of its subjects, millions of whom fought for it'.[19] 'The first age of globalisation, which Britain created, and like that of the twentieth century, had winners and losers, but to condemn it as wholly negative and exploitative is an ideological, not a historical judgement.' Tombs also questions whether coercion can have been so unremitting when the staff of the Colonial Office was only 300 and the Indian civil service 2,000 and that many countries applied to join the empire but were rebuffed. Many welcomed colonial rule, but these are inconvenient subjects for postmodern scholars.

Niall Ferguson goes further, arguing that the British Empire was a vehicle for globalisation and the dissemination of liberal institutions, the transmitter of capitalism and democracy, on balance good for colonised people and certainly better than alternative forms of imperial rule, and that though it could have been less bloody, on the whole the liberal empire worked. He concedes that the empire in India was nowhere near the success it was in Singapore, Canada, New Zealand and Australia, but adds that the colonised nations of the Soviet Empire have had much greater difficulty, since it ended, in adopting democratic and market-oriented institutions.

A quieter but fascinating set of observations is offered by Berny Sèbe, a historian of French extraction, brought up in the Sahara desert, but now professor of colonial and postcolonial studies at the University of Birmingham – another inhabitant of our floating world – who observes that in several African countries, former colonies, statues of colonial heroes have recently 'experienced a Phoenix-like rebirth', and that there has been throughout Africa a change in the narrative that these countries are reformulating about the birth of their independence. In places as diverse as Sudan, South Africa, Zambia and Congo, the roles and reputations of such figures as Cecil Rhodes and David Livingstone have undergone radical change, universities have been named after them and elsewhere the topography of these countries are unchanged: Lake Victoria is still Lake Victoria, Brazzaville is still Brazzaville, streets remain named after French presidents. Sèbe says there has been the development of 'neo-imperial' sites; this is partly because they are seen as tourist attractions for Western visitors, but also because of 'a more consensual approach to historical realities' in the former colonies and a willingness to see that there was in fact nothing less than a balance in imperial times, acknowledging 'the European men who gave African countries their modern shape as nation states', and that explorers in particular deserve to be remembered and honoured as 'founding fathers'.[20]

This lesser-known study was contained in a better-known and far more contentious article, Bruce Gilley's 'The Case for Colonialism'. This was published in the *Third World Quarterly* in 2017 and, though written in a conventional, even-handed academic manner, it provoked enormous controversy: thousands of academics demanded that it be retracted, that *TWQ* apologise and that the editor be dismissed. Fifteen of the journal's 34-member editorial board resigned in protest. The publishers explained that, despite accusations of poor – and even pseudo – scholarship, the article had been properly peer-reviewed. But then threats of violence against the editor caused the article to be withdrawn. It was reissued in *Academic Questions*, a journal which explores how ideology affects scholarship, in 2018. Gilley's argument, that there was and is a case for a new form of colonialism, that Western countries have successfully helped out non-Western ones (the Swiss helping Indonesia's customs service in the 1990s, the Australian police aiding the Solomon Islands, the British doing the same with Sierra Leone), is unlikely to find favour too widely, though the suggestion of Paul Romer, the World Bank's chief economist, that rich nations build 'charter cities' on vacant land in poor countries – the Hong Kong model – seems at least an imaginative way to move forward. Gilley also drew attention to the Nigerian writer Chinua Achebe (Chapters 29, 31 and 32) who, towards the end of his life, 'explicitly affirmed the positive contributions of colonialism to governance in his native Nigeria'.

The whole subject of imperial history is still riddled with contentious matter – notably, was slavery the source of Britain's wealth and the fuel of the industrial revolution? Profits from the slave trade undoubtedly made some individuals rich but accounted for between 1 per cent and 14 per cent of Britain's national income, according to which economists' calculations you accept. The industrial revolution's key element was in fact coal, of which Britain had plentiful supplies. But that is not the whole story.

There is another way of looking at 'balance' which is at least evidence-based. This finds expression in a long, mathematically technical paper by three American economists that can nevertheless be summed up simply in a few words of common sense.[21] Their paper looks at what several historians have noted, namely the 'reversal of fortune' of many countries which were colonised: that is to say countries which were among the richest nations in 1500 are now among the poorest, and vice versa. The answer, according to Daron Acemoglu and colleagues, is that the countries which were colonised could be divided, broadly, into two: thinly populated, non-urbanised poor nations, notably in what are now Canada, the United States, New Zealand and Australia, and the urbanised and prosperous established civilisations of Central America (the Aztecs, Incas and Mayans), the Ottoman Empire, India and China. In the former group, Europeans could settle in large numbers and develop institutions encouraging development.[22] In contrast with this, the large populations and relative prosperity of the second group made extractive institutions more profitable for the colonisers – despite their relatively advanced state, the huge technological and engineering gap which the Europeans had meant that the native population could be forced to work in mines or plantations.

A second factor that Acemoglu and his colleagues identify, and show in a series of graphs, is that the reversal did not take place until the end of the eighteenth century. In other words, the transformed prosperity of the formerly poor colonies did not arise from the 'plunder' of their resources by Europeans or because European diseases decimated productive capacity, but it occurred because of industrialisation, ideas imported from Britain. Therefore, it follows that Britain's industrialisation, whether or not it was helped by profits from the colonies, was actually the phenomenon that *brought* prosperity to large parts of empire (contrary to what Eric Williams, a future prime minister of Trinidad and Tobago, argued in his wartime *Capitalism and Slavery*). On these grounds, then, empire can be seen as broadly beneficial in what became the (white) settler dominions and the US, much less so in India, China and the Ottoman Empire. This obviously was crucial in the development of the Anglosphere.[23] The mature view now is that, contra Eric Williams, slave-run plantations remained profitable until the moment of abolition.[24]

All that said, the two sides in these 'imperial history wars' are unlikely to agree any time soon. But the second area of recent scholarship does add something fresh to our understanding. This is the investigation, rather late in the day, of trans-Saharan slavery, which now stands revealed as every bit as cruel and extensive – in sheer numbers – as the trans-Atlantic slaving voyages were.[25] Between 20 and 50 per cent of slaves are estimated to have died during the trans-Saharan passage, the bleached bones of those who died of thirst during the crossing being a common sight to other travellers.

There were great differences between trans-Saharan and trans-Atlantic slaves. The trans-Saharan slaves were predominantly women, traded for domestic work or as concubines, but there was also a significant number of eunuchs, whose fate was especially dire: *nine out of ten* eunuchs perished during surgery.

How far Britons of the eighteenth and nineteenth centuries would have been aware of these horrors is open to doubt, because scholarship is only just catching up with such archives as exist. But what it does show is that the British Empire was not worse than other polities in its shortcomings, that slavery was widespread and widely accepted, by Africans as much as by Europeans. An added criticism of contemporary academics is that they have concentrated almost exclusively on the post-1500 period of African history, intent on showing the extent of slavery for ideological reasons, but this means we are deficient in our understanding of what happened earlier, in particular how far back slavery existed on that continent, for how long it had been a fact of life, how coercive it was, so that we really cannot tell, even now, how important the 'colonial moment' was in African history. Put bluntly, as Richard Reid, professor of African history at Oxford, says, we have a hopelessly incomplete understanding of Africa's 'violent deeper past'.[26]

All this is important because, if we acknowledge, as Linda Colley points out, that even as late as 1730, the average British experience of slavery was of the *white* variety (Chapter 5), then the extent of what we might call the extreme 'culpability' of Britain in the slave trade, to accept the presentist point of view for a moment, was between that date, 1730, and 1787, when the first anti-slavery movement was organised – two or maybe three generations of Britons, though there were plenty of people throughout those years (Samuel Johnson, Edmund Burke, Granville Sharp, William Wilberforce, Hannah More) who were loudly opposed to the slave trade. That sounds a long time to us, today, but the science of anthropology was only begun in the early years of the eighteenth century (in France), so the change of thinking in Enlightenment Britain was, in the circumstances, remarkably swift. Two, at most three, generations.

And here is more context. The European empires of Holland, France, Spain, Portugal and Britain were different from other empires such as the Ottoman, the Chinese and the Russian, in that the latter were land-based. A land-based empire, where one power invades another contiguous to it, means by definition that those powers are much nearer to one another in developmental terms, in technology, in sociological organisation, in arms and weapons, in agricultural practices and so on. In a maritime empire, in contrast, the invaded country is much more likely (though not inevitably) to be at a very different stage of political, technological and social development, as is all too clear from the history of all the maritime empires of the European powers.

In such circumstances, early contacts are – or were – by no means necessarily hostile. One reason – and not enough has been made of this – is that for a while at the beginning of the 'sugar revolution', white indentured servants and political prisoners worked under the whip side by side with African slaves and, on occasion, were treated worse.[27] The biggest difference, so far as the British Empire was concerned, was that the indigenous peoples of the Americas, south Asia and Africa were not Christian. We hear time and time again about the role of Providence in the spread of the empire, a set of beliefs with which *we* are unsympathetic, but which was a commonplace until the very end of the nineteenth century. This combination of Providentialism and the lack of a modern anthropological perspective needs to be absorbed if we are to enter the minds of people of ages long gone. For example, it was only as recently as 1983 that Clifford Geertz, at Princeton, coined the phrases 'local knowledge' and 'thick description', processes devised to understand the signs and symbols of other cultures *on their own terms*. Given this very recent development, is it really so surprising, or so terrible, that, almost exactly 200 years before, David Hume should say, 'In rude, unpolished nations, neither learning nor trade could have developed in such conditions'? He was up to date in his reading and thinking, being familiar with the then-prevalent Scottish Enlightenment 'stadial' view that societies evolved through four stages – hunting, shepherding, agriculture, commerce. He also observed, rightly, that polytheistic religions are more tolerant than monotheistic ones. He was an intelligent and creative observer, not a bigot. John Locke, John Donne and John Milton were all regarded as jewels of British civilisation in their day and since, but all, in one way or another, would now be termed racist for their involvement in this or that aspect of empire. But of course they were among the most well-educated and informed individuals in their time, among the most understanding, and were they alive now, they would no doubt be among the most unprejudiced. Merchant William Smith's black assistant, who understood and could handle his master's navigational instruments (Chapter 5), had nothing but contempt for the Africans he encountered on his voyages because they could not cope as he could. Technological disparity was what counted, not race.

An added factor, which many contemporary historians appear blind to, is that people – if not historians – are often more than one thing. Isaac Newton, we know, was a hard-headed mathematician/physicist on the one hand, and a near-mystic on the other, who thought that Solomon's temple was 'the best guide to the topography of heaven'. Nearer to our theme is the case of Sir John Hawkins, one of Queen Elizabeth I's swashbuckling slave traders but also one of the team who designed the British fleet to withstand the Armada. Which of these achievements can we say is the more important in historical terms? Similarly, Edward Colston, whose statue was thrown into Bristol harbour in 2020 by aficionados of the Black Lives Matter movement, was, besides being a slave trader, a very observant Christian and a considerable philanthropist, founding a hospital, several schools and churches, workhouses and almshouses, and sponsoring a series of lectures. He spent his income from slavery on others rather than himself. Again, there were two Edward Colstons – which one should take precedence? Should either?

The white diaspora in the British settler dominions – Canada, Australia and New Zealand – though developed in each case at the expense of indigenous peoples, have proved to be successful, prosperous and stable polities. Had these territories not been invaded by the British, they would surely have been invaded by other European powers, but had they – by some miracle – not been 'discovered' at all, how would they have developed, alongside what was happening elsewhere? It hardly makes sense even to pose the question; by remaining as thinly populated territories, practising hunter-gathering or primitive agriculture, they could not have avoided being discovered and conquered sooner or later, for better or worse. As John Darwin has said, repeatedly, empire is the default mode in history: the British Empire was the largest, longest lasting and among the best documented, documentation which reveals its achievements and failings. Often those achievements and failings are one and the same because coercion lies at the heart of any empire but is likely to be effective over a longer term in maritime empires than in land-based empires, simply because of the considerable technological disparity that brought the maritime power to the shores of the invaded peoples. Add in the mix a desire for trade, and Christian Providentialism, and you have the (what were then entirely normal) ingredients for trouble, sooner or later, though it should by now be clear that imperial bureaucrats at the metropolitan centre were considerably less 'racist' than settlers in the distant colonies. That said, Cambridge professor Antony Hopkins, in a paper on imperialism, points out that imperial power came to realise that the needs of taxation, trade, strategy and civil order were frequently consistent with, 'indeed frequently required, the toleration and even the reinforcement of different ethnicities, religions and customs'. In other words, coercive power was needed but used much less than commonly thought. At the same time, he says, 'genuine advances across a wide range of issues, from medicine to engineering, were stimulated by the possession of empire, and ... in turn scientific knowledge was used to demonstrate Britain's superiority to others, while confirming it to ourselves'. These paradoxical truths surface everywhere.[28]

Arguably the most sensible summing up of Britain's colonial past comes in Sathnam Sanghera's *Empireworld*, published in 2024, in which he dismisses the idea of trying to achieve an overall 'moral reckoning' of empire, along the lines that Nigel Biggar and Niall Ferguson attempted, and instead encourages Britons 'to do some work' and face up to the terrible crimes of violence and coercion in the past, while at the same time acknowledging that good things came out of empire as well. His point is that no 'balanced' view can be achieved, the very idea is inappropriate. Massacres undoubtedly occurred, borders were drawn in unnatural straight lines on maps for convenience's sake, ignoring natural features that reflected traditional tribal contours, and the slave trade disrupted interethnic solidarity in Africa, which made interethnic patriotism more difficult to achieve.

Sanghera notes that in many areas the British were great builders (canals, railways, sewer and electrical systems, hospitals, telephones, paved roads) but at the same time were great demolishers, imposing a great social cost by destroying densely populated areas.

> The British empire both spread malaria and other diseases to millions and helped millions survive them. The British empire was an incubator and propagator of white supremacy, as well as a forum in which humanitarians founded campaigns that liberated people from crude ethnic classification . . . It brought communities together by giving them the common ground of the English language and alienated people from their own culture and traditions by insisting on the use of English . . . It resisted dissent with brutal violence and was also innately auto-critical.

He thinks that India's 2020 move to allow practitioners of *ayurveda*, the traditional Indian system of medicine, to perform surgery, was 'dismaying'. He thinks that the racist voting patterns in Mauritian elections perpetuate racism there. He notes that there are more English-literate people in Nigeria than in Britain itself, and that English literature has had a longer academic history in India than in Britain. But his overall conclusion, well into the book, is that

> whatever you say about the British empire, the opposite is almost always true to a certain degree . . . enough time has passed since colonialism to make it at least debatable about who exactly is responsible for, say, the violence in Nigeria, or the bribery in Nigeria, or the kidnapping in Nigeria . . . The past is a world where 'Liberals' were not liberal, where the 'Enlightened' were not enlightened, where abolitionists could be deeply racist, where people in favour of slavery could be kind to individual black people.

He does acknowledge one of the points being made here, that empire was an accelerant in history, but even here of course the effects were both good and the opposite. Sanghera, of Indian heritage, who grew up in Wolverhampton, in the British Midlands, has used the nuances of empire he acquired in his research to manage a dissatisfaction that might have been more acrimonious.[29] A good example of the way forward.

Science was one of the biggest differences between British travellers and the indigenous inhabitants of its empire, though as we have seen 'epistemic pluralism' has been stressed in recent scholarship, especially in regard to 'hybrid' Indian and African medicine, while there has for a time been a postmodern movement afoot to 'decentre' science from its European origins. Science, certainly, was one of the great beneficiaries of empire, as we have also seen: many sciences – botany, zoology, meteorology, cartography, medicine itself, astronomy, anthropology, marine studies and much more – could not have developed so well or so fully without the achievements and adventure of empire; indeed the inherently expansive nature of science was one of the factors that drove Britain to its 'blue-water destiny'.

So here, then, to end with, is a conundrum that highlights the impossibility of reconciling the 'imperial history wars'; it concerns perhaps the greatest scientific achievement of that blue-water destiny, and returns us to the idea with which we began this conclusion: evolution, or rather evolution by natural selection, as identified by Charles Darwin.

Darwin conceived his great idea as a result, very largely, of his voyage on the *Beagle*. The voyage took in Brazil and eventually Ecuador, in particular the Galápagos Islands, and he sailed home via Tahiti and New Zealand, and Brazil for a second time. It was his observations of ostriches in Brazil and finches in the Galápagos Islands that first provoked his ideas about populations which would lead to his grasp of natural selection. Darwin loathed the slavery he witnessed in Brazil but enjoyed his stopover in Tahiti, yet the point to make here is that without empire, without his travels, he would never have had his all-important ideas. Would the idea have occurred to anyone else? Not necessarily. Alfred Russel Wallace, a friend and colleague, came close but again that was after he had visited the Malay archipelago, also the title of one of his books, so here too empire played a crucial role.

And of course, evolution has been one of the two seminal scientific ideas that created modern life (the other being the conservation of energy, Chapter 19). Combined with the discovery of the gene by Gregor Mendel, Darwin's ideas have led directly to the science of genetics, without question the most profound level of understanding of ourselves, through the related discoveries of DNA, genetic fingerprinting, genetic engineering, the Human Genome Project, and even to the discovery and identification of the vaccines that helped the world recover from the Covid-19 pandemic of 2019–22. The understanding of molecular evolution and quantum biology is on the verge of transforming the treatment of that other great scourge, cancer, raising the possibility of a vaccine for the disease, unthinkable in the twentieth century.

We can't know if evolution and genetics would have emerged without Darwin, but we do know that his voyage on the *Beagle* was instrumental in the breakthrough, though he could not have anticipated the way his insights have themselves evolved. This is the way the world works, via accident and the prepared imagination. The empire's influence on the imagination of men and women was profound. The empire had many regrettable dimensions, not least the misuse of so-called Darwinian concepts in the late nineteenth and early twentieth centuries, but overall the intellectual mixture of empire and knowledge – from linguistics and philosophy, to biology and ecology, from the English language and sports, to astronomy and map-making – has added immeasurably to our stock of ideas and practices.

Zadie Smith said in one of her essays, 'One of the intellectual and moral responsibilities of being an adult, as I see it, is to be able to hold more than one reality in your head at the same time.' In thinking about Britain's empire – now long gone – and the knowledge revolution it unleashed, her adult sentiment strikes home.

ACKNOWLEDGEMENTS

In researching and writing this book, I have incurred a number of debts, and it is a pleasure to acknowledge them here. I thank the following for their input, insight, foresight and encouragement, for correcting errors and making suggestions for improvement: John Albery, Jim Al-Khalili, Ash Amin, Hugh Baker, Anne Baring, Peter J. Bowler, Michael Brent, Neil Brodie, Peter Burke, Christopher Chippindale, John Cornwell, Paul Davies, Frank Dikötter, Robin Duthy, Alex Eccles, Niles Eldridge, Alan Esterson, Amitai Etzioni, Charles Freeman, Robert Gildea, David Gill, Ian Graham, John Gribbin, Norman Hammond, P. M. Harman, David Henn, Peter Higgs, Ian Inkster, Derek Johns, John Keay, Robert Knox, Richard Leakey, Gwendolyn Leick, Gerard LeRoux, Johnjoe McFadden, Paul Mellars, Ben Murphy, Andrew Nurnberg, Joan Oates, Norman Palmer, Nicholas Postgate, Colin Renfrew, James Roundell, John Russell, James Sackett, Chris Scarre, Amartya Sen, B. F. Skinner, Roger Smith, Ian Stewart, Sam Stocker, Assallah Tahir, Kathy Tubb, Jonathan Wadman, Bernard Wasserstein, Keith Whitelam, Keith Whitelaw and Patricia Williams. Such errors, omissions or solecisms as remain are the author's responsibility alone.

Note: Materials incorporated from the author's previous books are specified below.

NOTES

Prologue: Smalltime Latecomer: Self-Inflicted Wounds; 'Despiser of Learning'

1 Alfred Crosby, *The Measure of Reality: Quantification and Western Society, 1250–1600*, Cambridge: Cambridge University Press, 1997, p. 3.

2 Bernard Lewis, *The Muslim Discovery of Europe*, London: Weidenfeld & Nicolson, 1982, p. 82.

3 Janet L. Abu-Lughod, *Before European Hegemony: The World System, AD 1250–1350*, New York: Oxford University Press, 1989, p. 316; Philip K. Hitti, *Islam: A Way of Life*, Minneapolis: University of Minnesota Press, 1970, p. 134.

4 Crosby, op. cit., p. 82.

5 Trevor Ross, 'Dissolution and the Making of the English Literary Canon: The Catalogues of Leland and Bale', *Renaissance and Reformation*, 1991, new series, vol. 15, no. 1, pp. 57–80.

Chapter 1: 'A More Intense Englishness'

1 Linda Shenk, *Learned Queen: The Image of Elizabeth I in Politics and Poetry*, Basingstoke: Palgrave Macmillan, 2010, p. 1.

2 Richard Helgerson, *Forms of Nationhood: The Elizabethan Writing of England*, Chicago: University of Chicago Press, 1992.

3 Ryan J. Stark, 'Protestant Theology and Apocalyptic Rhetoric in Ascham's *The Schoolmaster*', *Journal of the History of Ideas*, 2008, vol. 69, no. 4, pp. 517–32.

4 Alvin Vos, 'The Formation of Roger Ascham's Prose Style', *Studies in Philology*, 1974, vol. 71, no. 3, pp. 344–70.

5 J. W. Binns, *Intellectual Culture in Elizabethan and Jacobean England: The Latin Writings of the Age*, Leeds: Francis Cairns, 1990.

6 Lawrence Stone, 'The Educational Revolution in England, 1560–1640', *Past & Present*, 1964, no. 28, pp. 41–80.

7 Susan Doran and Norman Jones (eds), *The Elizabethan World*,

Abingdon: Routledge, 2011; E. E. Rich, 'The Population of Elizabethan England', *Economic History Review*, 1950, vol. 2, no. 3, pp. 247–65.

8 Daniel Javich, 'Poetry and Court Culture: Puttenham's Arte of English Poesie in the Light of Castiglione's Cortegiano', *MLN*, 1972, vol. 87, no. 7, pp. 865–88.

9 Doran and Jones (eds), op. cit., p. 881.

10 See Germaine Warkentin, review of *The Elizabethan Courtier Poets* by Stephen W. May, *Renaissance Quarterly*, 1993, vol. 46, no. 3, pp. 614–17.

11 See Stephen J. Greenblatt, review of *The Cult of Elizabeth* by Roy Strong, *Renaissance Quarterly*, 1978, vol. 31, no. 4, pp. 642–4.

12 Christina J. Faraday discusses the art of limning and its links to other forms of image in the work of John White in the New World, in 'Lively Limning: Presence in Portrait Miniatures and John White's Images of the New World', *British Art Studies*, 2020, no. 17, https://doi.org/10.17658/issn.2058-5462/issue-17/cfaraday

13 Constance Jordan, review of *Spencer's 'Faerie Queene' and the Cult of Elizabeth* by Robin Headlam Wells, *Renaissance Quarterly*, 1985, vol. 38, no. 3, pp. 564–6.

14 David Bregerson, review of *Entertainments for Elizabeth* by Jean Wilson, *Yearbook of English Studies*, 1983, vol. 13, pp. 304–5.

15 Greenblatt, op. cit., p. 642.

16 Jessica Winston, *Lawyers at Play: Literature, Law, and Politics at the Early Modern Inns of Court, 1558–81*, Oxford: Oxford University Press, 2016, p. 24.

17 Ibid., p. 26.

18 Ibid., p. 27.

19 Ibid., p. 33.

20 J. W. Tubbs, 'Custom, Time and Reason: Early Seventeenth-Century Conceptions of the Common Law', *History of Political Thought*, 1998, vol. 19, no. 3, pp. 363–406.

21 Winston, op. cit., p. 39.

22 W. R. Streitberger, *The Masters of the Revels and Elizabeth I's Court Theatre*, Oxford: Oxford University Press, 2016.

23 Winston, op. cit., p. 42.

24 R. J. Schoeck, review of *The Historical Revolution* by F. Smith Fussner, *Renaissance News*, 1963, vol. 16, no. 3, pp. 224–6.

25 Ibid.

26 Winston, op. cit., p. 42.

27 Francis Ames-Lewis, 'Introduction', in Francis Ames-Lewis (ed.), *Sir Thomas Gresham and Gresham College: Studies in the Intellectual History of London in the Sixteenth and Seventeenth Centuries*, Aldershot: Ashgate, 1999, p. xix.

28 Francis Johnson, 'Gresham College: Precursor of the Royal Society', *Journal of the History of Ideas*, 1940, vol. 1, no. 4, pp. 413–38.

29 Ames-Lewis, op. cit., p. xvii.

30 Ibid., p. 150.
31 William J. Thomas (ed.), *Anecdotes and Traditions, Illustrative of Early English History and Literature*, London: J. B. Nichols and Son, 1839, p. 125.
32 Helgerson, op. cit., p. 196.
33 Ibid., p. 199.
34 Ibid., p. 200.
35 Carla Mazzio, 'Shakespeare and Science, c. 1600', *South Central Review*, 2009, vol. 26, no. 1–2, pp. 1–23.
36 Helgerson, op. cit., p. 122.
37 Ibid., p. 212.
38 Ibid, pp. 236–40.
39 Ibid., p. 245.

Chapter 2: The Increasing Coherence of England

1 William Rockett, 'Topography and British History in Camden's *Britannia*', *Renaissance and Reformation*, 1991, new series, vol. 14, no. 1, p. 71.
2 Ibid., p. 72.
3 Ibid., p. 71.
4 Fritz Levy, 'William Camden as Teacher, Herald, and Scholar', *Huntington Library Quarterly*, 2009, vol. 72, no. 3, pp. 425–30.
5 Ibid., p. 426.
6 Rockett, op. cit., pp. 71–80.
7 Ibid., p. 74.
8 Ibid., p. 75.
9 Ibid., p. 77.
10 Ibid., p. 78; W. H. Herendeen, 'William Camden: Historian, Herald, and Antiquary', *Studies in Philology*, 1988, vol. 85, no. 2, pp. 192–210.
11 Herendeen, op. cit., p. 208.
12 Richard Helgerson, *Forms of Nationhood: The Elizabethan Writing of England*, Chicago: University of Chicago Press, 1992, p. 118.
13 Ibid., p. 130.
14 Ibid., p. 132.
15 Ibid., p. 135.
16 Ibid., p. 141.
17 Daniel Coquillete, *The Anglo-American Legal Heritage*: Durham: North Carolina Academic Press, 1999.

Chapter 3: London's Literacies Lead
England's 'Gathering Greatness'

1 Deborah E. Harkness, *The Jewel House: Elizabethan London and the Scientific Revolution*, New Haven, CT: Yale University Press, 2007.
2 Ibid., p. 8.
3 Ibid., p. 9.

4   Ibid.
5   Ibid., p. 12.
6   Ibid., pp. 38–41.
7   Ibid., p. 51.
8   Ibid., p. 65.
9   Ibid., p. 59.
10 Ibid., p. 95.
11 Ibid., p. 137.
12 Ibid., pp. 98–102.
13 Ibid., p. 108.
14 Ibid., p. 112.
15 Ibid., pp. 124–5.
16 Susan Rose, 'Mathematics and the Art of Navigation: The Advance of Scientific Seamanship in Elizabethan England', *Transactions of the Royal Historical Society*, 2004, vol. 14, pp. 175–84.
17 Harkness, op. cit., p. 242.
18 J. W. Binns, *Intellectual Culture in Elizabethan and Jacobean England: The Latin Writings of the Age*, Leeds: Frances Cairns, 1990.
19 D. M. Palliser, untitled article, *English Historical Review*, 1994, vol. 109, no. 431, pp. 435–6.
20 Ibid., p. 435.

Chapter 4: Bacon to Milton: Science, Equal Qualities and the Causes of Quarrel

1   Sarah Irving, *Natural Science and the Origin of the British Empire*, London: Pickering & Chatto, 2008.
2   Mark Rankin, 'Henry VIII, Shakespeare and the Jacobean Royal Court', *Studies in English Literature, 1500–1900*, 2011, vol. 51, no. 2, pp. 349–66.
3   Ibid., p. 358.
4   Ibid., p. 359.
5   Ibid., p. 362.
6   Patrick J. Murray, 'Shakespeare and His Contemporaries?', *Theatre Journal*, 2014, vol. 66, no. 1, pp. 151–9.
7   Ibid., p. 152.
8   Ibid., p. 153.
9   Ibid., p. 154.
10 Ibid., p. 155.
11 Patrick Cheney, review of *Shakespeare and the Poets' War* by James P. Bednarz, *Shakespeare Quarterly*, 2003, vol. 54, no. 1, pp. 98–103.
12 Ibid., p. 102.
13 Rankin, op. cit., p. 359.
14 Cheney, op. cit., p. 102.
15 Ibid., p. 103. See also Nancy Hickerson, review of *Shakespeare and Elizabethan Culture* by Philip K. Bock, *American Anthropologist*, 1986, vol. 88, no. 2, p. 512.

16 Fredson Thayer Bowers, 'Ben Jonson the Actor', *Studies in Philology*, 1937, vol. 34, no. 3, pp. 392–406.

17 Jane Rickard, *Authorship and Authority: The Writings of James VI and I*, Manchester: Manchester University Press, 2007.

18 James Loxley et al. (eds), *Ben Jonson's Walk to Scotland: An Annotated Edition of the 'Foot Voyage'*, Cambridge: Cambridge University Press, 2015.

19 A. J. Smith, *John Donne: The Critical Heritage*, London: Routledge & Kegan Paul, 1975.

20 Irving Lowe, 'John Donne: The Middle Way – The Reason–Faith Equation in Donne's Sermons', *Journal of the History of Ideas*, 1961, vol. 22, no. 3, p. 389.

21 Katherine Rundell, *Super-Infinite: The Transformations of John Donne*, London: Faber & Faber, 2022.

22 See for example Ben Saunders, *Desiring Donne: Poetry, Sexuality, Interpretation*, Cambridge, MA, and London: Harvard University Press, 2006, especially Part I.

23 Quentin Skinner, 'Thomas Hobbes and the Nature of the Early Royal Society', *Historical Journal*, 1969, vol. 12, no. 2, pp. 217–39.

24 Mark H. Curtis, 'The Alienated Intellectuals of Early Stuart England', *Past & Present*, 1962, no. 23, pp. 25–43.

25 John Bowle, *Hobbes and His Critics*, London: Jonathan Cape, 1951, p. 321.

26 The classic account is in William Locy, *The Story of Biology*, Garden City, NY: Garden City, 1925, pp. 180–96.

27 Catherine Gimelli Martin, '"What If the Sun Be the Centre of the World?": Milton's Epistemology, Cosmology, and Paradise of Fools Reconsidered', *Modern Philology*, 2001, vol. 99, no. 2, pp. 231–65.

28 J. Martin Evans, *Milton's Imperial Epic: Paradise Lost and the Discourse of Colonialism*, Ithaca, NY: Cornell University Press, 1996, esp. chapters 4–6.

29 Of the many accounts, see Margaret Kean (ed.), *John Milton's Paradise Lost: A Sourcebook*, Abingdon: Routledge, 2005.

30 See Richard Greaves, *Glimpses of Glory: John Bunyan and English Dissent*, Stanford, CA: Stanford University Press, 2002, where he considers the clinical evidence for depression in Bunyan.

Chapter 5: Early Thinking about 'Impire', Race and Slavery

1 Claire Jowitt, *The Culture of Piracy, 1580–1630: English Literature and Seaborne Crime*, Farnham: Ashgate, 2010, p. 82.

2 Barbara Fuchs, 'Faithless Empires: Pirates, Renegadoes and the English Nation', *ELH*, 2000, vol. 67, no. 1, pp. 45–69.

3 Susan Ronald, *Heretic Queen: Queen Elizabeth I and the Wars of Religion*, London: St Martin's Press, 2012.

4 David Armitage, 'The Elizabethan Idea of Empire', *Transactions of the Royal Historical Society*, 2004, series 6, vol. 14, pp. 269–77.

5 Ibid.

6 Emily C. Bartels, 'Imperialist Beginnings: Richard Hakluyt and the Construction of Africa', *Criticism*, 1992, vol. 34, no. 4, pp. 517–38.

7 Peter Mancall, *Hakluyt's Promise: An Elizabethan's Obsession for an English America*, New Haven, CT, and London: Yale University Press, 2007, p. 3.

8 Ibid., p. 72. For the map of the southern continent, see K. R. Andrews, 'The Aims of Drake's Expedition of 1577–1580', *American Historical Review*, 1968, vol. 73, no. 3, pp. 724–41.

9 Mancall, op. cit., p. 85.

10 Nicholas Canny (ed.), *The Oxford History of the British Empire, vol. 1: The Origins of Empire*, Oxford: Oxford University Press, 1998, p. 25.

11 Ibid., p. 8.

12 Alexandra Walsham, *Providence in Early Modern England*, Oxford: Oxford University Press, 1999.

13 Canny (ed.), op. cit., p. 52.

14 Alfred A. Cave, 'Canaanites in a Promised Land: The American Indian and the Providential Theory of Empire', *American Indian Quarterly*, 1988, vol. 12, no. 4, pp. 277–97; Ken Macmillan, 'Benign and Benevolent Conquest? The Ideology of Elizabethan Atlantic Expansion Revisited', *Early American Studies*, 2011, vol. 9, no. 1, pp. 32–72; Tzvetan Todorov, *The Conquest of America: The Question of the Other*, New York: Harper & Row, 1984.

15 Canny (ed.), op. cit., p. 43. See also Barbara Arneil, *John Locke and America: The Defence of English Colonialism*, Oxford: Clarendon Press, 1996.

16 Canny (ed.), op. cit., p. 44.

17 Ibid., p. 46.

18 Ibid., p. 47.

19 Ibid., p. 109; see also Macmillan, op. cit.

20 Sebastien Sobecki, 'New World Discovery', *Oxford Handbook Topics in Literature*, online ed., Oxford Academic, 16 December 2013, https://doi.org/10.1093/oxfordhb/9780199935338.013.141

21 Ibid., pp. 1–2.

22 Ibid., p. 3.

23 Andrews, op. cit, p. 736.

24 Helen Hackett, *The Elizabethan Mind: Searching for Self in an Age of Uncertainty*, New Haven, CT: Yale University Press, 2022, p. 145.

25 Ibid., p.145. See also Paul Stock, 'The Idea of Asia in British Geographical Thought, 1652–1982', *Transactions of the Royal Historical Society*, 2023, series 7, vol. 1, pp. 121–44: using an analysis of textbooks, Asia was seen as degenerate and corrupt, usually due to climatic decay.

26 These matters are considered in detail in Mark S. Dawson, *Bodies Complexioned: Human Variation and Racism in Early Modern English Culture, c.1600–1715*, Manchester: Manchester University Press, 2019.

27 Hackett, op. cit., p. 156.
28 Canny (ed.), op. cit., p. 156.
29 Katherine George, 'The Civilized West Looks at Primitive Africa, 1400–1800: a Study in Ethnocentrism', *Isis*, 1958, vol. 49, no. 1, pp. 62–72. See also Anna Neill, 'Buccaneer Ethnography: Nature, Culture, and Nation in the Journals of William Dampier', *Eighteenth-Century Studies*, 2000, vol. 33, no. 2, pp. 165–80, for how pirates and buccaneers affected views about race and race contact – in other words, non-elite views.
30 Canny (ed.), op. cit., p. 160.
31 Ibid., p. 161.
32 Hackett, op. cit., p. 164.
33 Ibid., p. 165.
34 Ibid., p. 167.
35 Ibid., p. 171.
36 Michael Adas, *Machines as the Measure of Men: Science, Technology, and Ideologies of Western Dominance*, Ithaca, NY: Cornell University Press, 1989, p. 2.
37 Ibid., p. 6.
38 Ibid., p. 7.
39 Ibid., p. 9.
40 Ibid., p. 24.
41 Ibid., pp. 38–9.
42 Ibid., p. 48.
43 Ibid., p. 54.
44 Ibid., p. 60.
45 Linda Colley, *Captives: Britain, Empire and the World, 1600–1850*, London: Jonathan Cape, 2002, p. 45. See also Don Jordan and Michael Walsh, *White Cargo: The Forgotten History of Britain's White Slaves in America*, Edinburgh: Mainstream, 2007.
46 Colley, op. cit., p. 52.
47 Ibid., p. 57.
48 Ibid., p. 63.
49 Ibid., p. 64.
50 Joseph C. Miller (ed.), *The Princeton Companion to Atlantic History*, Princeton, NJ: Princeton University Press, 2015 (a central reference), p. 426; see also Joseph Inikori, review of *Extending the Boundaries: Essays on the New Transatlantic Slave Trade Database* by David Eltis and David Richardson (eds), *Journal of Economic History*, 2011, vol. 71, no. 1, pp. 249–51; David Eltis et al. (eds), *Counting Slaves: The Trans-Atlantic Slave Trade – A Database on CD-ROM*, Cambridge: Cambridge University Press, 1999.
51 Miller (ed.), op. cit., pp. 426.
52 Ibid., p. 429.
53 Ibid., p. 430.

Chapter 6: Blue-Water Destiny

1   Christopher Hill, *Intellectual Origins of the English Revolution*, Oxford: Clarendon Press, 1965, p. 23.
2   Christopher Hill, *Reformation to Industrial Revolution: British Economy and Society, 1530-1780*, New York: Pantheon, 1968.
3   Hill, *Intellectual Origins*, p. 47.
4   Ibid., p. 58.
5   Charles Webster, *The Great Instauration: Science, Medicine and Reform, 1626–1660*, London: Duckworth, 1975, p. 18.
6   Hill, *Intellectual Origins*, p. 61.
7   Ibid., p. 65.
8   Webster, op. cit., p. 21.
9   Hill, *Intellectual Origins*, p. 79.
10 Ibid., p. 89.
11 Ibid., p. 93.
12 Ibid.
13 Ibid., p. 94.
14 Webster, op. cit., p. 111.
15 Hill, *Intellectual Origins*, p. 108.
16 Webster, op. cit., p. 70.
17 Ibid., p. 223.
18 Ibid., p. 294.
19 Ibid., p. 320.
20 Hill, *Intellectual Origins*, p. 111.
21 Ibid., p. 113.
22 Ibid.
23 Ibid., p. 114; Webster, op. cit., p. 499.
24 Webster, op. cit., p. 337.
25 Hill, *Intellectual Origins*, p. 115.
26 Richard F. Jones, 'Science and English Prose Style in the Third Quarter of the Seventeenth Century', *Proceedings of the Modern Languages Association*, 1930, vol. 45, no. 4, pp. 977–1009.
27 Hill, *Intellectual Origins*, p. 125.
28 Ibid., p. 131.
29 Ibid., p. 139.
30 Ibid., p. 140.
31 Ibid., p. 143.
32 Webster, op. cit., p. 172.
33 Hill, *Intellectual Origins*, p. 250.
34 Ibid., p. 228.
35 Ibid., p. 263.
36 Alexandre Koyré, *From the Closed World to the Infinite Universe*, Baltimore: Johns Hopkins University Press, 1968, p. 2.
37 Hill, *Intellectual Origins*, p. 62.
38 Webster, op. cit. p. 105.
39 Gerard Delanty, 'The Cosmopolitan Imagination: Critical Cosmopolitanism

and Social Theory', *British Journal of Sociology*, 2006, vol. 51, no. 1, pp. 25–47.

Chapter 7: Newton, Locke, Willis:
From Soul to Mind to Brain

1 J. D. Bernal, *Science in History, Vol. 2*, Cambridge, MA: MIT Press, 1971, p. 621.

2 J. D. Bernal, *The Extension of Man: A History of Physics Before 1900*, London: Weidenfeld & Nicolson, 1971, p. 212.

3 Shmuel Sambursky (ed.), *Physical Thought from the Presocratics to the Quantum Physicists: An Anthology*, London: Hutchinson, 1974, p. 312.

4 See Stevin Shapin, review of *Francis Bacon, the State and the Reform of Natural Philosophy* by Julian Martin, *British Journal for the History of Science*, 1993, vol. 26, no. 1, pp. 84–5; Peter Burke, *A Social History of Knowledge: From Gutenberg to Diderot*, Cambridge: Polity Press, 2000.

5 John Bowle, *Hobbes and His Critics*, London: Jonathan Cape, 1951, p. 361.

6 Daniel Boorstin, *The Creators*, New York: Random House, 1992, p. 180.

7 Bowle, op. cit., p. 364.

8 Boorstin, op. cit., p. 186; he says the works are 'laboured' and it is surprising they have been so influential.

9 Jacob Bronowski and Bruce Mazlish, *The Western Intellectual Tradition: From Leonardo to Hegel*, London: Hutchinson, 1960, p. 210.

10 Richard Popkin, *The Third Force in Seventeenth-Century Thought*, Leiden: Brill, 1992, pp. 102–3.

11 John Redwood, *Reason, Ridicule and Religion, 1660–1750*, London: Thames & Hudson, 1976, p. 150.

12 Richard H. Popkin, *The History of Scepticism from Erasmus to Spinoza*, Berkeley: University of California Press, 1979, pp. 215–16; Redwood, op. cit., p. 34.

13 Jonathan I. Israel, *Radical Enlightenment: Philosophy and the Making of Modernity, 1650–1750*, Oxford: Oxford: Oxford University Press, 2001, p. 81.

14 Carl Zimmer, *Soul Made Flesh: The Discovery of the Brain and How it Changed the World*, London: Heinemann, 2004, p. 19.

15 William Locy, *The Story of Biology*, Garden City, NY: Garden City, 1925, p. 155.

16 Charles Singer, *A History of Biology*, London and New York: Abelard-Schuman, 1959, pp. 82ff.

17 Locy, op. cit., p. 160.

Chapter 8: A New Home for Imagination

1 Barbara J. Shapiro, *Probability and Certainty in Seventeenth-Century England: A Study of the Relationships between Natural Science,*

Religion, History, Law, and Literature, Princeton, NJ: Princeton University Press, 1983.

2   Ibid., p. 173.
3   Ibid., p. 174.
4   Ibid., p. 143.
5   Ibid., p. 3.
6   Ibid., p. 236.
7   Ibid., p. 248.
8   Ibid.
9   Ibid., pp. 257–61.
10 Tita Chico, *The Experimental Imagination: Literary Knowledge and Science in the British Enlightenment*, Stanford, CA: Stanford University Press, 2018.
11 Shapiro, op. cit., p. 258.
12 Ibid., p. 259.
13 T. C. W. Blanning, *The Culture of Power and the Power of Culture: Old Regime Europe, 1660–1789*, Oxford: Oxford University Press, 2002, passim.
14 John Brewer, *The Pleasures of the Imagination: English Culture in the Eighteenth Century*, London: HarperCollins, 1997.
15 Jonathan Israel, *A Revolution of the Mind: Radical Enlightenment and the Intellectual Origins of Modern Democracy*, Princeton, NJ: Princeton University Press, 2010. See also Jonathan I. Israel, *Radical Enlightenment: Philosophy and the Making of Modernity, 1650–1750*, Oxford: Oxford University Press, 2001, chapter 7.
16 Blanning, op cit.
17 Arnold Hauser, *The Social History of Art, Vol. 1*, London: Routledge & Kegan Paul, 1951.
18 Blanning, op. cit.
19 Robin Valenza, *Literature, Language and the Rise of the Intellectual Disciplines in Britain, 1680–1820*, Cambridge: Cambridge University Press, 2009.
20 Ibid., p. 12.
21 Ibid., p. 26.
22 Shapiro, op. cit., p. 262.
23 Ian Watt, *The Rise of the Novel*, London: Chatto & Windus, 1957, p. 263.
24 Ilse Vickers, *Defoe and the New Sciences*, Cambridge: Cambridge University Press, 1996, pp. 4, 5.
25 Ibid., p. 38.
26 Ibid., p. 56.
27 Ibid., p. 59.
28 Ibid., p. 64.
29 Robert J. Allen, *The Clubs of Augustan London*, Cambridge, MA: Harvard University Press, 1933, pp. 158–9.
30 Ibid., p. 264.
31 Ibid., p. 265.

Chapter 9: Dryden, Dunciad, Defiant Daughters

1　Janet Todd, 'Behn, Aphra', *Oxford Dictionary of National Biography*, Oxford: Oxford University Press, 2004, https://doi.org/10.1093/ref:odnb/1961

2　Elliott Visconsi, 'A Degenerate Race: English Barbarism in Aphra Behn's "Oroonoko" and "The Widow Ranter"', *ELH*, 2002, vol. 69, no. 3, pp. 673–701.

3　Michael Werth Gelber, 'Dryden and the Battle of the Books', *Huntington Library Quarterly*, 2000, vol. 63, no. 1–2, pp. 139–56.

4　Ibid., p. 143.

5　Ibid., p. 144.

6　Ibid., p. 145.

7　Kenneth Craven, *Jonathan Swift and the Millennium of Madness: The Information Age in Swift's 'A Tale of a Tub'*, Leiden: Brill, 1992.

8　James Horowitz, '"Almost Normal", or Everything You Always Wanted to Know about Swift but Were Afraid to Ask', *Journal for Eighteenth-Century Studies*, 2020, vol. 43, no. 3, pp. 281–91.

9　Maynard Mack and Duncan Robinson, 'The World of Alexander Pope', *Yale University Library Gazette*, 1988, vol. 62, no. 3/4, pp. 87–157.

10　Elizabeth Kowaleski Wallace, 'The Things Things Don't Say: *The Rape of the Lock*, Vitalism, and the New Materialism', *Eighteenth Century*, 2018, vol. 59, no. 1, pp. 105–22.

11　Jonathan Pritchard, 'Pope, John Rackett, and the Slave Trade', *Studies in English Literature, 1500–1900*, 2005, vol. 45, no. 3, pp. 579–601.

12　See for example Katherine Mannheimer, 'Personhood, Poethood and Pope: Johnson's Life of Pope and the Search for the Man behind the Author', *Eighteenth Century Studies*, 2007, vol. 40, no. 4, pp. 631–49.

13　Wallace, op. cit., p. 115.

14　Diana Barnes, 'The Public Life of a Woman of Wit and Quality: Lady Mary Wortley Montagu and the Vogue for Smallpox Inoculation', *Feminist Studies*, 2012, vol. 38, no. 2, pp. 330–62; O. P. Sharma, 'Alexander Pope (1688–1744): His Spinal Deformity and His Doctors', *European Respiratory Journal*, 1999, vol. 14, no. 5, pp. 1235–7.

15　Jennifer Snead, 'Epic for an Information Age: Pope's *Dunciad in Four Books* and the Theater Licensing Act', *ELH*, 2010, vol. 77, no. 1, pp. 195–216.

16　Paddy Bullard, 'The Scriblerian Mock-Arts: Pseudo-Technical Satire in Swift and His Contemporaries', *Studies in Philology*, 2013, vol. 110, no. 3, pp. 611–36.

17　William A. McIntosh, 'Handel, Walpole, and Gay: The Aims of *The Beggar's Opera*', *Eighteenth-Century Studies*, 1974, vol. 7, no. 4, pp. 415–33.

18　Ibid., p. 429.

19　Ibid., p. 433.

20	See Brooke Allen, 'Augustan Satire Reconsidered', *Hudson Review*, 2013, no. 3, pp. 595–9.

21	Roger Lonsdale, review of *The Rhetorical World of Augustan Humanism* by Paul Fussell, *Review of English Studies*, 1967, vol. 18, no. 69, pp. 76–8.

22	James Anderson Winn, *John Dryden and His World*, New Haven, CT: Yale University Press, 1987.

23	Ophelia Field, *The Kit-Cat Club: Friends Who Imagined a Nation*, London: HarperPress, 2008.

24	Robert J. Allen, *The Clubs of Augustan London*, Cambridge, MA: Harvard University Press, 1933, p. 14.

25	D. Waddell, 'Charles Davenant (1656–1714): A Biographical Sketch', *Economic History Review*, 1958, vol. 11, no. 2, pp. 279–88.

26	Richard Coulton, '"The Darling of the Temple-Coffee-House Club": Science, Sociability, and Satire in Early Eighteenth-Century London', *Journal for Eighteenth-Century Studies*, 2012, vol. 35, no. 1, pp. 43–65.

27	Brian Cowan, 'Mr Spectator and the Coffeehouse Public Sphere', *Eighteenth-Century Studies*, 2004, vol. 37, no. 3, pp. 345–66.

28	Charles A. Knight, '*The Spectator*'s Moral Economy', *Modern Philology*, 1993, vol. 91, no. 2, pp. 161–79.

29	Ibid., p. 166.

30	Ibid., p. 167.

31	Ibid., p. 168.

32	Ibid., p. 170.

33	Ibid., p. 175.

34	Ibid., p. 176.

35	Ian Watt, *The Rise of the Novel*, London: Chatto & Windus, 1957, p. 19.

36	Jan Bloemendal, *Bilingual Europe: Latin and Vernacular Cultures, Examples of Bilingualism and Multilingualism, c.1300–1800*, Leiden: Brill, 2015.

37	Watt, op. cit., pp. 61–3.

Chapter 10: The Enormous Conceit: Britain – 'The Dread and Envy of Them All'

1	Roy Porter, *Enlightenment: Britain and the Creation of the Modern World*, London: Penguin, 2001, p. 19.

2	Linda Colley, *Britons: Forging the Nation, 1707–1837*, New Haven, CT: Yale University Press, 1992, p. 52.

3	Ibid., p. 12.

4	Ibid., p. 19.

5	Ibid.; see also David Cressy, *Bonfires and Bells: National Memory and the Protestant Calendar in Elizabethan and Stuart England*, London: Weidenfeld & Nicolson, 1989.

6	Colley, op. cit., p. 20.

7	Ibid., p. 43.

8   Ibid., p. 30.
9   Porter, op. cit., p. 31.
10 Ibid., p. 32.
11 Colley, op. cit., p. 108.
12 Ibid.
13 Paul Langford, *A Polite and Commercial People: England, 1727–1783*, Oxford: Clarendon Press, 1989, p. 242.
14 Porter, op. cit., pp. 21, 108.
15 Langford, op. cit., p. 293.
16 Porter, op. cit., p. 71.
17 Ibid., p. 40.
18 Ibid., p. 172.
19 Ben Dew, 'Spurs to Industry in Bernard Mandeville's *Fable of the Bees*', *Journal for Eighteenth-Century Studies*, 2005, vol. 28, no. 2, pp. 151–65.
20 Porter, op. cit., p. 201.
21 Ibid., p. 202.

Chapter 11: Dr Johnson's Microcosm of 'Conspicuous Men'

1   John Brewer, *The Pleasures of the Imagination: English Culture in the Eighteenth Century*, London: HarperCollins, 1997, p. 45.
2   Leo Damrosch, *The Club: Johnson, Boswell and the Friends Who Shaped an Age*, New Haven, CT, and London: Yale University Press, 2019.
3   A. D. Atkinson, 'Dr Johnson and the Royal Society', *Notes and Records of the Royal Society of London*, 1953, vol. 10, no. 2, pp. 131–8.
4   Anthony Burgess, 'The Dictionary Makers', *Wilson Quarterly*, 1993, vol. 17, no. 3, pp. 104–10.
5   Ibid., p. 105.
6   Roy Porter, *Enlightenment: Britain and the Creation of the Modern World*, London: Penguin, 2001, p. 271.
7   Damrosch, op. cit., p. 93.
8   Ibid., p. 83.
9   Ibid., pp. 84–8.
10 Adam Beach, 'The Creation of a Classical Language in the Eighteenth Century: Standardizing English, Cultural Imperialism, and the Future of the Literary Canon', *Texas Studies in Literature and Language*, 2001, vol. 43, no. 2, pp. 117–41.
11 Ibid., p. 118.
12 Ibid., p. 119.
13 Ibid., p. 123.
14 Ibid., p. 128.
15 Ellis Waterhouse, *Painting in Britain, 1530–1790*, Harmondsworth: Penguin, 1953, p. 219.
16 Ibid., p. 249.
17 Ibid., p. 257.

18 Ibid., p. 213.
19 P. J. Marshall, *Edmund Burke and the British Empire in the West Indies: Wealth, Power, and Slavery*, Oxford: Oxford University Press, 2019.
20 Anthony Quinton, 'Burke on the Sublime and Beautiful', *Philosophy*, 1961, vol. 36, no. 136, pp. 71–3.
21 Ibid., p. 72.
22 David Bromwich, 'Wollstonecraft as a Critic of Burke', *Political Theory*, 1995, vol. 23, no. 4, pp. 617–34; Susan Wolfson, *On Mary Wollstonecraft's 'A Vindication of the Rights of Woman': The First of a New Genus*, New York: Columbia University Press, 2022.
23 R. R. Fennessy, *Burke, Paine, and the Rights of Man: A Difference of Political Opinion*, The Hague: Martinus Nijhoff, 1963, p. 617.
24 Bromwich, op. cit.
25 Fennessy, op. cit., p. 619.
26 Ibid., p. 621.
27 Paul Langford, *A Polite and Commercial People: England, 1727–1783*, Oxford: Clarendon Press, 1989, p. 308.
28 Porter, op. cit., p. 309.
29 Brewer, op. cit., p. 327.
30 Porter, op. cit., p. 309.
31 Ibid., p. 332.
32 Langford, op. cit., p. 466.
33 Brewer, op. cit., p. 146.
34 Ibid.
35 Annick Cossic-Péricarpin, 'Fashionable Diseases in Georgian Bath: Fiction and the Emergence of a British Model for Spa Sociability', *Journal for Eighteenth-Century Studies*, 2017, vol. 40, issue 4, pp. 537–53.
36 Langford, op. cit., p. 479.
37 Ibid., p. 486.

Chapter 12: 'There Is No Colour in an Honest Mind'

1 Gretchen Gerzina, *Black England: Life before Emancipation*, London: John Murray, 1995, p. 48.
2 Ibid., p. 49.
3 John Gilmore, 'Williams, Francis', *Oxford Dictionary of National Biography*, Oxford: Oxford University Press, 2004, https://doi.org/10.1093/ref:odnb/57050
4 Ibid.
5 Vincent Caretta, 'Sancho, (Charles) Ignatius', *Oxford Dictionary of National Biography*, Oxford: Oxford University Press, 2004, https://doi.org/10.1093/ref:odnb/24609
6 Ibid.
7 Gerzina, op. cit., p. 70.
8 Caretta, op. cit.
9 Thomas Jefferson, *Notes on the State of Virginia*, Chapel Hill:

University of North Carolina Press, [1787] 1955, query xiv.

10 Derek Walvin, 'Equiano, Olaudah [Gustavus Vassa]', *Oxford Dictionary of National Biography*, Oxford: Oxford University Press, 2004, https://doi.org/10.1093/ref:odnb/57028. But see also the recent reprint of Equiano's own book, *The Interesting Narrative of the Life of Olaudah Equiano, or Gustavus Vassa, the African by Himself*, Philadelphia: Press at Toad Hall, 2007.

11 Ruth Paley, 'Somerset, James', *Oxford Dictionary of National Biography*, Oxford: Oxford University Press, 2004, https://doi.org/10.1093/ref:odnb/70057

12 Ibid.

13 A good recent source is Andrew Lyall, *Granville Sharp's Cases on Slavery*, Oxford: Hart, 2017.

14 Matthew Wyman-McCarthy, 'Perceptions of French and Spanish Slave Law in Late Eighteenth-Century Britain', *Journal of British Studies*, 2018, vol. 57, no. 1, pp. 29–52.

15 A good recent work is William Hague, *William Wilberforce: The Life of the Great Anti-Slave Trade Campaigner*, London: HarperPress, 2007.

Chapter 13: Eden in Edinburgh: Self-Interest, Sympathy and the 'Invisible Hand'

Some material from the author's *Ideas: A History from Fire to Freud*, London: Weidenfeld & Nicolson, 2005, is incorporated here.

1 James Buchan, *Capital of the Mind: How Edinburgh Changed the World*, London: John Murray, 2003, p. 5.

2 Ibid., pp. 275–86.

3 Ibid, pp. 1–2, 5.

4 Ibid., p. 151.

5 J. B. Morell, 'Science and Scottish University Reform: Edinburgh in 1826', *British Journal for the History of Science*, 1972, vol. 6, no. 1, pp. 39–56; see also George Elder Davie, *The Democratic Intellect: Scotland and Her Universities in the Nineteenth Century*, Edinburgh: Edinburgh University Press, 1962.

6 Buchan, op. cit., p. 153.

7 Geoffrey Hawthorn, *Enlightenment and Despair: A History of Social Theory*, Cambridge: Cambridge University Press, 1976, p. 32.

8 See in particular the sections on scepticism in Stephen Buckle, *Hume's Enlightenment Tract: The Unity and Purpose of 'An Enquiry Concerning Human Understanding'*, Oxford: Clarendon Press, 2001, pp. 14–15, 111–18, 167–8, 270–80.

9 Buchan, op. cit., p. 81.

10 Hawthorn, op. cit., pp. 32–3.

11 Ibid., p. 32.

12 Buchan, op. cit., p. 81.

13 Ibid., p. 224.

14 Ibid., p. 180.

15 Roger Smith, *The Norton History of the Human Sciences*, New York and London: Norton, 1997.

16 H. T. Buckle, *A History of Civilisation in England*, new ed., London: Longmans, Green, 1871, vol. 1, p. 194.

17 Ibid.

18 Buchan, op. cit., p. 154.

19 Craig Smith, *Adam Ferguson and the Idea of Civil Society: Moral Science and the Scottish Enlightenment*, Edinburgh: Edinburgh University Press, 2019.

20 Buchan, op. cit., p. 169.

21 Ibid., p. 292.

22 Deidre Dawson, 'Literature and Sentimentalism', in Alexander Broadie and Craig Smith (eds), *The Cambridge Companion to the Scottish Enlightenment*, 2nd ed., Cambridge: Cambridge University Press, 2019, p. 299; Gertrude Himmelfarb, *The Roads to Modernity: The British, French, and American Enlightenment*, New York: Knopf, 2004.

23 Dawson, op. cit., pp. 299–302.

Chapter 14: 'Agents of a Benevolent Providence': The Laboratory of Empire 1

1 Richard Drayton, 'Knowledge and Empire', in P. J. Marshall (ed.), *The Oxford History of the British Empire, Vol. II: The Eighteenth Century*, Oxford: Oxford University Press, 1998, pp. 211, 231.

2 Ibid., p. 232.

3 Ibid., p. 234.

4 Ibid., p. 233.

5 Ibid., p. 235.

6 Ibid., p. 236.

7 Brett M. Bennett and Joseph M. Hodge (eds), *Science and Empire: Knowledge and Networks of Science across the British Empire, 1800–1970*, Basingstoke: Palgrave Macmillan, 2011, pp. 48–9.

8 Drayton, op. cit., p. 235.

9 Ibid., p. 236.

10 James Delbourgo, *Collecting the World: Hans Sloane and the Origins of the British Museum*, Cambridge, MA: Belknap Press, 2017.

11 Ibid., p. 344.

12 Ibid., p. 345.

13 Kathleen S. Murphy, 'Collecting Slave Traders: James Petiver, Natural History, and the British Slave Trade', *William and Mary Quarterly*, 2013, 3rd ser., vol. 70, no. 4, pp. 637–70.

14 Ibid., p. 640.

15 Ibid., p. 667.

16 Edwin D. Rose, 'Specimens, Slips and Systems: Daniel Solander and the Classification of Nature at the World's First Public Museum, 1753–1768', *British Journal for the History of Science*, 2018, vol. 51, no. 2, pp. 205–37.

17 Drayton, op. cit., p. 251.

18 Ibid., p. 252.

19 Ibid., p. 239.

20 Anna Winterbottom, *Hybrid Knowledge in the Early East India Company World*, Basingstoke: Palgrave Macmillan, 2016.

21 Drayton, op. cit., p. 241.

22 Ibid., p. 242.

23 Patrick Turnbull, *Warren Hastings*, London: New English Library, 1975, pp. 199ff.

24 Raymond Schwab, *The Oriental Renaissance: Europe's Rediscovery of India and the East, 1680–1880*, New York: Columbia University Press, 1984, p. 35.

25 Garland Cannon, 'Sir William Jones, Sir John Banks, and the Royal Society', *Notes and Records of the Royal Society of London*, 1975, vol. 29, no. 2, pp. 205–30.

26 Ibid., p. 208.

27 Ibid.

28 Ibid., p. 210.

29 Ibid., p. 222.

30 Ibid.

31 Ibid., p. 225.

32 Ian Stewart, 'After Sir William Jones: British Linguistic Scholarship and European Intellectual History', *Journal of Modern History*, 2023, vol. 94, no. 4, pp. 808–46.

33 See for example Santibhusan Nandi, 'Controversy over Indo-European/ Aryan: Race Science versus Philology', *Current Anthropology*, 2000, vol. 41, no. 3, pp. 473–4.

34 Tony Ballantyne, *Orientalism and Race: Aryanism in the British Empire*, Basingstoke: Palgrave Macmillan, 2002.

35 Tony Ballantyne, *Science, Empire and the European Exploration of the Pacific*, Aldershot: Ashgate Variorum, 2004.

36 Richard Drayton, *Nature's Government: Science, Imperialism and the 'Improvement' of the World*, New Haven, CT, and London: Yale University Press, 2000, p. 161.

37 Ibid.

38 Ibid., p. 163.

39 Ibid.

40 Ibid., p. 164.

41 Ibid., p. 244.

42 Ibid., p. 247.

43 Ibid., p. 249.

44 Kapil Raj, 'Beyond Postcolonialism ... and Postpositivism: Circulation and the Global History of Science', *Isis*, 2013, vol. 104, no. 2, pp. 337–47. See also Helen Tilley, 'A Great (Scientific) Divergence: Synergies and Fault Lines in Global Histories of Science', *Isis*, 2019, vol. 110, no. 1, pp. 129–36; Toyin Falola and Christian Jennings (eds), *Africanizing*

Knowledge: African Studies across the Disciplines, New Brunswick, NJ: Transaction, 2002, p. 222; James Poskett, 'We must recognise science's unsung global pioneers to alter its future', *New Scientist*, 26 March 2022, p. 27.

45 Julia Bruce, 'Banks and Breadfruit', *RSA Journal*, 1993, vol. 141, no. 5444, pp. 817–20.

46 Drayton, op. cit., p. 250.

47 Bennett and Hodge (eds), op. cit., p. 60.

Chapter 15: Iron, Steam, Gaslight and Moonlight

Some material from the author's *Ideas: A History from Fire to Freud*, London: Weidenfeld & Nicolson, 2005, is included here.

1 Jacob Bronowski and Bruce Mazlish, *The Western Intellectual Tradition: From Leonardo to Hegel*, London: Hutchinson, 1960, p. 307. Depending on which scholar you listen to, there were many other 'revolutions' in the eighteenth century – for example, the demographic, the chemical and the agricultural among them.

2 David S. Landes, *The Wealth and Poverty of Nations: Why Some Are So Rich and Some So Poor*, New York: W. W. Norton, 1998, p. 42.

3 Bernal, *Science in History*, p. 520.

4 Peter Hall, *Cities in Civilisation: Culture, Innovation and Urban Order*, London: Weidenfeld & Nicolson, 1998, p. 310.

5 Ibid., p. 312.

6 Ibid., p. 315.

7 Ibid., p. 316.

8 Ibid., pp. 311–12.

9 Phyllis Deane, *The First Industrial Revolution*, 2nd ed., Cambridge: Cambridge University Press, 1979, p. 22.

10 Landes, op. cit., pp. 64–5.

11 Eric Hobsbawm, *The Age of Revolution: Europe, 1789–1848*, London: Weidenfeld & Nicolson, 1962, p. 63.

12 Landes, op. cit., p. 7.

13 Hall, op. cit., p. 308.

14 Landes, op. cit., p. 282.

15 Kleist is ignored in many histories, but see Michael Brian Schiffer, *Draw the Lightning Down: Benjamin Franklin and Electrical Technology in the Age of Enlightenment*, Berkeley: University of California Press, 2003, p. 46.

16 In turn, in the hands of André-Marie Ampère (1775–1836), Johann Karl Friedrich Gauss (1777–1855) and Georg Ohm (1787–1854), far more was learned about magnetic fields produced by currents and the way these flowed through conductors. Current electricity was now a quantitative science: see David S. Landes, *The Unbound Prometheus: Technological Change and Industrial Development in Western Europe from 1750 to the Present*, Cambridge: Cambridge University Press, 2003, p. 285. See also Jean-Pierre Poirier, *Lavoisier: Chemist, Biologist, Economist*,

Philadelphia: University of Pennsylvania Press, 1996, pp. 102ff for the new chemistry; pp. 105ff for the formation of acids; p. 107 for combustion; pp. 61ff for the calcinations of metals; and p. 150 for the analysis of water.

17 John Dalton, *A New System of Chemical Philosophy*, London: William Dawson, [1808–27] 1953, vol. 2, pp. 1ff, vol. 1, pp. 231ff. And see the diagrams facing p. 218.

18 Schiffer, op. cit., p. 34.

19 Bernal, op. cit., p. 620.

20 Bronowski and Mazlish, op. cit., p. 323.

21 Bernal, op. cit., p. 621.

22 Poirier, op. cit., pp. 72ff.

23 Dalton, op. cit., vol. 2, pp. 1ff, vol 1., pp. 231ff.

24 John Graham Gillam, *The Crucible: The Story of Joseph Priestley, LLD, FRS*, London: Robert Hale, 1954, p. 138.

25 Schofield, op. cit., p. 440.

26 Roy Porter, *Enlightenment: Britain and the Creation of the Modern World*, London: Penguin, 2001, p. 431.

27 E. P. Thompson, *The Making of the English Working Class*, London: Victor Gollancz, 1963, pp. 781ff.

28 Bronowski and Mazlish, op. cit., p. 339.

29 Landes, *Unbound Prometheus*, pp. 22–3.

30 R. W. Harris, *Romanticism and the Social Order*, London: Blandford, 1969, p. 78.

31 J. K. Galbraith, *A History of Economics: The Past as the Present*, London: Hamish Hamilton, 1987, p. 118.

32 Thompson, op. cit., pp. 807–8. Samuel Galton, grandfather of Francis, the founder of eugenics, was yet another who moved on from the Warrington Academy to the Lunar Society: he formed one of the earliest collections of scientific instruments. Thomas Day was most famous for his children's stories; he wrote 'pompously and vapidly', according to one account, but he lent money to the other members to support their activities (Robert Schofield, *The Lunar Society of Birmingham: A Social History of Provincial Science and Industry in Eighteenth-Century England*, Oxford: Clarendon Press, 1963, p. 53). James Keir, a former professional soldier, tried his hand at extracting alkalis from kelp (his method worked but the yield was too small) and then, having fought in France, and being fluent in French, translated Macquer's *Dictionary of Chemistry*, a distinguished (and highly practical) work, which helped establish the reputation of the Lunar Society.

Chapter 16: Deep Space, Deep Time, Darwin

Some material from the author's *Ideas: A History from Fire to Freud*, London: Weidenfeld & Nicolson, 2005, is included here.

1 Richard Holmes, *The Age of Wonder: How the Romantic Generation Discovered the Beauty and Terror of Science*, London: HarperPress,

2008, p. 60; Constance A. Lubbock (ed.), *The Herschel Chronicle: The Life-Story of Sir William Herschel and His Sister Caroline Herschel*, Cambridge: Cambridge University Press, 1933.

2   Holmes, op. cit., p. 87.

3   Ibid., p. 88.

4   Ibid., p. 91. For Flamsteed, see Francis Willmoth (ed.), *Flamsteed's Stars: New Perspectives on the Life and Work of the First Astronomer Royal, 1646–1719*, Woodbridge, Suffolk: Boydell Press, 1997.

5   Holmes, op. cit., p. 102.

6   Ibid.

7   Ibid., p. 123.

8   Ibid., p. 192.

9   Peter J. Bowler, *Evolution: The History of an Idea*, Berkeley: University of California Press, 1989, p. 40.

10 Ibid.

11 Mott T. Greene, *Geology in the Nineteenth Century: Changing Views of a Changing World*, Ithaca, NY: Cornell University Press, 1982, p. 36; Abraham Gottlob Werner, *Kurze Klassifikation und Beschreibung der verschiedenen Gebirgsarten*, New York: Haber, [1789] 1971; Rachael Laudan, *From Mineralogy to Geology: The Foundations of a Science, 1650–1830*, Chicago: University of Chicago Press, 1987, pp. 48ff. For Werner's theory of colour, see Patrick Syme, *Werner's Nomenclature of Colours*, Edinburgh: William Blackwood, 1821; Charles Gillispie, *Genesis and Geology: A Study of the Relations of Scientific Thought, Natural Theology, and Social Opinion in Great Britain, 1790–1850*, Cambridge, MA: Harvard University Press, 1951, p. 48.

12 Jack Repcheck, *The Man Who Found Time: James Hutton and the Discovery of the Earth's Antiquity*, London: Simon & Schuster, 2003, who says that Hutton's prose was 'impenetrable' and that, at the time, people were not very interested in the antiquity of the earth; J. J. O'Connor and E. F. Robertson, 'James Hutton', MacTutor, January 2004, https://mathshistory.st-andrews.ac.uk/Biographies/Hutton_James/

13 Gillispie, op. cit., p. 101.

14 Bowler, op. cit., p. 110.

15 Gillispie, op. cit., p. 133.

16 Bowler, op. cit., p. 138.

17 Ibid., p. 130.

18 Ibid.

19 Nicolaas A. Rupke, *The Great Chain of History: William Buckland and the English School of Geology (1814–1849)*, Oxford: Clarendon Press, 1983.

20 'Adam Sedgwick', UC Museum of Paleontology, 30 August 1996, https://www.ucmp.berkeley.edu/history/Sedgwick.html

21 Peter J. Bowler, *The Non-Darwinian Revolution: Reinterpreting a Historical Myth*, Baltimore: Johns Hopkins University Press, 1988, p. 13.

22 Ernst Mayr, *The Growth of Biological Thought: Diversity, Evolution, and Inheritance*, Cambridge, MA: Belknap Press, 1982, p. 590.

23 Ibid., p. 321.

24 James A. Secord, *Victorian Sensation: The Extraordinary Publication, Reception, and Secret Authorship of 'Vestiges of the Natural History of Creation'*, Chicago: University of Chicago Press, 2000, pp. 388, 526 (for the publishing histories of *Vestiges* and the *Origin* compared).

25 Jonathan Conlin, *Evolution and the Victorians: Science, Culture and Politics in Darwin's Britain*, London: Bloomsbury Academic, 2014.

26 Peter J. Bowler, *Charles Darwin, the Man and His Influence*, Oxford: Blackwell, 1990, p. 36.

27 For Wallace's trip to the Far East, see James T. Costa, *Wallace, Darwin, and the Origin of Species*, Cambridge, MA: Harvard University Press, 2014, pp. 223–31. For his interest in land reform, see Martin Fichman, *An Elusive Victorian: The Evolution of Alfred Russel Wallace*, Chicago: University of Chicago Press, 2004, pp. 145–6.

28 Bowler, *Charles Darwin*, p. 64; Peter Godfrey-Smith, *Darwinian Populations and Natural Selection*, Oxford: Oxford University Press, 2009.

29 Bowler, *Non-Darwinian Revolution*, p. 132.

30 Secord, op. cit., pp. 224, 230.

31 Ibid.

32 Bowler, op. cit, p. 47.

Chapter 17: Majesty with Menace

1 Jonathan I. Israel, *Radical Enlightenment: Philosophy and the Making of Modernity, 1650–1750*, Oxford: Oxford University Press, 2001, p. 668.

2 Ibid.

3 Ibid., pp. 665, 344.

4 John Bowle, *Hobbes and His Critics*, London: Jonathan Cape, 1951, p. 290.

5 Israel, op. cit., p. 344.

6 Roger Smith, *The Norton History of the Human Sciences*, New York: W. W. Norton, 1997, p. 337.

7 Isaiah Berlin, *The Sense of Reality: Studies in Ideas and Their History*, London: Chatto & Windus, 1996, p. 176.

8 Ibid., p. 168.

9 Ibid., pp. 181–2; see also Geoffrey Hawthorn, *Enlightenment and Despair: A History of Social Theory*, Cambridge: Cambridge University Press, 1976, pp. 238–9.

10 Chapter XII of Howard Mumford Jones, *Revolution and Romanticism*, Cambridge, MA: Belknap Press, 1974, is entitled 'The Romantic Rebels'.

11 Jones, op. cit., p. 274.

12 Arnold Hauser, *The Social History of Art, Vol. 1*, London: Routledge & Kegan Paul, 1951, p. 208.

13   Gerald N. Izenberg, *Impossible Individuality: Romanticism, Revolution, and the Origins of Modern Selfhood, 1787–1802*, Princeton, NJ: Princeton University Press, 1992, pp. 45–7, 142–3.

14   Robin Valenza, *Literature, Language and the Rise of the Intellectual Disciplines in Britain, 1680–1820*, Cambridge: Cambridge University Press, p. 142.

15   Hauser, op. cit., p. 188.

16   Ibid., p. 192.

17   Ibid., p. 210.

18   Jones, op. cit., p. 288.

19   Hauser, op. cit., p. 181.

20   Samar Attar, *Borrowed Imagination: The British Romantic Poets and their Arabic-Islamic Sources*, Lanham, MD: Lexington, 2014.

21   Andrew Wilton, 'Dr Thomas Monro and the Monro Academy', *Burlington Magazine*, 1976, vol. 118, no. 878, pp. 332–5.

22   Jonathan Mayne, 'English Romantic Water Colors', *Metropolitan Museum of Art Bulletin*, April 1962, new series, vol. 20, no. 8, p. 247.

23   Paul Miner, 'Blake's Word Play and Sir Joshua', *Notes & Queries*, 2017, vol. 64, no. 1, pp. 29–33.

24   See for example Michael Walker, 'John Martin: Visionary Artist', *Brontë Studies*, 2005, vol. 30, no. 1, pp. 53–60.

25   Donald Olson and Rolf Sinclair, 'The Origin of "Rain, Steam and Speed" by J. M. W. Turner', *The British Art Journal*, 2018, vol. 19, no. 1, pp. 42–8.

26   Marjorie Munsterberg, 'Ruskin's Turner: The Making of a Romantic Hero', *British Art Journal*, 2009, vol. 10, no. 1, p. 61.

27   William S. Rodner, 'Humanity and Nature in the Steamboat Paintings of J. M. W. Turner', *Albion*, 1986, vol. 18, no. 3, pp. 455–74.

28   Ibid., p. 456.

29   Ibid., p. 462.

30   Ibid, p. 474.

31   Maryanne C. Ward, 'Preparing for the National Gallery: The Art Criticism of William Hazlitt and P. G. Patmore', *Victorian Periodicals Review*, 1990, vol. 23, no. 3, pp. 104–10.

32   Claire Brock, 'William Hazlitt, on Being Brilliant', *Studies in Romanticism*, 2005, vol. 44, no. 4, pp. 493–513.

33   Frances Ferguson, 'Hazlitt's People', *Keats–Shelley Journal*, 2018, vol. 67, pp. 175–81.

34   William C. Wright, 'Hazlitt, Ruskin, and Nineteenth-Century Art Criticism', *Journal of Aesthetics and Art Criticism*, 1974, vol. 32, no. 4, pp. 509–23.

Chapter 18: 'Astronomy and Geology
Are Greater Muses than Love'

1   Rachel Dickinson, 'Ruskin and a Generation Worth Remembering', *Journal of Victorian Culture*, 2019, vol. 24, no. 3, pp. 303–10.

2 Frederic E. Faverty, 'The Brownings and Their Contemporaries', *Browning Institute Studies*, 1974, vol. 2, pp. 161–80.

3 Ibid., p. 173.

4 Charles H. Kegel, 'Carlyle and Ruskin: An Influential Friendship', *Brigham Young University Studies*, 1964, vol. 5, no. 3–4, pp. 219–29.

5 Ibid., p. 219.

6 Ibid., p. 220.

7 Ibid.

8 Rebecca Stott, 'Thomas Carlyle and the Crowd: Revolution, Geology and the Convulsive "Nature" of Time', *Journal of Victorian Culture*, 1999, vol. 4, no. 1, pp. 1–24.

9 Ibid., p. 10. But see also Adelene Buckland, '"The Poetry of Science": Charles Dickens, Geology, and Visual and Material Culture in Victorian London', *Victorian Literature and Culture*, 2007, vol. 35, no. 2, pp. 679–94.

10 Stott, op. cit., p. 11.

11 Richard Salmon, 'Thomas Carlyle and the Idolatry of the Man of Letters', *Journal of Victorian Culture*, 2002, vol. 7, no. 1, pp. 1–22.

12 Rodger L. Tarr, 'Emendation as Challenge: Carlyle's "Negro Question" from Journal to Pamphlet', *Papers of the Bibliographical Society of America*, 1981, vol. 75, no. 3, pp. 341–5.

13 Joseph Persky, 'Retrospectives: A Dismal Romantic', *Journal of Economic Perspectives*, 1990, vol. 4, no. 4, pp. 163–72.

14 Ibid., p. 167.

15 Ibid., p. 168.

16 Tarr, op. cit., p. 343.

17 David G. Reide, 'Tennyson's Poetic of Melancholy and the Imperial Imagination', *Studies in English Literature: 1500–1900*, 2000, vol. 40, no. 4, pp. 659–78.

18 See for example Catherine Hall, 'Top Boy', *History Workshop Journal*, 2010, vol. 70, pp. 282–92, especially p. 283.

19 Ibid., p. 284.

20 Ibid., p. 287.

21 Ibid., p. 288.

22 Ibid., p. 290.

23 Ibid., p. 291.

24 A recent study is Timothy Larsen, *John Stuart Mill: A Secular Life*, Oxford: Oxford University Press, 2018.

25 Duncan Bell, 'John Stuart Mill on Colonies', *Political Theory*, 2010, vol. 38, no. 1, pp. 34–64.

26 Alexandra Lewis (ed.), *The Brontës and the Idea of the Human, Science, Ethics, and the Victorian Imagination*, Cambridge: Cambridge University Press, 2019.

27 For a recent study, see Deborah Logan, *Harriet Martineau, Victorian Imperialism, and the Civilizing Mission*, Aldershot and Burlington, VT: Ashgate, 2010.

Chapter 19: A Significant New View of Nature

Some material from the author's *Convergence: The Idea at the Heart of Science*, London and New York, Simon & Schuster, 2016, is incorporated here.

1   Iwan Rhys Morus, *When Physics Became King*, Chicago and London: University of Chicago Press, 2005, p. 63; Thomas S. Kuhn, *The Essential Tension: Selected Studies in Scientific Tradition and Change*, Chicago: University of Chicago Press, 1977, p. 68.

2   Crosbie Smith, *The Science of Energy: A Cultural History of Energy Physics in Victorian Britain*, London: Athlone, 1998.

3   Kuhn, op. cit., pp. 97–8.

4   Smith, op. cit., p. 72.

5   Ibid., p. 8.

6   Ibid., p. 9.

7   John Theodore Merz, *A History of European Thought in the Nineteenth Century*, New York: Dover, [1904–12] 1965, vol. 1, pp. 23, 204.

8   Morus, op. cit., p. 65.

9   Peter M. Harman, *Energy, Force and Matter: The Conceptual Development of Nineteenth-Century Physics*, Cambridge: Cambridge University Press, 1982, p. 144; J. C. Poggendorff, *Annalen der Physik und Chemie*, Leipzig: J. A. Barth, 1824.

10 Basil Mahon, *The Man Who Changed Everything: The Life of James Clerk Maxwell*, Chichester: Wiley, 2003, p. 2; Raymond Flood et al. (eds), *James Clerk Maxwell: Perspectives on His Life and Work*, Oxford: Oxford University Press, 2014, p. 241.

11 Mahon, op. cit., p. 36.

12 Flood et al. (eds), op. cit., p. 14.

13 Mahon, op. cit., p. 69.

14 Ibid., p. 61.

15 John Gribbin, *Science: A History, 1543–2001*, London: Allen Lane, 2002, p. 432; Flood et al. (eds), op. cit., pp. 190–1.

16 Flood et al. (eds), op cit., p. 279.

17 Thomas Martin, 'Origins of the Royal Institution', *British Journal for the History of Science*, 1962, vol. 1, no. 1, pp. 49–63.

18 Christa Jungnickel and Russell McCormmach, *The Intellectual Mastery of Nature: The Theory of Physics from Ohm to Einstein, Vol. 1: The Torch of Mathematics, 1800–1870*, Chicago: University of Chicago Press, 1986, p. 164, quoted in Morus, op. cit., p. 147. See also Yehuda Elkana, *The Discovery of the Conservation of Energy*, London: Hutchinson, 1974.

19 Harman, op. cit., pp. 148–50. See Engelbert Broda, *Ludwig Boltzmann: Mensch, Physiker, Philosoph*, Vienna: Franz Deuticke, 1955, pp. 57–66, 74ff for Maxwell's views on heat death.

20 Carl B. Boyer, *A History of Mathematics*, 2nd ed., revised by Uta C. Merzbach, New York: Wiley, 1991, pp. 497.

Chapter 20: Darwin, Empire and the Pre-eminence of the English Novel

1 John Holmes, 'Pre-Raphaelitism, Science and Art in *The Germ*', *Victorian Literature and Culture*, 2015, vol. 43, no. 4, pp. 689–703.
2 Ibid., p. 689.
3 Ibid., p. 692.
4 Gillian Beer, *Open Fields: Science in Cultural Encounter*, Oxford: Clarendon Press, 1996, p. 203.
5 George Levine, *Darwin and the Novelists: Patterns of Science in Victorian Fiction*, Cambridge, MA: Harvard University Press, 1988.
6 Ibid., p. 155.
7 Ibid., p. 164.
8 Ibid., pp. 257–9.
9 Beer, op. cit., p. 203.
10 Ibid., pp. 205–7.
11 Ibid., p. 43.
12 Ibid., p. 48.
13 Ibid., p. 238.
14 Ibid., p. 237.
15 Ibid., p. 248.
16 Ibid., p. 260.
17 Edward W. Said, *Culture and Imperialism*, London: Chatto & Windus, 1993.
18 Corinne Fowler, 'Revisiting Mansfield Park: The Critical and Literary Legacies of Edward W. Said's Essay "Jane Austen and Empire" in *Culture and Imperialism* (1993)', *Cambridge Journal of Postcolonial Literary Inquiry*, 2017, vol. 4, no. 3, pp. 362–81.
19 Ibid., p. 363.
20 Ibid., p. 366.
21 Ibid., p. 369.
22 Ibid., p. 367.
23 Devoney Looser, 'Heroics all at sea', *Times Literary Supplement*, 8 July 2022, p. 5. For a more nuanced view of Orientalism, see: K. Humayun Ansari, 'The Muslim World in British Historical Imagination: "Re-thinking *Orientalism*"?', *British Journal of Middle Eastern Studies*, 2011, vol. 38, no. 1, pp. 73–93, where the author ranges wider than Said, and is more even-handed.
24 D. C. R. A. Goonetilleke, *Joseph Conrad: Beyond Culture and Background*, Basingstoke: Macmillan, 1990, pp. 15ff.
25 Richard Curle, *Joseph Conrad: A Study*, London: Kegan Paul, Trench, Trubner, 1914.

Chapter 21: The Intellectual Aristocracy

1 David Cannadine, *G. M. Trevelyan: A Life in History*, London: HarperCollins, 1992. Annan wrote several books on intellectuals at

various times, including *Selected Writings in British Intellectual History*, with Leslie Stephen, Chicago: University of Chicago Press, 1979.

2   Cannadine, op. cit., p. 245.

3   A useful introduction is John D. Fair, 'Walter Bagehot, Royal Mediation, and the Modern British Constitution, 1869–1931', *Historian*, 1980, vol. 43, no. 1, pp. 36–54.

4   Nicholas Murray, *A Life of Matthew Arnold*, London: Hodder & Stoughton, 1996, p. 52.

5   Stefan Collini, 'Arnold, Matthew', *Oxford Dictionary of National Biography*, Oxford: Oxford University Press, 2004, https://doi.org/ 10.1093/ref:odnb/679

6   Ibid.

7   An interesting assessment is to be found in Sherrin Berezowsky, 'Statistical Criticism and the Eminent Man in Francis Galton's *Hereditary Genius*', *Victorian Literature and Culture*, 2015, vol. 43, no. 4, pp. 821–39.

8   M. G. Bulmer, *Francis Galton: Pioneer of Heredity and Biometry*, Baltimore: Johns Hopkins University Press, 2003.

9   Cynthia Huff, 'The "Galton Family Books": Visual and Verbal Life Writing', *Forum for Foreign Language Studies*, 2016, vol. 52, no. 2, pp. 189–202.

10 Frans Lundgren, 'The Politics of Participation: Francis Galton's Anthropometric Laboratory and the Making of Civic Selves', *British Journal for the History of Science*, 2013, vol. 46, no. 3, pp. 445–66.

11 Chris Renwick, 'From Political Economy to Sociology: Francis Galton and the Social-Scientific Origins of Eugenics', *British Journal for the History of Science*, 2011, vol. 44, no. 3, pp. 343–69.

12 A useful introduction is Howard Ira Einsohn, 'Lifting the Millstones – So Spirits Can Soar', *Shaw*, 2017, vol. 37, no. 2, pp. 342–9.

13 Lisanne Radice, *Beatrice and Sidney Webb: Fabian Socialists*, New York: St Martin's Press, 1984.

14 An early history is David Mitrany, *The London School of Economics and Political Science*, London: Students' Union of the LSE, 1918.

15 Ray Monk, *Bertrand Russell*, London: Vintage, 1997, p. 46.

16 Ibid., p. 69.

17 Ibid., p. 193.

18 Ibid., p. 195.

Chapter 22: Learned Empire: A 'Higher Purpose' for Britain

1   Andrew Porter (ed.), *The Oxford History of the British Empire, Vol. 3: The Nineteenth Century*, Oxford: Oxford University Press, p. 256.

2   Ibid., p. 281.

3   A. D. Roberts, 'Livingstone, David', *Oxford Dictionary of National Biography*, Oxford: Oxford University Press, 2004, https://doi.org/ 10.1093/ref:odnb/16803

4   John Darwin, *After Tamerlane: The Global History of Empire*, London: Allen Lane, 2007, p. 23.

5 Ibid., p. 102.

6 Ronald Robinson et al., *Africa and the Victorians: The Official Mind of Imperialism*, New York: St Martin's Press, 1961, pp. 1–2.

7 Ibid., p. 3.

8 Richard Drayton, *Nature's Government: Science, Imperial Britain, and the 'Improvement' of the World*, New Haven, CT: Yale University Press, 2000, p. 93.

9 Bernard Porter, *Critics of Empire: British Radical attitudes to colonialism in Africa, 1895–1914*, London: Macmillan, 1968, p. 4.

10 Drayton, op. cit., p. 295.

11 Brett M. Bennett and Joseph M. Hodge (eds), *Science and Empire: Knowledge and Networks of Science across the British Empire, 1800–1970*, Basingstoke: Palgrave Macmillan, 2011, p. 6.

12 Drayton, op. cit., p. 196.

13 Ibid., p. 296.

14 Bennett and Hodge (eds), op. cit., p. 55.

15 Drayton, op. cit., p. 305.

16 Ibid., p. 311.

17 Lynn Zastoupil, 'J. S. Mill and India', *Victorian Studies*, 1988, vol. 32, no. 1, pp. 32–54.

18 Drayton, op. cit., p. 206.

19 Ibid., p. 211.

20 Ibid., p. 214.

21 Stewart J. Brown, 'Providential Empire? The Established Church of England and the Nineteenth-Century British Empire in India', *Studies in Church History*, 2018, vol. 54, pp. 225–59.

22 Drayton, op. cit., p. 225.

23 Brown, op. cit., p. 228.

24 Ibid., pp. 232–5.

25 Porter (ed.), op. cit., p. 667.

26 Richard Bourke, 'Liberty, Authority, and Trust in Edmund Burke's Idea of Empire', *Journal of the History of Ideas*, 2000, vol. 61, no. 3, pp. 453–71.

27 Andrew Porter, 'Evangelical Religions and Colonial Realities', *Journal of Imperial and Commonwealth History*, 2010, vol. 38, no. 1, pp. 145–55.

28 Bourke, op. cit., p. 455.

29 John Gallagher and Ronald Robinson, 'The Imperialism of Free Trade', *Economic History Review*, 1953, vol. 6, no. 1, pp. 1–15.

30 Porter (ed.), op. cit., p. 431.

31 Robinson et al., op. cit.

32 David Kopf, 'Fort William College and the Origins of the Bengal Renaissance', *Proceedings of the Indian History Congress*, 1961, vol. 24, pp. 296–303.

33 David Kopf, *British Orientalism and the Bengal Renaissance: The Dynamics of Indian Modernization, 1773–1835*, Berkeley: University of California Press, 1969, pp. 6, 45ff.

34 Ibid., p. 95.
35 Ibid., p. 8.
36 Ibid.
37 Ibid., p. 103.
38 Ibid., p. 19.
39 Robinson et al., op. cit., passim.
40 Sir J. R. Seeley, *The Expansion of England: Two Courses of Lectures*, 2nd ed., London: Macmillan, 1895.
41 See also David Armitage, 'Greater Britain: A Useful Category of Historical Analysis?', *American Historical Review*, 1999, vol. 104, no. 2, pp. 427–45; Elizabeth Thomson and E. A. Freeman, *A History of England*, London: Macmillan, 1875; J. A. Froude, *Oceana: Or England and Her Colonies*, London: Longmans, Green, 1886; Bennett and Hodge (eds), op. cit., pp. 61, 62. For the great wave of cultural nationalism in Bengal, see Partha Mitter, *Art and Nationalism in Colonial India, 1850–1922: Occidental Orientations*, Cambridge: Cambridge University Press, 1994, especially Part III. For a comprehensive view of British culture in the empire, see Holger Hoock, *Empires of the Imagination: Politics, War and the Arts in the British World, 1750–1850*, London: Profile, 2010.

Chapter 23: Britain as 'the Apex of Civilisation'

1 George W. Stocking, *Victorian Anthropology*, New York: Free Press 1987, p. 1.
2 Ibid., p. 3.
3 Gillian Beer, *Open Fields: Science in Cultural Encounter*, Oxford: Clarendon Press, 1996, p. 76.
4 Ibid., p. 77.
5 Ibid., p. 78.
6 Derek Freeman et al., 'The Evolutionary Theories of Charles Darwin and Herbert Spencer [and Comments and Replies]', *Current Anthropology*, 1974, vol. 15, no. 3, pp. 211–37.
7 On the other hand, see Stephen M. Stigler, 'Karl Pearson's Theoretical Errors and the Advances They Inspired', *Statistical Science*, 2008, vol. 23, no. 2, pp. 261–71.
8 For an assessment, see Mary Beard, 'Frazer, Leach, and Virgil, The Popularity (and Unpopularity) of *The Golden Bough*', *Comparative Studies in Society and History*, 1992, vol. 34, no. 2, pp. 203–24.
9 See for example Stan Smith, reviews of *The Golden Bough* by James George Frazer, *Sources for the Poetry of T. S. Eliot* by Anthony Hands and *T. S. Eliot at the Turn of the Century* by Marianne Thormählen, *Review of English Studies*, 1996, vol. 47, no. 188, p. 627.
10 Sarah Ogilvie, *The Dictionary People: The Unsung Heroes Who Created the Oxford English Dictionary*, London: Chatto & Windus, 2023, with early photos of Murray and colleagues.

Chapter 24: Hearts of Darkness, Hearts in Darkness

Some material from the author's *A Terrible Beauty: The People and Ideas That Shaped the Modern Mind*, London: Weidenfeld & Nicolson, 2000, is incorporated in the following chapters.

1 Philippa Gregory, *Normal Women: 900 Years of Making History*, London: William Collins, 2023, p. 403.
2 Ibid., p. 404.
3 Ibid., p. 444.
4 Robert Rhodes, *The Making of the Atomic Bomb*, New York: Simon & Schuster, 1986, p. 50.
5 Ibid., p. 43.
6 Ibid., p. 47.
7 Ibid., pp. 49–50.
8 Ibid., p. 50.
9 Helen Baron and Carl Baron, 'Introduction', in D. H. Lawrence, *Sons and Lovers*, Cambridge: Cambridge University Press, [1913] 1992, p. xviii.
10 Emanuel Miller (ed.), *The Neuroses in War*, London: Macmillan, 1940, p. 8.
11 Paul Fussell, *The Great War and Modern Memory*, Oxford: Oxford University Press, 1975, pp. 254ff.
12 Bernard Bergonzi, *Heroes' Twilight: A Study of the Literature of the Great War*, 2nd ed., London: Macmillan, 1980, p. 41.
13 Martin Seymour-Smith, 'Graves', in Ian Hamilton (ed.), *The Oxford Companion to Twentieth-Century Poetry in English*, Oxford: Oxford University Press, 1996, p. 194.
14 Jon Silkin, *Out of Battle: The Poetry of the Great War*, Oxford and New York: Oxford University Press, 1972, p. 232.
15 John Gribbin, *Companion to the Cosmos*, London: Phoenix, 1997, pp. 92, 571.
16 A. Vibert Douglas, *The Life of Arthur Stanley Eddington*, London: Thomas Nelson, 1956, p. 40.

Chapter 25: The Passions of Small Lives

1 R. H. Tawney, *Religion and the Rise of Capitalism*, London: John Murray, 1926.
2 Stephen Coote, *T. S. Eliot: 'The Waste Land'*, London: Penguin, 1985, pp. 12, 94.
3 Valerie Eliot (ed.), *The Letters of T. S. Eliot, Vol. 1: 1889–1922*, London: Faber & Faber, 1988, pp. 351–2.
4 Matthew Hollis, *The Waste Land: A Biography of a Poem*, London: Faber & Faber, 2022.
5 Declan Kibberd, 'Introduction', in James Joyce, *Ulysses*, Paris: Shakespeare & Co., 1922.
6 James Joyce, *Ulysses*, Paris: Shakespeare & Co., 1922, p. 595.

7   David Perkins, *A History of Modern Poetry, Vol. 1: From the 1890s to the High Modernist Mode*, Cambridge, MA: Belknap Press, 1976, p. 578.
8   A. Norman Jeffares, *W. B. Yeats: A New Biography*, London: Hutchinson, 1988, p. 275.
9   Virginia Woolf, *Jacob's Room*, Oxford: Oxford University Press, [1922] 1992, p. 37, quoted in Kate Flint, 'Introduction', ibid., pp. xiii–xiv.
10 Asa Briggs, *The History of Broadcasting in the United Kingdom, Vol. 1: The Birth of Broadcasting*, London: Oxford University Press, 1961, p. 65 and passim.
11 See for example Andy Beckett, 'PPE: the Oxford degree that runs Britain', *Guardian*, 23 February 2017.

Chapter 26: Auden, Orwell and the Age of Keynes

1   Humphrey Carpenter, *W. H. Auden: A Biography*, London: George Allen & Unwin, 1981, pp. 12–13.
2   See the discussion of 'Audenesque' in Bernard Bergonzi, *Reading the Thirties: Texts and Contexts*, London: Macmillan, 1978, pp. 40–1.
3   G. Rostrevor Hamilton, *The Tell-Tale Article: A Critical Approach to Modern Poetry*, quoted in Bergonzi, op. cit., p. 43.
4   Bergonzi, op. cit., p. 51.
5   See Carpenter, op. cit., for the writing of 'Spain' and Auden's direction of the royalties.
6   J. K. Galbraith, *The Age of Uncertainty*, London: BBC / André Deutsch, 1977, p. 218.
7   Ibid., p. 204.
8   Robert Lekachman, *The Age of Keynes*, Harmondsworth: Pelican, 1969, p. 72.
9   Ibid., pp. 80–4.
10 Robert Skidelsky, *John Maynard Keynes, 1883–1946: Economist, Philosopher, Statesman*, London: Macmillan, 2003, p. 572. According to Skidelsky, publication of *The General Theory* was followed by 'a war of opinion' among economists.
11 Ibid; Galbraith, op. cit., p. 221.

Chapter 27: The African Survey: The Laboratory of Empire 2

1   Helen Tilley, *Africa as a Living Laboratory: Empire, Development, and the Problem of Scientific Knowledge, 1870–1950*, Chicago: Chicago University Press, 2011, p. 70.
2   Ibid., p. 75.
3   John W. Cell, 'Lord Hailey and the Making of the African Survey', *African Affairs*, 1988, vol. 89, no. 353, pp. 481–505.
4   Ibid., p. 483.
5   Ibid., p. 482.
6   In addition to the many biographies of Rhodes, see George Walker,

'"So Much to Do": Oxford and the Wills of Cecil Rhodes', *Journal of Imperial and Commonwealth History*, 2016, vol. 44, no. 4, pp. 697–716.

7   Shula Marks and Stanley Trapido, 'Rhodes, Cecil', *Oxford Dictionary of National Biography*, Oxford: Oxford University Press, 2004, https://doi.org/10.1093/ref:odnb/35731

8   Tilley, op. cit., p. 79.

9   Ibid., p. 83.

10 Ibid., p. 71.

11 Ibid., p. 74.

12 Cell, op. cit., p. 486.

13 Tilley, op. cit., p. 137.

14 Ibid., p. 187.

15 Ibid., p. 189.

16 Ibid., p. 217.

17 Ibid., p. 219; Chloe Campbell, *Race and Empire: Eugenics in Colonial Kenya*, 2002, Manchester: Manchester University Press.

18 Ibid., p. 231.

19 Ibid., p. 236.

20 Ibid.

21 Ibid., p. 240.

22 Ibid., p. 330.

23 Ibid., p. 329.

24 David Mills, *Difficult Folk? A Political History of Social Anthropology*, New York: Berghahn, 2008, p. 71.

25 Ibid., p. 76.

26 Eric Williams, *Capitalism and Slavery*, Chapel Hill: University of North Carolina Press, 1944.

Chapter 28: Bletchley, the Bomb and Beveridge

1   See I. J. Good, 'Pioneering Work on Computers at Bletchley,' in N. Metropolis et al. (eds), *A History of Computing in the Twentieth Century*, New York: Academic Press, 1980, p. 33 for others who arrived at Bletchley at much the same time.

2   See Good, op. cit., pp. 35, 36 for excellent photographs of Enigma. For an excellent account of how the codes were broken, and the vital contribution of Harry Hinsley, using recently declassified documents, see Hugh Sebag-Montefiore, *Enigma: The Battle for the Code*, London: Weidenfeld & Nicolson, 2000.

3   Andrew Hodges, *Alan Turing: The Enigma*, London: Vintage, 1992, pp. 160ff.

4   Paul Strathern, *Turing and the Computer*, London: Arrow, 1997, pp. 46–7.

5   Ibid., pp. 63–4.

6   Guy Hartcup, *The Challenge of War: Scientific and Engineering Contributions to World War Two*, Newton Abbot: David & Charles, 1970, pp. 17ff.

7   Ibid., p. 91. For German progress, and some shortcomings of radar, see

Alfred Price, *Instruments of Darkness*, London: William Kimber, 1967, *circa* pp. 40–5.

8 Hartcup, op. cit., pp. 90, 107.

9 Ronald W. Clark, *The Life of Ernst Chain: Penicillin and Beyond*, New York: St Martin's Press, 1985, pp. 47ff.

10 Miles Weatherall, *In Search of a Cure; A History of Pharmaceutical Discovery*, Oxford: Oxford University Press, 1991, p. 168.

11 Ibid., pp. 175–6.

12 Robert Rhodes, *The Making of the Atomic Bomb*, New York: Simon & Schuster, 1986, p 319.

13 For more details about Peierls's calculations, see Ronald W. Clark, *The Birth of the Bomb*, London: Phoenix House, 1961, p. 118; also Rhodes, op. cit., p. 323.

14 Tizard's committee, extraordinarily, was the only body in wartime Britain capable of assessing the military uses of scientific discoveries: Clark, *The Birth of the Bomb*, p. 55.

15 Rhodes, op. cit., p. 379.

16 Nicholas Timmins, *The Five Giants: A Biography of the Welfare State*, London: Fontana, 1996, p. 23.

17 Paul Addison, *Churchill on the Home Front, 1900–1955*, London: Jonathan Cape, 1992, p. 51.

18 Timmins, op. cit., p. 20.

19 Ibid., p. 21, though this claim has been queried.

20 'Social Insurance and Allied Services: Report by Sir William Beveridge' (Cmd 6404, 1942), pp. 6–7.

21 Derek Fraser, *The Evolution of the British Welfare State*, London: Macmillan, 1973, p. 180, quoted in Timmins, op. cit., p. 33.

22 Allan Bullock, *Hitler and Stalin: Parallel Lives*, London: HarperCollins, 1991, p. 858.

23 Bernard Crick, *George Orwell: A Life*, London: Secker & Warburg, 1980, p. 316.

24 Robert Lekachman, *The Age of Keynes*, Harmondsworth: Pelican, 1969, p. 127.

25 Ibid., p. 152.

26 White had prepared his own proposal for an international bank: D. E. Moggridge (ed.), *The Collected Writings of John Maynard Keynes*, Vol. 24: *Activities, 1944–46: The Transition to Peace*, London: Royal Economic Society, 1979, p. 724.

Chapter 29: The Attack on the Intellectual Elite

1 Peter Ackroyd, *T. S. Eliot*, London: Hamish Hamilton, 1984, p. 291.

2 T. S. Eliot, *Notes Towards the Definition of Culture*, London: Faber & Faber, [1948] 1962, p. 31.

3 Ibid., p. 25.

4 Ian MacKillop, *F. R. Leavis: A Life in Criticism*, London: Allen Lane, 1995, pp. 15, 17ff.

5   Ibid., p. 111.
6   Michael Young, *The Rise of the Meritocracy, 1870–2033: An Essay on Education and Equality*, London: Thames & Hudson, 1958, p. xii. It was, however, poorly received by, among others, Richard Hoggart.
7   Paul Barker, 'The Ups and Downs of the Meritocracy', in Geoff Dench et al. (eds), *Young at Eighty*, Manchester: Carcanet Press, 1995, p. 161, cites reviewers who thought the book lacked 'the sound of a human voice'.
8   Colin MacInnes, *Absolute Beginners*, London: MacGibbon & Kee, 1959; Colin MacInnes, *Mr Love and Justice*, London: MacGibbon & Kee, 1960.
9   Oliver Neville, 'The English Stage Company and the Drama Critics', in Boris Ford (ed.), *The New Pelican Guide to English Literature, Vol. 8: From Orwell to Naipaul*, London: Pelican, 1983, p. 251.
10 Ibid., pp. 252–3.
11 Peter Mudford, 'Drama since 1950', in Martin Dodsworth (ed.), *The Penguin History of Literature, Vol. 7: The Twentieth Century*, London: Penguin, 1994, p. 395. See: Arnold Wesker's *Chicken Soup with Barley* (1956), Bernard Kops's *Hamlet of Stepney Green* (1957), John Arden's *Waters of Babylon* (1957) and David Brett's 1964 stage adaptation of Alan Sillitoe's 1958 novel *Saturday Night and Sunday Morning*.
12 Ibid., p. 346.
13 For the 'helpless bystander' quote, see Michael Kirkham, 'Philip Larkin and Charles Tomlinson: Realism and Art', in Ford (ed.), op. cit., pp. 286–9.
14 Richard Hoggart, *The Uses of Literacy*, London: Chatto & Windus, 1957.
15 For a good discussion, see Fred Inglis, *Cultural Studies*, Oxford: Blackwell, 1993, pp. 52–6; Fred Inglis, *Raymond Williams*, London: Routledge, 1995, pp. 162ff.
16 Stefan Collini, 'Introduction' to C. P. Snow, *The Two Cultures and the Scientific Revolution*, Cambridge: Cambridge University Press, 1959, p. viii.
17 Ibid., p 14.
18 MacKillop, op. cit., p. 320.

Chapter 30: Mothers and Genes: Biochemical Breakthrough

1   Published in book form as John Bowlby, *Child Care and the Growth of Love*, Harmondsworth: Pelican, 1953.
2   Bowlby, op. cit., pp. 161ff.
3   Paul Strathern, *Crick, Watson and DNA*, London: Arrow, 1997, pp. 37–8.
4   Ibid., p. 42.
5   Ibid., p. 49.
6   Ibid., pp. 50–3.
7   James D. Watson, *The Double Helix*, London: Weidenfeld & Nicolson, 1968, p. 123.

8   Ibid., p. 164.
9   Watson wrote an epilogue about Franklin in his book, praising her courage and integrity. He admitted too late that he had been wrong about her: ibid., pp. 174–5.
10 The classic account is: Georgina Ferry, *Dorothy Hodgkin: A Life*, London: Granta, 1998, but see also Guy Dodson, 'Dorothy Mary Crowfoot Hodgkin, OM, 12 May 1910–29 July 1994', *Biographical Memoirs of Fellows of the Royal Society*, 2002, vol. 48, pp. 179–219.
11 Richard Dawkins, *The Selfish Gene*, Oxford: Oxford University Press, 1976, p. 71.

Chapter 31: Peasants, Postmodernism and Poetry: Diversity and the 'Other'

1   Germaine Greer, *The Female Eunuch*, London: MacGibbon & Kee, 1971, pp. 273–82.
2   Ibid.
3   Juliet Mitchell, *Woman's Estate*, London: Penguin, 1971, p. 62.
4   Harvey J. Kaye, *The British Marxist Historians: An Introductory Analysis*, Cambridge: Polity Press, 1984, p. 86.
5   See for example Christopher Hill, *Change and Continuity in Seventeenth-Century England*, London: Weidenfeld & Nicolson, 1975, pp. 205ff.
6   E. P. Thompson, *The Making of the English Working Class*, London: Victor Gollancz, 1963, especially Part 2, 'The Curse of Adam', and p. 12 for the 'condescension' reference.
7   Christopher Hill, *The World Turned Upside Down: Radical Ideas during the English Revolution*, London: Temple Smith, 1972, chapters 3, 6, 7, 10.
8   Ibid., pp. 247ff.
9   Basil Davidson, *Old Africa Rediscovered*, London: Victor Gollancz, 1959, pp. 187–9. See also Basil Davidson, *The Search for Africa: A History in the Making*, London: James Currey, 1994.
10 See also Anthony Kirk-Greene, *The Emergence of African History at British Universities*, Oxford: WorldView, 1995.
11 David Harvey, *The Condition of Postmodernity: An Enquiry into the Origins of Social Change*, Oxford: Blackwell, [1980] 1990, pp. 8–9.
12 Ibid., p. 3.
13 Ibid., p. 156.
14 Ibid., p. 351.
15 Seamus Heaney, *The Government of the Tongue: the T. S. Eliot Memorial Lecture and Other Critical Writings*, London: Faber & Faber, 1988.

Chapter 32: Sir Salman, Sir Vidia and Soyinka's
Nobel: English as Lingua Franca

1 Marcus Cunliffe (ed.), *American Literature Since 1900*, London: Barrie & Jenkins, 1975, p. 373.

2 Salman Rushdie, *Midnight's Children*, London: Jonathan Cape, 1981; Salman Rushdie, *The Satanic Verses*, London: Viking, 1988; Catherine Cundy, *Salman Rushdie*, Manchester and New York: Manchester University Press, 1996, pp. 34ff.

3 Malise Ruthven, *A Satanic Affair: Salman Rushdie and the Rage of Islam*, London: Chatto & Windus, 1990, p. 15.

4 Ibid., pp. 20–5 passim.

5 Ibid., p. 25.

6 Each of these books was published by André Deutsch.

7 V. S. Naipaul, *Among the Believers: An Islamic Journey*, New York: Knopf, 1981.

8 V. S. Naipaul, *An Area of Darkness*, London: André Deutsch, 1964; V. S. Naipaul, *India: A Wounded Civilisation*, London: André Deutsch, 1977; V. S. Naipaul, *India: A Million Mutinies Now*, London: Heinemann, 1990. In particular, see *An Area of Darkness*, p. 53.

9 Wole Soyinka, *Myth, Literature and the African World*, Cambridge: Cambridge University Press, 1976, p. 42.

10 Jonathan Dollimore and Alan Sinfield (eds), *Political Shakespeare: Essays in Cultural Materialism*, Manchester: Manchester University Press, 1985. See also Peter Watson, 'Presume not that I am the thing I was', *Observer*, 22 August 1993, pp. 37–8.

11 Martin Bernal, *Black Athena: The Afroasiatic Roots of Classical Civilisation, Vol. 1: The Fabrication of Ancient Greece, 1785–1985*, London: Vintage, [1987] 1991.

12 Ibid., p. 239.

13 Ibid., pp. 18, 51, for example.

14 Ibid., p. 31.

15 Mary R. Lefkowitz and Guy MacLean Rogers, *Black Athena Revisited*, Chapel Hill: University of North Carolina Press, 1996.

16 Ibid., pp. 431–4.

17 Peter Fryer, *Staying Power: The History of Black People in Britain*, London: Pluto Press, 1984, p. 260.

18 Ibid., p. 267.

19 Ibid.

Chapter 33: The Promised Marriage of
Mathematics, Physics and Biology

1 John Maynard Smith and Eörs Szathmáry, *The Major Transitions in Evolution*, Oxford & New York: W. H. Freeman/Heidelberg: Spektrum, 1995.

2   Francis Crick, *The Astonishing Hypothesis: The Scientific Search for the Soul*, New York: Simon & Schuster, 1994.

3   John Maddox, *What Remains to Be Discovered: Mapping the Secrets of the Universe, the Origins of Life, and the Future of the Human Race*, London: Macmillan, 1998, p. 306.

4   John Cornwell (ed.), *Nature's Imagination: The Frontiers of Scientific Vision*, New York: R. S. Hederman, 1994; John Cornwell (ed.), *Consciousness and Human Identity*, New York: Oxford University Press, 1998, p. vi.

5   See for example Roger Penrose, *Shadows of the Mind: A Search for the Missing Science of Consciousness*, Oxford: Oxford University Press, 1994; Roger Penrose, *Fashion, Faith and Fantasy in the New Physics of the Universe*, Princeton, NJ: Princeton University Press, 2016.

6   Michael White and John Gribbin, *Stephen Hawking: A Life in Science*, New York and London: Viking, 1992, pp. 137–8.

7   Martin Rees, *Just Six Numbers: The Deep Forces That Shape the Universe*, London: Weidenfeld & Nicolson, 1999; White and Gribbin, op. cit., pp. 216–17.

8   Brian Greene, *The Elegant Universe: Superstrings, Hidden Dimensions and the Quest for the Ultimate Theory*, London: Jonathan Cape, 1999, pp. 174–6.

9   Ian Stewart, *Life's Other Secret: The New Mathematics of the Living World*, New York: Wiley, 1998, p. 66.

10 Ibid., pp. 89–90.

11 Ibid., pp. 95ff.

12 Ibid., pp. 96ff.

13 Ibid., p. 162.

14 Maddox, op. cit., p. 29.

15 Robert Wright, *The Moral Animal: Evolutionary Psychology and Everyday Life*, London: Little, Brown, 1995, p. 325.

Chapter 34: Our Floating World

1   See Norman Foster et al., *Rebuilding the Reichstag*, London: Weidenfeld & Nicolson, 2000; David Jenkins (ed.), *Norman Foster: Works*, Munich: Prestel, 6 vols, 2003–14.

2   A useful, accessible introduction to graphene and its significance is Terence Kemp, 'A Brief 100-Year History of Carbon', *Science Progress*, 2017, vol. 100, no. 3, pp. 293–8. See also Ben Clatworthy, 'First human trials of graphene brain implant to begin', *The Times*, 5 August 2024, https://www.thetimes.com/uk/science/article/first-human-trials-of-graphene-brain-implant-to-begin-xp3h5qxbr

3   See for example Ian Sample, 'Google's DeepMind predicts 3D shapes of proteins', *Guardian*, 2 December 2018, https://www.theguardian.com/science/2018/dec/02/google-deepminds-ai-program-alphafold-predicts-3d-shapes-of-proteins; Parmy Olson, *Supremacy: AI, ChatGPT and the Race That Will Change the World*, London: Macmillan, 2024.

4   Frank Close, *Elusive: How Peter Higgs Solved the Mystery of Mass*, London: Allen Lane, 2022.

5   'The Knowledge Quarter', *Sunday Times*, 22 October 2023, Business Section, p. 4.

6   Duncan Wilson, *The Making of British Bioethics*, Manchester: Manchester University Press, 2015.

7   See Eleanor Birne, 'At Tate Britain', *London Review of Books*, 2017, vol. 39, no. 21, p. 36, for a review of the 'triumphalist' show.

8   Kristian Shaw and Peter Sloane (eds), *Kazuo Ishiguro*, Manchester: Manchester University Press, 2023.

9   For an introduction to Gurnah's work, see Claire Chambers, *British Muslim Fictions: Interviews with Contemporary Writers*, Basingstoke: Palgrave Macmillan, 2011.

10 Besides her novels, see also Zadie Smith, *Changing My Mind: Occasional Essays*, London: Hamish Hamilton, 2009.

11 David Abulafia, *The Boundless Sea: A Human History of the Oceans*, London: Allen Lane, 2019.

12 John McAleer, review of *Islanders* by Nicholas Thomas, *International Journal of Nautical Archaeology*, 2012, vol. 41, no. 2, pp. 455–6.

13 See Jeff McMahan (ed.), *Principles and Persons: The Legacy of Derek Parfit*, Oxford: Oxford University Press, 2021.

14 For an introduction to transhumanism, see Peter Harrison and Joseph Wolyniak, 'The History of Transhumanism', *Notes and Queries*, 2015, vol. 62, no. 3, pp. 465–7.

15 John Gray, *The New Leviathans: Thoughts After Liberalism*, London: Allen Lane, 2023.

16 Dominic Sandbrook, *The Great British Dream Factory: The Strange History of Our National Imagination*, London: Allen Lane, 2015.

17 Hermione Lee, *Tom Stoppard: A Life*, London: Faber & Faber, 2020.

18 The best coverage of the affair was in the *Guardian*, which returned to the subject several times over several weeks and months in 2022 and 2023.

Conclusion: A Metaphysical Empire?

1   Daniel Dennett, *Darwin's Dangerous Idea, Evolution and the Meaning of Life*, London: Allen Lane, 1995, p. 21.

2   David Crystal, *English as a Global Language*, Cambridge: Cambridge University Press, 1998.

3   James Bennett, *The Anglosphere Challenge: Why the English-Speaking Nations Will Lead the Way in the Twenty-First Century*, Lanham, MD: Rowman & Littlefield, 2004, pp. 42–3, 289, to be read alongside Eric Kauffmann, *Whiteshift: Populism, Immigration and the Future of White Majorities*, London: Allen Lane, 2018.

4   Tamson Pietsch, *Empire of Scholars: Universities, Networks and the British Academic World, 1850–1939*, Manchester: Manchester University Press, 2013.

5   Dominic Sandbrook, *The Great British Dream Factory: The Strange*

History of Our National Imagination, London: Allen Lane, 2015, passim.

6 Lance E. Davis et al., *Mammon and the Pursuit of Empire: The Political Economy of British Imperialism, 1860–1912,* Cambridge: Cambridge University Press, 1986.

7 Alexander Motyl, 'Is Everything Empire? Is Empire Everything?', *Comparative Politics,* 2006, vol. 38, no. 2, pp. 229–49.

8 Philip Buckner, 'Canada and the End of Empire', in Philip Buckner (ed.), *Canada and the British Empire,* Oxford: Oxford University Press, 2008, pp. 107–26.

9 Buckner, op. cit., p. 111.

10 Ibid., p. 112.

11 Ibid., p. 113.

12 Ibid., p. 114.

13 See for example David Armitage, 'Greater Britain: A Useful Category of Historical Analysis?', *American Historical Review,* 1999, vol. 104, no. 2, pp. 427–45; Robert S. G. Fletcher et al., 'Making Connections: John Darwin and His Histories of Empire', *Journal of Imperial and Commonwealth History,* 2019, vol. 47, no. 5, pp. 801–14; Antoinette Burton, 'When was Britain? Nostalgia for the Nation at the End of the "American Century"', *Journal of Modern History,* 2003, vol. 75, no. 2, pp. 359–74.

14 Lorenzo Veracini, 'Decolonising Settler Colonialism; Kill the Settler in Him to Save the Man', *American Indian Culture and Research Journal,* 2017, vol. 41, no. 1, pp. 1–18.

15 James Belich, *Replenishing the Earth: The Settler Revolution and the Rise of the Anglo-World, 1783–1939,* Oxford: Oxford University Press, 2009.

16 Adam Kuper, *The Museum of Other People: From Colonial Acquisitions to Cosmopolitan Exhibitions,* London: Profile, 2023; 'Empire, Slavery & Scotland's Museums: Recommendations', Museums Galleries Scotland website, 2024, https://www. museumsgalleriesscotland.org.uk/project/empire-slavery-scotlands-museums/#recommendations; Stephen Howe, 'British Worlds, Settler Worlds, World Systems, and Killing Fields', *Journal of Imperial and Commonwealth History,* 2012, vol. 40, no. 4, pp. 691–725; Richard Drayton, 'Where Does the World Historian Write From? Objectivity, Moral Conscience and the Past and Present of Imperialism', *Journal of Contemporary History,* 2011, vol. 46, no. 3, pp. 671–85.

17 See for example Elizabeth Savage, *The Human Commodity: Perspectives on the Trans-Saharan Slave Trade,* London: Frank Cass, 1992; John Wright, *The Trans-Saharan Slave Trade,* Abingdon: Routledge, 2007; Terence Walz and Kenneth M. Cuno (eds), *Race and Slavery in the Middle East: Histories of Trans-Saharan Africans in Nineteenth-Century Egypt, Sudan, and the Ottoman Mediterranean,* Cairo: American University in Cairo, 2010.

18 Nigel Biggar, *Colonialism: A Moral Reckoning*, London: William Collins, 2023; Caroline Elkins, *Legacy of Violence: A History of the British Empire*, London: Bodley Head, 2022; Kehinde Andrews, *The New Age of Empire: How Racism and Colonialism Still Rule the World*, London: Penguin, 2021; Simon Gikandi, *Slavery and the Culture of Taste*, Princeton, NJ: Princeton University Press, 2014.

19 Robert Tombs, 'In defence of empire', *Spectator*, 8 May 2020.

20 Berny Sèbe, 'From Post-colonialism to Cosmopolitan Nation-Building? British and French Imperial Heroes in Twenty-First-Century Africa', *Journal of Imperial and Commonwealth History*, 2014, vol. 42, no. 5, pp. 936–68.

21 Daron Acemoglu et al., 'Reversal of Fortune: Geography and Institutions in the Making of the Modern World Income Distribution', *Quarterly Journal of Economics*, 2003, vol. 117, no. 4, pp. 1231–94.

22 Ibid., p. 1235.

23 Roger Anstey, 'Capitalism and Slavery: A Critique', *Economic History Review*, 1968, vol. 21, no. 2, pp. 307–20.

24 See David Richardson, 'Agency, Ideology and Violence in the History of Transatlantic Slavery', *Historical Journal*, 2007, vol. 50, no. 4, pp. 971–89.

25 Terence Walz, 'Egyptian-Sudanese Trade in the Ottoman Period to 1882', *Oxford Research Encyclopaedia of African History*, Oxford: Oxford University Press, 2018.

26 Richard Reid, 'Past and Presentisms: The "Precolonial" and the "foreshortening of African History"', *Journal of African History*, 2011, vol. 52, no. 2, pp. 135–55.

27 See Richard Drayton, 'Putting the British into Empire', *Journal of British Studies*, 2005, vol. 44, no. 1, pp. 187–93.

28 A. G. Hopkins, 'Viewpoint: Back to the Future: From National History to Imperial History', *Past & Present*, 1999, vol. 164, pp. 198–243.

29 Sathnam Sanghera, *Empireworld: How British Imperialism Has Shaped the Globe*, London: Viking, 2024, passim.

INDEX

528   THE BRITISH IMAGINATION